To my two sons,
Jeffrey and Andrew

A study of the history of opinion is a necessary preliminary to the emancipation of the mind.

—*John Maynard Keynes*

Ideas won by our intelligence, embodied in our outlook, and forged in our conscience, are chains from which we cannot tear ourselves away without breaking our hearts; they are demons we can overcome only by submitting to them.

—*Karl Marx*

Table of Contents

List of Tables and Figures

Tables

Figures

Foreword

I am exceedingly pleased that M.E. Sharpe Publishers are offering an updated second edition of E.K. Hunt's *History of Economic Thought: A Critical Perspective*. It is an excellent book on an important topic, and all students of economics would benefit from having a course based upon it.

There are probably no subjects in which truth filters down in undiluted form so that only the very latest vintages of work need to be consulted. But if there are, economics is certainly not among them. Some analytical problems have proved to be chronic. While earlier attempts at providing solutions sometimes contribute to knowledge, alterations in the structure or economic systems themselves make it uncertain as to the continuity of the relevant causal forces and thus pose the problem again. One example of this recurrence is the question of whether or not capitalist economies can stagnate, exhibiting persistent underutilization of capacity and constant or declining incomes. The answers have varied, depending on how capitalist systems have evolved and how economists believe economic forces operate in changed structures. Studying the history of economic thought helps one understand why economists seeking universal solutions to this problem, and many others too, can be misguided.

Being misguided is not always a purely individual deficiency. The development of economic theory responds to the influence of economic interests. Those groups who are dominant in a society foster analyses that represent their own roles and rewards in a favorable light, and they hinder the propagation of critical perspectives that are appreciated more by those with conflicting interests. Not surprisingly, economists have responded to the incentives, and mainstream economics has tended to be conservative in orientation. It is of great importance to illustrate how this has worked out in the history of economic thought. This is true even for conservatives who, like liberals and socialists, will be advantaged by an awareness of why they believe what they believe.

A closely related issue is the influence of ethical values on economic analysis. Most economists today assert that facts and values are logically separate matters, and they pride themselves on their endeavors leading to positive, value-free results. However, this position is easily subverted. All theories must focus on some aspect of economic relations and neglect others, and what is neglected cannot be subject to any kind of evaluation, positive or normative. These silences, of course, may be of ethical significance, as can be easily appreciated by considering the array of theorizations in intellectual history. Indeed, studying the history of economic thought can aid the development of this sort of awareness more efficiently than any other branch of economics.

There is another dimension relevant here. Contemporary economists have a marked propensity to forget what is inconvenient to remember. Thus, for example, the fact that the globalizing world economy of today has as much to do with imperialism as it does with voluntary contracting across borders—which is what orthodox economic theory wholly focuses upon—needs to be emphasized. It sheds much light on why economic development has been so unevenly distributed in the past and remains so today. The initial conditions of the countries involved in trade were very different, and so, too, have been the outcomes. Again, ignoring history, as much modern economics tends to do, creates systematic errors.

It is the great merit of Professor Hunt's book, *History of Economic Thought*, that none of this is suppressed or ignored. Instead, it is placed front and center; in doing so, Professor Hunt contributes greatly to educating economic students in the nature of their subject. The book deserves to be widely adopted and even more widely read.

M.C. Howard
Professor
Department of Economics
University of Waterloo
Ontario, Canada N2L 3G1

Preface

The writer of a history of economic thought must have, above all else, some principles of selectivity. Over the past 200-odd years, many hundreds of economic thinkers have written many thousands of books on economic theory and capitalism. The contemporary intellectual historian, in the space of one book, can, therefore, present only a limited number of the most important ideas of the most important thinkers.

But "importance" is not a scientific category upon which all historians of thought could agree. Every historian must have some criteria of selectivity. When one examines all of the histories of economic thought now in print, it seems that custom and tradition are the principal criteria. The ideas included in one generation's histories of thought seem to be restated by most of the historians of the next generation with few changes. To what degree the similarity is simply a question of the historians restating what they have found in previous secondary sources and to what degree it is a consequence of a common set of criteria for selection is difficult to say.

This book, however, is very different from any other history of thought now in print. It is therefore important to give the reader some idea of the fundamental intellectual preconceptions that underlie my criteria of selection. My criteria are based upon three general beliefs:

First, I believe that social theories and social-historical processes are reciprocally interconnected. Theories are based upon, grow out of, reflect, and attempt to explain ongoing social events and circumstances. Therefore, there is a sense in which it can be said that social theories are the products of the social and economic circumstances in which they are conceived. But it is equally true that human beings act, create, shape, and change their social and economic circumstances on the basis of ideas they hold about these circumstances. Therefore, there is a sense in which it can be said that social and economic circumstances are the products of ideas and social theories. Accordingly, despite the fact that this is a book about the history of economic thought, I have included several brief descriptions of some aspects of social and economic history that I believe will be useful in attaining an understanding of the ideas discussed.

Second, I believe that while social and economic change are continuous, and while today's capitalism is, in numerous respects, substantially different from capitalism of the late eighteenth century, nevertheless, there are important and fundamental institutional foundations that have continuously underlain capitalism throughout all of these changes, as obvious and striking as the changes are. Therefore, to the degree that economists have concerned themselves with these basic underlying features of capitalism, the various differences in points of view among late eighteenth- and nineteenth-century economists have their counterparts today in the writings of contemporary economists. Consequently, in writing this book I have tried to illuminate the nature of contemporary controversies in economic theory by examining their historical antecedents. This has affected my selection of theorists to examine. For example, most histories of economic thought do not discuss the ideas of Thompson, Hodgskin, and Bastiat. I have included them because I believe they are clear, cogently argued statements of points of view that, in only slightly modified form, are very important today.

Third, I believe that all economists are, and always have been, vitally concerned with practical, social, political, and moral issues. Consequently, their writings have both a cognitive, scientific element and emotive, moral, or ideological element. Moreover, I do not believe these two elements are entirely separable. Cognitive, scientific inquiry is always *directed* toward certain questions and problems, and the range of solutions to these questions and problems that any thinker will consider as "legitimate" is always *limited.* A thinker's moral feelings and ideological views give the direction to the cognitive, scientific inquiry and set the limits as to what will constitute the "legitimate" range of solutions for that thinker. Moreover, moral feelings and ideological views are based on, and are always defended by means of, the thinker's cognitive or scientific theories of how society actually functions. It follows that even though we can conceptually at least partially separate the scientific and ideological elements of a social theory, this separation can never be complete. We can never fully understand the cognitive, scientific element in an economist's theory without some understanding of the evaluative and ideological elements of the theory. Throughout this book I have tried to discuss both elements in the various theories considered.

The third belief is, perhaps, what differentiates this book most markedly from others of its kind. There is, in academic circles, a widely held view that science and value judgments are antithetical. According to this view, to the degree that value judgments creep into a work, the work is not scientific. Consequently, historians of this persuasion generally view their own work in the history of economic thought as "value free" and present the writings of those theorists whom they like as though they were "value free." Similarly, theorists whom they dislike, particularly Marx, are presented as having values in their writings and these values are (at least implicitly) held to partially vitiate the scientific value of the writings. In my view, all theorists, all historians, and all human beings (including myself, of course) have values that significantly interpenetrate all cognitive endeavors. Therefore, when I discuss the values and ideological aspects of the various theorists' writings, there is no intention of conveying the notion that the having of values, per se, is a basis for criticizing a thinker. I believe that the contention that some theorists are "value free" is either a self-deception or an attempt to deceive others. Judgments should not be made on the basis of whether or not a theorist had values—since every one of them did have values—but on the basis of the concrete nature of those values. For that reason, I have discussed some of the values underlying the theories presented, and I have concluded the book with a statement of some of my own values, which have affected the writing of this book.

Based upon these three beliefs, I have selected ideas that I believe were important in their time and continue to have importance today. One of the frequently recurring themes in the history of economic thought—a theme that is central to this book—is the issue of whether capitalism is a social system that conduces toward harmony or toward conflict. In the writings of Smith and Ricardo both views were developed. After Ricardo, most economists saw capitalism as either fundamentally harmonious or fundamentally conflictive. Each economist's view on this issue has been extremely significant in determining the scope, method, and content of his or her analysis. Another persistent theme is the debate over the inherent stability or instability of capitalism. There have also been persistent differences of opinion concerning the propriety of value judgments in economic theory.

Each of these and other issues are discussed at length in this book. One issue that perhaps deserves special mention in this preface is the question of the relationship between the pricing of consumer goods and the pricing of "the factors of production" or income distribution. The classical economists and Marx held that income distribution was an important determinant of the prices of commodities, whereas the neoclassical economists generally reversed the direction of causality. Most authors of histories of economic thought books have accepted the neoclassical version without question and have treated the classical-Marx version as a historically antiquated curiosum. The recent theoretical developments growing out of Piero Sraffa's *Production of Commodities by Means of Commodities* have turned the tables. The classical-Marx view now appears to rest on a much more secure theoretical foundation. The present book is, I believe, the first comprehensive history of economic thought to describe Sraffa's theoretical breakthrough and to reinterpret previous thinkers based upon Sraffa's insights, although, in a more limited manner, Maurice Dobb has insightfully dealt with this issue in the history of economic thought.

The book concludes with a discussion of differences among contemporary economic theories. It is hoped that the entire book contributes to a broader understanding of contemporary theory. No mathematics beyond a very few simple equations and graphs is included in the book. A person with no background in economic theory can read and understand the book. At the same time, I believe that because my perspective on the various theories discussed is sufficiently different from that of any other history of economic thought, many graduate students and professors in economics will find much that is original, informative, and stimulating.

My general intellectual debts are many. The teacher who most stimulated my interest in the history of economic thought was Lawrence Nabers. Writers who have significantly influenced me include Karl Marx, John Dewey, Thorstein Veblen, Leo Rogin, and Maurice Dobb. Helpful comments on the manuscript for this book were received from John Greenman and Professors James M. Cypher, Douglas Dowd, Howard Sherman, Norris C. Clement, and Warren Samuels. And many thanks are due to Mark Price for preparing the manuscript for the publisher. Most of all, I want to thank Ginger Alewine, without whose help this edition would have never been completed. She is a special person for whom I have both gratitude and great affection.

I wish to thank the publishers of various materials I have written for other publications for granting me permission to use some of the ideas or short excerpts from these writings.[1]

Finally, I wish to express my love and appreciation to my two sons, Jeffrey and Andrew, to whom this book is dedicated. The dedication to them is made with my deepest, most profound affection.

E.K. Hunt

Note

1. These include *Property and Prophets, the Evolution of Economic Institutions and Ideologies*, 6th ed. (New York: Harper and Row, 1990); "Marxian Labor Values, Prices, and Profits," *Intermountain Economic Review* (Spring 1978); "An Essay on the Criteria Defining Social Economics," *Review of Social Economics* (December 1978); "Value Theory in the Writings of the Classical Economists, Thomas Hodgskin and Karl Marx," *History of Political Economy* (Fall 1977); "Utilitarianism and the Labor Theory of Value," *History of Political Economy* (Spring 1980); permission to use some ideas or short excerpts of the two articles from *History of Political Economy* was granted by Duke University Press; "A Radical Critique of Welfare Economics," in *Value, Distribution and Growth: Essays in the Revival of Political Economy*, ed. E.J. Nell (New York: Cambridge University Press, 1978).

Acknowledgments

Excerpts from Paul A. Baran and Paul M. Sweezy, *Monopoly Capital*, are reprinted by permission of Monthly Review Press.

Excerpts from Frédéric Bastiat, *Economic Harmonies*, are reprinted by permission of the Institute for Humane Studies.

Excerpts from Harry Braverman, *Labor and Monopoly Capital: The Degradation of Work in the Twentieth Century*, are reprinted by permission of Monthly Review Press.

Excerpts from Martin Brofenbrenner, *Income Distribution Theory*, are reprinted by permission of Aldine Publishing Company and Macmillan, London and Basingstoke.

Excerpts from Maurice Dobb, *Theories of Value and Distribution since Adam Smith*, are reprinted by permission of Cambridge University Press.

Excerpts from C.E. Ferguson, *The Neoclassical Theory of Production and Distribution*, are reprinted by permission of Cambridge University Press.

Excerpts from Milton Friedman, *Capitalism and Freedom*, © 1962 by the University of Chicago, are reprinted by permission of the University of Chicago Press and Milton Friedman.

Excerpts from J.A. Hobson, *Imperialism: A Study*, are reprinted by permission of the University of Michigan Press.

Excerpts from John Maynard Keynes, *The General Theory of Employment, Interest and Money*, are reprinted by permission of Harcourt Brace Jovanovich and the Right Honorable Lord Kahn.

Excerpts from Richard B. McKenzie and Gordon Tullock, *The New World of Economics: Explorations in Human Experience*, are reprinted by permission of Richard D. Irwin.

Excerpts from Alfred Marshall, *Principles of Economics*, 8th ed., are reprinted by permission of Macmillan, London and Basingstoke.

Excerpts from Karl Marx, *Grundrisse: Foundations of the Critique of Political Economy*, Martin Nicolaus, tr., are reprinted by permission of Random House.

Excerpts from Ronald L. Meek, *Economics and Ideology and Other Essays*, are reprinted by permission of Chapman and Hall; excerpts from *Studies in the Labour Theory of Value*, rev. ed., © 1976 by Ronald L. Meek, are reprinted by permission of Monthly Review Press.

Excerpts from Carl Menger, *Principles of Economics*, are reprinted by permission of the Institute for Humane Studies.

Excerpts from D.M. Nuti, "Vulgar Economy in the Theory of Income Distribution," in *A Critique of Economic Theory*, ed. E.K. Hunt and Jesse G. Schwartz, are reprinted by permission of D.M. Nuti.

Excerpts from Paul A. Samuelson, "A Summing Up," *Quarterly Journal of Economics*, are reprinted by permission of John Wiley; excerpts from *Economics*, 10th ed., copyright 1976 McGraw-Hill, are reprinted by permission of McGraw-Hill.

Excerpts from Piero Sraffa, *Production of Commodities by Means of Commodities*, are reprinted by permission of Cambridge University Press.

Excerpts from Thorstein Veblen, *The Place of Science in Modern Civilisation, and Other Essays*, 1919, with a new preface by Joseph Dorfman, are reprinted by permission of Russell and Russell; excerpts from *Essays in Our Changing Order, Absentee Ownership and Business Enterprise in Recent Times, The Instinct of Workmanship, The Engineers and the Price System, The Theory of Business Enterprise*, and *The Theory of the Leisure Class* are all reprinted by permission of Augustus M. Kelley.

HISTORY
OF
ECONOMIC
THOUGHT

Chapter 1

Introduction

Modern economic theory is customarily said to have begun with Adam Smith (1723–1790). This book is concerned primarily with the economic ideas from Smith to the present. The common element in the ideas presented here is the concern to understand the nature of the capitalist economic system. The writers that we shall discuss all sought to understand what features were most essential to the functioning of capitalism, how the system functioned, what determined the volume of production, what was the source of economic growth, what determined the distribution of wealth and income, and many other questions as well. They also sought to evaluate capitalism: How adequately did the system fulfill human needs? How could it be changed to better fulfill these needs?

A Definition of Capitalism

It is, of course, simplistic to say that attempts to understand capitalism began with Adam Smith. Capitalism as the dominant social, political, and economic system, first of western Europe and later of much of the world, emerged very slowly over a period of several centuries. As it emerged people sought to understand it.

To survey the attempts to understand capitalism, it is necessary first to define it and then to review briefly the historical highlights of its emergence. It must be stated at the outset that there is no general agreement among economists or economic historians as to what the essential features of capitalism are. In fact, some economists do not believe that it is fruitful to define distinctly different economic systems at all; they believe in a historical continuity in which the same general principles suffice to understand all economic arrangements. Most economists would agree, however, that capitalism is an economic system that functions very differently from previous economic systems and from contemporary noncapitalist systems. This book is based on a methodological approach that defines economic systems according to the mode of production on which the system is based. The *mode of production* is, in turn, defined by the *forces of production* and the *social relations of production*.

The forces of production constitute what would commonly be called the productive technology of a society. These consist of the current state of productive or technical knowledge, skills, organizational techniques, and so forth, as well as the tools, implements, machines, and buildings involved in production. Within any given set of forces of production there are certain necessary costs that must be met in order to insure the system's continued existence. Some new resources, or raw materials, must be continuously extracted from the natural environment. Machinery, tools, and other implements of production wear out with use and must be replaced. Most important, the human beings who expend the effort necessary to secure raw materials and to transform these raw materials into finished products must have a minimum level of food, clothing, shelter, and other necessities to sustain social life.

Modes of production that have not satisfied these minimum requirements of continued production have vanished. Many historical modes of production successfully met these minimum requirements for a period of time and then, due to some change in circumstances, were unable to continue doing so, and, consequently, became extinct. Most modes of production that have continued to exist for very long periods of time have, in fact, produced enough to meet not only these necessary costs but also an excess, or social surplus, beyond these necessary costs. A social surplus is defined as that part of a society's material production that is left over after the necessary material costs of production have been deducted.

The historical development of the forces of production has resulted in a continuously increasing capacity for societies to produce larger social surpluses. In this historical evolution, societies have generally divided into two separate groups. The vast majority of people in every society has toiled to produce the output necessary to sustain and perpetuate the mode of production as well as the social surplus, while a small minority has appropriated and controlled it. In this book, social classes are distinguished accordingly; the social relations of production are defined as the relationships between these two classes. A mode of production, then, is the social totality of the technology of production (the forces of production) and the social arrangements by which one class uses these forces of production to produce all output including the surplus and another class appropriates the surplus (the social relations of production).

Within the context of this general set of definitions, we can define capitalism, the particular mode of production with which the thinkers surveyed in this book have been concerned. Capitalism is characterized by four sets of institutional and behavioral arrangements: market-oriented commodity production; private ownership of the means of production; a large segment of the population that cannot exist unless it sells its labor power in the market; and individualistic, acquisitive, maximizing behavior by most individuals within the economic system. Each of these features will be discussed briefly.

In capitalism, the products of human labor are valued for two distinct reasons. First, products have particular physical characteristics by virtue of which they are usable and satisfy human needs. When a commodity is valued for its use in satisfying our needs, it is said to have use value. All products of human labor in all societies have use value. In capitalism, products are also valued because they can be sold for money in the market. This money is desired because it can be exchanged for products that have a desired use value. Insofar as products are valued because they can be exchanged for money, they are said to have exchange value. Products of human labor have exchange value only in modes of production characterized by commodity production. A society must have a well-developed market in which products can be freely bought or sold for money in order for commodity production to exist. Commodity production exists when products are created by producers who have no immediate personal concern for the use value of the product but are interested only in its exchange value. Thus commodity production is not a direct means of satisfying needs. Rather, it is a means of acquiring money by exchanging the product for money, which, in turn, may be used to acquire products desired for their use value. Under such conditions, the products of human labor are commodities, and the society is described as a commodity-producing society.

Under commodity production, a person's productive activity has no direct connection to that person's consumption; exchange and the market must mediate the two. Furthermore, a person has no direct connection to the people who produce the commodities he or she consumes. This social relationship is also mediated by the market. Commodity production implies a high degree of productive specialization, in which each isolated producer creates only one or a few commodities and then must depend on other individuals, with whom he or she has no direct personal relations, to buy the commodities on the market. Once the person has exchanged the commodity for money, that person again depends on people with whom he or she has no direct personal relationship to supply on the market the commodities he or she must purchase in order to satisfy personal needs.

This type of economy is one in which extremely complex economic interrelationships and dependencies exist that do not involve direct personal interaction and association. The individual interacts only with the impersonal social institution of the market, in which the individual exchanges commodities for money and money for commodities. Consequently, what is in reality a set of complex social and economic relations among people appears to each individual to be merely so many impersonal relations among things—namely, commodities. Each individual depends on the impersonal forces of the market—of buying and selling or demand and supply—for the satisfaction of needs.

The second defining feature of capitalism is private ownership of the means of production. This means that society grants to private persons the right to dictate how the raw materials, tools, machinery, and buildings necessary for production can be used. Such a right necessarily implies that other individuals are excluded from having any say about how these means of production can be used. Early defenses of private property spoke in terms of each individual producer owning and therefore controlling the means of individual production. But very early in the evolution of capitalism things developed differently. In fact, the third defining feature of capitalism is that most producers do not own the means necessary to carry on their productive activity. Ownership came to be concentrated in the hands of a small segment of society—the capitalists. An owner-capitalist needed to play no direct role in the actual process of production in order to control it; ownership itself granted control. And it was this ownership that permitted the capitalist to appropriate the social surplus. Thus, ownership of the means of production is the feature of capitalism that bestows the power on the capitalist class by which it controls the social surplus, and, thereby, establishes itself as the dominant social class.

This domination, of course, implies the third defining feature of capitalism—the existence of a large working class that has no control over the means necessary to carry out their productive activity. In capitalism, most workers own neither the raw materials nor the implements with which they produce commodities. Consequently, the commodities that they produce do not belong to them but rather are owned by the capitalists who own the means of production. The typical worker enters the market owning or controlling only one thing—the capacity to work, that is, his or her labor power. In order to engage in productive activity, the person must sell his or her labor power to a capitalist. In return, the person receives a wage and produces commodities that belong to the capitalist. Thus, unlike any prior mode of production, capitalism turns human productive power itself into a commodity—labor power— and generates a set of conditions in which the majority of people cannot live unless they are able to sell their commodity, labor power, to a capitalist for a wage. With the wage, they are able to buy back from the capitalists only a portion of the commodities that they themselves have produced. The remainder of the commodities that they produce constitutes the social surplus and is retained and controlled by the capitalist class.

The fourth and final defining feature of capitalism is that most people are motivated by individualistic, acquisitive, maximizing behavior. This is necessary for the successful functioning of capitalism. First, in order to assure an adequate supply of labor and to facilitate the strict control of workers, it is necessary that working people produce commodities whose value is far in excess of the value of the commodities that they consume. In the earliest period of capitalism this was accomplished in two ways. First, workers were paid such low wages that they and their families were kept on the verge of extreme material deprivation and insecurity. The only apparent way of decreasing this deprivation and insecurity was to work longer and harder in order to obtain a more adequate wage and to avoid being forced to join the large army of unemployed workers, which has been an ever-present social phenomenon in the capitalist system.

As capitalism evolved, the productivity of workers increased. They began to organize themselves collectively into unions and workingmen's associations to fight for higher wages. By the late nineteenth and early twentieth centuries, after many hard battles and innumerable setbacks, these struggles began to have an impact. Since that time, the purchasing power of the wages of working people has been slowly and consistently increasing. In place of widespread physical deprivation, capitalism has increasingly had to rely on new types of motivation to keep working people producing the social surplus. A new social ethos, sometimes called consumerism, has become dominant, and is characterized by the belief that more income alone always means more happiness.

The social mores of capitalism have induced the view that virtually every subjectively felt need or unhappiness can be eliminated if one can buy more commodities. The competitive and economically insecure world within which workers function generally creates subjective feelings of anxiety, loneliness, and alienation. The cause of these feelings has been perceived by most working people as their inability to buy enough commodities to make them happy. But as workers have received higher wages and bought more commodities, the general unhappiness and anxiety have continued. The problem, they have tended to conclude, is that the increase in wages was insufficient. Misperceiving the root cause of their condition, they have frequently gotten aboard an Alice in Wonderland treadmill, where the more one gets the more needy one feels, the faster one runs the more inadequate one's pace appears to be, the harder one works the greater appears to be the need for even harder work in the future.

Capitalists have also been driven to acquisitive, combative behavior. The most immediate reason for this is the fact that capitalism has always been characterized by a competitive struggle among capitalists to secure larger shares of the social surplus. In this endless struggle the power of any given capitalist depends on the amount of capital that he or she controls. If a capitalist's competitors acquire capital—and hence size and economic strength—more rapidly than he or she does, then it becomes highly likely that he or she will face extinction. So continued existence as a capitalist depends on the ability to accumulate capital at least as rapidly as competitors. Hence, capitalism has always been characterized by the frantic effort of capitalists to make more profits and to convert these profits into more capital.

Consumerism among capitalists has also been important for the successful functioning of capitalism. In the process of production, after the workers have produced surplus value, the capitalists own this surplus value in the form of the commodities that the workers have produced. In order for this surplus value to be converted into monetary profit, these commodities must be sold on the market. The workers can usually be counted on to spend all of their wages on commodities, but their wages can purchase only some of the commodities (or else there would be no social surplus). Capitalists will purchase many of the commodities as investments to add to their accumulation of capital. But these two sources of demand have never been adequate to generate enough spending for the capitalists as an entire class to sell all of their commodities. Therefore, a third source of demand, ever-increasing consumption expenditures by capitalists, has also been necessary to assure adequate money demand to enable capitalists to sell all of their commodities.

When such demand has not been forthcoming, capitalism has experienced depressions in which commodities cannot be sold, workers are laid off, profits decline, and a general economic crisis ensues. Throughout its history, capitalism has suffered from recurring crises of this kind. A major concern of most of the economic thinkers discussed in this book has been to understand the nature and causes of these crises and to ascertain whether remedies can be found to eliminate or at least to alleviate the crises.

Precapitalist European Economy

In order to trace the outlines of the historical evolution of capitalism, it is necessary first to say a few words about feudalism—the socioeconomic system that preceded capitalism in western Europe. The decline of the western part of the old Roman Empire left Europe without the laws and protection that the empire had provided. The vacuum was filled by the creation of a feudal hierarchy, in which the serf, or peasant, was protected by the lord of the manor, who, in turn, owed allegiance to and was protected by a higher overlord. So the system went, ending eventually with the king. The strong protected the weak, but they did so at a high price. In return for payments of money, food, labor, or military allegiance, overlords granted the fief, or *feudum*—a hereditary right to use land—to their vassals. At the bottom was the serf, who tilled the land. The vast majority of the population raised crops for food or clothing or tended sheep for wool and clothing.[1]

Custom and tradition are the keys to understanding medieval relationships. In place of laws as we know them today, the custom of the manor governed. There was no strong central authority in the Middle Ages that could have enforced a system of laws. The entire medieval organization was based on a system of mutual obligations and services up and down the hierarchy. Possession or use of the land obligated one to certain customary services or payments in return for protection. The lord was as obligated to protect the serf as the serf was to turn over a portion of his crop to or perform extensive labor for the lord.

Customs were broken, of course; no system always operates in fact as it is designed to operate in theory. One should not, however, underestimate the strength of custom and tradition in determining the lives and ideas of medieval people. Disputes between serfs were decided in the lord's court according to both the special circumstances in each case and the general customs of the manor for such cases. Of course, a lord would usually decide in his own favor in a dispute between himself and a serf. Even in this circumstance, however, especially in England, an overlord would impose sanctions or punishments on a lord who, as the overlord's vassal, had persistently violated the customs in his treatment of serfs. This rule by the custom of the manor stands in sharp contrast to the legal and judicial system of capitalism. The capitalist system is based on the enforcement of contracts and universally binding laws, which are softened only rarely by mitigating circumstances and customs that often swayed the lord's judgment in medieval times.

The extent to which the lords could enforce their "rights" varied greatly from time to time and from place to place. It was the strengthening of these obligations and the nobleman's ability to enforce them through a long hierarchy of vassals over a wide area that eventually led to the emergence of modern nation-states. This process occurred during the period of transition from feudalism to capitalism. Throughout most of the Middle Ages, however, many of the lords' rights were very weak or uncertain because political control was fragmented.

The basic economic institution of medieval rural life was the manor, which contained within it two separate classes: noblemen, or lords of the manors, and serfs (from the Latin word *servus*, "slave"). Serfs were not really slaves. Unlike a slave, who was simply property to be bought and sold at will, the serf could not be parted from either his or her family or land. If the serf's lord transferred possession of the manor to another nobleman, the serf simply had another lord. In varying degrees, however, obligations were placed on the serfs that were sometimes very onerous and from which there was often no escape. Usually, they were far from being free.

The lord lived off the labor of the serfs who farmed his fields and paid taxes in kind and money according to the custom of the manor. Similarly, the lord gave protection, supervision, and administration of justice according to the custom of the manor. It must be added that although the system did rest on reciprocal obligations, the concentration of economic and political power in the hands of the lord led to a system in which, by any standard, the serf was exploited in the extreme.

The Catholic Church was by far the largest owner of land during the Middle Ages. Although bishops and abbots occupied much the same place as counts and dukes in the feudal hierarchy, there was one important difference. Secular lords might shift their loyalty from one overlord to another, depending on the circumstances and the balance of power involved, but the religious lords always had (in principle at least) a primary loyalty to the church in Rome. This was also an age during which the religious teaching of the church had a very strong and pervasive influence throughout western Europe. These factors combined to make the church the closest thing to a strong central government throughout this period.

Thus, the manor might be secular or religious (many times secular lords had religious overlords and vice versa), but the essential relationships between lords and serfs were not significantly affected by this distinction. There is little evidence that serfs were treated any less harshly by religious lords than by secular ones. The religious lords and the secular nobility were the joint ruling classes; they controlled the land and the power that went with it. In return for very onerous appropriations of the serf's labor, produce, and money, the nobility provided military protection, and the church provided spiritual aid.

In addition to manors, medieval Europe had many towns, which were important centers of manufacturing. Manufactured goods were sold to manors and sometimes traded in long-distance commerce. The dominant economic institutions in the towns were the guilds—craft, professional, and trade associations that had existed as far back as the Roman Empire. If anyone wanted to produce or sell any good or service, that person had to join a guild.

The guilds were as involved with social and religious questions as with economic ones. They regulated their members in all their activities: personal, social, religious, and economic. Although the guilds did regulate the production and sale of commodities very carefully, they were less concerned with making profits than with saving their members' souls. Salvation demanded that the individual lead an orderly life based on church teachings and custom. Thus, the guilds exerted a powerful influence as conservators of the status quo in the medieval towns.

But medieval society was predominantly an agrarian society. The social hierarchy was based on individuals' ties to the land, and the entire social system rested on an agricultural base. Yet, ironically, increases in agricultural productivity were the original impetus for a series of profound changes, occurring over several centuries, that resulted in the dissolution of medieval feudalism and the beginnings of capitalism. The most important technological advance in the Middle Ages was the replacement of the two-field system of crop rotation with the three-field system. Although there is evidence that the three-field system was introduced into Europe as early as the eighth century, its use was probably not widespread until around the eleventh century.

Yearly sowing of the same land would deplete the land and eventually make it unusable. Consequently, in the two-field system, half of the land was always allowed to lie fallow in order to recover from the previous year's planting. With the three-field system, arable land was divided into three equal parts. Rye or winter wheat would be planted in the fall in the first field. Oats, beans, or peas would be planted in the spring in the second field, and the third field would lie fallow. Every year there was a rotation of these positions. Any given piece of land would have a fall planting one year, a spring planting the next year, and none the third. A dramatic increase in agricultural output resulted from this seemingly simple change in agricultural technology. With the same amount of arable land, the three-field system increased the amount under cultivation at any particular time by as much as 50 percent.[2]

The three-field system led to other important changes. Spring sowing of oats and other fodder crops enabled the people to support more horses, which began to replace oxen as the principal source of power in agriculture. Horses were much faster than oxen, and, consequently, the region under cultivation could be extended. Larger cultivated areas enabled the countryside to support more concentrated population centers. Transportation of men, commodities, and equipment was much more efficient with horses. Greater efficiency was also attained in plowing: a team of oxen required three men to do the plowing; a horse-drawn plow could be operated by one man. The costs of transporting agricultural products were substantially reduced in the thirteenth century when the four-wheeled wagon with a pivotal front axle replaced the two-wheeled cart. These improvements in agriculture and transportation contributed to two important and far-reaching changes. First, they made possible a rapid increase in population growth. The best historical estimates show that the population of Europe doubled between 1000 and 1300.[3] Second, closely related to the expansion of population was a rapid increase in urban concentration. Before the year 1000, most of Europe, except for a few Mediterranean trade centers, consisted only of manors, villages, and a few small towns. By 1300, there were many thriving cities and larger towns.

The growth of towns and cities led to a growth of rural-urban specialization. With urban workers severing all ties to the soil, the output of manufactured goods increased impressively. Along with increased manufacturing and increased economic specialization came many additional gains in human productivity. Interregional, long-distance trade and commerce was another very important result of this increased specialization.

The Increase in Long-Distance Trade

Many historians have argued that the spread of trade and commerce was the single most important force leading to the disintegration of medieval feudalism. The importance of trade cannot be doubted, but it must be emphasized that this trade did not arise by accident or by factors completely external to the European economy, such as increased contact with the Arabs. On the contrary, it was shown in the previous section that this upsurge in trade was supported by the internal economic evolution of Europe itself. The growth of agricultural productivity meant that a surplus of food and handicrafts was available for local and international markets. The improvements in power and transportation meant that it was possible and profitable to concentrate industry in towns, to produce on a mass scale, and to sell the goods in a widespread, long-distance market. Thus, these basic agricultural and industrial developments were necessary prerequisites for the spread of trade and commerce, which then further encouraged industry and town expansion.

The growth of commerce cannot, however, be considered as the principal force in either the dissolution of feudalism or the creation of capitalism. While the transition from feudalism to capitalism coincided with increases in commerce in western Europe, and while commerce definitely was an important force in the dissolution of feudalism and the growth of capitalism there, increases in commercial activity in eastern Europe tended to contribute to the consolidation and perpetuation of feudal social and economic relationships.

These differing effects of commerce were due to the different stages of the historical development of feudalism in these two regions. In eastern Europe, feudalism was a relatively young and vigorous economic system with considerable potential for further development. In this context, commerce tended to be kept strictly subordinate to the interests of the feudal ruling class. In western Europe, feudalism had reached and possibly surpassed its full economic potential. Long before commerce became a significant part of western European life, feudalism had begun to dissolve. The initial impetus to its dissolution was the fact that, despite the increases in productivity, the social surplus became increasingly less adequate to support a rapidly growing ruling class. This led to increasingly severe and irreconcilable conflicts within the ruling class. Within the context of these acute conflicts among various segments of the nobility and the church, commerce became a corrosive, destabilizing force.[4] In our short summary, we shall confine ourselves to a discussion of western European feudalism, where commerce tended to accelerate the dissolution of feudalism and to establish many of the institutional foundations of capitalism.

The expansion of trade, particularly long-distance trade in the early period, led to the establishment of commercial and industrial towns to service this trade. The growth of these cities and towns, as well as their increased domination by merchant capitalists, led to important changes in both industry and agriculture. Each of these areas, particularly agriculture, weakened and ultimately dissolved the traditional ties that held together the feudal economic and social structures.

From the earliest part of the medieval period, some long-distance trade had been carried on throughout many parts of Europe. This trade was very important in southern Europe on the Mediterranean and Adriatic seas and in northern Europe on the North and Baltic seas. Between these two areas of commercialism, however, the feudal manorial system in most of Europe was relatively unaffected by commerce and trade until the later Middle Ages.

From about the eleventh century onward, the Christian Crusades gave the impetus to a marked expansion of commerce. Yet the Crusades themselves cannot be viewed as an accidental or external factor to European development. They were not undertaken for religious reasons, nor were they the result of Turkish molestation of pilgrims, for the Turks continued the Moslem policy of tolerance. Developments on the Moslem side did lead to increased attacks on Byzantium, but the West would normally have sent only token aid, because it had no great love for Byzantium. The basic reasons for the Crusades may be seen in the internal developments of France, where they had their most powerful backing. France had been growing stronger; it had more trade relations with an interest in the East; and it needed an outlet for social unrest at home. Additional propaganda for the Crusades came from the oligarchy of Venice, which wanted to expand its own eastern trade and influence.[5]

The development of trade with the Arabs—and with the Vikings in the north—led to increased production for export and to the great trade fairs that flourished from the twelfth through the late fourteenth centuries. Held annually in the principal European trading cities, these fairs usually lasted for one to several weeks. Northern European merchants exchanged their grain, fish, wool, cloth, timber, pitch, tar, salt, and iron for the spices, brocades, wines, fruits, and gold and silver that were the dominant items in southern European commerce.

By the fifteenth century, the fairs were being replaced by commercial cities where year-round markets thrived. The trade and commerce in these cities were incompatible with restrictive feudal customs and traditions. Generally the cities were successful in gaining independence from church and feudal lords. Within these commercial centers there arose complex systems of currency exchange, debt-clearing, and credit facilities, and modern business instruments like bills of exchange came into widespread use. New systems of commercial law developed. Unlike the system of paternalistic adjudication based on custom and tradition that prevailed in the manor, commercial law was fixed by precise code. Hence, it became the basis of the modern capitalist law of contracts, negotiable instruments, agency sales, and auctions.

In the manorial handicraft industry, the producer (the master craftsman) was also the seller. The industries that burgeoned in the new cities, however, were primarily export industries in which the producer was distant from the final buyer. Craftsmen sold their goods wholesale to merchants, who in turn transported and resold them. Another important difference was that the manorial craftsman was also generally a farmer. The new city craftsman gave up farming to devote himself to his craft, with which he obtained a monetary income that could be used to satisfy other individual needs.

The Putting-Out System and the Birth of Capitalist Industry

As trade and commerce thrived and expanded, the need for more manufactured goods and greater reliability of supply led to increasing control of the productive process by the merchant-capitalist. By the sixteenth century, the handicraft type of industry, in which the craftsman owned the workshop, tools, and raw materials and functioned as an independent, small-scale entrepreneur, had been largely replaced in the exporting industries by the putting-out system. In the earliest period of the putting-out system, the merchant-capitalist would furnish an independent craftsman with raw materials and pay him a fee to work the materials into finished products. In this way the capitalist owned the product throughout all stages of production, although the work was done in independent workshops. In the later period of the putting-out system, the merchant-capitalist owned the tools and machinery and often the building in which the production took place. The merchant-capitalist hired workers to use these tools, furnished them with the raw materials, and took the finished products.

The worker no longer sold a finished product to the merchant. Rather, the worker sold only his or her labor power. The textile industries were among the first in which the putting-out system developed. Weavers, spinners, fullers, and dyers found themselves in a situation where their employment, and hence their ability to support themselves and their families, depended on the merchant-capitalists, who had to sell what the workers produced at a price that was high enough to pay wages and other costs and still make a profit.

Capitalist control was, then, extended into the process of production. At the same time, a labor force was created that owned little or no capital and had nothing to sell but its labor power. These two features mark the appearance of the economic system of capitalism. Some writers and historians have defined capitalism as existing when trade, commerce, and the commercial spirit expanded and became more important in Europe. Trade and commerce, however, had existed throughout the feudal era. Yet, as long as feudal tradition remained the organizing principle in production, trade and commerce were really outside the social and economic system. The market and the search for monetary profits replaced custom and tradition in determining who would perform what task, how the task would be performed, and whether a given worker could find work to support him or herself. When this occurred, the capitalist system was created.[6]

Capitalism became dominant only when the relationship that existed between capitalists and workers in the sixteenth-century export industries was extended to most of the other industries in the economy. For such a system to evolve, the economic self-sufficiency of the feudal manor had to be broken down and manorial customs and traditions undermined or destroyed. Agriculture had to become a capitalist venture in which workers would sell their labor power to capitalists, and capitalists would buy labor only if they expected to make a profit in the process.

A capitalist textile industry existed in Flanders in the thirteenth century. When for various reasons its prosperity began to decline, the wealth and poverty it had created led to a long series of violent class wars, starting around 1280, that almost completely destroyed the industry. In the fourteenth century, a capitalist textile industry flourished in Florence. There, as in Flanders, adverse business conditions led to tensions between a poverty-stricken working class and their affluent capitalist employers. The results of these tensions were violent rebellions in 1379 and 1382. Failure to resolve these class antagonisms significantly worsened the precipitous decline in the Florentine textile industry, as it had earlier in Flanders.

In the fifteenth century, England dominated the world textile market. Its capitalist textile industry solved the problem of class conflict by ruralizing the industry. Whereas the earlier capitalist textile industries of Flanders and Florence had been centered in the densely populated cities, where the workers were thrown together and organized resistance was easy to initiate, the English fulling mills were scattered about the countryside. This meant that the workers were isolated from all but a small handful of other workers, and effective organized resistance did not develop.

The later system, however, in which wealthy owners of capital employed propertyless craftsmen, was usually a phenomenon of the city rather than of the countryside. From the beginning, these capitalist enterprises sought monopolistic positions from which to exploit the demand for their products. The rise of livery guilds, or associations of merchant-capitalist employers, created a host of barriers to protect these employers' positions. Different types of apprenticeships, with special privileges and exemptions for the sons of the wealthy, excessively high membership fees, and other barriers, prevented ambitious poorer craftsmen from competing with or entering the new capitalist class. Indeed, these barriers generally resulted in the transformation of poorer craftsmen and their sons into a new urban working class that lived exclusively by selling its labor power.

Decline of the Manorial System

Before a complete system of capitalism could emerge, however, the force of capitalist market relations had to invade the rural manor, the bastion of feudalism. This was accomplished as a result of the vast increase of population in the new trading cities. Large urban populations depended on the rural countryside for food and much of the raw materials for export industries. These needs fostered a rural-urban specialization and a large flow of trade between the rural manor and the city. The lords of the manors began to depend on the cities for manufactured goods and increasingly came to desire luxury goods that merchants could sell them.

 The peasants on the manor also found that they could exchange surpluses for money at the local grain markets; the money could be used to purchase commutation of their labor services.[7] Commutation often resulted in the peasant very nearly becoming an independent small businessman. The peasant might rent the land from the lord, sell the produce to cover the rent, and retain the remaining revenues. This system gave peasants a higher incentive to produce, and, thereby, increased their surplus marketings, which led to more commutations, more subsequent marketings, and so forth. The cumulative effect was a very gradual breaking down of the traditional ties of the manor, substituting the market and the search for profits as the organizing principle of production. By the middle of the fourteenth century, money rents exceeded the value of labor services in many parts of Europe.

Another force that brought the market into the countryside, which was closely related to commutation, was the alienation of the lords' demesnes. The lords who needed cash to exchange for manufactured goods and luxuries began to rent their own lands to peasant farmers rather than having them farmed directly with labor service obligations. This process led increasingly to a situation in which the lord of the manor was simply a landlord in the modern sense of that term. In fact, he very often became an absentee landlord, as many lords chose to move to the cities or were away fighting battles.

The breakup of the manorial system, however, stemmed more directly from a series of catastrophies in the late fourteenth and fifteenth centuries. The Hundred Years' War between France and England (1337–1453) created general disorder and unrest in those countries. The Black Death was even more devastating. On the eve of the plague of 1348–49, England's population stood at 4 million. By the early fifteenth century, after the effects of the wars and the plague, England had a scant 2.5 million population. This was fairly typical of trends in other European countries. The depopulation led to a desperate labor shortage, and wages for all types of labor rose abruptly. Land, now relatively plentiful, began to rent for less.

These facts led the feudal nobility to attempt to revoke the commutations they had granted and to reestablish the labor service obligations of the serfs and peasants (peasants were former serfs who had attained some degree of independence and freedom from feudal restrictions). They found, however, that the clock could not be turned back. The market had been extended into the countryside, and with it had come greater freedom, independence, and prosperity for the peasants. They bitterly resisted efforts to reinstate the old obligations, and their resistance did not go unchallenged.

The result was the famous peasant revolts that broke out over all of Europe from the late fourteenth through the early sixteenth centuries. These rebellions were extreme in their cruelty and ferocity. A contemporary French writer described a band of peasants who killed a "knight and putting him on a broach, roasted him over a fire in the sight of his wife and children. Ten or twelve of them ravished the wife and then forced her to eat of her husband's flesh. Then they killed her and her children. Wherever these ungracious people went they destroyed good houses and strong castles."[8] Rebellious peasants were ultimately slaughtered with equal or greater cruelty and ferocity by the nobility.

England experienced a series of such revolts in the late fourteenth and fifteenth centuries. But the revolts that occurred in Germany in the early sixteenth century were probably the bloodiest of all. The peasant rebellion in 1524–25 was crushed by the Imperial troops of the Holy Roman emperor, who slaughtered peasants by the tens of thousands. Over 100,000 persons probably were killed in Germany alone.

These revolts are mentioned here to illustrate the fact that fundamental changes in the economic and political structure of a social system are often achieved only after traumatic and violent social conflict. Any economic system generates a class or classes whose privileges depend on the continuation of that system. Quite naturally, these classes go to great lengths to resist change and to protect their positions. The feudal nobility fought a savage rearguard action against the emerging capitalist market system, but the forces of change ultimately swept them aside. Although the important changes were brought about by aspiring merchants and minor noblemen, the peasants were the pathetic victims of the consequent social upheavals. Ironically, they were usually struggling to protect the status quo.

Creation of the Working Class

The early sixteenth century is a watershed in European history. It marks the vague dividing line between the old, decaying feudal order and the rising capitalist system. After 1500, important social and economic changes began to occur with increasing frequency, each reinforcing the other and all together ushering in the system of capitalism. Among the most important of these changes were those creating a working class that was systematically stripped of any control over the production process and forced into a situation in which the sale of its labor power was its only means of survival. The population of western Europe, which had been relatively stagnant for a century and a half, increased by nearly one-third in the sixteenth century and stood at about 70 million in 1600.

The increase in population was accompanied by the enclosure movement, which had begun in England as early as the thirteenth century. The feudal nobility, in ever increasing need of cash, fenced off, or enclosed, lands that had formerly been used for communal grazing, using the lands to graze sheep to satisfy the booming English wool and textile industries' demand for wool. The sheep brought good prices, and a minimal amount of labor was needed to herd them.

The enclosure movement reached its peak in the late fifteenth and sixteenth centuries, when in some areas as many as three-fourths to nine-tenths of the tenants were forced out of the countryside and into the cities to try to support themselves. Subsequent waves of enclosure continued until well into the nineteenth century. The enclosures and the increasing population further destroyed the remaining feudal ties, creating a large new labor force—a labor force without land, without any tools or instruments of production, and with only labor power to sell. This migration to the cities meant more labor for the capitalist industries, more men for the armies and navies, more men to colonize new lands, and more potential consumers, or buyers, of products.

But the enclosures and the increase in population were by no means the sole source of the new working class. Innumerable peasants, yeomen, and minor nobility were bankrupted by exorbitant increases in monetary rents. Mounting debts that could not be repaid ruined countless others. In the cities and towns the guilds came to be more and more concerned with the income levels of their members. It was obvious to the craftsmen and merchants in the guilds that steps taken to minimize their number would serve to monopolize their crafts and to increase their incomes. Increasing numbers of urban producers came to be denied any means of independent production as the guilds became more exclusive. In this way, a considerable portion of the new working class was created within the towns and cities.

Many of the farmers and craftsmen who were thus uprooted and denied access to their former means of production became vagabonds and beggars. Even more attempted to secure a subsistence by squatting on marginal, unused lands where they could grow crops for their own use. Harshly repressive laws were passed against such farming and against being an unemployed vagabond.[9] Therefore, when force, fraud, and starvation were insufficient to create the new working class, criminal statutes and government repression were used.

Other Forces in the Transition to Capitalism

Other sources of change were also instrumental in the transition to capitalism. Among these was the intellectual awakening of the sixteenth century, which fostered scientific progress that was promptly put to practical use in navigation. The telescope and the compass, which enabled men to navigate much more accurately for much greater distances, ushered in the "Age of Exploration." Within a short period, Europeans had charted sea routes to India, Africa, and the Americas. These discoveries had a twofold importance: first, they resulted in a rapid and large flow of precious metals into Europe; and second, they ushered in a period of colonization.

Between 1300 and 1500, European gold and silver production had stagnated. The rapidly expanding capitalist trade and the extension of the market system into city and countryside had led to an acute shortage of money. Because money consisted primarily of gold and silver coin, the need for these metals was critical. Beginning around 1450, this situation was alleviated somewhat when the Portuguese began extracting metals from the African Gold Coast, but the general shortage continued until the middle of the sixteenth century. After that date there occurred such a large inflow of gold and silver from the Americas that Europe experienced the most rapid and long-lasting inflation in history.

During the sixteenth century, prices rose in Europe between 150 and 400 percent, depending on the country or region chosen. Prices of manufactured goods rose much more rapidly than either rents or wages. In fact, the disparity between prices and wages continued until late in the seventeenth century. This meant that both the landlord class (or feudal nobility) and the working class suffered, because their incomes rose less rapidly than their expenses. The capitalist class was the great beneficiary of the price revolution. It received larger and larger profits as it paid lower real wages and bought materials that appreciated greatly as it held the materials as inventories.

These larger profits were accumulated as capital. Capital refers to the materials that are necessary for production, trade, and commerce and consists of all tools, equipment, factories, raw materials, goods in process, means of transporting goods, and money. There are physical means of production in every kind of economic system, but they can become capital only in a social context in which the social relationships exist that are necessary for commodity production and private ownership. Thus, capital refers to more than simply physical objects; it refers to a complex set of social relations as well. In our earlier discussion, we saw that one of the defining features of the capitalist system is the existence of a class of capitalists who own the capital stock. It is by virtue of their ownership of this capital that they derive their profits. These profits are then plowed back or used to augment the capital stock. The further accumulation of capital leads to more profits, which leads to more accumulation, and the system continues in an upward spiral.

The term *capitalism* describes this system of profit seeking and accumulation very well. Ownership of capital is the source of profits and hence the source of further accumulation of capital. But this chicken-egg process had to have a beginning. The substantial initial accumulation, or primitive accumulation, of capital took place in the period under consideration. The four most important sources of the initial accumulation of capital were (1) the rapidly growing volume of trade and commerce, (2) the putting-out system of industry, (3) the enclosure movement, and (4) the great price inflation. There were several other sources of initial accumulations, some of which were somewhat less respectable and often forgotten—for example, colonial plunder, piracy, and the slave trade.

During the sixteenth and seventeenth centuries, the putting-out system was extended until it was common in most types of manufacturing. Although this was not yet the modern type of factory production, the system's increased degree of specialization led to significant increases in productivity. Technical improvements in shipbuilding and navigation also lowered transportation costs. Thus, during this period, capitalist production and trade and commerce thrived and grew very rapidly. The new capitalist class (or middle class or bourgeoisie) slowly but inexorably replaced the nobility as the class that dominated the economic and social system.

The emergence of the new nation-states signaled the beginning of the transition to a new dominant class. The new monarchs usually drew on the bourgeois capitalist class for support in their efforts to defeat feudal rivals and unify the state under one central power. This unification freed the merchants from the feudal maze of different rules, regulations, laws, weights and measures, and moneys; consolidated many markets; and provided military protection for commercial ventures. In return, the monarch relied on the capitalists for much needed sources of revenues.

Although England was nominally unified much earlier, it was not until Henry VII (1485–1509) founded the line of Tudor monarchs that England was unified in fact. Henry VIII (1509–1547) and Elizabeth I (1558–1603) were able to complete the work of nation building only because they had the support of Parliament, which represented the middle classes of the shires and boroughs. In the revolutions of 1648 and 1688, the supremacy of Parliament, or of the bourgeois middle classes, was finally established.

The other important early capitalist nation-states also came into existence during this period. In France, Louis XI (1461–1483) was the first king to unify France effectively since the time of Charlemagne. The marriage in 1469 of Ferdinand of Aragon and Isabella of Castile, and their subsequent defeat of the Moors, led to the unification of Spain. The Dutch republic, the fourth of the important early nation-states, did not win its independence until 1690, when it finally expelled its Spanish oppressors.

By the late sixteenth and early seventeenth centuries, most of the large cities in England, France, Spain, and the Low Countries (Belgium and Holland) had been transformed into thriving capitalist economies dominated by the merchant-capitalists, who controlled not only commerce but also much of the manufacturing. In the modern nation-states, coalitions of monarchs and capitalists had wrested effective power from the feudal nobility in many important areas, especially those related to production and commerce. This period of early capitalism is generally referred to as mercantilism.

Mercantilism

The earliest phase of mercantilism, usually called bullionism, originated in the period during which Europe was experiencing an acute shortage of gold and silver bullion, and, hence, did not have enough money to service the rapidly expanding volume of trade. Bullionist policies were designed to attract a flow of gold and silver into a country and to keep them there by prohibiting their export. These restrictions lasted from the late Middle Ages into the sixteenth and seventeenth centuries.

Spain, the country into which most of the gold from the Americas flowed, applied bullionist restrictions over the longest period and imposed the most severe penalty for the export of gold and silver: death. Yet the needs of trade were so pressing, and such large profits could be made by importing foreign commodities, that even in Spain merchant-capitalists succeeded in bribing corrupt officials or in smuggling large quantities of bullion out of the country. Spanish bullion rapidly found its way all over Europe and was to a large extent responsible for the long period of inflation described earlier. Spain did not legalize the export of gold and silver until long after the bullionist restrictions had been removed in England and Holland in the middle of the sixteenth century.

After the bullionist period, the mercantilists' desire to maximize the gold and silver within a country took the form of attempts by the government to create a favorable balance of trade, that is, to have more money coming into a country than was flowing out. Thus, exports of goods as well as things such as shipping and insuring (when performed by countrymen and paid for by foreigners) were encouraged, and imports of goods and shipping and insurance charges paid to foreigners were discouraged.

One of the most important types of policies designed to increase the value of exports and decrease that of imports was the creation of trade monopolies. A country like England could buy most cheaply (e.g., from a backward area) if only one English merchant bargained with the foreigners involved rather than having several competing English merchants bidding the price up in an effort to capture the business. Similarly, English merchants could sell their goods to foreigners for much higher prices if there was only one seller rather than several sellers bidding the price down to attract each other's customers.

The English government could prohibit English merchants from competing in an area where such a monopoly had been established. It was much more difficult, however, to keep out French, Dutch, or Spanish merchants. Various governments attempted to exclude such rival foreign merchants by establishing colonial empires that could be controlled by the mother country to ensure a monopoly of trade. Colonial possessions could thereby furnish cheap raw materials to the mother country and purchase expensive manufactured goods in return.

In addition to the creation of monopolies, all the western European countries (with the exception of Holland) applied extensive regulations to the businesses of exporting and importing. These regulations were probably most comprehensive in England, where exporters who found it difficult to compete with foreigners were given tax refunds, or, if that was not enough, subsidized. Export duties were placed on a long list of raw materials to keep them within England. Thus, the price that English merchant-manufacturers would have to pay for these raw materials would be minimized. Sometimes, when these items were in short supply for British manufacturers, the state would completely prohibit their export. The English textile industry received this type of protection. In the early eighteenth century it accounted for about half of England's exports. The English prohibited the export of most raw materials and semi-finished products, such as sheep, wool, yarn, and worsted, which were used by the textile industry.

Measures aimed at discouraging imports were also widespread. The importation of some commodities was prohibited, and other commodities had such high duties that they were nearly eliminated from trade. Special emphasis was placed on protecting England's principal export industries from foreign competitors attempting to cut into the export industries' domestic markets.

Of course, these restrictions profited some capitalists and harmed others. As would be expected, coalitions of special interest groups were always working to maintain the restrictions or to extend them into different areas in different ways. Attempts such as the English Navigation Acts of 1651 and 1660 were made to promote the use of British ships (British-made and British-manned) in both import and export trade. All these regulations of foreign trade and shipping were designed to augment the flow of money into the country while decreasing the outflow. Needless to say, many of the measures also stemmed from appeals and pressures by special interest groups.

In addition to these restrictions on foreign trade, there was a maze of restrictions and regulations aimed at controlling domestic production. Besides the tax exemptions, subsidies, and other privileges used to encourage larger output by industries that were important exporters, the state also engaged in extensive regulation of production methods and of the quality of produced goods. In France, the regime of Louis XIV codified, centralized, and extended the older decentralized guild controls. Specific techniques of production were made mandatory, and extensive quality control measures were enacted, with inspectors appointed in Paris charged with enforcing these laws at the local level. Jean-Baptiste Colbert, Louis XIV's famous minister and economic adviser, was responsible for the establishment of extensive and minute regulations. In the textile industry, for example, the width of a piece of cloth and the precise number of threads contained within it were rigidly specified by the government.

In England, the Statute of Artificers (1563) effectively transferred to the state the functions of the old craft guilds. It led to central control over the training of industrial workers, over conditions of employment, and over allocation of the labor force to different types of occupations. Regulations of wages, of the quality of many goods, and of other details of domestic production were also tried in England during this period.

It is not clear exactly how much of mercantilist thinking was honestly motivated by the desire to increase the power of the state and how much was merely thinly disguised efforts to promote the special interests of capitalists. The distinction is rather unimportant because most mercantilists believed that the best way to promote the interests of the state was to promote policies that would increase the profits of the merchant-capitalists. What is of much more interest are the mercantilist views on a question that will recur throughout this book: What are the nature and origins of profit? It is their thoughts on this question to which we turn in the next chapter.

Notes to Chapter 1

1. For a more complete discussion of the medieval economic and social system, see J.H. Chapman and Eileen E. Powers, eds., *The Agrarian Life of the Middle Ages,* 2d ed., *The Cambridge Economic History of Europe*, vol. 1 (London: Cambridge University Press, 1966).

2. Lynn White, Jr., *Medieval Technology and Social Change* (Oxford: Clarendon Press, 1962), pp. 71–72.

3. Harry A. Miskimin, *The Economy of Early Renaissance Europe, 1300–1460* (Englewood Cliffs, NJ: Prentice-Hall, 1969), p. 20.

4. For a concrete historical example of the growing conflicts within the feudal ruling class

and the resultant economic and social deterioration of feudalism prior to the growth of commerce, see Jane K. Beitscher and E.K. Hunt, "Insights into the Dissolution of the Feudal Mode of Production," *Science and Society,* 40, no. 1 (1976): 57–71.

5. For a more complete discussion of the rise of trade and commerce, see Dudley Dillard, *Economic Development of the North Atlantic Community* (Englewood Cliffs, NJ: Prentice-Hall, 1967), pp. 3–178.

6. See Maurice H. Dobb, *Studies in the Development of Capitalism* (London: Routledge and Kegan Paul, 1946), particularly ch. 4.

7. Commutation involved the substitution of money rents for the labor service required of the serf.

8. N.S.B. Gras, *A History of Agriculture in Europe and America* (New York: Appleton, 1940), p. 108.

9. See Dobb, *Studies in the Development of Capitalism,* ch. 6.

Chapter 2

Economic Ideas Before Adam Smith

In the early mercantilist period, most production was carried on by workers who still owned and controlled their own means of production. Capitalists were primarily merchants, and their capital consisted mostly of money and inventories of goods to be sold. It was only natural, therefore, that mercantilist writers looked to exchange, or buying and selling, as the source of profits. These profits were, of course, exchanged for commodities that constituted a portion of the surplus. But the merchants' share of the surplus was not, in this early period, acquired through control of the production process. The feudal lords still generally controlled production and expropriated the surplus. The result of exchange between the merchants and the lords was a sharing of the surplus by the two groups. Therefore, from the merchants' points of view, it was exchange and not production that generated their profits.

Merchant capital consists of ownership of the means of buying, transporting, and selling, while industrial capital consists of ownership of the means necessary for producing. During this period, industrial capital was still rather insignificant and inconspicuous, while merchant capital was widespread and significant. It was not, therefore, mental or theoretical inadequacy that caused mercantilist writers to look to buying and selling rather than production as the source of profits. Their ideas reflected the economic realities of the era in which they were writing.

Early Mercantilist Writing on Value and Profits

Profit accrues to merchant capital when the price at which the merchant sells a commodity is sufficiently high to cover the price the merchant pays for the commodity, plus all expenses for handling, storing, transporting, and selling the commodity, plus a surplus over and above these costs. This surplus is the merchant's profit. Therefore, an understanding of the determinants of the prices at which commodities were bought and sold was central to an understanding of the merchant's profits.

Earlier medieval thinkers had asserted that the price of a commodity had to be sufficient to cover a craftsman's direct costs of production and to yield the craftsman a return on the labor expended sufficient to maintain the craftsman in the style of life traditionally deemed appropriate. In other words, prices were determined by the costs of production, including an imputed, appropriate remuneration for the labor of the craftsmen.[1]

The early mercantilists generally abandoned this cost-of-production approach to the understanding of prices and focused on the point of sale to analyze exchange values. One scholar of mercantilist ideas has concluded that, despite a wide range of differences on specific issues, three important notions run through most early mercantilist writings on value theory. First, the "value" or "natural value" of commodities was simply their actual market price. Second, the forces of supply and demand determined market value. Third, mercantilist writers frequently discussed "intrinsic value" or use value as the most important factor determining demand, and, hence, as an important casual determinant of market value.[2]

Nicholas Barbon, one of the most important of the mercantilist writers, summed up these three points in his pamphlet, *A Discourse on Trade*:

1. The Price of Wares is the present Value. . . . The Market is the best Judge of value; for by the Concourse of Buyers and Sellers, the Quantity of Wares, and the Occasion for them are Best Known: Things are just worth so much, as they can be sold for, according to the Old Rule, *Valet Quantum Vendi Potest.*
2. The Price of Wares is the present Value, and ariseth by Computing the occasions or use for them, with the Quantity to serve that Occasion. . . . It is impossible for the Merchant when he has Bought his Goods, to know what he shall Sell them for: The Value of them, depends upon the Difference Betwixt the Occasion and the Quantity; tho' that be the Chiefest of the Merchants Care to observe, yet it Depends upon so many Circumstances, that it's impossible to know it. Therefore if the plenty of the Goods, has brought down the Price, the Merchant layeth them up, til the Quantity is consumed, and the Price riseth.
3. The Value of all Wares arise from their Use; Things of no Use, have no Value, as the *English* Phrase is, *They are good for nothing.* The Use of Things, are to supply the Wants and Necessities of Man: There are Two General Wants that Mankind is born with; the Wants of the Body, and the Wants of the Mind; To supply these two Necessities, all things under the Sun become useful, and therefore have a Value. . . . The Value of all Wares, arriveth from their Use; and the Dearness and Cheapness of them, from their Plenty and Scarcity.[3]

Barbon's pamphlet was written at a time during which economic attitudes were beginning to undergo rapid change. The passages just quoted reflect the attitudes of the earlier mercantilist who saw profits as originating primarily in the act of exchange. Their profits came largely from two sources. First, the inflation of the sixteenth and seventeenth centuries (discussed in the previous chapter) had created a situation in which there was generally a substantial appreciation of the value of the inventories held. Between the time at which the merchants purchased commodities and the time at which merchants sold them, the increases in the prices of these commodities resulted in windfall profits. Second, and more important, the differing conditions under which production took place in various regions of a country or various parts of the world, combined with the fact that there was very little mobility of resources, technology, and labor between these regions, resulted in substantially different relative prices of commodities in the various regions or countries. Merchants would buy a commodity in a region or country in which it was relatively inexpensive and sell it in a region or country in which it was relatively expensive.

Under these conditions, it is not surprising that merchants should have conceived of the value of a commodity in terms of its market price rather than its conditions of production. Moreover, it was only natural for them to see differences in market prices as resulting from differences in the willingness or desire to purchase particular commodities. Supply entered the picture only to the extent that the merchants saw that with a given level of desire to purchase a commodity, the price of a commodity would be high if this commodity was in short supply and low if its supply was abundant. It was for this reason that the large merchant companies sought state-created and enforced monopolies.

Competition among merchants inevitably led to a reduction in relative price differences and hence to a reduction of their profits. If a particular commodity commanded a very high price in a particular region, then the merchant who bought this commodity at a low price and transported it to this region would make a larger profit. This profit, however, would inevitably act as a lure inducing other merchants to sell the same commodity in the same region. But more merchants would mean a larger supply, which would lead to a lower price and lower profits. Thus, the great merchant companies went to great lengths to exclude competitors and to maintain their monopolistic privileges.

It appeared to the early mercantilists that control over the conditions affecting the supply of commodities was the principal means by which high profits could be attained and perpetuated. But the early mercantilist period had not yet experienced the change in social attitudes that was later to condone and justify the ceaseless quest for profits simply for the sake of profits. Governments' motivations and rationalizations for their policies of promoting merchant profits were very different from those motivations and rationalizations that were to be characteristic of capitalist governments in the nineteenth and twentieth centuries.

In the early mercantilist period, there was an ideological continuity between the intellectual defenses of mercantilist policies and the earlier ideologies that supported the medieval economic order. The latter relied on a Christian paternalist ethic that justified extreme inequalities of wealth on the assumption that God had selected the wealthy to be the benevolent stewards of the material welfare of the masses.[4] The Catholic Church had been the institution through which this paternalism was effectuated. As capitalism developed, the church grew weaker and the governments of the emerging nation-states grew stronger. In the early mercantilist period, economic writers increasingly came to substitute the state for the medieval church as the institution that should oversee the public welfare.

During the reign of Henry VIII, England broke with Roman Catholicism. This event was significant because it marked the final secularization (in England at least) of the functions of the medieval church. Under Henry, "the state in the form of God's monarchy assumed the role and the functions of the old universal church. What Henry had done in his own blunt way was to sanctify the processes of this world."[5] During his reign as well as the reigns of Elizabeth I, James I, and Charles I (1558–1649), there was widespread social unrest. The cause of this unrest was poverty; the cause of much of this poverty was unemployment; and the cause of much of this unemployment was the enclosure movement.

Another factor, however, was the decline in the export of woolens in the second half of the sixteenth century, which created massive unemployment in England's most important manufacturing industry. There were also frequent commercial crises similar to, but without the regularity of, the depression phase of later business cycles. In addition to these factors, seasonal unemployment put many workers out of work for as many as four months of the year.

The people could no longer look to the Catholic Church for relief from widespread unemployment and poverty. Destruction of the power of the church had eliminated the organized system of charity, and the state attempted to assume responsibility for the general welfare of society. In order to do this, "England's leaders undertook a general, coordinated program to reorganize and rationalize . . . industry by establishing specifications of standards of production and marketing."[6] All these measures were designed to stimulate English trade and alleviate the unemployment problem.

In fact, it appears that the desire to achieve full employment is the unifying theme of most policy measures advocated by mercantilist writers. The mercantilists preferred measures designed to stimulate foreign rather than domestic trade "because they believe it contributed more to employment, to the nation's wealth and to national power. The writers after 1600 stressed the inflationary effect of an excess of exports over imports and the consequent increase in employment which inflation produced."[7]

Among the other measures taken to encourage industry during this period was the issuance of patents of monopoly. The first important patent was granted in 1561, during the reign of Elizabeth I. Monopoly rights were given in order to encourage inventions and to establish new industries. These rights were severely abused, as might be expected. Moreover, they led to a complex system of special privileges and patronage and a host of other evils, which outraged most mercantilist writers every bit as much as similar abuses outraged late-nineteenth-century American reformers. The evils of monopoly led to the Statute of Monopolies of 1624, which outlawed all monopolies except those that involved genuine inventions or that would be instrumental in promoting a favorable balance of payments. Of course, these loopholes were large, and abuses continued almost unchecked.

The Statute of Artificers (1563) specified conditions of employment and length of apprenticeships, provided for periodic wage assessments, and established maximum rates that could be paid to laborers. The statute is important because it illustrates the fact that the Crown's paternalistic ethic never led to any attempt to elevate the status of the laboring classes. Monarchs of this period felt obliged to protect the working classes, but, like their predecessors in the Middle Ages, believed those classes should be kept in their proper places. Maximum wage rates were designed to protect the capitalists, and, furthermore, the justices who set these maximums and enforced the statute generally belonged to the employing class themselves. It is probable that these maximums reduced the real wages of laborers because prices generally rose faster than wages during the succeeding years.

Poor laws passed in 1531 and 1536 attempted to deal with the problems of unemployment, poverty, and misery then widespread in England. The first sought to distinguish between "deserving" and "undeserving" poor; only the deserving poor were allowed to beg. The second decreed that each individual parish throughout England was responsible for its poor and that the parish should, through voluntary contributions, maintain a poor fund. This proved completely inadequate, and the pauper problem grew increasingly severe.

Finally, in 1572, the state accepted the principle that the poor would have to be supported by tax funds and enacted a compulsory "poor rate." And in 1576, "houses of correction" for "incorrigible vagrants" were authorized and provisions made for the parish to purchase raw materials to be processed by the more tractable paupers and vagrants. Between that time and the close of the sixteenth century, several other poor-law statutes were passed.

The Poor Law of 1601 was the Tudor attempt to integrate these laws into one consistent framework. Its main provisions included formal recognition of the right of the poor to receive relief, imposition of compulsory poor rates at the parish level, and provision for differential treatment for various classes of the poor. The aged and the sick could receive help in their homes; pauper children who were too young to be apprenticed in a trade were to be boarded out; the deserving poor and unemployed were to be given work as provided for in the act of 1576; and incorrigible vagrants were to be sent to houses of correction and prisons.[8]

From the preceding discussion it is possible to conclude that the period of English mercantilism was characterized by acceptance, in the spirit of the Christian paternalist ethic, of the idea that "the state had an obligation to serve society by accepting and discharging the responsibility for the general welfare."[9] The various statutes passed during this period "were predicated upon the idea that poverty, instead of being a personal sin, was a function of the economic system."[10] These statutes acknowledged that those who were the victims of the deficiencies of the economic system should be cared for by those who benefited from it.

Later Mercantilist Writings and the Philosophy of Individualism

As capitalism developed, however, two economic developments increasingly rendered the mercantilist outlook unsatisfactory to the needs of the new system and most of the important capitalists of the time. First, despite the efforts of the great trading companies to maintain their monopolies, the spread of commerce and the growth of competition (especially within the nation-states themselves) continuously reduced the relative magnitude of price differences among different regions and nations. This correspondingly reduced the profits that could be made simply from taking advantage of these price differences.

The second change was closely related to the first: as potential profits from price differences alone were reduced, there occurred an integration of capitalist control over both the processes of production and commerce. This integration came from two sources. Initially, the merchants sought greater control over production by creating the putting-out system (as discussed in the previous chapter). Somewhat later, however, a new and ultimately much more revolutionary development occurred. As early as the sixteenth century, the craft guilds came to be relatively closed systems designed to protect the status and income of the guild masters by restricting the number of apprentices and journeymen who could become masters. Over time, in many of the guilds the masters increasingly came to be the organizers and controllers of the productive process rather than merely laborers working alongside the apprentices and journeymen. The masters came to be employers or capitalists, and the journeymen came to be simply hired workers with little or no prospects for becoming masters.

By the early seventeenth century, these producer-capitalists began moving into the arena of commerce. They soon constituted a major force in the economic life of England—a force that Dobb believes constituted "an important shift in the center of gravity in the English socioeconomic system."[11] The interests of this new segment of the capitalist class were, from the beginning, frequently opposed to the interests of the older merchant-capitalists.

These far-reaching economic changes led to two very important changes in economic ideas. First, there was a large segment of philosophers, economists, and other thinkers who rejected the older paternalist view of the state and state regulation and began to formulate a new philosophy of individualism. Second, there was a shift from the view that prices and profits were determined primarily by the forces of supply and demand and utility in particular, to the view that prices were determined by the conditions of production and that profits originated in the production process. Each of these two changes will be considered in turn.

By the late seventeenth century, an increasingly large number of capitalists, particularly those whose origins had been in the craft guilds, had come to be significantly inhibited in their quest for profits by the maze of mercantilist restrictions and regulations that had originally benefited the great trading companies; they sought relief from these constraints. They also disliked the mercantilist remnants of the older Christian paternalism that had condemned greed, acquisitive behavior, and the desire to accumulate wealth. The capitalist market economy, which was rapidly being extended into most significant areas of production and commerce, demanded self-seeking, acquisitive behavior to function successfully. In this context, new theories about human behavior began to emerge. Writers began to assert that selfish, egoistic motives were the primary if not the only ones that moved men to action.

This interpretation of man's behavior is expressed in the writings of many important thinkers of the period. Many philosophers and social theorists began to assert that every human act was related to self-preservation, and, hence, was egoistic in the most fundamental sense. The English nobleman Sir Robert Filmer was greatly alarmed by the large number of people who spoke of "the natural freedom of mankind, a new, plausible and dangerous opinion" with anarchistic implications.[12] Thomas Hobbes's *Leviathan*, published in 1651, trenchantly articulated a widely held opinion—that all human motives stem from a desire for whatever promotes the "vital motion" of the organism (man). Hobbes believed that all people's motives, even compassion, were merely so many disguised species of self-interest: "Grief for the calamity of another is pity, and ariseth from the imagination that the like calamity may befall himself; and therefore is called . . . *compassion*, and . . . fellow-feeling."[13]

Except for the few special interest groups that benefited from the extensive restrictions and regulations of commerce and manufacturing during this period, most capitalists felt constrained and inhibited by state regulations in their quest for profits. The individualist and egoistic doctrines were eagerly embraced by such men and began to dominate economic thinking, even among the mercantilists. One careful history asserts that "most of the mercantilist . . . policy assumed that self-interest governs individual conduct."[14]

The majority of mercantilist writers were either capitalists or privileged employees of capitalists, and, thus, it was quite natural for them to perceive the motives of the capitalists as universal. From the capitalists' views of the nature of humanity and their need to be free from the extensive economic restrictions grew the philosophy of individualism that provided the basis of classical liberalism. Against the well-ordered, paternalist view that Europe had inherited from the feudal society, they asserted "the view that the human person ought to be independent, self-directing, autonomous, free—ought to be, that is, an individual, a unit distinguished from the social mass rather than submerged in it."[15]

Protestantism and the Individualist Ethic

One of the most important examples of this individualist and middle-class philosophy was the Protestant theology that emerged from the Reformation. The new middle-class capitalists wanted to be free not only from economic restrictions that encumbered manufacturing and commerce, but also from the moral opprobrium that the Catholic Church had heaped on their motives and activities. Protestantism not only freed them from religious condemnation, but eventually made virtues of the selfish, egoistic, and acquisitive motives the medieval church had so despised.[16]

The principal originators of the Protestant movement were quite close to the Catholic position on questions like usury and the just price. On most social issues they were deeply conservative. During the German peasant revolt of 1524, Luther wrote a virulent pamphlet, *Against the Murdering Hordes of Peasants*, in which he said princes should "knock down, strangle and stab. . . . Such wonderful times are these that a prince can merit heaven better with bloodshed than another with prayer." Luther's advice contributed to the general atmosphere in which the slaughter of over 100,000 peasants was carried out with an air of religious righteousness.

Yet, despite the conservatism of the founders of Protestantism, this religious outlook contributed to the growing influence of the new individualist philosophy. The basic tenet of Protestantism, which laid the groundwork for religious attitudes that were to sanction middle-class business practices, was the doctrine that men were justified by faith rather than by works. The Catholic Church had taught that men were justified by *works*, which generally meant ceremonies and rituals. In the Catholic view no man could be justified on his own merit alone. "Justification by works . . . did not mean that an individual could save himself: it meant that he could be saved through the Church. Hence the power of the clergy. Compulsory confession, the imposition of penance on the whole population . . . together with the possibility of withholding absolution, gave the priests a terrifying power."[17] These powers also created a situation in which the medieval doctrines of the Catholic Church were not easily abandoned and in which the individual was still subordinated to society (as represented by the church).

The Protestant doctrine of justification by faith asserted that motives were more important than specific acts or rituals. Faith was "nothing else but the truth of the heart."[18] Each man had to search himself to discover if his acts stemmed from a pure heart and faith in God; each man had to judge for himself. This individualist reliance on each person's private conscience appealed strongly to the new middle-class artisans and small merchants:

> When the businessman of sixteenth and seventeenth century Geneva, Amsterdam or London looked into his inmost heart, he found that God had planted there a deep respect for the principle of private property. . . . Such men felt quite genuinely and strongly that their economic practices, though they might conflict with the tradi-

tional law of the old church, were not offensive to God. On the contrary: they glorified God.[19]

It was through this insistence on the individual's own interpretation of God's will that the "Puritans tried to spiritualize [the new] economic processes" and eventually came to believe that "God instituted the market and exchange."[20] However, it was only a matter of time before the Protestants expounded dogma that they expected everyone to accept. But the new dogma was radically different from medieval doctrines. The new doctrines stressed the necessity of doing well at one's earthly calling as the best way to please God, and emphasized diligence and hard work.

The older Christian distrust of riches was translated into a condemnation of extravagance and needless dissipation of wealth. Thus, the Protestant ethic stressed the importance of asceticism and abstemious frugality. A theologian who has studied the connection between religion and capitalism sums up the relationship in this way:

> The religious value set upon constant, systematic, efficient work in one's calling as the readiest means of securing the certainty of salvation and of glorifying God became a most powerful agency in economic expansion. The rigid limitations of consumption on the one hand and the methodical intensification of production on the other could have but one result—the accumulation of capital.[21]

Thus, although neither Calvin nor Luther was a spokesman for the new middle-class capitalist, within the context of the new religious individualism, the capitalists found a religion in which, over time, "profits . . . [came to be] looked upon as willed by God, as a mark of his favor and a proof of success in one's calling."[22]

Economic Policies of Individualism

Throughout the mercantilist period, this new individualism led to innumerable protests against the subordination of economic affairs to the will of the state. From the middle of the seventeenth century, almost all mercantilist writers condemned state-granted monopolies and other forms of protection and favoritism in the internal economy (as opposed to international commerce). Many believed that in a competitive market that pitted buyer against buyer, seller against seller, and buyer against seller, society would benefit most greatly if the price was left free to fluctuate and find its proper (market-equilibrating) level. One of the earliest mercantilist writers of importance, John Hales, argued that agricultural productivity could best be improved if husbandman were allowed to

> have more profit by it than they have, and liberty to sell it at all times, and to all places, freely as men may do their other things. But then no doubt, the price of corn would rise, specially at the first more than at length; yet that price would evoke

every man to set plough in the ground, to husband waste grounds, yes to turn the lands which be enclosed from pasture to arable land; for every man will gladder follow that wherein they see the more profit and gains, and thereby must need ensue both plenty of corn, and also much treasure should be brought into this realm by occasion thereof; and besides that plenty of other victuals increased among us.[23]

This belief—that restrictions on production and trade within a nation were harmful to the interests of everyone concerned—became increasingly widespread in the late seventeenth and early eighteenth centuries. Numerous statements of this view can be found in the works of such writers as Malynes, Petty, North, Law, and Child.[24] Of these men, perhaps Sir Dudley North (1641–1691) was the earliest clear spokesman for the individualist ethic that was to become the basis for classical liberalism. North believed that all men were motivated primarily by self-interest and should be left alone to compete in a free market if the public welfare was to be maximized. He argued that whenever merchants or capitalists advocated special laws to regulate production or commerce, "they usually esteem the immediate interest of their own to be the common Measure of Good and Evil. And there are many, who to gain a little in their own Trades, care not how much others suffer; and each man strives that all others may be forced in their dealings to act subserviently for his Profit, but under the cover of the Publick.[25] The public welfare would best be served, North believed, if most of the restrictive laws that bestowed special privileges were entirely removed.

In 1714, Bernard Mandeville published *The Fable of the Bees: or Private Vices, Publick Benefits*, in which he put forth the seemingly strange paradox that the vices most despised in the older moral code, if practiced by all, would result in the greatest public good. Selfishness, greed, and acquisitive behavior, he maintained, all tended to contribute to industriousness and a thriving economy. The answer to the paradox was, of course, that what had been vices in the eyes of the medieval moralists were the very motive forces that propelled the new capitalist system. And in the view of the new religious, moral, and economic philosophies of the capitalist period, these motives were no longer vices.

Many capitalists had struggled throughout the mercantilist period to free themselves from all restrictions in their quest for profits. These restrictions—from which only a relatively small number of the older, established, monopolistic merchant companies benefited—had resulted from the paternalist laws that were the remnants of the feudal version of the Christian paternalist ethic. Such an ethic simply was not compatible with the new economic system that functioned on the basis of strict contractual obligations between people rather than on traditional personal ties. Innumerable new merchants and capitalists sought to undermine the privileged positions of the older merchant monopolies and to create a sociopolitical system more conducive to free, uninhibited profit making. Merchants and capitalists who invested large sums in market ventures could not depend on the forces of custom to protect their investments. Nor could they effectively seek profits within the maze of government restrictions characteristic of the early mercantilist period.

Profit seeking could be effective only in a society based on the protection of property rights and the enforcement of impersonal contractual commitments between individuals. Within such an institutional framework, capitalists had to be allowed to pursue their quest for profits freely. The new ideology that was firmly taking root in the seventeenth and eighteenth centuries justified these motives and relationships between individuals. At the same time, an equally important change was taking place in the ways in which economic thinkers explained prices and the nature and origins of profits.

Beginnings of the Classical Theory of Prices and Profits

With the integration of production and commerce and the increasing difficulty of making profits by simply exploiting price differences came the beginnings of a new approach to understanding prices and profits. A leading scholar of this period has written: "In the late seventeenth century, particularly in Britain, the older producers' cost approach to value begins to show distinct signs of revival. More and more emphasis gradually comes to be laid on production costs, particularly in manufacture."[26]

With the creation of a "free" labor force—that is, a substantial number of producers denied any control over the necessary means for production and forced to sell their labor power in order to survive—it gradually became clear that control of these producers was the key to profit making. Typical of this view was the statement by Daniel Defoe in his *A General History of Trade* (1713) that "it is the labor and industry of the people that alone brings wealth and makes . . . trade profitable to the nation."[27] Another of the many statements of this view is found in William Petyt's *Britannia Language* (1680): "Sufficient stores of treasure cannot otherwise be got but by the industry of the people. . . . People are, therefore, the chiefest, most fundamental and precious commodity, out of which may be derived all sorts of manufacture, navigation, riches, conquests and solid dominion."[28]

Capitalist industry began to effect substantial increases in the productivity of labor by furthering the division of labor, in which different laborers specialized in only one or a few tasks; the economic thinkers of the early eighteenth century began to see two separate and important principles at work in this increased productivity. First, they saw that natural resources became commodities with exchange value only after labor had transformed them into products having use value. Second, with the increased specialization and division of labor, it became clear that an exchange of commodities could be seen as an exchange of the different specialized labor embodied in those commodities. This was most clearly seen by Bernard Mandeville:

As Providence has so ordered it, that not only different parts of the same country, have their peculiar most suitable productions; and like wise that different men have geniuses adapted to a variety of different arts and manufactures; therefore *commerce*, or the exchange of one commodity . . . for another, is highly convenient and beneficial to mankind . . . . To facilitate exchange, men have invented MONEY, properly called a *medium of exchange*, because through or by its means labor is exchanged for labor, or one commodity for another. . . . Trade in general being nothing else but the exchange of labor for labor, the value of all things is . . . most justly measured by labor.[29]

The clearest precursor of the classical economists' labor theory of value was the anonymous author of a pamphlet published in 1738 called *Some Thoughts on the Interest of Money in General*, who concluded that:

[T]he Value of . . . [commodities] when they are exchanged the one for the other, is regulated by the Quantity of Labour necessarily required, and commonly taken in producing them; and the Value or Price of them when they are bought and sold, and compared to a common Medium, will be govern'd by the Quantity of Labour employ'd, and the greater or less Plenty of the Medium or common Measure.[30]

From this point of view it is obvious that if labor is the most important determinant of prices generally, then labor must also be the source of profits because profits are made by buying and selling. When the profits are gotten through control of the production process, then they must reflect a difference in the prices paid for the inputs necessary for production and the output produced. Throughout this period numerous writers came to see profits as a *surplus* left after the laborers had been given the commodities necessary for their own consumption. In 1696, John Cary wrote that the commodities that are "exported are more or less profitable as the labor of the people adds to their value."[31] By 1751, this source of profits was being referred to as a surplus of production over the consumption needs of workers:

The source of wealth is from the number of its inhabitants . . . the more populous a country is, the richer it is or may be. . . . For the earth is grateful and repays their labour not only with enough but with an abundance. . . . Now whatever they have more than they consume, the surplus is the *riches* of the nation.[32]

But these thinkers failed to understand the process sufficiently clearly to show how it was possible for the quantity of labor embodied in a commodity to be simultaneously the determinant of prices and the source of surplus value and profits. Before this would be possible there had to emerge a clear recognition that profit on capital was a distinct category of class income that accrued to the owner of capital because ownership permitted him or her to control the employment of laborers and that accrued roughly in proportion to the exchange value of the owner's capital. Ronald L. Meek, an eminent historian of economic ideas, has concluded:

Profit on capital, and the social classes which came to receive incomes of this type, were of course the ultimate products of several centuries of economic development. But it was apparently not until the latter half of the eighteenth century that profit on capital, as a new generic type of class income, became so clearly differentiated from other types of income that economists were able to grasp its full significance and delineate its basic characteristics.[33]

In 1776, Adam Smith published his famous book *The Wealth of Nations*. This was the first systematic and extensive analysis of capitalism in which such an understanding of profit on capital was fully developed. In the next chapter we will examine Smith's ideas. Before doing so, however, it is necessary briefly to summarize the ideas of the Physiocrats, an eighteenth-century French school of economists whose writings were to exert considerable influence on the subsequent development of economic doctrines.

The Physiocrats as Social Reformers

The Physiocrats were a group of French social reformers who were intellectual disciples of François Quesnay (1694–1774). Most of their ideas came directly or indirectly from Quesnay's *Tableau économique*.[34] Their immediate influence in French economic and political affairs lasted about two decades and ended when their most politically influential member, Turgot, lost the office of comptroller general of finances in 1776.

The Physiocrats were interested in reforming France, which was experiencing economic and social disorder caused primarily from a motley combination of many of the worst features of feudalism and merchant capitalism. Taxation was disorderly, inefficient, oppressive, and unjust. Agriculture still used feudal technology, was small-scale and inefficient, and remained a source of feudal power that inhibited the advance of capitalism. The government was responsible for an extraordinarily extensive and complex maze of tariffs, restrictions, subsidies, and privileges in the areas of industry and commerce. The results were the social and economic chaos that culminated in the French Revolution.

The Physiocrats believed that societies were governed by natural law and that France's problems were due to the failure of her rulers to understand this natural law and to order production and commerce accordingly. Quesnay developed a simple model of how a society should be structured in order to reflect natural law, and, on the basis of this model, the Physiocrats advocated political reform: the abolition of guilds and the removal of all existing tariffs, taxes, subsidies, restrictions, and regulations that hindered industry and commerce. They proposed substituting large-scale, capitalist agriculture for the inefficient small-scale farming that prevailed. But the proposed reform for which they are most remembered was the recommendation that all government revenue be raised with a single, nationwide tax on agriculture (for reasons that will become clear in the following discussion).

The reforms were destined to be unattainable because the Physiocrats did not question the right of the feudal nobility to receive the rents from their lands, while the nobility perceived, quite correctly, that the Physiocratic schemes would lead to the impoverishment of the land-owning class and a takeover by the capitalist class. Social changes that require the displacement of one ruling class by another cannot be achieved by reforms. They require revolution, and France required the revolution of 1789 before changes similar to those advocated by the Physiocrats would be possible.[35]

The Physiocrats' influence was, therefore, primarily intellectual, not political. Some of the ideas expressed in Quesnay's *Tableau économique* were subsequently to become very important in economic literature. We will devote the remainder of this chapter to a discussion of three topics in which Quesnay's ideas were to have an important impact: (1) the notion of productive and unproductive labor and the economic surplus, (2) the mutual interdependencies of production processes, and (3) the circular flows of money and commodities and the economic crises that can result from hoarding money.

Quesnay's Economic Ideas

The *Tableau économique* is basically a model of an economy. The model shows the processes of production, circulation of money and commodities, and the distribution of income. The model assumes that production takes place in yearly cycles and that everything produced in one year is either consumed in that year or becomes the necessary inputs for the next year's production. The central focus is on agriculture. As an example, in one year the agricultural sector produces an output of 5 milliards.[36] The manufacturing sector produces an output of one milliard. Gross output is 6 milliards. One milliard immediately goes to replace the durable agricultural assets used up in production, leaving a net output of 5 milliards.

Agricultural output of 2 milliards is retained by the cultivators. This includes the seed grain for the next period as well as the wages of management (profit) for the capitalist farmers and wages for farm laborers. The entire stock of money (2 milliards) is in the hands of the capitalist farmers at the beginning of the period. They pay the 2 milliards of money to the landlord class as rent. This is the surplus income in the system. The landlords perform no economic function for which this is a payment.

These 2 milliards represent a surplus produced in the agricultural sector in excess of the consumption of the cultivators and the replacement costs of the assets used up in producing the agricultural output. The Physiocrats saw this surplus as a gift of nature and believed that only in dealing directly with nature in extractive or agricultural production could human labor produce a surplus. Cultivators were therefore referred to as the productive class. Producers of manufactured commodities were referred to as the sterile class, not because they did not produce but because the value of what they produced was presumed to be equal to the necessary costs of raw materials plus the necessary subsistence wages of the producers. No surplus or profits were thought to originate in manufacturing. There were therefore three classes: the productive class (capitalists and workers engaged in agricultural production), the sterile class (capitalists and workers engaged in manufacturing), and the idle class (the landlords who consumed the surplus created by the productive class).

After the landlord class receives its money rent, the *Tableau* goes through a long list of transactions that show how the products of the agricultural and manufacturing sectors are distributed or allocated and how the smooth circulation of money is necessary for this allocation. At the end of the entire process, if the transactions are aggregated, we see that the economy is restored to its initial state. Each period, the manufacturing sector reproduces the same value it uses up in inputs (raw materials and subsistence consumption from the agricultural sector); the agricultural sector reproduces the value of its inputs (seed grains, subsistence consumption, and durable agricultural assets used up) and a surplus value of 2 milliards, which is appropriated by the landlord class and consumed in the form of agricultural products and manufactured commodities.

The model illustrates that the two production sectors are interdependent, the output from each sector being a necessary input for the other. This technological interdependence of different industry ties (as we will discuss in a later chapter) was to form the foundation of future versions of the labor theory of value. The model also illustrates that the allocation of inputs and outputs requires the continuous circulation of money. The Physiocrats anticipated T.R. Malthus, Karl Marx, J.M. Keynes, and many other subsequent economists who showed how the hoarding of money or the development of bottlenecks or imbalances in the process of monetary circulation could disrupt the allocation of inputs and commodity outputs and create economic crises or depressions.

Finally, even though virtually all subsequent economists rejected the notion that the economic surplus was a gift of nature, the classification of those workers whose labor power creates surplus value as productive and those whose labor power does not create surplus value as unproductive was to become an important cornerstone of nineteenth-century economic analysis.

Conclusion

In general, it should be stated that very few of the economists prior to Adam Smith presented the same kind of coherent, elaborate analyses of the economic processes of capitalism that we will encounter in subsequent chapters. This was not because they were intellectually inferior to their successors, but because they were writing during a time of socioeconomic transition in which the features of the newly emerging capitalist system were intertwined with innumerable vestiges of the old system. By the late eighteenth century, the broad features of capitalism had become much more apparent. From that point onward, economic thinkers could perceive many of these features with increased clarity. Furthermore, once capitalism had clearly emerged as the dominant economic system in western Europe, each subsequent generation of economists could build on and refine the ideas of its predecessors.

Nevertheless, the reader will see that many of the ideas discussed in this chapter have recurred again and again up to the present. Despite the enormous changes that have occurred since the sixteenth century, capitalism continues to rest on many of the same social, political, legal, and economic foundations that were only dimly perceived during the period in which they were originally coming to dominate western European society.

Notes to Chapter 2

1. See Ronald L. Meek, *Studies in the Labour Theory of Value*, rev. ed. (New York: Monthly Review Press, 1976), pp. 12–14. Much of the first part of the present chapter relies heavily on chapter 1 in this very fine book.

2. Ibid., p. 15.

3. Quoted in ibid., pp. 15–16.

4. See E.K. Hunt, *Property and Prophets* (New York: Harper and Row, 1975), pp. 8–11.

5. William Appleman Williams, *The Contours of American History* (New York: Quadrangle, 1966), p. 36.

6. Ibid., p. 40.

7. William D. Grampp, *Economic Liberalism*, 2 vols. (New York: Random House, 1965), vol. 1, p. 59.

8. For an extension of this discussion of the poor laws, see Arthur Birnie, *An Economic History of the British Isles* (London: Methuen, 1936), ch. 12, 18.

9. Williams, *Contours of American History*, p. 41.

10. Ibid., p. 44.

11. Maurice H. Dobb, *Studies in the Development of Capitalism* (New York: International Publishers), p. 134.

12. Lee Cameron McDonald, *Western Political Theory: The Modern Age* (New York: Harcourt Brace Jovanovich, 1962), p. 29.

13. Quoted in Harry K. Girvetz, *The Evolution of Liberalism* (New York: Colliers, 1963), pp. 28–29.

14. Grampp, *Economic Liberalism*, vol. 1, p. 69.

15. McDonald, *Western Political Theory*, p. 16.

16. The classic studies of the relationship between Protestantism and capitalism are Max Weber, *The Protestant Ethic and the Spirit of Capitalism* (New York: Scribner, 1958), and Richard H. Tawney, *Religion and the Rise of Capitalism* (New York: Mentor Books, 1954).

17. Christopher Hill, "Protestantism and the Rise of Capitalism," in D.S. Landes, ed., *The Rise of Capitalism* (New York: Macmillan, 1966), p. 43.

18. Ibid., p. 43.

19. Ibid., pp. 46–47.

20. Ibid., p. 49.

21. Kemper Fullerton, "Calvinism and Capitalism: an Explanation of the Weber Thesis," in *Protestantism and Capitalism: The Weber Thesis and Its Critics*, ed. Robert W. Green (Lexington, MA: Heath, 1959), p. 19.

22. Ibid., p. 18.

23. Quoted in Grampp, *Economic Liberalism*, vol. 1, p. 78.

24. Ibid., pp. 77–81.

25. Quoted in Robert Lekachman, ed., *The Varieties of Economics*, 2 vols. (New York: Meridian, 1962), vol. 1, p. 185.

26. Meek, *Labour Theory of Value*, p. 18.

27. Quoted in Edgar S. Furniss, *The Position of the Laborer in a System of Nationalism* (New York: Augustus M. Kelley, 1965), p. 16.

28. Ibid., pp. 16–17.

29. Quoted in Meek, *Labour Theory of Value*, p. 41.

30. Ibid., pp. 42–43.

31. Quoted in Furniss, *Position of the Laborer*, p. 19.

32. William Hay, quoted in ibid., p. 19.

33. Meek, *Labour Theory of Value*, pp. 24–25.

34. François Quesnay, *Tableau économique* (London: H. Higgs, 1894); original privately printed (Versailles: 1758).

35. For a more elaborate defense of this assertion, see Leo Rogin, *The Meaning and Validity of Economic Theory* (New York: Harper and Row, 1957), pp. 14–50.

36. I am following the terminology in Rogin, *Economic Theory*, p. 20, not Quesnay's terminology.

Chapter 3

Adam Smith

Adam Smith (1723–1790) was born in Scotland, where he lived most of his life. He attended Glasgow and Oxford Universities (1737–46) and was a professor at Glasgow from 1751 to 1764. In 1759 he published one of his two major works, *The Theory of the Moral Sentiments*, a treatise on social and moral philosophy. He spent two years in France, from 1764 to 1766, where he interacted with many of the leading French intellectuals, including the Physiocrats Quesnay and Turgot. In 1776 he published his most important work, *An Inquiry into the Nature and Causes of the Wealth of Nations* (generally referred to as *The Wealth of Nations*).

Smith is distinguished from all prior economists not only by his scholarship and breadth of knowledge, but also by his development of a complete and relatively consistent abstract model of the nature, structure, and workings of the capitalist system. He clearly saw that there were important interconnections between the major social classes, the various sectors of production, the distributions of wealth and income, commerce, the circulation of money, the processes of price formation, and the process of economic growth. He based many of his policy recommendations on the conclusions derived from his model. Such systematic models of capitalism, whether considered as a whole or in part, have characterized the writings of most of the important economists since Smith. Smith's model is equally interesting whether one examines its logical consistencies or its contradictions. He was a seminal influence on modern economic thinking, and most of the nineteenth- and twentieth-century economists who have been in sharp intellectual conflict with each other can trace many of their important ideas to concepts first developed systematically in *The Wealth of Nations*.

Historical Context of Smith's Ideas

The capitalist mode of production, after it finally overcame the fetters of feudalism and the transitional period of mercantilism, reached its height and most clearly displayed its inherent socioeconomic features in the industrial revolution, which occurred first in England and Scotland roughly in the last three decades of the eighteenth century and in the early nineteenth century. It spread to many parts of western Europe in the early nineteenth century.

Between 1700 and 1770, the foreign markets for English goods grew much faster than England's domestic markets. During the period 1700–50, output of domestic industries increased by 7 percent, while that of export industries increased by 76 percent. For the period 1750–70, the respective figures are 7 percent and 80 percent. This rapidly increasing foreign demand for English manufactures triggered the industrial revolution, which ultimately proved to be one of the most fundamental transformations of human life in history.

Eighteenth-century England had an economy with a well-developed market, in which the traditional anticapitalist market bias in attitudes and ideology had been greatly weakened. In England at this time, larger outputs of manufactured goods produced at lower prices meant ever-increasing profits. Thus, profit seeking, stimulated by increasing foreign demand, was the motive that accounted for the virtual explosion of technological innovations that occurred in the late eighteenth and early nineteenth centuries—and that radically transformed all England and eventually most of the world.

The textile industry was most important in the early industrial revolution. In 1700, the woolen industry had persuaded the government to ban the import of Indian-made "calicoes" (cotton) and thus had secured a protected home market for domestic producers. As outlined earlier, rising foreign demand spurred mechanization of the industry.

More specifically, an imbalance between the spinning and weaving processes led to many of the innovations. The spinning wheel was not as productive as the handloom, especially after the 1730s, when the flying shuttle was invented and the weaving process was speeded up considerably. This imbalance was reversed by three later inventions: the spinning jenny, developed in 1769, with which one person could spin several threads simultaneously; the water frame, invented in 1775, which improved spinning by using rollers operating at different speeds; and the mule, developed in the late 1770s, which combined features of the other two and permitted the application of steam power. These new inventions could be used most economically in factories located near sources of water power (and later steam power). Richard Arkwright, who claimed to be the inventor of the water frame, raised sufficient capital to put many factories into operation, each employing anywhere from 150 to 600 people. Others followed his example, and textile manufacturing in England was rapidly transformed from a cottage to a factory industry.

The iron industry was also very important in the early drive to mechanized factory production. In the early eighteenth century, England's iron industry was quite inconsequential. Charcoal was still used for smelting and had been since prehistoric times. By this time, however, the forests surrounding the iron mines were almost completely depleted. England was forced to import pig iron from its colonies, as well as from Sweden, Germany, and Spain. In 1709 Abraham Darby developed a process for making coke from coal for use in the smelting process. Despite the relative abundance of coal near the iron mines, it was not until the latter part of the eighteenth century (when military demands on the arms and munitions industries were very great) that the iron industry began using coke extensively. This increased demand led to the development of the puddling process, which eliminated the excess carbon left by coke. A whole series of innovations followed, including the rolling mill, the blast furnace, the steam hammer, and metal-turning latches. All these inventions led to a very rapid expansion of the iron and coal-mining industries, which permitted the widespread use of machines made of iron in a wide variety of industries.

Entrepreneurs in many other industries saw the possibilities for larger profits if they could increase output and lower costs. In this period there was a "veritable outburst of inventive activity":

> During the second half of the eighteenth century, interest in technical innovations became unusually intensive. For a hundred years prior to 1760, the number of patents issued during each decade had reached 102 only once, and had otherwise fluctuated between a low of 22 (1700–1709) and a high of 92 (1750–1759). During the following thirty-year period (1760–1789), the average number of patents issued increased from 205 in the 1760s to 294 in the 1770s and 477 in the 1780s.[1]

Undoubtedly the most important of these innovations was the development of the steam engine. Industrial steam engines had been introduced in the early 1700s, but mechanical difficulties had limited their use to pumping water from mines. In 1769 James Watt designed an engine with such accurate specifications that the straight thrust of a piston could be translated into rotary motion. A Birmingham manufacturer named Boulton formed a partnership with Watt, and with Boulton's financial resources they were able to go into large-scale production of steam engines. By the turn of the century, steam was rapidly replacing water as the chief source of power in manufacturing. The development of steam power led to profound economic and social changes.

> With this new great event, the invention of the steam engine, the final and most decisive stage of the industrial revolution opened. By liberating it from its last shackles, steam enabled the immense and rapid development of large-scale industry to take place. For the use of steam was not, like that of water, dependent on geographical position and local resources. Whenever coal could be bought at a reasonable price a steam engine could be erected. England had plenty of coal, and by the end of the eighteenth century it was already applied to many different uses, while a network of waterways, made on purpose, enabled it to be carried everywhere very cheaply: the whole country became a privileged land, suitable above all others for the growth of industry. Factories were now no longer bound to the valleys, where they had grown up in solitude by the side of rapid flowing streams. It became possible to bring them nearer the markets where their raw materials were bought and

their finished products sold, and nearer the centers of population where their labor was recruited. They sprang up near one another and thus, huddled together, gave rise to those huge black industrial cities which the steam engine surrounded with a perpetual cloud of smoke.[2]

The growth in the major manufacturing cities was truly spectacular. For example, the population of Manchester rose from 17,000 in 1760 to 237,000 in 1831 and to 400,000 in 1851. Output of manufactured goods approximately doubled in the second half of the eighteenth century and grew even more rapidly in the early nineteenth century. By 1801, nearly 30 percent of the English workforce was employed in manufacturing and mining; by 1831, this figure had risen to over 40 percent. Thus, the industrial revolution transformed England into a country of large urban manufacturing centers, where the factory system was dominant. The result was a very rapid growth of productivity that vaulted England into the position of the greatest economic and political power of the nineteenth century.

The fact that Adam Smith wrote *The Wealth of Nations* in the period during which the industrial revolution was just getting under way attests both to the fact that many of the economic features that were to dominate the great industrial cities of the early nineteenth century were present in some form in some mid-eighteenth century English and Scottish cities (particularly Glasgow) and to the fact that Adam Smith was indeed a most perspicacious social scientist. A leading historian of this period has written, "Smith, looking at the economic organization of industry in his day, was apparently able to observe as something like a norm what many economic historians of today, looking back at the same period, have been able to observe only as an exception."[3]

By the mid-eighteenth century, in many commercial and industrial cities (including Glasgow), a significant amount of production took place in what have been called "manufactories." A manufactory was a center of production in which a capitalist owned the building, production equipment, and raw materials and hired wage laborers to do the work. It can be distinguished from the typical factory of the later stages of the industrial revolution in that the laborers generally used the older handicraft techniques of production rather than mechanized, assembly-line techniques.

In the manufactories, the capitalist manufacturer could be seen as economically distinct from both the merchant and the wage laborer. Furthermore, by Smith's time the great productive potential of the capitalist organization of production was clearly seen in these manufactories. Smith was greatly impressed with the degree to which they had carried the division of labor and the resulting increases in labor productivity.

Within this context, Smith was the first important economist to distinguish clearly between profits that accrued to industrial capital and wages, rents, and profits on merchant capital. He was also the first to appreciate the significance of the fact that the three principal functional categories of income—profits, rents, and wages—corresponded to the three most important social classes in the capitalist system of his day—capitalists, landlords, and the "free" laborers who could not live unless they sold their labor power for a wage. He also developed a historical theory in which he attempted to explain the evolution of this form of class society and a sociological theory to explain the power relations among the three classes.

Smith's Theories of History and Sociology

Smith's theories of history and sociology included an analysis of the origins and development of class conflict in society and an analysis of the manner in which power was wielded in the class struggle. There was, at the same time, a persistent theme in these theories that Smith discussed most elaborately in his economic theory; this theme was that even though individuals might act selfishly and strictly on their own behalf or on the behalf of the class of which they were a part, and even though individual conflict and class conflict seemed at first sight to be the result of these actions, there was operative in the "laws of nature" or in "divine providence" what Smith called an "invisible hand" that guided these seemingly conflict-creating actions into a benevolent harmony. The invisible hand was not the intentional design of any individual but was simply created by the systematic working out of natural laws. This was unquestionably the most important incongruity, if not contradiction, within Smith's writings. The same contradiction can be found in the writings of David Ricardo, as we will see in a later chapter. It is for this reason that the two major conflicting streams of economic thought in the nineteenth and twentieth centuries, one emphasizing its social conflicts, can both trace their intellectual roots to the writings of Smith and Ricardo.

Smith's theory of history began with the proposition that the way in which humans produced and distributed the material necessities of life was the most important determinant of any society's social institutions as well as of the personal and class relationships among its members.[4] The types of property relationships were of particular importance in determining the form of government in any society. Smith believed that there were four distinct stages of economic and social development: hunting, pasturage, agriculture, and commerce. At each stage, an understanding of a society's methods of producing and distributing economic necessities was key to understanding its social institutions and governments. The relationship between the economic base and the social and political superstructure was not, however, rigidly deterministic. Smith left room for local and regional variations due to geography and culture. All societies were primarily at one of these stages, although they might be undergoing a period of transition in which certain features of two of the stages were present. There was, however, no presumption that societies necessarily progressed from one stage to the next higher stage. Only when the appropriate set of geographical, economic, and cultural circumstances were present would progressive social evolution take place.

Smith defined the hunting stage as "the lowest and rudest state of society, such as we find it among the native tribes of North America."[5] In such societies, the poverty and precariousness of existence involved an equality in which no institutionalized forms of privilege and power existed because the economic basis necessary for such privilege and power was lacking. Therefore, "in this state of things there is properly neither sovereign nor commonwealth."[6]

The next higher stage was that of pasturage, "a more advanced state of society, such as we find it among the Tartars and Arabs."[7] In this stage, the economy supported larger social groupings. Production was based on the domestication of animals, and herding required a nomadic existence. In this type of society, we find for the first time a form of wealth that could be accumulated—cattle. Own partnership of cattle thus because the first form of property relationship and with it came the necessity of establishing institutionalized protection of privilege and power:

> The acquisition of valuable and extensive property, therefore, necessarily requires the establishment of civil government. Where there is no property . . . civil government is not so necessary.
>
> Civil government supposed a certain subordination. But as the necessity of civil government gradually grows up with the acquisition of valuable property, so the principal causes which naturally introduce subordination gradually grow up with the growth of that valuable property.[8]

Smith then went on to investigate the circumstances or causes that "give men . . . superiority over the greater part of their brethren."[9] He analyzed several particular circumstances that led to the institutionalized, coerced subordination of some people to others in various social settings, but he found one important circumstance to be common in all instances: "Civil government, so far as it is instituted for the security of property, is in reality instituted for the defence of the rich against the poor, or of those who have some property against those who have none at all."[10]

The third social state, that of agriculture, was seen in the medieval, feudal economy of western Europe. In this stage, societies permanently settled in one area, and agriculture became the most important economic activity. Accordingly, ownership of land became the most significant property relationship in differentiating classes according to their privileges and power. During this period all lands "were engrossed, and the greater part by a few great proprietors."[11]

Ownership of great estates was the source of social and political power. Therefore, society was divided into the ruled and the rulers. The rulers were nobility and were thought to be genetically superior to the ruled. The law of primogeniture prevented the great estates from being divided and thereby protected the power of the ruling class:

> When land was considered as the means, not of subsistence merely, but of power and protection, it was thought better that it should descend undivided to one. In

those disorderly times, every landlord was a sort of petty prince. His tenants were his subjects. He was their judge, and in some respects their legislator in peace and their leader in war.[12]

Smith believed that two features of agricultural society were particularly important. First, the wealthy nobility were severely limited in the ways in which they could use their wealth:

> In a country which has neither foreign commerce, nor any of the finer manufactures, a great proprietor, having nothing for which he can exchange the greater part of the produce of his lands which is over and above the maintenance of cultivators, consumes the whole in rustic hospitality at home. If this surplus is sufficient to maintain a hundred or a thousand men, he can make use of it in no other way than by maintaining a hundred or a thousand men. He is at all times, therefore, surrounded with a multitude of retainers and dependents, who having no equivalent to give in return for their maintenance, but being fed entirely by his bounty, must obey him, for the same reason that soldiers must obey the Prince who pays them.[13]

Second, this method of economic organization involved the wielding of absolute power by the nobility, with very few rights and very little freedom existing for the vast majority of people. The extension of the rights of and the increase in the freedom for the majority of producers were thought by Smith to be two of the most important improvements created by the advance to the highest or commercial state of society.

In Smith's view, the rise of European cities was the major force that led to the establishment of the commercial stage of social development. These cities were seen as dependent on foreign trade, and, to a great extent, economically independent of the medieval agricultural economy. The medieval lords permitted the growth of independent cities because of the rents and other benefits that they could derive from the cities. Within the cities a new political atmosphere evolved in which producers enjoyed more freedom than they had in any previous stage of social development. A much wider extension of the rights of property also developed, which permitted producers to aspire to create wealth for themselves rather than for an overlord. This greater freedom and security unleashed one of the most powerful of human motives, the desire to accumulate material wealth.

Smith believed that nature had everywhere created an illusion in people: that personal happiness came primarily from material wealth. Although Smith himself believed this illusion false, he was impressed with the economic and social effects of the desire for personal gain that this illusion created. In discussing nature's deception, Smith wrote:

> It is well that nature imposes upon us in this manner. It is this deception which rouses and keeps in continual motion the industry of mankind. It is this which first prompted them to cultivate the ground, to build houses, to found cities and commonwealths, and to invent and improve all the sciences and arts which ennoble and embellish human life.[14]

Here we see the theme that pervaded Smith's writings: the idea that people are led by an invisible hand to promote the social good when such a promotion was never a part of their intent or motive.

The growth of the cities, in Smith's view, transformed rural agriculture and created the commercial stage of society, capitalism, by creating markets where the feudal lords could exchange their agricultural surplus for manufactured goods. The desire for manufactured goods led to the enclosure movements. This was, Smith believed, because medieval agriculture had been very inefficient. The desire to buy more goods led the lords to increase efficiency by dismissing the unnecessary tenants and reducing the number of workers on the land "to the number necessary for cultivating it, according to the imperfect state of cultivation and improvement in those times."[15]

This also led to the feature that Smith considered most progressive about capitalism—the increase in freedom and security for the majority of producers. As landlords strove to increase economic efficiency, purely selfish motives led them to abolish the conditions of serfdom and slavery and to permit these former serfs and slaves to enjoy certain rights of property and security. Smith argued that "a person who can acquire no property, can have no other interest but to eat as much and to labour as little as possible."[16] Thus, what might seem an enlightened and moral act was in reality another example of the invisible hand or the "wisdom of God": "When by natural principles we are led to advance those ends which a refined and enlightened reason would recommend to us, we are very apt . . . to imagine that to be the wisdom of man which is in reality the wisdom of God."[17]

The increased efficiency of commercially oriented agriculture established the economic base for the expansion of the cities and for a continuous enlargement of profitable manufacturing. From that point, the development of industry and commerce promoted efficient, capitalist agricultural production, while the latter in turn spurred the greater development of the former. The growth of this mutually beneficial exchange created the commercial or capitalist society, which Smith believed to be the highest and most progressive form of human society. But again, this result was never intended by the people who created it. In the words of Andrew Skinner, a leading scholar of Smith's ideas:

> Thus, on the one hand, he [Smith] argued that the proprietors who used the produce of their lands in exchange for manufactures only sought to gratify "the most childish vanity"; while on the other, the merchants and artificers only acted on the (self-interested) principle of "turning a penny wherever a penny was to be got." He added: "Neither of them had either the knowledge or foresight of that great revolution which the folly of one, and the industry of the other was gradually bringing about." Once again, we find an example of the typical Smithian thesis, that man is led, as if by an Invisible Hand, to promote ends which were no part of his original intention.[18]

In a capitalist society Smith saw that differing conditions of property ownership were, once again, the basis of the major class divisions. Property ownership determined the source of an individual's income, and the source of income was the principal determinant of social class status:

> The whole annual produce . . . of every country . . . naturally divides itself . . . into three parts; the rent of land, the wages of labour, and the profits of stock; and constitutes a revenue to three different orders of people; to those who live by rent, to those who live by wages, and to those who live by profit. These are the three great, original and constituent orders of every civilized country.[19]

However, in a market society in which land and capital had not come to be owned by separate classes, that is, a society in which workers themselves controlled the means of production, "the whole produce of labour belongs to the labourer."[20] Smith had no doubt about the fact that of the three main social classes, labor was the sole creator of value or wealth: "The annual produce of the land and labour of any nation can be increased in its value by no other means, but by increasing either the number of productive labourers, or the productive powers of those labourers who had before been employed,"[21] and again, "It was not by gold or by silver, but by labour, that all the wealth of the world was originally purchased."[22]

But once a small class came to own the means of production, it acquired the power, through its property rights, of preventing the worker from producing unless it received a share of what the worker produced:

> As soon as stock has accumulated in the hands of particular persons, some of them will naturally employ it in setting to work industrious people . . . in order to make a profit by the sale of their work, or by what their labour adds to the value of the materials. . . . The value which the workmen add to the materials, therefore, resolves itself in the profits of their employer.[23]

The division of the produce of labor between wages and profits was determined in the struggle between laborers and capitalists over what the wage rate would be:

> What are the common wages of labour, depends everywhere upon the contract usually made between those two parties, whose interests are by no means the same. The workmen desire to get as much, the masters to give as little as possible. The former are disposed to combine in order to raise, the latter in order to lower wages of labour.[24]

But this struggle was by no means a struggle of equals. Smith had no doubt that the capitalists were the more powerful, dominant class in the conflict. The following passage, quoted at length, shows that Smith identified three sources of the capitalists' power to dominate workers. Their greater wealth enabled them to hold out much longer in industrial disputes; they were able to manipulate and control public opinion; and they had the incalculable advantage of having the government (which, it will be remembered, was "instituted for the defence of the rich against the poor") on their side. In their struggles, both capitalists and workers colluded among themselves (in Smith's words, they formed combinations) to better their position in the class struggle:

> It is not, however, difficult to foresee which of the two parties must, upon all ordinary occasions, have the advantage in the dispute and force the other into a compliance with their terms. The masters, being fewer in number, can combine much more easily; and the law, besides, authorizes, or at least does not prohibit their combinations, while it prohibits those of workmen. We have no acts of parliament against combining to lower the price of work; but many against combining to raise it. In all such disputes the masters can hold out much longer. A landlord, a farmer, a master manufacturer, or merchants, though they did not employ a single workman, could generally live a year or two upon the stocks which they have already acquired. Many workmen could not subsist a week, few could subsist a month, and scarce any a year without employment. . . . Masters are always and everywhere in a sort of tacit, but constant and uniform combination, not to raise the wages of labour. . . . We seldom, indeed, hear of this combination, because it is the usual, and one may say, the natural state of things which nobody ever hears of. Masters too sometimes enter into particular combinations to sink the wages of labour even below this rate. These are always conducted with the utmost silence and secrecy, till the moment of execution, and when the workmen yield, as they sometimes do, without resistance, though severely felt by them, they are never heard of by other people. Such combinations, however, are frequently resisted by a contrary defensive combination of the workmen. . . . But . . . their combinations . . . are always abundantly heard of. . . . They are desperate, and act with the folly and extravagance of desperate men, who must either starve, or frighten their masters into immediate compliance with their demands. The masters upon these occasions are just as clamorous upon the other side, and never cease to call aloud for the assistance of the civil magistrate, and the rigorous execution of those laws which have been enacted with so much severity against the combinations of servants, labourers, and journeymen. The . . . [workers'] combinations . . . generally end in nothing, but the punishment or ruin of the ring-leaders.[25]

Thus, Smith clearly recognized the central importance of the class conflict between capitalists and workers. He saw the principal basis of class differentiation to be the ownership of land and capital. He also saw that the power of capitalists came from several interrelated sources: their wealth, their ability to influence public opinion, and their control of the government.

Smith's Value Theory

Although Smith never presented a consistent labor theory of value, he did present many ideas that were to become the basis for the more sophisticated versions of the labor theory of value by David Ricardo and Karl Marx. The starting point of this theory is the recognition that in all societies the process of production can be reduced to a series of human exertions. Unlike some animals who live in a natural environment that is readily adaptable to their survival needs, humans generally cannot survive without exerting effort to transform the natural environment into a form that is more livable. Advances in human productivity have usually been associated with the extension or elaboration of the labor processes that culminate in the creation of some particular product. Most generally this increased productivity has resulted from producing new tools.

When these tools are subsequently used in production, it appears to some observers, particularly to certain schools of contemporary economic thinking, that the tools themselves are partly responsible for the subsequent production. Thus, it is said that both "capital" (i.e., tools or other means of producing) and labor are productive, that both contribute equally to subsequent production. Smith and other labor theorists, however, recognized the obvious fact that tools are the products of labor and that the contribution they make to production is, in reality, simply the human contribution made by the producers of the tools. A worker making a loom is really contributing one of the several series of labor expenditures that culminate in the production of cloth; viewed in this way, the loom is a kind of intermediate product that can be seen as so much partially produced cloth. This is the starting point of the labor theory of value and was emphasized by Smith: "Labour was the first price, the original purchase-money that was paid for all things. It was not by gold or by silver, but by labour, that all the wealth of the world was originally purchased."[26]

So Smith declared that the necessary prerequisite for any commodity to have value was that it be the product of human labor. But the labor theory of value goes beyond this. It asserts that the exchange value of a commodity is determined by the amount of labor embodied in that commodity, plus the relative allocation at different points in time of indirect labor (that labor which produced the means of production used in producing the commodity) and direct labor (that labor which uses the means of production to produce the commodity) used in production. Smith was able to see labor as the determinant of exchange value only in early precapitalist economies, where there were neither capitalists nor landlords:

> In that early and rude state of society which precedes both the accumulation of stock and the appropriation of land, the proportion between the quantities of labour necessary for acquiring different objects seems to be the only circumstance which can afford any rule for exchanging them for one another. If among a nation of hunters, for example, it usually costs twice the labour to kill a beaver which it does to kill a deer, one beaver should naturally exchange for or be worth two deer. It is natural that what is usually the produce of two days or two hours labour should be worth double of what is usually the produce of one day's or one hour's labour. . . .
> . . . In this state of things, the whole produce of labour belongs to the labourer; and the quantity of labour commonly employed in acquiring or producing any commodity is the only circumstance which can regulate the quantity of labour which it ought commonly to purchase, command, or exchange for.[27]

But when capitalists gained control of the means of production and landlords monopolized the land and natural resources, Smith believed that exchange value or price came to be a sum of three component parts: wages, profits, and rents. "As soon as stock has accumulated in the hands of particular persons," he wrote, then the laborer must in most cases share it [the produce of his labor] with the owner of the stock which employs him. Neither is the quantity of labour commonly employed in acquiring or producing any commodity, the only circumstance which can regulate the quantity which it ought commonly to purchase, command or exchange for. An additional quantity, it is evident must be due for the profits of stock. . . .

. . . As soon as the land of any country has all become private property, the landlords, like all other men, love to reap where they never sowed, and demand a rent. . . . [The laborer] must give up to the landlord a portion of what his labour either collects or produces. This portion, or what comes to the same thing, the price of this portion, constitutes the rent of land, and in the price of the greater part of commodities makes a third component part.[28]

Because profits and rents must be added to wages in order to determine prices, Smith's theory of prices has been called, by an eminent historian, "an 'Adding-up Theory'—a summation (merely) of three primary components."[29] The reason this theory differed from the labor theory that Smith believed to be applicable in the "early and rude state of society" was that the profit component of a price did not have any necessary relationship to the labor embodied in the commodity. Smith realized that competition tended to equalize the profits earned on capitals of the same value, that is, if a capitalist owned $100 worth of looms and received $40 per year profit on these looms, competition and the search for maximum profits would tend to lead to a situation in which $100 worth of any other kind of capital would also yield $40 per year profit:

The profits of stock, it may perhaps be thought, are only a different name for the wages of a particular sort of labour, the labour of inspection and direction. They are, however, altogether different, are regulated by quite sufficient principles, and bear no proportion to the quantity, the hardship, or the ingenuity of this supposed labour of inspection and direction. They are regulated altogether by the value of the stock employed, and are greater or smaller in proportion to the extent of this stock.[30]

It followed from this principle that prices could remain proportional to the amounts of labor embodied in commodities only if the value of capital per worker was the same in different lines of production. If this condition held, then profits based on the value of capital would stand in the same proportion to wages in each line of production, and wages added to profits would yield a sum (or a price if rent is ignored) proportional to the labor embodied in the production of the commodities. But if the value of capital per worker differed among the various sectors of the economy, then the addition of profits to wages would yield a sum that would not be proportional to the labor embodied in the production of the commodities. Smith accepted as an obvious empirical fact the assertion that the value of capital per worker differed from industry to industry. He could not see any way of showing how the labor embodied in production determined exchange value in these circumstances. It remained for David Ricardo to show the general nature of the relationship between the labor embodied in commodities and their exchange values under these circumstances, and for Karl Marx and subsequent theorists to work out a complete and logically coherent labor theory of value.

Smith's cost-of-production theory of prices was not intended to explain the actual day-to-day fluctuations of prices in the market. He distinguished between market price and natural price. The market price was the actual commodity price that existed at any particular point in time in a particular market. He believed that it was regulated by the relationship between the amount of the commodity that sellers wished to sell and the quantity that buyers wished to buy at various prices. In other words, the market price was determined by the forces of supply and demand. If supply was small relative to demand, then the small supply would be allocated to those purchasers willing to pay a high price. If supply was large relative to demand, then the price would have to be lowered to induce buyers to purchase the entire amount. The natural price was that price where the proceeds of the sale were just sufficient to provide the landlord, the capitalist, and the workers with rent, profit, and wages equivalent to the ordinary or socially average rates of rent, profits, and wages.

There was, however, a very important connection between the market price and the natural price. The natural price was a kind of equilibrium price around which day-to-day changes in the market price fluctuated, and it was the forces of supply and demand that tended to push the market price toward the natural price. If demand was large relative to supply and the market price was higher than the natural price, then profits would exceed the socially average rate of profit. These high profits would attract other capitalists who were constantly looking for industries in which they could make higher profits. As these new capitalists began producing and selling the commodity, it would increase the supply of, and thereby reduce the price of, the commodity. As long as the market price remained above the natural price, this process would continue. But when the market price had been forced down to the natural price, the profits earned in that industry would be equal to the socially average rate of profit, and there would no longer be any incentive for capitalists to expand the supply of the commodity.

If demand was small relative to supply and the market price was lower than the natural price, then profits would fall short of the socially average rate. These low profits would induce some of the capitalists to leave the industry and invest their capital in other industries where the profit rate was higher. This would reduce the supply and thereby increase the price of the commodity. Again, this process would continue until the market price had been pushed up to the natural price.

Thus, the natural price was an equilibrium price determined by the costs of production but established in the market by the forces of supply and demand, and fluctuations in the market price would tend to occur around the natural price. In Smith's theory of prices, the amount of demand would allocate society's capital among the various industries and thereby determine the composition or the relative quantities of the different commodities that were produced. But the cost of production alone would determine the equilibrium or natural price that would tend to prevail in any market.

There were two major weaknesses in Smith's theory of prices. First, the three components of prices—wages, profits, and rents—were themselves either prices or derived from prices. A theory that explains prices on the basis of other prices cannot explain prices in general. If to understand one price we have to know what other prices are, the question immediately arises as to how those other prices are explained. And if they also must be explained in terms of still other prices, we become involved in an endless chain in which the ultimate determinants of prices can never be explained.

Smith vaguely understood this difficulty and devoted chapters 8, 9, and 11 of Book I of *The Wealth of Nations* to attempts at explaining the levels of wages, profits, and rents in terms of the historical and institutional circumstances of the capitalist system of his time. These attempts, while filled with important insights, were not successful, and Smith's theory of prices must be judged to have contained an element of circularity (explaining prices in terms of other prices) from which he was never completely able to extricate himself. As we will see in later chapters, only two theories of value have really succeeded in breaking out of this circularity and explained all prices on the basis of an external determinant. The first was the labor theory of value, which Smith was unable to formulate in situations in which the value of capital per worker differed in different sectors of the economy. The second was the utility theory of value, which made prices dependent on use value, or utility.

Smith's rejection of use value as a possible determinant of prices was explicit:

> The word VALUE, it is to be observed, has two different meanings, and sometimes expresses the utility of some particular object, and sometimes the power of purchasing other goods which the possession of that object conveys. The one may be called "value in use," the other "value in exchange." The things which have the greatest value in use have frequently little or no value in exchange; and on the contrary those which have the greatest value in exchange have frequently little or no value in use. Nothing is more useful than water: but it will purchase scarce anything; scarce anything can be had in exchange for it. A diamond, on the contrary, has scarce any value in use; but a great quantity of other goods may frequently be had in exchange for it.[31]

Economists having a utility theory of value generally refer to this passage as "the water-diamond paradox."[32] Smith did not, however, see it as a paradox, but simply as a statement that use value and exchange value were not systematically related to each other. Later utility theorists were to explain this by differentiating between the total utility of diamonds (to which Smith was referring) and their marginal utility.[33] The utility theory of value will be discussed in later chapters. For now, it must suffice to say that Smith explicitly rejected both the utility and the labor theories of price determination and was left with a theory having an unresolved element of circularity.

The second major weakness of Smith's cost-of-production theory of prices, which was to be the focal point of Ricardo's critique of Smith, was that it yielded conclusions about the general *level* of all prices (or, what amounts to the same thing, about the purchasing power of money) rather than the relative values of different commodities. In Smith's theory, if anything happened to increase any of the three cost components of a commodity, then the value of the commodity had to increase. This was particularly true of wages, because they represented the major part of the costs of producing all commodities. Smith and all of the classical economists believed that wages would tend to be at or near the subsistence level. The major part of a worker's subsistence was foodstuffs, which in Smith's time were mostly products produced from grains (or "corn," as grains were called at that time). It therefore followed that if the price of corn was high, then the money wages necessary to keep laborers at subsistence would also have to be high. But if wages were high, the price of all commodities would have to be high because wages constituted the largest component of costs in all production.

From this line of reasoning, Smith concluded that a tax that was used to subsidize the export of corn would immediately raise the domestic money price of corn. The ultimate effect of such a tax would be

> not so much to raise the real value of corn as to degrade the real value of silver; or to make an equal quantity of it exchange for a smaller quantity, not only of corn, but of all other home-made commodities: for the money price of corn regulates that of all other home-made commodities. . . . The money price of labour, and of everything that is the produce either of land or labour, must necessarily either rise or fall in proportion to the money price of corn.[34]

The practical political significance of the contemporary British government's taxes and subsidies affecting the price of corn will be discussed in the chapters on Malthus and Ricardo. At this point we are interested in the implications of this view for a theory of value. The idea that the value of silver did not, as with other commodities, depend on its costs of production but rather on the value of corn would seem to be a paradox requiring an explanation. Furthermore, it is clear that price changes for any commodity that was widely used as a productive input would have the same impact on the value of silver as did changes in the value of corn. Therefore, Smith's theory could be reduced to the assertion that the value of silver depends on the value of the commodities that are widely used as productive inputs.

But this introduced special problems. Silver (or money) was the commonly used measure of exchange value (or the *numeraire* in terms of which relative exchange values were expressed). It was clear to Ricardo and other critics of Smith that if the price of corn or any other widely used productive input increased, then the effects on the values of various commodities would differ. For some commodities corn would be a very significant input (they can be called corn-intensive commodities), while for others it would be relatively insignificant. It was obvious that the money price of the corn-intensive commodities would increase much more than the money prices of those commodities in which corn was a less significant input. This meant that there would be a change in the exchange ratios between the two sets of commodities. The corn-intensive commodities would be relatively higher in value, and the other commodities relatively lower. But in Smith's theory, the value of all commodities would be higher simply because the measuring rod of value (the value *numeraire*, or money) had changed. Smith gave no argument to support the notion that an increase in the price of corn would decrease the relative value of silver. Moreover, if the commodity in which corn was the very most intensively used as an input was used as a measuring rod, then it would have been the case that the value of all commodities would have decreased (because this commodity would have increased in value relative to all other commodities).

It followed, then, that in Smith's theory the impact of a change in the price of corn on the values of other commodities would depend on which commodity was chosen as a *numeraire*. But Smith, the other classical economists, and Marx were all interested in developing a value theory in which they not only could explain relative prices but also calculate the total value of output in a manner that would not reflect the ambiguity of an arbitrarily chosen measuring rod. If the composition of output was changing, and relative exchange ratios and the value of the measuring rod were also changing, then the value of total output could increase or decrease depending on the measuring rod chosen.

For those economists who developed the labor theory of value, this was a particularly important problem, as we will see in the chapters on Ricardo and Marx. Ricardo's version of the labor theory of value required a measuring rod independent of price changes that he could use to compare the total social output with the total of necessary inputs in order to arrive at the total surplus value. Surplus value, in turn, became the basis for calculating the rate of profit, which, in turn, was necessary to explain the pattern of relative prices. This will be discussed at greater length later, but for now it will suffice to explain why the classical economists searched for an "invariant measure of value" and why Ricardo, in particular, criticized this deficiency in Smith's price theory.

Although Smith's inability to show how a labor theory of value could explain prices in a capitalist economy indicated that he did not attach the same importance to finding an invariant measure of value as did Ricardo and Marx, nevertheless, he did try to find a measuring rod that would be the best measure of value. He began by rejecting gold and silver because the conditions under which they were produced varied and hence they would be variable measuring rods. He insisted that "a commodity which is itself continually varying in its own value, can never be an accurate measure of the value of other commodities."[35] The best measure of value, in his opinion, was the amount of labor any commodity could command in exchange. When a person owned a commodity, Smith argued, the power which that possession immediately and directly conveys to him, is the power of purchasing; a certain command over all the labour, or over all the produce of labour which is then in the market. His fortune is greater or less, precisely in proportion to the extent of this power; or to the quantity either of other men's labour, or, what is the same thing, of the produce of other men's labour, which it enables him to purchase or command. The exchangeable value of everything must always be precisely equal to the extent of this power which it conveys to its owner.[36]

This choice, however, was not a good one. Just as the price of gold or silver can vary, so can the wages of labor. And because the wage rate represents the price at which labor can be purchased, Smith's measure of value is variable. It is obvious that the price of any commodity can and does vary. Therefore, the amount of any commodity that can be purchased depends both on its own value and the value of the object being exchanged for it and can vary as either or both of these vary. Therefore, the amount of any commodity obtainable in exchange can never be an invariant standard of value.

Sometimes we can gain understanding by analyzing the errors that a great thinker makes as well as by studying his or her scientifically valid propositions. Smith's choice of labor commanded as an invariant measure of value is such an error. It can give us insights into the general social perspective through which Smith frequently tended to view the economic processes of his day. The historian Ronald L. Meek has written:

> From the point of view of a capitalist employer, who organizes the production of commodities not because he wishes to consume them himself or to exchange them for subsistence goods but because he wishes to sell them at a profit and accumulate capital, the most appropriate measure of the "real value" of these commodities may well appear to be the amount of wage-labour which the proceeds of their sale enable him to command in the next period of production. The larger the quantity of wage-labour which the commodities will command, the larger will be the addition he is able to make to his labour force, and the larger, therefore, will be the amount which can be accumulated.[37]

In concluding our discussion of Smith's theory of value, it should be stated that here, as well as in many other parts of his social and economic theories, there are perplexing ambiguities. He explicitly stated that when capitalists monopolized the ownership of the means of production and landlords monopolized the ownership of land, the amounts of labor embodied in the production of different commodities no longer regulated the value of these commodities; yet in many of his discussions, he wrote as though the labor theory of value still sufficed to explain prices. The following three quotations are examples of his use of the labor theory:

> As it cost less labour to bring those metals from the mine to the market, so when they were brought thither they could purchase or command less labour.[38]

> In a country naturally fertile, but of which the far greater part is altogether uncultivated, cattle, poultry, game of all kinds, &c. as they can be acquired with a

very small quantity of labour, so they will purchase or command but a very small quantity.[39]

It cost a greater quantity of labour to bring the goods to market. When they were brought thither, therefore, they must have purchased or exchanged for the price of a greater quantity.[40]

Smith's Theory of Economic Welfare

Smith's economic theory was, above all else, a normative or policy-oriented theory. His principal concern was to ascertain what social and economic forces were most conducive to increasing human welfare, and, on the basis of this, to recommend policies that would best promote human happiness. Smith's definition of economic welfare was fairly simple and straightforward. Economic welfare depended on the amount of the annual "produce of labour" and "the number of those who are to consume it."[41] Another criterion of welfare, not explicitly stated by Smith but important in many of his discussions, was that welfare could be increased as the composition of productive output conformed more to the needs and desires of those who purchased and used the output.

In analyzing the forces that tended to increase economic welfare, Smith developed a model that delineated the most important social and economic components of capitalism and made explicit the principal motivation that propelled the system. Capitalism was divided into two primary sectors of production—agriculture and manufacturing. The production of commodities required three distinctive groups of inputs—land (including natural resources), labor, and capital. Corresponding to these three groups of inputs were the three principal social classes of capitalism—landlords, laborers, and capitalists. The legal and social bases of this class division were the laws of property ownership and the distribution of actual ownership among the people. The three social classes each received a distinct form of monetary return—rent, wages, and profits. These forms of class income, as we have seen, corresponded to the three component parts of production costs and determined the prices of commodities. Smith assumed that selfish, acquisitive motives characterized all economic behavior (despite his admission that in noneconomic behavior people had other motives, including those considered altruistic). The assumption that all economic behavior is based on selfish, acquisitive motives was to become the foundation of neoclassical economics in the late nineteenth and the twentieth centuries.

Within the context of Smith's theory of history, capitalism represented the highest stage of civilization, and capitalism would reach its greatest height when it had evolved to a state in which the government had adopted a laissez-faire policy, allowing the forces of competition and the free interplay of supply and demand to regulate the economy, which would be almost entirely unhindered by government restrictions or interventions. The entire structure of *The Wealth of Nations* builds toward Smith's laissez-faire conclusions. The first third of the book (Books I and II) develops Smith's own economic concepts and theories. Book III details Smith's views on the historical rise of capitalism. Book IV is devoted primarily to a discussion of the policies and theories of the mercantilists (chapters 1 through 8) and the Physiocrats (chapter 9).

Toward the end of chapter 9 of Book IV, all of the threads of analysis come together. On the basis of his own analyses, Smith rejected the theories and policies of both the mercantilists and the Physiocrats and then stated what system would maximize economic welfare. This statement is the main conclusion of the book: Laissez-faire capitalism, or, as Smith calls it, "the obvious and simple system of natural liberty," is asserted to be the best possible economic system.

> All systems either of preference or of restraint, therefore, being thus completely taken away, the obvious and simple system of natural liberty establishes itself of its own accord. Every man . . . is left perfectly free to pursue his own interest in his own way, and to bring both his industry and capital into competition with those of any other man, or order of men. The sovereign is completely discharged from . . . the duty of superintending the industry of private people, and of directing it towards the employments most suitable to the interest of the society.[42]

We shall now summarize some of the arguments by which Smith arrived at this ultimate conclusion.

The level of production in any society depended, in Smith's view, on the number of productive laborers and the level of their productivity. Productivity, in turn, depended on specialization, or the extent of the division of labor: "The greatest improvement in the productive powers of labour, and the greater part of the skill, dexterity, and judgment with which it is anywhere directed, or applied, seem to have been the effects of the division of labor."[43] The extent of the division of labor was governed by two circumstances. First, there had to be a well-developed market, or a commercial exchange economy, in order for extensive specialization to take place. When a market economy existed, the degree of specialization would depend on the size of the market. "As it is the power of exchanging that gives occasion to the division of labour, so the extent of this division must always be limited by the extent of that power, or, in other words, by the extent of the market."[44]

The most important or fundamental division of labor was that between rural agriculture and urban manufacturing. "There are some sorts of industry," Smith wrote, "which can be carried on nowhere but in a great town."[45] The natural order of economic development was agriculture first, then urban manufacturing, and then foreign commerce. "The great commerce of every civilized society is that carried on between the inhabitants of the town and those of the country. It consists in the exchange of rude for manufactured produce."[46]

When a commercial society had developed to a point where this urban-rural specialization was possible, then the second circumstance governing the extent of the division of labor became more important:

As the accumulation of stock must, in the nature of things, be previous to the division of labour, so labour can be more and more subdivided in proportion only as stock is more and more accumulated. The quantity of materials which the same number of people can work up, increases in a great proportion as labour comes to be more and more subdivided; and as the operations of each workman are gradually reduced to a greater degree of simplicity, a variety of new machines come to be invented for facilitating and abridging those operations . . . therefore . . . a greater stock of materials and tools . . . must be accumulated.[47]

When we compare, therefore, the state of a nation at two different periods, and find, that the annual produce of its land and labour is evidently greater at the latter than at the former, that its lands are better cultivated, its manufactures more numerous and more flourishing, and its trade more extensive, we may be assured that its capital must have increased during the interval.[48]

The accumulation of capital, then, was the principal source of economic progress, and profits were the source of new capital. Given this central significance of profits and capital accumulation, Smith placed a great deal of emphasis on his distinction between productive and unproductive labor. He was concerned with countering the Physiocrats' argument that labor expended in manufacturing was sterile or unproductive. He realized that such labor was a source of profits and further accumulation, and, hence, a source of economic progress.

Smith advanced two definitions of productive labor. First, he argued that laborers were productive when their labor resulted in revenues, accruing to capitalists, that were sufficient to repay wage costs and still leave a profit. Second, he argued that laborers whose labor was embodied in a tangible, vendible commodity were productive. In both cases he was attempting to distinguish those laborers who contributed to the process of capital accumulation from those who merely sold their services to either wealthy persons or the government. The latter he viewed as a variety of "menial servants," whose services, however desirable, did not result in the generation of profits or the accumulation of capital and, hence, did not further economic progress. Such services he regarded as unproductive labor.

It is obvious from our contemporary vantage point that Smith's two definitions of productive labor were inconsistent. But, as Maurice Dobb has observed:

[I]t can reasonably be supposed that Adam Smith saw no conflict between the two definitions because he did not suppose it to be possible for there to be a profit or surplus-value *unless* the labour in question produced a vendible commodity. Over a large area, no doubt, the two notions amount to the same thing. But as Marx . . . observed, actors, musicians, dancing masters, cooks and prostitutes may all create a surplus or profit for an employer if they happened to be employed by "an entrepreneur of theaters, concerts, brothels, etc."[49]

The important point was that productive labor was the labor that furthered the accumulation of capital. The new capital increased economic welfare because it increased the productivity of labor.

Smith argued, however, that capital was more productive in some employments than in others. Capital employed in agriculture was the most productive, manufacturing was next, then came domestic trade, and last was foreign trade.[50] The reader will recall that this ranking of the productivity of capital corresponds with what Smith believed to be the natural order of economic development. If governments did nothing either to encourage or to discourage the investment of capital in any particular sector, then the capitalists' selfish quest for maximum profits would cause economic development to take place in accordance with this natural and socially beneficial order. "If human institutions had never thwarted . . . [man's] natural inclinations," Smith wrote, then that "order of things . . . is . . . promoted by the natural inclinations of man."[51] In the natural order of economic development, agriculture came first. If the market was free and there was no government intervention, "most men will choose to employ their capitals rather in the improvement and cultivation of land, than either in manufacturers or in foreign trade."[52]

After agricultural production was developed in a "system of natural liberty," capital would flow into manufacturing. Still, at this stage of development, domestic industry contributed more to human welfare than to foreign commerce. In describing the flow of capital into domestic industry, under a "system of natural liberty," Smith formulated the most famous statement of his thesis that in a free market the selfish actions of individuals are directed, as though by an invisible hand, in such a way as to maximize economic welfare:

> Every individual who employs his capital in the support of domestic industry, necessarily endeavours so to direct that industry, that its produce may be of the greatest possible value.
>
> The produce of industry is what it adds to the subject or materials upon which it is employed. In proportion as the value of this produce is great or small, so will likewise be the profits of the employer. But it is only for the sake of profit that any man employs a capital in the support of industry; and he will always, therefore, endeavour to employ it in the support of that industry of which the produce is likely to be of the greatest value, or to exchange for the greatest quantity either of money or of other goods.
>
> But the annual revenue of every society is always precisely equal to the exchangeable value of the whole annual produce of its industry. . . . As every individual, therefore, endeavours as much as he can both to employ his capital in the support of domestic industry, and so to direct that industry that its produce may be of the greatest value; every individual necessarily labours to render the annual revenue of the society as great as he can. He generally, indeed, neither intends to promote the public interest, nor knows how much he is promoting it. By preferring the support of domestic to that of foreign industry, he intends only his own security; and by directing that industry in such a manner as its produce may be of the greatest value, he intends only his own gain, and he is in this, as in many other cases, led by an invisible hand to promote an end which was not part of his intention. Nor is it always the worse for the society that it was no part of it. By pursuing his own interest he frequently promotes that of the society more effectually than when he really intends to promote it.[53]

Thus, Smith concluded that government interventions, regulations, grants of monopoly, and special subsidies all tended to misdirect capital and to diminish its contribution to economic welfare. Furthermore, such government actions tended to restrict markets and thereby to reduce the rate of capital accumulation, to decrease the extent of the division of labor, and, accordingly, to reduce the level of social production.

Not only would free, competitive markets direct the employment of capital to those industries in which it would be most productive, but they would also result, again through the invisible hand directing selfish profit-maximizing into socially beneficial channels, in those commodities being produced that people need and desire most intensely:

> It is not from the benevolence of the butcher, the brewer, or the baker, that we expect our dinner, but from their regard to their own interest. We address ourselves, not to their humanity but to their self-love, and never talk to them of our own necessities but of their advantages.[54]

The influence of Smith on the socially conservative economic doctrines of the past two centuries lies primarily in his belief that, in a competitive, laissez-faire, capitalist economy, the free market channeled all self-seeking, acquisitive, profit-oriented actions into a socially beneficial, harmonious "obvious and simple system of natural liberty." He declared that the appropriate duties of governments ought to be strictly limited:

> The statesman who should attempt to direct private people in what manner they ought to employ their capitals, would not only load himself with a most unnecessary attention, but assume an authority which could safely be trusted, not only to no single person, but to no council or senate whatever, and which would nowhere be so dangerous as in the hands of a man who had folly and presumption enough to fancy himself fit to exercise it.[55]

The government ought to be given only three duties:

> [F]irst, the duty of protecting the society from violence and invasion of other independent societies; secondly, the duty of protecting, as far as possible, every member of the society from the injustice or oppression of every other member of it, or the duty of establishing an exact administration of justice; and, thirdly, the duty of erecting and maintaining certain public works and certain public institutions, which it can never be for the interest of any individual, or small number of individuals, to erect and maintain; because the profit would never repay the expense to any individual or small number of individuals, though it may frequently do much more than repay it to a great society.[56]

Class Conflict and Social Harmony

It is clear that Smith's "obvious and simple system of natural liberty" was envisioned as an economic system in which harmony prevailed. Of course, Smith was aware that selfish, acquisitive motives led to individual and class conflicts. But within the social context of competitive capitalism, these conflicts were only apparent and not ultimately real. The invisible-hand automatically resolved superficial or apparent conflicts in a manner most conducive to human happiness.

Smith's writings strike the reader as extremely ambiguous, if not contradictory, however, on the issue of class conflict versus social harmony within capitalism. A central argument, which will recur in later chapters of this book, is that proponents of the labor theory of value view class conflict to be of fundamental importance in understanding capitalism, while the utility theory of value sees social harmony as fundamental and leads inevitably to some version of Smith's invisible-hand argument. Only insofar as Smith abandoned the labor theory of value was he able to argue for the invisible hand and social harmony.

But much of Smith's analysis flows from his labor theory perspective. Thus, he was able to argue that labor was the only original creator of value, that the laborers had to share the produce of their labor with two classes whose source of power and claim to income came not from creating commodities but from property ownership, that property ownership gave some people "the right to reap where they did not sow," and that the government's protection of property rights was primarily a "defence of the rich against the poor."

Furthermore, as we have seen, Smith believed that wages were determined by an economic, social, and political struggle between workers and capitalists, in which the capitalists nearly always had the upper hand. He was also aware that businessmen used every means at their disposal to avoid competition and to secure monopolies, as is evidenced by the two following quotations:

> People of the same trade seldom meet together, even for merriment and diversion, but the conversation ends in a conspiracy against the public, or in some contrivance to raise prices.[57]

> The interest of the dealers, however, in any particular branch of trade or manufactures, is always in some respects different from, and even opposite to, that of the public. . . . To narrow the competition is always the interest of dealers. .... But to narrow the competition must always be against . . . [the interests of the public], and can serve only to enable the dealers, by raising their profits above what they naturally would be, to levy, for their own benefit, an absurd tax upon the rest of their fellow-citizens.[58]

In analyzing the effects of capitalism, the accumulation of capital, and its attendant division of labor on the majority of workers, the following two quotations are equally revealing:

> The difference of natural talents in different men is, in reality, much less than we are aware of. . . . The difference between the most dissimilar characters, between a philosopher and a common street porter, for example, seems to arise not so much from nature, as from habit, custom and education. When they came into the world, and for the first six or eight years of their existence, they were, perhaps, very much alike, and neither their parents nor playfellows could perceive any remarkable difference. About that age, or soon after, they come to be employed in very different occupations.[59]

In the progress of the division of labour, the employment of the far greater part of those who live by labour, that is, of the great body of the people, comes to be confined to a few very simple operations, frequently to one or two. But the understandings of the greater part of men are necessarily formed by their ordinary employments. The man whose whole life is spent in performing a few simple operations, of which the effects too are, perhaps, always the same, or very nearly the same, has no occasion to exert his understanding, or to exercise his invention in finding out expedients for removing difficulties which never occur. He naturally loses, therefore, the habit of such exertion, and generally becomes as stupid and ignorant as it is possible for a human creature to become. The torpor of his mind renders him, not only incapable of relishing or bearing a part in any rational conversation, but of conceiving any generous, noble, or tender sentiment, and consequently of forming any just judgment concerning many even of the ordinary duties of private life.[60]

For such workers, the value of the invisible hand and the "obvious and simple system of natural liberty" seem rather far removed. Moreover, when one considers that government exists to "protect the rich from the poor," that the use of the government is a principal means by which capitalists overpower laborers in their struggles over wage rates, and that capitalists use every means at their disposal, including government, to secure and protect monopolies, then one wonders how Smith even hoped to achieve the "system of natural liberty" in which the government had only three duties and in which the invisible hand channeled all selfish, acquisitive actions into a mutually beneficial, harmonious whole.

Considering these difficulties and the many insightful analyses in *The Wealth of Nations*, it is not surprising that Smith's intellectual influence can be seen in two rival traditions in nineteenth- and twentieth-century economic thinking, one that emphasizes the labor theory of value and class conflict and another that emphasizes the utility theory of value, social harmony, and the invisible hand.

Notes to Chapter 3

1. Reinhard Bendix, *Work and Authority in Industry* (New York: Harper and Row, 1963), p. 27.

2. Paul Mantoux, *The Industrial Revolution in the Eighteenth Century* (New York: Harcourt Brace Jovanovich, 1927), pp. 344–45.

3. Ronald L. Meek, "Adam Smith and the Classical Theory of Profit," in *Economics and Ideology and Other Essays* (London: Chapman and Hall, 1967), p. 25. The next three paragraphs rely on this essay by Meek.

4. For useful summaries of Smith's theory of history, see Ronald L. Meek, "The Scottish Contribution to Marxist Sociology," in *Economics and Ideology,* pp. 34–50, and Andrew Skinner's introduction to *The Wealth of Nations,* ed. Andrew Skinner (Baltimore: Penguin, 1970), sect. 2, pp. 29–43. For a useful summary of Smith's sociology, see Warren J.S. Samuels, "Adam Smith and the Economy as a System of Power," *Review of Social Economy* 31, no. 2 (1973): 123–37.

5. Adam Smith, *An Inquiry into the Nature and Causes of the Wealth of Nations* (New York: Modern Library, 1937), p. 653.

6. Ibid., p. 653.

7. Ibid., p. 653.

8. Ibid., p. 670.

9. Ibid., p. 670.

10. Ibid., p. 674.

11. Ibid., p. 361.

12. Ibid., pp. 361–362.

13. Ibid., p. 385.

14. Quoted in Skinner's introduction to *Wealth of Nations*, p. 23.

15. Ibid., p. 39.

16. Ibid., p. 39.

17. Ibid., pp. 26–27.

18. Ibid., p. 40

19. Smith, *Wealth of Nations*, p. 248.

20. Ibid., p. 47.

21. Ibid., p. 326.

22. Ibid., p. 30

23. Ibid., p. 48.

24. Ibid., p. 66.

25. Ibid., pp. 66–67.

26. Ibid., p. 30.

27. Ibid., pp. 47–48.

28. Ibid., pp. 48–49.

29. Maurice Dobb, *Theories of Value and Distribution since Adam Smith* (Cambridge, UK: Cambridge University Press, 1973), p. 46.

30. Smith, *Wealth of Nations*, p. 48.

31. Ibid., p. 28.

32. See, for example, Mark Blaug, *Economic Theory in Retrospect* (Homewood, IL: Irwin, 1968), p. 41.

33. Ibid., p. 43.

34. Smith, *Wealth of Nations*, pp. 476–77.

35. Ibid., pp. 32–33.

36. Ibid., p. 31.

37. Ronald L. Meek, *Studies in the Labour Theory of Value* (New York: Monthly Review Press, 1973), pp. 65–66.

38. Smith, *Wealth of Nations*, p. 32.

39. Ibid., p. 186.

40. Ibid., p. 246.

41. Ibid., p. lvii.

42. Ibid., p. 651.

43. Ibid., p. 3.

44. Ibid., p. 17.

45. Ibid.

46. Ibid., p. 356.

47. Ibid., p. 260.

48. Ibid., p. 326.

49. Maurice Dobb, *Theories of Value and Distribution*, p. 61.

50. Smith, *Wealth of Nations*, pp. 341–55.

51. Ibid., p. 357.

52. Ibid., pp. 357–58.

53. Ibid., pp. 422–23.

54. Ibid., p. 14.

55. Ibid., p. 423.

56. Ibid., p. 651.

57. Ibid., p. 128.

58. Ibid., p. 250.

59. Ibid., p. 15.

60. Ibid., pp. 734–35.

Chapter 4

Thomas Robert Malthus

Thomas Robert Malthus (1766–1834) was the son of a comfortably well-to-do English family. He was educated at Cambridge University and in 1805 was appointed to the faculty of the East India Company's college at Harleybury. He held the first British professorship of political economy and continued in that post until his death in 1834.

Malthus lived in tumultuous times of intense class conflicts, and his writings reflect his positions on these conflicts. There were two principal conflicts, each of which will be briefly discussed here. First, the industrial revolution was made possible only through immense, widespread sacrifice and suffering by the working class. The workers did not always meekly accept these sacrifices and consequently suffered from not only social and economic distress, but also legislative and political oppression. Second, during the late eighteenth and early nineteenth centuries, the older land-owning class still had effective control of the British Parliament, and an intense class conflict was waged between this class and the new industrial, capitalist class. This conflict was fought over the control of Parliament, but the ultimate issue was whether England was to remain a relatively self-sufficient agricultural economy or to become an island devoted primarily to industrial production.

Class Conflicts óf Malthus's Times

The industrial revolution brought about increases in human productivity without precedent in history. The widespread construction of factories and the extensive use of machinery constituted the mechanical basis for this increase. In order to channel the economy's productive capacity into the creation of capital goods, however, it was necessary to devote a relatively much smaller part of this capacity to the manufacture of consumer goods. Capital goods had to be purchased at a social cost of mass deprivation. Although technological change increased productivity and thereby mitigated somewhat this social cost, its effects were by no means sufficient to provide for the growing volume of accumulated capital.

Historically, in all cases in which society has had to force a bare subsistence existence on some of its members, it has always been those with the least economic and political power who have made the sacrifices. And so it was in the industrial revolution in England. The working class lived near the subsistence level in 1750, and their standard of living (measured in terms of the purchasing power of wages) deteriorated during the second half of the eighteenth century. The trend of working-class living standards in the first several decades of the nineteenth century is a subject of dispute among historians. The fact that many eminent scholars find sufficient evidence to argue that the living standard failed to increase, or even decreased, leads to the conclusion that any increase during this period was slight at best.

Throughout the period of the industrial revolution, there is no doubt that the standard of living of the poor fell precipitously in relation to the standards of the middle and upper classes. A detailed analysis shows that the

> relatively poor grew poorer, simply because the country, and its rich and middle class, so obviously grew wealthier. The very moment when the poor were at the end of their tether . . . was the moment when the middle class dripped with excess capital, to be wildly invested in railways and spent on the bulging opulent household furnishings displayed at the Great Exhibition of 1851, and on palatial municipal constructions . . . in the smoky northern cities.[1]

There can be no doubt about which class paid the social costs in terms of the sacrificed consumption that was necessary for industrialization.

Yet, the costs in terms of decreased consumption were by no means the only, and perhaps not even the worst, hardships forced on the laboring class by the industrial revolution. The new factory system completely destroyed the laborers' traditional way of life, throwing them into a nightmare world with which they were completely unprepared to cope. They lost the pride of workmanship and close personal relationships that had existed in handicraft industries. Under the new system their only relationship with their employer was through the impersonal market, or *cash nexus*. They lost direct access to the means of production and were reduced to mere sellers of labor power totally dependent on market conditions for their livelihood.

Perhaps worse than any of these was the monotonous, mechanical regularity imposed on the worker by the factory system. In preindustrial Europe, a worker's tasks were not so specialized. The worker went from one task to another, and the work was interrupted by variation in the seasons or the weather. When the worker felt like resting or playing or changing the pace of the work routine, he or she had a certain amount of freedom to do so. Factory employment brought the tyranny of the clock. Production was mechanized, and absolute regularity was necessary to coordinate the complex interaction of processes and to maximize the use of new, expensive machinery. The pace of work was no longer decided by the worker but by the machine.

The machine, which had formerly been an appendage to the worker, was now the focal point of the production process. The worker became a mere appendage to the cold, implacable, pacesetting machine. During the late eighteenth and early nineteenth centuries, a spontaneous revolt against the new factory system saw bands of workers smashing and destroying machines and factories, which they believed were responsible for their plight. These revolts, called the Luddite revolts, ended in 1813 when large numbers of workers were hanged or deported for their activities.

The extensive division of labor in the factory made much of the work so routine and simple that untrained women and children could do it as well as men. Because women and children could be hired for much lower wages than men, and because in many cases entire families had to work in order to earn enough to eat, women and children were widely employed. Many factory owners preferred women and children because they could be reduced to a state of passive obedience more easily than men. The widespread ideology in this period that the only good woman was a submissive woman was a great help to their employers.

Children were bound to factories by indentures of apprenticeship for seven years, or until they were twenty-one. Almost nothing was given the children in return for long hours of work under the most horrendous conditions. Poor-law authorities could indenture the children of paupers, which led to "regular bargains . . . [where] children . . . were dealt with as mere merchandise . . . between the spinners on the one hand and the Poor Law authorities on the other. Lots of fifty, eighty or a hundred children were supplied and sent like cattle to the factory, where they remained imprisoned for many years."[2]

These children endured the cruelest servitude. They were totally isolated from anyone who might take pity on them and were thus at the mercy of the capitalists or their hired managers, whose main concern was the challenge of competitive factories. The children's workday lasted from fourteen to eighteen hours or until they dropped from complete exhaustion. The foremen were paid according to how much the children produced and therefore pushed them mercilessly. In most factories the children had hardly more than twenty minutes a day for their main (and often only) meal. "Accidents were very common, especially towards the end of the overlong day, when the exhausted children almost fell asleep at their work. The tale never ended of fingers cut off and limbs crushed in the wheels."[3] The children were disciplined in such savage and brutal ways that a recitation of the methods would appear completely incredible to the reader of today.

Women were mistreated almost as severely. Work in a factory was long, arduous, and monotonous. Discipline was harsh. Many times the price of factory employment was submission to the sexual advances of employers and foremen.[4] Women in the mines toiled fourteen to sixteen hours a day, stripped to the waist, working with men and doing the work of men. There were reports of women who came out of the mines to bear children and were back in the mines within days after giving birth. Many accounts have been written of the fantastically cruel and dehumanizing working conditions for women during this period. And, of course, the men who worked were not much better off than the women or the children.

Another important consideration in assessing the living standard of the working class during the period of capitalist industrialization was the rapid urbanization that took place at that time. In 1750, only two cities in Britain had populations over 50,000. In 1850, there were twenty-nine. By the latter date, nearly one person in three lived in a city with over 50,000 inhabitants.

Conditions in the cities of this period were terrible:

> And what cities! It was not merely that smoke hung over them and filth impregnated them, that the elementary public services—water supply, sanitation, street-cleaning, open spaces, etc.—could not keep pace with the mass migration of men into the cities, thus producing, pace especially after 1830, epidemics of cholera, typhoid and an appalling constant toll of the two great groups of nineteenth-century urban killers—air pollution and water pollution, or respiratory and intestinal diseases. . . . The new city populations . . . [were] pressed into overcrowded and bleak slums, whose very sight froze the heart of the observer. "Civilization works its miracles" wrote the great French liberal de Tocqueville of Manchester, "and civilized man is turned back almost into a savage."[5]

Included in these slums was a district in Glasgow that, according to a report of a government commissioner, housed

> a fluctuating population of between 15,000 and 30,000 persons. This district is composed of many narrow streets and square courts and in the middle of each court there is a dunghill. Although the outward appearance of these places was revolting, I was nevertheless quite unprepared for the filth and misery that were to be found inside. In some bedrooms we visited at night, we found a whole mass of humanity stretched on the floor. There were often 15 to 20 men and women huddled together, some being clothed and others being naked. There was hardly any furniture there and the only thing which gave these holes the appearance of a dwelling was fire burning on the hearth. Thieving and prostitution are the main sources of income of these people.[6]

The total destruction of the laborers' traditional way of life and the harsh discipline of the new factory system, combined with deplorable living conditions in the cities, generated social, economic, and political unrest. Chain reactions of social upheaval, riots, and rebellion occurred in the years 1811–13, 1815–17, 1819, 1826, 1829–35, 1838–42, 1843–44, and 1846–48. In many areas these uprisings were purely spontaneous and primarily economic in character. In 1816, one rioter was reported to have shouted: "Here I am between Earth and Sky, so help me God. I would sooner lose my life than go home as I am. Bread I want and bread I will have."[7] In 1845, an American named Colman reported that the working people of Manchester were "wretched, defrauded, oppressed, crushed human nature lying in bleeding fragments all over the face of society."[8]

There can be no doubt that industrial capitalism was erected on the base of the wretched suffering of a laboring class denied access to the fruits of the rapidly expanding economy and subjected to the most degrading of excesses to increase the capitalists' profits. The basic cause of the great evils of this period was

> the absolute and uncontrolled power of the capitalist. In this, the heroic age of great undertakings, it was acknowledged, admitted and even proclaimed with brutal candor. It was the employer's own business, he did as he chose and did not consider that any other justification of his conduct was necessary. He owed his employees wages and once those were paid the men had no further claim on him.[9]

From the earliest introduction of factory production in the textile industries, workers tried to band together to protect their interests collectively. In 1787, during a period of high employment, the Glasgow muslin manufacturers attempted to lower the piece rates that they were paying. The workers resisted collectively, refused to work below a certain minimum rate, and organized a boycott of the manufacturers who would not pay the minimum rate. The struggle led to open rioting and shooting, but the workers proved to be a strong and well-disciplined group, and they built a strong union. In 1792, a union of weavers forced a collective agreement on Bolton and Bury Manufacturers.

Labor organizations spread rapidly in the 1790s. As a result of this and the concurrent growth of social and economic discontent, the upper classes became very uneasy. The memory of the French Revolution was fresh in their minds, and they feared the power of united workers. The result was the Combination Act of 1799, which outlawed any combination of workers whose purpose was to obtain higher wages, shorter hours, or the introduction of any regulation constraining the free action of their employers. Proponents couched their arguments in terms of the necessity of free competition and the evils of monopoly—cardinal tenets of classical liberalism—but did not mention combinations of employers or monopolistic practices of capitalists. The effects of this legislation have been summarized as follows:

> The Combination Laws were considered as absolutely necessary to prevent ruinous extortions of workmen, which, if not thus restrained, would destroy the whole of the trade, manufactures, commerce and agriculture of the nation. . . . So thoroughly was this false notion entertained, that whenever men were prosecuted to conviction for having combined to regulate their wages or the hours of working, however heavy the sentence passed upon them was, and however rigorously it was inflicted, not the slightest feeling of compassion was manifested by anybody for the unfortunate sufferers. Justice was entirely out of the question: They could seldom obtain a hearing before a magistrate, never without impatience or insult. . . . Could an accurate account be given of proceedings, of hearings before magistrates, trials at sessions and in the Court of King's Bench, the gross injustice, the foul invective, and terrible punishments inflicted would not, after a few years have passed away, be credited to any but the best evidence.[10]

Another cause for which the proponents of laissez-faire capitalism campaigned vigorously was the abolition of the Speenhamland system of poor relief that had come into existence in 1795. This system was (continuing in the tradition of the Elizabethan Statute of Artificers) the result of the Christian paternalist ethic. It held that unfortunates would be entitled to a certain minimum living standard whether employed or not. To be sure, the system had serious drawbacks: it actually depressed wages below the relief level in many cases (with the parish taxes making up the difference) and severely limited labor mobility at a time when greater mobility was needed. But most of the arguments were not confined to these features of the Speenhamland system. They were opposed to any government aid to the poor, and many of their arguments were based on the ideas of Malthus.

During the 1790s, the plight of workers had deteriorated sharply. The wars in which England was fighting had cut off much of its food imports, and the price of grains rose very substantially. Wheat, for example, cost 31 shillings per quarter of a ton in 1750. By 1775, the price was 46 shillings, and over the next twenty-five years it soared to 128 shillings. While money wages rose during the period, the amount of food a worker could buy with his or her pay declined.

Of equal importance was the fact that the prices of manufactured goods generally did not rise as fast as wages (some even fell during the period), much less as fast as agricultural prices. In 1815, with the long series of wars over, the corn laws became one of the most critical political issues facing the British Parliament. The landlord class used all of its social, intellectual, and political influences to obtain a new set of tariffs on agricultural products. It wanted to raise the tariffs high enough to keep foreign grains, which could be imported at prices far lower than those prevailing in Britain, from entering the country. This would sustain British agricultural prices at a high rate and assure continuation of the equally high incomes that landlords had enjoyed throughout the war years.

The British industrial capitalists, however, opposed the corn laws for two fundamental reasons. First, because grains and products made from grains constituted the largest part of the necessary subsistence of laborers, the high price of grains forced the capitalists to pay workers a higher money wage in order for the workers and their families to subsist. This higher money wage cut into the capitalists' profits. Thus, the high agricultural prices had the effect of transferring much of the surplus value created by the workers from the profits of the capitalists to the rents of the landlords. Second, by the early nineteenth century, British manufacturing had become much more efficient than its continental competitors, and, hence, the prices of British manufactured goods were much lower than those of the other countries of Europe. This meant that if all tariffs could be abolished and free international trade could be established, British manufacturers could undersell their European competitors. For Britain to sell manufactured goods to continental Europe, however, it had to buy some commodities there. If Britain imported grain from continental Europe, this would place British pounds in the hands of Europeans, which would then permit those Europeans to buy British manufactured commodities.

The ultimate issue at stake was tremendously important. The landlords wanted Britain to remain a predominantly agricultural economy in order to perpetuate their position, income, and power. The industrial capitalists wanted Britain to specialize in manufacturing in order to expand their income and power and to reduce the portion of surplus value that was accruing to the landlords. What in fact was occurring was the last battle between two antagonistic elements of the British ruling class. The landlords were the last vestige of the feudal ruling class, and, like the feudal nobility, their power came from control of the land. The capitalists' power came from their control over labor and the production process. The surplus value created by workers was shared by capitalists and landlords, who were each fighting to become the controlling faction of the ruling class of capitalism.

In 1815, the landlords won a round in the fight. A corn law was passed that prohibited all grain importation until certain relatively high domestic prices had been reached. Wheat, for example, could not be imported until the British price reached 80 shillings per quarter. The industrial capitalists had economic dominance, but the landlords still controlled Parliament. This situation could not be maintained indefinitely, however. The dominant economic class has always eventually extended its economic dominance to political dominance. So the struggle continued, and finally, in 1846, Parliament voted for the total abolition of the corn laws. The event dramatized the final political dominance of the industrial capitalists.

The Theory of Population

Malthus wrote many books, pamphlets, and essays during his lifetime. His writings can be separated into two periods, each characterized by its own overriding social concern and theoretical approach. During the 1790s and early 1800s, his chief concerns were the unrest of labor and the schemes being advocated by radical intellectuals to restructure society in order to promote the welfare and happiness of workers. These schemes, Malthus correctly perceived, could attempt to promote the cause of laborers only by eroding the wealth and power of the two classes of proprietors, capitalists and landlords. Malthus was an outspoken champion of the wealthy, and his theory of population provided the framework within which he defended them. In 1798 he published *An Essay on the Principle of Population as It Affects the Future Improvement of Society, with Remarks on the Speculations of Mr. Godwin, M. Condorcet, and Other Writers*, generally referred to as the first *Essay on the Principle of Population.* In 1803, he published a revised edition in which the revisions were so extensive that it was, in reality, a new book. This book is generally referred to as the second *Essay on the Principle of Population.* He later published *A Summary View of the Principles of Population.*[11]

From about 1814 onward, Malthus's chief concerns became the corn laws and the struggle between the landlords and the capitalists. During this period he was a consistent defender of the interests of the landlord class. The intellectual foundation for this defense of the landlords is contained in his *Principles of Political Economy Considered with a View to Their Practical Application*, first published in 1820.[12] In the *Principles*, the most important theoretical basis for his defense of the landlords was his theory of economic "gluts," or depressions.

The abject conditions of the working class and the labor unrest of the late eighteenth century had spawned many intellectual champions of the working class. Particularly influential among these were the Frenchman Marie Jean Antoine Nicholas de Caritat, Marquis de Condorcet (1743–1794), and the Englishman William Godwin (1756–1836). It was primarily against the ideas of these two men that Malthus's first *Essay* was directed.

Condorcet had been an important influence in the first phases of the French Revolution. But after the Jacobins had come to dominate the Convention, he argued that the Republic should abolish the death penalty, protested the execution of the King and the arrest of the Girondins, and told the Convention that Robespierre lacked both ideas and human feelings. As a consequence, Condorcet was sentenced to death. He went into hiding where he wrote the *Esquisse d'un tableau historique des progrès de l'espirit humain*, his most famous work. In this book, he argued that there was a natural order of human progress, which was to reach its highest stage during the period following the French Revolution. In this stage, humans could develop morally, spiritually, and intellectually far beyond the level that had been possible previously.

The most important prerequisites for such development, however, were greater economic equality and security. Condorcet advocated two basic reforms to achieve these goals. First, while accepting the existing class divisions of society, he argued that the precariousness of the incomes of the working poor could be eliminated by the government establishing a fund for the welfare of the aged and of women and children who had lost their husbands and fathers. Second, he believed that the power and wealth of capitalists could be reduced by government regulation of credit. By limiting the amount of credit available to the powerful capitalists and by extending credit to ordinary working people, he believed that laborers could slowly become more independent of capitalists and that much greater social and economic equality would result.

William Godwin was much more radical than Condorcet. While most British conservatives as well as many classical liberal reformers were bemoaning the natural laziness and depravity of the working class, Godwin argued that the defects of the working class were attributable to corrupt and unjust social institutions. The capitalist society, in his opinion, made fraud and robbery inevitable: "If every man could with perfect facility obtain the necessaries of life . . . temptation would lose its power."[13] Men could not always obtain the necessities because the laws of private property created such great inequalities in society. Justice demanded that capitalist property relations be abolished and that property belong to that person whom it would benefit most:

> To whom does any article of property, suppose a loaf of bread, justly belong? To him who most wants it, or to whom the possession of it will be most beneficial. Here are six men famished with hunger, and the loaf is, absolutely considered, capable of satisfying the cravings of them all. Who is it that has a reasonable claim to benefit by the qualities with which the loaf is endowed? They are all brothers perhaps, and the law of primogeniture bestows it exclusively to the eldest. But does justice confirm this award? The laws of different countries dispose of property in a thousand different ways; but there can be but one way which is most conformable to reason.[14]

That one way, of course, must be based on the equality of all men. To whom could the poor turn to correct the injustices of the system? In Godwin's opinion, it most certainly would not be the government. With economic power went political power. The rich are "directly or indirectly the legislators of the state; and of consequence are perpetually reducing oppression into a system."[15] The law, then, is the means by which the rich oppress the poor, for "legislation is in almost every country grossly the favorer of the rich against the poor."[16]

These two ideas of Godwin's were to be voiced again and again by nineteenth century socialists: (1) that capitalist social and economic institutions, particularly private property relations, were the causes of the evils and suffering within the system, and (2) that the government in a capitalist system would never redress these evils because it was controlled by the capitalist class. But Godwin had an answer to this seemingly impossible situation. He believed human reason would save society. Once men became educated about the evils of the situation, they would reason together and arrive at the only rational solution. As Godwin saw it, this solution entailed the abolition of government, the abolition of laws, the abolition of private property and social classes, and the establishment of economic, social, and political equality.

Again, Malthus's first *Essay* was directed against the ideas of Condorcet and Godwin. A man subscribing to such ideas, Malthus believed,

> equally offends against the cause of truth. With eyes fixed on a happier state of society, the blessings of which he paints in the most captivating colours, he allows himself to indulge in the most bitter invectives against every present establishment, without applying his talents to consider the best and safest means of removing abuses and without seeming to be aware of the tremendous obstacles that threaten, even in theory, to oppose the progress of man towards perfection.[17]

Throughout the first *Essay* there were two recurring dominant themes. The first is an argument that no matter how successful reformers were in their attempts to alter capitalism, the present class structure of wealthy proprietors and poor laborers would inevitably reemerge. Such a class division was, Malthus believed, the inevitable consequence of natural law.

Malthus devised elaborate arguments to show that even if Godwin and his disciples were able to reconstruct society according to their ideals, such

> a society constituted according to the most beautiful form that imagination can conceive, with benevolence for its moving principle, instead of self-love, and with every evil disposition in all its members corrected by reason and not force, would, from the inevitable laws of nature, and not from any original depravity of man, in a very short period degenerate into a society constructed upon a plan not essentially different from that which prevails in every known state at present; I mean a society divided into a class of proprietors, and a class of labourers, and with self-love the main-spring of the great machine.[18]

The second theme pervading his population theory was that abject poverty and suffering were the inevitable lot of the majority of people in every society. Furthermore, attempts to alleviate the poverty and suffering, no matter how well intentioned they might be, would make the situation worse, not better:

> It has appeared, that from the inevitable laws of our nature some human beings must suffer from want. These are the unhappy persons who, in the great lottery of life, have drawn a blank.[19]

> No possible sacrifices of the rich, particularly in money, could for any time prevent the recurrence of distress among the lower members of society, whoever they were.[20]

We "should reprobate specific remedies for human suffering," Malthus argued, and we should also reprobate "those benevolent, but much mistaken men, who have thought they were doing a service to mankind by projecting schemes for the total extirpation of particular disorders."[21]

The population theory on which Malthus based these conclusions was relatively simple. He believed that most people were driven by an insatiable desire for sexual pleasure and that consequently rates of reproduction, *when unchecked*, would lead to geometric increases in population; specifically, population would double at each generation. "All animals," he argued, "must have a capacity of increasing in a geometrical progression.[22] In this regard, humans were no different from other animals:

> Elevated as man is above all other animals by his intellectual facilities, it is not to be supposed that the physical laws to which he is subject should be essentially different from those which are observed to prevail in other parts of animated nature.[23]

> It may be safely asserted therefore, that population, when unchecked, increases in a geometrical progression of such a nature as to double itself every twenty-five years.[24]

It was obvious to Malthus that in no society had population grown at this rate for very long, because within a relatively short period of time every square foot of the earth would have been inhabited. Thus, the central question to which he addressed himself was what forces had operated to check population growth in the past and what forces were likely to operate in the future.

The most immediate and obvious answer was that the population in any given territory was limited by the available food there. While Malthus was aware that by applying more labor or better methods of food production, humans could increase the level of food production, he asserted that in all probability the increases from each generation to the next would become successively smaller within a given territory. At best, he believed that food production could be increased at an arithmetic rate, that is, each generation could only increase production by roughly the same amount as the previous generation had:

> By the laws of nature in respect to the powers of a limited territory, the additions which can be made in equal periods to the food which it produces must, after a short time, either be constantly decreasing, which is what would really take place; or, at the very most, must remain stationary, so as to increase the means of subsistence only in arithmetical progression.[25]

So if there were no other checks, ultimately, starvation would limit population growth to the maximum rate at which food production could be increased. But there were many other checks. Sometimes Malthus classified these checks into two categories, preventive and positive. Preventive checks reduced the birth rate; these included such things as sterility, sexual abstinence, and birth control. Positive checks increased the death rate; these included famine, misery, plague, war, and the ultimate inevitable check of starvation. The population was always checked by some combination of these so that it was kept within the bounds of the available food supply. If preventive checks were inadequate, then positive checks were inevitable; and if there was an insufficiency of disease, war, and natural catastrophes, then starvation would always check population growth.

Malthus also had a second classificatory scheme, which gets us much closer to an understanding of the normative side of his theory. The positive and preventive "checks which repress the superior power of population, and keep its effects on a level with the means of subsistence, are all resolvable into moral restraint, vice and misery."[26] Within this scheme of classification, Malthus was able to argue that if the wealth and income of everyone in society were increased, the vast majority would respond by having so many children that they would very soon be pushed back to bare subsistence living; only the morally virtuous could escape this fate. "Moral restraint" was defined very simply as "the restraint from marriage which is not followed by irregular gratifications."[27] It is obvious, however, throughout Malthus's writings, that he believed such moral restraint was found only in the persons who had all of the other moral virtues that he valued. It is also obvious that Malthus believed that the lack of sexual restraint would be found among those who squandered every penny that they received above their subsistence on "drinking, gaming, and debauchery."[28]

Thus, in Malthus's theory, the ultimate difference between the rich and the poor was the high moral character of the former and the moral turpitude of the latter. He considered birth control to be a vice that a good Christian would hardly mention, much less advocate. Furthermore, he associated it exclusively with premarital or extramarital sexual intercourse:

> A promiscuous intercourse to such a degree as to prevent the birth of children seems to lower, in the most marked manner, the dignity of human nature. It cannot be without its effect on men, and nothing can be more obvious than its tendency to degrade the female character, and to destroy all its most amiable and distinguishing characteristics.[29]

The conclusion seemed obvious to Malthus when he observed "that carelessness and want of frugality . . . [predominates] among the poor." He noted that "even when they have an opportunity of saving they seldom exercise it, but all that is beyond their present necessities goes, generally speaking, to the ale-house."[30] Any Christian gentleman, such as Malthus, had to conclude that where moral restraint was absent, population would be checked by either vice or misery. Therefore, a good Christian must virtuously denounce vice and then realistically accept the inevitable misery necessary to keep population from outstripping subsistence.

Malthus therefore rejected all schemes that would redistribute wealth or income. Such redistributions would merely increase the number of poor workers and push them all back to subsistence. Sometimes Malthus even argued that such a redistribution would not even raise workers' welfare for the brief period until they were able to have children:

> Suppose that by a subscription of the rich the eighteen pence a day which men earn now was made up five shillings, it might be imagined, perhaps, that they would then be able to live comfortably and have a piece of meat every day for their dinners. But this would be a very false conclusion. . . . The receipt of five shillings a day, instead of eighteen pence, would make every man fancy himself comparatively rich and able to indulge himself in many hours or days of leisure. This would give a strong and immediate check to productive industry, and, in a short time, not only the nation would be poorer, but the lower classes themselves would be much more distressed than when they received only eighteen pence a day.[31]

Malthus also opposed virtually every attempt to legislate some form of relief for the suffering of the poor.

> The poor laws of England tend to depress the general condition of the poor in these two ways. Their first obvious tendency is to increase population without increasing the food for its support. . . . Secondly, the quantity of provisions consumed in workhouses upon a part of the society that cannot in general be considered as the most valuable part diminishes the shares that would otherwise belong to more industrious and more worthy members.[32]

The most valuable members of society were, of course, the wealthy class of proprietors, whose value was both economic and cultural. To illustrate the economic value of the wealthy, Malthus argued that in any society the only possible escape from anarchy and total insecurity was the establishment of property rights and marriage. Once these institutions were established, then those persons of high moral character would begin to accumulate, while most of the members of society would dissipate their property in riotous living.

At this point, the lower classes would have no means to continue their existence unless the moral, wealthy elite shared their accumulated funds. But there would be so many poor persons that the wealthy elite would have to choose with whom to share their funds.

> And it seems both natural and just that . . . their choice should fall upon those who were able, and professed themselves willing, to exert their strength in procuring a further surplus produce; and thus at once benefiting the community, and enabling these proprietors to afford assistance to greater numbers. . . .
> On the state of this [proprietors'] fund, the happiness, or degree of misery, prevailing among the lower classes of people in every known state at present chiefly depends.[33]

This statement is followed by the previously quoted assertion that the "inevitable laws of nature" decree that all societies will be "divided into a class of proprietors and a class of labourers."

The social and cultural value of the wealthy class of proprietors was even greater. Malthus believed that the private property system and the class inequality that it created were responsible for all of the great cultural achievements of humanity:

> It is to the established administration of property and to the apparently narrow principle of self-love that we are indebted for all the noblest exertions of human genious, all the finer and more delicate emotions of the soul, for everything, indeed, that distinguishes the civilized from the savage state; and no sufficient change has as yet taken place in the nature of civilized man to enable us to say that he either is, or ever will be, in a state when he may safely throw down the ladder by which he has risen to this eminence. . . .
> It should be observed that the principal argument of this *Essay* only goes to prove the necessity of a class of proprietors and a class of labourers.[34]

Sometimes Malthus went beyond merely opposing redistributions of wealth and income and legislative attempts to mitigate the harshness of poverty:

> It is an evident truth that, whatever may be the rate of increase in the means of subsistence, the increase in population must be limited by it, at least after the food has once been divided into the smallest shares that will support life. All the children born, beyond what would be required to keep up the population to this level, must necessarily perish, unless room be made for them by the deaths of grown persons.
> . . . To act consistently therefore, we should facilitate, instead of foolishly and vainly endeavouring to impede, the operation of nature in producing this mortality; and if we dread the too frequent visitation of the horrid form of famine, we should sedulously encourage the other forms of destruction, which we compel nature to use. Instead of recommending cleanliness to the poor, we should encourage contrary habits. In our towns we should make the streets narrower, crowd more people into

the houses, and court the return of the plague. In the country, we should build our villages near stagnant pools, and particularly encourage settlements in all marshy and unwholesome situations. But above all, we should reprobate specific remedies for ravaging diseases; and those benevolent, but much mistaken men, who have thought they were doing a service to mankind by projecting schemes for the total extirpation of particular disorders. If by these and similar means the annual mortality were increased . . . we might probably every one of us marry at the age of puberty, and yet few be absolutely starved.[35]

Perhaps Malthus sensed that even the most hard-hearted conservative might find his policy suggestions a little too harsh, so he ended the first *Essay* with a sanctimonious appeal to religion and God's will. Near the conclusion of the last chapter he reassured his readers:

Life is, generally speaking, a blessing. . . . The partial pain, therefore, that is inflicted by the supreme Creator, while he is forming numberless beings to a capacity of the highest enjoyments, is but as the dust of the balance in comparison of the happiness that is communicated, and we have every reason to think that there is no more evil in the world than what is absolutely necessary as one of the ingredients in the mighty process.[36]

Malthus's population theory was to have tremendous intellectual influence. It inspired Charles Darwin to formulate his theory of evolution, and variations of this population theory are widely accepted today—especially in theories dealing with economically less-developed countries. The normative orientation of the theory remains now, as with Malthus, to convince us that poverty is inevitable, that little or nothing can be done about it, and that poverty is, generally speaking, due to the weakness or moral inferiority of the poor.

Economics of Exchange and Class Conflict

During and after the second decade of the nineteenth century, Malthus's concern shifted from the class conflict between the proprietors and laborers to the conflict between the two antagonistic classes of proprietors—the capitalists and the landlords. Most of his theoretical writings during the period were incorporated into his *Principles of Political Economy*, and the remainder of this chapter will be devoted to a discussion of the ideas contained in that work.

Malthus lacked Smith's appreciation of history. In his rather culture-bound, egocentric view, there were only two states of society: the rude, uncivilized state and the civilized state. He had gone to great lengths in his *Essay on the Principle of Population* "to prove the necessity of a class of proprietors and a class of laborers" in every civilized society. But such a class division presupposed not only a money-exchange, commodity-producing society, but one in which labor power had become a commodity. With such an ahistorical view, it is not surprising that, unlike Smith, Malthus was unable to compare the methods of appropriating the economic surplus that had been utilized in precapitalist societies with those utilized in capitalism. Had he made such a comparison, he, like Smith, would have realized that the surplus is created in the production process and that, in order to understand the creation of the surplus, one must examine the process of production, *not* the process of the circulation of money and commodities; that is, the processes of exchange, or market supply and demand, can never furnish insights into the nature and origins of surplus value.

When Smith examined capitalism from the vantage point of production, he was led to a class conflict view of the economy; when he examined it from the vantage point of exchange, he was led to a social harmony view. Malthus, while forcefully aware of the class conflicts that characterized British society, adopted the exchange or supply-demand vantage point. Consequently, it seemed to him that existing conflicts were based on ignorance of how the capitalist economy worked. When a proper understanding was achieved, Malthus believed that all classes would see their common, harmonious interests.

The reason the exchange vantage point generally supports a view of social harmony is that it takes for granted existing laws of ownership and the existing distribution of property rights. The production vantage point (or the labor theory of value) on the contrary, considers these as elements of the economy to be explained by the theory and generally sees them as the legal manifestation of class division. When the laws of ownership and the distribution of property rights are taken for granted, then every exchange can be seen as mutually beneficial to both parties involved. The laborer who has nothing to sell but labor power is better off if he or she can find a buyer—no matter how low the wage—than if he or she starves. Therefore, all exchange is beneficial to capitalist and laborer alike, particularly if one accepts the inevitability of a class of proprietors and a class of laborers.

The universal beneficence of exchange, which we will see in later chapters was to become the normative core of neoclassical economics, was succinctly stated by Malthus:

> Every exchange which takes place in a country, effects a distribution of its produce better adapted to the wants of society. It is with regard to both parties concerned, an exchange of what is wanted less for what is wanted more, and must therefore raise the value of both the products.[37]

This is the foundation of theories that stress social harmony. Therefore, Malthus had to show that apparent class conflicts in his society were, in fact, amenable to harmonious solution. He did this by constructing an argument in which, despite superficial appearances to the contrary, the ultimate, long-run interests of both capitalists and laborers would best be promoted by the promotion of the immediate, short-run interest of the landlords: "It may be safely asserted that the interest of no other class in the state is so nearly and necessarily connected with its [the state's or general society's] wealth, prosperity, and power as the interest of the landowner."[38]

The exchange vantage point entered Malthus's analysis from the outset. Whereas Smith had defined wealth as the produce of labor, Malthus wrote, "I should define wealth to be material objects, necessary, useful, or agreeable to man, which are voluntarily appropriated by individuals or nations."[39] In a footnote to this definition, he stated that "an object might be considered as wealth which had no labor employed upon it."[40] He defined productive labor as that labor that produced material wealth. He objected, however, to the term *unproductive labor* because he believed it connoted that such labor was so-cially unimportant. He preferred "to substitute the term *personal services* for unproductive labor."[41]

Like Smith, Malthus believed that the quantity of labor commanded was the best measure of value. He also accepted the cost-of-production theory of value. The natural price was the sum of the wages, rent, and profits when each of these costs yielded their recipients the "normal" rate of return on their labor, land, and capital. His discussion of the cost-of-production theory of value differed from Smith's, however, in two very important ways. First, unlike Smith, who saw labor as the only absolutely necessary social cost of production, Malthus argued that wages, rent, and profits were all equally necessary. Second, Malthus did not believe that the market forces of supply and demand would necessarily move the market price toward the natural price. Both of these differences were significant, and we will discuss each at length.

From the production vantage point, one can abstract from the particular social institutions whereby the economic surplus is appropriated, that is, from the forms of property relations prevailing in a given economy. When one does this, production is seen as a sequence through time of labor exertions directed toward the transformation of natural resources into useful products. This is true for every mode of production. It was from this vantage point that Smith asserted that labor was the only necessary social cost of production, and that prior to the private appropriation of land and capital, labor received the total of what it produced.

From Malthus's exchange vantage point, property ownership was taken as "natural" and inevitable. Production was viewed as an exchange of produc-tive inputs. Each class owned a different but equally necessary input. In the *Principles*, as in his *Essay*, Malthus was fond of referring to a "lottery" where some just happened to come into the ownership of only their own labor, while others happened to come into the ownership of capital and land. The funda-mental principle of ownership was, he believed, the same in all three cases (i.e., because laborers were not owned by others, or were not slaves, they were on the same socioeconomic or legal footing as the owners of the means of production). One "cannot imply," he asserted, "that the labourer or farmer, who in the lottery of human life has not drawn a prize of land, suffers any hardship of injustice in being obliged to give something in exchange for the use of what belongs to another."[42]

Each class owned a unique type of commodity, and each had to be remunerated if it was to give permission to use its commodity in production. "It is not, therefore, correct," Malthus insisted, "to represent as Adam Smith does, the profits of capital as a deduction from the produce of labour."[43] Furthermore, "in speaking of the landlords, Adam Smith's language is again exceptionable. He represents them, rather invidiously, as loving to reap where they have not sown."[44] All three components of the natural price had the same basis in property ownership:

> The possessors of land . . . conduct themselves, with regard to their possessions, exactly in the same way as the possessors of labour and of capital, and let out or exchange what they have for as much money as the demanders are willing to give them for it.
>
> The . . . compensation which . . . [forms] the ordinary price of any exchangeable commodity, may be considered as consisting of three parts; that which pays the wages of the labourers employed in its production; that which pays the profits of the capital, including the advances to the labourers, by which such production has been facilitated; and that which pays the rent of land, or the compensation for those powers attached to the soil which are in the possession of the landlord; the price of each of these component parts being determined exactly by the same causes as those which determine the price as a whole.[45]

Because production could not take place without natural resources, the products of past labor, and present labor, and because the owners of each of these just happened to draw that particular type of property "in the lottery of human life," each class was equally entitled to a compensation representing the contribution to the production process of its property. From this exchange vantage point, which was later to dominate neoclassical economics, the distinctly human contribution to production was owning property—not a productive activity but a legal relationship. Furthermore, owning nothing but one's own labor power was, in principle, no different from owning the means of production.

Malthus's justification of profits as a return to a productive contribution of capitalists was simple. Workers could produce more when they had tools and machinery than when they had none. This added productivity was caused by the capitalists allowing their tools and machinery to be used. Therefore, Smith was wrong, and capitalists did contribute to production. Malthus entirely missed Smith's point that tools and machinery were simply the present embodiment of past labor exertions.

In Malthus's defense of the landlords' rent as also constituting remuneration for their contribution to production, he was concerned to refute the then widely held notion that rent was either the return to a monopoly or some form of unearned income. As early as 1815, he published a pamphlet entitled *An Inquiry into the Nature and Causes of Rent, and the Principles by Which It Is Regulated.* In this pamphlet, he developed a theory of rent that was very similar to a theory being simultaneously developed by David Ricardo (and others) and that subsequently came to be associated primarily with Ricardo. Malthus's ideas on rent will be very briefly summarized here. A more complete discussion of what has come to be known as "Ricardian rent" is in the next chapter.

Malthus equated income from a monopoly with income resulting from artificially created restraints of supply. He insisted that "rent is the natural result of a most inestimable quality in the soil, which God has bestowed on Man—the quality of being able to maintain more persons than are necessary to work it."[46] But all soil did not furnish an equal bounty. "Diversities of soil and situation must necessarily exist in all countries. All land," he argued, "cannot be the most fertile."[47] Rent existed because of the differences in the fertility of the soil.

When a country's population was small, its need for food could be satisfied by farming only the most fertile land. As capital was accumulated and the population grew, however, it would necessitate the farming of increasingly less fertile land. With inferior land, the profit and wage costs of producing a given quantity of agricultural produce would increase. Therefore, to make farming profitable on inferior lands, agricultural prices would have to rise to sufficiently high levels to cover these increased costs. But the costs of producing a given quantity of agricultural produce on the most fertile land would remain lower. It followed that the increasing agricultural prices would yield a larger surplus of price over costs of production on those crops grown on the most fertile land. It was this surplus, created by differences in the fertility of land, that was the basis of rent. Thus, rent was not the return to an artificially created restraint on supply; it was due to the differences in nature's gifts to man. Again, Malthus did not question the rights of property ownership but considered it quite appropriate to consider nature's gifts as the personal contributions to production of the landowners. In addition to the rent based on differences in natural soil fertility, Malthus argued that some differences in fertility were due to the landlord's improvement of the soil. Rent also had a special social value, which profits did not. Increased food production permitted a larger population to subsist and thereby created its own demand because the additional people had to eat. Increased manufacturing did not provide the necessities for a larger population, he argued, and, therefore, did not create any additional demand. In his theory of gluts, or depressions, as we will see, this created demand was an important social benefit of agriculture.

In discussing the economic causes of high rents, Malthus concluded that high profits, economic prosperity, and population growth were generally the forces that led to increased agricultural production. Increased agricultural production must bring successively less fertile land under cultivation and thereby increase rents. Therefore, high rents were both the result of and the best single indicator of general economic and social prosperity.

> Rents are the reward of present valour and wisdom, as well as of past strengths and abilities. Every day lands are purchased with the fruits of industry and talents. They

afford the great prize, the *"otium cum dignitate"* to every species of laudable exertion; and, in the progress of society, there is every reason to believe, that, as they become more valuable from the increase of capital and population, and the improvements in agriculture, the benefits which they yield may be divided among a much greater number of persons.

In every point of view, then, in which the subject can be considered, that quality of land which, by the laws of our being, must terminate in rent, appears to be a boon most important to the happiness of mankind.[48]

The Theory of Gluts

Malthus's second qualification to Smith's theory of prices was his insistence that the market forces of supply and demand do not automatically push the market price toward the natural price. "The worth of a commodity, in the place where it is estimated," wrote Malthus, "is its market price, not its natural price."[49] When market prices differed from natural prices, then the former were "determined by the extraordinary or accidental relations of supply and demand."[50] It was in his analysis of such extraordinary or accidental relations of supply and demand that Malthus made his most important and lasting contribution to economic theory—his theory of gluts, or depressions.

Whereas the production vantage point permitted Smith and Ricardo to develop much more sophisticated understandings of the nature of surplus value than that developed by Malthus, the latter's exchange vantage point was, perhaps, a factor that led him to investigate in a more thorough and sophisticated manner the process of the circulation of money and commodities. Malthus was aware that for the natural value of all produced commodities to be realized through money exchange, there would have to be a total "effectual" (or "effective," as it is now generally labeled) money demand for these commodities that was equal in value to the natural value of the commodities. Because the component costs of the natural value of all commodities also represented the incomes to the three classes in society, it followed that, in any given period, the total costs, making up the aggregate natural value of all commodities produced, had to equal the aggregate income accruing to the three classes for that period. Therefore, the necessary condition for effectual demand to equal the value of all commodities produced was that the three classes, taken together, had to be willing and able to spend all of their collective income on the commodities produced in each production period.

There were two ways in which income could be spent. The first was in the acquisition of commodities for consumption. The second was in the acquisition of commodities that were accumulated as capital. The classical economists (and nearly all economists to the present) defined saving as that income remaining after expenditures for consumption have been deducted. It followed that for all income to be spent, the expenditures for commodities to be accumulated as capital would have to be equal to the amount of income that was saved. (Modern economists define the purchase of currently produced commodities for the purpose of capital accumulation as investment. Therefore, the necessary condition for aggregate supply and aggregate demand to be equal is that investment equals saving.)

Adam Smith had been aware of this necessary condition for the smooth, continuous circulation of money and commodities. He had assumed, however, that no person saved unless that person desired to provide for the future. With this saving, a person could accumulate capital that would return the original saving plus a profit, or he or she would lend it to a capitalist in return for a portion of the capitalist's profits, paid as interest. In either case, the person would get more in the future than if that person had let the money sit idle. Smith had thus concluded:

> Whatever a person saves from his revenue he adds to his capital, and either employs it himself in maintaining an additional number of productive hands, or enables some other person to do so, by lending it to him for an interest, that is, for a share of the profits. . . .
> What is annually saved is as regularly consumed as what is annually spent, and nearly in the same time too; but it is consumed by a different set of people.[51]

Therefore, Smith and nearly all of the other classical economists argued that capitalism would never experience the difficulty of having insufficient aggregate demand for all of the produced commodities to be sold. But the capitalist system did have and always has had such problems.

From the very beginning, wherever the market forces of supply and demand have been relied on to regulate the production of commodities and the allocation of resources, the result has always been recurring economic crises, or depressions. In such depressions, businessmen have always had problems finding buyers for their commodities, productive capacity has gone unused, unemployment among workers has been much worse than usual, and increases in poverty and social distress have been the inevitable results.

In Britain in late 1818, there was a sharp decline of agricultural prices, followed by a general depression in 1819. The depression resulted in severe unemployment, a resurgence of labor militancy, and general social unrest. In August of that year, thousands of workers demonstrated in the streets of Manchester. The British government called out the armed forces and the demonstrators were brutally suppressed. Ten demonstrators were killed and many hundreds were severely injured in what came to be known as the "Peterloo Massacre." This occurred just one year before the publication of the first edition of Malthus's *Principles*. Malthus was extremely aware that depressions not only could but did happen in a capitalist economy; he was also well aware of the potential revolutionary danger of such labor uprisings. His single most important goal in writing the *Principles* was to promote an understanding of these crises, or gluts, and to propose policies to mitigate them. These policies were, of course, always consistent with his belief that "the interest of no other class in the state is so nearly and necessarily connected with its wealth, prosperity, and power as the interest of the landowner."[52]

It seemed obvious to Malthus that the cause of a general glut of commodities was the periodic insufficiency of effectual demand. In order to understand the source of, and remedy for, this lack of demand, he analyzed the patterns of expenditure of each of the three classes. Laborers of necessity spent all of their incomes on their subsistence. Capitalists were driven by a passion to accumulate capital and had neither the inclination nor the time to spend much of their profits on consumption or on personal services. He concluded that

> such consumption is not consistent with the actual habits of the generality of capitalists. The great object of their lives is to save a fortune, both because it is their duty to make a provision for their families, and because they cannot spend an income with so much comfort to themselves, while they are obliged perhaps to attend a counting-house for seven or eight hours a day.[53]

Landlords, however, were gentlemen of leisure. Being assured of a continual income from rents, they spent all of their income on comfortable surroundings, servants, and patronizing the arts, universities, and other institutions of culture. They always spent all of their income on consumer goods, or "personal services," and in the process promoted "all the noblest exertions of human genius, all the finer and more delicate emotions of the soul."[54]

Each of the three classes attempted to spend all of their income. But the capitalists attempted to spend all of their profits for new capital. The problem, Malthus believed, was that, as capitalism progressed, there was a tendency for capitalists to receive too much income. They could not profitably invest in capital all of the money that they saved. "Almost all merchants and manufacturers save, in prosperous times," he wrote, "much more rapidly than it would be possible for the national capital to increase, so as to keep up the value of the produce."[55]

The important question that Malthus had to answer was why the capitalists could not, as Smith had suggested, continually employ more workers and make more profits as they expanded their capital at whatever rate they were able. Malthus gave two answers to this question. Either the new capital would embody the same technology as the old, or it would embody technical innovations that rendered workers more productive. In either case, he believed that problems would develop.

In a period of prosperity, if profits were invested in new capital that embodied the same technology as the old capital, then any given quantity of new capital would employ the same number of workers as that same quantity of old capital. This would require, in order for sufficient workers to be available, that the work force grow at the same rate as capital. The problem was that with the advent of prosperity, capital would begin to grow immediately. But Malthus insisted that it was "obvious . . . that from the very nature of population, and the time required to bring full-grown labourers into the market, a sudden increase of capital and produce cannot effect a proportionate supply of labour in less than sixteen or eighteen years."[56] Therefore, when this new capital outstripped the labor supply, two things would happen. First, some capital would find no labor to employ and would remain idle. Second, there would be a temporary shortage of labor. "If the market were comparatively understocked with labor," Malthus wrote, "the landlords and capitalists would be obliged to give a larger quantity of produce to each workman."[57] In this case, "wages . . . would continue progressively to rise . . . as long as capital continued to increase."[58] In either case, capitalists would prefer to hold their income in barren cash rather than continuing to reduce profits on existing capital by accumulating more capital. Thus, capitalists would cease spending all of their income, and there would be an insufficiency of effectual demand.

Such imbalances in the circulation of money and commodities undoubtedly do occur, and Malthus made an important contribution to economic understanding when he analyzed their effects. The analysis, however, appears to contradict his population theory. Although it is true that if the rate of capital accumulation was to "suddenly increase," the size of the mature labor force could not suddenly increase. What is not clear, given his population theory, is why there should ever be a sudden increase in capital that would require the sudden increase in population. No matter what the rate of profit and consequent rate of accumulation, once they were historically established, it would appear that the rate of population growth should adjust to the rate of accumulation. Thus, if capital was accumulated at an annual rate of 10 percent every year, then one year's 10 percent population growth would supply the laborers for the 10 percent growth in capital that would take place in sixteen years. Similarly, if that rate had been maintained for some time, the increase in population sixteen years ago would have been sufficient to meet the current demand for labor. The difficulty, in the present writer's opinion, lies not in Malthus's theory of gluts but in his population theory.

The second possible type of accumulation involved technical change that augmented the productivity of labor. This new labor-saving capital would act as a substitute for labor. The same quantity of produce could be produced with more capital and less labor. But the displacement of workers would reduce demand. Therefore,

> if the substitution of fixed capital were to take place much faster than an adequate market could be found for the more abundant supplies derived from it and for the new products of the labour that had been thrown out of employment, a slack demand for labour and distress among the labouring classes of society would be universally felt.[59]

Thus, in either case the ultimate cause of gluts was excessive profits leading to an unsustainable rate of capital accumulation. The only answer to the problem, in Malthus's opinion, was to pursue policies that would alter the distribution of income, leaving the capitalists with lower profits and some other class with more income to spend on consumption. The relationship between Malthus's theory of gluts and the controversy surrounding the corn laws now becomes apparent. In Malthus's words:

> There must therefore be a considerable class of persons who have both the *will* and power to consume more material wealth than they produce, or the mercantile classes could not continue profitably to produce so much more than they consume. In this class the landlords no doubt stand preeminent.[60]

The landlords themselves would not consume all of the excess material produce. They would, Malthus believed, hire large numbers of servants and other unproductive laborers, or providers of "personal services," who would spend their incomes on the material commodities produced in the manufacturing sector. Thus Malthus's solution entailed the creation of an army of unproductive workers who were the servants of the landlords. They would consume material wealth without producing it and thereby eliminate the problem of inadequate aggregate demand.

The only way to assure adequate effectual demand, then, was through some redistributional device, such as the corn laws, that would permit the landlords to receive more rent, and, thereby, through their own expenditures and those of their servants, to contribute more to aggregate demand without contributing to further increased production. Once again the economic welfare of all society depended on promoting the interests of the landlords. To further cement his case, after showing that landlords were economically and culturally indispensable to England, Malthus argued that their political power in Parliament was also in the best interest of all of society:

> It is an historical truth which cannot for a moment be disputed, that the first formation and subsequent preservation and improvement of our present constitution, and of the liberties and privileges which have so long distinguished Englishmen, are mainly due to a landed aristocracy.[61]

One final question remains: how did Malthus argue against a redistribution that would increase wages in order to increase aggregate demand? From his *Essay on the Principle of Population*, one might suppose that he would have argued that no social benefit would come of this because increases in the number of workers would simply push the workers back to the subsistence level. But as we have seen, in his theory of gluts, Malthus abandoned his population theory, at least in the short run. Or, again from the *Essay*, one might suppose that he would argue that the increase in wages "would make every man fancy himself comparatively rich" and thereby create "a strong and immediate check to productive industry."[62] Although there were hints of the latter argument in the *Principles*, Malthus's primary case against increased wages was contained in the following passage:

> It is indeed most important to observe that no power of consumption on the part of
> the labouring classes can ever . . . alone furnish an encouragement to the employ-
> ment of capital. No one will ever employ capital merely for the sake of the demand
> occasioned by those who work for him. Unless they produce an excess of value
> above what they consume . . . it is quite obvious that his capital will not be employed
> in maintaining them. . . . As a great increase of consumption among the working
> classes must greatly increase the cost of production, it must lower profits, and di-
> minish or destroy the motive to accumulate.[63]

This passage is interesting because it illustrates a point made in the previous chapter of this book: When a significant and powerful thinker makes a
seemingly obvious error of logic, it frequently illustrates the degree to which
the social orientation or the class loyalty of the thinker, rather than pure logic,
determines his or her conclusions. Because the categories of class income
were identical to the three components of the cost of production, any political
measure, such as the corn laws, that resulted in an increase of either rents or
wages would have the effect of lowering profits. Malthus correctly assumed
that the objections that the capitalists had against reforms to reduce profits by
increasing *wages* were identical to the objections they had against reforms to
reduce profits by increasing *rents*.

David Ricardo, the leading intellectual spokesman for the capitalist class
of that time, immediately and clearly understood the error of Malthus's conclusion. He wrote:

> A body of unproductive labourers are just as necessary and as useful with a view to
> future production, as a fire, which should consume in the manufacturer's warehouse
> the goods which those unproductive labourers would otherwise consume. . . . What
> advantage can it be to me that another man who returns nothing to me shall consume
> my goods? How does such a consumption enable me to realize my profits? . . . To
> enable the capitalists to continue their habits of saving, says Mr. Malthus, "they
> must either consume more or produce less." . . . Commodities consumed by unpro-
> ductive consumers are given to them, not sold for an equivalent. . . . Will the taking
> of 100 pieces of cloth from a clothier's manufactury, and clothing soldiers and sail-
> ors with it, add to his profits? Will it stimulate him to produce?—yes, in the same way
> as a fire would. . . . What would be more wise if Mr. Malthus' doctrine be true than to
> increase the army and double the salaries of all the officers of the government?[64]

Who was correct in this debate between Malthus and Ricardo? In the present
writer's opinion, they were both partially correct, but each was oblivious to
the partial truth of the other's argument. Capitalism does tend to generate
imbalances in the circulation of money and commodities. These imbalances
are frequently manifested as crises, in which aggregate demand is insufficient
to purchase all of the commodities that have been produced. In such a situation, it is in the interests of capitalists, taken collectively as a class, to find
some source of increased demand. However, each capitalist, taken individually, realizes that his or her own production costs do not directly affect the
demand for his or her product in any significant manner. His or her costs do,
however, significantly affect profits. He or she therefore has a strong motiva-

tion to keep production costs as low as possible. But the costs of production of capitalists, taken collectively, generate the incomes that are used to buy their products. Therefore, it would be ideal for each capitalist, taken individually, to keep costs as low as possible while all other capitalists paid high rates of wages and rents, thereby generating a high demand for the individual capitalist's products.

There is, in short, a contradiction between the needs of any capitalist, taken individually, and the needs of all capitalists, taken collectively. Malthus and Ricardo were each clearly aware of one horn of the dilemma, but each tried to solve the problem by ignoring or denying the other horn. No such solution was or is possible. We will discuss this dilemma more fully in the chapter on John Maynard Keynes, where we evaluate the impact of his ideas on post–World War II capitalist economies.

Notes to Chapter 4

1. E.J. Hobsbawm, *Industry and Empire: An Economic History of Britain Since 1750* (London: Weidenfeld and Nicolson, 1968), p. 72. Several of Hobsbawm's ideas appear in this chapter.

2. Paul Mantoux, *The Industrial Revolution in the Eighteenth Century* (New York: Harcourt Brace Jovanovich, 1927), pp. 410–11.

3. Ibid., p. 413.

4. Ibid., p. 416.

5. Hobsbawm, *Industry and Empire*, pp. 67–68.

6. Quoted in F. Engels, *The Condition of the Working Class in England in 1844* (New York: Macmillan, 1958), p. 46.

7. Quoted in Hobsbawm, *Industry and Empire*, p. 74.

8. Ibid., p. 75.

9. Mantoux, *Industrial Revolution*, p. 417.

10. Quoted in ibid., p. 449.

11. The first *Essay* and the *Summary View* are published together in one volume, T.R. Malthus, *An Essay on the Principle of Population and a Summary View of the Principles of Population*, ed. A. Flew (Baltimore: Penguin, 1970). The second *Essay* is published in two volumes: T.R. Malthus, *An Essay on the Principle of Population* (New York: Dutton, 1960).

12. The second edition of the *Principles* was published in 1836. All references in this chapter will be to this second edition: T.R. Malthus, *Principles of Political Economy* (New York: Augustus M. Kelley, 1964).

13. Quoted in Alexander Gray, *The Socialist Tradition* (London: Longmans, 1963), p. 119.

14. Ibid., p. 131.

15. Ibid., p. 119

16. Ibid., p. 119.

17. Malthus, first *Essay*, pp. 68–69.

18. Ibid., p. 144.

19. Ibid., p. 143.

20. Malthus, second *Essay*, vol. 2, p. 39.

21. Ibid., vol. 2, p. 179.

22. Malthus, *Summary View*, p. 226.

23. Ibid., p. 225.

24. Ibid., p. 238.

25. Ibid., p. 242.

26. Malthus, second *Essay*, vol. 1, p. 19.

27. Ibid., vol. 1, p. 14.

28. Ibid., vol. 2, p. 13.

29. Ibid., vol. 1, p. 13.
30. Malthus, first *Essay*, p. 98.
31. Ibid., pp. 94–95.
32. Ibid., p. 97.
33. Ibid., pp. 143–44.
34. Ibid., pp. 176–77.
35. Malthus, second *Essay*, vol. 2, pp. 179–80.
36. Malthus, first *Essay*, pp. 215–16.
37. Malthus, *Principles of Political Economy*, pp. 282–83.
38. Ibid., p. 206.
39. Ibid., p. 33.
40. Ibid., p. 34.
41. Ibid., p. 35.
42. Ibid., pp. 76–77.
43. Ibid., p. 76.
44. Ibid., p. 76.
45. Ibid., p. 77.
46. Ibid., p. 148.
47. Ibid., p. 149.
48. Ibid., pp. 216–17.
49. Ibid., p. 78.
50. Ibid.
51. Adam Smith, *An Inquiry into the Nature and Causes of the Wealth of Nations* (New York: Modern Library, 1937), p. 321.
52. Malthus, *Principles*, p. 206.
53. Ibid., p. 400.
54. Malthus, first *Essay*, pp. 176–77.
55. Malthus, *Principles*, p. 400.
56. Ibid., p. 280.
57. Ibid., p. 279.
58. Ibid., p. 277.
59. Ibid., p. 238.
60. Ibid., p. 400.
61. Ibid., p. 380.
62. Malthus, first *Essay*, p. 95.
63. Malthus, *Principles*, pp. 404–5.
64. Quoted in Sydney H. Coontz, *Productive Labour and Effective Demand* (New York: Augustus M. Kelly, 1966), pp. 45–46.

Chapter 5

David Ricardo

David Ricardo (1772–1823) was the son of a wealthy English capitalist who had made a fortune on the stock exchange after migrating to England from Holland. The younger Ricardo was even more successful on the stock exchange than his father had been, becoming a very wealthy man before he was thirty. In 1799 he read Adam Smith's *The Wealth of Nations*, and from that time until his death he divided his time between studying and writing about issues in political economy and enlarging his fortune. It is generally agreed that he was the most rigorous theoretician of the classical economists. His ability to construct an abstract model of how capitalism worked and then to depict all of its logical implications was unsurpassed in his own time. Furthermore, his economic theorizing established a style of abstract deductive economic models that has dominated economic theory down to the present. Like Adam Smith, he was to exert a powerful influence on both the radical Marxist and the conservative neoclassical traditions of economic theorizing throughout the remainder of the nineteenth and twentieth centuries. Unquestionably, he has been one of the five or six most influential economists of modern times.

Ricardo lived through the same turbulent era as Malthus, and, like the latter, was influenced by the French Revolution, the industrial revolution, the increasing unrest of the working class, and the struggle between the English capitalists and landlords. His attitude toward the working class was not essentially different from that of Malthus. Ricardo accepted Malthus's population theory and Malthus's conclusions regarding the nature and causes of laborers' poverty. Ricardo wrote:

> Of Mr. Malthus's *Essay on Population* I am happy in the opportunity here afforded me of expressing my admiration. The assaults of the opponents of this great work have only served to prove its great strength; and I am persuaded that its just reputation will spread with the cultivation of that science of which it is so eminent an ornament.[1]

He was, however, a life-long intellectual antagonist, although close personal friend, of Malthus. The primary social issue on which they differed
was the conflict between the capitalists and the landlords. Ricardo was a
consistent defender of the interests of the capitalist class. The principal theoretical issues on which they differed were the theory of value and Malthus's
theory of gluts.

In the preface to his *Principles of Political Economy and Taxation*, Ricardo
stated what he saw as the central problem of political economy:

> The produce of the earth—all that is derived from its surface by the united applica-
> tion of labour, machinery, and capital, is divided among three classes of the commu-
> nity, namely, the proprietor of the land, the owner of the stock of capital necessary
> for its cultivation, and the labourers by whose industry it is cultivated.
>
> To determine the laws which regulate this distribution is the principal problem in
> Political Economy.[2]

Malthus published *An Inquiry into the Nature and Causes of Rent* in 1815,
and Ricardo read it immediately after publication. He recognized that Malthus's
rent theory complemented a theory of profits on which he had been working
for some time.[3] He had already concluded that the price of corn, relative to
the prices of manufactured commodities, was regulated by the tendency for
labor and capital, applied to successively less fertile lands, to be less and less
productive of corn. He had also concluded that the rate of profit was governed
by the diminishing productivity of agricultural labor. Malthus's theory of rent
therefore gave explicit statement to ideas that were already implicit in Ricardo's
theory of profit. Three weeks after the publication of Malthus's pamphlet,
Ricardo published *An Essay on the Influence of a Low Price of Corn on the
Profits of Stock, Showing the Inexpediency of Restrictions on Importation.* In
it, he first developed the essentials of his theory of distribution.

Ricardo's theory of rent in the *Principles* was a consistent elaboration of
the view contained in his *Essay* of 1815. He defined rent as "that portion of
the produce of the earth which is paid to the landlord for the use of the original and indestructible powers of the soil."[4] His theory of the determination of
rent was based on two assumptions: first, that land differed in its fertility and
that all lands could be arrayed along a spectrum from the most fertile to the
least fertile; and second, that competition always equalized the rate of profit
among the capitalist farmers who rented land from the landlords. His theory
of rent cannot be summarized better than he himself summarized it. His discussion of the determination of rent shall therefore be quoted at length. Before reading this quotation, however, it is necessary for the reader to understand
Ricardo's definition of net produce. Net produce was the total quantity produced minus all of the necessary costs of production, including the replacement of capital used up in production and the wages of workers. Net produce
was therefore the total of the surplus value, created by labor, which could go
to either profit or rent. Ricardo's theory of rent follows in his own words:

It is only . . . because land is not unlimited in quantity and uniform in quality, and because, in the progress of population, land of an inferior quality . . . is called into cultivation, that rent is ever paid for the use of it. When, in the progress of society, land of the second degree of fertility is taken into cultivation, rent immediately commences on that of the first quality, and the amount of that rent will depend on the difference in the quality of these two portions of land.

When land of the third quality is taken into cultivation, rent immediately commences on the second, and it is regulated as before by the difference in their productive powers. At the same time, the rent of the first quality will rise, for that must always be above the rent of the second by the difference between the produce which they yield with a given quantity of capital and labour. With every step in the progress of population, which shall oblige a country to have recourse to land of a worse quality, to enable it to raise its supply of food, rent, on all the more fertile land, will rise.

Thus suppose land—No. 1, 2, 3—to yield with an equal employment of capital and labour a net produce of 100, 90, and 80 quarters of corn. . . . As soon as population had increased as to make it necessary to cultivate No. 2 . . . rent would commence on No. 1; for either there must be two rates of profit on agricultural capital, or ten quarters . . . must be withdrawn from the produce of No. 1 for some other. Whether the proprietor of the land, or any other person, cultivated No. 1, these ten quarters would equally constitute rent; for the cultivator of No. 2 would get the same result with his capital whether he cultivated No. 1, paying ten quarters rent, or continued to cultivate No. 2, paying no rent. In the same manner it might be shown that when No. 3 is brought into cultivation, the rent of No. 2 must be ten quarters . . . whilst the rent of No. 1 would rise to twenty quarters; for the cultivator of No. 3 would have the same profits whether he paid twenty quarters for the rent of No. 1, ten quarters for the rent of No. 2, or cultivated No. 3 free of all rent.[5]

It was competition among capitalist farmers that assured that rent would progress in this way. Suppose that the farmer on number 1, in Ricardo's example, paid only 15 quarters rent after number 3 was brought into cultivation. In that event, he would be making 85 quarters profit (100 quarters net produce minus 15 quarters rent) on the same capital with which the other two capitalist farmers were making only 80 quarters profit. The other two capitalist farmers could increase their profits by offering to pay landlord number 1 more rent, say 18 quarters, to allow them to farm his land. But as long as the rent on land number 1 was below 20 quarters, capitalists would continue to have an incentive to bid the rent up. Only when the rent was bid up to 20 quarters would they no longer have such an incentive. At that point, the rate of profit would be the same for all capitalist farmers. Ricardo believed that, in general, competition would tend to equalize the rate of profit for all capitalists. The "restless desire on the part of all the employers of stock," he wrote, "to quit a less profitable for a more advantageous business has a strong tendency to equalize the rate of profits of all."[6]

Ricardo's theory of rent was so important to the conclusions of his economic model that we shall give two illustrations of it. In Figure 5.1, the geometrical areas of each of the three bars represent the net produce in Ricardo's example. Net produce is comprised of profit plus rent; that is, it is the same as total produce less wages and replacement of capital used up in production. If only number 1 is farmed, the capitalist farmer makes 100 quarters profit. If

Figure 5.1 **Net Produce and Rent on Three Tracts of Land**

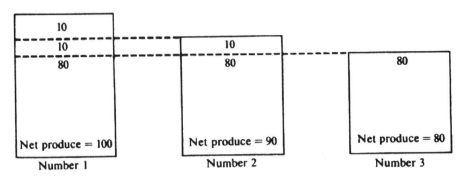

number 2 is brought into cultivation, competition bids the rent up to 10 quarters in number 1, and each capitalist earns 90 quarters profit. If number 3 is brought into cultivation, competition bids the rent up to 10 quarters on number 2 and to 20 quarters on number 1, and each capitalist earns 80 quarters profit.

As additional land is brought into cultivation, the quantity of land that we label as a parcel is arbitrary. Therefore, since we have assumed that land gets continuously less fertile, we could subdivide the land into smaller and smaller parcels, each successive parcel yielding a smaller net produce than the previous parcel. Putting the bars onto a quadrant whose axes indicate the number of parcels of land being farmed and the net produce per parcel, we might get something resembling Figure 5.2. As the size of the parcels gets smaller and smaller, the steplike tops of the bars come closer and closer to being a simple downward sloping line. We can assume that each land unit is so small that a straight line can be used to show the diminishing fertility of land. In Figure 5.2, *NP* is such a line. It shows that net produce per small unit of land diminishes as the quantity of land under cultivation increases. If we assume that wages are the only cost of production, then wages paid per unit of land farmed can be added to line *NP* in Figure 5.2 to show total produce. The result, in Figure 5.3, is a line, *P*, showing total produce for any quantity of land as the amount of land in cultivation is increased. While line *NP* shows only net produce (profit plus rent), line *P* shows total produce (profit plus rent plus wages). If *x* units of land are under cultivation, then *y* will be the total produce on the last (or no-rent) small unit of land brought into cultivation. The area of triangle *a* will be the total amount of rent received by the landlord class; the area of rectangle *b* will be the total profits and wages received by the capitalists and laborers in agriculture. This diagram will be used below to illustrate one of the most important conclusions of Ricardo's model.

Ricardo's theory of profits was, perhaps, the most crucial and central element of his overall theory. In his first approach to his profit theory, he assumed a simple economy, consisting of landlords, capitalists, and laborers, which produced only corn. Ricardo saw profits as a surplus. We have already seen that competition equated the profits of all of the capitalist farmers culti-

Figure 5.2   **Diminishing Productivity in Agriculture**

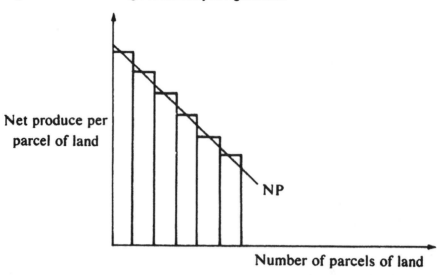

vating the superior grades of land with those accruing to the capitalist farmer cultivating the no-rent, marginal land. Therefore, profits would be determined by the determinants of the profit of the capitalist cultivating the no-rent land.

Ricardo accepted Malthus's population theory and its most important corollary that population growth would tend to force the wages of labor to the subsistence level. Therefore, the level of profit on the no-rent land was the total produce of that land minus the subsistence of the labor working on that land. In other words, profit was simply what was left over after paying wages. In this single commodity model, the capital consisted simply of the corn, which the capitalist "advanced" to the laborers as wages. Accordingly, the rate of profit was the ratio of the net produce on the no-rent land to wages, both expressed in corn. It followed that as long as the net produce was decreasing with each less fertile plot of land brought under cultivation, and as long as the corn-wage rate remained the same, the rate of profit (the net produce in corn over the wage in corn) had to decrease.

This view of profits has been called Ricardo's "Corn Theory of Profit."[7] Ricardo believed that the model could easily be expanded to include manufactured commodities. For if population increases decreased the rate of profit in agriculture, and if the rate of profit was determined solely by the productivity of labor and capital on the no-rent land, and if competition equalized all rates of profit, then it followed that the rate of profit in the manufacturing sector as well as in agriculture depended solely on productivity on the no-rent land.

Economic Basis of Conflict Between Capitalists and Landlords

We can now use the graph in Figure 5.3 to demonstrate Ricardo's contention in the *Essay* that "the interest of the landlord is always opposed to the interest

Figure 5.3   **Separation of Rent from Profits and Wages**

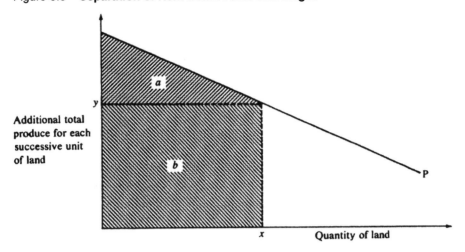

of every other class in the community."[8] Ricardo identified economic prosperity with capital accumulation and the economic growth and prosperity that
this accumulation fostered (as did all of the classical economists). When capitalists earned profits they accumulated capital, which would result in an increased demand for labor. The increased demand for labor led to an increase
of the market wage rate above the natural wage rate (subsistence), which led
to an increase in population. As long as capitalists continued to make profits,
this sequence could repeat itself over and over again. As long as the sequence
repeated itself, the economy would be growing, there would be general prosperity, and the wages of labor would be above the subsistence level. But the
economy ran into difficulty because of diminishing productivity in agriculture, which caused rents to squeeze out profits.

Ricardo's reasoning is illustrated in Figure 5.4. This figure is the same as
Figure 5.3, except that the line labeled w has been added to show the subsistence wage that must be paid to the laborers farming one unit of land, and the
double line w^* has been added to show the somewhat higher wage that will
prevail as long as capital accumulation is occurring. Various points on the
graph have been lettered to permit us to illustrate our point.

Assume that we observe the economy at a point where x_1 units of land are
under cultivation. Assume also that accumulation has taken place in the past
and the wage rate is at w^*. Now at x_1 the total quantity of the produce going to
rents would be the area of the triangle *abc*. Wages would be the area of the
rectangle *Ohed* (with the rectangle *fged* representing the excess of wages over
the amount necessary for subsistence). Profits would be the residual, or the
area of rectangle *debc*. With wages at w^*, above subsistence, population growth
will take place. This will require that more land be brought under cultivation.

Now suppose that population has grown to the point where x_2 is the amount
of land under cultivation. At this point, wages are now given by the area of the

rectangle *Omld*, rent is the area of triangle *akj*, and profits are the area of rectangle *dlkj*. Notice that while the wage rate has remained the same, total profits as a share of the total product, as well as the rate of profit, have declined substantially.

It is easy to see in Figure 5.4 that there is an ultimate limit to this economic growth. Once the economy has brought x_3 amount of land under cultivation, wages will have been pushed back to subsistence (w); rent will be the area of triangle *anf*, and wages will be the area of rectangle *Oqnf*. There will be no profits, and, thus, wages will be back at the subsistence level.

This explains why, in the struggle of the landlords and capitalists for the surplus or net product, Ricardo believed that diminishing productivity in agriculture would cause profits to be squeezed out steadily by higher and higher rents. Thus, in his *Essay*, Ricardo stated that rent was "in all cases a portion of the profits previously obtained on the land. It . . . [was] never a new creation of revenue, but always a part of a revenue already created."[9]

In Ricardo's model, rent was not directly responsible for squeezing out profit. Rather, it was the increases in the cost of labor created by the increase in the cost of corn, labor's principal staple for subsistence. Ricardo had to show how the increase in wages redistributed a larger and larger share of the net product from profit to rent. To do this he assumed a constant *average* level of prices (or a constant purchasing power of money). With his belief that competition equalized all rates of profit, then it followed that when the prices of corn and labor increased, prices would have to adjust to equalize the rate of profit in the different sectors of the economy. The labor embodied in producing corn had increased because labor became less productive as the margin of cultivation was extended. This lowered profits in the agricultural sector. But the productivity of labor remained the same in manufacturing, and, therefore, the labor embodied in manufactured goods did not change. In order for competition to equate the rates of profit, it would therefore be necessary for the prices of most manufactured goods to decline relative to corn. With Ricardo's assumption of a constant average level of prices, the increase in the prices of agricultural products would have to be offset by a decrease in the prices of at least some manufactured goods. The effect of these price changes would be the reestablishment of a uniform rate of profit in both sectors but at a lower profit rate. Each increase in the margin of cultivation would thus result in a further decline in the general price level of manufactured goods (all prices, including agricultural prices, again remaining at the same average level) and a decline in the general rate of profit. The decline of profits meant a decline in the rate of accumulation and, hence, a retardation of economic growth and a decrease in general social welfare.

On the basis of these arguments, Ricardo opposed the corn laws. By prohibiting the importation of grains, the British government was causing the agricultural sector to bring successively less fertile land under cultivation. This process was reducing profits and would, if continued long enough, bring

Figure 5.4   **Changes in the Distribution of Income as the Margin of Cultivation Is Extended**

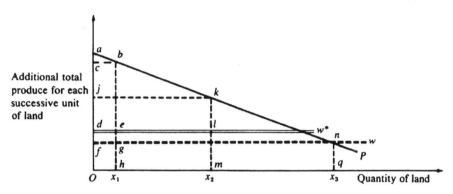

Note: P = additional product per successive unit of land; w = subsistence wage per unit of land; w^* = wage with accumulation.

economic progress to a halt. In their debate over the corn laws, Ricardo's argument was certainly more coherent and logical than that of Malthus, even though it generally failed to impress most of the members of Parliament who represented the interests of the landlords.

Malthus, however, found several grounds on which to attack Ricardo's argument. In particular, one of his objections was taken very seriously by Ricardo. Malthus wrote that

> profits depend upon the prices of commodities, and upon the cause which determines these prices, namely the supply compared with the demand . . . [while Ricardo's] theory of profits depends entirely upon the circumstance of the mass of commodities remaining at the same price, while money continues of the same value, whatever may be the variation in the price of labor. . . . We can infer nothing respecting the rate of profits from a rise of money wages, if commodities, instead of remaining of the same price, are very variously affected, some rising, some falling, and a very small number indeed remaining stationary.[10]

Ricardo realized that to defend his model against this criticism, he needed to work out a more adequate theory of prices. In his *Principles* he did just that.

The Labor Theory of Value

Ricardo began his *Principles* by stating that while all commodities having value had to have utility, or they would otherwise not be marketable, utility did not regulate value. He stated: "Possessing utility, commodities derive their exchangeable value from two sources: from their scarcity, and from the quantity of labour required to obtain them."[11] On the next page he stated that scarcity was important only for those commodities that were not freely reproducible. Some commodities, such as "rare statues and pictures, scarce books and coins, [and] wines of a peculiar quality" had a value that "is wholly independent of the quantity of labour originally necessary to produce them, and varies with the varying wealth and inclinations of those who are desirous to possess them."[12]

These commodities were, however, quite unimportant in Ricardo's opinion. The vast majority of commodities, he insisted, "may be multiplied . . . almost without assignable limit, if we are disposed to bestow the labor necessary to obtain them."[13] It was only such freely reproducible commodities with which his theory of value was concerned.

One argument that was to be advanced by later proponents of the utility theory of value was that their theory was more general than Ricardo's. The utility theorists were to make all prices ultimately dependent on "the varying wealth and inclinations of those who are desirous to possess them." The advantage of this greater generality of the utility theory would not have impressed Ricardo, however. He did not believe that these few nonreproducible luxuries had any importance in determining the laws that affect the distribution of the "produce of the earth . . . among the three classes of the community,"[14] and hence, they were unimportant in their effect on the accumulation of capital. The accumulation of capital was the principal determinant of the welfare of a country. "In proportion as the capital of a country is diminished," wrote Ricardo, "its productions will be necessarily diminished; . . . with a constantly diminishing reproduction, the resources of the people and the state will fall away with increasing rapidity, and distress and ruin will follow."[15]

The labor theory of value permitted Ricardo to focus on those forces affecting the accumulation of capital. The utility theory has never contributed to an understanding of such forces (for reasons that will be discussed in later chapters). Therefore, Ricardo would not have been impressed by the fact that the utility theory could explain those few prices of nonreproducible luxuries while the labor theory could explain the prices of only the freely reproducible commodities. In later chapters, it will be argued that the labor theory focuses on the *social aspects of commodity production and exchange* while the utility theory focuses on the *individual aspects of exchange* only. The latter theory's greater generality is purchased at a rather high price.

"If the quantity of labour realized in commodities regulates their exchangeable value," wrote Ricardo, "every increase of the quantity of labour must augment the value of that commodity on which it is exercised, as every diminution must lower it."[16] Of the importance of this he had no doubt: "That this is really the foundation of the exchangeable value of all things, excepting those which cannot be increased by human industry, is a doctrine of the utmost importance in political economy."[17]

Ricardo developed the theory by first stating it as the simplified hypothesis that the prices of commodities were strictly proportional to the labor embodied in them in the production process. He then went to some length to describe how this simple principle would have to be modified due to a variety of special circumstances. He believed that these modifications were fully explainable in a systematic and coherent way and, therefore, did not constitute arguments against the labor theory of value, but rather showed the complexity and realism of the theory.

Ricardo began by approvingly quoting Adam Smith's previously cited assertion:

> If among a nation of hunters, for example, it usually costs twice the labour to kill a beaver which it does to kill a deer, one beaver should naturally exchange for or be worth two deer. It is natural that what is usually the produce of two days or two hours labour should be worth double of what is usually the produce of one day's or one hour's labour.[18]

Unlike Smith, he believed that this assertion was as valid for a capitalist society as it had been in the "early and rude" state of society. In capitalist society, however, several qualifications and modifications of the assertion of simple proportionality of labor embodied and prices were necessary. Before making these modifications, Ricardo discussed and then dismissed two objections to the labor theory of value. These were, first, that one could not combine different types of labor having differing skills and differing rates of wages; and second, that the labor theory did not account for the increased productivity made possible by natural resources and capital. These objections have been made repeatedly from the time of the first formulations of the labor theory until the present time. Therefore, Ricardo's answers to these objections are of considerable interest.

In considering the problem of differing skills and wage rates among laborers, Ricardo was mainly interested in the *variations* of relative prices over time; that is, he was interested in why agricultural prices would increase through time relative to the prices of manufactured goods. With only this objective, he was quite correct in asserting that the general structure of varying labor skills and wage rates "when once formed is liable to little variation."[19] From this he drew a valid conclusion:

> In comparing, therefore, the value of the same commodity at different periods of time, the consideration of the comparative skill and intensity of labour required for that particular commodity needs scarcely to be attended to, as it operates equally at both periods.[20]

But when the labor theory is used to explain the exact structure of relative prices at one particular time, this solution to the problem is insufficient. In one sentence Ricardo mentioned, in passing, the crucial idea that was to form the basis for later adequate solutions to this problem: "whatever the . . . time necessary for the acquirement of one species of manual dexterity more than another, it continues nearly the same from one generation to another."[21] Later developments in the labor theory of value took this notion that differences in skills could be reduced to time spent acquiring these skills and showed that skilled labor was itself created by the exertions of labor. Skilled labor could thereby be reduced to a multiple of simple unskilled labor in calculating the total labor embodied in a commodity. The main reason that Ricardo did not work out this solution, while Marx later did, was that Ricardo did not consider labor power itself to be a commodity whose value was determined in the same manner as that of other commodities. Marx's recognition of the fact that labor power was a commodity whose price could be explained in the same way as other commodity prices constituted one of his principal advances over Ricardo in developing the labor theory of value.

Ricardo's answer to the charge that the labor theory did not consider increases in productivity made possible by land and capital, however, was more adequate and remains to the present time an integral part of the labor theory of value. Tools and machinery, he argued, were *intermediate* products of labor, created only because they contributed to the ultimate end of producing a commodity for consumption. Production was a series of labor exertions that effected a transformation of natural resources from the unusable forms in which they existed prior to human activity into forms that had use value. Without an environment to transform, production could not take place; that is, human beings could not even exist. But to consider the environment itself to be productive was to attribute human activity to inert matter. Production, and hence the creation of exchange value, was a strictly human endeavor involving only labor. Ricardo insisted that the resources found in nature

> are serviceable to us, by increasing the abundance of productions, by making men richer, by adding value in use; but as they perform their work gratuitously, as nothing is paid for the use, of air, of heat and of water, the assistance which they afford us adds nothing to value in exchange.[22]

Now Ricardo was certainly aware that rent was paid to the owners of natural resources; indeed, as we have seen, a large portion of his *Principles* was devoted to analyzing rent. But rent was strictly a social method of distributing the produce of labor. Production remained solely an activity of human beings. In terms of human costs, he was certainly correct in stating that natural resources perform "their work gratuitously." He quoted, with complete agreement and approval, the following sentences from Adam Smith: "The real price of everything . . . is the toil and trouble of acquiring it. . . . Labour was the first price—the original purchase money that was paid for all things."[23]

Natural resources, then, were the objects that labor transformed in production. But they were simply gratuitously there and were not a social cost of production. Capital was merely so many products of human labor, representing resources that were only partially transformed into their ultimately usable forms. A loom, for example, was produced by labor only to aid in the further production of cloth. Therefore, a loom embodied some of the labor that was ultimately to be embodied in the cloth. In this light, a loom could be seen as merely so much partly produced cloth. To produce was a human activity. Instead of saying, as later neoclassical economists were to say, that the weaver and the loom each contributed to the production of cloth, Ricardo said that the weaver and the laborer who produced the loom each contributed to the production of cloth. We shall let Ricardo speak for himself on this matter:

> In estimating the exchangeable value of stockings, for example, we shall find that their value, comparatively with other things, depends on the total quantity of labour necessary to manufacture them and bring them to market. First, there is the labour necessary to cultivate the land on which the raw cotton is grown; secondly, the labour of conveying the cotton to the country where the stockings are to be manufactured, which includes a portion of the labour bestowed in building the ship in which it is conveyed, and which is charged in the freight of the goods; thirdly, the labour of the spinner and the weaver; fourthly, a portion of the labour of the engineer, smith, and carpenter, who erected the buildings and machinery, by the help of which they are made; the labour of the retail dealer, and of many others, whom it is unnecessary further to particularize. The aggregate sum of these various kinds of labour determines the quantity of other things for which these stockings will exchange, while the same consideration of the various quantities of labour which have been bestowed on those other things will equally govern the portion of them which will be given for the stockings.[24]

In his recognition of the fact that the contribution of machinery to production was really only the contribution of past labor, Ricardo was repeating Smith's insight, an insight that has always served as the starting point of the labor theory of value. But Ricardo had an ahistorical view of capitalism, in which he saw the social relationships of capitalism as natural or eternal. He therefore saw all previous history as simply the development of the institutions of capitalism. As a result, he made a fundamental error in asserting that capital was everywhere and always identical with tools, machinery, and other produced means of production. "Capital," he wrote, "is that part of the wealth of a country which is employed in production, and consists of food, clothing, tools, raw materials, machinery, etc., necessary to give effect to [the] labourer."[25] Thus, he asserted that "even in that early state to which Adam Smith refers, some capital, though possibly made and accumulated by the hunter himself, would be necessary to enable him to kill his game."[26] Ricardo believed that if workers made and owned their own capital, it would not result in a different system of prices than that which would prevail when "all the implements necessary . . . [for production] belong to one class of men, and the labour employed . . . be furnished by another class."[27]

In arriving at this conclusion, Ricardo reasoned that when laborers owned their own capital, their incomes would consist partly of profits and partly of wages. The system of pricing would work in exactly the same manner, but each person would be simultaneously a laborer and a capitalist. Ricardo's error was in not realizing that although tools had always been used in production, profits had never accrued to anyone from merely owning tools, and people had never even imagined or mentally conceived of profits from the simple ownership of capital until one class had gained a monopoly on the ownership of the means of production and another class evolved that had no means of existing except by selling the commodity of labor power in the market. Capital, then, only came into existence when this class relationship developed. But tools have existed as long as humans have produced. It remained for Thomas Hodgskin, whom we will discuss in chapter 7, to recognize that the truly essential feature of capital was that it reflected a particular social relationship.

Having obviated the two previously mentioned objections to the labor theory of value, Ricardo next considered the objection that had caused Adam Smith to abandon the theory. Because Ricardo considered only agricultural production at the no-rent margin of cultivation along with manufacturing, all prices were resolvable into wages and profits. Rents, it will be remembered, were a residual income determined by the price of agricultural products (which, in turn, depended on the extent of cultivation). Rents were not, therefore, a component part of the costs that determined prices but, rather, were a residual determined by prices. Hence, in analyzing the costs of production that would determine the natural price of a commodity, Ricardo considered only profits and wages. His definitions of natural prices and market prices were identical to Smith's, with the exception that rent was not a component of the necessary costs of production. His discussion of how supply and demand, by equalizing all rates of profit, tended to push the market price into equality with the natural price was also much the same as Smith's. The problem for the labor theory of value was to show how the natural prices, each being the sum of wage costs and profit costs, were determined by the labor embodied in the production of commodities.

Price Determination with Differing Compositions of Capital

Smith, it will be recalled, had realized that in order for prices to be proportional to the quantities of labor embodied, it was necessary for the ratio of profits to wages to be the same for every commodity. But because competition tended to equalize the rate of profits on different capitals, then an equal ratio of profits to wages necessarily implied an equal ratio of capital to labor in the production of each commodity. He had realized that amount of capital per worker differed widely from industry to industry, and it was likely that such differences would always exist. He therefore abandoned the notion that the quantity of labor embodied in a commodity determined its value. He then used a simple cost-of-production theory of prices.

Both Ricardo and Marx believed that competition tended to equalize the rates of profit on different capitals. They also believed that the natural price (or equilibrium price) was equal to the cost production when labor and capital received the socially average rates of wages and profits. But both men realized that because both wages and profits are either prices or derived from other prices, one could not explain prices in general without finding a cause or a determinant that was not itself a price. In our discussion of Adam Smith's theory in chapter 3, it was explained why his theory of prices in general was circular and therefore not adequate. For Ricardo and Marx, the labor embodied in commodities served as that casual factor or determinant that was not a price. The labor theory of value and the utility theory of value (which will be discussed in later chapters) are the only consistent theories that have worked out solutions to this problem.

Ricardo, then, had to show that even with differing ratios of capital to labor, the labor theory could be modified to show a systematic connection between the labor embodied in a commodity and the exchange value of that commodity. The problem can be easily seen if one imagines two capitalist firms. In the first, the owner's capital consists almost entirely of a fund to pay workers' wages during the production period before the commodity being produced can be sold. In the second, the owner's capital consists primarily of expensive machines, with only a small portion consisting of a fund with which to pay wages. If in the first period of production each firm employs 100 workers, the price of the first firm's commodity will then have to be equal to the wages of the 100 workers plus the profits of, say, 10 percent on the fund from which the capitalist paid the wages. The price of the second firm's commodity will be higher. The second commodity contains the labor of the 100 workers plus some of the labor of the workers who produced the expensive machines. The second price will then include the wages of the 100 workers, plus the 10 percent profit on the capitalist's wages fund, plus the cost of the machines that are used up in production, plus the 10 percent profit on the money the capitalist has invested in the machines. Let us assume that when these costs are totaled, the price of the second commodity is twice that of the first.

Now let us assume that in the next production period, for whatever reasons, the wage rate increases. Given the same level of output and the same employment of labor using the same productive techniques, it is obvious that the higher wages will result in a decrease in profits. But if the labor embodied in the commodities is the only determinant of their prices, the relative prices should remain the same, insofar as the labor embodied did not change.

But consider the new prices. Wages constituted roughly 90 percent of the first commodity's cost, and profits constituted 10 percent. The increase in wages will have a very large effect on the new price, and the decrease in the rate of profit will have a relatively small effect. The first commodity's price will undoubtedly go up substantially. Wages constituted a relatively small percent of the second commodity's cost, so the impact of the increased wages on its total costs will be relatively small. The costs of the machinery it uses may go up or down, depending on the impact of the wage increase on the firm that produces these machines. But included in the costs of the second commodity are the profits on both the wages fund and the expensive machinery used in its production. Therefore, the effect of the new lower rate of profits will be much greater on the costs of the second commodity than on those of the first commodity.

Three possibilities emerge regarding the change in the price of the second commodity. First, the smaller increase in its wage costs may still more than offset the decline in its costs caused by the lower rate of profit. In this case, its price will rise, but by a much smaller percentage than the increase in the price of the first commodity. Second, its increased wage costs may be exactly equal to its decreased profit costs, in which case the price will remain unchanged. Third, the decrease in profit costs may be greater than the increase in wage costs, in which case the price will decline. (For the sake of simplicity, we have ignored any changes in the prices the second firm would have to pay for its machinery as a consequence of the change in the wage rate.)

In each of these three cases one fact emerges: whether the price of the second commodity goes up or down, the price of the first commodity will increase much more than the price of the second commodity. Therefore, the price ratio will no longer be 2:1; the first commodity will have a relatively higher price. The ratio may go to 1.5:1, for example. All that we can deduce from this example is that the second commodity must still have a higher value (because it has the same wage costs but also has machinery costs), while the difference between the two prices must decline (because the price of the first commodity increases relative to the price of the second commodity). The most important point to note is that *the price ratio has changed while the quantities of labor embodied in the two commodities have remained unchanged.* This was what motivated Adam Smith to abandon the labor theory of value.

Ricardo's task was to explain under what conditions a change in the wage rate would lead to a change in relative prices, even though the amounts of labor embodied in commodities remained unchanged. This was particularly important for Ricardo because he had argued that extending the margin of agricultural cultivation would increase corn prices, that increased corn prices would necessitate higher wages to keep the laborers at subsistence, and that higher wages would always decrease the general rate of profits as well as decrease the average price level of manufactured goods. He had to use the labor theory of value to demonstrate how all of these effects followed from an extension of the margin of cultivation. There were, he stated, three situations in which a change in the wage rate would alter relative prices, that is, three situations in which prices would not be proportional to labor embodied.

First, the "proportions . . . in which the capital that is to support labour, and the capital that is invested in tools, machinery, and buildings, may be variously combined."[28] This was the case in our example above, where the ratio of the capitalists' wages funds to the value of their machinery differed. Ricardo divided capital into fixed capital and circulating capital. In circulating capital he included the money for wages, the raw materials, and generally all capital that was used up immediately within one production period. Fixed capital was all capital having greater durability. If the two were in different proportions in two production processes, then the prices would not be proportional to the labor embodied. Second, "the tools, implements, buildings, and machinery employed in different trades may be of various degrees of durability."[29] In this case, even if the direct labor used in production and the cost of the machinery actually used up in production were equal, the capitalist who had much more durable machinery would have more money invested in machinery. An equal rate of profit would mean that this capitalist would receive profits that would be higher in relation to the labor embodied in production than those received by the capitalist having less durable machinery. Therefore, the two prices would not be proportional to the labor embodied in production. The third situation was one in which there was "unequal rapidity with which . . . [the capital of different capitalists was] returned to its employer."[30] A capitalist who had his capital tied up for a longer period would receive profit that was more than proportionally higher than a capitalist using the same labor inputs over a shorter period.

Actually, all three of Ricardo's special cases are merely different ways of looking at the same phenomenon. Because this phenomenon is very important in every version of the labor theory of value from Ricardo to the present, we will discuss it at length.

Each of Ricardo's three cases can be characterized in either of two ways. First, if we consider capital to be merely previously produced commodities that are used as production inputs, then, in each case, the ratio of commodities to labor used in production is different. Remembering that Ricardo saw capital as merely the embodiment of past labor in commodity inputs currently being used in production, we could restate this: in each of the three cases, the ratio of past labor (embodied in commodities) to present labor is different. Second, as soon as we introduce the words *past* and *present*, we introduce a time dimension into production. In Ricardo's three cases, it is also true that if production is seen as a time sequence of labor inputs, then there are differing time sequences of labor inputs in each. Both ways of stating the common element in each of Ricardo's three cases are equivalent.

We will now illustrate the effect of differing ratios of capital to labor (or past labor to present labor). First, in Figure 5.5, we see how capital can be reduced to a series of time-dated labor inputs. The bars on the top row represent the productive inputs of labor (l) and previously produced commodities (c). The commodities were produced in the previous period by labor (l_1) and commodities (c_1). These commodities were in turn produced in the period before that by labor (l_2), and commodities (c_2), and so on. In each case, the bar representing commodities is constructed with a dotted line to indicate that these commodities can be replaced by labor and commodities used in the previous period.

In Figure 5.6, we have simply removed the dotted rectangles representing commodities. This removal reflects the fact that each of the commodity bars has been reduced to prior labor and commodities. At some point, the remaining commodities have become sufficiently small that they can be ignored. All that remains in the production process is a series of time-dated labor. In Figure 5.6, the present labor is labeled l; past labor has a subscript, indicating how many periods into the past the labor was exerted.

Figure 5.5   **Reduction of Capital to Past Labor**

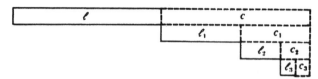

We get at the root of the difficulty when we realize that profit is received on capital for the entire period during which the capitalist has funds tied up in the production process. In the process symbolized in Figure 5.6, for example, the capitalist hired labor, represented by l_3, three years previously (assuming each period is one year). The labor embodied in the commodities produced by l_3 does not come to fruition in a finished *consumer* commodity until the present period ends. Three years ago the capitalist paid the wages of l_3. At the end of that year, the value of the intermediate goods produced by l_3 was the labor costs plus the profits earned by the capitalist because he or she had money tied up in this production process. At the end of the following year (two years previously), the capitalist again calculated profits, this time on the original wage costs and the profits of the last period that were still tied up in production. The same process is repeated each year, so that the initial costs three years ago grow at a *compounded rate* each year.

For example, if the wage costs of l_3 are $100 and the rate of profit is 10 percent throughout the period, then the capitalists have two choices. They can invest the $100 at the beginning of a series of one-year production processes and then reinvest each year the entire amount, including all profits earned in the previous period; or they can invest in the four-year project illustrated in Figure 5.6. If the capitalist chooses the first alternative, he or she will receive $110 at the end of the first year. Reinvesting the entire amount, he or she will receive $121 at the end of the second year and $133.10 at the end of the third. Therefore, if the four-year project is to be equally profitable, the commodities representing that part of capital embodying the labor l_3 must be valued at $133.10 at the beginning of the final year, and the profits in the final year's production must be $13.31 on this portion of capital. So the labor l_3, which originally costs the capitalist $100, finally results in $146.41 being added to the price of the commodity. Of this, $100 repays the capitalist the initial $100 wage expense, and $46.41 is considered profit for having $100 in capital tied up for four years. The capitalist ends up with the same amount if he or she invests in four separate one-year ventures with a return of 10 percent profit, provided that each year the capitalist reinvests the original $100 plus all profits earned to that point.

This is why, in Ricardo's terms, either more capital per worker or a longer period of production would give the same result. If the capitalist had $100 tied up for only two years, the value of that capital at the beginning of the final year would be $110 ($100 plus $10 profit from the preceding year);

Figure 5.6   **Sequence of Time-Dated Labor**

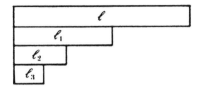

whereas if the capitalist had $100 tied up for four years, the value of that capital at the beginning of the final year would be $133.10 ($100 plus $10 profit the first year, plus $11 profit the second year, plus $12.10 profit the third year). Thus, the value of capital is greater in the four-year process than in the two-year process, even though the initial wage costs (and hence the original labor embodied in the capital) were the same in each case.

A Numerical Example of Price Determination

Although numerical examples of price determinations are rather tedious, most readers can understand the principle more easily if such examples are used rather than relying solely on abstract mathematical formulas. We will therefore go through a numerical illustration of (1) how differing capital-to-labor ratios result in prices that are not proportional to labor embodied, and (2) how changes in the wage rate alter such prices. In Figure 5.7, two production processes are illustrated. In part (a), 400 units of embodied labor produce 100 units of commodity x, and in part (b), 400 units of embodied labor produce 100 units of commodity y. It requires 100 units of present labor (labeled l) and 300 units of past labor (labeled c), applied uniformly at the rate of 75 units per year over the four previous years, to produce x. It requires 300 units of present labor and 100 units of past labor, applied at the rate of 50 units per year over the two previous years, to produce y. Obviously, if prices were proportional to labor embodied, the two prices would be equal. However, commodity x has both more past labor and a longer period of production; it therefore has a higher ratio of capital to present labor. We assume that all of the commodity inputs are used up at the end of each production process.

We will make two simple computations using the production formulas of Figure 5.7. In the first, we assume that the wage rate is $1.00 per labor unit and the profit rate is 50 percent. In the second, we assume that the wage rate is $2.00 per labor unit and the profit rate is reduced to 10 percent. (The examples are computed with very large changes in the rates of profit and wages in order to illustrate the point dramatically.)

We can see from Table 5.1 that, at these particular profit and wage rates, the price of x is more than double the price of y, even though they both have 400 units of labor embodied in 100 units of the commodity. The difference is entirely in the greater profits that went into the cost of x at each stage of the production process.

Figure 5.7   **Two Production Processes Have the Same Quantity of Labor but Differing Compositions of Capital**

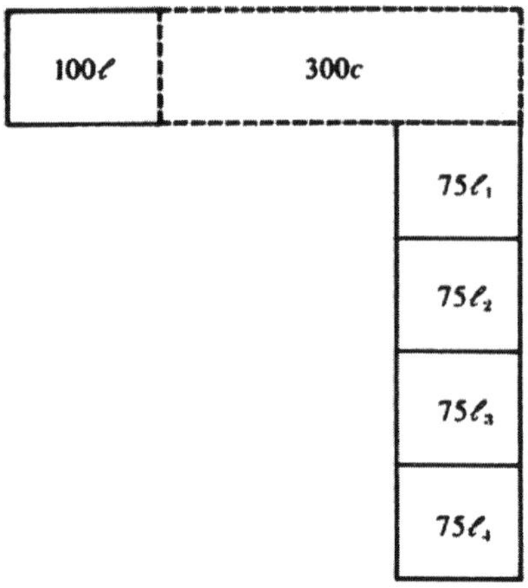

| 100ℓ | 300c |
| | |

	75ℓ_1
	75ℓ_2
	75ℓ_3
	75ℓ_4

(a) Labor units necessary to produce 100 units of commodity *x*. (400 units of labor over a period of five years.)

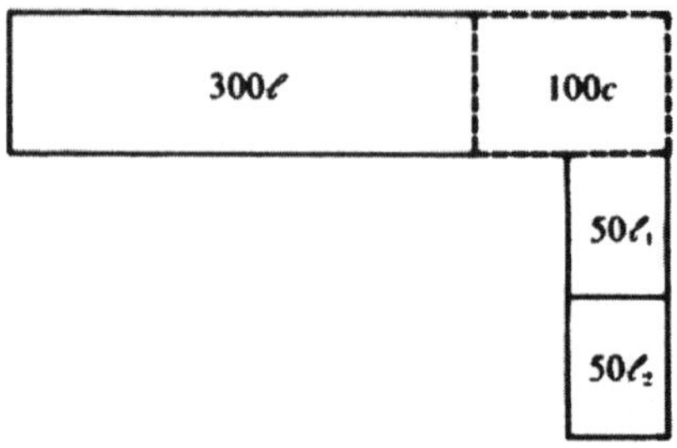

| 300ℓ | 100c |

| | 50ℓ_1 |
| | 50ℓ_2 |

(b) Labor units necessary to produce 100 units of commodity *y*. (400 units of labor over a period of three years.)

Now we will assume that the wage rate goes up to $2.00 per unit of labor. With the same quantity of production being divided between capitalists and laborers, it follows that the profit rate must go down. We have assumed that the profit rate falls to 10 percent. When Ricardo made the assertion that higher wage rates always mean lower profit rates, he was always comparing two situations in which the techniques of production and the quantities of output were the same. Table 5.2 shows the computations at these new rates.

Three important observations can be made in comparing the results in Tables 5.1 and 5.2. First, changing the wage rate substantially alters the relative prices of *x* and *y*; whereas the price of *x* is more than double that of *y* in Table 5.1, it is only slightly higher in Table 5.2. This illustrates the fact that it is the difference in profits that causes prices not to be proportional to labor embodied. In Table 5.2, profits are much smaller, and, hence, the deviation of the price ratio from the labor ratio is also much smaller. If the wage rate would rise to the point where there are no profits, the prices of *x* and *y* would be equal, reflecting the equal total labor embodied in them.

The second point to note is that the tables illustrate why Ricardo rejected Adam Smith's assertion that an increase in wages always increases the prices of all commodities produced by labor. In Table 5.2 the price of commodity *x* has declined from $15.21 to $10.62 as a consequence of doubling the wage rate. Smith's error was his failure to consider the fact that at any level of output, the capitalists and the laborers are antagonistically competing for the produce of labor. When the technique of production remains unchanged and the quantity of output remains unchanged, an increase in the wage rate can be achieved only through a decrease in the profit rate. This point was central to

Table 5.1

Costs and Prices When Wage Rate Is $1.00 and Profit Rate Is 50 Percent (in dollars)

	A. Labor cost (cost (number of labor units times wage rate)	B. Cost of machinery of past labor' compounded each year by the rate of profit)	C. Profit cost (rate of profit times the sum of A and B)	D. Total cost (A+B+C)	E. Price per unit (D divided by 100)
Commodity *x*	100.00	914.08	507.04	1,521.12	15.21
Commodity *y*	300.00	187.50	243.75	731.25	7.31

Table 5.2

Costs and Prices When Wage Rate Is $2.00 and Profit Rate Is 10 Percent (in dollars)

	A. Labor cost (number of labor units times wage rate)	B. Cost of machinery (cost of past labor compounded each year by the rate of profit)	C. Profit cost (rate of profit times the sum of A and B)	D. Total cost (A+B+C)	E. Price per unit (D divided by 100)
Commodity x	200.00	765.78	96.58	1,062.36	10.62
Commodity y	600.00	231.00	83.10	914.10	9.14

Ricardo's argument. If the wage rate increases, the consequent decrease in the profit rate will lower the prices of those commodities in which the profit component of costs is large.

The third important point illustrated in the two tables is this: as long as the rate of profit is positive, commodity x will always have a higher price than commodity y. Commodity x also has a higher ratio of capital to labor than commodity y. This furnished Ricardo with two systematic rules for predicting the deviation of price ratios from labor ratios. First, as long as the profit rate is positive, price ratios will diverge from labor ratios in the same direction that the ratios of capital per worker diverge. In other words, of two production processes embodying the same quantity of labor, that process having more capital per present laborer will always have a higher price. By more capital per present laborer is meant the same thing to which Ricardo was referring when he characterized a production process as having a higher ratio of durable to circulating capital, or greater durability of machinery, or a longer period before a capitalist's capital was returned to him.[31] Second, the higher the rate of profit, the larger will be the deviation of price ratios from labor ratios.

Distribution of Income and the Labor Theory of Value

We can now return to Ricardo's discussion of value theory and see how his value theory was tied to the conclusions that he had reached in his earlier model of the simple corn theory of profits. In the simpler model, only corn was produced, and the rate of profit was given by the ratio of the net produce per worker on the marginal no-rent land (or the net produce minus rents per worker on all lands) to the quantity of the produce per worker required for labor's subsistence, all expressed in terms of corn. The place of Ricardo's labor theory of value in his general theory of distribution has been succinctly stated by Maurice Dobb, a leading scholar of Ricardo's ideas:

> In using the Labour Theory of Value. . . . Ricardo in effect was substituting Labour for Corn as the quantity in terms of which product, wages and surplus were alike expressed. Profit was now conceived as the surplus, or residual difference, between the amount of labour required to produce subsistence for the labour-force and the total labour-force.[32]

In Ricardo's words, of the total value produced by labor, some

> proportion of what remains of that value, after paying rent is consumed by the producers, and it is this, and this alone, which regulates profits. . . .
> Thus we again arrive at the same conclusion which we have before attempted to establish: that in all countries, and at all times, profits depend on the quantity of labour requisite to provide necessaries for the labourers on that land or with that capital which yields no rent.[33]

It was thus the total value of what was produced and its division among the three main classes of society that interested Ricardo. Value depended on the labor embodied in commodities, but differences in the value of capital per man would cause variations of prices. "In estimating . . . the causes of the variations in the value of commodities," he wrote, "although it would be wrong wholly to omit the consideration of the effect produced by a rise or fall of [the wages of] labour, it would be equally incorrect to attach much importance to it."[34]

These variations were relatively unimportant for two reasons. First, Ricardo believed that they would be quite small.[35] Second, when considering the aggregate quantities, with which his theories of distribution and accumulation were concerned, the variations of price ratios from labor ratios would cancel out. It was obvious that if all production processes had the same composition of capital, these ratios would be equal. By the same reasoning, any commodities that were produced by processes having the *socially average composition of capital* would always have prices proportional to the labor embodied in them. Commodities produced with more capital than the social average would have their prices "fall as wages rise, and rise as wages fall," while those with less capital than the social average would have their prices "rise as wages rise, and fall as wages fall."[36] It followed from the definition of an average that deviations above the average exactly cancelled deviations below the average. It also followed that any commodity "produced with precisely the same combinations of fixed and circulating capital as all other things," or the same combination as the social average, "would be a perfect measure of value"[37] because its price would depend only on the labor embodied in it.

When Ricardo considered a complex economy, the aggregates of net product and wages were composed of many commodities. In order to measure these aggregates and arrive at a rate of profit, Ricardo had to find a commodity whose price did not vary when wages and profits varied. The other commodities could then be measured in terms of this commodity, and the value of the aggregates would be invariant to changes in wages and profits. If he could not find such a commodity, his aggregates would reflect not only the quantities of actual commodities produced by labor but also the distribution of income. Furthermore, as we have seen in our previous numerical example, a knowledge of the extent to which the price of a commodity would vary from being proportional to the labor in it when its production involved a composition of capital that deviated from the social average depended on a prior knowledge of the rate of profit. In other words, Ricardo's theory of prices required that the rate of profit be ascertained before one could calculate the deviation of price ratios from ratios of labor embodied.

For these reasons, it was very important for Ricardo to find a commodity that was produced under socially average conditions to serve as an "invariable measure of value."[38] While both Smith and Malthus had searched for such a measure, it was Ricardo who first understood the full importance of finding it. Such a measure has been an important concern of theorists having a labor theory of value to this day. Ricardo, unfortunately, was unable to find any commodity that he was prepared to defend as an invariable measure of value. He simply tentatively and provisionally took gold to be this measure, knowing that in reality it was not.

On the basis of his labor theory of value, Ricardo was able to give a much more sophisticated theoretical basis for the simple distributional model that was illustrated in Figure 5.4. The essence of his theory can be extracted, in his own words, from the following quotations:

> The natural tendency of profits then is to fall; for, in the progress of society and wealth, the additional quantity of food required is obtained by the sacrifice of more and more labour.[39]

> But suppose corn to rise in price because more labour is necessary to produce it; that cause will not raise the price of manufactured goods in the production of which no additional quantity of labour is required. . . . But if, as is absolutely certain, wages should rise with the rise of corn, then profits would necessarily fall.[40]

> Every rise of wages . . . would lower the relative value of those commodities which were produced with a capital of a durable nature, and would elevate those which were produced with capital more perishable.[41]

> In estimating . . . the causes of variations in the value of commodities . . . it would be . . . incorrect to attach much importance to [variations caused by the increase in wages]. . . . All the great variations which take place in the relative value of commodities . . . [are] produced by the greater or less quantity of labor which may be required . . . to produce them. [42]

> Commodities . . . will be subject to . . . a minor variation . . . from the rise or fall of wages and profits. . . . But those profits would be unequal if the prices of the goods did not vary with a rise or fall in the rate of profits.[43]

> If a manufacturer always sold his goods for the same money, his profits would depend on the price of the labour necessary to manufacture those goods. . . . In proportion then as wages rose would profits fall. But if the price of raw produce would increase, it may be asked whether the farmer at least would not have the same rate of profits, although he should pay an additional sum for wages? Certainly not: for he will not only have to pay, in common with the manufacturer, an increase of wages to each labourer he employs, but he will be obliged either to pay rent, or to employ an additional number of labourers to obtain the same produce; and the rise in the price of raw produce will be proportioned only to that rent, or that additional number, and will not compensate him for the rise of wages.[44]

> [As profits fell, eventually] there would be no motive for accumulation; for no one accumulates but with a view to make his accumulation productive, and it is only when so employed that it operates on profits. Without a motive there could be no accumulation.[45]

The result of this cessation of accumulation would be a halt of economic progress, a sinking of the market wage rate down to the subsistence level, and general social distress and poverty. This was Ricardo's stationary state. Some historians have said that Ricardo's theory was pessimistic and gloomy because his model seemed to imply that this stationary state was inevitable.

Others have said that his theory was wrong because it did not foresee the technological changes that were to occur in agricultural production during the nineteenth and twentieth centuries, changes that were to result in a more or less continuous increase in productivity in agriculture. Both of these assessments of Ricardo's theory are based on misunderstandings.

Ricardo saw society from the labor theory or production perspective. He focused sharply on the two major class conflicts of his era, and, in his theory, the interests of workers and capitalists were opposed. "If wages should rise," he repeatedly stated, "then . . . profits would necessarily fall."[46] Similarly, the interests of capitalists and landlords were always opposed. His theory was not an attempt to predict what was, in fact, going to happen over the next century. It was an attempt to influence Parliament on issues and policies that were currently being debated. In particular he wanted to see the corn laws abolished.

In looking at the three antagonistic classes, Ricardo argued, as did Malthus, that because of their tendency to increase the size of their families when their income increased, workers would always be near or at the subsistence level. In the conflict between the landlords and the capitalists, Ricardo wanted to show that the interests of the landlords were always opposed to the general well-being of society, while those of the capitalists were always in accord with the general well-being of society.

England did not face a crisis of food production in the nineteenth and twentieth centuries. But this was because England repealed the corn laws and allowed the free importation of foodstuffs, and because agricultural productivity increased throughout the period. Considering the following two quotations from Ricardo's *Principles*, it is obvious that he was aware of these remedies:

> This tendency . . . [for profits to fall] is happily checked at repeated intervals by the improvements in machinery connected with the production of necessaries, as well as by discoveries in the science of agriculture.[47]

> A small but fertile country, particularly if it freely permits the importation of food, may accumulate a large stock of capital without any great diminution in the rate of profits, or any great increase in the rent of land.[48]

Ricardo was simply attempting to persuade legislators that the landlord's interests were opposed to both of these sources of improvement in England's social and economic well-being. The legislators' opposition to the free importation of foodstuffs was, of course, obvious. He also argued that improvements in agricultural technology would have the immediate effect of lowering the labor content of corn and lowering agricultural prices. The immediate effect would be a reduction in rent, even though further increases in cultivation might eventually restore these rents and more. The landlords generally opposed anything that would immediately reduce rent. He concluded that:

> [T]he interest of the landlord is always opposed to that of the consumer and manufacturer. . . . The dealings between the landlord and the public are not like the deal-

ings in trade, whereby both the seller and buyer may equally be said to gain, but the loss is wholly on one side, and the gain wholly on the other.[49]

The Impossibility of Gluts

Malthus's theory that inadequate aggregate demand was the cause of periodic gluts or depressions was the basis on which he had recommended that the landlords ought to receive a larger share of national production. Accordingly, Ricardo opposed this theory. First, as we have seen in the previous chapter, he argued that for the capitalist to subsidize the unproductive consumption of the landlord would be as profitable to the capitalist as having a fire in the capitalist's warehouse that destroyed some of his commodities. Second, Ricardo argued that the forces of supply and demand would automatically adjust prices and the composition of aggregate output so that a general glut would be impossible. In this latter argument, he advanced an analysis that was, in its essentials, the same as one argued by the French economist J.B. Say. The analysis is usually associated with Say (in fact, it is called Say's law) and will be explained in somewhat more detail in the next chapter. It has been an influential doctrine and has had many devotees down to the present time.

The argument is relatively simple. It asserts that capitalists produce what they themselves do not need only because they intend to exchange it for something that they do need. Money mediates the exchange, but money is not desired for itself. A producer produces a commodity to exchange for a different commodity. When the producer exchanges the commodity for money, he or she intends to exchange the money for the other commodity. Because money itself does not have any useful property other than the fact that it can purchase another commodity, no one desires to hoard it. Therefore, production creates its own demand. For each dollar in commodities a capitalist produces, he or she has a one-dollar demand for other commodities. Ricardo stated the argument very succinctly:

> No man produces but with a view to consume or sell, and he never sells but with an intention to purchase some other commodity, which may be immediately useful to him, or which may contribute to future production. By producing, then, he necessarily becomes either the consumer of his own goods, or the purchaser and consumer of the goods of some other person.[50]

> Commodities are always bought by commodities, or by services; money is only the medium by which the exchange is effected. Too much of a particular commodity may be produced, of which there may be such a glut in the market as not to repay the capital expended on it; but this cannot be the case with respect to all commodities.[51]

But Ricardo was aware that the decade prior to the appearance of the third edition of his *Principles* had been one of generally depressed business conditions and widespread unemployment. The explanation he advanced was similar to those that would be advanced over the following 160 years by theorists who wanted to believe that capitalism automatically created full employment, despite the persistence of cyclical crises and depressions:

> A great manufacturing country is peculiarly exposed to temporary reverses and contingencies, produced by the removal of capital from one employment to another. . . . The demand for any particular manufactured commodity is subject, not only to the wants, but to the tastes and caprice of the purchasers. . . . [When demand for a commodity decreases] considerable distress, and no doubt some loss, will be experienced by those who are engaged in the manufacture of such commodities; and it will be felt, not only at the time of the change, but through the whole interval during which they are removing their capitals, and the labour which they can command, from one employment to another.[52]

He thus explained the depressions of his era as simply the necessary adjustment to the abnormal patterns of supply and demand during the preceding war years.

Machinery as a Cause of Involuntary Unemployment

In the course of his debate with Malthus, however, Ricardo made a major concession in the third edition of his *Principles*. He added chapter 31, entitled "On Machinery." This chapter discussed the possibility that new machinery, which displaced labor in the production process, could be injurious to workers. In the first chapter, he had discussed the effects of introducing new types of machinery that could lower the capitalist's costs of production. He had assumed that this would result in increased production and lower prices for the commodities produced by this machinery. Therefore, he had concluded, all of society benefited from this machinery.

> The manufacturer . . . who . . . can have recourse to a machine which shall . . . [decrease the costs] of production on his commodity, would enjoy peculiar advantages if he could continue to charge the same price for his goods; but he . . . would be obliged to lower the price of his commodities, or capital would flow to his trade till his profits had sunk to the general level. Thus then is the public benefited by machinery.[53]

Ricardo's belief that the public would always benefit from the introduction of machinery was based on the assumption that market prices would smoothly and rapidly decline and that labor would be relocated smoothly and rapidly so as to increase the volume of production. His debates with Malthus, however, convinced him that this was not necessarily so. In the third edition of the *Principles*, Ricardo began his new chapter 31 by stating:

> Ever since I first turned my attention to questions of political economy, I have been of the opinion that . . . an application of machinery to any branch of production as should have the effect of saving labour was a general good, accompanied only with that portion of inconveniences which in most cases attends the removal of capital and labour from one employment to another. It appeared to me that . . .

the landlords . . . would be benefited by the reduction in the prices of some of the commodities on which . . . [their] rents were expended. . . . The capitalist, I thought, was eventually benefited precisely in the same manner. He, indeed who made the discovery of the machine . . . would enjoy an additional advantage by making great profits for a time; but in proportion as the machine came into general use, the price of the commodity produced would, from the effects of competition, sink to its cost of production, when the capitalist would get the same money profits as before . . . [but he would be] enabled, with the same money revenue, to command an additional quantity of comforts and enjoyments. The class of labourers also, I thought, was equally benefited . . . as they would have the means of buying more commodities with the same money wages.[54]

Ricardo then stated that he still believed capitalists and landlords would benefit by such a change in productive technology, but "that the substitution of machinery for human labor is often very injurious to the interests of the class of labourers."[55] This was because laborers initially would be diverted from the production of wage goods to the production of capital goods. In the following period, there would be fewer wage goods and hence a reduced demand for labor because the demand for labor was limited by the availability of wage goods. When the new machinery was put into use, it would require some laborers, but not nearly as many would be put back to work as were previously fired, because the machinery was constructed only in order to reduce the number of laborers necessary to produce a given output and hence to reduce the capitalist's wage costs and increase profits. Thus, the net income of society (profits and rents) could be increased while the gross income (profits, rents, and wages) was being reduced. In that case, many laborers would "be thrown out of employment," and a large part of the working class would "become redundant compared with the funds which are to employ it."[56]

Ricardo concluded "that the opinion entertained by the labouring class, that the employment of machinery is frequently detrimental to their interests, is not founded on prejudice and error, but is conformable to the correct principles of political economy."[57] Such a conclusion meant that he agreed with Malthus that the market might not be very effective in reallocating resources when a change in the conditions of production took place, and that the result could be a chronic depression in the labor market that would reduce the total produce of the economy. It also meant that Ricardo's faith in the accumulation of capital as the principal force that would increase the economic welfare of all society was unfounded. But his main sympathy was clearly with the capitalist class, not with society as a whole. He concluded the chapter by asserting: "The statements which I have made will not, I hope, lead to the inference that machinery should not be encouraged."[58] This hope was *not* based on a plan to ameliorate the conditions of workers. For he had stated, and he still believed, that like "all other contracts, wages should be left to the fair and free competition of the market, and should never be controlled by the interference of the legislature."[59]

The Theory of Comparative Advantage and
International Trade

Ricardo was the first economist to argue consistently that free international trade could benefit two countries, even though one country produced all of the traded commodities more efficiently than the other. He was also one of the first economists to argue that, because capital was relatively immobile between nations, a separate theory of international trade, as distinct from international trade, was needed.

Ricardo argued that a country need not have an *absolute advantage* in the production of any commodity in order for international trade between it and another country to be mutually beneficial. By absolute advantage was meant greater efficiency in production, or the use of less labor in production. Two countries could both benefit from trade if each had a *relative advantage* in production. By relative advantage was meant simply that the ratio of the labor embodied in two commodities differed between two countries, such that each country would have at least one commodity where the relative amount of labor embodied would be less than that of the other country. Table 5.3 is a reproduction of Ricardo's example to illustrate the principle of comparative advantage. In this table, Portugal has an absolute advantage in the production of both wine and cloth; that is, fewer labor hours are required to produce either commodity in Portugal than are required in England. If we assume that the prices of wine and cloth are proportional to the labor embodied in them in both England and Portugal, then the ratios of the two prices in each country will be the same as the ratio of labor hours required to produce the commodities in each country.

In Portugal it takes ninety hours to produce one unit of cloth and eighty hours to produce one unit of wine. This means that wine requires only 88 percent as much labor as cloth and that the price of wine is only 88 percent that of cloth. In England, the labor embodied in and the price of wine are both 120 percent that of cloth. Thus, Portugal uses relatively less labor to produce wine, and the price is relatively lower. On the other hand, Portugal uses 112 percent as much labor to produce cloth as wine, and the price of cloth in that country is 112 percent that of wine. England uses only 83 percent as much labor to produce cloth as wine, and, again, the price of cloth is only 83 percent that of wine. Thus, England uses relatively less labor to produce cloth, even though it uses absolutely more labor; therefore, England has a relative advantage in producing cloth.

Now suppose that the Portuguese have been producing only wine (the commodity in which they have a comparative advantage) and decide that they want cloth as well. They have two ways of getting the cloth—diverting some labor from the production of wine to the production of cloth or trading wine with England for cloth. Suppose that if trade takes place it does so at the price ratio prevailing in England. To produce one unit of cloth will require ninety

Table 5.3

Number of Hours Required to Produce One Unit of Cloth and Wine in England and Portugal

	Cloth	Wine	Ratio of price of wine to price of cloth	Ratio of price of cloth to price of wine
England	100	120	1.20	0.83
Portugal	90	80	0.88	1.12

working hours. This means that the Portuguese must discontinue producing 1.12 units of wine for every unit of cloth they produce. But if they trade with England at the English price ratio, they need only give up 0.83 units of wine for each unit of cloth. Obviously, trading would leave them a greater combined total of wine and cloth than would the production of both commodities.

Similarly, if England has been producing only cloth but could trade at the price ratio prevailing in Portugal, then it should not produce wine. To do so would require that it give up 1.2 units of cloth for each unit of wine produced, while it could give up only 0.88 units of cloth for one unit of wine if it trades with Portugal.

It is obvious that both countries could benefit if each could trade at the price ratio prevailing in the other country. But both countries could benefit if they trade at a price ratio that is between the ratios prevailing in each country. The ratio of the price of wine to the price of cloth is 1.2 in England and 0.88 in Portugal. If both countries trade on a one-to-one basis, one unit of cloth for one unit of wine, both could consume a larger combined total of wine and cloth than if they each produce both commodities.

This, then, explains Ricardo's theory of comparative advantage. On this basis, he argued that free trade would be beneficial to both countries. Every extension of trade would "very powerfully contribute to increase the mass of commodities and the sum of enjoyments."[60] Every restriction on trade would likewise reduce the "sum of enjoyments." This principle, then, was another link in Ricardo's general attack on the corn laws.

Social Harmony and Class Conflict

Ricardo's particular choice of words clearly illustrates a main theme of the present book: the utility theory of value, or any approach to economics that tends to equate prices and utility, usually supports the view that social harmony prevails through the "invisible hand" of the free market. When Ricardo asserted that free trade would increase the "sum of enjoyments" of each country, he was merely restating Adam Smith's principle that free exchange increases the utility or "enjoyments" of both parties to the exchange. When this principle becomes the focal point of economic analysis, the remedy to nearly all problems of human material deprivation becomes one of extending the market or making exchange and trade freer. If this policy is followed, it appears as if everyone would benefit, and hence all interests would be harmonious.

In order for Ricardo's conclusion to follow from his premises, he had to assume that if England imported the relatively more expensive commodity, then the higher price of that commodity would be a reasonable index of the increase in the "sum of enjoyments." In other words, suppose wine were drunk only by landlords and capitalists and that laborers did not have enough clothing to keep themselves warm. The labor theory perspective would tend to focus on the circumstances that resulted in so much of the produce of labor being expropriated as rent and profit. The utility theory, however, generally assumes the laws of property ownership and the distribution of wealth to be fixed, or "natural," and, consequently, would tend to focus on the fact that capitalists and landlords would prefer having their surplus in both cloth and wine rather than in cloth alone. Free trade would increase the enjoyments of those who had the wealth and purchasing power but not necessarily the enjoyments of the working class.

Ricardo could have suggested, for example, that the importation of wine be prohibited until every worker had adequate clothing. Some would certainly argue that this would increase social welfare more than importing more wine for the capitalists and the landlords would. But he did not do so, instead insisting that free trade would maximize the "sum of enjoyments."

This point illustrates that the same contradiction that we have discussed concerning Adam Smith's writings was present in Ricardo's theories. Most of Ricardo's *Principles* is based on the labor theory, or production vantage point. The book is filled with discussions of the basic class conflicts among the three classes. "Can any point be more clearly established," he asked, "than that profits must fall with a rise in wages?"[61] Or again, "the interest of the landlord is always opposed to that of the consumer and manufacturer."[62] Most of his book was an analysis of the factors underlying these conflicts.

Adam Smith's theory of history stopped with capitalism, which he considered the highest possible stage of social evolution. For that reason, Smith tended to take the property relationships and the distribution of wealth prevailing in capitalism as given and fixed. Only when these class differences were taken as given and fixed could Smith argue for the beneficence of the invisible hand. Ricardo's approach to understanding capitalism was much more ahistorical than Smith's. He considered the property relationships, distribution of wealth and power, and class relationships of capitalism to be eternal, unchanging, and natural. The labor theory of value sees society from a perspective that focuses on conflict, as Ricardo's *Principles* so clearly illustrates. But conflict implies change. And change implies that socioeconomic systems, such as feudalism or capitalism, have a life process of their own: they are born; they grow to maturity; and they decay and die. It was precisely this part of the labor theory perspective that Ricardo denied. In one of his most illuminating passages he wrote:

> It must be remembered . . . that the retrograde condition is always an unnatural state of society. Man from youth grows to manhood, then decays, and dies; but this is not the progress of nations. When arrived to a state of the greatest vigour, their further advance may indeed be arrested, but their natural tendency is to continue for ages to sustain undiminished their wealth and their population.[63]

Within the context of this ahistorical view, it is not surprising that Ricardo did not consider policies that would increase the "sum of enjoyments" by altering the distributions of wealth, privilege, or power. When these distributions are accepted as natural or eternal, the enjoyments of those who have the purchasing power generally are thought to be synonymous with the overall social welfare. From this, a belief that the free market acts as an invisible hand to maximize everyone's welfare nearly always follows. Thus, Ricardo wrote the following defense of free trade:

> Under a system of perfectly free commerce, each country naturally devotes its capital and labour to such employments as are most beneficial to each. This pursuit of individual advantage is admirably connected with the universal good of the whole. By stimulating industry, by rewarding ingenuity, and by using most efficaciously the peculiar powers bestowed by nature, it distributes labour most effectively and most economically: while, by increasing the general mass of productions, it diffuses general benefit, and binds together, by one common tie of interest and intercourse, the universal society of nations throughout the civilized world.[64]

The invisible hand operated locally, nationally, and internationally, harmonizing everyone's interests.

But Ricardo's advocacy of the interests of the capitalists had been best served by taking a labor theory perspective. It was therefore inevitable that his writings should involve contradictions on the issue of whether capitalism creates conflict or a harmony of interests. We have already encountered an example where the invisible hand did not work: "The dealings between the landlord and the public are not like dealings in trade, whereby both the seller and buyer may equally be said to gain, but the loss is wholly on one side, and the gain wholly on the other."[65] Similarly, in discussing international trade, as soon as he did not take the balance of real, coercive power to be given, it became obvious to Ricardo that conflict, not harmony, was the result. It was clear to him, for example, that

> a mother country may . . . sometimes be benefited by the restraints to which she subjects her colonial possessions. Who can doubt . . . that if England were the colony of France, the latter country would be benefited by a heavy bounty paid by England on the exportation of corn, cloth and any other commodities?[66]

Again, four pages later, he stated: "It is evident, then, that trade with a colony may be so regulated that it shall at the same time be less beneficial to the colony, and more beneficial to the mother country, than a perfectly free trade."[67]

Every argument that Ricardo gave showing how coercive restrictions in the free market could benefit the mother country at the expense of the colony could just as easily demonstrate how exchange between capitalists and laborers could be regulated by coercive restrictions that benefited the capitalist at the expense of the laborer (or vice versa, as many of the leaders in the rising labor movement of Ricardo's time hoped).

Given Adam Smith's assertion that "civil government, so far as it is instituted for the security of property, is in reality instituted for the defence of the rich against the poor, or of those who have some property against those who have none at all,"[68] it behooved both Smith and Ricardo to show why government would not be used by capitalists in exactly this way. Without such a demonstration, the invisible-hand argument would inevitably be used simply to justify any observed outcome in a market, capitalist system.

It seems obvious that this central contradiction in the doctrines of Smith and Ricardo would result in a cleavage of their doctrines into two antagonistic schools of thought. In the next chapter, we will examine the writings of Jeremy Bentham, J.B. Say, and Nassau Senior, the three men who began the process of substituting the utility perspective for the labor perspective in the doctrines of Smith and Ricardo. Chapter 7 will discuss the writings of William Thompson and Thomas Hodgskin, who attempted to push the labor theory to its ultimate implicit conclusions.

Notes to Chapter 5

1. David Ricardo, *The Principles of Political Economy and Taxation* (London: Dent, 1962), p. 272. This is Ricardo's principal work in economic theory. It was first published in 1817; a second edition appeared in 1819, and a third edition in 1821. The Dent edition cited here is a reprint of the third edition.

2. Ibid., p. 1.

3. See Maurice Dobb, *Theories of Value and Distribution since Adam Smith* (Cambridge, UK: Cambridge University Press, 1973), pp. 67–69. Much of the present chapter relies heavily on this excellent book. If the reader wishes to understand the conceptual and analytical issues as well as the ideological issues at stake in the ongoing debate between the proponents of the labor theory of value and the utility theory, the present writer believes that Dobb's book is by far the best single source.

4. Ricardo, *Principles*, p. 33.

5. Ibid., pp. 35–36.

6. Ibid., p. 48.

7. Dobb, *Theories of Value and Distribution*, p. 70.

8. Quoted, ibid., p. 72.

9. Quoted, ibid., p. 71.

10. Quoted, ibid., p. 74.

11. Ricardo, *Principles*, p. 5.

12. Ibid., p. 6.

13. Ibid.

14. Ibid., p. 1.

15. Ibid., p. 95.

16. Ibid., p. 7.

17. Ibid.

18. Ibid.

19. Ibid., p. 12.

20. Ibid.

21. Ibid.

22. Ibid., p. 191.

23. Ibid., p. 6.

24. Ibid., pp. 14–15.

25. Ibid., p. 53.

26. Ibid., p. 13.

27. Ibid., pp. 13–14.

28. Ibid., p. 18.

29. Ibid.

30. Ibid., p. 24.

31. The issue is more complicated than our discussion suggests, however. In a very important book, published in 1960, a present-day disciple of Ricardo has shown that when comparing two production processes, it is possible that their time patterns of dated labor inputs can be such that throughout some range of wage rates (or profit rates), one process will have a higher value of capital per worker, while in another range of wage rates (or profit rates) the other process will have a higher value of capital per worker; Piero Sraffa, *The Production of Commodities by Means of Commodities* (Cambridge, UK: Cambridge University Press, 1960), pp. 1–95. We will discuss some of the important results of Sraffa's book in chapter 16.

32. Dobb, *Theories of Value and Distribution*, p. 74.

33. Ricardo, *Principles*, pp. 75–76.

34. Ibid., pp. 22–23.

35. Ibid., pp. 23, 26.

36. Ibid., p. 27.

37. Ibid., p. 28.

38. Ibid., pp. 27–30.

39. Ibid., p. 71.

40. Ibid., p. 64.

41. Ibid., p. 25.

42. Ibid., pp. 22–23.

43. Ibid., pp. 26–27.

44. Ibid., pp. 64–64.

45. Ibid., pp. 72–73.

46. Ibid., p. 64.

47. Ibid., p. 71.

48. Ibid., p. 76.

49. Ibid., p. 225.

50. Ibid., pp. 192–93.

51. Ibid., p. 194.

52. Ibid., p. 175.

53. Ibid., p. 26.

54. Ibid., pp. 263–64.

55. Ibid., p. 264.

56. Ibid., p. 266.

57. Ibid., p. 267.

58. Ibid., p. 267

59. Ibid., p. 61.

60. Ibid., p. 77.

61. Ibid., p. 68.

62. Ibid., p. 225.

63. Ibid., p. 177.

64. Ibid., p. 81.

65. Ibid., p. 225.

66. Ibid., p. 227.

67. Ibid., p. 231.

68. Adam Smith, *An Inquiry into the Nature and Causes of the Wealth of Nations* (New York: Modern Library, 1937), p. 674.

Chapter 6

Rationalistic Subjectivism: The Economics of Bentham, Say, and Senior

Capitalist commodity production, as we have seen in chapter 1, necessarily involved certain socioeconomic institutions, modes of human behavior, and human self-perceptions as well as perceptions of others. The insatiable quest for profit led to an extensive division of labor and productive specialization; specialization meant an increase in social interdependence; but this increased interdependence was not experienced as a dependence on other human beings but as a personal, individual dependence on a nonhuman social institution—the market. Those who dominated and controlled markets were motivated by the acquisition of profits; but while capitalists, taken collectively, dominated and controlled markets, they did not experience or perceive this domination and control personally or subjectively. The intense competitive struggle for profits was experienced by individual capitalists as an impersonal, social force over which they generally had little or no personal control; the forces of market competition were seen as natural, immutable laws, similar in every way to the laws of nature.

Social Origins of the Premises of Utility Theory

There are several human consequences of this competitive process. While these consequences are the particular results of the capitalist mode of production, they are most frequently perceived as general human conditions, existing in all societies, in all places and times. At several points throughout the previous three chapters, we have stressed the distinction between the labor theory of value, or the production perspective, and the utility theory of value, or the market perspective, in analyzing the capitalist economy. The intellectual foundations of the utility theory are (1) the mental awareness of these special human conditions engendered by the capitalist mode of production and (2) the universal projection or generalization of these conditions as pervasive, unalterable, natural characteristics of all human beings in all societies. We will discuss five particularly important features of capitalism and how they have been perceived by those within the utility tradition in economic theory.

First, the specialization of labor and the isolation of producers led individuals to see themselves not as integral parts of an interconnected, interdependent socioeconomic whole, but as isolated, independent, atomistic units, each concerned with his or her own survival against the impersonal, immutable forces of the market. To a considerable extent, individuals felt alone, isolated, and alienated in their humanness; other individuals were not seen as integrally connected, mutual sharers of a common humanity, but merely as so many facets, aspects, or embodiments of the impersonal forces of the market.

Thus, each person came to be seen as fundamentally egoistic and as a natural antagonist or combatant of every other person. This new point of view can be seen most clearly in the writings of Thomas Hobbes, who lived when capitalist relations were first being perceived as the increasingly dominant form of human relations in England. His *Leviathan*, published in 1651, trenchantly articulated a widely held opinion—that all human motives stemmed from an egoistic desire for whatever promotes the "vital motion" of the individual organism (person). He believed that all human motives, even compassion, were so many disguises for egoistic self-interest: "Grief for the calamity of another is *pity*," he wrote, "and ariseth from the imagination that the like calamity may befall himself; and therefore is called . . . *compassion*, and . . . fellow-feeling."[1]

In the absence of social restraints, Hobbes believed that this innate egoism inevitably led to a "natural state" of war, with each person pitted against all others. In this "state of nature," the life of each person was "solitary, poor, nasty, brutish, and short." The only escape from brutal combat, Hobbes argued, was the establishment of some source of absolute power—a central government—to which each person submitted in return for protection from all other persons.[2]

Hobbes was writing in a period during which the features of capitalism were still mixed with those of the medieval social order. While he advocated submission to an absolute monarch as the means of escaping the brutal conflict among people, later writers accepting his view of human nature advocated the "invisible hand" of the market as the means of reconciling the conflicts arising from the natural combativeness and competitiveness of human nature.

Second, accepting that human nature was competitive and egoistic, how did the thinkers in the utility tradition conceive the basis, or essential source, of human motivation? Increasingly, they came to see all human motives as stemming from the desire to achieve pleasure and avoid pain. This belief is called utilitarianism and is the philosophical basis of the utility theory of value and modern neoclassical economics (although in the twentieth century neoclassical economists have gone to some lengths, as we shall see, to disguise the utilitarian basis of their theories). Utilitarianism received its most distinctive, classical formulation in the writings of Jeremy Bentham, whom we will consider below.

Third, economic specialization necessarily created a complete dependence, both individual and social, on the successful functioning of the market. Individual specialized producers could not live if they could not sell their commodity for money and then buy the assortment of commodities, each produced by other specialized producers, that was necessary for them to sustain themselves. A relatively freely functioning market was, therefore, a necessary part of the capitalist mode of production—as unnecessary as it might have been for previous modes of production or as it may be for future modes of production.

But most economists within the utility theory tradition in economics have always taken the capitalist mode of production for granted. Therefore, when these economists evaluated the market, they saw no necessity of evaluating the entire capitalist mode of production of which it was but one necessary part. Accepting capitalism as natural and eternal, they were powerfully impressed with how much better off all people were when the market functioned well than when it functioned poorly, or with how much better off all people were with a market than they would be without one. The market, then, was seen as a universally beneficial social institution.

When one begins by accepting capitalism as eternal, it is obvious that not only capitalists but also workers and all other people in society benefit from a market. Indeed, within a capitalist system, hardly anyone could continue to exist without it. This universal dependence on the market has always been the foundation of the perceived social harmony of all persons' interests within the tradition of the utility theory of value. We have already encountered the intellectual rationalization of this universal dependence in the invisible-hand argument of Smith and in the ideas of Malthus and Ricardo.

In the writings of Smith and Ricardo, however, this social harmony perspective frequently contradicted the class conflict conclusions implicit in their labor theory of value approach. The three writers considered in this chapter each contributed to the abandonment of the labor theory of value—and hence its class conflict conclusions—in favor of the orthodox, conservative economics of most of the nineteenth century. Their influence helped to remove the contradictions inherent in the ideas of Smith and Ricardo and to make orthodox economics essentially a theory of social harmony.

Fourth, the most important prerequisite for productive specialization was the creation and accumulation of new and more complex tools, machinery, and factories, that is, the accumulation of capital. It is obvious that, in any society, the means of production can themselves be produced and accumulated only if a significant portion of the society's productive capacity is devoted to producing these tools and machinery rather than to producing food, shelter, clothing, and other consumption goods.

Therefore, capital accumulation, or industrialization, must involve the forgoing of some consumption goods that otherwise could have been produced; this is a universally necessary social cost of industrialization. In capitalism, where a small capitalist class owns and controls the means of production, this means that profits must increase relative to wages (or, to say the same thing differently, wages must decrease relative to profits) in order that profits be large enough to maintain the consumption of the capitalist class, and, simultaneously, to finance industrialization. If capital accumulation were not financed by profits, the capitalist class would lose its control of the means of production, and the economic system would cease being a capitalist system. Therefore, capitalist industrialization necessarily means capital accumulation financed by profits.

But whether the capitalist class or the working class pays the real social cost of decreased consumption necessary for industrialization depends on what happens to the relative magnitudes of profits and wages during the process. In the actual history of capitalism there is no question but that the working class paid most of these real social costs. Economic historians generally agree that the purchasing power of wages fell in the last third of the eighteenth century in England; however, the direction of the change in the purchasing power of wages in the first half of the nineteenth century is disputed. Some historians have argued that *real wages* (the purchasing power of wages) increased in this period; some have argued that they decreased; and some have maintained that they remained unchanged. Obviously, the historical evidence is contradictory, and the issue cannot be clearly decided. However, it is clear that, at best, any increase in real wages was relatively much smaller than the increase in the total amount produced in this period.

Therefore, throughout the period of English industrialization, real wages declined in relation to the size of profits. It is thus true that the real social costs of industrialization were paid by the working class. What this meant in terms of the poverty and suffering of the working class was described briefly in chapter 4.

But when a theorist takes the capitalist system for granted and assumes that the market determination of wages and profits is natural and just, then it inevitably appears as though capitalists paid the social costs of industrialization. When one does not question the initial division of income between wages and profits, then the fact that capital accumulation was financed out of profits seems to be de facto evidence that capitalists paid these social costs. The theorists in the social harmony, or utility, tradition have always taken the class distribution of income for granted. Thus, beginning with Nassau Senior, whose ideas we will examine in this chapter, they have usually attempted to justify profits morally on the basis of the sacrifices made by capitalists.

Fifth, as the capitalist market system developed, the intensity of competition among capitalists increased. Profit making was no casual, relaxed, idyllic affair. Each capitalist was faced with competitors trying to undercut prices, outsell, and in general destroy him or her economically. Making profits depended on achieving some measure of calculated, rational, and predictable control over raw materials, labor power, expenses of production and transportation, and final sales in the market. Double-entry bookkeeping, complex systems of accounting, uniform and codified laws of private property, contractual commitments, and commercial laws generally all originally came into existence during the period of early capitalism, and all were indispensable in the capitalists' quest to control the processes of production and exchange.

This aspect of capitalists' behavior, entirely necessary within a capitalist system, came to be seen by the theorists within the utilitarian tradition as being at the core of all human decision-making processes. Human behavior was never explained as merely habitual, capricious, accidental, superstitious, religious, altruistic, or as simply emotional and nonrational. All human acts came to be seen as the consequence of rational, calculated decisions in which the individual acted much like an accountant, weighing all of the benefits (pleasures) that would come from any particular act, deducting all the costs (pains) of that act, and then rationally choosing the action that would maximize the surplus of pleasure over pain. Thus, in modern neoclassical textbooks on microeconomic theory, all human behavior is reduced to rational, calculated attempts to maximize either profits or utility. And profit maximization is frequently reduced to merely an indirect form of utility maximization (although, as we will see, the word *utility* is sometimes dropped in favor of a synonym such as "preference ordering").

These five aspects of human behavior and self-perception under capitalism—atomistic individualism, egoistic utilitarianism, dependence on markets, the financing of industrialization out of profits, and calculating rationalism—became the intellectual foundation of the neoclassical theory of utility and social harmony in the late nineteenth and twentieth centuries. Bentham, Say, and Senior formulated most of the ideas that later economists were to use in extricating the concepts of the social harmony and the social beneficence of the market from the labor theory of value perspective, in which these concepts had so uncomfortably rested in the writings of Smith and Ricardo.

Jeremy Bentham on Utility

Jeremy Bentham (1748–1832), an Englishman whose career as a writer and influential social theorist spanned over sixty years, wrote numerous articles, essays, and pamphlets on economic topics.[3] The work that exerted the most powerful influence on nineteenth-century economic theory, however, was *An Introduction to the Principles of Morals and Legislation*, published in 1780, about six years before he turned his attention to the immediate issues of economic theory. The *Introduction* was intended to be a part of a general preface to a complete code of law. Although it does not deal directly with economic theory, it contains an elaborate statement of the utilitarian social philosophy, which was to become the philosophical basis of neoclassical economics during the last several decades of the nineteenth century.

Chapter 1 of the *Introduction* begins with this statement:

> Nature has placed mankind under the governance of two sovereign masters, *pain* and *pleasure*. It is for them alone to point out what we ought to do, as well as to determine what we shall do. . . . They govern us in all we do, in all we say, in all we think. . . . The *principle of utility* recognizes this subjection, and assumes it for the foundation of [its social theory].[4]

Thus, he began with the assertion that all human motivation, in all times and all places, can be reduced to a single principle: the desire to maximize one's utility.

> By utility is meant that property in any object, whereby it tends to produce benefit, advantage, pleasure, good, or happiness (all this in the present case comes to the same thing), or (what comes again to the same thing) to prevent the happening of mischief, pain, evil, or unhappiness to the party whose interest is considered.[5]

All of these various motivations, Bentham believed, were merely manifestations of the desire for pleasure and the avoidance of pain. Because pain was merely negative pleasure, Bentham's principle of utility could be restated as "all human activity springs from the desire to maximize pleasure."

By reducing all human motives to a single principle, Bentham believed that he had found the key to the construction of a science of human welfare or happiness that could be stated mathematically and might someday be worked out with the same numerical exactitude as the science of physics. "Pleasures . . . and the avoidance of pains are . . . *ends*," he argued, which can be numerically quantified such that we can "understand their *value*."[6]

He suggested a possible method for quantifying pleasures:

> To a number of persons, with reference to each of whom the value of a pleasure or pain is considered, it *will* be greater or less, according to seven circumstances: . . . *viz.*
>
> 1. Its *intensity.*
> 2. Its *duration.*
> 3. Its *certainty* or *uncertainty.*
> 4. Its *propinquity* or *remoteness.*
> 5. Its *fecundity.*
> 6. Its *purity.*
> 7. Its *extent.*[7]

He then went into a discussion of the specific ways in which these circumstances might suggest how one could rationally calculate the values of pleasures and pains.

Bentham not only conceived of human beings as calculating maximizers of pleasure, he also saw them as being fundamentally individualistic. "In the general tenor of life," he wrote, "in every human breast, self-regarding interest is predominant over all other interests put together. . . . Self-preference has place everywhere."[8] People were also, he believed, essentially lazy. Any kind of exertion or work was viewed as painful, and, therefore, work would never be undertaken without the promise of greater pleasure or the avoidance of greater pain. "Aversion," he insisted, "is the emotion—the only emotion— which *labour*, taken by itself, is qualified to produce. . . . In so far as *labour* is taken in its proper sense, *love of labour* is a contradiction in terms."[9]

Each of these ideas of Bentham was to become important in the subsequent development of the utility theory of value. Smith, it will be remembered, rejected the notion that utility could be systematically related to exchange value. Although Smith, Ricardo, and Marx all realized that commodities had to have use value in order to have exchange value, they did not believe that one could find a scientific explanation of the magnitude of exchange value by examining a commodity's use value. Smith had used the example of water and diamonds to illustrate the absence of such a systematic connection. The later proponents of the utility theory of value were to reject Smith's illustration by arguing that it was not the *total utility* of a commodity that determined its exchange value, but rather its *marginal utility*, that is, the additional utility derived from a small, marginal increase in the commodity. Here, again, Bentham was an important precursor of the later utility theorists:

> The terms *wealth* and *value* explain each other. An article can only enter into the composition of a mass of wealth if it possesses some value. It is by the degrees of that value that wealth is measured.
>
> All value is founded on utility. . . . Where there is no use, there cannot be any value.[10]

Smith and Ricardo would have agreed that use value was a necessary condition for exchange value. But, as Ricardo insisted, when one sees value as created by labor, then an increase in the productivity of labor *lowers* the value of a commodity while *increasing* the general wealth. When Bentham stated that "it is by the degree of that value that wealth is measured," he was speaking from the utility theory perspective, in which an increase in utility increases a commodity's value and hence increases its owner's wealth.

Somewhat later in the same essay, Bentham criticized Smith's diamond-water illustration and consequently came very close to explicitly developing the principle of *marginal* utility, which was later to become the cornerstone of neoclassical economics:

> Value in use is the basis of value in exchange. . . . This distinction comes from Adam Smith but he has not attached to it clear conceptions. . . .
> Water is the example he has chosen of that sort of article which has great value with a view to use but none with a view to exchange. In order to realize how erroneous the latter assertion is, he would only have had to consult in London the New

River Board, and to remember that at Paris he had seen it sold retail by those who carry it into the houses.

He gives *diamonds* as an example of that sort of article which has great value with a view to exchange and none with a view to use. This example is as ill chosen as the other . . . .

The value [in use] of diamonds . . . is neither essential nor invariable like that of water: but this is no reason why its utility with regard to enjoyment should be doubted. . . .

The reason why water is found not to have any value with a view to exchange is that it is equally devoid of a value with a view to use. If the whole quantity required is available, the surplus has no kind of value. It would be the same in the case of wine, grain, and everything else. Water, furnished as it is by nature without any human exertion, is more likely to be found in that abundance which renders it superfluous: but there are many circumstances in which it has a value in exchange superior to that of wine.[11]

Thus, Bentham not only formulated the philosophical foundation of the later tradition of neoclassical economics but also came very close to developing a theory of the relationship between marginal utility and price. The development of his ideas also foreshadowed an important split in the orthodox utility approach to economics. In the late eighteenth century, he was an ardent spokesman for a laissez-faire policy, believing that the free market would allocate resources and commodities in the most socially beneficial manner possible. In his later writings, he fundamentally altered his position.

Bentham as a Social Reformer

In Bentham's earlier writings, he accepted Smith's argument that a competitive free market would allocate productive resources to those industries in which they would be the most productive. He therefore believed that government interference in the free market might very likely diminish the level of production. At best, such interference could not possibly increase production: "Therefore no regulations nor any efforts whatsoever, either on the part of subjects or governors, can raise the quantity of wealth produced during a given period."[12]

Bentham also accepted, during this early period, the notion that nearly all of the economists of his generation, except Malthus and a few lesser-known writers, believed to be true—that aggregate supply would always equal aggregate demand in a free market. In such a market there need never be a depression or any involuntary unemployment because any saving was automatically converted into more capital with which to employ more labor. "Whoever saves money," Bentham asserted, "adds proportionately to the general mass of capital."[13]

However, by 1801, Bentham's opinions about government intervention in the economy had undergone a change:

I have not . . . any horror, sentimental or anarchical, of the hand of government. I leave it to Adam Smith and the champions of the rights of man (for confusion of ideas will jumble together the best subjects and the worst citizens upon the same ground) to talk of invasions of natural liberty, and to give as a special argument against this or that law, an argument the effect of which would be to put a negative upon all laws. The interference of government, as often as . . . [it results in] the smallest . . . advantage . . . is an event I witness with . . . satisfaction.[14]

This change of opinion was prompted by two principal concerns, each of which was later to become an important argument against complete laissez faire. First, Bentham, like Malthus, came to see that saving might not be matched by new investment. In this event, production would diminish, unemployment would be created, and the free market would not be functioning in the best interests of the public. "Suppose an increase in the habit of frugality," he wrote. "Its first effect will be to diminish the mass of expenditure on consumption.[15] Its ultimate effect would depend on how the saving was used. Suppose, he continued, that the money, "instead of being put into circulation, is for an indefinite time put into a chest and kept there."[16] In that case, saving would lead to decreased prices and production; profits would decline and so would investment. In such a case, Bentham argued, if the government increased the amount of money in circulation, "then the money introduced . . . becomes a source of increasing wealth."[17]

The second reason for government interference in the market was to lessen the socially harmful effects of great inequalities of wealth and income. Bentham believed that a person's capacity to get enjoyment from money declined as he got more money. In modern utility terminology, he believed in a diminishing marginal utility of money. Therefore, all other things being equal, a government measure that redistributed money from the rich to the poor would increase the total of society's aggregate utility:

> Take, for example, on the one hand, a labouring man, who, for the whole of his life, has a bare but sure subsistence. . . . Take, on the other hand, the richest man in the country. . . . [Suppose the richest man receives an income] 50,000 times as great as that received, in the same time, by the labourer. This supposed, the quantity of pleasure in the breast of the . . . [rich man] will naturally be greater than the quantity in the breast of the labourer: Be it so. But by how much—by how many times greater? Fifty thousand times? This is assuredly more than any man would take it upon himself to say. A thousand times then?—a hundred?—ten times?—five times? . . . *Five* times the labourer's seems a very large, not to say excessive allowance: even twice, a liberal one.[18]

Bentham was by no means an advocate of complete equality. If redistributions of wealth and income were made, he believed, a point would be reached where their beneficial effects would be more than offset by harmful effects. Particularly harmful would be the effects of decreasing the workers' inducement to labor. The ideal degree of inequality, he believed, "should be that which has place in the *Anglo-American United States:* meaning always those in which slave-holding has no place."[19] To the modern reader this might seem a rather minimal reform for Bentham to have advocated. But when these words were written, the degree of inequality in those states to which he was referring was substantially less than the inequality in England. This criterion would have meant a very radical reform indeed.

Thus, over Bentham's lifetime, there was a split or antagonism between his earlier extreme laissez-faire attitude and his later reformist attitude. This same split was to be reflected later in the neoclassical tradition, which was constructed on the foundation of Bentham's utilitarian philosophy.

In addition, an inadequacy that was to be pervasive in the neoclassical approach can be seen clearly in Bentham's reformist phase: If the government carried out reforms that increased the general welfare by redistributing wealth and income from the rich to the poor, then it was necessary for the government to have no narrow or special interests of its own. It had to be a benevolent, impartial institution, equally interested in every individual's welfare. However, the government was not made up of angels, or "philosopher kings," but of ordinary persons, who, in accordance with "general human nature," were egoistic and interested in maximizing their own pleasure. If one asks the question of whether legislators were more likely to receive material benefits by promoting the interests of the poor or the interests of the rich, the inherent difficulty in Bentham's belief in beneficial social reform by a fair and impartial government becomes obvious.

Jean-Baptiste Say on Utility, Production, and Income Distribution

J.B. Say (1767–1832) considered himself to be a disciple of Adam Smith. He claimed to be simply systematizing Smith's ideas and correcting certain minor errors that Smith had made. The correction of minor errors, however, ultimately resulted in the abandonment of some of Smith's most important ideas and the laying down of a foundation for a quite different tradition of economic theory. One historian has summarized Say's relation to Smith in this way: "Say put Smith's theory in order in the same way that a cautious spouse puts her husband's trousers in order when she turns them upside down and empties them of all their valuables. It is much safer that way. So Say 'purged' Smith of 'dangerous thoughts.'"[20]

In the introduction to his *A Treatise on Political Economy*, Say praised Smith for his contributions to political economy and then concluded with a passage that is the key to understanding most of Say's writings:

> After having shown . . . the improvement which the science of political economy owes to Dr. Smith, it will not, perhaps, be useless to indicate . . . some of the points on which he erred. . . .
>
> To the labour of man alone he ascribes the power of producing values. This is an error.[21]

The price, or exchange value, of any commodity, Say asserted, depends entirely on its use value, or utility:

> The value that mankind attaches to objects originates in the use it can make of them. . . . [To the] inherent fitness or capability of certain things to satisfy the various wants of mankind, I shall take leave to affix the name utility. . . . The utility of things is the ground-work of their value, and their value constitutes wealth. . . .
>
> Although price is the measure of the value of things, and their value the measure of their utility, it would be absurd to draw the inference, that, by forcibly raising their price, their utility can be augmented. Exchangeable value, or price, is an index of the recognized utility of a thing.[22]

In rejecting the notion that labor was the source of value and insisting that only utility created values, Say not only departed sharply from the ideas of Smith and Ricardo. He also placed the utility approach in the context of a methodological approach and a social philosophy that show him to be, along with Nassau Senior, the most important of the forerunners of the neoclassical tradition that came to dominate economics in the late nineteenth and the twentieth centuries. In the writings of Smith and Ricardo, it is clear that labor incomes are fundamentally different from the incomes that accrue from ownership of the means of production. In recognizing the source of this difference, they were led to the conclusion that class conflict characterized capitalism. We have seen, however, that when they reverted to the exchange or utility approach to economic theory, they were led to the conclusion that free market capitalism was inherently a system of social harmony.

Say resolved this dilemma by rejecting completely the production perspective or labor theory of value approach to economic theory. Within his utility framework, he totally obliterated the theoretical distinction between the incomes of the different social classes. Instead of seeing the process of production as a series of human exertions applied to transform natural raw materials into usable goods, Say asserted the existence of different "productive agencies" that combined together to produce goods. What these productive agencies were ultimately producing was "utility," and each agency was coequally responsible for the production of the utility. These productive agencies included "human industry, with the aid of capital and of natural agents and properties," and altogether they created "every kind of utility, which is the primary source of value."[23] In other words, there was no qualitative difference, in the creation of utility, between the *exertion* of human labor, on the one hand, and the *ownership* of capital, land, and property, on the other.

Say attempted to defend the essential similarity between working and owning by arguing that commodities were "invested with value by the necessity of giving something to obtain them."[24] Objects of wealth were obtained only by human sacrifice. The sacrifice given up by the workers who produced the commodities was obvious. Say wanted to show that owners of the means of production received their incomes from similar sacrifices. He asserted that frugality was the source of capital ownership, and frugality involved as much sacrifice as working. He wrote:

> Perhaps it is scarcely necessary to remark, that property in that class of productive means, which has been called human industry, and in that distinguished by the general name of capital, is far more sacred and indisputable, than in the remaining class of natural powers and agents. The industrious faculties of man, his intelligence, muscular strength, and dexterity, are peculiar to himself and inherent in his nature. And capital, or accumulated produce, is the mere result of human frugality and forbearance to exercise the faculty of consuming, which, if fully exerted, would have destroyed products as fast as they were created, and these never could have been the existing property of any one; wherefore, no one else, but he who has practised this self-denial, can claim the result of it with any show of justice. Frugality is next of kin to the actual creation of products, which confers the most unquestionable of all titles to the property in them.[25]

Having thus argued that working and owning capital involved similar sacrifices and that workers and capitalists had similar moral justifications for their incomes, Say anticipated the neoclassical theory of distribution by totally revising the relationship that Smith and Ricardo had seen between income distribution and commodity values. Whereas Smith and Ricardo had argued that commodity prices reflected the rate of wages and the rate of profits (even though for Ricardo this was an influence of secondary significance) and that these rates were determined by other social and technical considerations (namely, the subsistence of workers and the total productivity of labor), Say argued that wage and profit rates were determined by the relative contributions to utility creation made by labor and capital. In Say's words:

> The value of products is not founded upon that of productive agency [that is, not the rates of profit and wages], as some authors have erroneously affirmed; . . . since the desire of an object, and consequently its value, originates in its utility, it is the ability to create the utility . . . that gives value to a productive agency; which value is proportionate to the importance of its co-operation in the business of production.[26]

This theory of income distribution, which we will see in chapter 12 was fully developed by John Bates Clark, had the ideological advantage of showing that each person received as income an amount determined solely by the importance of his or her sacrifices in creating the utility enjoyed by all of society. Not only were profits and wages paid for very similar reasons, but also there was an important sense of social justice in the notion that each person received from society an amount determined only by his or her own (or his or her capital's) contribution to society's well being.

It is not surprising that within this utility approach to value and distribution theory, all notions of class conflict disappeared. A central purpose of Say's *Treatise* was to demonstrate that social harmony and not class conflict was the natural result of a capitalist economy. Once these ideas were widely understood, "people, becoming more enlightened as to their true interests, will perceive that these interests are not at variance with each other."[27] The greatest value would be attached to studying political economy, he believed, when it was realized that political economy "proves that the interest of the rich and poor . . . are not opposed to each other, and that all rivalships are mere folly."[28]

Say's ideas were founded on an unquestioned acceptance of capitalist property relationships. He asserted that property ownership was "sacred and indisputable" and that the question of "whether the actual owner . . . or the person from whom he derived its possession, has obtained it by prior occupancy, by violence, or by fraud, can make no difference whatever in the business of the production and distribution of its product or revenue."[29]

Say's Law of Markets

Another important aspect of Say's writings was his belief that a free market would always adjust automatically to an equilibrium in which all resources—including labor—were fully utilized, that is, to an equilibrium with full employment of both labor and industrial capacity. Although, as we have seen, Smith, Ricardo, and Bentham (in his earliest writings) had argued that a free, competitive market automatically created full employment, this belief in the automaticity of the market subsequently came to be known as "Say's law." Economists who rejected this "law" have included Malthus, Bentham (in his later writings), Karl Marx, and John Maynard Keynes.

In a lengthy and famous exchange of letters with Malthus, Say defended his belief that there could never be a general glut or a depression involving involuntary unemployment. He argued that a market economy is one in which specialized producers exchanged their products. Money had no inherent importance but was merely a means of facilitating exchange. No one would produce, Say argued, unless that person wanted to exchange his or her production for someone else's production. Therefore, *a supply creates a demand of the same magnitude*. "Produce opens a vent for produce,"[30] he maintained. If this was true for each producer taken individually, it must be true of the aggregates of supply and demand; that is, aggregate supply must equal aggregate demand.

There could be, Say argued, a *temporary* glut of *some* commodities, but this would result from the fact that market equilibrium had not been attained. Some prices would be too low and others too high. In this case, there would be a glut of those commodities whose prices were too high and simultaneously a shortage of those commodities whose prices were too low. The gluts and shortages would exactly cancel out in the aggregate. Furthermore, those capitalists selling commodities at too low a price would receive a low profit, while those selling them at too high a price would receive high profits. The search for maximum profits would then cause capitalists to leave the low-priced industries and enter the high-priced industries. This migration of capitalists would have two effects. First, it would alter the prices, raising the prices that were too low (because less would be produced and sold, and buyers would bid up the prices in their attempt to secure their share of the diminished produce) and lowering the prices that were too high (because more would be produced and sold, and sellers would bid down the prices in their effort to find buyers for the additional produce). Second, it would lower the quantity produced of the commodities for which there was a glut, and it would increase the quantity produced of commodities for which there was a shortage. Thus, throughout the entire process, aggregate supply would always equal aggregate demand, but individual shortages and surpluses would be eliminated by price changes and the migration of capitalists from low-profit industries to high-profit industries.

In Say's words,

> If there is an overstock, of many kinds of goods, it is because other goods are not produced in sufficient quantities.[31]
> That [commodity] which sells above its cost of production will induce a part of the producers of the other commodity to the production of . . . [the higher-priced commodity] until the productive services are equally paid by both.[32]

This, then, will assure that aggregate demand not only equals aggregate supply, but that demand and supply for each and every commodity will be equal. Thus, the market can *never* have a glut of all commodities. Furthermore, temporary shortages and surpluses among different commodities will be eliminated automatically by the free, competitive market. These conclusions constitute Say's law and are still accepted by many economists today.

Nassau Senior's Social Orientation

Nassau Senior (1790–1864), like Bentham and Say, was an important precursor of modern neoclassical economics. Like Say, he carefully selected certain ideas of prior classical economists, modified some of them, and added ideas of his own to develop a consistent theoretical justification of the status quo of nineteenth-century capitalism. His ideas about the appropriate methodology of economic theory, the place of utility in explaining value, and the moral and intellectual justification of profit and rent constitute the most important areas in which he influenced the later neoclassical tradition.

Senior was a lawyer with a strong interest in social, economic, and political issues. He was an intimate friend of many of the most prominent members of the Whig party and was the party's general adviser on social and economic questions. In 1825, he was appointed to the first chair of political economy at Oxford University. The social and economic problems that most consistently commanded his attention were the general condition of the working class and the causes and consequences of poverty. Senior's ideas about the working class and poverty underwent a dramatic change in 1830, and, in the period after 1830, he produced the ideas that were to have the most influence both intellectually and politically.

Prior to 1830, Senior was a politically conservative man with a keen sympathy and benevolent concern for the poverty of the working class. His *Introductory Lecture on Political Economy* was published in 1826, and his *Two Lectures on Population* was published in 1828. In these early works, he showed an optimism about the future of the working class. He did not believe that Malthus's population theory could legitimately lead one to the conclusion that working people would always be at a subsistence level. He believed, rather, that increases in productivity could be accompanied by improvements in the moral character of workers, and, consequently, the standard of living of most workers would rise. He actively supported efforts that he believed would uplift the intellectual and moral status of the poor, and he saw moral education as the only hope for eliminating poverty. However, his views were to change in 1830.

Between 1829 and 1842, England experienced a long series of labor difficulties. Industrialization had reduced the English working class to an almost subhuman level of exploitation and degradation. In the 1820s and 1830s, the working class fought back. After 1829, there were many massive efforts to organize labor, which frequently met with harsh repression. The consequence was widespread strikes, riots, and industrial sabotage, all of which profoundly frightened Senior. Particularly important in changing some of his views were what he called "the fires and insurrections which terrified the south of England in the frightful autumn of 1830."[33] Senior became convinced that the poor laws and the government's dole to the poor and the unemployed were the principal causes of poverty and a great threat to the very existence of English capitalism.

In 1830, he published *Three Lectures on the Rate of Wages*, written in the early part of that year; after the "frightful autumn of 1830," he added a preface entitled "The Causes and Remedies of the Present Disturbances." In this preface, he argued that capitalists had a "fund for the maintenance of labourers" (this notion came to be known in economic literature as the "wages fund doctrine").[34] He asserted that the size of this fund was determined solely by labor's productivity. Therefore, improving the living standard of workers required either an increase in their productivity or a decrease in the number of workers among whom the wages fund was divided. There were, he stated, two ways of increasing labor's productivity: first, the removal of all restrictions on free commerce and accumulation of capital, and second, the abolition of the poor laws, which had "made wages not a matter of contract between the master and the workman, but a right for the one, and a tax on the other."[35]

In the preface, it is clear that Senior was no longer concerned with the misery caused by poverty, but with "the threat of an arrogant laboring class, resorting to strikes, violence, and combinations [unions], a threat to the foundations not merely of wealth but of existence itself."[36] The great danger, in Senior's eyes, was that labor unions would fight to maintain and extend the notion that wages should reflect the needs of each worker's family rather than the free play of the forces of supply and demand. The poor laws were based on a system of family allowances for the unemployed and the destitute. Such laws, Senior believed, decreased workers' incentives to work and created the arrogant attitude of workers that their families had a right to exist even if the workers themselves did not or could not find work. This created an "unnatural" relationship between capitalists and workers. When the capitalist worker relationship was in "the natural state," Senior wrote,

> greater exertion and severer economy are . . . [the laborer's] resources in distress; and what they cannot supply, he receives with gratitude from the benevolent. The connexion between him and his master has the kindliness of a voluntary association, in which each party is conscious of benefit, and each feels that his own welfare depends . . . on the welfare of the other. But the instant wages cease to be a bargain—the instant the labourer is paid, not according to his *value*, but his *wants*, he ceases to be a free man. He acquires the indolence, the improvidence, the rapacity, and the malignity, but not the subordination of a slave. He is told that he has a right to wages. . . . But who can doubt that he will measure his rights by his wishes, or that his wishes will extend with the prospect of gratification? The present tide may not complete the inundation, but it will be a dreadful error if we mistake the ebb for a permanent receding of the waters. A breach has been made in the sea-wall, and with every succeeding irruption they will swell higher and spread more widely. What we are suffering is nothing to what we have to expect.[37]

The unchecked anger, arrogance, and fanaticism of the poor, Senior argued, would ultimately lead to a situation in which "rent, tithes, profit, and capital, are all eaten up, and pauperism produces what may be called its natural effects—for they are the effects which, if unchecked, it must ultimately produce—famine, pestilence, and civil war."[38]

In this period, the ideas of radicals and socialists were spreading fast. Thomas Hodgskin and William Thompson had written books in the 1820s in which they argued that profits were generally unearned income coercively expropriated from workers.[39] These ideas were being widely disseminated and discussed. The socialist doctrines of Robert Owen were also rapidly becoming influential. Senior deplored socialist ideas, calling them a mistaken belief that the conditions creating inequality could be remedied. Such a mistaken belief he called "the political economy of the poor," and he argued that these ideas had a natural appeal to the uneducated. Equality can only involve extreme misery, he argued, because "though it is in the power of human institutions to make everybody poor, they cannot make everybody rich; . . . they can diffuse misery, but not happiness."[40]

Senior believed that every educated, knowledgeable person would understand the utter futility and great danger of socialist ideas. Discussing the futility of socialist ideas, he wrote:

> Among philosophers . . . [an understanding of the futility] is a conviction; among the higher and middle classes . . . [it] is a prejudice founded partly on . . . their own apparent interest. But the apparent interest of the lower classes is the other way. They grossly miscalculate the number and value of the prizes in the lottery of life,

they think that they have drawn little better than blanks, and believe those who tell them that if all the high lots were abolished everybody might have a hundred-pound prize.

As long as this is the political economy of the poor, there seem to be only three means of governing a densely peopled country in which they form the large majority. One is to exclude them from political life. This is our English policy. . . . Another is the existence among them of a blind devotion to the laws and customs of the country. . . . A third plan is to rely on military power—to arm and discipline the higher and middle classes, and to support them by a regular army trained to implicit obedience.[41]

With his connections to the most powerful members of the Whig party, Senior was able to put some of his ideas into practice. In 1832, he was appointed a member of the Poor Law Inquiry Commission, which was to study existing poor laws and methods of dealing with poverty and to recommend reforms designed to make the system of poor relief function more effectively and economically. According to reliable sources, the report that the commission issued in 1834 was largely Senior's work, and it became the basis of a new poor law, passed also in 1834. The new poor law reflected the following commission views: (1) workers should accept any job the market offered, regardless of the working conditions or pay involved; (2) any person who would not or could not find work should be given just barely enough to prevent physical starvation; and (3) the dole given to such a person should be substantially lower than the lowest wage offered in the market, and his general situation should be made so miserable and should so stigmatize him as to motivate him to seek any employment, irrespective of the pay or conditions.

One present-day economic and social historian has written that the poor law Senior was so influential in creating was

an engine of degradation and oppression more than a means of material relief. There have been few more inhuman statutes than the Poor Law Act of 1834, which made all relief "less eligible" than the lowest wage outside, confined it to the jail-like workhouse, forcibly separated husbands, wives and children in order to punish the poor for their destitution, and discourage them from the dangerous temptation of procreating further paupers.[42]

Such was the social philosophy underlying, and the policies that grew out of, Senior's economic analysis of capitalism.

Senior's Theoretical Methodology

Senior's economic analysis was most completely developed in his *An Outline of the Science of Political Economy*, first published in 1836. The first chapter of the *Outline* contains a statement of his methodology that is important for three reasons: first, it is the first explicit statement of a particular methodological approach that has subsequently been very influential among economists and other social scientists of a conservative bent down to the present; second, it is a methodology that, we will argue (both in this chapter and in chapter 18 on the Chicago School of economics), attempts to hide and obscure the conservative normative foundations of Senior's (and the later conservative economists') economic theory; and third, it appears to give Senior's (and the later conservative economists') ideas the authority of a detached, objective, neutral, and scientific foundation, removed from the supposed stigma of defending the interests of any particular persons or classes.

Senior believed that so much controversy existed in theories of political economy because economists had concerned themselves with *social welfare* rather than merely analyzing *wealth*. When one considered social welfare, one was immediately involved in normative or ethical statements reflecting the positions of varying contending groups involved in social conflicts. It was thus inevitable that intellectual conflicts would arise. Ethical statements, Senior declared, were not subject to either scientific confirmation or disproof. Therefore, as long as they remained a part of economic theorizing, scientific advancement could never result in agreement among theoreticians. If political economy was to become a science, it was first necessary to eliminate all of the unscientific, ethical premises contained within it. After these were eliminated, a few clearly established empirical principles of economic life would remain. Then, using deductive logic, economists would be able to explore scientifically all of the theoretical and practical implications of these few empirically substantiated principles. The use or application of these conclusions would not be the concern of the economist as scientist, but rather of the moralist or the legislator. Political economics would be a value-free, neutral, "pure science." Senior wrote:

> The subject treated by the Political Economist . . . is not Happiness, but Wealth; his premises consist of a very few general propositions, the result of observation, or consciousness, and scarcely requiring proof, or even formal statement, which almost every man, as soon as he hears them, admits as familiar to his thoughts, or at least as included in his previous knowledge; and his inferences are nearly as general, and, if he has reasoned correctly, as certain as his premises. Those which relate to the Nature and Production of Wealth are universally true. . . . But his conclusions, whatever be their generality and their truth, do not authorize him in adding a single syllable of advice.[43]

The difficulty with Senior's methodology is that the ongoing empirical reality of a capitalist social and economic system is composed of a nearly infinite number of interconnected and interrelated empirical "facts." Nothing inherent in experience per se suggests to us that any particular "few general propositions" are of central importance in understanding capitalism. The process of constructing a social theory is one in which we abstract from or ignore innumerable "facts" and simultaneously isolate and focus on a few others that we believe to have explanatory power.

If one believes his or her theory to have any importance whatsoever (and Senior as well as the later economists using his methodology always clearly believed their theories to be important), that person must believe that he or she has abstracted from, or ignored, irrelevant or unimportant facts and focused on relevant and important ones. But the questions of relevance and importance have no meaning at all unless one asks, relevant or important with respect to what problem? Thus, the social or economic issue or problem to which a theory is addressed is crucial in determining what aspects of reality the theoretician ignores and what aspects he or she focuses on in a "few general propositions." But what constitutes an important problem or an important issue is a judgment based entirely on the values of the theoretician.

Thus, values stand at the very foundation of the process of theorizing. They dictate not only what a theoretician will consider an important social issue but also what types of solutions to social problems would be acceptable. Social theories are generally addressed to problems that the theoretician considers important. Furthermore, the "few general propositions" selected are generally chosen in a manner so that the theory will produce conclusions that are acceptable within the context of the theoretician's values. Similarly, the "few general propositions" generally preclude theoretical conclusions that are morally or ethically unacceptable. Such was definitely the case with Senior, and such has been the case with virtually all later theorists who repeated Senior's claim to have elevated economic theory to a higher plane, where it was supposedly uncontaminated by moral or ethical values.

It is also very clear that Senior wanted his theory to be seriously considered by those who had decision-making power in the most important social, political, and moral issues of his era. In fact, given his social and moral values, he believed that it would be disastrous if legislators did not act in accordance with the conclusions of his theory. This is clearly illustrated in the following sentence, contained in his discussion of methodology: "The business of a Political Economist is neither to recommend nor to dissuade, but to state general principles, which it is fatal to neglect."[44]

In what sense did Senior mean it would be "fatal to neglect" his principles? Surely he could not have meant that such neglect would have led to the physical extinction of the human race, in that the human race had existed for untold centuries without having his principles to guide it. The only possible meaning of the phrase was that he believed a failure to follow his principles would lead to consequences that he judged to be morally bad.

So much for Senior's attempted separation of the scientific and the normative. We shall see that later theoreticians who followed Senior in attempting this separation generally did so for the same reasons as Senior, and that their attempts have been no more successful than his.

Senior's Four Propositions

After stating his methodological approach, Senior listed four general propositions that he considered to be self-evidently true from ordinary experience and introspection. He wrote:

We have already stated that the general facts on which Political Economy rests, are comprised in a few general Propositions, the result of observation or consciousness. The Propositions to which we have alluded are these:—

1. That every man desires to obtain additional Wealth with as little sacrifice as possible.
2. That the Population of the world . . . is limited only by moral or physical evil, or by a fear of a deficiency of those articles of wealth which the habits of the individuals of each class of its inhabitants lead them to require.
3. That the powers of Labour, and of the other instruments which produce wealth, may be indefinitely increased by using their Products as the means of further production.
4. That, agricultural skill remaining the same, additional Labour on the land within a given district produces in general a less proportionate return, or, in other words, that though, with every increase of the labour bestowed, the aggregate return is increased, the increase of the return is not in proportion to the increase of the labour.[45]

It was on the basis of these four supposedly value-free propositions, which Senior believed to be obviously scientifically valid, that he attempted to construct the science of political economy. We will examine his treatment of each of the four propositions both to understand what he saw as the implications of these premises and to see how free from moral considerations his conclusions, based on these principles, really were.

Senior on Utility Maximization, Prices, and Gluts

In the development of the first proposition, Senior expressed clearly two of the themes discussed in the first section of the present chapter. First, he believed that introspection would prove that all economic behavior was calculating and rationalistic, and, like Bentham, he saw this behavior as ultimately reducible to the maximizing of utility. He spoke of maximizing wealth, but in explaining the nature of wealth he wrote: "Of the . . . qualities which render anything an article of Wealth, or, in other words, give it Value, the most striking is the power, direct or indirect, of producing pleasure. . . . *Utility* . . . comes nearest to [expressing this quality]."[46] The first proposition stated that people always desired to increase wealth with as little sacrifice as possible. In our discussion of Senior's third proposition, we will see that all means of acquiring wealth did, in his view, involve a sacrifice or a disutility (or negative utility). Therefore, as with Bentham, we can speak of maximizing utility or minimizing disutility. But both these amount to simple utility maximization. Senior differed with Bentham, however, on the basic assumption whereby the latter argued for his egalitarian reform. Bentham, it will be recalled, believed that as wealth or income increased, the utility of each successive, or marginal, increment declined.

The diminishing marginal utility of wealth was the basis of Bentham's argument that wealth taken from the richest people and given to the poorest people in a society would increase social utility. Two premises seem to underlie Bentham's belief—first, that people can acquire so much wealth that they become satiated, and thus a slight increment or decrement to their wealth has very little, if any, effect on the total utility that they derive from their wealth; and second, that the utilities that any two people derive from their wealth can be compared. Later utility theorists were generally much more conservative than Bentham, so it was necessary for them to deny these two egalitarian premises. Senior explicitly denied both of them.

Senior asserted that no matter how unequally wealth might be distributed, "no person feels his whole wants to be adequately supplied; . . . every person has some unsatisfied desires which he believes that additional wealth would gratify."[47] Furthermore, "the nature and urgency of each individual's wants are as various as the differences in individual character."[48] Therefore, we cannot make comparisons among individuals as to the amount of utility that they would receive or lose from an increment or a decrement in their wealth.

The second important theme of this chapter, expressed in Senior's discussion of his first proposition, is that prices reflect individuals' utilities derived from consuming the various commodities rather than the labor embodied in commodities. Although he did not develop a theory of how utility determined prices, Senior repeatedly stated that commodities "exchange in proportion to the force or weakness of the causes which give utility to them."[49] In response to Ricardo's labor theory of value he wrote that

> if all the commodities used by man were supplied by nature without any intervention whatever of human labor, but were supplied in precisely the same quantities as they now are, there is no reason to suppose either that they would cease to be valuable, or would exchange in any other than their present proportions.
>
> The reply to Mr. Ricardo is . . . that the articles of wealth which do not owe the principal part of their value to the labour which has been bestowed on their respective actual production, form, in fact, the bulk of wealth, instead of a small and unimportant portion of it.[50]

Finally, Senior's first proposition was used against Malthus to argue that economic gluts or depressions were impossible. He believed that if the desire for wealth were insatiable, then there could never be a general glut of commodities. And because common observation "proved" the desire for wealth to be insatiable, the belief that depressions or general gluts had existed or would exist in the future must be false. He argued that

> the only . . . hypothesis on which the existence of a general glut can be supposed is that of a general satiety, that all men may be so *fully* provided with the precise articles which they desire as to afford no market for each other's superfluities. And this doctrine is opposed to the proposition which we set out, that every man desires to obtain additional wealth.[51]

Senior appears to be more extreme than either Ricardo or Say in his rejection of the possibility of gluts. The latter two theorists at least recognized that there had been recurring periods of general economic distress but argued that a competitive market would automatically alleviate this distress and restore a proper balance in the various industries in disequilibrium. Senior, in his various writings, does not appear to have recognized the very existence of such periodic crises. But, as we said above, values frequently dictate those aspects of reality from which theoreticians will abstract, and, by implication, those aspects that they will ignore as being unimportant.

Senior's Views on Population and Workers' Welfare

Senior's second proposition nearly restated Malthus's views on population. Like Malthus, he believed that unless the moral character of the poor was improved, misery would be their inevitable lot. Prior to 1830, however, he believed that the moral character of England's poor was improving, and he was optimistic that it would improve even more in the future. After the "frightful autumn of 1830," his views changed. In the preface to the 1831 edition of *Three Lectures on the Rate of Wages*, he argued that there was only one "effectual and permanent means" of alleviating poverty—"to raise the moral and intellectual character of the labouring population." But, whereas he had formerly believed that workers' characters had already been improved considerably, he now went on to say it was necessary "to improve, or I fear we must say, to create habits of prudence, of self-respect, and of self-restraint."[52] It is obvious that when he said these habits had to be created, he was asserting that, in fact, English workers lacked them entirely.

Thus, in the statement of his second proposition, Senior stressed that the only alternative to "moral and physical evil" in controlling population was the "fear of deficiency." Senior believed it to be absolutely necessary to keep the working class living in a constant and extreme "fear of deficiency," and he believed that the older poor laws had lessened this fear by giving workers a minimal level of security. His objection to this and his belief in the importance of maintaining extreme fear and insecurity were to become the foundations of the 1834 poor law. But Senior, like Malthus, believed that the attainment of the ultimate good of society frequently required suffering (inevitably it was the poor whom they believed had to suffer). "Nature has decreed," he wrote, "that the road to good shall be through evil—that no improvement shall take place in which the general advantage shall not be accompanied by partial suffering."[53]

Senior on Capital Accumulation and Abstinence

Senior's third proposition was, on the surface, a denial that there would be diminishing returns in manufacturing. As the amount of labor devoted to manufacturing increased, the output of manufactured goods *could* increase at least proportionately if not more than proportionately, depending on whether the products of labor and capital were accumulated as additions to the capital stock, thus augmenting the productivity of labor. Senior agreed with Say that capital was productive in the same way as labor. In fact, Senior frequently argued as though capital was much more important than labor in creating commodities. But he had read the writings of Thompson and Hodgskin (to be discussed in the next chapter) and was aware of the popular appeal of these writers, who had focused on the fact that work is a human activity that is absolutely necessary if production is to occur. Capital, they had insisted, is simply a fact of legal ownership. As such, capital is a legal or social relationship between different classes of people, and it is not necessary to production. Labor, they had argued, is a *real human cost* of production and capital is not. Therefore, wages can be morally justified as the remuneration for a real human exertion, and profits cannot be so justified.

Senior disagreed. And despite his claim that morality had no place in scientific political economy, he proceeded to give the moral justification for profits that is still usually given by conservative economists today. It was not enough to attempt to show that physical capital was productive, because physical capital and capitalists were not the same. Senior had to show how the ownership of capital involved a real human cost analogous to working if he was to give profits the same moral justification as wages. This is exactly what he attempted to do:

> According to the usual language of Political Economists, Labour, Capital, and Land are the three instruments of production; Labourers, Capitalists, and Landlords are the three classes of Producers; and the whole Produce is divided into Wages, Profit, and Rent. . . . We approve, on the whole, of the principles on which this classification is founded, but we have been forced, much against our will, to make considerable alterations in the language in which it has been usually expressed.[54]

The principal changes in terminology that he referred to were, not surprisingly, the terms *capital, capitalist,* and *profit.*

> These terms express the instrument, the person who employs or exercises it, and his remuneration; but there is no familiar term to express the act, the conduct of which profit is the reward, and which bears the same relation to profit which labour does to wages. To this conduct we have already given the name of Abstinence. . . . Abstinence expresses both the act of abstaining from the unproductive use of capital, and also the similar conduct of the man who devotes his labour to the production of remote rather than of immediate results.[55]

Thus, the capitalist abstains from the unproductive use of his capital, and this is the contribution that entitles him to receive a profit. Senior, like Bentham, thought that working was painful, and, therefore, it required a wage to bribe a worker to endure the pain. Similarly, he asserted: "To abstain from the enjoyment which is in our power, or to seek distant rather than immediate results, are among the most painful exertions of the human will."[56] Thus, capitalists, like laborers, had to be paid for enduring pain, and therefore they had to receive profits. There were, then, no really important differences in the nature of or justification for wages and profits.

Only by carefully protecting the rights of private property, and, thereby, protecting capital and profits, could the government be assured that men would engage in abstinence and thus accumulate capital. The final and most important conclusion of Senior's third proposition was that only capital accumulation could assure a country that its manufacturing capacity would grow at least as fast as its population. Thus, the most important source of a nation's prosperity was ultimately the abstinence of its capitalists.

Senior on Rent and Class Distribution of Income

Senior's fourth and last proposition would appear to be a mere restatement of Ricardo's assertion of diminishing returns in agricultural production. Senior's interests, however, were very different from Ricardo's.

First, Senior was not really interested in what happened when "agricultural skill remained the same." Like Malthus, he stressed improvements in agricultural skills that would more than offset the diminishing productive returns that would result without the improvements. He believed that such improvements had actually resulted in increasing productive returns in Great Britain's agriculture over the previous century: "The total amount of the annual agricultural produce of Great Britain has much more than doubled during the last hundred years; but it is highly improbable that the amount of labour annually employed has also doubled."[57] Here, again, Great Britain owed its prosperity and its escape from the Ricardian specter of the stationary state to the beneficial effects of abstinence and the accumulation of capital in the agricultural sector of the economy.

Senior's modification of the notion of differential rent was his second important difference from Ricardo in the development of this fourth proposition. Rent was defined by Senior as "an advantage derived from the use of a natural agent not universally accessible."[58] It was a return to any ownership that conveyed monopoly power because the object owned could not be freely reproduced. It might therefore be supposed that, unlike wages and profits, rent could not be morally justified in Senior's theory. This was not the case. Agricultural rent, he argued, was the only "means by which the population of a country is proportioned to the demand for labour. In this as in many other cases, nature has provided that the interests of the landlord and the interests of the public shall coincide.[59]

The most important part of Senior's discussion of rent, however, was his assertion that much of what were normally called wages and profits contained an important component of rent. If any worker or capitalist enjoyed an advantage that could not be reproduced by his rivals, then a part of his wages or profits was really rent. Variations in the fertility of land, he argued, were not different in principle from variations in the productive abilities among workers or machines. This was important because it was the initial step in a chain of reasoning whereby Senior eliminated the distinctions between the incomes of the various classes and made all types of income virtually identical. If the sources of all incomes were the same, then the distinguishing features of different classes became economically unimportant—and eventually, among thinkers influenced by Senior, the belief evolved that capitalism was essentially a classless society. This was a central development in the social harmony tradition of economic theory, because with class distinctions being either unimportant or nonexistent, class conflict also became either unimportant or nonexistent.

Senior's elimination of the distinctions among the incomes of the three classes was summarized in the following quotation:

> We have defined RENT to be *the revenue spontaneously offered by nature or accident*; WAGES, *the reward of labour*; and PROFIT, *that of abstinence*. At a distance these divisions appear clearly marked, but when we look into the details, we find them so intermingled that it is scarcely possible to subject them to a classification which shall not sometimes appear to be inconsistent, and still more frequently to be arbitrary. . . . [For] all useful purposes, the distinction of profit from rent ceases as soon as the capital, from which a given revenue arises, has become, whether by gift or by inheritance, the property of a person to whose abstinence and exertions it did not owe its creation. . . .
>
> [The] extraordinary remuneration of the labourer, which is assisted by extraordinary talents . . . might be termed, with equal correctness, rent, which can be received only by a labourer, or wages, which can be received only by the proprietor of a natural agent. . . .
>
> It is still more difficult to draw the line between Profit and Wages. . . . And, as a general rule, it may be laid down that capital is an instrument which, to be productive of profit, must be employed, and that the person who directs its employment must *labour*, that is, must to a certain degree conquer his indolence, sacrifice his favourite pursuits, and often incur other inconveniences.[60]

Thus, class differences were, he believed, largely illusory. "In the natural state," the relationship between a worker "and his master has the kindliness of a voluntary association."[61] Their interests were in harmony and were best promoted by a free market and the protection of private property.

Social Harmony Versus the Political Economy of the Poor

The doctrine that classes were naturally antagonistic and that the working class might benefit from actions that harmed the interests of landlords and capitalists was labeled by Senior as "the political economy of the poor." Such ideas were believed only by those "whose reasoning faculties are either uncultivated, or perverted by their feelings or their imagination."[62] The correct doctrine was that all interests were in harmony and were promoted by a free market and the accumulation of capital. "Among philosophers," he wrote, "this is a conviction; among the higher and middle classes . . . this is a prejudice founded partly on . . . their own apparent interest."[63] Only when laborers saw that the prejudice founded on the "apparent interest" of the rich coincided with the ultimate truth of which philosophers (such as Senior) had a conviction, would they abandon their false notions of class conflict and begin to support the "economics of the rich" (which ultimately promoted the welfare of all of society).

Most later proponents of what Senior called "the political economy of the poor" accepted the notion that the distinction between rents and profits had become unimportant by the middle of the nineteenth century. During the seventeenth and eighteenth centuries, the landlord class had retained many of its characteristics as the old ruling class of feudalism. In this era, their interests frequently clashed with those of the capitalist class (as we have seen in the chapters on Malthus and Ricardo). By the mid-nineteenth century, industrial capital had clearly established its supremacy. As a result, increasing numbers of capitalists ceased functioning as entrepreneurs or organizers of production and began to rely on hired managers to perform those functions. Increasingly, profits, like rents, became a return to passive ownership alone. Consequently, the distinction between landlords and capitalists, or between rents and profits, became unimportant.

The advocates of "the political economy of the poor" have continued, however, to insist on the importance of the distinction between income from working and income from owning. These two sources of income, they believe, form the basis of a fundamental, ongoing class antagonism. It is therefore not surprising that these theorists have persistently attacked Senior's notion that abstinence is a social cost of production borne by capitalists.

These critics of Senior have insisted that the origins of capital were almost never capitalists' abstinence (see chapter 9 on Marx). Moreover, most capital in modern capitalist society is inherited, and, hence, an accident of birth. When abstinence is defined, as Senior frequently defined it, as "abstaining from the unproductive use of capital,"[64] it merely means that a capitalist uses his factory (or other physical capital) as a means of making profit and accumulating more capital rather than as a place of personal enjoyment (if one can imagine how a factory could be used as a consumption good for one's personal enjoyment). This means that using capital to make profit is simply defined as painful and the profit is justified by that pain. Even Senior, in many of his passages, showed a recognition of the absurdity of this notion. Contrary to what one would expect from Senior's theory of abstinence, in capitalism, capitalists enjoy making profits. In fact, it is generally a passion that dominates their lives. Senior admitted that vanity encouraged the upper classes to save rather than spend, and among the educated classes vanity was "the most powerful of human passions."[65] Furthermore, capitalists

> can show their wealth by the magnitude of their concerns and by the firmness of their credit. Ostentation would rather lower than raise them in the estimation of the

class whose opinion they value. They go on producing and amassing and leave the task of expending to their heirs.[66]

Finally, Senior considered the "desire of wealth for its own sake" to be "instinctive," it seemed "to be implanted in us by nature as a counterbalance to the strong propensities to indolence and to expenditure."[67]

Thus, when he was not directly attempting to justify profits morally, Senior made many observations that would appear to refute his assertion that abstinence was "among the most painful exertions of the human will."[68]

Notes to Chapter 6

1. Quoted in Harry K. Guvetz, *The Evolution of Liberalism* (New York: Colliers, 1963), pp. 28–29.

2. Thomas Hobbes, *Leviathan*, in *Ethical Theories*, ed. A.I. Melden (Englewood Cliffs, NJ): Prentice-Hall, 1955), pp. 192–205.

3. Most of Bentham's writings on economic topics are collected in Jeremy Bentham, *Jeremy Bentham's Economic writings*, 3 vols., ed. W. Stark (London: Allen and Unwin, 1954).

4. Jeremy Bentham, *An Introduction to the Principles of Morals and Legislation*, in *A Bentham Reader*, ed. M.P. Mack (New York: Pegasus, 1969), p. 85.

5. Ibid., p. 86.

6. Ibid., p. 96.

7. Ibid., p. 97.

8. Jeremy Bentham, *Jeremy Bentham's Economic Writings*, vol. 3, p. 412.

9. Ibid., vol. 3, p. 428.

10. Ibid., vol. 3, p. 83.

11. Ibid., vol. 3, pp. 87–88.

12. Ibid., vol. 1, p. 201.

13. Ibid., vol. 1, p. 196.

14. Ibid., vol. 3, pp. 257–58.

15. Ibid., vol. 3, p. 120.

16. Ibid., vol. 3, p. 123.

17. Ibid., vol. 3, p. 124.

18. Ibid., vol. 3, p. 441.

19. Ibid., vol. 3, pp. 442–43.

20. Leo Rogin, *The Meaning and Validity of Economic Theory* (New York: Harper and Row, 1957), p. 209.

21. Jean-Baptiste Say, *A Treatise on Political Economy* (Philadelphia: Lippincott, 1863), p. xi. This translation is from the fourth French edition, which was published in 1821.

22. Ibid., p. 62.

23. Ibid., p. 284.

24. Ibid., p. 286.

25. Ibid., p. 293.

26. Ibid., p. 287.

27. Ibid., pp. lii–liii.

28. Ibid., p. lix.

29. Ibid., p. 293.

30. Jean-Baptiste Say, *Letters to Thomas Robert Malthus on Political Economy and Stagnations of Commerce* (London: George Harding's Bookshop, 1936), p. 3.

31. Ibid., p. 5.

32. Ibid., p. 24.

33. Nassau Senior, *Industrial Efficiency and Social Economy*, 2 vols. (New York: Holt, 1928), vol. 2, p. 156.

34. Nassau Senior, *Three Lectures on the Rate of Wages* (New York: Augustus M. Kelley, 1966), p. iv.

35. Ibid., p. v.

36. Rogin, *Meaning and Validity*, p. 251.

37. Senior, *Three Lectures*, pp. x–xi.

38. Ibid., p. xiii.

39. See chapter 7.

40. Nassau Senior, *Journals Kept in France and Italy*, 2 vols., 2d ed. (London: Henry S. King, 1871), vol. 1, p. 150.

41. Ibid., pp. 150–52.

42. E.J. Hobsbawn, *Industry and Empire: An Economic History of Britain since 1750* (London: Weidenfield and Nicolson, 1968), pp. 69–70.

43. Nassau Senior, *An Outline of the Science of Political Economy* (London: Allen and Unwin, 1938), pp. 2–3.

44. Ibid., p. 3.

45. Ibid., p. 26.

46. Ibid., p. 6.

47. Ibid., p. 27.

48. Ibid.

49. Ibid., p. 14.

50. Ibid., p. 24.

51. Ibid., p. 29.

52. Senior, *Three Lectures*, p. v.

53. Ibid., pp. xiv–xv.

54. Senior, *Science of Political Economy*, p. 88.

55. Ibid., p. 89.

56. Ibid., p. 60.

57. Ibid., p. 86.

58. Ibid., p. 115.

59. Nassau Senior, *Journals, Conversations and Essays Relating to Ireland*, 2 vols. (London: Longmans, Green, 1868), vol. 1, p. 153.

60. Senior, *Science of Political Economy*, pp. 128–30.

61. Senior, *Three Lectures*, pp. ix, x.

62. Senior, *Journals Kept in France and Italy*, vol. 1, p. 4.

63. Ibid., p. 150.

64. Senior, *Science of Political Economy*, p. 89.

65. Senior, *Industrial Efficiency and Social Economy*, vol. 1, pp. 67, 69.

66. Ibid., vol. 1, p. 69.

67. Ibid., vol. 1, p. 68.

68. Senior, *Science of Political Economy*, p. 60.

Chapter 7

Political Economy of the Poor: The Ideas of William Thompson and Thomas Hodgskin

The "frightful autumn of 1830," which created in Nassau Senior a terror of working-class mass actions, was merely one of a series of strikes, riots, and rebellions through which laborers expressed their hatred of what the industrial revolution was doing to them and their families. Industrialization resulted in the total destruction of the laborers' traditional way of life. Harsh discipline in the factories and deplorable living conditions in the cities were the fruits of finding and keeping a job. High unemployment made finding and keeping a job very uncertain. Moreover, with most of the important changes in productive technology came forced, technologically related job losses for large numbers of workers. The three evils that galvanized the most worker resistance, then, were low wages, bad working and living conditions, and economic insecurity.

Workers' Resistance to Industrialization

In the earliest attempts to resist the effects of capitalist industrialization, workers very frequently tried to form combinations or unions. In chapter 4, we mentioned the early successes of some of these workers' combinations in the textile industry. In England, the decade of the 1790s was one of widespread labor unrest and frequent attempts to form combinations. Wealthy Englishmen, the memory of the French Revolution fresh in their minds, became increasingly alarmed by both the combination movement and the growing influence of many radical writers such as Godwin. Their response to the workers' movement was the Combination Act of 1799.

The employers realized that individually a worker was powerless against them. With a large reserve of unemployed laborers, any "arrogant" or recalcitrant worker could be immediately and easily replaced. Such a replacement would serve as an example to increase the insecurity and hence the docility of the remaining workers. But laborers had significantly more power when bargaining collectively. The Combination Act was enacted for only one purpose: the complete destruction of the combination movement and the preservation of the powerlessness of workers. Although it did not ultimately succeed, for twenty-five years it dealt a very severe blow to the labor movement. Enforcement of the law was incredibly harsh. Frequently, the prosecution's argument was little but foul invective, the evidence was sparse if not fabricated, and the punishments were terrifying and cruel.

Another form of worker rebellion was the destruction of machinery. Laborers often did not realize that it was not machinery per se that put them out of work but the ways in which it was used in the capitalists' quest for maximum profits. In 1758, English laborers destroyed many of the first mechanical wool-shearing machines. The result was something near mass panic, and Parliament passed a law threatening execution for any worker caught destroying a factory or a machine. But machine wrecking continued as workers continued to face economic insecurity and material deprivation.

After the passage of the Combination Act, workers had no means of legal resistance and machine wrecking became even more widespread. From 1811 onward, the rebellion grew rapidly in numbers and intensity. Chain reactions occurred in the years 1811–13, 1815–17, 1819, 1826, 1829–35, 1838–42, 1843–44, and 1846–48. Most of these upheavals were spontaneous manifestations of the utter wretchedness and desperation of the working class. Despite the poignant opposition of Lord Byron in 1812, the British government repeatedly sought to solve the problem by making machine breaking a capital offense.

By the 1820s, however, many defenders of working-class interests were clearly aware that the machines were not the source of the evil. The plight of working people, they argued, was the outcome of economic, legal, social, and political institutions. Therefore, any substantial improvement in the conditions of the poor would require a transformation of these institutions. Thus, the working class would have to understand the institutional basis of oppression and organize collectively to create a better society.

Robert Owen, a humane middle-class capitalist, became the most influential leader of this movement in the 1830s. Born in 1771, Owen served as a draper's apprentice from the age of ten. At age twenty, he was the manager of a large mill. Wise business decisions and good luck soon resulted in the acquisition of a considerable fortune. He acquired a factory at New Lanark, which became known throughout England because he insisted on decent working conditions, livable wages, and education for working-class children.

He was a man of benevolent sentiments who was appalled by the suffering and hardships endured by workers. At first he hoped to show other capitalists, by the example of his factory at New Lanark, that their treatment of workers was shortsighted and ignorant. The capitalists could, he believed, get more productivity out of workers and, consequently, make more profits if they treated their workers more humanely.

He found, however, that almost no capitalists were interested in following his example, and so he became convinced that the answer lay in the formation of voluntary "cooperatives," in which the producers themselves would jointly control their own economic destinies. He believed that a system of cooperatives could coexist and compete with existing capitalist enterprises and eventually replace them entirely.

The cooperatives were to be self-governing industrial and agricultural communities in which private ownership of the means of production would be abolished and the selfish quest for profits eliminated.

> One portion of mankind will not, as now, be trained and placed to oppress, by force and fraud, another portion, to the great disadvantage of both; neither will one portion be trained in idleness, to live in luxury on the industry of those whom they oppress, while the latter are made to labor daily and to live in poverty. Nor yet will some be trained to force falsehood into the human mind and be paid extravagantly for so doing while other parties are prevented from teaching the truth, or severely punished if they make the attempt.[1]

Owen's cooperative movement and the ideas behind it became very influential in the English labor movement of the 1820s, particularly after the repeal of the Combination Act in 1824 once again made labor organizations legal. It is therefore not surprising that several theorists of this period who were sympathetic to the labor movement combined many of the ideas of the Owenite cooperative movement with the class conflict perspective of the labor theory of value found in the writings of Adam Smith and David Ricardo. Two of the most interesting and influential of these theorists were William Thompson and Thomas Hodgskin.

Thompson's Utilitarianism and Labor Theory of Value

William Thompson (1775–1833) published several books and pamphlets, the two most important being *An Inquiry into the Principles of the Distribution of Wealth Most Conducive to Human Happiness* (1824) and *Labour Rewarded, The Claims of Labour and Capital Conciliated* (1827). The three principal intellectual influences on Thompson were the labor theory of value of the classical political economists, the Owenite philosophy of the cooperative movement, and the utilitarianism of Jeremy Bentham.

In the previous chapter, we asserted that Bentham's utilitarianism furnished the philosophical foundation for later neoclassical economics and the utility theory of value. We also asserted that the utility theory of value proceeds from and intellectually reinforces a social harmony perspective, which usually culminates in an ideological justification of the status quo of free market capitalism. But, as was discussed in the previous chapter, during the last few decades of his career, Bentham was an advocate of fairly far-reaching social, political, and economic reforms. Thompson advocated reforms that were much more radical than Bentham's. As we will see in the next chapter, John Stuart Mill considered himself a disciple of Bentham and believed that legal reforms should restrict the domain of free market capitalism.

Therefore, in this discussion of Thompson's ideas, we will attempt to show that whenever Bentham's utilitarianism is used (whether by Bentham, Mill, or Thompson) to justify reforms, restrictions, or abolition of free market capitalism, irreconcilable contradictions are involved. It is our opinion that only the conservative neoclassical devotees of laissez-faire capitalism have developed the implications of Bentham's utilitarianism with logical consistency, and that Bentham's philosophy will support only their conservative defense of capitalism.

Thompson was an avowed disciple of Bentham. Like Bentham, he espoused both psychological hedonism and ethical hedonism, although, as we will see, he also held social theories that were incompatible with his utilitarianism. His psychological hedonism is evident in passages such as the following:

> Our organization has made us *sentient* beings, that is to say, capable of experiencing pleasure and pain from various sources. The only rational motive to exertion of any sort, whether to acquire wealth or for any other purpose, is to increase the means of happiness or to remove or lessen causes of annoyance, immediate or in prospect.[2]

Thompson did not defend his ethical hedonism. He simply asserted that utilitarian ethical theory, in the writings of Bentham, had been "developed and established forever, to the exclusion of all other pretended tests of morals."[3]

Thompson believed that the distribution of wealth was the most important determinant of how much pleasure and happiness the various members of society could attain. He also believed that as a person's wealth increased, equal increments of wealth would give that person successively smaller increments of pleasure.[4] Moreover, he believed that if all members of society were treated equally, they would have equal capacities to experience pleasure and happiness.[5] These beliefs were very similar to those of Bentham discussed in the previous chapter.

Thompson also accepted the labor theory of value. He believed that only labor created wealth and that the quantity of labor bestowed on a commodity was the chief determinant of the value of that commodity:

> *Without labour there is no wealth.* Labour is its distinguishing attribute. The agency of nature constitutes nothing an object of wealth. Labour is the *sole* parent of wealth. . . .
> Land, air, heat, light, the electric fluid, men, horses, water, *as such* are equally unentitled to the appellation of wealth. They may be objects of desire, of happiness; but, till touched by the transforming hand of labour they are not wealth.[6]

Thompson's Argument for Egalitarian, Market Socialism

Thompson concluded from his utilitarian premises that "in all cases where human effort has not been concerned in production, equality of distribution is the rule of justice."[7] There was, he believed, only one defense of any inequality whatsoever:

> Without security—which means the exclusive possession by every man of all the advantages of his labour—labour would not be called forth. Therefore, in the distribution of such articles where labour is employed, called articles of wealth, and in these alone, equality must be limited by security, because in no other case are equality and production incompatible with each other.[8]

Thompson's description of the only possible defense of inequality was similar to Bentham's. But Thompson was much more radical than Bentham. Whereas Bentham had believed that the distribution of wealth and income in England was significantly more unequal than was necessary, he nevertheless believed that the existing capitalist economy was quite compatible with a just distribution of wealth and income. Thompson strongly disagreed. He did not believe that capitalism could ever be a "system of security" in which each person had the fruits of his or her labor secured: "The tendency of the existing arrangement of things as to wealth is to enrich a few at the expense of the mass of producers, to make the poverty of the poor more hopeless."[9]

Capitalism had far greater extremes of wealth and poverty than could be justified in utilitarian philosophy, Thompson believed. Within capitalism, he asserted,

> to inequality of wealth there is no bound: it becomes the ruling passion: the distinction which it confers, the envy which it excites, urge men to acquire it by any means. Every expedient which force and cunning can use to appropriate the fruits of other men's labour, and with this view to turn the mass of mankind into ignorant contented drudges, is erected into a custom or a law. A universal and always vigilant conspiracy of capitalists . . . exists everywhere . . . to cause the labourers to toil for the lowest possible wage, and to wrest as much as possible of the products of their labour to swell the accumulations and expenditures of capitalists. Yet such is the rage of these men for distinction, for expenditure as an instrument of distinction rather than of any direct enjoyment, that the products of the labour of thousands are swallowed up for no other end than to gratify such unsubstantial desires. What accumulated wealth there is in such a community is gathered into the hands of a few; and as well from its bulk as from its contrast with the surrounding poverty, it strikes every eye. The productive labourers, stript of all capital, of tools, houses, and materials to make their labour productive, toil from want, from the necessity of existence, their remuneration being kept at the lowest, compatible with the existence of industrious habits.[10]

Moreover, under capitalism the wealth of the capitalists "engenders positive vices in the possessors of these excessive shares of wealth,"[11] while at the same time it "excites the admiration and the imagination [of the poor], and in this way diffuses the practice of the vices of the rich, amongst the rest of the community."[12]

As a result of capitalist property relations, the capitalist class coercively expropriated "at least one-half of the products of labour from the use of the producer."[13] Moreover, capitalism was inherently unstable. The instability resulted in depressions that created unemployment, economic waste, and widespread suffering:

> The *ordinary* wants and comforts of society remain through the ages nearly the same; the food, and clothing, form and mode of constructing dwellings, change but slowly. . . . The nature and form of the productions to which they give rise, partake, of course, of their steadiness of character. . . .
>
> But there exists, in the very nature of things, a constant source of caprice in the demand for all those extra articles of luxury called for by excessive wealth. . . . The urgency of the caprice enhances the demand . . . for the article in request; and this naturally induces many to leave other lines of industry, and engage in the more liberally paid new branch. At length, however, the sickly ardour of fashion relaxes— the bauble becomes old and familiar, ceases to please, and the trade in the superfluity, so lately active, is now comparatively at a stand. On the fixed and moveable capital employed during the great demand, there must be more or less of loss in transferring it to other employment. . . . The inclination, the ability to work, remain as before; but the employment, without any fault of the labourers, is taken away from them.[14]

Thompson concluded that capitalism was inevitably a system of exploitation, degradation, instability, suffering, and grotesque extremes of wealth and income. He believed that utilitarianism would always lead a thoughtful inquirer to the same conclusions. Ironically, Thompson accepted nearly all of the utilitarian arguments that have been used to morally justify competitive, free market capitalism. He asserted that voluntary exchange would always benefit both parties to the exchange because each party would receive more utility than he gave up: "All *voluntary* exchanges of the articles of wealth, implying a preference on both sides, of the thing received to the thing given, tend to the increase of happiness from wealth, and thence to increase the motives to production."[15] This passage was identical to the utilitarian defense of capitalism. It was with just such a defense of free exchange that utilitarians could argue that the market harmonized the interests of everyone, capitalists and workers included.

Thompson was able to argue against this conservative, utilitarian defense of capitalism because he denied the assertion that laborers *freely* sell their labor power under capitalism. He maintained that when workers did not own the tools and materials with which to produce, they were unfree. The selling of their labor power was not a free exchange, but was coerced. The threat of starvation was as coercive as a threat of death by violent means.

Therefore, Thompson concluded that in a fair, competitive, exchange society "all the products of labour ought to be secured to the producers of them."[16] This meant that an owner of capital should be able to live only "in equal comfort with the more actively employed productive labourers."[17] If this rule were enforced, then Thompson concluded that, within a generation, all workers would, either individually or within groups, own their own capital and retain all of the fruits of their labor.[18]

Thus, in order for free exchange to harmoniously benefit all exchangers, Thompson believed that two very stringent conditions were necessary. First, workers would have to have their own capital and materials necessary for production in order for them to produce freely rather than under coercion. Because no single worker used substantially more capital than any other worker, such a society would have a substantially more equal distribution of wealth than capitalism—even though there would still be some inequality. Second, if competition was to be universally beneficial, then all restrictions on free competition would have to be removed. To remove these restrictions would require the repeal of all laws that restricted or directed production, established or maintained monopolistic advantage in any market, levied taxes on or gave subsidies for production, permitted the government to regulate the money supply, or permitted the acquisition of wealth through inheritance.[19]

The system Thompson was describing resembled very closely many twentieth-century theoretical models or intellectual visions of egalitarian, market socialism. It was Thompson's belief that any consistent utilitarian would arrive at similar conclusions.[20]

Thompson's Critique of Market Socialism

Having attempted to use utilitarian moral arguments to show the superiority of competitive, market socialism over capitalism, Thompson then posed the question:

> May there not be found a mode of labour consistent with security which will not only obviate the evils of individual competition, but which will afford its peculiar benefits—abundant production and development of all the faculties—to a greater, an incalculably greater extent, than the best arrangements of individual competition could afford?[21]

To answer this question, he outlined five evils that "seem to be inherent" in "the *very principle* of individual competition."[22]

The first evil of competitive, market socialism was that every "labourer, artisan and trader [saw] a competitor, a rival in every other." Moreover, each saw "a second competition, a second rivalship between . . . [his or her profession] and the public."[23] Hence, the "principle of selfishness necessarily . . . [dominated] in all ordinary affairs of life."[24] For example, under competitive, market socialism, it would be "in the interest of all medical men that diseases should exist and prevail, or their trade would be decreased ten, or one hundred, fold."[25] It would never be in the interest of medical men to practice social, preventative medicine. Many other professions could reap similar benefits by contriving to create or induce a strong need for their products or services even in cases where society would benefit when such products or services were not needed. Such an evil was irremediable under market socialism because individual remuneration is . . . opposed at every step to the principle of benevolence; and the only remedy to the public evil which the system admits, is private competition between individuals of the same calling, mitigating the evils on a large scale, by developing them on a smaller. . . . From the pursuit of self-interest in the acquisition of individual wealth, proceed almost all vices and crimes. These vices and crimes must, to a certain extent, continue, til the interest of self ceases to be opposed to the interests of others.[26]

The second evil inherent in the individualistic pursuit of wealth even in a market socialist economy was the systematic oppression of women. This oppression was an evil in itself, and it also led to enormous economic waste. The individualistic pursuit of wealth, Thompson believed, was compatible only with individual nuclear families. Within an individual family "all the little items of domestic drudgery" must be "done at stated hours." Women could be relieved of this drudgery if "numbers of families adjoining each other . . . [formed] a common fund for preparing their food and educating their children."[27] But such a cooperative arrangement would be impossible to sustain if, in all other aspects of their lives, they continue to function in an individualistic competition reminiscent of capitalism. Either a "mutual benevolence . . . [would] be engendered by it" and it would lead to a complete system of "mutual cooperation and equality of enjoyment of the products of united labor," or selfishness would prevail and "the love of individual expenditure and enjoyment" would destroy the arrangement and reinstitute the nuclear family.[28]

Within a system of individualistic competition, the "animal, physical advantages" of greater strength, combined with a forced inequality of "knowledge and of civil and political rights," would ensure that women would

continue to be condemned to the seclusion and drudgery of . . . [economically wasteful] slaves, all their actions liable to the control of other human beings, their exertions and duties limited to looking after the domestic comforts . . . of their masters and children . . . [and never rising] in the scale of social existence.[29]

But this was purely the result of the system of individualistic competition and not inherent differences between the sexes. With industrial technology, physical strength was very rarely a source of greater productivity, and "women, if equally trained . . . [would] be as productively employed . . . as men."[30] But this productive equality, which Thompson saw as a necessary precondition for social equality, would require a society based on cooperation and mutual sharing rather than individualistic competition.

Thompson's account of the repression of women was most remarkable. His understanding of its nature and effects was, in many respects, superior to that voiced by John Stuart Mill nearly a half century later. Unfortunately, Mill's analysis of sexual oppression has been widely acclaimed, and that of Thompson nearly forgotten. Some of the flavor of Thompson's writings on this topic is revealed in the following quotation:

> Under no head, perhaps, so appropriate as that of field or domestic slavery, can be introduced the institutions, almost universally prevailing, whether in despotisms or republics, respecting that half of the human race which hypocritical sensuality calls the most lovely, the most innocent, and the best portion of it—women. Man is to woman the most lovely and joy-exciting creature in the universe, as woman is to man; therefore as to loveliness, and similar nonsense the account is balanced. Nature has given woman less strength, and has subjected her to enormous physical inconveniences and pain, from which men are exempt. Are these reasons why men should add to these natural and unavoidable evils, artificial restraints and evils that may be avoided?[31]

This quotation was followed by a lengthy and extraordinarily insightful discussion of the ways in which the oppression of women destroyed not only women's well-being but ultimately men's well-being, too. His analysis was intended to show that the happiness and "the general intellect of the whole community, male and female . . . [was] stinted or perverted" by the ways in which sexual inequality was maintained.[32]

The third evil of market competition—whether capitalistic or socialistic— was the economic instability caused by the anarchy of the market. While socialism would eliminate the capriciousness of the luxurious tastes of the capitalists as a source of crises and depressions, as long as the competitive market allocated resources, economic instability, unemployment, waste, and social suffering would result.

> The third evil here imputed to the very principle of individual competition is, that it must occasionally lead to unprofitable or injudicious modes of individual exertion, from the limited field of judgment open to individual minds. . . . Under equal security, every man becoming possessed of the physical and mental means necessary to make his labour productive, every labourer being also a capitalist, the great mass of these evils would doubtless disappear. But, still while individual competition exists, every man must judge for himself as to the probability of success in the occupation which he adopts. And what are his means of judging? Every one, doing well in his calling, is interested in concealing his success, lest competition should reduce his gains. What individual can judge whether the market, frequently at a great distance, sometimes in another hemisphere of the globe is overstocked, or likely to be so, with the article which inclination may lead him to fabricate? . . . And should any *error* of judgment . . . lead him into an uncalled for, and, therefore, unprofitable line of exertion, what is the consequence? A mere error of judgment . . . may end in severe distress, if not in ruin. Cases of this sort seem to be unavoidable under the scheme of individual competition in its best form.[33]

The fourth evil of competitive, market socialism was that it would not eliminate many of the insecurities of capitalism that came from reliance on the market. The selfishness and egotism fostered by a competitive market society would create a situation in which there would be "no adequate . . . resource for malformation, sickness, or old age, or for numerous accidents incident to human life."[34]

The fifth evil of market competition was that it retarded the advance and dissemination of knowledge by making the acquisition of knowledge subsidiary to greed and personal gain. "Concealment, therefore, of what is new or excellent from competitors, must accompany individual competition . . . because the strongest personal interest is by it opposed to the principle of benevolence."[35]

Thus, Thompson concluded that while competitive, market socialism would be a dramatic improvement over capitalism, the reliance on the market would still involve numerous social evils. The best form of society, he argued, would be a planned, cooperative socialist society. Such a society would consist of mutually coordinated, self-governing, cooperative communities, each having from 500 to 2,000 members.

In such communities, people could freely get the necessities of life from a common store. Children would be cared for communally and sleep in common dormitories, while adults would live in small apartments. There would be common kitchen facilities for everyone. There would be no sexual division of labor—cooking, child rearing, and other forms of women's drudgery would be shared by everyone on a rotational basis. All persons would become skilled in a variety of occupations and would regularly alternate employments to eliminate the monotony of work. Every adult member of each community would participate regularly in the necessary coordinating or governing bodies. The finest education would be freely available to everyone. Absolute political, intellectual, and religious freedom would be guaranteed. And finally, all wealth would be communally controlled and shared so that no invidious distinctions could result from the distribution of material wealth.[36] Thompson's view of a cooperative, socialist community reflected, in general, the views of most of the people in the Owenite movement of his era. He was, throughout the history of that movement, its most influential spokesman after Owen. Thompson's description of a planned, cooperative, socialist society was one of the earliest and the most fully elaborated in the history of socialist ideas.

Thompson was not, however, a revolutionary socialist. He abhorred violence and believed that his scheme of cooperative socialism would, if widely understood, have a nearly universal appeal. Once the majority of people realized the benefits that could come from such a society, they would, he was convinced, voluntarily and peacefully create it.

A Critique of Thompson's Utilitarianism

A central theme of the present book is that utilitarianism provides the philosophical foundation for the neoclassical utility theory of value and that the latter theory supports a general view of the harmony of all interests. This intellectual tradition represents the most elaborate and profound intellectual defense for, or ideology in support of, the status quo of market capitalism. Therefore, just as conservative theorists, such as Ricardo, became involved in contradictions when they combined elements of the labor theory of value with elements of the utility theory, so radical social critics of capitalism, such as Thompson, necessarily became involved in similar contradictions as a result of combining the same two viewpoints. In this section, we shall attempt to show why utilitarianism cannot support radical reform of society and why it inherently tends to support the status quo.

Utilitarianism is both a psychological theory of how people behave and an ethical theory of how they ought to behave. We have seen that, in at least some of his assertions, Thompson accepted both elements of utilitarianism. To him (as to John Stuart Mill whom we will discuss in the next chapter), utilitarianism seemed to support his egalitarian sentiments. It seemed to be a democratic philosophy because it stated that one should not count the pleasures only of an aristocracy (whether of birth or of wealth) in forming a moral judgment, but the pleasures of all people—the economically least advantaged and most oppressed included. But this apparent egalitarian and democratic character of utilitarianism can be seen, on closer examination, to be illusory.

The problem is that in utilitarianism, individuals' pleasures and pains are the *only* moral criteria of good and bad. Pleasures and pains, however, are subjectively felt sensations. The immediate experience of pleasure or pain is by its very nature private to the individual. Although an individual might be able to compare or rank his own subjective pleasures, there is no direct means of comparing the intensity of one individual's pleasures with those of another individual. Moreover, the private, subjective, relative rankings of any individual's pleasures is likely to differ substantially from the rankings of other individuals'. Because individual pleasures are the ultimate moral criteria in utilitarianism, there is no way one can make moral judgments between the pleasures of two individuals. Bentham recognized this when he wrote "quantity of pleasure being equal, pushpin is as good as poetry."

Therefore, utilitarianism will not furnish any argument in favor of egalitarian market socialism over capitalism. Had he been a consistent utilitarian, Thompson should have stated: "I prefer egalitarian, market socialism over capitalism because the former would give me more pleasure than the latter." But any capitalist could respond by stating his preference for capitalism over egalitarian, market socialism. Then, for a consistent utilitarian, the dispute would be no different from one in which Thompson stated his preference for poetry over pushpin and the capitalist stated his preference for pushpin over poetry. Each would be correct for *him* or *herself* in both disputes, but neither would be correct in general. Utilitarianism offers no criterion higher than personal preferences by which one can judge among different preferences which is best.

But Thompson believed that an equal distribution of wealth would increase the total of all pleasure in society. Will utilitarianism support this view? The answer is no. In order to arrive at this conclusion, we would have to quantitatively compare all individuals' personal, private, subjective capacities for experiencing pleasure. No one has ever suggested how one might go about making such comparisons. Thompson himself realized this when he wrote the following passage:

Suppose that these capabilities, or susceptibilities, of enjoyment were . . . different in different individuals . . . [A] difficulty, of a practical nature, and insurmountable, occurs. Who are to be the *measurers* of these susceptibilities? The rich or the poor, the young or the old, the studious or the illiterate? . . . We must dismiss, then, as altogether unworthy of consideration, the notion of influencing the distribution of wealth by speculations as to the capacities for enjoyment of different individuals.[37]

How then did Thompson arrive at the conclusion that an equal distribution of wealth was morally superior to a highly unequal distribution? He did this by *starting* with the assumption of an initial distribution that was equal. He then argued that since we cannot show that some people have greater capacities for pleasure than other people, we cannot defend a *change* from an initially equal distribution to an unequal distribution on utilitarian grounds. But his conclusion depended entirely upon his assumption of an initially equal distribution.

Thompson's difficulty lay in not realizing that just as we cannot demonstrate that people have unequal capacities for pleasures, so we cannot demonstrate that they have equal capacities. Insofar as any redistribution of wealth from any status quo involves taking wealth from some and giving it to others, we cannot morally evaluate redistributions because we would have to quantitatively compare the pleasure lost by the persons losing wealth with the pleasure gained by the persons gaining wealth. And, by Thompson's own admission, such comparisons are impossible.

Therefore, utilitarianism will always support whatever the existing distribution of wealth actually is. If the distribution is equal, as Thompson assumed, it will support equality. But, as later conservative neoclassical economists were to realize, if the distribution is unequal, it will support inequality. Such support is, of course, only an indirect support. Utilitarianism does not demonstrate that the status quo is superior to any alternative. It merely demonstrates that no change from the status quo can be supported on utilitarian grounds alone. But because utilitarians have no other moral criteria beyond utilitarianism, this always means that no change from the status quo can be morally defended.

Because the status quo of capitalism is one of grotesque inequality, as Thompson was so passionately aware, utilitarianism turns out to be a highly conservative philosophy that justifies such inequality as actually exists. This is because within utilitarianism our inability to quantitatively compare different persons' subjective states renders us unable to judge morally between any two situations where disagreement or conflict exists. Utilitarianism can thus be seen as an extraordinarily restrictive or narrow philosophy that permits judgments only where unanimity exists.

If one accepts the existing distribution of wealth and income, then market exchange is one of the only social situations where such unanimity exists. Both parties to an exchange desire what they are getting in the exchange more than what they are giving up in the exchange. Therefore, when we look only at the exchange, unanimity exists and harmony prevails. This is why utilitarianism can be identified with the exchange perspective in economic theory, and this is why the exchange perspective always sees capitalism as a system of social harmony.

The most important normative difference between the labor theory perspective and the utility or exchange perspective is now clear. When a penniless worker, for example, exchanges his labor power for a paltry wage and bad working conditions, the labor theory perspective focuses on the fact that only labor transforms nature into useful products to be consumed. The immediate focus is on the historically evolved property relations that force producers to live wretchedly while property owners, having no necessary part in the production process, amass great wealth. Conflict is at the center of the labor perspective. The utility perspective, however, takes the distribution of wealth (that is, the distribution of property rights) as given and focuses on the harmonious, mutually beneficial aspects of the same exchange: the worker prefers a low wage to starvation and the capitalist prefers more profits to less profits. Hence, both laborer and capitalist benefit from the exchange and harmony is seen to prevail.

From the foregoing discussion we can conclude that Thompson's utilitarianism gave him no reason to prefer competitive, egalitarian, market socialism over capitalism. When we look at his preference of planned, cooperative socialism over either market socialism or capitalism, Thompson's utilitarianism involved him in even worse difficulties.

His main argument for cooperative socialism over competitive individualism was that the former system would promote benevolent motives whereas the latter system would promote antisocial, selfish motives. This view is wholly incompatible with Thompson's utilitarian psychology, which rested on the assumption that all motives can be reduced to the rational pursuit of self-interest. In Bentham's words: "In the general tenor of life, in every human breast, self-regarding interest is predominant over all other interests put together. . . . Self-preference has place everywhere."[38] The impossibility of Thompson's argument for cooperative socialism within a utilitarian philosophy is obvious.

We will conclude our discussion of Thompson's writings by stating that while his writings are among the most interesting and profound of the early socialist writers, and while his economic theories may truly be called "the political economy of the poor," it is nevertheless true that his utilitarian philosophy involved him in insolvable contradictions because utilitarianism most consistently supports the status quo.

Thomas Hodgskin's View of the Source of Profit

Thomas Hodgskin (1787–1869) was another writer who exerted considerable influence on the British working-class movement around the 1820s.[39] He developed a theory of capital and profits that was clearly within the labor theory of value tradition. Hodgskin's influence and the radical conclusions of his theory were undoubtedly major factors in causing Nassau Senior and most other conservative economists of the late 1820s and the 1830s to abandon Ricardo's labor theory of value. Conservatives came to associate Ricardo's theory with Thompson, Hodgskin, and the labor movement generally. One eminent historian of economic ideas has written:

> Thomas Hodgskin was a name to frighten children with in the days following the repeal of the Combination Laws in 1824. It was probably inevitable, therefore, that many of the more conservative economists should come to regard Ricardo's theory of value not only as logically incorrect but also as socially dangerous.[40]

Hodgskin had a long and varied career as a writer. Most of his books and articles were devoted to economic and political issues.[41] In his first two books he denounced as unjust the income that people received from property ownership. In *An Essay on Naval Discipline*, published in 1813, he wrote that property exerts an "unjust and injurious influence."[42] This was so because property "absolutely ... takes from the daily labourer to give to the idle gentleman."[43] There is very little argument supporting such assertions, however, and no attempt to understand the origin of either value or profit.

During the years 1818 and 1819, Hodgskin wrote *Travels in the North of Germany*. Again one finds in this book condemnations of profit and rent: "The landlord and the capitalist produce nothing. Capital is the produce of labour, and profit is nothing but a portion of that produce, uncharitably exacted for permitting the labourer to consume a part of what he has himself produced."[44]

Although the notion that "capital is the produce of labour" contains the seed of a labor theory of value, such a theory was not developed in this work. Rather, profit and rent were seen as legal robbery. Hodgskin explained them as being the results of a class-divided society in which the rich controlled the legislative processes and thus perpetuated their influence, wealth, and power:

> Laws ... are everywhere a trap for the unwary, an instrument employed by a particular class to enrich themselves at the expense of other men .[45]

> It is not enough, in the eyes of legislators, that wealth has of itself a thousand charms, but they have ... given it a multitude of privileges. In fact, it has now usurped all the power of legislation, and most penal laws are now made for the mere protection of wealth .[46]

The cure for this social injustice that Hodgskin advocated was the elimination of governments and laws. Although in *Travels in the North of Germany* Hodgskin did not mention the writers who might have influenced him, his ideas seem to reflect the influence of Godwin and Smith:

There are many testimonies at present to the evil of numerous laws. There is a diseased desire to legislate common to this age, which crowds the statute-books of every European nation with numerous and contradictory enactments.[47]

Men seek wealth by legitimately oppressing the labourer, that they may figure as makers of benevolent laws, or as the chiefs of charitable societies. Miserable is the nation where either is much needed. Nature has created each individual with powers to provide for its own wants. She has placed the welfare of millions in their own hands, and has not subjected them to one or a few men like themselves. Our senses and our knowledge extend only to the little circle about us; and it is not only vain, but ridiculous, to wish that our power and our influence may be more widely extended. We can only obtain means to pour the oil of gladness into the bosoms of the sorrowful, by first of all condemning them to sorrow. It cannot be too often repeated, that it is the exactions of one class and the interference of legislators, which have made that poverty and misery these persons are sometimes so anxious to mitigate. Benevolence and vanity conspire to make men oppress and rule their brethren. The doctrines of selfishness are in truth full of love as well as of wisdom; and no sentiment deserves so much to be scouted, as that benevolence which curses with its care.[48]

There is no evidence that Hodgskin had any theory of value to supplement his theory of profits as "legislated robbery" until he began studying Ricardo's *Principles of Political Economy and Taxation* shortly after its publication in 1817. Hodgskin's initial response to Ricardo was negative and antagonistic.[49] In a letter written on May 28, 1820, to Francis Place, Hodgskin wrote, "I dislike Mr. Ricardo's opinions because they go to justify the present political situation of society, and to set bounds to our hopes of future improvement. . . . This is the source of . . . my prejudices against them which I thus honestly and openly confess."[50] In this same letter, he sketched a theory of value, derived from Adam Smith, that he considered to be a refutation of Ricardo's theory of value. The following initial statement of Hodgskin's value theory is important because it was never altered but only developed and elaborated in his subsequent three books on political economy. Speaking of Ricardo's theory of price determination, Hodgskin wrote:

Mr. R[icardo] has involved this part of the subject in considerable confusion by *supposing* the buyers . . . are different from the three great classes, to wit landlords, capitalists and labourers, among whom he divides the produce of the earth. . . . Adam Smith . . . in all which he says on the subject of rent and profits increasing prices . . . evidently supposes the society to be composed of these three classes. In fact both he and Mr. Ricardo make the *real natural price* of all things to be paid by *labour*, and it is therefore self-evident that whatever diminishes the *value* of labour or makes a greater quantity necessary to obtain an equal quantity of any commodity enhances *its price*. . . . Rent . . . enhances price by the whole amount of rent. Profit, by being in like manner a diminution to the labourer of the value of his produce, enhances the price of everything into which it enters to the labourer. It is in this sense in which A. Smith says rent and profit enhance price. . . . In proportion therefore, as rent and profits increase . . . the price the labourer must pay for commodities will . . . increase. . . . Rent and profit do not enter into price if Mr. Ricardo's account . . . be true. . . . I hold this . . . to be the ground of the difference in the opinions of A. Smith and Mr. Ricardo.[51]

In *Labour Defended against the Claims of Capital*, published in 1825, Hodgskin devoted himself primarily to an attempt to refute the claim that profit was a return earned from the productivity of capital. His analysis of price determination was brief and merely repeated the idea contained in the above quotation from his letter to Place.[52] In 1827, in his *Popular Political Economy*, Hodgskin again elaborated his version of Smith's theory of value.[53] In this work, however, he elaborated on a distinction that had been implicit in all of his earlier writings on value theory and that, perhaps, explains in part the erroneous identification of Hodgskin's value theory with that of Ricardo. The distinction was between "natural price" and "social price."

> *Natural* or necessary price means . . . the whole quantity of labour nature requires from man that he may produce any commodity. . . . Nature exacted nothing but labour in time past, she demands only labour at present, and she will require merely labour in all future time. Labour was the original, is now and ever will be the only purchase money in dealing with Nature. There is another description of price, to which I shall give the name of *social*; it is natural price enhanced by social regulations.[54]

"Social regulations" by which the natural price was "enhanced" to form the social price were the laws that yielded unearned income to landlords and idle capitalists. Social price therefore had to include rent and profit as well as wages. Hodgskin was absolutely clear about the fact that his "natural price" was a normative concept describing a situation that could obtain only if existing governments and laws, which Hodgskin saw as unnatural, were abolished. "By his [the worker's] labour, and by nothing else, is natural price measured, but he never obtains commodities for the labour of producing them. At present, therefore, all money price is not natural but social price."[55]

Therefore, unlike Ricardo, Hodgskin did not believe that in contemporary capitalist society the labor embodied in the production of commodities determined their value. Rather, he asserted, following Adam Smith, that prices were determined by the summation of wages, rent, and profits. Unlike Smith and most of Smith's more conservative disciples, however, Hodgskin held that the laws of private property, through which rents and profits were extracted, were unnatural and hence inherently unjust.

Hodgskin's Conception of Capital

According to Hodgskin, profit and rent were coercively imposed, unnatural costs of production that raised prices, despite the fact that they were socially unnecessary. They were unnecessary in that they represented merely a tribute paid by producers to those who had coercive power over them and did *not* represent a payment for anything inherently *necessary* for the production process to take place. In order to demonstrate this, Hodgskin felt it necessary to refute the idea that capital was a separate, independent factor of production.

His refutation was based on an examination of the nature of capital. Following the convention of classical economics, he examined first the nature of circulating capital and then the nature of fixed capital. Circulating capital, he asserted, was supposed to be a fund of accumulated means of subsistence, without which laborers could not subsist during the period when their labor was coming to fruition in the form of a finished commodity.[56] Hodgskin then proceeded to argue that in reality no such fund existed, or at most it was very small and inconsequential.[57] He concluded by stating:

> All classes of men carry on their daily toils in full confidence that while each is engaged in his particular occupation some others will prepare whatever he requires, both for his immediate and future consumption and use. I have already explained that this confidence arises from that law of our nature by which we surely expect the sun will rise tomorrow, and that our fellowmen will labour on the morrow and during the next year as they have laboured during the year and the day which have passed. I hope I have also satisfied the reader that there is no knowledge of any produce of previous labour stored up for use, that the effects usually attributed to a stock of commodities are caused by coexisting labour, and that it is by the command the capitalist possesses over the *labour of some men*, not by possessing a stock of commodities, that he is enabled to *support* and consequently employ other labourers.[58]

By "fixed capital" Hodgskin meant "the tools and instruments the machinery . . . and the buildings he [the worker] uses either to facilitate his exertions or to protect their produce."[59] He argued, first, "that all instruments and machines are the produce of labour";[60] second, that they are useless without the application of labor, that is, by themselves they can produce nothing;[61] third, that they require the regular application of labor for their maintenance;[62] and fourth, that most fixed capital does not represent an accumulation in the hands of capitalists but is perpetually being used up and recreated by coexisting labor.[63]

Therefore, Hodgskin argued, capital is merely so many different aspects of the process of laboring, the relations among laborers, and the products of labor. But these are aspects of any production process and are present in all societies. In the western European economies of the 1820s, Hodgskin believed that calling these universal aspects of the production process "capital" tended to obscure the most essential feature of capital as it really existed and functioned in the economies of his time:

> Capital which thus engrosses the whole produce of a country, except the bare subsistence of the labourer . . . is "the produce of labour," "is commodities," "is the food the labourer eats and the machines he uses," so that we are obliged to give that enormous portion of the whole produce of the country which remains, after we have been supplied with subsistence, . . . for the privilege of eating the food we have ourselves produced, and of using our skill in producing more.[64]

> Capital is a sort of cabalistic word, like Church or State, or any other of those general terms which are invented by those who fleece the rest of mankind to conceal the hand that shears them.[65]

Hodgskin's Utilitarianism

Despite the fact that Hodgskin believed that capital was essentially a social relationship involving the coercive power of one class to expropriate the produce of another class, he was not a socialist. He asserted that private ownership of the means of production was decreed by nature. The distinction between the existing forms of unnatural property ownership and those forms that would be natural and just was the topic of his last book, *The Natural and Artificial Rights of Property Contrasted*, published in 1832. He wrote, "Nature bestows on every individual what his labour produces, just as she gives him his own body."[66] Capital, when conceived of as merely the produced means of production, was both a product of past labor and a necessary aid to present and future labor. As such, the natural ownership of capital should fall to the laborer who both produces it and then produces with it. It was the ownership of capital by those who did not produce that Hodgskin believed to be unnatural and to lie at the heart of most social ills. Any law that allowed one, because of idle ownership, to take a part of what he did not produce was unnatural. Hodgskin railed against the defenders of existing property rights:

> The right of property which they call natural, and which they can perceive no motives to respect, is merely legal, and is established and sanctioned by the law-giver only. . . . The power of making laws was long vested in those—and still is vested in their descendents—who followed no trade but war, and knew no handicraft but robbery and plunder. . . . The present legislators of Europe are the descendents of these men—cherishing their opinions and habits, and acting on their principles—who were unacquainted with any wealth creating arts, and who lived by appropriating the produce of others. On them nature bestowed no property; all which they possessed they took, by force, from those on whom she bestowed it.[67]

The ideal society was, for Hodgskin, one in which income from idle ownership would be impossible. Only those who worked could own capital, and they could own only the capital that aided them personally in their productive activities.[68] Only in such a society would there be no necessity to calculate profit and rent into each price. Therefore, only under these circumstances would the natural price and the social price be equal, because only then would the laborer receive all of his product. It is only in this ideal society that Hodgskin believed the Ricardian value theory would hold true.[69] He believed that the self-education of workers would be sufficient to bring about these reforms,[70] and he sometimes wrote as if he believed this reform process was well under way in his own time.[71]

In this ideal society, all production would be for exchange in the market. Hodgskin's defense of the beneficence of a free market was identical to Thompson's, and it simply relied on the argument that both parties in a voluntary exchange got something with a greater utility for them than the utility of the object that they gave up. This standard utilitarian defense of the desirability of free exchange pervaded all of Hodgskin's writings. In keeping with most utilitarianian defenders of the invisible hand of a free market, he advocated the abolition of any restrictions on supply and demand, whether imposed by government, private individuals, or groups. Thus, his ideal society was virtually identical to Thompson's system of "security with individual competition"; that is, it was competitive capitalism without capitalists.

The principal area in which Hodgskin's analysis was superior to Thompson's was in its description of the nature of capital as both the produced means of production and a coercive social relationship. Utilitarianism, however, ultimately furnished Hodgskin with no better defense for his ideal system of competitive capitalism without capitalists than it had furnished for Thompson. Not surprisingly, Thompson was one of Hodgskin's most outspoken critics. The latter's *Labour Defended* was published in 1825. In 1825, Thompson wrote his *Labour Rewarded*, which was a critique of Hodgskin's book. In *Labour Rewarded*, all of the shortcomings of the "system of individual competition" that Thompson had catalogued in his earlier *Distribution of Wealth* were repeated. His purpose, of course, was to demonstrate that competitive individualism in a market economy, even when there were no capitalists expropriating the produce of laborers, was socially and morally inferior to a system of cooperative socialism.

Notes to Chapter 7

1. Robert Owen, "The Book of the New Moral World," reprinted in part in *Communism, Fascism and Democracy*, ed. Carl Cohen (New York: Random House, 1962), pp. 47–48.

2. William Thompson, *An Inquiry into the Principles of the Distribution of Wealth Most Conducive to Human Happiness* (London: William S. Orr, 1850), p. 15.

3. Ibid., p. 1.

4. Ibid., p. 144.

5. Ibid., p. 17.

6. Ibid., p. 6.

7. Ibid., p. 111.

8. Ibid.

9. Ibid., p. xxix.

10. Ibid., p. 133.

11. Ibid., p. 145.

12. Ibid., p. 147.

13. Ibid., p. 126.

14. Ibid., pp. 155–57.

15. Ibid., p. 35.

16. Ibid., p. 137.

17. Ibid., p. 128.

18. Ibid., p. 454.

19. Ibid., pp. 250–53.

20. Ibid., pp. vii–xxxii.

21. Ibid., p. 255.

22. Ibid., p. 258.

23. Ibid., p. 259.

24. Ibid., p. 257.

25. Ibid., p. 259.

26. Ibid., pp. 259–60.

27. Ibid., p. 260.

28. Ibid.

29. Ibid., p. 261.

30. Ibid.

31. Ibid., pp. 213–14.

32. Ibid., p. 214. Thompson's discussion of sexism follows on the next several pages. Sexism is also discussed in his *Labour Rewarded, The Claims of Labour and Capital Conciliated* (New York: Augustus M. Kelly, 1969), which was first published in 1827. He wrote a book, devoted entirely to an analysis of the oppression of women, entitled *Appeal of One-Half of the Human Race, Women*, and published in 1825.

33. Ibid., pp. 261–63.

34. Ibid., p. 263.

35. Ibid., p. 267.

36. Ibid., pp. 269–367.

37. Ibid., p. 19.

38. Jeremy Bentham, *Jeremy Bentham's Economic Writings*, vol. 3, ed. W. Stark (London: Allen and Unwin, 1954), p. 421.

39. For a comparison of Hodgskin's ideas with those of Smith, Ricardo, and Marx, see E.K. Hunt, "Value Theory in the Writings of the Classical Economists, Thomas Hodgskin and Karl Marx," *History of Political Economy* 9, no. 3 (Fall 1977): 322–45.

40. Ronald L. Meek, *Studies in the Labour Theory of Value* (New York: Monthly Review Press, 1973), p. 124.

41. He wrote five books: *An Essay on Naval Discipline, Showing Part of Its Evil Effects on the Mind of the Officers and the Minds of the Men and on the Community; with an Amended System by Which Pressing May Be Immediately Abolished*, published in 1813; *Travels in the North of Germany, Describing the Present State of Social and Political Institutions, the Agriculture, Manufactures, Commerce, Education, Arts and Manners in That Country, Particularly in the Kingdom of Hanover*, published in 1820; *Labour Defended against the Claims of Capital; or the Unproductiveness of Capital Proved with Reference to the Present Combinations amongst Journeymen*, published anonymously in 1825; *Popular Political Economy*, published in 1827; and *The Natural and Artificial Rights of Property Contrasted*, published in 1832. He also wrote scores of articles, the majority of which appeared between 1844 and 1857 in *The Economist*.

42. Thomas Hodgskin, *An Essay on Naval Discipline, Showing Part of Its Evil Effects on the Minds of the Officers and the Minds of the Men and on the Community* (London: Hurst Robinson, 1813), p. 173.

43. Ibid., p. 192.

44. Thomas Hodgskin, *Travels in the North of Germany, Describing the Present State of Social and Political Institutions, the Agriculture, Manufactures, Commerce, Education, Arts and Manners in That Country, Particularly in the Kingdom of Hanover* (Edinburgh: Archibald Constable, 1820), vol. 2, p. 97.

45. Ibid., p. 27.

46. Ibid., p. 228.

47. Ibid., p. 466.

48. Ibid., pp. 107–8.

49. In June 1819, Hodgskin wrote a letter to Francis Place criticizing Ricardo's theory. See Francis Place, *Private Correspondence*, vol. 2 (British Museum), add. MSS 35, 153, F142 ff.

50. Francis Place, *Private Correspondence*, vol. 2 (British Museum), add. MSS 35, 153, F67.

51. Ibid.

52. Thomas Hodgskin, *Labour Defended against the Claims of Capital* (London: Labour, 1922), pp. 75–76.

53. Thomas Hodgskin, *Popular Political Economy* (New York: Augustus M. Kelley, 1966), pp. 219–35.

54. Ibid., pp. 219–20.

55. Ibid., p. 233.

56. Hodgskin, *Labour Defended*, pp. 35–36.

57. Ibid., pp. 38–50.

58. Ibid., pp. 51–52.

59. Ibid., p. 52.

60. Ibid., p. 54.

61. Ibid., pp. 56–58.

62. Ibid., pp. 59–60.

63. Ibid., p. 54.

64. Ibid., pp. 31–32.

65. Ibid., p. 60.

66. Thomas Hodgskin, *The Natural and Artificial Rights of Property Contrasted* (London: B.S. Fabernoster Row, 1832), p. 28.

67. Ibid., p. 32.

68. This idea is expressed in each of Hodgskin's last three books: *Labour Defended*, pp. 86–105; *Popular Political Economy*, pp. 243–57; *Rights of Property Contrasted*, p. 101.

69. See *Popular Political Economy*, pp. 26–29, 98–102.

70. *Labour Defended*, pp. 26–29, 98–102.

71. *Rights of Property Contrasted*, p. 101.

Chapter 8

Pure Versus Eclectic Utilitarianism:
The Writings of Bastiat and Mill

We have seen how the combination of both the utility theory and labor theory perspectives, in the writings of Smith and Ricardo, seemed to lead to conclusions suggesting that capitalism was characterized both by social harmony and by class conflict. Say and Senior "sanitized" classical political economy by rejecting the labor theory perspective and arguing that a knowledge of the true principles of political economy would show that the interests of all classes were in harmony. They explained all existing conflicts as resulting from ignorance and misunderstanding. The doctrines of Say and Senior (and Malthus as well) attempted to show how the ultimate or hidden interests of the poor, when understood in the light of "scientific" political economy, were identical to the immediate and obvious interests of the propertied, wealthy, and powerful.

Thompson and Hodgskin adopted the labor theory perspective. They believed that as long as the immediate producers of wealth—the workers—did not have any control over the means of production, class conflict would be inherent in capitalism. Both men identified with the cause of working people, and both advocated social change designed to transform the class structure of capitalism. Both of these writers, however, by basing many of their ideas on the utilitarian philosophy, were involved in contradictions not unlike those of Smith and Ricardo.

The radical or socialist influence of the labor theory perspective of classical political economy spread rapidly between 1820 and 1850. Socialists began exerting considerable influence on the growing working class movements during this period. Conservatives, therefore, began to look with more and more urgency for new versions of political economy based on pure utilitarianism. The two most significant books on economic theory to appear around the mid-nineteenth century were John Stuart Mill's *Principles of Political Economy* (published in 1848) and Frédéric Bastiat's *Economic Harmonies* (published in 1850). Mill's book was the last great effort to retain both the utility and labor perspectives within the same body of economic doctrines. Bastiat's book represented the final product, in most essential respects, of pure economic utilitarianism pushed to its logical conclusions.

The Spread of Socialist Ideas

Socialist economic ideas unquestionably had their principal intellectual roots in English classical political economy. Through the writings of Thompson and Hodgskin, these economic doctrines found their way into the Owenite movement in England, exerting considerable influence in the 1830s. However, socialist ideas grew fastest in France, having their greatest influence in the 1830s and 1840s.

Socialism could be said to have derived equally from both English and French ideas, even though its economic doctrines originated mostly in England. The left wing of the French revolutionary movement in the eighteenth century produced many socialist ideas. One of its leaders was Gracchus Babeuf (1760–1797). After the fall of Robespierre, he masterminded a conspiracy to topple the French government and replace it with one dedicated to equality and brotherhood. The plot was betrayed and Babeuf was executed.

In his writings, Babeuf argued that nature made all people equal in rights and needs. Therefore, the inequalities of wealth and power that had developed should be redressed by society. Unfortunately, most societies did the opposite: they set up a coercive mechanism to protect the interests of the property holders and the wealthy. For Babeuf, the presence of inequality meant the presence of injustice. Capitalist commerce existed, he said, "for the purpose of pumping the sweat and blood of more or less everybody, in order to form lakes of gold for the benefit of the few."[1] The workers who created the wealth of society got the least; and until private property was eliminated, the inequalities in society could never be redressed.

Henri de Saint-Simon (1760–1825) was also influential. He came from an impoverished family of nobility and had an aristocrat's disdain for the antisocial egoism of the wealthy capitalists of his era. He condemned the pernicious moral effects of individualistic competition and stressed the social value of planned cooperative production. He also condemned the large number of idle rich who lived off the industriousness of working people. He sanctioned private property when it was used to promote the welfare of the masses, but he insisted that only extensive government intervention in production, distribution, and commerce could ensure this.

Many of Saint-Simon's followers were more radical, however. They wrote endless pamphlets and books exposing the abuses of capitalism, attacking private property and inheritance, denouncing exploitation, and advocating government ownership and control of economic production in the interest of the general welfare.

Socialist cooperatives were popularized in France by Charles Fourier in the 1830s. He believed that in a capitalist economy only about one-third of the people really did socially useful work. The other two-thirds were directed, by the corruption and distortion caused by the market system, into useless occupations or were useless, wealthy parasites. He urged the productive members of society to escape this oppression and tyranny by voluntarily forming cooperatives (or "phalanxes," as he called them). He was also one of the first socialists to perceive that competition among capitalists would inevitably lead to monopoly:

> Among the influences tending to restrict man's industrial rights, I will mention the formation of privileged corporations which, monopolizing a given branch of industry, arbitrarily close the doors of labour against whomsoever they please. . . . Extremes meet, and the greater the extent to which anarchical competition is carried, the nearer the approach to *universal monopoly*, which is the opposite excess. . . . Monopolies, . . . operating in conjunction with the great landed interest, will reduce the middle and labouring classes to a state of commercial vassalage. . . . The small operators will be reduced to the position of mere agents, working for their mercantile coalition. We shall then see the reappearing of feudalism in an inverse order, founded on mercantile leagues, and answering to the Baronial Leagues of the Middle Ages.[2]

In the 1840s, and for several decades thereafter, the most influential French socialist was Pierre Joseph Proudhon (1809–1865). In his well-known book *What Is Property?* he answered the question posed in the title with the slogan that made him famous: "Property is theft." He believed that property was "the mother of tyranny." Because property rights were simply sets of special privileges for the few and general restrictions and prohibitions for the masses, they necessarily involved coercion in order to be established and continually enforced. Hence, the primary function of the state was to coerce.

Property rights were the source not only of tyranny and coercion but also of economic inequality. Whereas the amount of labor expended determined how much was produced in a capitalist society, ownership of property determined the division of the produce so that those who produced got almost nothing and those who owned property could use the laws of private ownership to "legally steal" from the workers. Proudhon's ideal society rejected not only capitalist property relations but industrialization as well. He envisioned a golden age of small-scale agriculture and handicraft production in which each farmer and worker owned individual capital and no one lived through property ownership alone.

Foundation and Scope of Bastiat's Utilitarian Economics

In the 1840s the influence of French socialism was rapidly expanding. Within this context, Frédéric Bastiat (1801–1850) attempted to establish the sanctity of private property, capital, profit, and the existing distribution of wealth—in general, competitive laissez-faire capitalism. He did this by consistently extending the principles of utilitarianism into economic theory (although, as we will see, the utility theory of value was not given its final, modern formulation until more than two decades later, in response to the growing influence of socialist ideas).

The title of Bastiat's most important book, *Economic Harmonies*, showed the importance he placed on refuting the notion that class conflict was inherent in capitalism. In defense of his doctrines, he (like Senior) claimed the authority of *Science*. In discussing the distinction between "scientific" political economy (where his favorites were clearly Say and Senior) and socialism (where his most despised opponent was clearly Proudhon) he wrote:

> What makes the great division between the two schools is the difference in methods. Socialism, like astrology and alchemy, proceeds by way of imagination; political economy, like astronomy and chemistry, proceeds by way of observation.
>
> Two astronomers observing the same phenomenon may not reach the same conclusion. Despite this temporary disagreement they feel the bond of a common method that sooner or later will bring them together. . . . But between the astronomer who observes and the astrologer who imagines, there stretches an unbridgeable gulf. . .
>
> The same is true of political economy and socialism.
>
> The economists observe man, the laws of his nature and the social relations that derive from these laws. The socialists conjure up a society out of their imagination and then conceive of a human heart to fit this society.[3]

He (like Malthus) also placed the authority of religion in defense of his doctrines:

> Proclaiming in the name of faith, formulating in the name of science, the divine laws . . . of our dynamic moral order, we utterly reject the . . . institutions that some men in their blindness would heedlessly introduce into this admirable mechanism. It would be absurd for an atheist to say: *Laissez faire!* Leave it to chance! But we, who are believers have the right to cry: *Laissez passer!* Let God's order and justice prevail. *I believe in God.*[4]

> Indeed, if this work differs . . . from the works of the socialists, it is because they say: "We do indeed pretend to believe in God, but in reality we believe only in ourselves, since we want nothing to do with *laissez faire*, and each and every one of us offers his social plan as infinitely superior to that of Providence.[5]

Having thus established the scientific and religious superiority of his ideas, Bastiat began a consistent development of utilitarian economics. We saw in the preceding chapter that utilitarianism provides no basis for judging two situations if the utility of one individual is decreased in the second situation, even though the utility of all other persons increases. We also saw that if we accept the existing distribution of wealth as ideal and just (or if we ignore the distribution completely), voluntary market exchanges are the paradigm of an instance in which total utility unambiguously increases between two situations. The utility of both individuals is increased after the exchange from what it had been; unanimity prevails. Bastiat quoted with approval from

Condillac: "The very fact that an exchange takes place is proof that there must necessarily be profit in it for both the contracting parties; otherwise it would not be made. Hence, every exchange represents two gains for humanity."[6]

Utilitarianism requires unanimity. Once one accepts the initial distribution of "exchangeable things," voluntary exchange is one of the few aspects of social life in which such unanimity exists between socially interacting persons. Both the requirement of unanimity and its fulfillment in the act of exchange are of great importance to modern neoclassical economics. In neoclassical utilitarian economics, all economic, social, and political interactions among human beings are reduced to acts of exchange. Once such a reduction is made, the result is obvious. Utilitarian economic theory reduces to this syllogism:

> *All exchanges are mutually beneficial to all parties.*
> *All human interactions can be reduced to exchanges.*
> *Therefore, all human interactions are beneficial to all parties.*

It was in the writings of Bastiat that the utility approach was first consistently developed so as to reduce all economic theory to a mere analysis of market exchange. "Exchange is political economy," Bastiat declared, "it is society itself, for it is impossible to conceive of society without exchange or exchange without society."[7]

When Bastiat proclaimed that "exchange is political economy," he had certainly gone a good distance from Adam Smith, who had devoted only a few dozen pages to exchange in the nearly 1,000 pages of *The Wealth of Nations*, or from David Ricardo, who had defined political economy as the study of the laws regulating the distribution of the economy's produce among the three great classes of society.

Smith's few pages devoted to a description of the "invisible hand" had, with Bastiat, become the whole of political economy. The sanitizing job was complete. Making the claims that "exchange is political economy" and that "political economy is restricted to the area we call *business*, and business is under the influence of *self-interest*,"[8] Bastiat set out to prove that "all men's impulses, when motivated by legitimate self-interest, fall into a harmonious social pattern."[9] He addressed his book to all classes and promised to prove that laissez-faire capitalism was the best possible economic system for everyone:

> Property owners, however vast may be your possessions, if I prove that your rights, which people today so vehemently contest, are confined, as are those of the simplest manual worker, to receiving services in return for real services performed by you or your forefathers, then these rights of yours will henceforth be beyond challenge. . . .

> Capitalists and laborers, I believe that I can establish the law: "In proportion as capital accumulates, the *absolute* share of capital in the total returns of production increases and its relative share decreases; labor also finds that its *relative* share increases and that its *absolute* share increases even more sharply. The opposite

effect is observed when capital is frittered away." If this law can be established, it is clear that we may conclude that the interests of workers and employers are harmonious.[10]

Utility and Exchange

Bastiat's demonstration of the universal harmony of capitalism relied on several "scientific laws" that he believed would be readily confirmed by casual observation. "We cannot doubt," he declared, "that self-interest is the mainspring of human action."[11] The immediate motives to action were human wants. Human desires or wants were insatiable, but the means to satisfy them were limited: "*Desire* runs ahead, while the *means* limp along behind."[12] Satisfaction of wants yields pleasure: "If we give the name of utility to everything that effects the satisfaction of wants, then there are two kinds of utility. One kind is given us by Providence without cost to ourselves; the other kind insists, so to speak, on being purchased through effort."[13] Thus, the universal principle of human action was this: "Our *self-interest* is such that we constantly seek to increase the sum of our satisfactions in relation to our efforts."[14] This was simply a restatement of Bentham's principle of utility maximization, and it has stood at the heart of conservative economic theory from Bastiat to the present.

Bastiat's separation of utility into two kinds represented his attempt to make prices depend on utility and to obviate Smith's water-diamond paradox. Had he read Bentham more carefully, he might have developed the marginal utility concept of later neoclassical economists. However, he argued that nature gave us some utility, such as that gratuitously gotten from water, whereas most utility, such as that gotten from diamonds, required effort or pain. This latter utility he called "onerous utility." The objects that yielded onerous utility were those requiring human effort to produce. Such productive human effort he called "service." Central to Bastiat's approach was his insistence that labor was only one type of service that was not qualitatively different from other productive services performed by landlords and capitalists.

An isolated individual would perform all productive services for him or herself. But that individual's existence would be precarious and his or her material welfare meager. People lived in societies because they could then divide their labor, specialize, increase production, and exchange the fruits of the increased production. In society, then, people performed services (i.e., undertook productive effort) for others. Exchange was, in reality, an exchange of services that inevitably increased people's utility above what they could obtain by providing productive services only for themselves. Thus in an exchange society, service was defined by Bastiat as "*effort* on the part of one man, whereas the *want* and the *satisfaction* are another's."[15]

The above definition of service is important to an understanding of the social class orientation of Bastiat's writings. Productive effort, he insisted, was painful. People could satisfy needs "only by an effort that we call *taking pains.*"[16] Such productive effort, having already been defined as painful, was equated with service. Therefore, service meant pains endured by people in order for production to take place.

One of the major inconsistencies of Bastiat's writings, which recurred again and again, was that once he had defined service as a human pain endured for the sake of production, he repeatedly referred to services as the use of those qualities in *material objects* that render such objects desirable.

A theme to which we have returned several times in this book is that a thinker's inconsistencies are often the most fruitful indication of the thinker's class bias. This is because such class bias is often more consistent than a thinker's logic. So it was with Bastiat. His principal objective was to defend the private ownership of capital. In doing so, like Say and Senior, he desired to make the contribution of the capitalist and landlord to production appear similar to the contribution of the laborer. He insisted that the capitalist and landlord both provided services and thus both endured pain. But as we shall see, the services for which capitalists and landlords were paid frequently turned out simply to be allowing others to use the tools and land that were necessary for production. At such points in Bastiat's discussions, one is at a loss to see how the capitalist and landlord suffer pain.

For example, after defining service as human productive pain and then extolling the importance of the division of labor and exchange, Bastiat wrote:

> Once it is admitted that exchange is both the cause and the effect of the division of labor, once it is admitted that the division of labor multiplies *satisfactions* in relation to *effort*, . . . the reader will readily understand the services money has rendered humanity by the mere fact that it facilitates the act of making an exchange.[17]

We see then that *money rendered an important service.* The owner of money, of course, received *interest.* But how are owning money and receiving interest painful in a way that promotes society's productivity?

Having established that selfish individuals found specialization and the exchange of productive services and commodities to be the most effective way to maximize utility, Bastiat went on to discuss exchange value. Nature's contributions to utility, he insisted, were never priced. Human contributions, in the form of productive services, were priced in proportion to the utility derived from them by their buyer:

> Say's axiom was this: the basis of value is utility.
>
> If it were a question here of utility as related to human services, I should have no argument with him. . . . The word service is so completely included in the area of utility that it is simply the translation . . . of the Latin word *uti*, to *serve.*[18]

> Since products and services are interchanged, they must necessarily have something in common, something against which they can be compared and appraised, namely, *value.*[19]

> Value is not transmitted from the material object to the service, but from the service to the material value.[20]

In viewing the utility of services as the origin of the utility and hence of the value of products, Bastiat reversed the line of causality that was to become standard in neoclassical utility theory. In this respect, Say was much closer to the later neoclassical school than was Bastiat, but Bastiat's theory was directly conducive to the achievement of his principal aim—to show that landlords and capitalists created value and wealth in the same way that labor did. Having said that utility is the source of value and having equated the value of products with the value of the services required to produce them, Bastiat never developed a theory of exactly how utility determined the value of services and thereby determined the value of products. Such a theory was not to be worked out until the early 1870s, after Marx's radical version of the labor theory of value had begun to exert widespread influence.

Bastiat's Defense of Private Property, Capital, Profits, and Rent

Bastiat set out to defend private ownership of land and capital, explain the nature of the services provided by landlords and capitalists, show that everyone benefited from the rigid enforcement of the laws of ownership and from free exchange, and show that the unfettered accumulation of capital benefited the laborers as much as it benefited the capitalists, if not more. On the basis of these suppositions, he was convinced that laissez-faire capitalism was a harmonious system that universally benefited all people.

Bastiat first defended the sanctity of the laws of private property. His defense was simple: private property was a *natural law* created by God and existing before any man-made laws. Therefore, human laws that recognized this conformed to natural law and God's will; human laws that infringed on property rights were unnatural and contrary to God's will. "Property does not exist because there are laws," he insisted, "but laws exist because there is property."[21]

To Bastiat, property was a necessary consequence of the nature of man:

> In the full sense of the word, man *is born a proprietor*, because he is born with wants whose satisfaction is necessary to life, and with organs and faculties whose exercise is indispensable to the satisfaction of these wants. Faculties are only an extension of the person; and property is nothing but an extension of the faculties. . . .
> That is why we believe that property has been divinely instituted, and that the object of human law is its *protection* or *security.*[22]

But it was not enough to insist on the sacredness of property. Hodgskin would have agreed with the above quotation, but he would have insisted that it was *unnatural* and *unjust* that the land and tools, which were extensions of people's productive faculties, were nearly all owned by those who did not *use* them as such, that is, by those who did not produce with them. Therefore, Hodgskin would have agreed that property ownership was natural but would have asserted that *capitalist property ownership* was unnatural because it was the means by which the idle robbed the industrious.

Recognizing this, Bastiat went further. He began by giving the wealthy the following reassurance:

> Men of property and leisure . . . you are still strangely disturbed. Why? Because the sweet-smelling but deadly perfume of utopia threatens your way of life. There are men who say, who rant, that . . . [your fortune] has been acquired at the expense of your brethren. They say that you . . . have exacted a tribute . . . in the name of property, of interest, of rent, and hire. . . .
> But I say no . . . all that has passed . . . [to] you has been *compensation* for mental and physical effort, for sweat and toil expended, for dangers faced, for skills contributed, for sacrifices made, for pains taken, for *services rendered and received*. You thought only of yourselves, perhaps, but even your own self-interest has become in the hands of an infinitely wise and all-seeing Providence an instrument for making greater abundance available to all men.[23]

In defense of profits on capital, Bastiat first pointed to the obvious necessity for workers to use previously produced means of production. Then he asked how these means of production had come into existence. A labor theory of value would have led to the conclusion that, like all other commodities, they were the result of human labor exerted in the transformation of natural resources. But, taking capitalist property relations as eternal and sacred, Bastiat insisted that they were the result of pain suffered by capitalists:

> Capital has its roots in three attributes of man: foresight, intelligence, and thrift. For him to resolve to lay aside capital funds, . . . [a capitalist] must sacrifice the present for them, [and] exercise control over himself and his appetites. . . . To accumulate capital is to provide for the subsistence, the protection, the shelter, the leisure, the education, the independence, the dignity of generations to come. None of this can be done without putting into practice all our most social virtues, and, what is harder, without making them our daily habit.[24]

Bastiat never even considered the socialists' belief that an ordinary worker earned in wages just enough (and sometimes less) for his or her family's subsistence; that there was utterly no possibility for him or her to save the millions necessary to become a capitalist from the meager paycheck received; that in actual fact the origins of most capitalists' fortunes were deceit, treachery, fraud, coercion, and bribery; and that once capitalism was established, after a generation or two, the origin of most capitalists' fortunes was inheritance. From the profits on their capital, capitalists, whether they were virtuous or vicious, intelligent or stupid, thrifty or profligate, could devote a portion to the accumulation of more capital—for more future wealth, income, and power—and devote a portion to luxury and extravagant consumption.

The only sacrifice capitalists would have to make, the only pain they would have to endure, was twofold: first, they had to use their capital to make more profits rather than, for example, simply letting their factory stand idle; and second, they could not become so extravagant and profligate that they killed the goose that laid their golden eggs—that is, they had to live off their profits, interest, and rents and not dissipate the inherited fortune that gave them their power. Such were the sufferings and privations that Bastiat believed morally entitled capitalists to their profits, interests, and rents.

It was no accident that Bastiat did not look at the actual, historical origins of the great family fortunes of his day, for this would have destroyed his argument for the absolute sacredness of inheritance laws. After stressing the naturalness, holiness, and sacredness of property rights, he wrote:

> The same holds true of inheritance. No theory, no flights of oratory can succeed in keeping fathers from loving their children. The people who delight in setting up imaginary societies may consider this regrettable but it is a fact. A father will expend as much *effort*, perhaps more, for his children's satisfactions as for his own. If, then, a new law contrary to Nature should forbid the bequest of private property, it would not only in itself do violence to the rights of private property, but it would also prevent the creation of new private property by paralyzing a full half of human *effort*.[25]

Thus, eliminating inheritance laws would paralyze the moral virtue that underlay the pain and effort required to allow a capitalist's factory to be a source of profits to him or her, rather than to let it sit idle or to burn it down. Thus, love rather than self-interest was the motive defended by Bastiat and attacked by the socialists! It will be remembered that one of Thompson's arguments for a society of mutual cooperation was that only in such a society could all children (not just those fortunate enough to have been born of wealthy parents), as well as all others who for various legitimate reasons could not contribute to production, be spared the insecurity of competitive capitalism.

Bastiat's defense of private ownership of land was equally simple: no rent accrued to landowners simply by virtue of the natural, untouched, virgin qualities of the earth. All rent was due to human improvements of the soil. Therefore, land was simply capital that could not be moved about in the same manner as tools and machinery:

> The land as a means of production, insofar as it is the work of God, produces *utility*, and this utility is gratuitous; it is not within the owner's power to charge for it. The land, as a means of production, insofar as the landowner has prepared it, worked on it, enclosed it, drained it, improved it, added other necessary implements to it, produces *value*, which represents human *services* made available, and this is the only thing . . . [the landlord] charges for.[26]

Bastiat offered no theory whatsoever to show, contrary to Smith and Ricardo, that no rent was paid for the use of the original qualities existing on and in the earth; he simply asserted it.

Furthermore, Bastiat's claim that he looked at facts while socialists constructed their theories from fancy and imagination is strained to the breaking point in this argument. Did he look around at the wealthy, powerful landowners, living in palatial mansions in Paris and other French cities, and see them donning their work clothes and trudging out to their fields to prepare them, work on them, enclose them, drain them, and improve them? If he had gone to the fields, he would have observed peasants doing this work and paying rents to absentee landlords, or wage workers doing this work for capitalist farmers who were paying rents to absentee landlords.

Ultimately, the pain and efforts of the landlords were similar to those of the capitalists: they endured having their land worked by others in order to receive rents, rather than letting their lands lie unused.

Bastiat's View of Exchange, Social Harmony, and the Role of Government

Having established the sacredness of private property and the "productive pains" endured by landlords and capitalists, the universal beneficence of exchange followed. Labor could not produce without natural resources and capital. Wealthy people had to suffer pain to let these resources and capital be used in production. All of society was better off if production took place than if it did not. Therefore, when, through exchange, workers sold their labor power and capitalists and landlords extracted their profits and rents, everyone benefited and social harmony prevailed. Bastiat was fond of stressing the freedom that existed in such a system. Workers had a choice of starving or exchanging their labor power for a subsistence wage. They freely engaged in such an exchange, and, therefore, exchange benefited them as well as the capitalists and landlords.

To be sure, Bastiat stressed the notion that for exchange to be universally beneficial, competition had to prevail. He saw the government, however, as the principal source of barriers to such competition. So he appealed to government to restrict itself to "the maintenance of liberty, property, and individual rights."[27] Thus, the government was to restrict itself to the protection of all the privileges of private property as well as the liberty or individual right to engage in exchange. He recognized that "government action involves coercion by its very nature,"[28] but both Nature and God join to give people an absolute right "to defend, *even by their joint force*, the individual's liberty and property."[29]

Bastiat never asked himself why governments created conditions of monopoly and other impediments to free competition. If he had, he would have discovered that it was because a monopoly is more profitable than a competitive enterprise. Insofar as everyone was motivated by self-interest, it was more advantageous for government officials to take the bribes or campaign contributions from the wealthy than to follow Bastiat's prescription. The capitalists and the government officials merely engaged in an exchange: bribes for legislation protecting monopoly power. As Bastiat's own theory would have predicted, both parties to the exchange benefited. Individuals in government obtained the financing necessary to remain in power and to lead a "commodious" life, while capitalists obtained the legal restrictions necessary to make more profits than the mere enforcement of their property rights would have made possible. Both parties to the exchange benefited, but the public suffered. It is no wonder that, in his system of harmony, Bastiat ignored this type of exchange. He was much more concerned with socialists than he was with capitalists bribing government officials.

Bastiat was struck with the esthetic beauty of capitalism and its political economy: "Political economy does . . . have its own special poetry. Whenever there is order and harmony, there is poetry."[30] But he was not unaware that workers did sometimes suffer hardship or deprivation: "Suffering," he wrote, "has a role to play in the life of the individual and, consequently in that of society as well."[31] But here, again, the harmony of laissez-faire capitalism came to the rescue. To reassure workers, he wrote:

> Therefore, having established that every increase in capital is necessarily accompanied by an increase in the general welfare, I venture to present as incontrovertible the following axiom relating to the distribution of this prosperity:
>   *As capital increases, the capitalists' absolute share in the total production increases while their relative share decreases. On the other hand, the workers' share increases both relatively and absolutely.*[32]

The "proof" of this proposition was simple, Bastiat asserted: "*The more plentiful capital is, the lower its interest rate.* Now this point is not open to question, nor has it been questioned."[33]

This was a logical error. The belief that there is a tendency for the rate of profit to fall as capital is accumulated has been one of the most consistently held opinions among economic theorists, from Smith and Ricardo to Marx, and, in the twentieth century, John Maynard Keynes. But a decline in the rate of profit accompanying an increase in the amount of capital in the hands of capitalists does *not* necessarily indicate a decrease in the relative share of production going to capitalists. If the percent increase in capital sufficiently exceeds the percent decrease in the rate of profit, then the capitalists' relative share of production will increase and the laborers' relative share will decrease. Once again, a logical error clearly indicates the class bias of a theorist.

In summary, Bastiat's answer to the socialists' assertion that there were "fundamental antagonisms . . . between the property owner and the worker, between capital and labor, between the common people and the bourgeoisie"[34] was simple. "Men's interests are harmonious; therefore, the answer lies entirely in this one word: *freedom.*"[35] Freedom of exchange and the protection of property—such was Bastiat's ultimate answer to all social ills. Such freedom was, of course, the freedom to prevent workers coercively from producing unless wealthy property owners were permitted to extract the profits, rents, and interests that resulted from owning the means of production.

Mill's Utilitarianism

The last great attempt to integrate the labor theory of value and the utilitarian perspective was made by John Stuart Mill in his *Principles of Political Economy*, first published in 1848. Mill claimed to be a disciple of both Bentham and Ricardo. His writing, however, nearly always had one distinctive characteristic: he tried to be fair-minded and judicious in his presentation of any doctrine and, consequently, presented modifications, extensions, and numerous qualifications to nearly every principle he asserted. Frequently the modifications were so significant—as in the case of his development of both Bentham's utilitarianism and Ricardo's labor theory of value—that the doctrine he ended with was totally different from the doctrine that he first asserted. Ultimately, however, Mill was neither a utilitarian nor a proponent of the labor theory of value. It was also frequently the case that his qualifications of any principle were so extensive and so persuasively argued that their cumulative effect was to suggest to the reader—and frequently to give a lucid and convincing defense for—the validity of principles quite contradictory to those espoused by him. As a result, both Mill's social philosophy and his economic theory were eclectic and often inconsistent.

The contrast between Mill and Bastiat could not be more striking. They are discussed in the same chapter because they are the first two clear representatives of a polar bifurcation of utilitarian economics. Bastiat was the precursor of the later Austrian and the contemporary Chicago schools—proponents of extreme conservatism and rigid, uncompromising defenders of laissez-faire capitalism. Mill was the precursor of the much more moderate Marshallian school of neoclassical economics—frequently advocates of liberal reform and government intervention. Mill was Bastiat's superior both as a theoretician and as a scholar. Mill's *Principles* had a breadth of scholarship and an urbane style that put it in a class with Smith's *The Wealth of Nations*. His polished, fair-minded style contrasted sharply with Bastiat's doctrinaire, sanctimonious, and arrogant style. Yet Mill was the eclectic whose doctrines contain major inconsistencies, while Bastiat was the consistent developer of the conclusions implicit in utilitarian psychology and ethics.

Mill began the *Principles* with an assertion that contradicted most economic theorists prior to him and that contradicts contemporary neoclassical economics. "The production of wealth," he wrote, "is evidently not an arbitrary thing. It has necessary conditions."[36] By this, he meant that the laws of matter and the material consequences of given physical techniques of production were the same in all societies. "Unlike the laws of Production," he continued, "those of Distribution are partly of human institution: since the manner in which wealth is distributed in any given society, depends on the statutes or usages therein obtaining."[37] By this he meant that the laws of property and other institutions that affected the distribution of wealth were human institutions that had been changed in the past and would, he believed, be changed in the future.

Unlike Bastiat, he did not believe that Nature or God instituted private property. It was a human convention and thus was "wholly a question of general expediency. When private property . . . [was] not expedient, it . . . [was] unjust."[38] With this rejection of the notion that private property was sacred and the additional rejection of the two most fundamental axioms of utilitarianism (which we will discuss below), it is not surprising that Mill refused to make exchange the heart of political economy: "Exchange is not the fundamental law of the distribution of . . . produce, no more than roads and carriages are the essential laws of motion, but merely a part of the machinery for effecting it. To confound these ideas seems to me not only a logical, but a practical blunder."[39]

For all consistent utilitarians, from Bastiat to the present, exchange has been the central focal point of all economic theory. Mill's rejection of this approach followed from his rejection of two of the central tenets of utilitarianism. He always professed to be a disciple of Bentham, and one of Mill's best-known works was entitled *Utilitarianism*. Chapter 2 of that work defined utilitarianism, but it obviously contradicted Bentham's definition. If Bentham's philosophy and its intellectual offspring in the history of economic ideas is to be called utilitarianism, Mill's philosophy cannot be; they are radically different. The two fundamental axioms of Benthamite utilitarianism are that (1) all motives can be reduced to the self-interested quest for pleasure, and (2) each person is the sole judge of his own pleasures, and, therefore, interpersonal comparisons of pleasure are impossible (as we argued in the preceding chapter). The second axiom was epitomized in Bentham's statement that if the quantity of pleasure was the same, pushpin was as good as poetry. Benthamite utilitarianism permits no invidious comparisons of qualitatively different sorts of pleasure.

Mill, as we will see later in our discussion, did not believe that all actions were motivated by self-interest. He believed only that most people whose personalities were molded by a competitive capitalist culture acted out of self-interest in their economic behavior. He looked forward, however, to the future, when, in a socialist or communist society, people would act from "higher" or "nobler" motives. Such an invidious comparison of motives is totally alien to utilitarianism, which reduces all motives to self-interest and views such judgments as merely reflective of personal, subjective biases.

Mill also insisted that some pleasures could be judged as morally superior to other pleasures. If this is true, and the present writer certainly agrees with Mill here, then there must be some higher principle than the pleasure principle of utilitarianism whereby moral judgments among different pleasures become possible. Obviously, this higher principle, and not the utilitarian pleasure principle, would be the source of ethical judgments. Mill repeatedly asserted that "some *kinds* of pleasure are more desirable and more valuable than others."[40] In other words, regardless of the quantity of pleasure involved, poetry may be judged to be more desirable and more valuable than pushpin.

Obviously this is contrary to utilitarianism. Pleasure, in this view, is not the ultimate normative criterion. Mill had no doubt that it was "better to be a Socrates dissatisfied than a fool satisfied."[41] This utterly destroys the basis on which utilitarian economists since Bastiat have constructed normative economic theories, and have attempted to show the universal beneficence of exchange. We must, therefore, conclude that despite the fact that Mill claimed to espouse a utilitarian point of view, and despite the fact that utilitarianism significantly influenced his views, he was certainly not a consistent utilitarian.

Mill's Theory of Value

Mill began chapter 1 of Book 1 of the *Principles* with a statement of the labor theory perspective; that is, production consisted simply of labor transforming natural resources: "The requisites of production are two: labour and appropriate natural objects. . . . In all but . . . [a] few . . . unimportant cases, the objects supplied by nature are only instrumental to human wants, after having undergone some degree of transformation by human exertion."[42] In keeping with his claim of being a disciple of Ricardo, Mill started with something very close to a labor theory of value:

> What the production of a thing costs its producer, or its series of producers, is the labour expended in producing it. . . . At the first glance indeed this seems to be only a part of . . . [a capitalist's] outlay, since he has not only paid wages to labourers, but has likewise provided them with tools, materials, and perhaps buildings. These tools, materials, and buildings, however, were produced by the labour and capital; and their value . . . depends on cost of production, which again is resolvable into labour. . . .
> . . . The value of commodities, therefore, depends principally (we shall presently see whether it depends solely) on the quantity of labour required for their production.[43]

Thus, according to his claim of being a disciple of Ricardo, Mill appeared to have stated a labor theory of value. But the last sentence of the above quotation is important. He went on to claim that while labor was the most important determinant of value, it was not the only determinant. Just as his qualifications of Bentham's pleasure principle ultimately constituted an antagonistic critique of utilitarianism, so his qualifications of the labor theory of value culminated in a rejection of that theory.

The labor theory of value held, Mill argued, only when the ratios of capital to labor were the same in all industries; in that case, the costs of production would be proportional to the labor embodied in the various commodities. But this was not the case for most commodities. For example, wine and cloth produced by equal quantities of labor would have different values because wine was "called upon to yield profit during a longer period of time than the other."[44] Furthermore, "all commodities made by machinery are assimilated, at least approximately, to the wine in the preceding example."[45]

Ricardo, of course, had been well aware of these causes of prices deviating from proportionality to labor values. He had, however, considered them of secondary importance and believed that they could be systematically accounted for while still retaining the labor theory of value. Mill disagreed. He reverted back to Smith's "adding-up" cost-of-production theory, which, it will be remembered, Ricardo had opposed for good reason.

Mill's eclecticism, however, led to persistent inconsistencies. Sometimes his view of profits was identical to Ricardo's; profits were simply the surplus produce of labor over and above the produce necessary to sustain laborers. This view was clearly stated in the following quotation:

> The cause of profit is, that labour produces more than is required for its support.... To vary the form of the theorem: the reason why capital yields a profit, is because food, clothing, materials, and tools, last longer than the time which was required to produce them; so that if a capitalist supplies a party of labourers with these things, on condition of receiving all they produce, they will, in addition to reproducing their own necessaries and instruments, have a portion of their time remaining, to work for the capitalist. We thus see that profit arises, not from the incident of exchange, but from the productive power of labour.[46]

In Mill's simple adding-up cost-of-production theory, however, market price was determined by supply and demand. Over time, the market price would approximate the natural price (as was the case in Smith's theory), which was equal to the summation of the three components of cost: the price of land, the price of labor, and the price of capital. This view was antithetical to the labor theory because it assumed that *profit was the natural price of capital*, rather than a surplus or a residual. Furthermore, profit was a *price* paid in an *exchange* for some *service* of a capitalist. Thus, contrary to the above quotation from Mill, the adding-up cost-of-production theory saw profit originating because of exchange, not production.

When Mill shifted to his adding-up cost-of-production theory, the effect on his view of profits was obvious:

> As the wages of the labourer are the remuneration of labour, so the profits of the capitalist are properly, according to Mr. Senior's well-chosen expression, the remuneration of abstinence. They are what he gains by forbearing to consume his capital for his own uses, and allowing it to be consumed by productive labourers for their uses. For this forbearance he requires a recompense.[47]

This view, rather than Ricardo's, dominated Mill's *Principles*. He unequivocally stated that profit was the remuneration for services and that there was a minimum or natural rate of profit:

> The gross profits from capital ... must ... afford a sufficient equivalent for abstinence, indemnity for risk, and remuneration for the labour and skill required for superintendence.... The lowest rate of profit which can permanently exist, is that which is barely adequate ... to afford an equivalent for the abstinence, risk and exertion implied in the employment of capital.[48]

Thus, in this view profit did arise in exchange and not in production. Profit was the remuneration, through exchange, for abstinence, risk, and exertion.

Mill believed that nearly all natural prices were determined by his adding-up cost-of-production theory. Unlike Ricardo and Marx, he abandoned the notion that labor underlay the exchange value of a commodity. Value for Mill meant simply exchange value, or relative price. He had no notion of labor value. He therefore did not understand why Ricardo had sought an invariable measure of value (see chapter 5) and dismissed Ricardo's search as both impossible and irrelevant to value theory.[49]

Mill discussed several exceptions to the rule that the costs of production determine natural prices. Two of his exceptions were of particular importance: the cases of international prices and the price of labor, or wages. Mill's theory of the determination of international prices was perhaps one of his most significant original contributions to economic theory. With modifications, it remains today the principal orthodox theory of international prices. We will discuss this theory only very briefly here. In the next section of this chapter, we shall discuss his writings on the determination of wages.

Ricardo showed (see chapter 5) that when two countries had different ratios of costs in the production of two commodities, both countries could benefit from specializing in the production of the commodity that they produced *relatively* more cheaply. This mutual benefit would depend on the international ratio of exchange (i.e., the international price ratio), which would fall somewhere between the two ratios of costs prevailing in the two countries. But Ricardo made no attempt to explain how international prices were actually determined.

Within one country, Mill argued, prices were equal to the costs of production because competition tended to equalize these costs (including an equalization of the rate of profit) and to force prices into equality with costs. The factors of production could not, however, move freely between countries. Therefore, competition would not equalize wage or profit rates between different countries; price ratios would not be equalized; and international prices would depend exclusively on supply and demand—not on costs of production.

Mill proposed that international supply and demand could be analyzed on the supposition that each country would always be forced to balance its international payments, that is, the income from exports would have to equal the outlay for imports. Therefore, at each possible price (between the limits of the cost ratios prevailing in the two countries), each country would offer a certain quantity of its exports in exchange for a certain quantity of the other country's exports. As the price varied, the quantities offered and demanded would vary. On a graph, a curve could be constructed depicting the various quantities a given country would export and import, always keeping international payments equal to receipts, at every price falling between the ratios of production costs in the two countries. Such a curve has come to be known as an "offer curve." Each country would have such an offer curve. If these curves crossed at a particular price, then that price would equate the value of the imports the first country demanded with the value of the exports the second country supplied and vice versa. Then, prices that fulfilled this condition would be equilibrium prices, whereby the "produce of a country exchanges for the produce of other countries, at such values as are required in order that the whole of her exports may exactly pay for the whole of her imports."[50]

Mill on Wages

In chapter 6 we saw that Senior used the wages fund doctrine to argue that the wages of labor were determined by the size of the fund that capitalists had set aside to pay wages and the number of workers among whom this fund had to be divided. Nearly all of the classical economists had accepted some version of the wages fund doctrine, and, in his *Principles*, Mill accepted it. "The demand for labour," he asserted, "is constituted solely by the funds directly set apart for the use of labourers."[51] This meant that wages would depend on the supply of labor, or the number of workers sharing this fund. Mill, like Malthus and most of the classical economists, believed that the most effective way of raising the wages of labor was through education, which would decrease the size of laborers' families.

Malthus had concluded that laborers did not have the "moral character" to practice sexual abstinence and were therefore condemned to misery and vice, or, ultimately, starvation. Mill, however, did not consider birth control to be a vice. He believed that through education workers would increasingly make use of various methods of birth control, which would limit the size of their families and raise their standard of living.

Senior used the wages fund doctrine to argue for the uselessness of labor combinations. Mill arrived at a very different conclusion, however. "Experience of strikes" made possible by combinations, he asserted, "has been the best teacher of the labouring classes on the subject of the relation between wages and the demand and supply of labour."[52]

In 1869, however, in a review of a book by William T. Thornton, Mill repudiated the wages fund doctrine. In this review, Mill argued that wages were not limited by the amount that capitalists had previously set aside to pay for labor. Rather, the limit was the total profits of capitalists minus what the capitalists needed "to maintain themselves and their families."[53] Therefore, wages would not be determined by the wages fund but by a competitive struggle between laborers and capitalists. Mill had reversed the wages fund doctrine: now the size of the wages fund was determined by the rate of wages, which was determined by class struggle. If a capitalist "has to pay more for labour, the additional payment comes out of his own income."[54]

Thus, Mill came to see combinations and labor strikes as not only educational but also potentially important in redistributing income from profits to wages. Unlike Malthus, Say, Senior, and Bastiat, Mill's sympathy was with the workers:

Having regard to the greatly superior numbers of the labouring class, and the inevitable scantiness of the remuneration afforded by even the highest rates of wages which, in the present state of the arts of production, could possibly become general; whoever does not wish that the labourers may prevail and that the highest limit, whatever it be, may be attained, must have a standard of morals, and a conception of the most desirable state of society, widely different from those of either Mr. Thornton or the present writer.[55]

Mill's recantation of the wages fund doctrine was important in influencing his opinion of the possible gains to the working class of combining into unions and struggling collectively against the capitalists. It did not, however, change his earlier position, stated in the *Principles*, that the price of labor—wages— was *not* determined by the costs of production. In fact, repudiating the wages fund doctrine strengthened his view that wages were determined more by social and political factors than by narrowly defined economic factors.

Tendency for the Rate of Profit to Fall

One area in which Mill considered himself a disciple of Ricardo was his theory of the long-run decline in the rate of profit. He expressed agreement with Ricardo's view in one sentence: "The effect of accumulation, when attended by its usual accompaniment, an increase of population, is to increase the value and price of food, to raise rent and to lower profits."[56] Here, as in so many other parts of Mill's writings, the qualifications were more important than the original principle. He discussed several circumstances that would counteract the tendency for the rate of profit to fall. Of those counteracting forces, two were particularly important—the export of capital and periodic commercial crises.

Mill's discussion of the export of capital is important because it is very similar to that of Marx and that of Lenin, the latter of which was developed after European imperialism had become a major world force. For Mill, the export of capital was one of the most important

counter-forces which check the downward tendency of profits, in a country whose capital increases faster than that of its neighbours and whose profits are therefore nearer to the minimum. This is the perpetual overflow of capital into colonies or foreign countries, to seek higher profits than can be obtained at home. . . . It has a twofold operation. In the first place, it does what a fire, or an inundation, or a commercial crisis would have done: it carries off a part of the increase of capital from which the reduction of profits proceeds. Secondly, the capital so carried off is not lost, but it is chiefly employed . . . in founding colonies, which become large exporters of cheap agricultural produce. . . . It is to the emigration of English capital, that we have chiefly to look for keeping up a supply of cheap food and cheap materials of clothing, proportional to the increase in our population; thus enabling an increasing capital to find employment in . . . [our] country, without a reduction in profit. . . . Thus, the exportation of capital is an agent of great efficacy in extending the field of employment for that which remains; and it may be said truly that . . . the more capital we send away, the more we shall possess and be able to retain at home.[57]

The second counteracting force was "one which is so simple and so conspicuous, that some political economists . . . have attended to it almost to the exclusion of all others. This is, the waste of capital in periods of over-trading and rash speculation, and in the commercial revulsions by which such times are always followed."[58] Thus, Mill argued that periodic business crises destroyed capital and stemmed the downward tendency of the rate of profit. From this, it would appear that Mill could be classed with Malthus and Marx as a nineteenth-century theorist who rejected Say's law that market capitalism automatically tends to produce full employment. He asserted that there were recurring periods of "over-trading" and "rash speculation" during which "mines are opened, railways or bridges made, and many other works of uncertain profit commenced." More important, "factories are built and machinery erected beyond what the market requires, or can keep in employment."[59] Inevitably, after "a few years have passed over without a crisis, so much additional capital has been accumulated, that it is no longer possible to invest it at the accustomed profit."[60] When that happened,

> establishments are shut up, or kept working without any profit, hands are discharged, and numbers of persons in all ranks, being deprived of their income . . . find themselves, after the crisis has passed away, in a condition of more or less impoverishment. Such are the effects of a commercial revulsion: and that such revulsions are almost periodical, is a consequence of the very tendency of profits which we are considering.[61]

But despite this insightful analysis of depressions and business cycles, Mill defended Say's law.

When he considered Malthus's doctrine "that there may be a supply of commodities in the aggregate surpassing the demand," he concluded, "The doctrine appears to me to involve so much inconsistency in its very conception, that I feel considerable difficulty in giving any statement of it which shall be at once clear, and satisfactory to its supporters."[62]

Mill's objection to Malthus's doctrine and his defense of Say's law rested on two points, one definitional and one theoretical. First, Mill simply insisted on labeling what others called "an overproduction of commodities" or a "general glut" as an "under-supply of money": "At such times there is really an excess of all commodities above the money demand: in other words there is an undersupply of money."[63] But neither Malthus nor any other theorist had ever stated that there was an oversupply of goods relative to human needs or desires. They had only said exactly what Mill had stated: that an oversupply of goods relative to money demand frequently existed. Mill's definitional quibble hardly elucidated a glaring inconsistency that would render the principle hard to state clearly.

Second, Mill's theoretical objection to Malthus's doctrine, and consequent defense of Say's law, was simply a statement that, *in the long run,* market capitalism would automatically pull out of depressions and ultimately attain full employment. He agreed that these "derangements of markets" were a social "evil" but insisted that they were "temporary."[64] The most famous twentieth-century elaborator of Malthus's doctrine, John Maynard Keynes, was to say in response to Mill's and subsequent neoclassical economists' defenses of Say's law: "In the long run we are all dead." Meanwhile, as Mill himself said, each crisis left innumerable people "in a condition of more or less impoverishment."

Mill on Socialism

Mill, unlike Say, Senior, and Bastiat, did not defend private ownership of the means of production as sacrosanct. Unlike Senior and Bastiat, he had read widely in actual history and did not conjure up a "history" of private property and wealth whereby the thrifty, industrious, and virtuous had supposedly accumulated capital and the profligate sinners had squandered everything to the point where they and their families had nothing. He wrote:

> The social arrangements of modern Europe commenced from a distribution of property which was the result, not of just partition, or acquisition by industry, but of conquest and violence: and notwithstanding what industry has been doing . . . to modify the work of force, the system still retains many and large traces of its origin. The laws of property have never yet conformed to the principles on which the justification of private property rests.[65]

Moreover, Mill morally condemned the effects of the concentration of the ownership of nearly all of the means of production in the hands of a small capitalist class. He realized that this created a tiny parasitic class, living in luxury, whose income had no necessary connection to productive activity. The existing class structure was, he believed, "by no means a necessary or permanent state of social relations":

> I do not recognize as either just or salutary, a state of society in which there is any "class" which is not labouring; any human beings, exempt from bearing their share of the necessary labours of human life, except those unable to labor, or who have fairly earned rest by previous toil. So long, however, as the great social evil exists of a non-labouring class, labourers also constitute a class.[66]

Mill not only morally rejected the capitalist class structure of his time, because of its extremes of wealth and poverty, he also believed it would ultimately be abolished. "It is not to be expected," he wrote, "that the division of the human race into two hereditary classes, employers and employed, can be permanently maintained."[67] The principal question that concerned Mill was the direction and speed of the social change by which capitalism would evolve into some form of socialist or communist society. There was no question in his mind about whether a communist society would be morally superior to the capitalist society of his era:

> If, therefore, the choice were to be made between Communism with all its chances, and the present state of society with all its sufferings and injustices; if the institution of private property necessarily carried with it as a consequence, that the produce of labour should be apportioned as we now see it, almost in an inverse ratio to the labour the largest portion to those who have never worked at all, the next largest to those whose work is almost nominal, and so on in a descending scale, the remuneration dwindling as the work grows harder and more disagreeable, until the most fatiguing and exhausting bodily labour cannot count with certainty on being able to earn even the necessaries of life; if this or Communism were the alternative, all the difficulties, great or small, of Communism would be but as dust in the balance.[68]

However, despite Mill's beliefs that either socialism or communism was morally preferable to the capitalism of his era and that a society divided "into two hereditary classes" could not "be permanently maintained," it is questionable whether he could properly be called a socialist. On this point, his anti-utilitarian judgments of different character types—or different kinds of desires and pleasures—became important. Socialism would become a possibility when, and only when, people's characters had been elevated. A socialist society, he insisted, was "at present workable only by the *elite* of mankind."[69]

In the meantime, the competitive "struggle for riches" was all that was possible for the majority of society:

> That the energies of mankind should be kept in employment by the struggle for riches . . . until the better minds succeed in educating the others into better things, is undoubtedly more desirable than that they should rust and stagnate. While minds are coarse they require coarse stimuli, and let them have them. In the meantime, those who do not accept the present very early stage of human improvement as its ultimate type, may be excused for being comparatively indifferent to the kind of economic progress which excites the congratulations of ordinary politicians; the mere increase of production and accumulation.[70]

Mill advocated the encouragement of small cooperatives, such as those proposed by Owen and Fourier. "Whatever may be the merits or defects of these various schemes," he argued, "they cannot be truly said to be impracticable."[71] Over a long period of time, if these cooperatives prove to be economically and socially successful, then "there can be no doubt . . . that the relation of masters and workpeople will be gradually superseded by partnership, in one of two forms: in some cases, association of the labourers with the capitalist; in others, and perhaps finally in all, association of labourers among themselves."[72] But this was to be a spontaneous, voluntary process that would undoubtedly take a very long time. Mill advocated that

> in the meantime we may, without attempting to limit the ultimate capabilities of human nature, affirm that the political economist, for a considerable time to come, will be chiefly concerned with the conditions of existence and progress belonging to a society founded on private property and individual competition; and that the object to be principally aimed at, in the present stage of human improvement, is not the subversion of the system of individual property, but the improvement of it, and the full participation of every member of the community in its benefits.[73]

Mill's Interventionist Reformism

Despite his sympathy for socialist ideas, Mill's real objective was to promote the reform of capitalism. Against those, such as Bastiat, who believed in the sacredness of existing property rights, Mill argued that "society is fully entitled to abrogate or alter any particular right of property which on sufficient consideration it judges to stand in the way of the public good."[74] In accordance with this view of property, Mill stated that

> it is not admissible that the protection of persons and that of property are the sole purposes of government. The ends of government are as comprehensive as those of social union. They consist of all the good and all the immunity from evil, which the existence of government can be made either directly or indirectly to bestow.[75]

Mill believed that the government should intervene to modify the socially adverse effects of the free market in three principal areas. First, as a result of free market capitalism, "the immense majority are condemned from their birth to a life of never-ending, never-intermitting toil, requited by a bare, and in general a precarious, subsistence."[76] Second, the natural complement of this extreme poverty was "that a small minority of mankind . . . [was] born to the enjoyment of all the external advantages which life can give, without earning them by any merit or acquiring them by any exertion of their own."[77] Third, there were many businesses that could

> only be advantageously carried on by a large capital, this in most countries limits so narrowly the class of persons who can enter into the employment, that they are enabled to keep their rate of profit above the general level. A trade may also, from the nature of the case, be confined to so few hands, that profits may admit of being kept up by a combination of the dealers. . . . [78]

> The monopolist can fix the value as high as he pleases, short of what the consumer either could not or would not pay; but he can only do so by limiting the supply.[79]

Thus, in spite of Mill's insistence that "*laissez faire* . . . should be the general practice" and that "every departure from it, unless required by some great good, is a certain evil,"[80] he advocated active government intervention in each of these three areas.

In his proposed measures to eradicate poverty, we can see how far Mill was from agreeing with the utilitarian dictum that "quantity of pleasure being equal, pushpin is as good as poetry." We have seen that the principle involved in that dictum—and the principle is at the very heart of utilitarianism—is that every individual is always the best judge of his or her own welfare. Remembering the earlier quotation from Mill comparing a "dissatisfied Socrates" and a "satisfied fool," it is not surprising that he wrote:

> The individual who is presumed to be the best judge of his own interests may be incapable of judging . . . for himself. . . . In this case the foundation of the *laissez*

faire principle breaks down entirely. The person most interested is not [always] the best judge of the matter, nor a competent judge at all.[81]

The poor, he argued, were frequently not in a position to judge properly what would best promote their interests. To alter the characters, habits, and judgments of the poor, Mill believed:

> There is need of a twofold action, directed simultaneously upon their intelligence and their poverty. An effective national education of the children of the labouring class, is the first thing needful; and, coincidentally with this, a system of measures which shall . . . extinguish extreme poverty for one whole generation.[82]

The principal means suggested by Mill for extinguishing extreme poverty for an entire generation were, first, "a grant of public money, sufficient to remove at once, and establish in the colonies, a considerable fraction of the youthful agricultural population," and second, the devotion of "all common land, hereafter brought into cultivation . . . to the benefit of the poor."[83]

Against those who believed that the financing of such schemes would drastically curtail the accumulation of capital, Mill asserted that "the funds . . . would not be drawn from the capital employed in maintaining labour, but from that surplus which cannot find employment . . . and which is therefore sent abroad for investment, or wasted at home in reckless speculations."[84]

An interesting inconsistency in Mill's ideas may be noted here: If such excess capital was to be more or less continuously available for an entire generation, then how could Mill maintain that it was only because of the existing rate of profit that people saved and practiced abstinence? Once again, this inconsistency is an important clue to the social class orientation of Mill's writings. He was an eclectic humanitarian whose aversion to injustice and the extremes of wealth and poverty, however strong it was, was not sufficient to cause him to abandon entirely the ideological rationale for capitalists' receipt of profits.

In addition to the above, Mill advocated laws protecting the rights of working people to form unions, laws preventing the abuse or overworking of children in any hired employment,[85] and laws limiting the number of hours a worker may be employed.[86] Laws limiting the length of the working day were necessary because of the powerlessness of a single worker when bargaining with a capitalist. As long as capitalists could easily replace any given worker, then no single worker or small group of workers would ever have the power to decrease the length of the working day, regardless of how beneficial such a reduction would be to all society. A similar argument could be made for laws enforcing minimum safety standards in all factories. Finally, the government should, Mill believed, provide a minimum subsistence for all those unable or unwilling to work. In this regard, he defended Senior's philosophy that underlay the Poor Law of 1834. Assistance to the indigent was good, Mill argued, only "if, while available to everybody, it leaves to everyone a strong motive to do without it if he can. . . . This principle, applied to a system of public charity, is that of the poor law of 1834."[87]

The principal reform whereby Mill sought to diminish the extremes of wealth was a tax on inheritances:

> The power of bequeathing is one of the privileges of property which are fit subjects for regulation on grounds of general expediency; and . . . as a possible mode of restraining the accumulation of large fortunes in the hands of those who have not earned them by exertion, [there should be] a limitation of the amount which any person should be permitted to acquire by gift, bequest, or inheritance.[88]

The final major area in which Mill advocated government intervention into the market was where a natural monopoly or a monopolistic control by a few colluding sellers resulted in harm to society's well being. "There are many cases," he wrote, "in which a practical monopoly, with all the powers it confers of taxing the community, cannot be prevented from existing."[89] In such cases,

> the community needs some other security . . . than the interest of the managers; and it is the part of the government, either to subject the business to reasonable conditions for the general advantage, or to retain such power over it that the profits of the monopoly may at least be obtained by the public.[90]

A Critique of Mill's Reformism

One central theme of the present book is that utilitarianism—particularly the utility theory of value and exchange—when consistently developed, generally provides a powerful intellectual justification for the status quo of market capitalism. Mill, however, was a reformer who claimed to be a utilitarian. But as we have seen, his views contradicted two of the cardinal tenets of utilitarianism: the notion that all motives are reducible to self-interest and the notion that each individual's desires or pleasures are synonymous with his or her well-being; that is, each individual is always the best judge of his or her own welfare.

Had Mill been a consistent utilitarian, his reformist views would be easy to dismiss. Not only does utilitarianism preclude the possibility of invidious comparisons of the desires of different individuals (which is, as discussed in the previous chapter, the basis of its severely restricted applicability to only those situations in which unanimity prevails), it is so extremely individualistic that its own social ethic can be shown to be incompatible with its individual ethic. The proof of this statement is simple: if something is good only because it is desired by, or gives pleasure to, a particular individual, then a maximum of total social utility is good only if it is desired by a particular individual. If all individuals desire maximum social utility, then the utilitarian unanimity requirement is satisfied and there are no problems. But let there be even one misanthrope in society and contradiction appears. The misanthrope derives pleasure from the pain of others. The optimum situation for him or her would be a maximum of human pain, or a maximum social disutility, or a minimum of social utility. But pushpin is as good as poetry. We have no basis in utilitarianism for elevating the desires of a philanthropist (if indeed there can be such people who act exclusively from self-interest) above those of the misanthrope. Where, then, does this leave the utilitarian social ethic? It requires unanimity or it is nonexistent.

But suppose we grant utilitarianism both its individualistic ethic and its social ethic on the grounds that the foundations, or first principles, of any philosophical system ought not to be used as a basis for rejecting that philosophy itself. Utilitarianism still leaves no room for us to hope that a government will institute reforms designed to maximize utility. There are two reasons for this: first, the government would have to restrict itself to those reforms that had the unanimous support of every person. If a minority opposed the reform, then the government would be left in the position of comparing the increased pleasures of some people with the decreased pleasures of others. When discussing twentieth-century neoclassical welfare economics, we will see that, down to the present time, utilitarians have never found an escape from their unanimity requirement. If the good depends exclusively on subjective states of individuals' consciousnesses, then unanimity is required because such states can never be directly compared.

The second reason utilitarianism cannot be the intellectual basis for advocating reforms was mentioned above in our discussions of both Bastiat and Bentham: governments are made up of people. If all people act exclusively from self-interest, then we must endeavor to find what would be in the self-interest of politicians in a capitalist system. To ask the question is to answer it. Money is, and always has been, the lifeblood of politics in a capitalist system. To come to political power requires money and money perpetuates such power. The laws of private property and contracts as well as the innumerable legal privileges of monopoly, subsidies, and tax exemptions all support and perpetuate the existing extremes of wealth and poverty. It is difficult to imagine an exchange that would be of more mutual benefit to the parties involved than that between the politicians in a capitalist system and those who derive their massive wealth and incomes from the legal foundations of capitalism.

While this second critique is decisive against utilitarian reformism, it merely poses an extraordinarily difficult obstacle for other reformers who do not accept the utilitarian philosophy. In this respect, Mill's rejection of utilitarianism simply meant that the possibility of his reforms was not precluded by his view of human nature. Had he been a consistent utilitarian, he would have had to believe that every politician was only interested in his own welfare. A politician acting in accordance with the utilitarian view of human nature would support political reforms designed to promote the welfare of the poor at the expense of the rich only if such a change was more profitable for that politician. But having rejected two of the most fundamental tenets of utilitarianism, it was possible for Mill to hope that a public-spirited, benevolent politician who was primarily concerned with the general public welfare might come to power.

Thus, the problem for Mill was not one of an impossibility (insofar as he rejected Benthamite utilitarianism) but rather an improbability. The problem for Mill was that he was a part of a capitalist system in which money was power and power begot more money. In Mill's own words, in capitalism "the energies of mankind" were "kept in employment by the struggle for riches." And "while minds are coarse they require coarse stimuli."[91]

Mill was not totally unaware of this difficulty. He realized that as long as the capitalists and workers viewed themselves as antagonistic classes, politics would be an arena of class struggle in which, under normal circumstances, capitalists could be expected to dominate. He hoped, however, that the "struggle for riches" might eventually subside among the wealthy. They might become satisfied with what they already had. If this happened, the prospects for reform would indeed be improved. Under these circumstances, Mill wrote, "where the rich are content with being rich, and do not claim as such any political privileges, their interest and that of the poor are generally the same."[92]

Unfortunately for the poor, in the 143 years since the publication of Mill's *Principles of Political Economy*, the rich have seldom been "content with being rich" and have never renounced their claim to "political privileges." Rereading Mill's quotation on page 196, one wonders where he would stand today.

Notes to Chapter 8

1. Quoted in Alexander Gray, *The Socialist Tradition* (London: Longmans, 1963), p. 105.

2. Quoted in Sydney H. Coontz, *Productive Labor and Effective Demand* (New York: Augustus M. Kelley, 1966), p. 54.

3. Frédéric Bastiat, *Economic Harmonies* (Princeton, NJ: D. Van Nostrand, 1964), p. xxv.

4. Ibid., p. 569.

5. Ibid., p. 487.

6. Ibid., p. 66.

7. Ibid., p. 59.

8. Ibid., p. 81.

9. Ibid., p. xxi.

10. Ibid., pp. xxxiii–xxxiv.

11. Ibid., p. 27.

12. Ibid., p. 46.

13. Ibid., p. 27.

14. Ibid.

15. Ibid., p. 33.

16. Ibid., p. 27.

17. Bastiat, *Economic Harmonies*, p. 75.

18. Ibid., p. 134.

19. Ibid., p. 148.

20. Ibid., p. 150.

21. Frédéric Bastiat, *Selected Essays on Political Economy* (Princeton, NJ: D. Van Nostrand, 1964), p. 97.

22. Ibid., p. 99.

23. Bastiat, *Economic Harmonies*, p. 200.

24. Ibid., p. 196.

25. Ibid., p. 29.

26. Ibid., p. 253.

27. Ibid., p. 459.

28. Ibid., p. 455.

29. Ibid., p. 457.

30. Ibid., p. 26.

31. Ibid., p. 36.

32. Ibid., p. 192.

33. Ibid., p. 193.

34. Ibid., p. xxiv.

35. Ibid., p. xxxvii.

36. John Stuart Mill, *Principles of Political Economy* (New York: Augustus M. Kelley, 1965), p. 21.

37. *Ibid.*, p. 21.

38. *Ibid.*, p. 233.

39. *Ibid.*, pp. 435–436.

40. John Stuart Mill, "Utilitarianism," in *Utilitarianism, Liberty, and Representative Government* (New York: Dutton, 1951), p. 10.

41. Ibid., p. 12.

42. Mill, *Principles*, p. 22.

43. Ibid., pp. 457–58.

44. Ibid., p. 463.

45. Ibid.

46. Ibid., pp. 416–17.

47. Ibid., p. 404.

48. Ibid., pp. 406–7.

49. Ibid., pp. 564–68.

50. Ibid., p. 592.

51. Ibid., p. 80.

52. Ibid., p. 936.

53. John Stuart Mill, *Dissertations and Discussions*, 5 vols. (New York: Henry Holt, 1874), vol. 5, p. 49.

54. Ibid., vol. 5, p. 50.

55. Ibid., vol. 5, p. 75.

56. Mill, *Principles*, p. 842.

57. Ibid., pp. 738–39.

58. Ibid., pp. 733–34.

59. Ibid., p. 734.

60. Ibid.

61. Ibid.

62. Ibid., pp. 556–57.

63. Ibid., p. 561.

64. Ibid.

65. Ibid., p. 208.

66. Ibid., pp. 752–53.

67. Ibid., p. 761.

68. Ibid., p. 208.

69. John Stuart Mill, "Socialism," in *Socialism and Utiltarianism* (Chicago: Belfords, Clarke and Co., 1879), pp. 123–24.

70. Mill, *Principles*, p. 749.

71. Ibid., p. 204.

72. Ibid., pp. 763–64.

73. Ibid., p. 217.

74. Mill, "Socialism," p. 136.
75. Mill, *Principles*, pp. 804–5.
76. Mill, *Dissertations and Discussions*, vol. 3, p. 59.
77. Ibid., 3:59.
78. Mill, *Principles*, p. 410.
79. Ibid., p. 449.
80. Ibid., p. 950.
81. Ibid., p. 957.
82. Ibid., p. 380.
83. Ibid., pp. 381–82.
84. Ibid., p. 382.
85. Ibid., p. 958.
86. Ibid., pp. 963–64.
87. Ibid., p. 968.
88. Ibid., p. 809.
89. Ibid., p. 962.
90. Ibid.
91. Ibid., p. 749.
92. Mill, *Dissertations and Discussions*, vol. 2, p. 114.

Chapter 9

Karl Marx

Very few thinkers in history have formulated ideas, both in intellectual matters and in practical affairs, that have had an impact equal to those of Karl Marx (1818–1883). The intellectual, political, economic, and social influences of his ideas are sufficiently well known as to need no elaboration here. Like most intellectual geniuses, from the time of the ancient Greeks to the present, he formulated a complete, integrated intellectual system, which included elaborate conceptions of ontology and epistemology, of human nature, of the nature of society and the individual's relationship to the social whole, and of the nature of the process of social history.

Because his intellectual system was an integrated whole, it can be argued that no part of the system can be understood fully except by putting it into its proper context within the whole system. While the present writer has some sympathy toward this argument, it is not possible to do this within the limited scope of this book. We will therefore neglect many aspects of Marx's writings entirely and touch on others only very briefly when necessary in our discussion of his ideas concerning the nature, origins, and mode of functioning of a capitalist economy. Only these latter ideas will constitute the focus of this chapter.

Marx's analysis of capitalism was most fully developed in his three-volume work, *Capital*, of which only the first volume was published in his lifetime (in 1867). Rough drafts and notes, which were to have been rewritten and published as volumes 2 and 3, were written mostly in the mid-1860s (before the completion of volume 1) and remained unfinished when Marx died in 1883. They were edited, pieced together, and published by Frederick Engels (volume 2 in 1885 and volume 3 in 1894). Marx wrote many other books, pamphlets, and articles containing analyses of capitalism; of particular importance is a series of seven notebooks, written in 1857 and 1858, which were rough drafts of many of the analyses that were to be developed in *Capital* and other topics that Marx had intended to include in an even larger work, of which *Capital* was to be the first part. These notebooks were published in German under the title *Grundrisse der Kritik der Politischen Ökonomie* (Foundations of the Critique of Political Economy). The English translation of these notebooks was published under the title *Grundrisse*. It is a useful supplement to *Capital* as the chief source of Marx's economic ideas.

Marx's Critique of Classical Economics

Marx's relationship to the thinkers we have discussed in previous chapters was complex. He was deeply influenced by the theories of value and profits of Smith and Ricardo—and, in some respects, his theory can be seen as an extension, refinement, and elaboration of their ideas. Concerning other aspects of their theories, however, Marx considered himself an antagonistic critic. He also quoted frequently and approvingly from the writings of Thompson and Hodgskin, but here, again, Marx was highly critical of many of their ideas. He took Mill seriously as an intellectual opponent but was nearly entirely critical and contemptuous of Malthus, Bentham, Senior, Say, and Bastiat.

The greatest deficiency of most of these thinkers, in Marx's opinion, was their lack of historical perspective (although this criticism applied least to Smith). Had they studied history more thoroughly, Marx insisted, they would have discovered that production is a social activity that can take many forms or modes, depending on the prevailing forms of social organization and their corresponding techniques of production. European society had passed through several distinct historical epochs, or modes of production, including slave society and feudal society, and was currently organized in a historically specific form: capitalism.

Had these economic writers made a detailed study of these various modes of production, they would have discovered that "all epochs of production have certain common traits, common characteristics."[1] But as indispensable to production as some of these characteristics were, the first step toward understanding any one mode—such as capitalism—was to isolate the features that were both essential to and particular to that mode of production:

> The elements which are not general and common, must be separated out from the . . . (features common to all) production as such, so that in their unity—which arises already from the identity of the subject, humanity, and of the object, nature, their essential difference is not forgotten. The whole profundity of those modern economists who demonstrate the eternity and harmoniousness of the existing social relations lies in this forgetting.[2]

This failure to differentiate between those characteristics of production that were common to all modes of production and those that were specific to capitalism led to innumerable confusions and distortions. Two of these confusions were particularly important, in Marx's opinion: the first was the belief that capital was a universal element in all production processes, and the second was that all economic activity could be reduced to a series of exchanges. Nearly all of the previous economists had been guilty of the first confusion (with the exception, as we have seen, of Hodgskin). Most of the economists writing after Ricardo (particularly Senior and Bastiat) had been guilty of the second confusion.

The misidentification of capital stemmed from the fact that capital had one feature that was universal in all production and one feature particular to capitalism. "Production," Marx admitted, was not "possible without an instrument of production," nor could there be

> production without stored-up past labour. . . . Capital is, among other things, also an instrument of production, also objectified, past labour. Therefore capital is a general, eternal relation of nature; that is, if I leave out just the specific quality which alone makes "instrument of production" and "stored-up labour" into capital.[3]

That specific quality was the *power of capital to yield profits* to a special social class. Only in capitalism were "instruments of production" and "stored-up labour" the source of the income and power of the dominant social class. Marx, in contrast to the economists that he criticized, sought to understand how this aspect of capital came into existence and then how it was perpetuated.

Most economists prior to Marx had believed that property was sacrosanct (Mill, of course, was an exception to this). Furthermore, they had identified property in general with its existing form as capitalist private property. Marx objected to this; he also objected to Mill's total separation of production and distribution. There were innumerable forms of property, Marx insisted, and each particular mode of production had its particular forms of property, and these forms of property determined distribution. Thus, production and distribution were not, as Mill had believed, independent of each other:

> All production is appropriation of nature on the part of an individual within and through a specific form of society. In this sense it is a tautology to say that property (appropriation) is a precondition of production. But it is altogether ridiculous to leap from that to a specific form of property, e.g., private property. . . . History rather shows common property (e.g., in India, among the Slavs, the early Celts, etc.) to be the more original form, a form which long continues to play a significant role in the shape of communal property. . . .
>
> Every form of production creates its own legal relations [types of property], form of government, etc. . . . All the bourgeois economists are aware of is that production can be carried on better under the modern police than e.g., on the principle of might makes right. They forget only that this principle [might makes right] is also a legal relation, and that the right of the stronger prevails in their "constitutional republics" as well, only in another form.[4]

When the bourgeois economists (to use Marx's term) accepted existing capitalist property rights as universal, eternal, and sacrosanct and viewed capital as common to all production, the institutions that in Marx's opinion were the distinguishing features of capitalism were put outside the purview of their analyses. What, then, was left for them to analyze in their quest to understand capitalism? The answer was simple. In Bastiat's words, "political economy *is* exchange." All economic phenomena were reduced to acts of buying and selling commodities. The entire focus was on exchange, or the sphere of the circulation of money and commodities.

In exchange, individuals began with commodities that they owned. The commodities were seen simply as the embodiment of an exchange value. When a worker's labor was viewed simply as a commodity, having exchange value like any other commodity, then all economic, social, and political distinctions among individuals disappeared. A kind of abstract equality (and very nearly an identity) among individuals appeared:

> Indeed, insofar as the commodity or labour is conceived of only as exchange value, and the relation in which the various commodities are brought into connection with one another is conceived of as the exchange of these exchange values . . . then the individuals . . . are simply and only conceived of as exchangers. As far as the formal character is concerned, there is absolutely no distinction between them. . . . Each of the subjects is an exchanger; i.e., each has the same social relation towards the other that the other has towards him. As subjects of exchange, their relation is therefore that of *equality*. It is impossible to find any trace of distinction, not to speak of contradiction, between them; not even a difference.[5]

> A worker who buys commodities for 3s. appears to the seller in the same function, in the same equality—in the form of 3s.—as the King who does the same. All distinction between them is extinguished. The seller, *qua* seller appears only as owner of a commodity of the price of 3s., so that both are completely equal; only that the 3s exist here in the form of silver, there again in the form of sugar, etc.[6]

Hence, on superficial appearance, a system of exchange appears to be a system of equality.

Given bourgeois economists' total neglect of the features differentiating capitalism from other modes of production, an exchange economy also appeared as one in which human freedom prevailed. In the exchange relationship

> there enters, in addition to the quality of equality, that of *freedom*. Although individual A feels a need for the commodity of individual B, he does not appropriate it by force, nor vice versa, but rather they recognize one another reciprocally as proprietors. . . . No one seizes hold of another's by force. Each divests himself of his property voluntarily.[7]

Finally, an exchange economy also appeared as a system in which actions motivated by pure, egoistic self-interest were channeled, "as though by an invisible hand," into a socially harmonious whole. The motive to exchange clearly presupposed that individuals did not produce or own what they desired or needed. "Only the differences between their needs and between their production gives rise to exchange," Marx wrote.[8] The appearance of harmony was, thus, inevitable:

> Individual A serves the need of individual B by means of the commodity *a* only insofar as and because individual B serves the need of individual A by means of the

commodity *b*, and vice versa. Each serves the other in order to serve himself; each makes use of the other, reciprocally, as his means. . . . As such it is irrelevant to each of the two subjects in exchange . . . that this reciprocity interests him only insofar as it satisfies his interest . . . without reference to that of the other. That is, the common interest which appears as the motive of the act as a whole is recognized as a fact by both sides; but as such, it is not the motive.[9]

Thus, the economic harmony of capitalism was only visible when one accepted "the assertion that there exists only one single economic relation—exchange."[10] Marx's conclusion was obvious:

It is in the character of the money relation—as far as it is developed in its purity to this point, and without regard to more highly developed relations of production—that all inherent contradictions of bourgeois society appear extinguished in money relations as conceived in a simple form; and bourgeois democracy even more than bourgeois economists takes refuge in this aspect . . . in order to construct apologetics for the existing economic relations.[11]

Commodities, Value, Use Value, and Exchange Value

Marx was interested in explaining the nature of the social relationship between capitalists and laborers. In terms of economic theory, this meant explaining the relationship between wages and profits. When one looked only at the sphere of exchange, or circulation, wages and profits both appeared to be the consequences of the simple exchange of commodities. So Marx began volume 1 of *Capital* (subtitled *A Critical Analysis of Capitalist Production*) with an analysis of commodities and the sphere of circulation.

Capitalism was a system in which wealth appeared as "an immense accumulation of commodities, its unit being a single commodity."[12] A commodity had two essential characteristics: first, it was "a thing that by its properties satisfies human wants."[13] The particular physical qualities of a commodity, from which people derived utility, made the commodity a *use value*. The particular physical qualities that rendered a thing useful did not, in Marx's opinion, have any definite or systematic connection to "the amount of labour required to appropriate its useful qualities."[14] Second, commodities were, "in addition, the material depositories of *exchange-value*."[15] The exchange value of a commodity was a ratio of how much of that commodity one could get in exchange for a given amount of some other commodity or commodities.

Exchange value was usually expressed in terms of the money price of a commodity; that is, it was expressed in terms of how much of the commodity money one could get in exchange for one unit of the commodity in question. Thus, if the price of a pair of shoes was $2, then it simply meant that one pair of shoes would exchange for two units of the money commodity (in this case $2), or for a quantity of any other commodity that could be exchanged for $2. Money, then, was a special commodity that was generally used as a *numeraire*, in terms of which exchange values were generally stated, and that also functioned as a universal exchange equivalent. As a universal exchange equivalent, it functioned as a medium of exchange; that is, it was used in nearly every purchase or sale. It was the universal use of money as an exchange equivalent that differentiated a money-exchange economy from a barter-exchange economy. Money was also a means of holding wealth when hoards of wealth were desired in the form of pure exchange value rather than in the form of use values. As we will see later, money could also, under certain circumstances, be a part of capital.

Exchange value was the means by which all commodities could be directly and quantitatively compared. Exchange values presupposed a common element in all commodities by virtue of which such comparisons could be made. In addition to their exchange value, commodities had two other characteristics in common: they all had use values, and they were all produced by human labor alone.

Each of these two common characteristics, as we have asserted earlier in this book, has been assumed to be the determinant of exchange value by different traditions in economic theory. Marx, however, rejected use value as a possible determinant of prices. He wrote, "As use-values, commodities are, above all, of different qualities, but as exchange-values they are merely different quantities."[16] Moreover, use values were primarily relations between particular individuals and material things. Exchange value, however, existed only in very specific social circumstances. Because of this, Marx believed that the foundations of exchange value would have to involve some aspect of the social relations peculiar to those social circumstances. Thus, Marx asserted that the infinite variety of physical qualities that gave commodities their use value, or utility, were neither directly comparable in any quantitative sense nor reflective of the social relations peculiar to capitalist society. Use value could not be the basis of exchange value.

Therefore, the only element that was common to all commodities, directly quantitatively comparable, and an integral part of capitalist social relations, was the labor time required for their production. It would seem that labor is a universal element in all social production and not specific to capitalist social relations. The labor that created the exchange value of commodities, however, had qualitative aspects, which we will discuss below, that were specifically the consequences of capitalist social relations. When Marx considered commodities abstractly, ignoring all differences and peculiarities, they reduced to the material embodiments of labor expended in production. Commodities, so considered, were defined as *values* by Marx. "Human labor is in them. When looked at as crystals of this . . . [human labor], common to them all they are—Values."[17]

Marx used "value" in a way that is usually misunderstood because the word "value" had been frequently used by economists writing before Marx, and came to be used almost exclusively by later economists, to mean simply exchange value, or price. In reading *Capital*, it is necessary to keep Marx's definition clearly in mind in order to avoid confusion. Value is a qualitative social relation with a quantitative dimension. Value exists historically only when productive labor is not immediately social. That is, in such a society, even though you consume the product that I have produced, and, hence, we are mutually interdependent, we have no consciousness of a social relation between us. I produce only in order to exchange and you exchange in order to consume. For you, my social labor exists in the form of the commodities in which it is embodied, that is, only as a value. Thus, the qualitative dimension of value is this particular social relation. But value also has a quantitative dimension. This dimension is simple: "The value of one commodity is to the value of any other, as the labour time necessary for the production of the one is to that necessary for the production of the other."[18] The labor being quantified was not, however, the immediately perceived, empirically observable labor that one might simply measure while observing a production process. It was what Marx called "abstract labor." We will examine the nature of abstract labor in the next section.

This confusion is easily compounded because in volume 1 *Marx was not concerned with any theory designed to explain actual prices*. Rather, he was trying to explain the nature of capital and the origins of profit. For this purpose, he found it convenient to take Ricardo's view that the labor embodied in production was the primary determinant of exchange values. For Ricardo, factors such as differences in the ratio of machinery to labor or in the length of the production processes among different industries were *secondary* influences on prices. Such secondary influences were both relatively unimportant and fully explainable by subsidiary principles in Ricardo's value theory. In volume 1, Marx took this view and abstracted away from these secondary influences. To explain the nature and origins of capital and profit, he assumed as an abstract first approximation that values (labor embodied) were the only determinants of exchange values. At that level of abstraction, as we have seen in the chapters on Smith and Ricardo, exchange values were always proportional to values (as Marx defined values). Therefore, throughout volume 1 Marx used the terms *value* and *exchange value* interchangeably. While this was quite appropriate given this level of theoretical abstraction, it nevertheless has compounded the confusion for students of Marx's writings. Marx was well aware of the distinctions between values and exchange values and prices. "We must perceive, at first sight," he wrote, "the deficiencies of the elementary form of value: it is a mere germ, which must undergo a series of metamorphoses before it can ripen into the price-form."[19]

It was not until volume 3 of *Capital* that Marx extended his labor theory to explain actual prices, that is, to take account of the secondary influences on prices that we mentioned above. Unfortunately, volume 3 was never finished by Marx, and his discussion of the relation between values and actual prices, while conceptually quite adequate, generally has been misunderstood.

Having noted the possible sources of confusion in understanding Marx's use of the terms *value* and *exchange value*, we now return to his discussion of commodities and their exchange values.

Useful Labor and Abstract Labor

When Marx asserted that labor time determined exchange values, he defined this labor time as consisting of simple homogeneous labor, in which all specific differences among different types of work processes were abstracted away: "The labour . . . that forms the substance of value is homogeneous human labour, expenditure of one uniform labour-power."[20] This led Marx to distinguish between two different ways of viewing labor and the process of working. When one looked at the specific *characteristics* of specific *work processes*, one saw that their particular differentiating qualities were necessary to produce the particular use values of the different commodities involved. Labor looked at in this way was defined as *useful labor*, and, as such, it produced the particular use values of different commodities. Thus, useful labor was the cause of commodities having use value:

> The coat is a use value that satisfies a particular want. Its existence is a result of a special sort of productive activity, the nature of which is determined by its aim, mode of operation, subject, means, and result. The labour, whose utility is thus represented by the value in use of its product, or which manifests itself by making its product a use value, we call useful labour.[21]

The labor that created exchange value, however, was *abstract labor*, where the differences in the qualities of various kinds of useful labor were abstracted away

> Productive activity, if we leave out of sight its special form, viz., the useful character of the labour, is nothing but the expenditure of human labour-power. . . . The value of a commodity represents human labour in the abstract, the expenditure of human labour-power. . . . The value of a commodity represents human labour in the abstract, the expenditure of human labour in general.[22]

When he asserted that abstract labor determined exchange value, Marx had two important qualifications. First, it was only the *socially necessary* labor time that counted: "The labour-time socially necessary is that required to produce an article under normal conditions of production, and with the average degree of skill and intensity prevalent at the time."[23] He was also aware that some types of production required that workers expend considerable time in the acquisition of special skills, whereas other work processes could be performed by simple unskilled workers. In this case, the computation of values would require that skilled labor be reduced to a simple multiple of unskilled labor:

> Skilled labour counts only as simple labour intensified, or rather, as multiplied simple labour, a given quantity of skilled [labor] being considered equal to a greater quantity of simple labour. Experience shows that this reduction is constantly being made. . . . The different proportions in which different sorts of labour are reduced to unskilled labour as their standard, are established by a social process that goes on behind the backs of the producers, and, consequently, appear to be fixed by custom.[24]

When we describe Marx's theory of the price of labor power (or wages) we will describe how he saw the determination of the wage differentials by which skilled labor was reduced to simple labor.

Having thus established the connection between the exchange value of a commodity and "the amount of the labour-time socially necessary for its production," Marx, consistent with his earlier critique of bourgeois economists, showed the specific historical social conditions necessary in order for the products of human labor to be commodities.

Social Nature of Commodity Production

Products of human labor were commodities only when they were produced solely for exchange for money in the market and not for the immediate use or enjoyment of the producers or anyone directly associated with the producers. "The mode of production in which the product takes the form of a commodity, or is produced directly for exchange," Marx wrote, "is the most general and most embryonic form of bourgeois production."[25] Commodity production is not the characteristic form of social production until workers do not produce the products for their own subsistence, but must purchase them from capitalists. This is the source of the capitalists' power over workers in a commodity-producing society:

> Definite historical conditions are necessary that a product may become a commodity. It must not be produced as the immediate means of subsistence of the producer himself. . . . Production and circulation of commodities can take place, although the great mass of objects produced are intended for the immediate requirements of the producers, are not turned into commodities, and consequently social production is not yet by a long way dominated in its length and breadth by exchange-value.[26]

In order for a society to have been "dominated in its length and breadth by exchange-value," that is, in order for it to have been primarily a commodity-producing society, three historical prerequisites were necessary: First, there had to evolve a degree of productive specialization such that each individual producer continuously produced the same product (or portion of a product). Second, such specialization necessarily required the complete "separation of use-value from exchange-value."[27] Because life was impossible without the consumption of innumerable use values, a producer could relate to his or her own product only as an exchange value and could only acquire his or her necessary use values from the products of other producers. Third, a commodity-producing society required an extensive, well-developed market, which required the pervasive use of money as a universal value equivalent mediating every exchange.

In a commodity-producing society, any given producer worked in isolation from all other producers. The producer was, of course, socially and economically connected, or related, to other producers: many of them could not continue their ordinary daily patterns of consumption without the given producer creating a commodity, which the other producers consumed; and the producer could not continue this pattern of consumption unless the innumerable other producers continuously created the commodities that the initial producer needed. Thus, there was a definite, indispensable social relationship among producers.

Each producer, however, produced only for sale in the market. With the proceeds of the sale, the producer bought the commodities that he or she needed. The producer's well-being appeared to depend solely on the quantities of other commodities for which the producer could exchange his or her commodity. "These quantities vary continually," wrote Marx, "independently of the will, foresight and action of the producers. To them their own social action takes the form of the action of objects, which rule the producers, instead of being ruled by them."[28] Thus, what social relationships there were among producers appeared to each producer as simply a relationship between the individual and an impersonal, immutable social institution—the market. The market appeared to involve simply a set of relationships among material things—commodities. "Therefore, the relations connecting the labour of one individual with that of the rest appear," Marx concluded, "not as direct social relations between individuals at work, but as . . . relations between things."[29]

Thus, in a commodity-producing society, the use values produced by useful labor could *not* be consumed and enjoyed without the successful functioning of market exchange. But it was still only useful labor that produced the use values that sustained human life and generated all of the utility derived from consumption. The great naivete of Smith's invisible-hand argument, and all of the apologetic variations constructed by other bourgeois economists, derived from its shortsightedness. Looking only superficially at the act of exchange and the sphere of circulation, bourgeois economists believed that such utility was generated in exchange itself. Exchange, therefore, seemed to them to be universally benevolent and to harmonize every individual's interests with those of all other individuals. The simple truth was that useful labor was always the source of all utility derived from commodities and that exchange was merely the necessary prerequisite for the very functioning of a commodity-producing society. Bourgeois economists had been unable to visualize anything but a commodity-producing society, so the appearance of the market as a harmonizing, mutually beneficial institution merely masked the underlying fact that in such a society no one could enjoy the utility created by useful labor unless the market functioned. But this fact in itself gave no clue as to the nature of social relations among the various classes in a capitalist society or to whether these relations were harmonious or conflicting.

Simple Commodity Circulation and Capitalist Circulation

The historical conditions necessary for commodity production were not, Marx argued, identical to those necessary for the existence of capitalism. He was interested in understanding the specific historical and social nature of capital as the source of profits. He maintained that the "historical conditions of its [capital's] existence are by no means given with the mere circulation of money and commodities."[30]

In simple commodity production in a noncapitalist system, commodities were produced for sale in order to acquire other commodities to *use*. In such a system, Marx wrote,

> the exchange of commodities is . . . accompanied by the following changes in their form.
>
> Commodity—Money—Commodity
> C—M—C.
>
> The result of the whole process is . . . the exchange of one commodity for another, the circulation of materialized social labour. When this result is attained, the process is at an end.[31]

In contrast, in a capitalist system it could readily be observed that for one segment of society—the capitalists—the process of exchange was very different:

> The simplest form of circulation of commodities is C-M-C the transformation of commodities into money, and the change of the money back again into commodities; or selling in order to buy. But [in capitalism] alongside of this form we find another specifically different form: M-C-M, the transformation of money into commodities, and the change of commodities back again into money; or buying in order to sell. Money that circulates in the latter manner is thereby transformed into, becomes capital, and is already potentially capital.[32]

It was obvious, Marx continued, that the *M-C-M* circulation "would be absurd and without meaning if the intention were to exchange by this means two equal sums of money, £100 for £100. The miser's plan would be far simpler and surer; he sticks to his (pounds) 100 instead of exposing it to the dangers of circulation."[33] It was clear that the only possible intention of such a circulation was "buying in order to sell dearer."[34] Therefore, this circulation process could better be described as *M-C-M'*, where *M'* is greater than *M*. Unlike the *C-M-C* circulation, the *M-C-M'* circulation ended with a greater value than it had at the beginning.

Surplus Value, Exchange, and the Sphere of Circulation

The difference between *M'* and *M* was *surplus value*. To Marx, the quest for ever greater quantities of surplus value was the motive force propelling the entire capitalist system:

> As the conscious representative of this movement, the possessor of money becomes a capitalist. His person or rather his pocket, is the point from which money starts and to which it returns. The expansion of value . . . becomes his subjective aim, and

it is only in so far as the appropriation of ever more and more wealth in the abstract becomes the sole motive of his operations, that he functions as a capitalist, that is, as capital personified and endowed with consciousness and a will. Use-values must therefore never be looked upon as the real aim of the capitalist; neither must the profit on any single transaction. The restless never-ending process of profit-making alone is what he aims at. This boundless greed after riches, this passionate chase after exchange-value, is common to the capitalist and the miser; but while the miser is merely a capitalist gone mad, the capitalist is a rational miser. The never-ending augmentation of exchange-value, which the miser strives after, by seeking to save his money from circulation, is attained by the more acute capitalists, by constantly throwing it afresh into circulation.[35]

Marx concluded that *M-C-M'* was "therefore, in reality, the general formula of capital as it appears prima facie within the sphere of circulation."[36] The central question to Marx was if the essential feature of capitalism that gave rise to surplus value, the excess of *M'* over *M* could be found within the sphere of circulation. Exchange of a commodity could take place at its value, above its value, or below its value. If the exchange took place at the value of the commodity, then equivalents would be exchanged and obviously no surplus value would arise. If the commodity was exchanged above its value, then the seller would gain exchange value but the buyer would lose an equal amount of exchange value. Obviously, there would be no net gain in surplus value between the two parties. Similarly, if the exchange took place below the value of the commodity, then the buyer's gain would be identical to the seller's loss. Again, the transaction would create no net increase in surplus value. The conclusion was clear: "Turn and twist then as we may, the fact remains unaltered. If equivalents are exchanged, no surplus-value results, and if non-equivalents are exchanged, still no surplus-value results. Circulation, or the exchange of commodities, begets no value."[37]

Thus Marx concluded that the essential feature of capitalism that gave rise to surplus value, or profit, could not be found in the sphere of circulation, and he turned his attention to the sphere of production:

> We therefore take leave for a time of this noisy sphere [of circulation], where everything takes place on the surface and in view of all men, and . . . [go] into the hidden abode of production, on whose threshold there stares us in the face "No admittance except on business." Here we shall see not only how capital produces, but how capital is produced. We shall at last force the secret of profit making.
>
> This sphere that we are deserting . . . is in fact a very Eden of the innate rights of man. There alone rule Freedom, Equality, Property and Bentham. Freedom, because both buyer and seller of a commodity . . . are constrained only by their own free will. They contract as free agents. . . . Equality, because each enters into relation with the other, as with a simple owner of commodities, and they exchange equivalent for equivalent. Property, because each disposes only of what is his own. And Bentham, because each looks only to himself. The only force that brings them together, and puts them in relation with each other, is the selfishness, the gain and private interest of each. Each looks to himself only, and no one troubles himself above the rest, and just because they do so, do they all, in accordance with the pre-established harmony of things, or under the auspices of an all-shrewd providence, work together to their mutual advantage, for the common weal and in the interest of all.

On leaving this sphere of simple circulation or of exchange of commodities, which furnishes the "Free-trader Vulgaris" with his views and ideas, and with the standard by which he judges a society based on capital and wages, we think we can perceive a change in the physiognomy of our dramatis personae. He, who before was the money-owner, now strides in front as the capitalist; the possessor of labour-power follows as his labourer. The one with an air of importance, smirking, intent on business; the other, timid and holding back, like one who is bringing his own hide to market and has nothing to expect but—a hiding.[38]

Circulation of Capital and the Importance of Production

The fact that surplus value was created in the sphere of production could be ascertained if one carefully examined the process of the circulation of capital. In the *M-C-M'* formula, it was clear that the process of profit making that was being described was that of merchant capital: "The circuit *M-C-M'*, buying to sell dearer, is seen most clearly in . . . merchants' capital."[39] In the course of both his historical investigation and his extensive analysis of circulation, Marx had come to the conclusion that neither merchant capital nor interest-bearing money capital was involved in the process of the actual creation of surplus value. Early in volume 1 he wrote: "In the course of our investigation, we shall find that both merchants' capital and interest bearing capital are derivative forms, and at the same time it will become clear, why these two forms appear in the course of history before the modern standard form of capital."[40]

Both these forms of capital were essentially parasitic. They did not constitute a part of the process whereby surplus value was created. Rather, they could attach themselves to whatever mechanism was being used for the creation and expropriation of an economic surplus. After this attachment, merchants and moneylenders could gain a share of the surplus even though their capital had not been directly involved in the creation of this surplus. It was for this reason that both these forms of capital could appear in the feudal mode of production and share in its surplus.

Industrial capital was the form of capital that was most representative of the capitalist mode of production. It constituted the mechanism by which surplus value was both created and expropriated in capitalism. In Marx's scheme of circulation, industrial capital could be depicted in three stages:

> *First stage:* The capitalist appears as a buyer; . . . his money is transformed into commodities. . . .
> *Second stage:* Productive consumption of the purchased commodities by the capitalists. He acts as the capitalist producer of commodities; his capital passes through the process of production. The result is a commodity of more value than that of the elements entering into its production.
> *Third stage:* The capitalist returns to the market as a seller; his commodities are turned into money. . . .
> Hence the formula for the circuit of money-capital is: $M - C \ldots P \ldots C' - M'$, the dots indicating that the process of circulation is interrupted, and C' and M' designating C and M increased by surplus-value.[41]

The *P* in Marx's formula indicated the process of production. It is clear in this formula that *M'* exceeded *M* because *C'* exceeded *C*. In addition, the surpluses in both cases were equal.

Thus, the origin of surplus value was due to the fact that capitalists bought one set of commodities and sold an entirely different set. The first set of commodities (*C*) consisted of the ingredients for production. The second set of commodities (*C'*) was the output of the production process. In the act of production, the capitalist used up, or consumed, the use value of the productive inputs that he or she bought as commodities:

> In order to be able to extract value from the consumption of a commodity, our friend, Moneybags [Marx's epithet for a capitalist], must be so lucky as to find, within the sphere of circulation, in the market, a commodity whose use-value possesses the peculiar property of being a source of value, whose actual consumption, therefore, is itself an embodiment of labour, and, consequently, a creation of value. The possessor of money does find on the market such a special commodity in capacity for labour or labour-power.
>
> By labour-power or capacity for labour is to be understood the aggregate of those mental and physical capabilities existing in a human being, which he exercises whenever he produces a use-value of any description.[42]

Labor, Labor Power, and the Definition of Capitalism

Labor power, then, was the capacity to work, or potential labor. When labor power was sold as a commodity, its use value was simply the performance of work—the actualizing of the potential labor. When the work was performed it became embodied in a commodity, thus giving the commodity value. Therefore, the only possible source of surplus value was the difference between the value of the labor power as a commodity (or potential labor) and the value of the commodity produced, which embodied the actualized labor (or the consumed use value of the labor power). Labor power was an absolutely unique commodity: its consumption or use created new value large enough both to replace its original value and to yield a surplus value. Obviously labor power was a commodity that had to be examined more carefully.

The existence of labor power as a commodity depended on two essential conditions. First,

> labour-power can appear upon the market as a commodity, only if, and so far as, its possessor, the individual whose labour-power it is, offers it for sale, or sells it, as a commodity. In order that he may be able to do this he . . . must be the untrammelled owner of his capacity for labour, i.e., of his person. . . . The owner of the labour-power . . . [must] sell it only for a definite period, for if he were to sell it rump and stump, once and for all, he would be selling himself, converting himself from a free man into a slave, from an owner of a commodity into a commodity. . . .
>
> The second essential condition . . . is . . . that the labourer instead of being in the position to sell commodities in which his labour is incorporated, must be obliged to offer for sale as a commodity that very labour-power, which exists only in his living self.

> In order that a man may be able to sell commodities other than labour-power, he must of course have the means of production, such as raw materials, implements, etc. No boots can be made without leather. He requires also the means of subsistence. . . .
>
> For the conversion of his money into capital, therefore, the owner of money must meet in the market with the free labourer, free in the double sense, that as a free man he can dispose of his labour-power as his own commodity, and that on the other hand he has no other commodity for sale, is short of everything necessary for the realization of his labour-power.[43]

This, then, was capitalism's defining feature, differentiating it from a simple commodity-producing society. Capitalism existed when, in a commodity-producing society, one small class of people—capitalists—had monopolized the means of production, and where the great majority of the direct producers—workers—could not produce independently because they had no means of production. Workers were "free" to make one of two choices: starve or sell their labor power as a commodity.[44] Thus, capitalism was neither inevitable nor natural and eternal. It was a specific mode of production that evolved under specific historical conditions and that had a ruling class that ruled by virtue of its ability to expropriate surplus value from the producers of commodities:

> One thing . . . is clear—Nature does not produce on the one side owners of money or commodities, and on the other men possessing nothing but their own labour-power. This relation has no natural basis, neither is its social basis one that is common to all historical periods. It is clearly the result of a past historical development, the product of many economic revolutions, of the extinction of a whole series of older forms of social production.[45]

After explaining how surplus value was created and expropriated, Marx devoted several hundred pages of volume 1 to a description of the historical forces that created capitalism. We will follow the same sequence, first discussing his explanation of the creation and realization, through production and exchange, of surplus value, and then briefly mentioning some of the forces that he considered important in the evolution of capitalism.

The Value of Labor Power

We have seen that the difference between the value of labor power and the value of the commodity produced when that labor power became actualized was the source of surplus value. Marx therefore had to begin his discussion of surplus value by explaining this difference. In this regard, the distinction between labor power and labor expended, or embodied, in production was of crucial significance. Labor power was merely potential labor. This was what the laborer sold as a commodity. The use value of labor power was actual labor expended. The importance of this distinction will become even clearer after we examine Marx's explanation of the value of the labor power as a commodity:

> The value of labour-power is determined, as in the case of every other commodity, by the labour-time necessary for the production, and consequently also the reproduction of this special article. . . . Given the individual, the production of labour-power consists in . . . his maintenance. For his maintenance he requires a given quantity of the means of subsistence. . . . The labour-power withdrawn from the market by wear and tear and death, must continually be replaced. . . . Hence the sum of means of subsistence necessary for the production of labour-power must [also] include the means necessary for the labourer's substitutes, i.e., his children.[46]

The value of labor power was equal to the value of the subsistence of a worker's family. Therefore, the labor embodied in labor power was identical to the labor embodied in the commodities comprising this subsistence. This subsistence was not a biological or physiological minimum subsistence but a "product of historical development" that depended on "the habits and degree of comfort" to which the working class was accustomed.[47]

The wage differences among various occupations reflected the fact that "special education or training" was required for some occupations. "The expenses of this education" entered "into the total value" of the various types of labor power.[48] By calculating the labor costs of the various education and training requirements of different occupations, all labor could be reduced to some multiple of simple labor. This, of course, permitted the summation of labor hours exerted by different types of laborers in order to compute the value of any commodity produced by labor of varying skills.

"In a given country, at a given period, the average quantity of means of subsistence necessary for the labourer" was fairly easy to ascertain.[49] Taking, say, the yearly amounts of commodities necessary for one worker's family, one could calculate the amount of labor embodied in these commodities. Dividing by 365, one could find the labor embodied in the means of subsistence for one family for one day. This amount of labor was the value of labor power for one day. Thus, if the various laborers who were producing food, clothing, and shelter for workers collectively expended an average of four hours to produce those commodities necessary to sustain a worker's family for one day, then the value of the use of one person's labor power for one day would be four hours.

Now, if each worker worked only four hours a day, then total production would just meet the subsistence needs of workers. There would be no surplus. Each worker would create commodities embodying four hours' labor, while his or her labor power was also a commodity embodying four hours' labor. Each worker would create the value equivalent of his or her subsistence, and hence the value equivalent of his or her own labor power, by working four hours a day.

Necessary Labor, Surplus Labor, and the Creation and Realization of Surplus Value

The significance of the distinction between labor power and labor should now be much clearer. Labor power was the *capacity* to work. The upper limit of a human being's capacity to work was, depending on the type of work, fourteen to eighteen hours a day. Therefore, the quantity of actual labor that could be extracted from one day's labor power (and, hence, the value of the commodities produced by one day's actual labor) depended on the length of the working day. "The working day is thus not a constant," Marx wrote, "but a variable quantity."[50] If the length of the working day was such that "the value paid by the capitalist for the labour-power is replaced by an exact equivalent, it is simply a process of producing value; if, on the other hand, it be continued beyond that point, it [then] becomes a process of creating surplus-value."[51]

"That portion of the working day," Marx wrote, during which the production of the value of labor power "takes place, I call 'necessary' labour-time, and the labour expended during that time I call '*necessary*' labour."[52] But in capitalism the working day always extended beyond this necessary labor time. This extended "portion of the working day," he continued, "I name surplus labour-time, and to the labour expended during that time, I give the name of surplus labour."[53] Thus, just as value was "a congelation of so many hours of labour, . . . nothing but materialized labor," so surplus value was "a mere congelation of surplus labour-time, . . . nothing but materialized surplus-labour."[54]

We can now return to the formula for the circulation of industrial capital:

$$M - C \ldots P \ldots C' - M'.$$

The capitalist began with money capital (a fund of value embodied in money). He or she bought three different kinds of commodities: raw materials, tools, and labor power (his or her capital had now changed to a fund of value embodied in these three types of commodities). Next came production.

For the sake of simplicity, we will assume that all of the tools and raw materials were used up in one period of production. This assumption merely simplifies but does not change the basic logic of the analysis. Marx devoted approximately 200 pages of volume 2 of *Capital* to a discussion of the effects of the "turnover time," or durability, of capital. In our short account we will have to omit this complication (although it does affect Marx's theory of price determination, which we will discuss below).

During the production process, the capital was transformed into finished goods (capital then became a fund of value embodied in finished goods). The value of the finished goods came from three sources: the raw materials, the tools, and the labor power. First, then, there are the raw materials and tools. As commodities, raw materials and tools had values determined by the labor already embodied in them. They were produced originally only in order to make possible the production of the final commodities. For example, the raw material might be wool, the tools might be spinning wheels and looms, and the final commodity might be cloth. The labor involved in raising the sheep and shearing the wool was first embodied in the wool. But as the wool was transformed into cloth, the material embodiment of that original labor changed from wool to cloth.

After the final production of cloth, the cloth embodied all of the labor involved in producing the wool. The wool could not transfer to the cloth any more labor than was already embodied in it. Therefore, the value of the wool (its labor content) was transferred exactly in its original amount to the cloth. Similarly, the labor embodied in the spinning wheels and looms was transferred to the cloth as these tools were used up in production. Following our assumption that all tools were used up in each period of production, it is obvious that the tools could transfer to the cloth only that amount of labor already embodied in them. Thus, they transferred all (and no more) of their value to the value of the cloth.

It was different, however, with labor power. Using our previous assumption about the value of the commodities necessary for a worker's subsistence, let us say that the labor embodied in one day's labor power was four hours. Now, assume that the working day was ten hours. One day's labor power, therefore, had a value of four hours, but when the work was actually performed, the labor added a value of ten hours to the cloth. Each day a worker labored, the capitalist used up the commodity labor power having an exchange value determined by four hours of embodied labor. But the actual labor extracted from one day's labor power created an exchange value in the wool determined by the full ten hours worked.

Thus, after production, the capitalist's capital was a fund of value embodied in commodities (in our example, cloth). This was the C in Marx's formula $M - C \ldots P \ldots C' - M'$.

It is now clear, from the foregoing discussion, that the value of the commodities C' (cloth) exceeded the value of the commodities C (wool, spinning wheels, looms, and labor power) by an amount exactly equal to the excess of the length of the working day over the necessary labor time required to produce the laborers' subsistence. (This assumes that the capitalist bought only one day's labor power. If the capitalist bought fifty days of labor power, then the surplus of value of C' over C would be this difference multiplied by fifty.) This was why Marx insisted that the commodity labor power was the only source of surplus value.

In the last stage of the circulation, the commodities C' (cloth) were exchanged for an equivalent amount of money M'. The capital had completed a full cycle, going from money to commodities, through production to a new set of commodities, and finally back to money. M' exceeded M by exactly the same amount that C' exceeded C. Only exchanges of value equivalents had taken place, but now the capitalist had a fund of money capital that was of greater value than the original fund. The capitalist was now in a position to begin the process again, only this time on an expanded scale with more capital.

Capitalism represented a never-ending repetition of this process. Capital created surplus value, which was the source of more capital, and, in turn, more surplus value, and so on, in an endless, ceaseless drive to accumulate more capital. The credo of capitalism was: "Accumulate, accumulate! That is Moses and the prophets!"[55]

Constant Capital, Variable Capital, and the Rate of Surplus Value

When the capitalist spent his or her money capital to buy the commodities necessary for the production process, the resultant capital (in the form of commodities) was divided by Marx into constant capital and variable capital. *Constant capital* was defined as all tools, machines, buildings, and raw materials—all nonhuman means of production. It was called constant because these commodities transferred only their own value to the value of the final product. Hence, the value embodied in these means of production remained constant when transmitted into a product. *Variable capital* was defined as the labor power that the capitalist purchased. Its value was increased when the potential labor purchased became actual labor embodied in a produced commodity. Alternatively, when capital took its money form, it could also be similarly divided into these two categories:

> The capital C is made up of two components, one, the sum of money c laid out upon the means of production, and the other, the sum of money v expended upon labour-power; c represents the portion that has become constant capital, and v the portion that has become variable capital. At first then, C = c + v. . . . when the process of production is finished, we get a commodity [C'] whose value = (c + v) + s, where s is the surplus value.[56]

Marx then defined the rate of surplus value, a ratio that was to reappear many times in his analysis:

> Since, on the one hand, the values of the variable capital and of the labour-power purchased by that capital are equal, and the value of this labour-power determines the necessary portion of the working day; and since, on the other hand, the surplus-value is determined by the surplus portion of the working day, it follows that surplus-value bears the same ratio to variable capital that surplus labour does to necessary labour, or in other words, the rate of surplus-value

$$\frac{s}{v} = \frac{\text{surplus labour}}{\text{necessary labour}}$$

> Both ratios . . . express the same thing in different ways; in the one case by reference to materialized, incorporated labour, in the other, by reference to living, fluent labour. The rate of surplus-value is therefore an exact expression for the degree of exploitation of labour-power by capital, or of the laborer by the capitalist.[57]

The rate of surplus value tells us how many hours the laborer worked to create profits for the capitalist for each hour the laborer worked to create the value equivalent of his or her own subsistence. In our previous example, the working day was ten hours, four hours of which replaced the value of the labor power (or created the value equivalent of the worker's subsistence). The rate of surplus value was therefore 6 / 4, or 1.5. This means that the laborer worked one and one-half hours producing profits for the capitalist for each hour that the laborer worked for him or herself (i.e., for each hour the laborer spent creating the value equivalent of his or her own subsistence).

The difference between labor and labor power was clearly the source of surplus value. As Marx was later to show, profits, interest, and rents (and all other nonwage incomes) were merely the divisions of surplus value among the capitalist class. Throughout the remainder of volume 1, Marx continued to treat surplus value and profit as though they were identical, in order to elucidate and explain the origins and magnitude of income derived solely from ownership of property. All forms of capital that did not employ workers who created surplus value by providing surplus labor were merely parasitic. They shared in the surplus value in the same way in which merchant capital and interest-bearing capital had been able to share in the economic surplus that was produced in the feudal mode of production. Only capital that employed productive workers made possible the creation of surplus value in the capitalist mode of production.

Length of the Working Day

The magnitude of the difference between labor and labor power depended (given the subsistence requirements of workers) primarily on the length of the working day. In volume 1 of *Capital*, Marx devoted the seventy-two pages of chapter 10 to a detailed historical account of the actual struggle between capitalists and workers to determine the length of the working day. As long as laborers procreated and thereby produced their own replacements, he argued, capitalists would struggle to extend the length of the working day to the limit of human endurance.

Marx's description of the history of this struggle was rich in detail and cannot be summarized here. His historical survey led him to the following view of the motives of the capitalists engaged in this struggle:

> In its blind unrestrainable passion, its were-wolf hunger for surplus-labour, capital oversteps not only the moral, but even the merely physical maximum bounds of the working-day. It usurps the time for growth, development, and healthy maintenance of the body. It steals the time required for the consumption of fresh air and sunlight. It haggles over a meal-time, incorporating it where possible with the process of production itself, so that food is given to the labourer as to a mere means of production, as coal is supplied to the boiler, grease and oil to the machinery. It reduces the sound sleep needed for the restoration, reparation, refreshment of the bodily powers to just so many hours of torpor as the revival of an organism, absolutely exhausted, renders essential. It is not the normal maintenance of the labour-power which is to determine the limits of the working day; it is the greatest possible daily expenditure of labour-power, no matter how diseased, compulsory, and painful it may be. . . . Capital cares nothing for the length of life of labour-power. All that concerns it is simply and solely the maximum of labour-power, that can be rendered fluent in a working-day. It

attains this end by shortening the extent of the labourer's life, as a greedy farmer snatches increased produce from the soil by robbing it of its fertility.[58]

Marx was aware that capitalists were not always able to exploit labor to this extreme. But it was only through persistent struggle that labor was sometimes able to protect itself from the ravages of capital. "The establishment of a normal working day," he wrote, was "the result of centuries of struggle between capitalist and labourer."[59] In every instance of this conflict, capital was "reckless of the health or length of life of the labourer, unless under compulsion from society."[60]

The Labor Theory of Value and the Transformation Problem

Marx's concept of value is generally misunderstood. The labor theory of value is at the heart of Marx's economic theory and it follows from nearly all of the different components of his economic theory as well as provides a foundation that shows the interconnections of these components. For Marx, a commodity was anything that was produced in order to be sold in the market. A commodity had both use value and value. A commodity's use value consisted of its physical and chemical properties by virtue of which it could be put to certain human uses. These properties were the same in all societies (e.g., wheat had the same physical and chemical properties whether it was produced in a slave economy, a capitalist economy, or any other economy). A commodity's value, however, had no physical or chemical basis and was entirely the outcome of the specific historical and social circumstances in which it was produced.

In all societies, in all times, production was a social process of interdependent producers, organized socially to undertake the physical and mental exertions necessary to transform their natural environment in order to make that environment sustain human, social life. This interdependence and the resultant necessity for social coordination of labor meant that in all societies, laboring, or producing, was both a set of activities and a set of social relations.

Value was an aspect of a produced object that reflected social relations that were specific to the capitalist, commodity producing society within which the object was produced as a commodity. Value was the consequence of something that Marx took to be an essential fact of capitalism—that within this system, interdependent labor was only *indirectly* social and was not seen by the participants as being a social relation at all.

In a precapitalist economy, the dependence of one producer on other producers had been immediate and obvious. The leather maker, for example, had seen himself or herself as working to provide the shoemaker with leather, and the shoemaker as working to provide him or her with shoes. The shoemaker had seen the same interdependent social relation. The labor of each of these producers had been immediately social. Producing leather had been identical to producing leather for a shoemaker.

In capitalism, this relation was no longer direct and immediate. Each individual producer produced only for the market. One neither knew nor cared who would consume one's commodity or who would produce the commodities one consumed. More important, the social relations among producers were not direct and immediate. In capitalism, the leather maker might be unable to sell his or her leather in the market. In that event, the labor with which the leather was produced *would not* be social; it would be a private folly, a private misfortune that contributed nothing to society.

The labor became social only when the commodity was sold in the market. The purchase and sale of the commodity, at some specific price, transformed some quantity of private labor into social labor. When the sale took place, the value of a commodity assumed the empirical form of a specific price defining the ratio that money would exchange for one unit of the commodity. The substance of the value was some specific quantity of private labor that could be transformed into social labor only through the sale of the commodity. This substance had no empirically observable form other than the price of the commodity.

Corresponding to the distinction between the use value and the value of a commodity was a distinction between useful labor and abstract labor in Marx's analysis. Useful labor was the actual empirically observable, concrete, physiological exertions of a particular person in a particular situation. The laws of physics and chemistry dictated that only certain kinds of exertions performed on certain raw materials would create certain use values. These specific exertions constituted useful labor.

In capitalism, however, the capitalist was not ultimately concerned about use values, only value through sale in the market. The worker was hired to produce a commodity to be sold in order that the capitalist would receive a profit. The identity of the specific worker made no difference to the capitalist. The capitalist also had little or no knowledge of the specific useful labor that would create specific use values. The capitalist was hiring workers to produce commodities only to yield value in exchange, in order that part of this value would accrue to the capitalist as surplus value, or profit.

If the production of one commodity did not yield sufficient value and surplus value, the capitalist directed his or her laborers to produce a different commodity because the capitalist did not care about use value, only about value. The capitalist did not care which workers performed labor or what concrete exertions created use values; the capitalist cared only about abstract labor—the labor of any laborer in general, producing any commodity in general—that would yield value and surplus value. Marx stressed that abstract labor, not useful labor, is the substance of value.

In order to understand Marx's labor theory of value, one must realize that Marx belonged to the school of science that sees a distinction between the immediately given, empirically manifested appearance of a social phenomenon and the deeper, less visible, but more important substance or essence that underlies this appearance. Studied in this tradition, scientific explanation consists of identifying the essence of a phenomenon and then showing how that essence is manifested in the phenomenon's appearance.

For Marx, it was often the case that the essential aspect of any human relation tended to be the most general aspect of the behavior involved in that relation. Although this general aspect was common to nearly all societies or modes of production, it nevertheless took on a very different appearance from one historical epoch to another, or from one society to another. It is nevertheless the case that this general, essential aspect of human behavior remained relatively constant through these changes of appearance.

For example, human procreation is necessary for the continuance of the species generally and for any society specifically. Within different societies, however, the social relations that lead to and make possible procreation take many different empirically observable forms. No specific human activity or relation (including sexual intercourse) is always, in every empirical instance in which it occurs, a part of the process of the social relations of procreation. Nor does procreation always involve any specific human activity or relation. (Artificial insemination, for example, can be accomplished in a wide variety of ways.)

In any society, the immediate causes of the behavior of individuals involved in that society's dating and courtship rituals are varied religious beliefs, peer approval, economic constraints, and the like. Understanding of these rituals is advanced, however, when one can mentally go beneath or behind these observable, empirical causes. One can see that the substance or essence of the rituals is the universal human necessity of procreation, regardless of the variety of their immediate causes.

Similarly, for Marx, the social allocation of labor was a universal necessity in all societies. In capitalism, this was accomplished through the sale of the products of labor. There were several specific, empirical causes of the magnitudes of money prices. These included the costs of production, market structures, the magnitude and composition of the demands of consumers, and others. Within the context of capitalist social relations, these prices had to be realized (i.e., the commodities had to be sold), however, if individual private labor was to be transformed into social labor. The transformation of private labor into social labor through the sale of commodities at specific prices in a market was the particular form that the universally necessary, social allocation of labor took in a capitalist society. Succinctly, abstract labor (that has been rendered social through the sale and purchase of a commodity) was the substance or essence of value, while the price was the empirical manifestation of that substance or essence within the historical conditions of capitalist commodity production.

A theory of the immediate, superficial, empirical determinants of prices and of the relation between these determinants and labor values was important to Marx because it was necessary in order to make persuasive the argument that abstract labor was the substance of value. Prices, despite the diversity of causes influencing them, were the actual empirical form this substance took. Because actual, existing prices had several empirically observable, immediate causes, there was no obvious, immediately observable, quantitative connection between values and prices.

The "transformation problem" is a problem of sorting out these causes and their effects on prices in order to find mentally the quantitative relationship between the substance (value) and its empirical manifestation (price).

With these distinctions in mind, one can turn to the analysis of the transformation problem. To Marx, the value of a commodity consisted of the labor embodied in the means of production that were used up in the production of the commodity (sometimes called "dead labor" by Marx) and the labor expended in the current production period (called "living labor"). Thus,

$$W = L_d + L_l, \tag{9.1}$$

where W is value, L_d is dead labor, and L_l is living labor. Living labor can be separated into necessary labor L_n and surplus labor L_s. Necessary labor is that proportion of living labor that creates the value equivalent of the worker's wages. Surplus labor is the remaining living labor time during which the value equivalent of surplus value is created. Thus equation (9.1) becomes:

$$W = L_d + L_n + L_s \tag{9.2}$$

In the actual pricing process, Marx believed that capitalists summed up the costs of production and then added a percentage markup, which was determined by the socially average rate of profit. Thus, the formula for actual pricing was:

price of production =	cost of commodities used in production	+	cost of labor used in production (constant capital)	+	profit markup (surplus capital) (variable capital)

Using p for the price of production, c for constant capital, v for variable capital, and r for the rate of profit, one obtains:

$$p = c + v + r(c + v) \tag{9.3}$$

where, $r = \{s / (c + v)\}$ and $r(c + v) \{s / (c + v)\} \{c + v\} = s$.

The general correspondence between the various types of labor and cost-components of price is obvious:

$$W = L_d + L_n + L_s$$
$$\updownarrow \quad \updownarrow \quad \updownarrow \quad \updownarrow$$
$$P = C + V + r(c + v) \tag{9.4}$$

Price corresponds to value; constant capital corresponds to dead labor; variable capital corresponds to necessary labor; and profit or surplus value corresponds to surplus labor. This is the logic by which money prices correspond to, and indeed are, the empirical manifestation of abstract labor.

The most important reason why this correspondence is not proportional, or one-to-one, however—and hence the origin of the transformation problem—can be seen by dividing both the numerator and the denominator of the formula for the rate of profit by v.

$$r = \frac{s}{c+v} = \frac{s/v}{(c/v)+1} \quad r = \frac{s}{c+v} = \frac{s/v}{(c/v)+1} \tag{9.5}$$

Marx called s / v the "rate of surplus value" and c / v the "organic composition of capital" (which is the quantity of means of production per laborer). Within capitalism, competition among workers and among employers tended to equalize both the length of the working day and the wage rate among all of the various sectors of the economy. Because the rate of surplus value is derived from the length of the work day and the wage rate, it followed that it tended to be equal among different sectors. Competition and the mobility of capital also tended to equalize the rate of profit among all sectors of the economy. Therefore, looking at equation (9.5), it is clear that in order for both r and s / v to be equal among all sectors, it is logically necessary for c / v, the organic composition of capital, to be equal among all sectors.

Marx knew that c / v varied significantly from sector to sector. Yet, his theory requires the equality of r and s / v among the various sectors and hence has an apparent contradiction. Marx's solution to this apparent contradiction was to differentiate between the creation or production of surplus value in the "sphere of production" on the one hand and the realization of surplus value through the sale of commodities in the "sphere of circulation" (the market) on the other hand.

Marx insisted that the ratio *surplus labor/necessary labor* would always tend to be equal, regardless of differences in the organic compositions of capital. When the rate of surplus value is expressed in that form, it has meaning only within the sphere of production. However, when the ratio is stated as *surplus value/variable capital*, it can refer either to the surplus value *created* within the sphere of production or to the surplus value *realized* through the sale of the commodity in the sphere of circulation.

When *surplus value/variable capital* refers to surplus value created, then it can be equated to the ratio *surplus labor/necessary labor*. The numerator and denominator have a clear meaning within the sphere of production. The ratio of the two in any industry tends toward equality with the ratios in all other industries, *regardless of differences in the organic compositions of capital.*

When *surplus value/variable capital* refers to surplus value realized through market sale, then it has its meaning within the sphere of circulation. When the organic compositions of capital differ, the very forces of competition that equate the rates of profit among different industries assure that *surplus value/variable capital* (conceived of in this way) will *not* be equal. But, ail of Marx's arguments for the equality of *surplus value/variable capital* among all industries clearly show that only surplus value created in the sphere of production was being considered.

Marx believed that in the earliest phases of capitalism, prices roughly corresponded to values, and different profit rates prevailed. But, as the market developed and the economy became a more integrated whole, competition also developed, and capital became much more mobile. In their quest for higher profits, capitalists from low-profit industries moved their capital into high-profit industries, raising the profit rate in the former and lowering the rate in the latter. Thus, Marx believed "the rates of profit prevailing in the various branches of production are originally very different. These different rates of profit are equalized by competition to a single general rate of profit, which is the average of all these different rates of profits."[61]

The only way in which competition could equalize the rates of profit was through price changes brought about by changes in supply and demand. The changes in supply and demand were brought about by capital being transferred from low-profit industries (thereby decreasing the supply and increasing the prices in those industries) to high-profit industries (thereby increasing the supply and decreasing the prices in those industries). These price changes, which equalize the rates of profit, caused the equilibrium prices of production to deviate from values. But Marx, following Ricardo, believed that these deviations would follow a definite pattern and, hence, were fully explainable. Like Ricardo, he believed that in industries with a higher than average organic composition of capital, prices of production would be higher than values. In industries with a lower than average organic composition, prices of production would be lower.

Marx believed that when competition equated the rates of profit among different industries by causing prices to deviate from values, the inevitable result would be a *redistribution of some surplus value* from industries in which it was created to other industries. Surplus value was created by surplus labor and, hence, was created in each industry in proportion to the variable capital employed.

But the competitive price changes that equalized the rate of profit transferred some surplus value from all industries having lower than average organic compositions of capital to all industries having higher than average organic compositions of capital. It was only through such a transference that rates of profit could be brought into equality. Hence, after commodities were sold in the market at the prevailing prices of production, the ratio *s / v* (when surplus value is interpreted as profit actually realized in the market) was *different* in every industry.

There is absolutely no inconsistency in recognizing this inevitable inequality while still insisting that in the sphere of production, surplus value is created in strict proportion to the quantity of living labor employed (or variable capital). This simply means that s/v, interpreted as surplus value created, remains equal among all industries.

The erroneous charge of a logical error in Marx's analysis nevertheless remains common among critics of Marx. That Marx saw the matter as just described is unequivocally clear in the following passage from *Capital*:

> Thus, although in selling their commodities, the capitalists in the various spheres of production recover the value of the capital consumed in their production, *they do not secure the surplus-value, and consequently the profit, created in their own sphere by the production of these commodities.* What they secure is only as much surplus-value, and hence profit, as falls, when uniformly distributed, to the share of every aliquot part of the total social capital from the total social surplus value, or profit, produced in a given time by the social capital in all spheres of production.[62]

In volume 3 of *Capital*, Marx illustrated this by constructing a table illustrating a situation in which prices were proportional to values, but the organic compositions of capital differed from sector to sector. The proportionality of prices and value required different profit rates in each sector. Marx then computed the average rate of profit for the economy as a whole and constructed a second table in which prices had been altered.

Tables 9.1 and 9.2 are slightly rearranged versions of Marx's tables. Table 9.1 shows that differing profit rates would obtain if each industry sold its output at a price just sufficient to realize all of the surplus value created in the industry. After competition among business firms had equalized the rates of profits among all of the sectors, the situation was transformed to that depicted in Table 9.2.

The following conditions then obtained: (1) Each sector had a rate of profit equal to the aggregate or socially average rate of profit. (2) The increases and decreases in prices (between the first and second tables) in the various sectors precisely offset each other such that the total of all prices (or the average price level) was the same in both tables. (3) Because of the changes in prices, surplus value was increased in some sectors and decreased in others, but the aggregate surplus value remained unchanged between Table 9.1 and Table 9.2.

Marx's tables were intended to illustrate the argument, summarized above, that differences in the organic compositions of capital cause prices to deviate from values in such a way as to rearrange existing quantities of surplus value that have been created previously in the production process. Marx's illustration, however, was incomplete. The problem was that while he transformed output prices, he left input prices proportional to values. Thus, each commodity had two different prices, one price as an output and another price as an input.

Shortly after the publication of volume 3 of *Capital*, a mathematical solution was found that transformed both output and input prices.[63] In the initial solution, however, only two of Marx's three conditions held: the sectoral profit rates were equal, and the total amount of surplus value in transformed prices was equal to the total in transformed prices. However, the transformation of

Table 9.1

Rates of Profit When Prices Equal Values

Industry	1 Total capital (column 2 + column 4)	2 Total constant capital	3 Constant capital used up (c)	4 Variable capital (v)	5 Surplus value (s)	6 Cost of production ($c + v$)	7 Value of commodities ($c + v + s$)	8 Rate of profit (column 5 ÷ column 1)
I	100	80	50	20	20	70	90	20%
II	100	70	51	30	30	81	111	30%
III	100	60	51	40	40	91	131	40%
IV	100	85	40	15	15	55	70	15%
V	100	95	10	5	5	15	20	5%
Total	500	390	202	110	110	312	422	—
Average	100	78	—	22	22	—	—	22%

Table 9.2

The Deviations of Prices from Values with Equal Profit Rates

Industry	1 Total capital	2 Rate of profit	3 Profit	4 Cost of production	5 Price of production (column 4 + column 3)	6 Surplus value	7 Deviations of profit from surplus value (column 3 – column 6)	8 Value	9 Deviation of prices of production from value (column 5 – column 8)
I	100	22%	22	70	92	20	+2	90	+2
II	100	22%	22	81	103	30	–8	111	–8
III	100	22%	22	91	113	40	–18	131	–18
IV	100	22%	22	55	77	15	+7	70	+7
V	100	22%	22	15	37	5	+17	20	+17

prices altered the average price level (i.e., the total of transformed prices diverged from the total of untransformed prices).

Subsequent solutions showed it was generally true that various mathematical solutions that transformed both input and output prices left only two of Marx's three equalities intact. A voluminous literature has offered numerous mathematical formulations, each usually claiming to be closer than the others to the spirit of Marx.

As seen above, the various categories of expenses of production correspond to Marx's categories of abstract labor. If they corresponded exactly, prices would be proportional to value. Various causes can disturb the strict proportionality, but abstract labor remains the underlying substance that is empirically manifested (albeit in a distorted way) as prices. The real issues involved in the transformation problem all relate to the general persuasiveness of the argument that private labor only becomes social in a capitalist economy by becoming abstract labor and taking the form of a price of a commodity that is sold in the market and the persuasiveness of the explanation of why money prices are not perfect, proportional reflections of abstract labor. It is beyond the scope of this chapter to review the relative merits of the various solutions to the transformation problem.

Private Property, Capital, and Capitalism

Marx had thus formulated answers to the initial questions that he had asked about the nature and origins of surplus value. He had shown that, through a series of exchanges in which all commodities exchanged at their proper values, surplus value arose not through exchange but in the production process. He had shown that surplus value could be realized in exchange only in a socioeconomic system where the "free" laborer sold his or her labor power to the owner of capital. Thus, "free laborers" who owned no significant means of producing were a prerequisite for the existence of capital. Thus, capital had to involve a very specific set of social relationships.

But orthodox economic theorists during Marx's time had (and have continuously to the present) simply identified capital as the previously produced means of production, that is, as a collection of "things." Marx recognized that capital involved, at least partially, the mere produced means for further production; this *partial* aspect of capital could be said to exist in all societies and in all historical epochs. But capital did not exist in all epochs. It was peculiar to capitalism. Similarly, insofar as production always consisted of the appropriation and transformation of natural resources, it followed that *some type of property relations* existed in all societies and in all historical epochs. What interested Marx, however, was the question of what features of property were peculiar and specific to capitalism and how these property relations transformed the produced means of production into capital. Such knowledge was necessary to understand capitalism.

> Capital comes more and more to the fore as a social power, whose agent is the capitalist. This social power no longer stands in any possible relation to that which the labour of a single individual can create. It becomes an alienated, independent, social power, which stands opposed to society as an object, and as an object that is the capitalist's source of power.[64]

The legal foundation of capital was the law of private property as it existed in the capitalist mode of production:

> At first the rights of property seemed to us to be based on a man's own labour. At least, some such assumption was necessary since only commodity-owners with equal rights confronted each other, and the sole means by which a man could become possessed of the commodities of others, was by alienating [giving up in exchange] his own commodities; and these could be replaced by labour alone. Now, however, property turns out to be the right, on the part of the capitalist, to appropriate the unpaid labour [by which Marx meant surplus labor] of others or its product, and to be the impossibility on the part of the labourer, of appropriating his own product. The separation of property from labour has become the necessary consequence of a law that apparently originated in their identity.[65]

Capital and the laws of private property had become the mechanism, within the capitalist mode of production, by which a ruling class coercively expropriated the economic surplus created by the working class.

Primitive Accumulation

Once capital and free labor have come into existence, capital makes more surplus value possible and more surplus value makes more capital possible. The process was a continuous upward spiral. To really understand capital, however, one had to go behind this continuous spiral and uncover the real beginnings of the process.

The historical origins of capital were not, Marx argued, the thrifty, frugal, abstemious behavior of a moral elite (as Malthus, Say, Senior, Bastiat, and even Mill had argued). The capitalist system presupposed a propertyless working class and a wealthy capitalist class. Marx gave the name "primitive accumulation" to the actual historical process by which these two classes had been created. Referring to the above-mentioned economists' view of the origins of capital, he wrote:

> This primitive accumulation plays in Political Economy about the same part as original sin in theology. Adam bit the apple, and thereupon sin fell on the human race. Its origin is supposed to be explained when it is told as an anecdote of the past. In times long gone by there were two sorts of people; one, the diligent, intelligent, and above all, frugal elite; the other, lazy rascals, spending their substance, and more, in riotous living. . . . Thus it came to pass that the former sort accumulated wealth, and the latter sort had nothing to sell except their own skins. And from this original sin dates the poverty of the great majority that, despite all its labour, has up to now nothing to sell but itself, and the wealth of the few that increases constantly although they have long ceased to work. Such insipid childishness is every day preached to us in the defence of property. . . . As soon as the question of property crops up, it becomes a

sacred duty to proclaim the intellectual food of the infant as the one thing fit for all stages of development. In actual history it is notorious that conquest, enslavement, robbery, murder, briefly force, play the part. . . . The methods of primitive accumulation are anything but idyllic.[66]

Primitive accumulation could be looked at from two different vantage points (although it was one general socioeconomic process): as the process of either the creation of the propertyless, economically helpless, and dependent working class, or the creation of a wealthy capitalist class having monopolistic control over the means of production. From either vantage point, its history was "written in the annals of mankind in letters of blood and fire."[67] Marx devoted sixty-two pages of volume 1 of *Capital*, as well as parts of three chapters of volume 3, to a detailed historical description of the events that created these two principal classes of capitalism.

The precapitalist feudal society had been predominantly agricultural. Therefore, the creation of the working class involved the destruction of the feudal social ties by which most laboring people had been guaranteed access to the land and thus had maintained their ability to produce. When feudal property relationships were destroyed and transformed into modern private property, the tillers of the soil had been forcefully and violently driven off the lands to which feudal traditions had guaranteed them and their ancestors access:

> The spoliation of the Church's property, the fraudulent alienation of the State domains, the robbery of common lands, the usurpation of feudal and clan property, and its transformation into modern private property under circumstances of reckless terrorism, were just so many idyllic methods of primitive accumulation. They conquered the field for capitalist agriculture, made the soil part and parcel of capital, and created for the town industries the necessary supply of a "free". . . proletariat.[68]

When these thousands of "free" laborers were initially created, there were, of course, no preexisting jobs awaiting them. Even where there were industrial jobs, such employment required a rigid discipline to which they were not accustomed. As a consequence, "they were turned *en masse* into beggars, robbers and vagabonds . . . in most cases from stress of circumstances."[69] Marx described the cruel and barbarous legislation enacted during the transition from feudalism to capitalism to control this growing population of displaced people. These people were "whipped, branded, tortured by laws grotesquely terrible," until they were sufficiently remolded to accept "the discipline necessary for the wage system."[70]

In addition to the land becoming a part of capital, it was necessary for large fortunes to be accumulated that could be transformed into industrial capital. Marx's account of some of the most important sources of such capital is summarized in the following:

> The discovery of gold and silver in America, the extirpation, enslavement and entombment in mines of the aboriginal population, the beginning of the conquest and looting of the East Indies, the turning of Africa into a warren for the commercial hunting of

black-skins, signaled the rosy dawn of the era of capitalist production. These idyllic proceedings are the chief momenta of primitive accumulation. On their heels treads the commercial war of the European nations, with the globe for a theatre. . . .

The different momenta of primitive accumulation distribute themselves now, more or less in chronological order, particularly over Spain, Portugal, Holland, France and England. In England at the end of the seventeenth century they arrive at a systematical combination, embracing the colonies, the national debt, the modern mode of taxation, and the protectionist system. These methods depend in part on brute force, e.g., the colonial system. But they all employ the power of the State, the concentrated organized force of society, to hasten, hothouse fashion, the process of transformation of the feudal mode of production into the capitalist mode, and to shorten the transition. Force is the midwife of every old society pregnant with a new one.[71]

Thus, in describing the entire process of primitive accumulation, Marx wrote that in the period of its initial creation, "capital comes dripping from head to foot, from every pore, with blood and dirt."[72]

Capitalist Accumulation

Once capitalism came into being, however, all of this changed. The power of the capitalists, Marx maintained, came to be guaranteed by the new laws of private property. When capitalists became the ruling class, they and their spokesmen became advocates of "law and order"—the law of private property and the order of the capitalist mode of production and circulation both perpetuated their power. The separation of workers from all means of production was sufficient to start capitalism moving according to its own "laws of motion." "As soon as capitalist production is once on its own legs, it not only maintains this separation, but reproduces it on a continually extending scale."[73]

Given the social, legal, and economic foundations of the capitalist system, its "laws of motion" reflected the motive force that propelled the system—the ceaseless, unending drive to accumulate capital. The capitalist's social standing, prestige, and economic and political power depended on the size of the capital he or she controlled. The capitalist could not stand still; but was beset on every side by fierce competition. The system demanded that he or she accumulate and grow more powerful in order to outdo competitors, or else these very competitors would force him or her to the wall and take over his or her capital. Competitors were constantly developing new and better methods of production. Only by the accumulation of new and better capital could this challenge be met. Thus, Marx believed that the capitalist

shares with the miser the passion for wealth as wealth. But that which in the miser is a mere idiosyncrasy, is in the capitalist the effect of the social mechanism of which he is but one of the wheels. Moreover, the development of capitalist production makes it constantly necessary to keep increasing the amount of capital laid out in a given industrial undertaking, and competition makes the immanent laws of capitalist production to be felt by each individual industrial capitalist as external coercive laws. It compels him to keep constantly extending his capital, in order to preserve it, but extend it he cannot except by means of progressive accumulation.[74]

It was this ceaseless drive to accumulate and the fierce competition among capitalists that underlay the patterns of development, or the "laws of motion," of capitalism.

We will discuss four important consequences of competition and accumulation according to Marx: economic concentration, the tendency for the rate of profit to fall, sectoral imbalances and crises, and the alienation and increasing misery of the proletariat (working class).

Economic Concentration

As capitalism developed, Marx argued, wealth and power would become concentrated in the hands of fewer and fewer capitalists. This concentration was the result of two forces. First, competition among capitalists tended to create a situation in which the strong either crushed or absorbed the weak. "Here competition rages in direct proportion to the number, and in inverse proportion to the magnitudes, of the antagonistic capitals. It always ends in the ruin of many small capitalists, whose capitals partly pass into the hands of their conquerors, partly vanish."[75]

Second, as technology improved, there was "an increase in the minimum amount of . . . capital necessary to carry on a business under its normal conditions." In order to remain competitive, a firm would constantly have to increase the productivity of its laborers. The "productiveness of labour . . . [depended] on the scale of production."[76] Thus, changing technology as well as competition among capitalists created an inexorable movement of the capitalist system toward larger and larger firms owned by fewer and fewer capitalists. In this way, the gulf between the small class of wealthy capitalists and the great majority of society, the proletariat, continually widened.

Tendency for the Rate of Profit to Fall

Marx considered "the composition of capital and the changes it undergoes in the course of the process of accumulation" to be one of the "most important factors" in his theory.[77] The composition of capital was "determined by the proportion in which it is divided into constant capital or value of the means of production, and varible capital or value of labour-power, the sum total of wages."[78] He defined the ratio of constant capital to variable capital (c/v) as the *organic composition of capital*. He believed that ceaseless accumulation would have the effect, over time, of persistently increasing the organic composition of capital; that is, the value of the means of production would tend to increase at a faster rate than the value of the labor power purchased to operate those means of production. One of the consequences of this increase would be a persistent tendency for the rate of profit to fall.

Whereas surplus value was created by variable capital alone, the capitalist based his rate of profit on all of his capital.

The surplus-value, whatever its origin, is thus a surplus over the advanced total capital. The proportion of this surplus to the total capital is therefore expressed by the fraction $\dfrac{s}{C}$, in which C stands for total capital. We thus obtain the rate of profit $\dfrac{s}{C} = \dfrac{s}{(c+v)}$ as distinct from the rate of surplus-value $\dfrac{s}{v}$.[79]

When we divide the numerator and the denominator of the rate of profit $\dfrac{s}{(c+v)}$ by v, we get $\dfrac{(s/v)}{(c/v)+(v/v)}$ or $\dfrac{(s/v)}{(c/v)+1}$. It is obvious that the rate of profit was equal to the ratio of the rate of surplus value over the organic composition of capital plus one. Therefore, increases in the rate of surplus value (taken by themselves) would always increase the rate of profit. This was why the capitalist class had always tried to maximize the length of the working day, according to Marx. Increases in the organic composition of capital (again, taken by themselves) would always decrease the rate of profit. This latter effect might not seem as directly obvious as the effect of increases in the rate of surplus value, however. Remembering that only variable capital produced surplus value, one can see that if the rate of surplus value remained unchanged, while the organic composition of capital increased, then the surplus value created by a given quantity of labor power would have to be spread over a *larger* quantity of total capital to arrive at the rate of profit. Hence, increases in the organic composition of capital would decrease the rate of profit if the rate of surplus value remained constant.

Marx believed that capitalists' efforts to increase the rate of surplus value must hit some practical limits. When that happened, "the gradual growth of constant capital in relation to variable capital must necessarily lead to *a gradual fall of the general rate of profit*."[80] Marx thus joined Smith, Ricardo, and Mill, and was later to be joined by Keynes, in theorizing that the accumulation of capital produced a tendency for the rate of profit to fall (indeed this notion has been shared by more economic theorists than has nearly any other).

A falling rate of profit did not, of course, mean either a fall in total profit or a fall in the profit share of total output (in that total profit depended on both the rate of profit and the total quantity of capital).[81] After stating this obvious fact, Marx went on to indicate his belief that total profit generally would increase even when the rate of profit was falling.[82] Moreover, when capitalists felt the downward pressures on the rate of profit, they took steps to reverse this trend. There were, therefore, several "counteracting influences" that could halt or even reverse this tendency for various periods of time. For this reason, the decline in the profit rate did "not manifest itself in an absolute form, but rather as a tendency toward a progressive fall."[83]

Marx discussed five such counteracting influences (two of which appear to be basically the same, so we will mention only four). First, capitalists could increase the "intensity of exploitation" by "lengthening the working-day and intensifying labour."[84] Having already discussed the struggle over the length of the working day, Marx limited the discussion of this counteracting influence to methods of speeding up workers, scientific management, or what in the late nineteenth and early twentieth centuries came to be called "Taylorism." All these forms of increasing the exploitation of labor tended to raise the profit rate by "effecting a rise in the rate of surplus-value."[85]

Second, Marx mentioned all influences that could lead, for various lengths of time, to a "depression of wages below the value of labour-power."[86] This category would seem to include Marx's fourth counteracting influence—a "relative overpopulation" of workers—because overpopulation could increase profits only by depressing the wage rate.

Third, Marx listed the "cheapening of the elements of constant capital." This occurred when technological change in the methods of producing constant capital "prevents the value of constant capital, although it continually increases, from increasing at the same rate as its material volume."[87]

The last counteracting influence was foreign trade. Here Marx's analysis was very similar to Mill's. "Capital invested in foreign trade can yield a higher rate of profit," he asserted. Furthermore, it cheapened "the necessities of life for which variable capital . . . [was] exchanged" and thereby caused "the variable capital to shrink in relation to the constant capital."[88] To the extent that this happened it would offset the increase in the organic composition of capital caused by accumulation. It would also increase the rate of surplus value.

Marx devoted only three pages to a discussion of foreign trade as a counteracting influence on the fall of the rate of profit (his discussion was neither as extensive nor as sophisticated as Mill's). This was, however, to become one of the bases for the theories of imperialism formulated by disciples of Marx in the early twentieth century (which we will discuss in a later chapter). He did, even though very briefly, state a principle that was to become central to these later doctrines: "The expansion of foreign trade, although the basis of the capitalist mode of production in its infancy, has become its own product, however, with the further progress of the capitalist mode of production, *through the innate necessity of this mode of production, its need for an ever-expanding market.*"[89]

Thus, Marx's assertion that the profit rate tended to fall was *not* an empirical prediction. It was merely a theoretical, or taxonomical, device for identifying various forces that could, at any given time, be producing opposite results in the actual historical trend of the rate of profit. Of the influence of the forces tending to depress profits, Marx wrote: "It is only under certain circumstances and only after long periods that . . . [their] effects become strikingly pronounced."[90] It seems probable, in retrospect, that the most glaring deficiency in Marx's analysis of this tendency was his failure to discuss the relationship between the rate of surplus value and the organic composition of capital. An increase in the organic composition of capital meant that techniques of production were changing. With technological change, it was possible that increased efficiency in the production of the commodities consumed by workers could permit a simultaneous increase in the real wages of workers and an increase in the rate of surplus value. Thus, the change in the organic composition of capital could create its own counteracting influence, which might even be powerful enough to result in an increase in the rate of profit. It appears probable that something like this has actually happened over certain periods during the century since Marx formulated his theory. It is also probable that much of the technological change that has occurred in the twentieth century has, in Marx's terms, "cheapened the elements of constant capital." Such technological change involves what contemporary economists call "capital saving" innovations. To the degree that this has happened, it is possible that the organic composition of capital has not increased (or has increased only very slightly) even though the physical mass of capital goods has undoubtedly increased enormously.

Sectoral Imbalances and Economic Crises

When Marx asserted that wages would tend toward the subsistence level, he was in agreement with nearly all of the classical economists who had preceded him. When he stipulated that this subsistence was culturally and not biologically determined, he was in agreement with Mill. He disagreed with all of these economists, however, as to the social mechanism by which wages were kept at that level. He totally rejected Malthus's principle of population. "Every special historic mode of production," he argued, "has its own special laws of population historically valid within its limits alone."[91] The tendency of wages toward the socially defined subsistence was a result of the fact that

> a surplus labouring population is a necessary product of accumulation . . . on a capitalist basis. . . . It forms a disposable industrial reserve army, that belongs to capital quite as absolutely as if the latter had bred it at its own cost. Independently of the limits of the actual increase of population, it creates for the changing needs of the self-expansion of capital a mass of human material always ready for exploitation.[92]

Competition among workers kept wages near subsistence because members of the "industrial reserve army" of unemployed workers usually lived *below* the subsistence level and always strove to take jobs that would pay a mere subsistence. As accumulation took place, however, a boom period would create such a sharp increase in the demand for labor that the ranks of the reserve would be quickly depleted. When this happened, the capitalist would find that he had to pay higher wages to get enough labor.

Because the individual capitalist took the wage level as given and beyond any one power to change, he or she attempted to make the most of the situation. The most profitable course of action seemed to be to change the techniques of production by introducing new labor-saving machinery so that each laborer would then be working with more capital and output per worker could be increased. This labor-saving accumulation of capital would enable the capitalist to expand output with the same or an even smaller workforce. When all or most of the capitalists, acting individually, did this, the problem of high wages was temporarily alleviated as the reserve army was replenished by workers displaced by the new techniques of production. The creation of technological unemployment saved the day, but not without introducing new problems and dilemmas.

Labor-saving expansion permitted increases in total production without increasing the wages paid to workers. Therefore, while new commodities were flooding the market, workers' wages were being restricted, with the result that consumer demand was limited. The workers were still creating surplus value embodied in commodities, but the capitalists could not transform these commodities into money, or realize their profits by selling these commodities in the market, because of lack of consumer demand.

In order to clarify this process further, Marx divided the capitalist economy into two sectors, one producing consumer goods and the other producing capital goods.[93] Smooth, continuous expansion of the economy required that the exchange between these two sectors be balanced. That is, the consumption goods demanded by the workers and capitalists in the sector producing capital goods had to balance the demand for capital goods by the capitalists in the sector producing consumer goods. If this did not occur, supply would not equal demand in either sector.

But the relative size of the productive capacities of the two sectors had been at least roughly determined in the period preceding the introduction of the labor-saving technology. Consequently, after the restriction of workers' wages, the relative productive capacities did not correspond to the new redistribution of income between wages and profits, and the sector producing consumer goods found itself with excess capacity—or inadequate market demand for its products.

In this situation, the capitalists in the consumer goods industry would certainly *not* want to add immediately to their production facilities. They would, therefore, cancel any plans to add to their already excessively large capital stock. These decisions would, of course, significantly reduce the demand for capital goods, which would result in a decrease in the production of the capital-goods sector. Unlike some early underconsumptionist theories of business crises (or depressions), Marx's theory posited as the originating cause of a depression a structural imbalance between the productive capacities of the two sectors and the distribution of income between wages and profits (which tended to determine the demand for the output of the two sectors). When this imbalance occurred, the first obvious sign of a depression might appear in either sector.

When the production of capital goods decreased, workers were fired, total wages declined, and, consequently, consumer demand decreased. This led to reduced production in the consumer-goods industry, more layoffs, less demand, and so forth, in a declining spiral. The result was a general glut, or surfeit of commodities, in both sectors—a general economic collapse into depression. In the process, of course, the industrial reserve army of the unemployed was more than replenished:

> The course characteristic of modern industry, viz., a decennial cycle (interrupted by smaller oscillations), of periods of average activity, production at high pressure, crisis and stagnation, depends on the constant formation, the greater or less absorption, and the re-formation of the industrial reserve army or surplus-population. In their turn, the varying phases of the industrial cycle recruit the surplus-population, and become one of the most energetic agents of its reproduction. This peculiar course of modern industry . . . occurs in no earlier period of human history.[94]

Alienation and the Increasing Misery of the Proletariat

The process of primitive accumulation created a class of workers with nothing to sell but their labor power. That which workers produced—capital—came to control them. The further process of accumulation extended the domain of capital over increasing numbers of workers and intensified the control of capital over all wage laborers. In Marx's opinion, the entire process had extraordinarily pernicious effects on workers. It systematically prevented them from developing their potentialities. They could not become emotionally, intellectually, or esthetically fully developed human beings.

Human beings differed from animals because they created and worked with tools to shape and control the natural environment. Human senses and intellect were developed and refined through working. Through one's relations with what one produced, an individual achieved both pleasure and self-realization. In precapitalist social systems like feudalism, an individual could at least partially achieve this self-realization through work, despite an exploitative class structure. Because the exploitative social relations were also personal and paternalistic, work involved more than merely selling one's labor power as a commodity. This changed with capitalism in Marx's opinion:

> The bourgeoisie, wherever it has got the upper hand, has put an end to all feudal patriarchal, idyllic relations. It has pitilessly torn asunder the motley feudal ties that bound man to his "natural superiors," and has left remaining no other nexus between man and man than naked self-interest, than callous "cash payment." It has drowned the most heavenly ecstasies of religious fervor, of chivalrous enthusiasm, of philistine sentimentalism, in the icy water of egotistical calculation. It has resolved personal worth into exchange value.[95]

In a capitalist society, the market separated and isolated exchange value, or money price, from the qualities that shaped man's relations with things as well as with other human beings. This was especially true in the work process. To the capitalist, wages were merely another expense of production to be added to the costs of raw materials and machinery in the profit calculation. Labor became a mere commodity to be bought if a profit could be made.

Whether the laborer could sell his or her labor power was completely beyond the laborer's control. It depended on the cold and totally impersonal conditions of the market. The laborer's product was likewise totally outside the laborer's life, being the property of the capitalist.

Marx used the term *alienation* to describe the condition of men and women in this situation. They felt alienated or divorced from their work, from their institutional and cultural environment, and from their fellow workers. The conditions of work, the object produced, and, indeed, the very possibility of working were determined by the numerically small class of capitalists and their profit calculations, not by human needs or aspirations. The effects of this alienation can best be summarized in Marx's own words:

> What, then, constitutes the alienation of labour? First, the fact that labour is external to the worker, i.e., it does not belong to his essential being; that in his work, therefore, he does not affirm himself but denies himself, does not feel content but unhappy, does not develop freely his physical and mental energy but mortifies his body and ruins his mind. The worker therefore only feels himself outside his work, and in his work feels outside himself. He is at home when he is not working, and when he is working he is not at home. His labour is therefore not voluntary but coerced; it is *forced labour.* It is therefore not the satisfaction of a need; it is merely a *means* to satisfy needs external to it. Its alien character emerges clearly in the fact that as soon as no physical or other compulsion exists, labour is shunned like the plague. External labour, labour in which man alienates himself, is a labour of self-sacrifice, or mortification. Lastly, the external character of labour for the worker appears in the fact that it is not his own, but someone else's, that it does not belong to him, that in it he belongs, not to himself, but to another. . . . As a result, therefore, man (the worker) no longer feels himself to be freely active in any but his animal functions—eating, drinking, procreating, or at most in his dwelling and in dressing up, etc.; and in his human functions he no longer feels himself to be anything but an animal. What is animal becomes human and what is human becomes animal.[96]

It was this degradation and total dehumanization of the working class, thwarting man's personal development and making an alien market commodity of man's life-sustaining activities, that Marx most thoroughly condemned in the capitalist system. Furthermore, he argued that the progressive accumulation of capital worsened the worker's alienation. The counterpart of the law of the increasing concentration of capital was what Marx called the "law of the increasing misery" of the proletariat. In Marx's words:

> Within the capitalist system all methods for raising the social productiveness of labour are brought about at the cost of the individual labourer, all means for the development of production transform themselves into means of domination over, and exploitation of, the producers; they mutilate the labourer into a fragment of a man, degrade him to the level of an appendage of a machine, destroy every remnant of charm in his work and turn it into hated toil; they estrange from him the intellectual potentialities of the labour-process in the same proportion as science is incorporated in it as an independent power; they distort the conditions under which he works, subject him during the labour-process to a despotism the more hateful for its meanness; they transform his life time into working time, and drag his wife and child beneath the wheels of the Juggernaut of capital. But all methods for the production

of surplus-value are at the same time methods of accumulation; and every extension of accumulation becomes again a means for the development of those methods. It follows therefore that in proportion as capital accumulates, the lot of the labourer, be his payment high or low, must grow worse. The law . . . establishes an accumulation of misery, corresponding with accumulation of capital. Accumulation of wealth at one pole is, therefore, at the same time accumulation of misery, agony of toil, slavery, ignorance, brutality [and] mental degradation at the opposite pole.[97]

It should be noted that Marx asserted that the laborer would become worse off even if wages increased. It is necessary to stress this point because many writers have interpreted the law of increasing misery as meaning that the volume of material commodities that workers would be able to consume would consistently decline. Although Marx did once make such a statement in his youth, he later changed his mind. We do not find any argument in his mature writings to suggest that he believed wages would continuously decline. On the contrary, in *Capital* he clearly stated that he believed wages would actually rise as accumulation proceeded. As capital was accumulated, he wrote,

a larger part of their own surplus . . . comes back to . . . [workers] in the shape of means of payment, so that they can extend the circle of their enjoyments; can make some additions to their consumption-fund of clothes, furniture, etc., and can lay by small reserve-funds of money. But just as little as better clothing, food and treatment, and a larger peculium, do away with the exploitation of the slave, so little do they set aside that of the wage-worker. A rise in the price of labour, as a consequence of accumulation of capital, only means, in fact, that the length and weight of the golden chain the wage-worker has already forged for himself, allow of a relaxation of the tension of it. . . . Such an increase only means at best a quantitative diminution of the unpaid labour that the worker has to supply. This diminution can never reach the point at which it would threaten the system itself.[98]

Therefore, when Marx wrote "as capital accumulates, the lot of the labourer, be his payment high or low, must grow worse,"[99] he definitely was not asserting that wages were going to decline. He clearly was referring to an increase in alienation and general misery. As capital was accumulated, he believed, the creative, emotional, aesthetic, and intellectual potential of workers would be systematically thwarted. Marx undoubtedly would have taken as evidence of this the statement of a twentieth-century psychoanalyst who wrote that the managers of modern corporations "strip the worker of his right to think and move freely. Life is being denied; need to control, creativeness, curiosity, and independent thought are being balked, and the result, the inevitable result, is flight or fight on the part of the worker, apathy or destructiveness, psychic regression."[100]

The important point in this psychoanalyst's statement is that when capital inflicts "psychic regression" on the worker, the result is either "apathy or destructiveness." Marx believed that the result would ultimately be destructiveness—the worker would destroy the capitalist system:

Along with the constantly diminishing number of magnates of capital, who usurp and monopolize all advantages of this process of transformation, grows the mass of misery, oppression, slavery, degradation, exploitation; but with this too grows the revolt of the working-class, a class always increasing in numbers, and disciplined, united, organized by the very mechanism of the process of capitalist production itself. The monopoly of capital becomes a fetter upon the mode of production, which has sprung up and flourished along with, and under it. Centralization of the means of production and socialization of labour at last reach a point where they become incompatible with their capitalist integument. This integument is burst asunder. The knell of capitalist private property sounds. The expropriators are expropriated.[101]

But this destructiveness would, he believed, also constitute an historic act of creativity. From the shell of the old exploitive system, workers would create a new socialist system in which cooperation, planning, and human development would take the place of competition, anarchy of the market, and human degradation, exploitation, and alienation.

Workers have arisen in struggle after struggle with capitalists during the more than 100 years since Marx wrote *Capital*. But such struggles have generally been confined to local areas and have usually been brutally repressed in the advanced industrial capitalist economies. It was only in these economies, with their industrial bases and enormous productivity, that Marx believed a humane socialist system could be established by the workers.

The success of capitalism and its apparent viability to the present reflect a development that Marx did not foresee: the brutal repression of workers' struggles had the effect of channeling their misery and alienation into the nonviolent forms of apathy, despair, emotional malaise, anxiety, isolation, and loneliness,

Marx's analysis of the nature, origins, and "laws of motion" of capitalism, however, stands quite independently of his belief that workers would, within a relatively short period of time, replace capitalism with a new mode of production that they operated for their own benefit. Capitalism has survived many subsequent prophecies of its impending demise made by disciples of Marx. We cannot expect Marx, or any other thinker for that matter, to have been an infallible seer of the exact sequence and timing of future events. Capitalism—or any other social mode of production—is simply too complex to permit crystal-ball predictions. Marx did, however, provide a framework of analysis, as well as innumerable concrete theoretical and historical insights, that have continued to prove highly useful to this day in providing an understanding of the structure and functioning of capitalism.

Events in the Soviet Union and other East European countries from 1989 to early 1991 have led, once again, to the view, widely propagated in some academic circles and in the press, that "Communism has died" and Marx and Marxism are now disproved and obsolete. Marx was, above all else, a theorist who sought to understand capitalism. Nothing that has occurred in these countries that have called themselves Communist countries can possibly detract from Marx's brilliant insights into the nature and laws of motion of capitalism. If Marx had anticipated economies such as those that have existed in Eastern Europe and had written about their nature and laws of motion, then it is conceivable that recent events in that region could have proved him wrong. But he wrote about capitalism, and only events in capitalist economies could possibly prove him wrong and render his ideas obsolete. Those events have yet to occur. Marx's ideas will undoubtedly survive this and other attempts in the future to diminish their impact as long as capitalism continues to function essentially as Marx described it.

Notes to Chapter 9

1. Karl Marx, *Grundrisse*, tr. Martin Nicolaus (New York: Vintage Books, 1973), p. 85.
2. Ibid.
3. Ibid., pp. 85–86.
4. Ibid., p. 242.
5. Ibid., p. 241.
6. Ibid., p. 246.
7. Ibid., p. 243.
8. Ibid., p. 242.
9. Ibid., pp. 243–44.
10. Ibid., p. 249.
11. Ibid., pp. 240–41.
12. Karl Marx, *Capital*, 3 vols. (Moscow: Foreign Languages, 1961), vol. 3, p. 35.
13. Ibid.
14. Ibid., vol. 1, p. 36.
15. Ibid.
16. Ibid., vol. 1, pp. 37–38.
17. Ibid., vol. 1, p. 38.
18. Ibid., vol. 1, pp. 39–40.
19. Ibid., vol. 1, p. 62.
20. Ibid., vol. 1, p. 39.
21. Ibid., vol. 1, p. 41.
22. Ibid., vol. 1, p. 44.
23. Ibid., vol. 1, p. 39.
24. Ibid., vol. 1, p. 44.
25. Ibid., vol. 1, p. 82.
26. Ibid., vol. 1, pp.169–70.
27. Ibid., vol. 1, p. 170.
28. Ibid., vol. 1, p. 75.
29. Ibid., vol. 1, p. 73.
30. Ibid., vol. 1, p. 170.
31. Ibid., vol. 1, pp. 105–6.
32. Ibid., vol. 1, pp. 146–47.
33. Ibid., vol. 1, p. 147.
34. Ibid., vol. 1, p. 155.
35. Ibid., vol. 1, pp. 152–53.
36. Ibid., vol. 1, p. 155.
37. Ibid., vol. 1, p. 163.
38. Ibid., vol. 1, p. 176.
39. Ibid., vol. 1, p. 63.
40. Ibid., vol. 1, p. 165.
41. Ibid., vol. 2, p. 23.
42. Ibid., vol. 1, p. 167.
43. Ibid., vol. 1, pp. 168–69.
44. Ibid., vol. 1, p. 170.
45. Ibid., vol. 1, p. 169.
46. Ibid., vol. 1, pp. 170–72.
47. Ibid., vol. 1, 171.
48. Ibid., vol. 1, p. 172.

49. Ibid., vol. 1, p. 171.

50. Ibid., vol. 1, p. 232.

51. Ibid., vol. 1, p. 195.

52. Ibid., vol. 1, pp. 216–17.

53. Ibid., vol. 1, p. 217.

54. Ibid.

55. Ibid., vol. 1, p. 595.

56. Ibid., vol. 1, p. 212.

57. Ibid., vol. 1, pp. 217–18.

58. Ibid., vol. 1, pp. 264–65.

59. Ibid., vol. 1, p. 270.

60. Ibid.

61. Ibid., vol. 3, p. 156.

62. Ibid.

63. L. Bortkeiwicz, "Value and Price in the Marxian System," *International Economic Papers*, 2 (1937).

64. Marx, *Capital*, vol. 3, p. 259.

65. Ibid., vol. 1, pp. 583–84.

66. Ibid., vol. 1, pp. 713–14.

67. Ibid., vol. 1, p. 715.

68. Ibid., vol. 1, pp. 732–33.

69. Ibid., vol. 1, p. 734.

70. Ibid., vol. 1, p. 737.

71. Ibid., vol. 1, p. 751.

72. Ibid., vol. 1, p. 760.

73. Ibid., vol. 1, p. 714.

74. Ibid., vol. 1, p. 592.

75. Ibid., vol. 1, p. 626.

76. Ibid.

77. Ibid., vol. 1, p. 612.

78. Ibid.

79. Ibid., vol. 3, p. 42.

80. Ibid., vol. 3, p. 208.

81. Ibid., vol. 3, p. 219. This citation is given here because both of these assertions are frequently and erroneously attributed to Marx.

82. Ibid., vol. 3, p. 226.

83. Ibid., vol. 3, p. 209.

84. Ibid., vol. 3, p. 227.

85. Ibid., vol. 3, p. 228.

86. Ibid., vol. 3, p. 230.

87. Ibid., vol. 3, p. 231.

88. Ibid., vol. 3, p. 232.

89. Ibid., italics added.

90. Ibid., vol. 3, p. 233.

91. Ibid., vol. 1, p. 632.

92. Ibid.

93. Ibid., vol. 2, chs. 20–21.

94. Ibid., vol. 1, pp. 532–33.

95. Karl Marx and Frederick Engels, "The Communist Manifesto," in *Essential Works of Marxism*, ed. Arthur P. Mendel (New York: Bantam, 1965), p. 15.

96. Karl Marx, *Economic and Philosophic Manuscripts of 1844* (Moscow: Progress, 1959), p. 69.

97. Marx, *Capital*, vol. 1, p. 645.

98. Ibid., vol. 1, pp. 618–19.

99. Ibid., vol. 1, p. 645.

100. Quoted from Erich Fromm, *The Sane Society* (New York: Premier Books, 1965), p. 115.

101. Marx, *Capital*, vol. 1, p. 763.

Chapter 10

The Triumph of Utilitarianism: The Economics of Jevons, Menger, and Walras

The period from the mid-1840s to 1873 (the year that marked the beginning of the Long Depression in Europe) was one of rapid economic expansion throughout most of Europe. Industrialization was taking place in continental Europe as well as in the United States. England experienced a surge of industrial growth, with heavy industry, and particularly the capital goods industry, leading the way.

In the entire North Atlantic capitalist sphere, this rapid industrial growth was accompanied by an ever increasing degree of concentration of capital, industrial power, and wealth. In some cases, this growing concentration was the result of aggressive and destructive competition that eliminated small or weak competitors. In other cases, large, powerful competitors, seeing the potentially mutual destructiveness of such ruthless rivalry, combined in cartels, trusts, and mergers in order to ensure their survival.

During this period, there were also revolutionary changes in transportation and communication. These changes also furthered industrial concentration, because they made it possible for ever-widening markets to be supplied efficiently by a small number of giant companies or corporations. The joint-stock company, or corporation, became an effective means by which a single business organization could gain control over vast amounts of capital. A large, well-organized money market evolved in Europe and North America that successfully channeled the smaller capital holdings of thousands of individuals and small businesses into the hands of large corporations.

Thus, by the early 1870s, capitalism was beginning to take on a modified form—an economic system dominated by anywhere from several hundred to a thousand or so colossal corporations in the important spheres of industry, finance, transportation, and marketing. Although this concentration was to become significantly more severe by the early twentieth century, the new form of capitalism was emerging quite clearly by the 1870s.

Social relations among people in this new form of capitalism began to assume two distinct and drastically different forms. Within the giant corporation, social relations took on a hierarchical, bureaucratic form. Corporations were pyramidal social organizations in which each stratum was rigidly controlled and coordinated by the stratum above it. The entire pyramid was controlled from the top by a small group of owners or managers. All individual actions and economic or production processes within the corporation were integrated and coordinated in a rational, calculated manner. Elaborate systems of cost accounting, quality control, and scientific management were among the methods by which this rational control was exercised. The objective of the capitalists, of course, remained unchanged: to maximize profit and to accumulate more capital.

In its relationship to the remainder of the capitalist economy, however, the corporation was in no different a position than had been the smaller, individual capitalist of earlier decades. Among the giant corporations, the thousands of much smaller and less important business enterprises, and the tens of millions of workers, the older social relations of commodity production still prevailed. A massive, intricate system of mutual interdependence among all of these institutions and individuals continued to be mediated only by the blind, impersonal forces of the market.

Within this historical context, it might seem that economists would abandon Adam Smith's "invisible hand" conception of a capitalist economy, which had been based on the analysis of an economy composed of many small enterprises. In such an economy, no individual enterprise could exercise a significant influence on the overall market. The actions of any firm were dictated by consumer tastes, as registered in the marketplace, and by the competition of innumerable other small firms, each vying for consumers' dollars.

We have seen that this view of a capitalist economy combined quite naturally with the individualism and moral hedonism of utilitarianism to create the conclusion that capitalism was an economic system in which social harmony naturally prevailed. While the writings of Smith and Ricardo combined this view with a labor theory of value perspective that led to quite different conclusions, Bentham, Say, Senior, and Bastiat had gone far in freeing the individualistic, utilitarian perspective from the "dangerous," class conflict conclusions of the labor theory perspective.

If one believed that the history of economic theories should reveal nothing but a continuous and progressively closer approximation of economic theories to the existing reality of the evolving capitalist system, then it would appear that one would expect the individualistic, utilitarian perspective of Say, Senior, and Bastiat to be slowly replaced by one that reflected the changing economic and social forms of capitalism.

Such was not the case. During the early 1870s, at precisely the time when the drive toward the economic concentration of corporate capitalism was gaining momentum, three very famous economics texts were published. William

Stanley Jevons's *The Theory of Political Economy*[1] and Carl Menger's *Grundsatze der Volkswirtschaftslebre* (Principles of Economics)[2] both appeared in 1871, and three years later Leon Walras's *Elements d'economie politique pure* (Elements of Pure Economics) was published.[3] Although there were many differences in the analyses of these men, the similarities in both the approaches and contents of these books were striking.

Each represented a continuation of the individualistic, utilitarian perspective of Say, Senior, and Bastiat. Each independently worked out a logically consistent solution to the water-diamond paradox that had led Smith to the conclusion that no direct relation between utility and exchange value could be found. This paradox had never been adequately resolved by Say, Senior, or Bastiat, even though these three thinkers had insisted that utility was the determinant of exchange value.

Jevons, Menger, and Walras formulated the version of the utility theory of value that remains at the heart of neoclassical orthodoxy to this day. They also added certain refinements and extensions to the ideas of Say, Senior, and Bastiat—the most important extension being Walras's conception of general economic equilibrium, which constituted one of the most important conceptual or analytical developments in the history of economic thought, and of which more will be said below. It is unquestionably because they were the first thinkers to provide a consistent theory of value within the general utilitarian philosophical perspective that later conservative economists have referred to their theories as a "revolution" in economic thinking, and have referred to the 1870s as a watershed separating old-fashioned classical economics from modern, scientific neoclassical economics.

The significance of the "marginalism" that was introduced into economic theory by these three thinkers would seem to depend on the historian's view of contemporary economic theory. A segment of the academic economics profession has evolved that appears to put great emphasis on the logical and mathematical rigor of a theory, quite independently of its content or the practical importance of its conclusions. Among economists of this bent, a theorist is admired to the extent that he or she can cast his or her theory in the most esoteric, complex, and rigorously mathematical form.

The notion of declining marginal utility (developed independently by each of the thinkers discussed in this chapter) permitted Jevons, Menger, and Walras and their successors to show concretely and explicitly how utility determined values (something that Bentham, Say, Senior, and Bastiat believed but could not demonstrate). Although this was definitely a major improvement over the doctrines of the earlier utility theorists, the major significance of Jevons, Menger, and Walras lay in how they changed the form of utilitarian economics and did *not* make any major change in its content. Marginalism permitted the utilitarian vision of human nature, which was considered to consist exclusively of the rational, calculating maximization of utility, to be formulated in terms of differential calculus. This then constituted the real beginning of the trend toward esoteric mathematical formulation of economic theories (although Menger himself disliked the use of mathematics to express economic theory). It is probably for this reason that economists who value mathematical rigor for its own sake see Jevons and Walras as being the most important forebears of modern economic theory.

While these three thinkers' development of the principle of marginal utility unquestionably furnished an important link in completing the chain of the arguments of Say, Senior, and Bastiat, it hardly seems significant enough to view their ideas either as revolutionary or as a watershed dividing the history of economic theories. Their corrections to the formulation of the already widely held utilitarian notion that utility determines prices seem comparable in importance to those of later theorists who successfully worked out Marx's "transformation problem." Beyond this refinement of utilitarian price theory, only Walras—in his theory of general economic equilibrium—appears to have formulated a truly significant addition to the utilitarian tradition in economics (although the Physiocrats and Say had developed simpler versions of a general economic equilibrium, Walras went far beyond their sketchy, suggestive treatments).

Jevons's Theory of Marginal Utility and Exchange

William Stanley Jevons (1835–1882) wrote on a wide variety of topics, ranging from meteorology to logic to economic theory. His *Theory of Political Economy* was his most important work in the last field. In 1860, in a letter to his brother, he wrote: "in the last few months I have fortunately struck out what I have no doubt is the *true Theory of Economy*, so thorough-going and consistent that I cannot read other books on the subject without indignation."[4] This "true theory" was finally published in 1871.

In the preface to the *Theory*, Jevons stated that "Bentham's ideas . . . are . . . the starting point of the theory given in this work."[5] He had no doubt that utilitarianism was the only possible foundation for scientific economic theory: "In this work I have attempted to treat economy as a·calculus of pleasure and pain, and have sketched out . . . the form which the science . . . must ultimately take."[6] The ultimate truth, on the basis of which he had felt such indignation toward other theories, was "*that value depends entirely upon utility.*"[7]

When Jevons used the term *value*, he always meant simply exchange value, or price. Whereas labor theorists, such as Marx, had defined value as the labor embodied in a commodity, Jevons contemptuously rejected such a definition:

> A student of economics has no hope of ever being clear and correct in his ideas of the science if he thinks of value as at all a *thing* or an *object*, or even as anything which lies in a thing or object. . . . The word value, so far as it can be correctly used, merely expresses *the circumstance of its exchanging in a certain ratio for some other substance.*[8]

Thus, Jevons was interested only in prices. He avowedly and proudly restricted his economic analysis to the sphere of circulation, the market. As Marx had pointed out some years before, within the sphere of the market all people are essentially identical. When Jevons wrote of people, he assiduously avoided any real discussion of superordinate or subordinate social relations. People, in Jevons's view, had only two characteristics that defined them as economic agents; moreover, every person had both of these characteristics. Hence, there was an abstract, implicit equality among all persons. The first characteristic was that they derived utility from consuming commodities: "Anything which an individual is found to desire . . . must be assumed to possess for him utility. In the science of economics we treat men not as they ought to be, but as they are."[9] The second characteristic was that every person was a rational, calculating maximizer. And rational, calculating, maximizing behavior was the only element of human action to be studied by economics: "To satisfy our wants to the utmost with the least effort—to procure the greatest amount of what is desirable at the expense of the least that is undesirable—in other words, to *maximize pleasure*, is the problem of economics."[10]

People received utility from consuming commodities. The error of previous economists, Jevons believed, lay in their failure to distinguish between the *total utility* a person derived from the consumption of a given quantity of some commodity and the "final degree of utility" (or, what in later neoclassical terminology came to be called the "marginal utility") that the person derived from consuming the *last small increment* of that commodity. Although it was often true that total utility might continue to become greater as one consumed an increased quantity of a commodity, the final "degree of utility . . . ultimately decreases as that quantity increases."[11] It was this "final degree of utility," or marginal utility, that concerned Jevons. This principle of diminishing marginal utility was to become the cornerstone of the neoclassical restatement of utilitarianism.

By introducing the notion of marginalism into utilitarian economics, Jevons had found a way in which the utilitarian view of human beings as rational, calculating maximizers could be put into mathematical terms. If the total utility one received from consuming a commodity depended on the quantity consumed, then this could be written as a mathematical function, $TU = f(Q)$, which simply says total utility (TU) has some concrete mathematical relationship to the quantity (Q) consumed. In calculus, the first derivative of a function tells one how much the dependent variable (in this case, total utility) changes as a consequence of an infinitesimally small change in the independent variable (in this case, the quantity consumed). The first derivative of the total utility function gives one the *marginal utility* at any particular quantity consumed. The logic of maximization could be easily formulated in terms of calculus. The total utility function was maximized when the quantity was increased to that point at which marginal utility was equal to zero. This was not very profound. It simply meant that to maximize one's utility from consuming a particular commodity, one should consume the commodity (if there were no costs of consumption) until one was satiated, that is, until one could derive no more utility from another small increment of the commodity.

When consumption involved costs, those costs could be stated in mathematical form. For example, if one possessed a commodity y and could only get another commodity x by giving up some y in exchange, then one could compare the ratios of one's marginal utilities for the two commodities, MU_x / MU_y and the prices of the two commodities, P_x / P_y. If MU_x / MU_y was higher than P_x / P_y, then our individual could gain utility by trading some of his y for some x. If the process continued until the individual had exhausted the gains from exchange, he or she would have traded to the point at which $MU_x / MU_y = P_x / P_y$. To put the same thing differently, the ratio MU_x / P_x would tell one how much additional utility one would get (or give up) if one purchased (or sold) an additional dollar's worth of commodity x. The two individuals would, Jevons asserted, buy and sell the commodities until the marginal utilities of each commodity had changed to the point where $MU_x / P_x = MU_y / P_y$. At that point, the last dollar's worth of either x or y yielded the same increment to the individual's total utility. If for an individual the ratio MU_x / P_x was greater than MU_y / P_y, then that individual would sell y and buy x, thereby losing less utility for giving up a dollar's worth of y than he or she gained from the additional dollar's worth of x. But as he or she gave up y and gained x, the principle of diminishing marginal utility meant that MU_y would increase and MU_x would decrease until $MU_x / P_x = MU_y / P_y$. At that point, no further gains from exchange could be realized. The reverse but identical process would have occurred if MU_y / P_y had been greater than MU_x / P_x.

All prior utilitarian theorists had realized that in voluntary exchange, an individual bought or sold as long as what he or she purchased gave more utility than the utility lost in what he or she sold. This had always been the basis for advocating free exchange and for the belief that exchange harmonized everyone's interests. Jevons's only addition to the theory had been to give this principle a mathematical formulation and to make explicit the distinction between total utility and marginal utility.[12] Thus Jevons's major addition to the ideas of the previous utilitarian economists can be summed up in his own words: "The nature of wealth and value is explained by the consideration of indefinitely small amounts of pleasure and pain."[13] "I contend that all economic writers must be mathematical so far as they are scientific at all."[14]

Jevons attempted to show how marginal utility determined prices. But in doing so he tried to show how two "trading bodies" could arrive at equilibrium prices for two commodities. But the theoretical problem as he set it up did not yield any determinate solution, and it was left to other neoclassical economists to demonstrate how the marginal-utility theory could become a theory of prices. Jevons simply demonstrated how consumers arranged their exchanges, once prices were known, in order to maximize their individual utilities.

Jevons did not, however, derive from the Benthamite notion of diminishing marginal utility the egalitarian conclusions of Bentham. In our critique of Thompson's utilitarianism, we argued that interpersonal comparisons of the relative intensities of the utility of wealth or income were impossible because pleasure was a purely subjective, personal experience. From this we concluded that utilitarianism could ethically compare two social situations only when unanimity prevailed among all participants. This, we argued, gave utilitarianism its highly conservative bent. The situations before and after an exchange are among the few situations in any social setting where such unanimity prevailed. If both parties participated in the exchange voluntarily, then it could be assumed that both benefited. This seemingly trivial conclusion has always been the basis of the utilitarian belief in the natural harmony of market capitalism.

Unlike Bentham, Thompson, and Mill, Jevons clearly recognized (and appreciated) this limitation of utilitarianism:

> The reader will find . . . that there is never, in any single instance, an attempt made to compare the amount of feeling in one mind with that in another. I see no means by which such comparison can be accomplished. The susceptibility of one mind may, for what we know, be a thousand times greater than that of another. . . . Every mind is thus inscrutable to every other mind, and no common denominator of feeling seems to be possible.[15]

Not surprisingly, Jevons felt certain that social harmony and not class conflict was the natural state of market capitalism. He asserted that "the supposed conflict of labour with capital is a delusion."[16] Appealing to universal brotherhood, he added: "We ought not look at such subjects from a class point of view," because "in economics at any rate [we] *should regard all men as brothers*."[17] This "brotherhood" of social harmony arose, of course, because all people appear essentially equal and in the same light when seen exclusively as exchangers:

> Each labourer must be regarded, like each landowner and each capitalist, as bringing into the common stock one part of the component elements, bargaining for the best share of the produce which the conditions of the market allow him to claim successfully.[18]
>
> He who pays a high price must either have a very great need of that which he buys, or very little need of that which he pays for it; on either supposition there is gain by exchange. In questions of this sort there is but one rule which can be safely laid down, namely that no one will buy a thing unless he expects advantage from the purchase; *and perfect freedom of exchange, therefore, tends to the maximizing of utility.*[19]

Again the utility perspective had arrived at a new appreciation of the "invisible hand" that now, with Jevons's new "scientific" and "mathematical" formulation, could be shown to maximize everyone's utility in a world of brotherhood and harmony.

Jevons also developed a theory of capital that, like those of Ricardo and

Marx, stressed the temporal dimension of production. A highly similar theory of capital was to become central to the later Austrian and Chicago schools of neoclassical economics (both of which grew out of the influence of Menger and reflected the spirit of Bastiat). This capital theory was developed only a few years later by a disciple of Menger—Eugen von Böhm-Bawerk. Because Böhm-Bawerk's version was superior to that of Jevons, and because the theory is usually associated with Böhm-Bawerk, we will postpone a discussion until we consider his ideas in the next chapter.

The principal objective of Jevons's capital theory was to refute Ricardo's conclusion that the rate of profit varied inversely to the rate of wages. Ricardo's conclusion obviously demonstrated the fundamental antagonism between capital and labor, and Jevons did not like it. Discussing Ricardo's theory, Jevons wrote:

> We thus arrive at the simple equation—
>   produce = profit + wages
> A plain result also is drawn from the formula; for we are told that if wages rise profits must fall, and vice versa. But such a doctrine is radically fallacious. . . . The wages of a working man are ultimately coincident with what he produces, after the deduction of rent, taxes and the interest of capital.[20]
>
> It is the proper function of capitalists to sustain labour before the result is accomplished, and as many branches of industry require a large outlay long previous to any definite result being arrived at, it follows that capitalists must undertake the risk of any branch of industry where the ultimate profits are not accurately known. . . . The amount of capital will depend upon the amount of anticipated profits, and the competition to obtain the proper workmen will strongly tend to secure to the latter all their legitimate share in the ultimate produce.[21]

Since competition would secure to the worker his "legitimate share," Jevons hoped the trade unionist, who saw the capitalist as a class enemy, would "cease his exclusive strife against his true ally, his wealthy employer."[22] Because the accumulation of capital benefited all workers, Jevons believed that the laborer should view the capitalists as "the trustee who holds his capital rather for the good of others than himself."[23] The common interest of both the wealthy "trustee" and the laborer who "benefited" from the trustee's wealth were both promoted by free exchange. Bastiat had asserted that economics was exchange—pure and simple. Jevons wrote:

> Exchange is so important a process in the maximizing of utility . . . that some economists have regarded their science as treating of this operation alone. . . . I am perfectly willing to agree with the high importance attributed to exchange. It is impossible to have a correct idea of the science of economics without a perfect comprehension of the theory of exchange.[24]

Jevons, however, did not want economics to be seen as explaining only exchange. Both Thompson and Hodgskin had argued, on utilitarian grounds, that exchange would be even more beneficial in an economy where workers owned their own means of production. Jevons did not want anyone to forget that capitalists' ownership of capital was sacrosanct and that "it is the proper function of capitalists to sustain labour."[25] Therefore, he extended Bastiat's definition of economics (in a way with which Bastiat surely would have agreed): "Economics, then, is not solely the science of exchange or value: it is also the science of capitalization."[26]

It is not surprising that Jevons's indignation toward prior economists, which he had expressed to his brother in the letter written in 1860, did not extend to all prior economists, but was directed primarily toward Ricardo and Mill:

> When at length a true system of economics comes to be established, it will be seen that that able but wrong-headed man, David Ricardo, shunted the car of economic science on to a wrong line—a line, however, on which it was further urged toward confusion by his equally able and wrong-headed admirer, John Stuart Mill. There were economists, such as Malthus and Senior, who had a far better comprehension of the true doctrines.[27]

Jevons's *The Theory of Political Economy* is replete with condemnations of Ricardo and Mill and laudatory statements describing the doctrines of Malthus, Say, Senior, and Bastiat. "J.B. Say has correctly . . . defined utility,"[28] he wrote, and the doctrine was correctly developed by Senior "in his admirable treatise" and by "Bastiat, for instance, in his *Harmonies of Political Economy*."[29] In another essay, while discussing Malthus's theory of population, Jevons referred to Malthus as "one of the most humane and excellent of men."[30]

One of John Maynard Keynes's favorite quotations from Malthus's writings shows quite clearly what type of man Jevons considered to be "most humane and excellent." The quotation is from Malthus's *Essay on Population*, and it was in the context of discussing Malthus's population theory that Jevons expressed his admiration of Malthus.

> A man who is born into a world already possessed, if he cannot get subsistence from his parents on whom he has a just demand, and if the society does not want his labour, has no claim of *right* to the smallest portion of food, and, in fact, has no business to be where he is. At nature's mighty feast there is no vacant cover for him. She tells him to be gone, and will quickly execute her own orders, if he does not work upon the compassion of some of her guests. If these guests get up and make room for him, other intruders immediately appear demanding the same favour. The report of a provision for all that come, fills the hall with numerous claimants. The order and harmony of the feast is disturbed, the plenty that before reigned is changed into scarcity; and the happiness of the guests is destroyed by the spectacle of misery and dependence in every part of the hall, and by the clamorous importunity of those, who are justly enraged at not finding the provision which they had been taught to expect. The guests learn too late their error, in counteracting those strict orders to all intruders, issued by the great mistress of the feast, who, wishing that all her guests should have plenty, and knowing that she could not provide for unlimited numbers, humanely refused to admit fresh comers when her table already was full.[31]

One wonders what a person would have to have done or said for Jevons to have considered that person inhumane.

Rereading the doctrines of the four economists whom Jevons most admired, it strikes one as rather strange that Jevons's ideas are frequently referred to as constituting a revolution in economic theory that marks a watershed dividing older from more modern views. The fundamental differences between the utility-theory perspective and the labor-theory perspective were clear before Jevons wrote anything, and his contribution was primarily to show that marginalism permitted the doctrines of Malthus, Say, Senior, and Bastiat to be stated with mathematical elegance and greater logical consistency. But the theoretical and ideological essence of the utility perspective remained unchanged.

Menger's Theory of Marginal Utility, Prices, and Income Distribution

Carl Menger (1840–1921) achieved eminence through his writings both in economic theory (the *Principles of Economics* being his principal work) and in methodology (some of his writings on methodology exist in English translation under the title *Problems of Economics and Sociology*).[32] In his economic theory, he rejected the use of mathematical equations and expressed his theories verbally with the aid of numerical examples.

His description of total utility and marginal utility was similar to that of Jevons. He illustrated the principle with a table of numbers. Table 10.1 reproduces the numbers from Menger's table with some labels added for clarification.[33] In the table, to find the marginal utility of some commodity (say type II) one goes to the second column and then reads down to the number of units consumed. If six units of commodity II were consumed, for example, the marginal utility of the sixth unit would be 4. The total utility (not illustrated in the table) can be calculated simply by summing the marginal utilities down to the number of units consumed. For example, six units of commodity II yield a total utility of 39.

The relationship between total utility and marginal utility can be graphed (assuming that the units of commodities can be subdivided and therefore that the lines relating utility to quantities consumed are smooth and continuous). Figure 10.1 illustrates the relationship between the marginal utility and the total utility of commodity II in Menger's table. This general relationship between total quantities and marginal quantities recurs in neoclassical economics, and several types of maximizing problems can be analyzed in a similar manner.

Menger used his table to illustrate how a consumer maximized his or her utility. We quote Menger's own explanation of the table:

> Suppose that the scale in column I expresses the importance to some one individual of satisfaction of his need for food, this importance diminishing according to the degree of satisfaction already attained, and that the scale in column V expresses similarly the importance of his need for tobacco. It is evident that satisfaction of his need for food, up to a certain degree of completeness, has a decidedly higher impor-

Table 10.1

An Illustration of Declining Marginal Utility

Number of units consumed	Type of commodity									
	I	II	III	IV	V	VI	VII	VIII	IX	X
1	10	9	8	7	6	5	4	3	2	1
2	9	8	7	6	5	4	3	2	1	0
3	8	7	6	5	4	3	2	1	0	
4	7	6	5	4	3	2	1	0		
5	6	5	4	3	2	1	0			
6	5	4	3	2	1	0				
7	4	3	2	1	0					
8	3	2	1	0						
9	2	1	0							
10	1	0								
11	0									

tance to this individual than satisfaction of his need for tobacco. But if his need for food is already satisfied up to a certain degree of completeness (e.g., if a further satisfaction of his need for food has only the importance to him that we designated numerically by the figure 6), consumption of tobacco begins to have the same importance to him as further satisfaction of his need for food. The individual will therefore endeavor, from this point on, to bring the satisfaction of his need for tobacco into equilibrium with the satisfaction of his need for food.[34]

Menger believed that the equilibrium at which the individual maximized his or her utility was achieved when the individual equated the marginal utility derived from any one commodity to the marginal utility derived from each of the other commodities he or she consumed. This statement of the maximizing condition was inferior to that of Jevons because Menger neglected prices. Menger's maximizing solution would hold only if the price per unit of each of his types of commodities were equal to the price per unit of every other type. In that case Jevons's equation $MU_x / P_x = MU_y / P_y$ would have the same number in the denominator of each ratio, and the equality of the ratios would require that the numerators (or the marginal utilities) be equal. Jevons's formulation was the correct one, and Menger's formulation was, although he did not realize it, a special, highly unlikely case.

Menger's discussion of price determination, however, was superior to Jevons's. Menger explained prices on the basis of supply and demand. All of the classical economists had explained short-run market prices on the basis of supply and demand. So, in this respect, the classical, Marxist, and neoclassical economists have never differed. The differences have been in their explanations of what underlies supply and demand. Smith, Ricardo, and Marx sought to find explanations of rent, wages, and profit that were outside the realm of prices. Rent, wages, and profits were both the components in the class distri-

Figure 10.1   **Relationship of Total Utility and Marginal Utility**

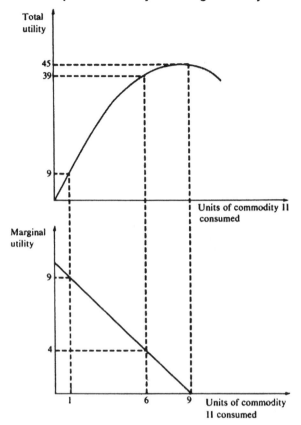

bution of income for the total society and the components of cost for an individual firm's output. As cost components, their summation was Smith's "natural price" or Marx's "price of production" of a commodity. When an industry was in equilibrium, the market price, as determined by supply and demand, would equal the natural price, or price of production. This was the nature of the pricing process when viewed from the labor-theory perspective—the distribution of income was independent of prices, and, in fact, determined them.

The utility perspective viewed the pricing process in an entirely different manner: supply and demand determined prices, and supply and demand were, in turn, explained by utility. Therefore, utility was the ultimate determinant of the prices of consumer goods. The prices of the "factors of production"— land, labor, and capital—were also determined by their supply and demand. Their supply was determined by the calculations of utility on the part of their owners, and their demand by *their productivity* in producing consumer goods as well as by the utility consumers derive from consuming these goods. Thus, in the utility perspective, wages, rent, and profit were at least partially determined by the prices of consumer goods. The difference in the two views of the pricing process was indeed distinct. Menger's superiority over Jevons lay in the way in which he described this pricing process from his utility-theory perspective.

Menger explained demand for consumer goods by showing that when a particular good had a high price in relation to the marginal utility that most consumers could get from that commodity, most consumers would get more utility by keeping their money than by spending it on that good. But as the price of the good dropped, more consumers would find that the marginal utility derived from consuming that commodity exceeded the utility that they lost by giving up the smaller amount of money. Moreover, as the price dropped, consumers who were already consuming the good would find that utility maximization required them to buy more of the good. Thus, from Menger's principle of diminishing marginal utility, he derived the law of demand: The quantity of a commodity that people were willing to purchase depended on the price of the commodity, and the quantity demanded and the price were inversely related to each other.[35]

Menger's discussion of supply was less adequate. He usually treated supply as a preexisting quantity already in the hands of the seller. The seller, using utility maximization as a guide, decided what quantities he or she wished to sell at any given price. The combination of the desires to buy and sell (all determined by utility considerations) determined prices. Menger went on to show that a monopolist selling a commodity would charge higher prices and sell smaller quantities than would have obtained if the commodity had been sold by many competitive sellers.[36] Menger, therefore, extolled the benefits of free competition.

Menger called commodities produced for consumption "goods of first order," and the factors of production he called "goods of higher order."[37] He wished to demonstrate two relationships between these two kinds of goods. First, a variety of goods of higher order was necessary to produce "goods of lower order," and, therefore, capital and land were as necessary to production as was labor.[38] In this assertion, as we have seen, he did not differ from the labor theory of value. Second, he wanted to show, in direct contradiction to the labor theory, that "the value of goods of higher order is always and without exception determined by the prospective value of the goods of lower order in whose production they serve."[39] In this regard, he considered the labor theory of value to be "among the most egregious of the fundamental errors that have had the most far-reaching consequences in the previous development of our science."[40]

Menger included labor, raw materials, and tools as goods of higher order. Like Jevons, his conception of capital involved more than simply the tools and materials of production; it focused primarily on the time dimension of production. He argued that the "satisfaction of our needs is . . . dependent on the command of quantities of economic goods for certain periods of time (on capital services). . . . For this reason, capital services are objects to which we attribute value."[41] Because Menger believed that no good of higher order could produce a consumption good by itself—that is, that goods of higher order were complementary and had to be used together—he had a difficult time demonstrating how one could measure the productivity of a single good of higher order. Like nearly every thinker in the utility tradition, he believed that the price paid each individual productive input reflected the size of each input's productive contribution. Measuring that productive contribution was, therefore, very important.

Menger's solution to this problem of measurement was summarized in this way:

> Assuming in each instance that all available goods of a higher order are employed in the most economic fashion, the value of a concrete quantity of a good of higher order is equal to the difference in importance between the satisfactions that can be attained when we have command of the given quantity of the good of higher order whose value we wish to determine and the satisfactions that would be attained if we did not have this quantity at our command.[42]

Menger's analysis was suggestive but inadequate. If, for example, the firm being considered was a farm, and the good of higher order being considered was seed grain, then without the seed grain, production would be impossible. Using his method, Menger would have to conclude that the seed grain produced all of the value of the output, despite the use of land, tractors, fertilizers, and so on. Needless to say, this was not Menger's intention. A consistent theory of input pricing within the utility perspective required that inputs be at least partially substitutable and that one examine the effect on output of a small marginal increment of one input. This, in fact, was the method adopted in the marginal-productivity theory, which we will discuss in the next chapter.

Having established that inputs were paid according to their productivity, Menger made an assertion that was to characterize most versions of marginal utility economics: When each input was paid the value of its productive contribution, the value of the total output that had been produced would be exactly exhausted. Therefore, *there was no surplus for any person or class to expropriate*. The economic, social, political, and ideological implications of this assertion—antithetical to the doctrines of Smith, Ricardo, Thompson, Hodgskin, and Marx—are obvious. In Menger's words:

> The aggregate present value of all the complementary quantities of goods of a higher order (that is, all the raw materials, labor services, services of land, machines, tools, etc.) necessary for the production of a good of . . . first order is equal to the prospective value of the product. But it is necessary to include in the sum not only the goods of higher order technically required for its production but also the services of capital and the activity of the entrepreneur. For these are as unavoidably necessary in every economic production of goods as the technical requisites already mentioned.[43]

Menger felt no need to justify profits by claiming that capitalists engaged in painful abstemious behavior. He simply stated that "the harmony of the needs that the individual households attempt to satisfy is reflected in their property."[44] Then he reassuringly affirmed that "the entire sum of goods at an economizing individual's command for the satisfaction of his needs, we call his *property*. His property is not, however, an arbitrarily combined quantity of goods, but a direct reflection of his needs."[45] He continued:

> Human economy and property have a joint economic origin since both have, as the ultimate reason for their existence, the fact that goods exist whose available quantities are smaller than the requirements of men. Property, therefore, like human economy, is not an arbitrary invention but rather the only practically possible solution of the problem that is, in the nature of things, imposed upon us by the disparity between requirements for, and available quantities of, all economic goods.[46]

We will see in the next section that Menger believed society was an organic whole that had evolved with an inherent, deterministic necessity to its existing state. Social institutions and laws, he believed, could not and should not be tampered with. Thus, the necessity of property was, for him, a necessity of the particular property relations of existing capitalist society.

After developing this theory of income distribution (or input pricing) and making these assertions about private property, Menger felt no need to justify rent and profit (or interest, which he conceived to be the total return to the ownership of capital). Such income was *absolutely necessary* and *absolutely inevitable*, he believed. Why condemn or justify the necessary and the inevitable? Just accept its inevitability and be happy about the harmony existing in the situation:

> One of the strangest questions ever made the subject of scientific debate is whether rent and interest are justified from an ethical point of view or whether they are "immoral.". . . Wherever the services of land and of capital bear a price, it is always as a consequence of their value, and their value to men is not the result of arbitrary judgments, but a necessary consequence of their economic character. The prices of these goods (the services of land and of capital) are therefore the necessary products of the economic situation under which they arise, and will be more certainly obtained the more developed the legal system of a people and the more upright its public morals.[47]

Menger, of course, was doing everything in his power to give a scientific foundation to the efforts to create and maintain "upright . . . public morals."

Menger's Arguments on Methodology

Menger was one of the most important participants in an extensive debate over the proper methodology for the social sciences. The debate occupied the attention of many of the leading German-speaking intellectuals in the late nineteenth century and has come to be known as the *Methodenstreit*. We will not attempt to summarize the issues involved in the debate; instead, we will merely discuss two of the central assertions that Menger attempted to defend.

His first assertion was that "pure science" was always value free. Normative, moral, or ethical values were, he believed, completely foreign to science. In their values, individuals were influenced by their personal circumstances, class position, and emotions, and hence widespread agreement was never very likely on ethical questions. Science, however, was the description and understanding of actual reality—not reality as one wished it to be. Therefore, to the degree that scientists purged their theories of values, they could eventually come to complete and universal agreement.

Economics, then, to the extent that it was a science, was value free. Menger believed that many of the confusions in the writings of earlier economists had been the result of their failure to understand that ethical judgments had no place in pure economic theory. "The so-called 'ethical orientation' of political economy," he wrote, "is thus a vague postulate devoid of any deeper meaning both in respect to the theoretical and the practical problems of the latter, a confusion in thought."[48]

This, of course, was a repetition of Nassau Senior's methodological assertion. In our discussion of Senior, we argued that all theorizing—especially in the social sciences—is based on value judgments. Senior honored his own methodological argument only in the breach; all of his writings were intended to persuade the reader of his correctness on important ethical issues. While Menger and the many twentieth-century neoclassical economists who have expressed reverence for Senior's methodological argument have been considerably more subtle in their pervasive and persistent violations of the principle, these violations are nevertheless relatively easy to uncover in their writings. Menger's attempt to put the laws of private property and the distribution of income above either theoretical or moral dispute constitutes a most important violation of the principle of value-free social science.

Menger's second methodological principle was that economists could scientifically understand only individual households or business firms (Menger called these "individual economies"). They could never develop a similar scientific understanding of social aggregates such as classes or nations. Menger disliked the term "national interest," which was so frequently used to justify proposals for national reform, because he believed that its use was based on the false belief that a national economy with its own interests, separate and distinct from "individual economies" and their individual interests, could be identified and studied. The error of these reformers, he insisted, was that they saw the nation "itself as a large individual economy in which the 'nation' is to represent the needing, economic and consuming subject."[49] The "scientific" doctrine was then juxtaposed to this erroneous view:

> That phenomenon, which is commonly designated by 'national economy,' always presents itself to us, rather, merely as an organized complex of individual economies, as a multiplicity of economies joined together into a higher unity which is nevertheless not an economy itself in the strict meaning of the word.[50]

In our discussions of Bentham, Thompson, and Mill, we argued that utilitarianism has an extreme individualist orientation. As a result, moving from the notion that individual desires are the only criteria of good and bad to the notion that the social welfare is promoted by policies that maximize the total of all pleasures, entails innumerable logical and practical difficulties. Menger correctly perceived that reform based on utilitarian principles was inconsistent with utilitarian individualism. He therefore rejected the notion that there could possibly be such a thing as total national pleasure that could be increased through reform.

But we have also seen that the social conservatism of the utility theory, or the market-exchange perspective in economic theory, has always been based on a belief or faith that the existing laws of property ownership are natural, eternal, or above question. Therefore, in order for Menger's individualism to culminate in the ethical conclusions that characterize all of his writings, he had to have some sort of moral defense of the existing laws of private property, which he did.

Although the national economy could not be scientifically understood in the same manner as individual economies, Menger insisted that we could have some form of understanding of it. The national economy, he asserted, was "an *organism of economies*."[51] He praised the German "historical school of jurists" (as opposed to the German historical school of economists, whom he attacked), who had recognized that a nation and the laws that defined its particular institutional arrangements constituted

> an "organic" structure which cannot and must not be arbitrarily shaped by individuals or by single generations, that is a structure which, on the contrary, is opposed as something higher to the arbitrariness of the individual, of the entire age, of human wisdom. . . . [The] "subconscious wisdom" which is manifested in the political institutions that came about organically stands high above meddlesome human wisdom.[52]

Menger concluded that "law is *not a chance affair*, but, both in terms of its essential idea and its particular content, it is something *implicitly* given essentially by human nature and the particularity of conditions."[53]

Menger expressed regret that there had not evolved

> a historical school of economists comparable to the historical school of jurists, which would have defended existing economic schools and interests against the exaggerations of reform thought in the field of economy, but especially against socialism. [Such a school] would have fulfilled a certain mission in Germany and prevented many a later setback.[54]

Thus, we see that Menger's methodological individualism and his belief that his theories were value free led to the belief that existing institutions and laws were above reform; reform efforts were, in his opinion, unscientific and socially harmful. His individualism ended in an appreciation of the "benevolence" of the "subconscious wisdom" of the "organic whole." His value-free "science" ended in an assertion of the moral importance of defending existing economic interests against the "exaggerations" of socialists.

It is not surprising, therefore, that in his *Principles of Economics*, after discussing what he believed to be the determinants of the distribution of income, Menger wrote:

> It may well appear deplorable to a lover of mankind that possession of capital or a piece of land often provides the owner a higher income for a given period of time than the income received by a laborer for the most strenuous activity during the same period. Yet the cause of this is not immoral.[55]

It is, of course, no less an ethical judgment to say that something is not immoral than to say that it is immoral.

The ethical orientation of all Menger's writings (as was the case for Senior and for most twentieth-century neoclassical economists professing to have value-free theories) was revealed in his consistent defense of existing economic interests against reformers and socialists:

> The agitation of those who would like to see society allot a larger share of the available consumption goods to laborers than at present . . . [is based on] a view of providing them with a more comfortable standard of living and achieving a more equal distribution of consumption goods and of the burdens of life. A solution of the problem on this basis, however, would undoubtedly require a complete transformation of our social order.[56]

Given Menger's faith in the benevolence of the "subconscious wisdom" embodied in the existing social, economic, and legal institutions, such a social transformation was morally unthinkable.

Walras's Theory of General Economic Equilibrium

Walras's independent development of the theory of diminishing marginal utility (he used the term *rareté* for marginal utility) and his discussion of the equation that gave the maximum utility a consumer could achieve through exchange need not be summarized here, because we have examined similar contributions in the writings of Jevons and Menger. Walras's most important and lasting contribution to economic theory was his theory of general economic equilibrium.

Although most previous economic theorists had discussed interrelationships between different markets, no economist prior to Walras set out a general conceptual and theoretical structure within which to examine the multiplicity of relationships among different markets. He realized that the forces of supply and demand in any one particular market depended in varying degrees on the prices prevailing in innumerable other markets.

For example, the demand of a consumer for a particular good depended, as Jevons and Menger had argued, on the marginal utilities the consumer would derive from consuming various quantities of that good and the price of that good. But the condition for utility maximization showed that the consumer would purchase that particular good up to the point at which the ratio of its marginal utility over its price was equal to the same ratio for all other goods available for purchase. Therefore, the consumer's demand for that good depended also on the prices of all other consumer goods.

Now, insofar as the price of any good was, for the utility theorists, determined solely by the supply and demand for that good, and insofar as the demand for any good was determined by *both* all consumers' utilities from consuming that good *and the prices* of all consumer goods, it followed that to determine the price of the good, the prices of all other goods would have to be known. But the demand for those other goods (and hence their price) also depended on the price of the good in question. Therefore, a general theory of price determination was required. In such a theory, all prices would have to be determined simultaneously by both the total of all consumer utilities and the interrelations that existed among all markets.

However, such interrelationships did not exist only in the demand for consumer goods. They also existed in the supply of consumer goods, as well as in the demands and supplies of the other types of commodities or assets that were exchanged. Walras attempted to formulate a general theoretical framework within which he could show how, through the interactions of all markets, all prices could be determined simultaneously.

The purely logical requirement for such a general equilibrium theory was (as in all theoretical systems where several unknown variables must be determined simultaneously) that the number of unknown variables must equal the number of independent equations designed to determine the variables. There are additional logical conditions that must be fulfilled to guarantee the existence of a solution to this system of simultaneous equations, to guarantee that this solution be meaningful—that is, that it not contain solutions such as negative prices, which contradict some of the premises on which the theory is constructed—and to guarantee that the solution is unique. Walras, however, was primarily concerned to show that a theoretical system could be constructed in which the number of independent equations was sufficient to solve for the number of unknowns.

But if this had been his only concern, he could simply have posited any number of equations (which are, after all, not difficult to concoct). But he wanted his equations to have economic meaning and to describe what he considered real market forces that were important in determining prices. Therefore, before going on to describe Walras's system of equations, we must discuss the notion of general-equilibrium analysis in economics.

Needless to say, no theory can explain everything simultaneously. This would require an omniscience by which the entire universe was completely understood. Obviously all "general" theories are partial theories in the sense that there are innumerable phenomena that they do not purport to explain. The difference between general-equilibrium theory and partial-equilibrium theory in economics is that whereas the former usually attempts to explain all prices and quantities exchanged within an entire economy for a given period, the latter takes as *given* all prices and quantities exchanged except for one or two and attempts to explain those one or two markets within the context of these given prices and quantities. In the next chapter, we will discuss the partial-equilibrium theory of Alfred Marshall.

In Walras's general-equilibrium theory, all prices and quantities exchanged were to be explained. This meant, of course, that they had to be explained on the basis of their relationships to some other elements in the social and economic environment. There had to be, in his theory, a description of some features of the social and economic setting of the market situation that could be used to explain prices and quantities exchanged.

In his equations, therefore, prices and quantities exchanged would constitute the dependent variables, and those features of the socioeconomic setting would constitute the independent variables (which could then, of course, be seen as the determinants of the dependent variables). The precise form of the equations would reflect the real economic relationship that Walras believed existed between the given features of the socioeconomic setting (his independent variables) and the prices and quantities exchanged in the market (his dependent variables).

The institutional setting of Walras's theory was competitive capitalism in which "there are land-owners, workers, and capitalists."[57] These three classes functioned in two economically important ways: first, as owners of productive services (land, labor, and capital), they supplied these services in the market; second, as consumers, they demanded consumer goods in the market. Walras took the existing distribution of ownership of "productive services" (i.e., the existing class division of society) for granted—as have nearly all the economists in the utility tradition. Taking class distinctions—and hence, different people's various roles in the production process—for granted, the most important element within the socioeconomic context was, for Walras, people's *subjective desires*, or their schedules of marginal utilities.

There were three important institutional factors, therefore, in Walras's theory. The first was the acceptance of the existing laws of and distribution of property as morally right and just. Here he simply stated that "the *ownership* of property . . . is legalized appropriation, or appropriation in conformity with justice."[58] Although he sometimes added that he intended to show why existing property rights embodied justice,[59] he never did. Rather, he repeatedly asserted the justness of existing property relations. For example, eleven pages after the above quotation, he wrote: "Property consists in fair and rational appropriation, or rightful appropriation."[60] Second, he assumed that the economy was made up exclusively of small, relatively powerless business firms, and perfect competition prevailed. Although he realized that "the principle of free competition is not generally applicable . . . [to] monopolies,"[61] he ignored monopolies entirely throughout his general equilibrium discussion. Only after this discussion, and in the next to last chapter of his book, did he devote a few pages to a discussion of monopolies. He never attempted to tie this latter discussion back into his discussion of general equilibrium. Third, people were simply assumed to have measurable marginal utility schedules. There was no discussion of how these utility schedules came into existence or how they changed over time. He simply assumed that during the time period under analysis "the utility . . . remains *fixed* for each party."[62] Thus, utility was a metaphysically given, ultimate datum, in terms of which everything was to be explained.

While Walras did admit that people's utility schedules would change over time, he simply assumed that when such changes occurred, one simply had the new but essentially identical problem of finding a general equilibrium solution for a new time period. This was much more than a mere analytical simplification. Walras's utilitarian ideology justifying market capitalism depended on his conclusion that equilibrium prices accurately reflected people's *needs* or utilities, and, thereby, human satisfaction was maximized.

The conservative ideology embodied in the utility perspective loses what force it has if one admits desires are either socially determined or in a state of constant flux. Either of these possibilities leads to the question of a higher standard by which to judge desires themselves—a question that utilitarianism never considers. It is therefore not surprising that Walras asserted that "any value in exchange, once established, partakes of the character of a natural phenomenon, natural in its origins, natural in its manifestations and natural in essence."[63] By contrast, the labor theory of value stresses the view that prices are *social*.

After assuming the existing distribution of ownership, a perfectly competitive market, and metaphysically given, fixed utility schedules, Walras developed his system of equations to show what quantities of the various commodities were exchanged and how their prices were determined. He posited n productive services, m consumer goods, n prices of productive services, and $m - 1$ prices of consumer goods (one consumer good was taken as the *numeraire* so that its price was one, by definition). Therefore, there were $m + n$ quantities of productive services and consumer goods exchanged, and $m + n - 1$ prices at which they were exchanged. The total number of dependent variables, then, was $2m + 2n - 1$.

There were four sets of equations that Walras set up to solve for the magnitudes of his dependent variables.

In the first set, the supply of each of the n productive services depended on the prices of every productive service and every consumer good. Thus, n equations were derived, relating the quantity supplied of each productive service to all prices in the system. The particular mathematical form of each equation would depend on the marginal utility schedules of all owners of productive services. At any particular set of the $m + n - 1$ prices, they could make all of the appropriate utility calculations and decide exactly how much of their productive services to sell in order to buy consumer goods so as to maximize their utilities. Therefore, the owners of any given productive service would have a particular amount that they wished to supply at each and every possible set of prices. There would be a separate equation relating these quantities supplied of each of the n factors to all possible sets of prices.

In the second set, the demand for each of the m consumer goods depended on all of the $m + n - 1$ prices. Thus, m equations were derived. The reasoning was identical to that in the first set of equations. Productive service owners sold their services in order to buy consumer goods, and utility maximization would dictate exactly how much of the services that they supplied and how much of each consumer good that they would buy for each and every possible set of all of the $m + n - 1$ prices.

In the third set, in order for the economy to be in equilibrium, the demand for each productive service would have to equal the supply. Full employment of resources was assumed as a condition of equilibrium. This furnished one equation (equating supply and demand) for each of the n productive services.

In the fourth set, Walras believed that the assumption of perfect competition would assure that the price of each consumer good would have to equal its cost of production. The cost of production would depend on the "technical coefficients" of production (or technical recipes for production) and the prices of the productive services.

Therefore, Walras had $2m + 2n$ equations—m from each of the second and fourth sets of equations and n from each of the first and third sets of equations—to solve for $2m + 2n - 1$ unknowns. In the next several paragraphs, we will discuss what has come to be known as "Walras's law," which proves that if all markets but one are in equilibrium, then the last market must also be in equilibrium. This means that one of Walras's equilibrium equations was not an independent equation, because if all of the other equations were simultaneously solved, it would automatically be solved also. Therefore, he ended up with $2m + 2n - 1$ independent equations—the same number as the unknowns that had to be solved.

Walras's law is really a definitional identity. It states that with any given set of prices, the total demand for all things exchanged must equal the total supply of all things exchanged. It follows from the definition of supply and demand because, at some set of prices, the desire to exchange definitionally implies the desire to acquire something at those prices (demand) by giving up something (supply) of equal value. Therefore, every individual demand is simultaneously a supply of the same magnitude, and so if these individual demands and supplies are aggregated, the totals must be equal. Walras (using the word *offer* where we have used *supply*) stated the principle in this way:

> The effective demand for or offer of one commodity in exchange for another is equal respectively to the effective offer of or demand for the second commodity multiplied by its price in terms of the first. . . . Indeed, demand ought to be considered as the principal fact and offer as the accessory fact where two commodities are exchanged for each other in kind. No one ever makes an offer simply for the sake of offering. The only reason one offers anything is that one cannot demand anything without making an offer. Offer is only a consequence of demand.[64]

Walras's law is obviously true by definition. However, many defenders of Say's law have appeared to confuse it with Walras's law. Say's law implies that there will be a demand for all newly produced commodities. This does not follow from Walras's law. People might produce in order to exchange this output for some limited quantity of previously existing assets, such as money. There may not be as much money in existence as people desire to own at the existing set of prices. In such a case, there would be an excess supply of newly produced output, just matched by an excess demand for money. There would, therefore, be a general "glut" of commodities (to use Malthus's term), even though Walras's law still held. In fact, at any set of prices, Walras's law always holds even when *every single individual market is out of equilibrium.*

But Walras's law tells us something useful, even though it is merely definitional. It proves that in any disequilibrium, the total of excess demand (in all of those markets where demand exceeds supply) *must be exactly equal to* the total of excess supply (in all those markets where supply exceeds demand). It tells us that if any good is in excess supply, then one or more other goods must be in excess demand, and that overall the excess demand and excess supply will have identical magnitudes. It must be kept in mind, however, that this law refers not only to goods currently produced but also to money, securities, and, in general, all previously existing assets that could be exchanged.

We can see now why one of Walras's equations could be dropped in our discussion of his system of equations. If one market is out of equilibrium, then one or more other markets must simultaneously be out of equilibrium for excess demand to equal excess supply. Therefore, if all markets but one are in equilibrium, then the last market must also be in equilibrium. Therefore, the equations giving equilibrium conditions in all markets contain one unnecessary equation.

It is very difficult to grasp intellectually the real meaning of a general equilibrium from a discussion of equations. It is even more difficult if one merely looks at $2m + 2n - 1$ actual equations (particularly if this represents a very large number). Therefore, we will graphically present a simple three-commodity general-equilibrium model. This will help to illustrate the nature of the general-equilibrium model and serve to introduce the problem of how equilibrium may or may not be attained when the economy starts from a position of disequilibrium. Our model will have no distinction between productive services and consumer goods. It is simply a model of exchange—not production—in which one commodity serves as a *numeraire*. There are five unknowns—the quantities exchanged of commodities a, b, and c, as well as the price of $a(P_a)$ and the price of $b(P_b)$, both stated in terms of the numeraire, commodity c.

Our equations are:

$$ED_b = 0,$$
$$ED_a = f(P_a, P_b), \qquad\qquad (10.1)$$

that is, the excess demand (ED) for a depends on both prices. This simply means that for any set of the two prices, one of three situations will arise in the market for a: $ED_a = 0$, that is, the supply of and demand for a will be equal; $ED_a > 0$, that is, the demand for a will exceed the supply; or $ED_a < 0$, that is, the demand for a will be less than the supply of a; negative excess demand is identical to excess supply.

$$ED_b = (P_a, P_b), \tag{10.2}$$

that is, the excess demand for b depends on both prices; the meaning of this function that was given for commodity a applies equally to commodities b and c.

$$ED_c = f(P_a, P_b), \tag{10.3}$$

that is, excess demand for c also depends on both prices.

$$ED_a = 0 \tag{10.4}$$

that is, excess demand for a must be zero, as a condition of equilibrium.

$$ED_b = 0 \tag{10.5}$$

the same equilibrium conditions must apply for commodity b.

We now have five unknowns and five equations. Walras's law assures us that if a and b are in equilibrium, c will also be in equilibrium. We could just as well have had eight unknowns and eight equations—the unknowns would have been the two prices and the individual supply and demand functions for each of the three commodities. Actually, Equations 10.1, 10.2, and 10.3 are each really the combination of a supply equation and a demand equation. They are combined because in equilibrium the quantity of the supply of any good equals its demand, and both equal the quantity exchanged.

We can now illustrate general equilibrium with the use of simple supply and demand curves taken from partial equilibrium analysis. We do it in the following way: in the market for a, we can *assume* a price for b and then construct supply and demand curves showing how much of a would be supplied and demanded at different prices of a, given the assumed price of b. We next assume a *different* price for b, which gives us two entirely different supply and demand curves for a, under the same assumption. If we were to continue to vary the price of b, we get a family of supply and demand curves for a. These curves, together with the different prices of b that generate them, give us the information implicit in Equation 10.1. For any price of b, there will be one supply curve and one demand curve for a. At some particular price of a, those curves will cross; at that price, Equation 10.4 is solved, *given the assumed price of b*. The assumed price of b and the corresponding price of

a that satisfies Equation 10.4, that is, which equates supply of and demand for a, will give us *one set* of prices that satisfies Equation 10.4. Each time we vary the price of b, we will get another set of prices that satisfy Equation 10.4.

Figure 10.2 illustrates the foregoing explanation. The first supply and demand curves (solid lines) are constructed with a given price of b, P_{b1}, and the second set of curves (broken lines) are constructed with a second given price P_{b2}.

In part (a) of Figure 10.2, we see that with the supply and demand curves for a corresponding to P_{b1}, the equilibrium of supply and demand is at P_{a1}. Similarly, with those corresponding to P_{b2}, the equilibrium is at P_{a2}. Thus, we have two sets of prices for a and b that satisfy Equation 10.4. If we continued this process, we could get a whole series of price sets that satisfy Equation 10.4. Part (b) of Figure 10.2 is a graph depicting *all* sets of prices satisfying Equation 10.4.

The line labeled $ED_a = 0$ is the locus of all points satisfying Equation 10.4. The graph in part (b) shows prices of a (on the vertical axis) and prices of b (on the horizontal axis). Any point on the line $ED_a = 0$ gives two prices that will equilibrate the supply and demand for a. Point 1 on that line corresponds to the first set of supply and demand curves (in solid lines) in part (a), and point 2 corresponds to the second set of supply and demand curves (in broken lines) in part (a).

One further point should be made about part (b) of Figure 10.2. All points in the space above and to the right of the $ED_a = 0$ line correspond to sets of prices for a and b that will result in a negative excess demand (or an excess supply) for a. All points below and to the left of the line are price sets that will result in excess demand (or a negative excess supply) for a.

Figure 10.3 illustrates exactly the same things for commodity b. Parts (a) and (b) of the graph have exactly the same rationale as those of Figure 10.2. In Figure 10.4 we have combined the part (b) graphs from both Figures 10.2 and 10.3. Here we see in the same graph all sets of prices that will equilibrate the supply and demand for both commodities. We see that only $\overline{P}_a$ and $\overline{P}_b$ will result in an *equilibrium in both markets*. All points not on the $ED = 0$ lines are divided into four regions. The excess demand conditions for both a and b at every point in each of these four regions are summarized to the right of the graph in Figure 10.4.

On the basis of the information illustrated in Figure 10.4 and Walras's law, we can construct another line giving all sets of prices for which the excess demand for $c(ED_c)$ will equal zero. First, from Walras's law, we know that the point $(\overline{P}_a, \overline{P}_b)$ at which the $ED = 0$ lines of a and b intersect must be a point where $ED_c = 0$. We did not need an equation (in our original five equations of our general equilibrium system) for the equilibrium of commodity c, because we knew that if all other commodities were in equilibrium, then commodity c had to be in equilibrium. For c to be in disequilibrium would require that at least one of the other two commodities be in disequilibrium, because total demand must equal total supply by Walras's Law. Therefore, point $(\overline{P}_a, \overline{P}_b)$ is a point on the $ED_c = 0$ line.

Figure 10.2 **Prices Equilibrating the Supply of and Demand for Commodity** *a*

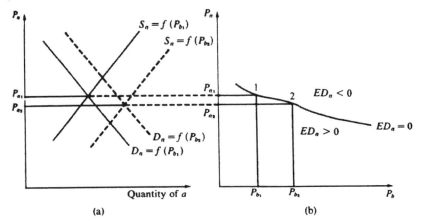

But there must be other sets of prices where $ED_c = 0$, and the locus of all points representing these sets of prices will give us the $ED_c = 0$ line. We know that at any set of prices other than $(\overline{P}_a, \overline{P}_b)$, either the *a* market or the *b* market or both will be in a state of disequilibrium (because $\overline{P}_a$ and $\overline{P}_b$ constitute the only set of prices that will equilibrate *both* the *a* market and the *b* market). Therefore, all sets of prices on the $ED_c = 0$ line other than $(\overline{P}_a, \overline{P}_b)$ must involve an equilibrium in the *c* market and a disequilibrium in both the *a* and *b* markets (because from Walras's law we know that it is impossible for only one market to be in disequilibrium).

Moreover, from Walras's law, we know that at all points on the $ED_c = 0$ line other than $(\overline{P}_a, \overline{P}_b)$ the disequilibriums in the *a* and *b* markets must offset each other exactly in order that total demand remain equal to total supply. Therefore, at any such point on the $ED_c = 0$ line, if $ED_a > 0$, then it must be the case that $ED_b < 0$, and the magnitude of the excess demand for *a* must equal the magnitude of the negative excess demand (excess supply) for *b*. Similarly, if $ED_a < 0$, then it must be the case that $ED_b > 0$, and the magnitudes of the excess demand and excess supply must again be equal.

Looking back at Figure 10.4, we see that the $ED_c = 0$ line cannot pass through regions *F* or *H*, because in these regions the markets for *a* and *b* both have either excess supply (region *F*) or excess demand (region *H*). Only in regions *J* and *G* is it possible for the *c* market to be in equilibrium and for the disequilibriums in the *a* and *b* markets to offset each other.

Therefore, if we find every set of prices in region *J* where the excess supply of *a* exactly equals the excess demand for *b*, and every set of prices in region *G* where the excess demand for a exactly equals the excess supply of *b*, the resulting locus of points will constitute the $Ed_c = 0$ line.

Figure 10.5 illustrates the lines giving the sets of equilibrium prices for each of the three commodities. The prices $\overline{P}_a$ and $\overline{P}_b$ equilibrate all three markets. They are therefore the general equilibrium prices. Two of our original five unknowns are now solved and known. With these two prices we can

Figure 10.3 **Prices Equilibrating the Supply of and Demand for Commodity *b***

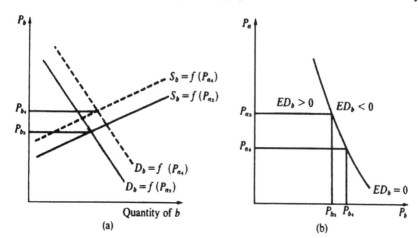

go back to our supply and demand curves for each commodity (as illustrated in part (a) of both Figures 10.2 and 10.3) and see exactly how much of each commodity is exchanged. We did not illustrate the supply and demand curves for commodity *c*. They would be exactly the same as those of *a* and *b* with one difference: because the price of *c* is defined as the *numeraire* (and is therefore always equal to one), we could either make the demand and supply schedules for *c* depend on the price of *a* with the price of *b* given (and then vary the price of *b* to generate new supply and demand schedules), or make the supply and demand schedules for *c* depend on the price of *b* with the price of *a* given (and then vary the price of *a* to generate new supply and demand schedules). Both methods would yield identical results.

Therefore, starting with five unknowns and five equations, we have seen how to determine the general equilibrium solutions for both prices and the quantities exchanged of each of the three commodities. We can appreciate the complexity of a general equilibrium theory explaining the prices and quantities exchanged of a large number of both consumer goods and productive services by understanding the complexity of our simple three-commodity general-equilibrium model.

Figure 10.5 illustrates all three *ED* = 0 lines. We now divide the space between these three lines into six regions. At the right of the graph, the excess demand and supply conditions in each of these regions are summarized.

Stability of General Equilibrium

A central issue in general-equilibrium theory is whether market forces will *automatically* correct a disequilibrium, that is, whether when a disequilibrium set of prices actually exists, the market forces of supply and demand will automatically change these prices until equilibrium is established. If one believes this to be true, then there remains the very significant issue of how

Figure 10.4 **Equilibrium in the *a* and *b* Markets and the Four Regions of Disequilibrium**

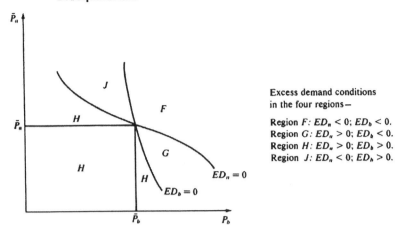

Excess demand conditions
in the four regions—

Region *F*: $ED_a < 0$; $ED_b < 0$.
Region *G*: $ED_a > 0$; $ED_b < 0$.
Region *H*: $ED_a > 0$; $ED_b > 0$.
Region *J*: $ED_a < 0$; $ED_b > 0$.

long this will take and what sorts of human costs or human suffering will be involved.

At stake in these issues are the different policy orientations of thinkers such as Bentham (in his later writings), Malthus, Marx, Hobson, and Keynes— all of whom argued that reliance on the market would involve enormous human costs and that, therefore, steps ought to be taken to mitigate these costs (although they advocated very different remedies)—and Say, Ricardo, Senior, Bastiat, and nearly all neoclassical economists—all of whom had a faith that such market adjustments would be fast and effective and should be relied on completely.

If we look back at Figure 10.5 and assume that commodity *c* is money, then at all points in region *M* there will be a glut of all consumer commodities—all consumer commodity markets will have excess supply (matched by an excess demand for money). What will result in this situation? The answer to this question has divided economists from the time of Malthus and Say to the present. Walras stood squarely on the side of Say and all other proponents of extreme laissez-faire in maintaining that the market would automatically and relatively without cost create the appropriate full-employment equilibrium prices.

Walras described the process of the market attaining an equilibrium as a process of *tâtonnement* or "groping." In most of his discussions of this problem, he assumed that the economy *started* at a position of equilibrium, which was disturbed by a change in the demand for one commodity.[65] He always assumed that a situation of excess demand would immediately lead to a price increase and a situation of excess supply would immediately lead to a price decrease. These price changes would automatically reestablish equilibrium, either through altering the quantities people wished to exchange or through a reallocation of resources as enterprises rapidly converted from the excess supply industries to the excess demand industries: "The upward and downward movements of prices in conjunction with the effective flow of entrepreneurs

Figure 10.5   **Equilibrium in the *a*, *b*, and *c* Markets and the Six Regions of Disequilibrium**

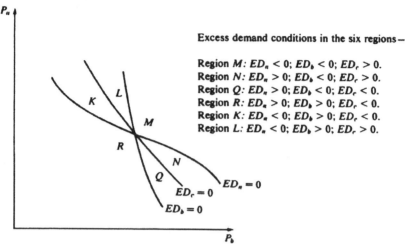

Excess demand conditions in the six regions—

Region M: $ED_a < 0$; $ED_b < 0$; $ED_c > 0$.
Region N: $ED_a > 0$; $ED_b < 0$; $ED_c > 0$.
Region Q: $ED_a > 0$; $ED_b < 0$; $ED_c < 0$.
Region R: $ED_a > 0$; $ED_b > 0$; $ED_c < 0$.
Region K: $ED_a < 0$; $ED_b > 0$; $ED_c < 0$.
Region L: $ED_a < 0$; $ED_b > 0$; $ED_c > 0$.

from enterprises showing a loss to enterprises showing a profit is purely and simply a method of groping towards a solution of the equations involved in these problems."[66]

There were several problems with Walras's solution (which have never been satisfactorily resolved to the present time). First, for the ideological conclusions of his theory, as we shall see, Walras required the assumption of perfect competition. But in the neoclassical vision of perfect competition every firm is a *price taker*. Prices are first established in the market and then firms respond to those prices. How then do the new prices get established? Neoclassical economists have always had a most difficult time with this question.

To deal with this problem, Walras had to assume an auctioneer or "crier" to announce all prices to everyone:

> The markets which are best organized from the competitive stand point are those in which purchases and sales are made by auction, through the instrumentality of . . . criers acting as agents who centralize transactions in such a way that the terms of every exchange are openly announced and an opportunity is given to sellers to lower their prices and to buyers to raise their bids.[67]

But Walras's imaginary crier was not enough. Suppose the crier announced a set of prices and exchange took place. If this set of prices was *not* the equilibrium set, then excess demand and supply would result in many markets. Then the next set of prices proclaimed by our crier would find all individuals trying to achieve an equilibrium in terms of these new prices but also trying to rectify the mistakes made on the basis of the wrong prices previously announced. Unless by pure luck, the new set of prices will also be a disequilibrium set. All new exchanges and corrections of past mistakes result in a new round of mistakes. All traders compound mistake upon mistake, and the situation seems at least as likely to move away from equilibrium as toward it.

Walras had only two choices: either his crier could be omniscient (that is, be God) and know in advance what the equilibrium set of prices would be, or his crier would have to be the equivalent of a socialist central planning agency with many high-speed computers at its disposal. In this latter case, the crier could announce the price set and then every exchanger could respond by telling the crier *their intentions* to buy and sell at those prices. Then no one would act until the central planning agency fed all of this data into its computers and computed the total demand and supply for every market. When the crier with the aid of the central planning agency found some markets to have potential excess demands, the crier would adjust those prices upward. Similarly, markets with potential excess supply would have their prices adjusted downward. This process would continue as a series of gropings in which exchangers held their commodities until the crier discovered the equilibrium set of prices. Only then could they exchange.

Despite his aversion to socialism, Walras chose this crier and central planning agency model as a means of avoiding the issue of the "anarchy of the market" (to use the socialist phrase):

> Once the *prices* or the ratios of exchange of all these goods and services have been cried at random . . . each party to the exchange will *offer* at these prices those goods or services of which he thinks he has relatively too much, and will demand those articles or services of which he thinks he has relatively too little. . . . The quantities of each thing effectively demanded and offered having been determined in this way, the prices of those things for which the demand exceeds the offer will *rise*, and the prices of those things of which the offer exceeds the demand will *fall*. New prices having now been cried, each party to the exchange will offer and demand new quantities. And again prices will rise or fall until the demand and the offer of each good and each service are equal. Then the prices will be *current equilibrium prices* and [only then] exchange will effectively take place.[68]

Walras realized, of course, that such a crier did not exist. But he had a faith—and it was never anything more than faith—that the actual working of the market would be similar to this. One problem (but by no means the worst problem) for Walras's faith was that whenever any one price changed, the change affected not just the supply and demand in that one market, but those in numerous other markets as well. Thus, suppose all markets but two were in equilibrium. In those two, one had excess demand and one had an equivalent excess supply. By Walras's reasoning, the price would rise in the excess demand market and fall in the excess supply market. If these were the only markets affected, and if supply and demand curves had the shapes that Walras had theorized, and if in fact the only response to the disequilibriums was that predicted by Walras, then the market would indeed establish a general equilibrium.

But these ifs must be rejected. First, the whole point of Walras's general equilibrium analysis was to show that price changes in any one market affected supply and demand in innumerable other markets. Thus, as the two prices began to change, many other supply and demand curves would shift (as illustrated in part (a) of Figures 10.2 and 10.3). The initial disequilibrium would spread to many markets. As these other prices began to change, nearly all supply and demand curves would begin to shift again. Thus, disequilibrium in two markets could rapidly become a disequilibrium in all markets. How then would equilibrium ever be established?

Walras escaped this dilemma by asserting that a given price change would have a *primary effect* only in the market of the affected commodity. Its effects on other markets would be *secondary*. He then asserted his faith that "these secondary effects, however, will be less appreciable than the primary effect if there are a great many commodities . . . on the market."[69]

Subsequent disciples of Walras have shown that with all of Walras's assumptions, if the secondary effects are sufficiently small, then the market will indeed automatically achieve an equilibrium. But they have never shown that these secondary effects must, in reality, be that small.

Furthermore, several of Walras's other assumptions are also highly questionable. He assumed that because the economy was perfectly competitive, the small, relatively powerless business firms would always react to a situation of excess supply by lowering their prices. Experience has taught us, however, that large, powerful business firms that have some control over prices tend to reduce their level of output and attempt to maintain their price in the face of an excess supply that they view as temporary. This reduction in output reduces incomes, which further reduces demand for other products. If these producers react to the resultant excess supply in their market by reducing output, then a general glut, economic crisis, or depression would seem to be the only possible result.

Moreover, Walras assumed that all exchangers would react to any set of prices as if they expected those prices to be the equilibrium prices that would continue to prevail. Again, experience shows that exchangers frequently behave otherwise, exchanging on the basis of prices that they expect to obtain in the future. John Maynard Keynes showed, as we will see in a later chapter, that these expectations can frequently make the achievement of a full-employment general equilibrium impossible.

We can conclude that Walras's belief that the market would automatically create a full-employment general equilibrium was as much a matter of pure faith as had been Say's belief—and both beliefs were equally unjustifiable on either theoretical or empirical grounds.

Walras's theoretical framework for his general equilibrium model was and still remains significant. If we drop his highly unrealistic faith in the automaticity of the market, his system of market interrelationships shows just how difficult it would be for a capitalist market system ever to achieve a full-employment general equilibrium. The theory can also show how, once a crisis starts, it spreads to all sectors of the economy and becomes a general crisis or depression. Walras's general-equilibrium framework is the best theoretical context within which to analyze the anarchy of the market. Many underconsumption theorists would have avoided innumerable logical and theoretical inadequacies had they formulated their theories within some framework akin to Walras's general-equilibrium theory. Therefore, Walras's theory of general equilibrium must be judged as one of the most significant theoretical achievements in the history of economic ideas. The theory can be easily extricated both from Walras's naive faith in the automaticity of the market and from his conservative, utilitarian ideology with which he justified competitive, laissez-faire capitalism.

Walras's Ideological Defense of Capitalism

Walras shared several characteristics with nearly all the economic theorists writing in the utility tradition, from Say and Senior to the present. First, he viewed the economy almost entirely from the exchange perspective. Even when he wrote about production, like most utility theorists, he viewed production primarily as a series of *exchanges* and never from the perspective of the class relationships involved in production. Thus, his analysis remained in what Marx called the sphere of circulation.

Walras's denial of the class relationships in the production process can be seen most clearly in his discussion of the entrepreneur. There were three types of productive services—capital, land, and labor. The pattern of ownership of these services was taken for granted. Each and every individual, acting identically as maximizers of utility, sold some quantity of productive services to an entrepreneur in order to buy some consumer goods—the whole process being merely an exercise in utility maximization through exchange. Each productive service was paid by the entrepreneur exactly the value of what it contributed to production. Interest was the payment to capital, rent to land, and wages to labor. In equilibrium, these productive payments exactly exhausted the value of what was produced; *there was no surplus value and there was no profit*; profit was only present when disequilibrium existed (and was matched by an equal loss somewhere else in the system).

In this view, who chose to be the entrepreneur was purely accidental. It might be a capitalist, who would then pay for labor services and land services and have a remaining residual (in equilibrium) exactly equal to the interest on the services of his or her capital. It might just as well be a laborer, who would then pay for capital services and land services and have a remaining residual exactly equal to the wages for his or her labor services. Similarly, it could be a landlord or a person owning some combination of productive services who acted as an entrepreneur. Because profits were zero in equilibrium, it did not matter who was the entrepreneur: "Thus, in a state of equilibrium in production, entrepreneurs make neither profit nor loss. They make their living not as entrepreneurs, but as land-owners, labourers or capitalists in their own or other businesses."[70]

Therefore, all individuals were simply utility-maximizing exchangers with

various initial "endowments" of exchangeable things. There was no difference between a Henry Ford and the poorest, lowest-paid worker on his assembly line. Both were maximizing exchangers, and production was merely
a species of exchange. Such is the essence of Walras's theory, which has numerous adherents in contemporary academic economics.

Bastiat had declared that "Political Economy *is* exchange." After developing a much more elaborate and sophisticated theory than Bastiat, Walras came
to an identical conclusion:

> Thus: The exchange of two commodities for each other in a perfectly competitive
> market is an operation by which all holders of either one, or both, of the two com-
> modities can obtain the greatest possible satisfaction of their wants consistent with
> the condition that the two commodities are bought and sold at one and the same rate
> of exchange throughout the market.
>   The main object of the theory of social wealth is to generalize this proposition by
> showing, first, that it applies to the exchange of several commodities for one another
> as well as to the exchange of two commodities for each other, and secondly, that
> under perfect competition, it applies to production as well as to exchange. The main
> object of the theory of production of social wealth is to show how the principle of
> organization of agriculture, industry and commerce can be deduced as a logical
> consequence of the above proposition. *We may say, therefore, that this proposition
> embraces the whole of pure and applied economics.*[71]

He made similar statements throughout his book. At one point, for example, he
asserted that "everyone competent in the field knows that the theory of exchange . . . constitutes the very foundation of the whole edifice of economics."[72]

Like Senior, Bastiat, and nearly all neoclassical economists, Walras thought
he saw a clear distinction between moral values and science. His writings
were, he assured the reader, pure science, not defiled or vitiated by any value
judgments. In the first chapter of the *Elements* he proclaimed: "Indeed the
distinguishing characteristic of a science is the complete indifference to consequences, good or bad, with which it carries on the pursuit of pure truth."[73]
Like Senior, Bastiat, and nearly all neoclassical economists, Walras honored
this proclamation only in the breach. On the next page, he began immediately
to show where "pure truth" stood in relation to controversial social issues: "It
has been observed . . . that in times gone by, industry languished and stagnated under a system of guilds, trade regulations and price fixing. It is evident
today that under the opposite system of freedom of enterprise and freedom of
trade, industry grows and prospers."[74]

The principal problem was that socialists had failed to understand the beneficence, prosperity, and harmony of capitalism. While prior economists who
had advocated and defended laissez-faire capitalism had performed a valuable service to society by countering the claims of socialists, they had unfortunately formulated the correct defense of capitalism inadequately in Walras's
opinion. For example, in his criticism of the Physiocrats, he concluded:
"Mingled with their errors are found views of extraordinary profundity and
accuracy; . . . [one] of enduring value . . . declares that for the production of

wealth free competition is the best rule, subject to exceptions only when they can be justified."[75]

In discussing the superiority of his own theory of interest over those of the "English School" (by which he meant Ricardo and Mill), Walras wrote: "The theory of interest . . . has been a favourite target for socialists; and the answer which economists have given to these attacks has not, up to the present, been overwhelmingly convincing."[76] Similarly, while sympathetically criticizing J.B. Say and other economists who had taken Say's view, he wrote: "Such a point of view was particularly useful to them in their controversy with the socialists. . . . Unfortunately, convenient as this point of view is, it is mistaken."[77]

Walras's conception of his role in combating the ideas of socialists was again expressed in the following quotation:

> The equations we have developed do show freedom of production [Walras's phrase meaning capitalism] to be the superior general rule. Freedom procures, within certain limits, the maximum of utility. . . . Unfortunately, it must be said that up to the present economists have been less concerned with establishing proofs for their arguments in favour of *laisser-faire*, *laisser-passer* than they have been with using them as weapons against the socialists.[78]

Finally, Walras left no question as to the use to which his "pursuit of pure truth" should be put. In discussing communism and capitalism he wrote:

> It is a question of the relation of ethics to economics which was hotly debated by Proudhon and Bastiat, among others, around 1848. In his *Contradictions Economiques*, Proudhon argued that there is a conflict between justice and material well-being [Walras's euphemism for capitalism]. Bastiat in his *Harmonies Economiques* defended the opposite thesis. I think that neither proved his point. I shall take up Bastiat's proposition again and defend it in a different way.[79]

Much of Walras's *Elements* consisted of an elaborate defense of Bastiat's thesis that in the existing capitalist society, free exchange maximized total utility, and, hence, laissez-faire capitalism was the best of all possible worlds.

Beginning with his assumption that "the ownership of property . . . is . . . in conformity with justice,"[80] Walras went on to show that all problems in economics could be reduced to problems of exchange: "Exchange of several commodities for one another in a market ruled by free competition is an operation by which all holders of one, several or all of the commodities exchanged can obtain the greatest possible satisfaction of their wants."[81]

This statement appeared in various forms at least twenty times in Walras's *Elements*. It is clear that he believed that competitive capitalism inevitably maximized social welfare and that this was a mere scientific deduction from postulates that represented "pure truth," uncontaminated by value judgments. Ironically, certain isolated passages in Walras's own writings contain the germ of a devastating moral critique of his own utilitarianism. Bentham's statement that "quantity of pleasure being equal, pushpin is as good as poetry" finds its equivalent in the following statement by Walras:

> From other points of view the question of whether a drug is wanted by a doctor to cure a patient, or by a murderer to kill his family is a very serious matter, but from our point of view, it is totally irrelevant. So far as we are concerned, the drug is useful in both cases, and may even be more so in the latter case than in the former.[82]

Thus, in the utility perspective, total social satisfaction may be maximized when all of the drug goes to the murderer to kill his family and none goes to the doctor to cure his patients. Walras could have shown with the same Benthamite logic that milk being used for a rich person's beauty bath contributes more to the social welfare than milk for a starving baby of poor parents.

Intellectual Perspective of Neoclassical Marginalism

At the beginning of this chapter, we described the process of the concentration and centralization of industry that was occurring during the period in which neoclassical marginalism received its first significant formulations (the early 1870s). During the last three decades of the nineteenth century, the concentration of industry grew at an accelerated pace and neoclassical marginalism (as first formulated by Jevons, Menger, and Walras) came to dominate completely the orthodox, conservative tradition in economic theory. The concurrence of this change in the socioeconomic structure of capitalism and the emergence of marginalism in economic theory do not seem to be totally unrelated.

During the initial phases of the industrial revolution (from the middle of the eighteenth century through the first few decades of the nineteenth century), industrial capitalists engaged in a prolonged struggle against the landed interests and merchant capitalists for economic and political supremacy. During this period, industrial capitalists usually were personally involved in directing, coordinating, and overseeing the actual processes of production. The central focus or objective of their endeavors had been the rapid accumulation of industrial capital, and their main intellectual concern had been to understand the source of capital accumulation. The labor theory of value perspective had furnished the most serviceable insights into the process of capital accumulation, focusing on the distinction between productive and unproductive labor. It had shown how productive labor was the source of the surplus labor that made the expansion of capital possible. Thus, in its earliest formulations, the labor theory of value reflected the perspective of, and was serviceable in the fulfillment of the objective needs of, the industrial capitalist class.

During this same period, merchant capitalists and landlords received their incomes from ownership and market exchange. Their situation could best be served by economic theories that sanctioned private ownership of capital and land, while extolling the social beneficence of exchange. The exchange or utility perspective, as represented in the writings of Malthus, Say, and Senior, had serviced their needs best.

With the growth of the corporation as the principal form of industrialization and the growing industrial concentration described at the beginning of this chapter, there was an important change in both the nature of the accumulation of industrial capital and the role of the industrial capitalist. The accumulation became systematized, institutionalized, and regularized. Increasingly, corporate managers were hired to direct and oversee industrial enterprises and to channel profits automatically as part of a perpetual accumulation process. The role of the individual capitalist entrepreneur in the industrial production processes became increasingly less significant.

The owners of industrial capital came more and more to resemble, in social and economic functions, the landlord class. Increasingly, profits and interest came to be the result of passive ownership. Therefore, the theoretical and ideological needs of the owners of industrial capital became identical with those of the landlords and merchant capitalists. They all needed a theory that sanctioned their ownership and proclaimed the virtues of an exchange economy.

Therefore, at the very time when the labor theory of value, in the writings of Karl Marx, was becoming identified with the interests of the working class, the utility theory or market perspective began to serve the interests of all elements of the class owning the means of production (whether land, merchant capital, finance capital, or industrial capital).

The individual as a rational, calculating maximizer, as portrayed in neoclassical marginalism, has never been an accurate reflection of the behavior of most people in a capitalist society. Most working-class people have grown up in families where their consumption patterns were socialized so as to become habitual and relatively standardized. To be sure, if a commodity that they habitually consumed rose sharply in price, their limited purchasing power would force them to adjust their consumption patterns. But the thought of rationally calculating marginal utilities, comparing utility ratios to price ratios, and adjusting their purchases so as to attain a "maximum of pleasure" has always been utterly foreign to the mental processes of most working-class people.

This view of the individual as a rational, calculating maximizer who buys at this margin and sells at that margin in a constant quest to maximize is, however, quite descriptive of one group in a capitalist economy: the functionless owner of a broad portfolio of investment assets. Such an individual owns a variety of stocks, bonds, land, and other assets yielding income to ownership alone. Such an individual, usually working through specialized exchange brokers, is constantly selling some of this stock, buying some of that stock, shifting from short-term bonds to long-term bonds, or making perpetual *marginal adjustments* to his or her portfolio of assets in an unceasing effort to calculate rationally the combination of property holdings that will maximize either income through time or the rate of growth in the value of owned assets. This is the type of individual best described by neoclassical marginalism, and neoclassical marginalism culminates in ideological conclusions that best service the needs of this type of individual.

Notes to Chapter 10

1. William Stanley Jevons, *The Theory of Political Economy*, 2d ed., ed. R.D. Collison Black (Baltimore: Penguin, 1970).

2. Carl Menger, *Principles of Economics* (New York: Free Press, 1950).

3. Leon Walras, *Elements of Pure Economics* (Homewood, IL: Irwin, 1954).

4. William Stanley Jevons, *Letters and Journal of W. Stanley Jevons*, ed. Harriet A. Jevons (London: Macmillan, 1886), p. 151.

5. Jevons, *Theory of Political Economy*, p. 55.

6. Ibid., p. 44.

7. Ibid., p. 77.

8. Ibid., p. 127.

9. Ibid., pp. 101–2.

10. Ibid., p. 101.

11. Ibid., p. 111.

12. Jevons used different symbols than we have used. The meanings of his formulas were, however, identical to those used here (see Ibid., pp. 142–43). We have used the standard contemporary form of the equation to avoid confusing the reader.

13. Ibid., p. 44.

14. Ibid., p. 52.

15. Ibid., p. 85.

16. William Stanley Jevons, *The State in Relation to Labour* (London: Macmillan, 1882), p. 98.

17. Ibid., p. 104.

18. Jevons, *Theory of Political Economy*, pp. 68–69.

19. Ibid., p. 173.

20. Ibid., p. 256.

21. Ibid., pp. 257–58.

22. Jevons, *State in Relation to Labour*, p. 127.

23. William Stanley Jevons, *Methods of Social Reform and Other Papers* (London: Macmillan, 1883), p. 108.

24. Jevons, *Theory of Political Economy*, p. 126.

25. Ibid., p. 257.

26. Ibid., p. 225.

27. Ibid., p. 72.

28. Ibid., p. 101.

29. Ibid., p. 103.

30. Jevons, *Methods of Social Reform*, p. 196.

31. Quoted in John Maynard Keynes, *Essays in Biography* (London: Macmillan, 1933), pp. 126–27.

32. Carl Menger, *Problems of Economics and Sociology* (Urbana: University of Illinois Press, 1963).

33. Menger, *Principles of Economics*, p. 127.

34. Ibid.

35. Ibid., ch. 5.

36. Ibid., pp. 222–25.

37. Ibid., pp. 80–87.

38. Ibid., p. 85.

39. Ibid., p. 150.

40. Ibid., p. 149.

41. Ibid., p. 156.

42. Ibid., pp. 164–65.

43. Ibid., p. 161.

44. Ibid., p. 75.

45. Ibid., p. 76.
46. Ibid., p. 97.
47. Ibid., pp. 173–74.
48. Menger, *Problems of Economics and Sociology*, p. 237.
49. Ibid., p. 194.
50. Ibid., p. 195.
51. Ibid., p. 194.
52. Ibid., p. 91.
53. Ibid., p. 230.
54. Ibid., pp. 91–92.
55. Menger, *Principles of Economics*, p. 174.
56. Ibid., p. 174.
57. Walras, *Elements of Pure Economics*, p. 42.
58. Ibid., p. 67.
59. Ibid., pp.75, 80.
60. Ibid., p. 78.
61. Ibid., pp. 115–17.
62. Ibid., p. 117.
63. Ibid., p. 69.
64. Ibid., p. 89.
65. Ibid., pp. 146–47, 178–79.
66. Ibid., p. 44.
67. Ibid., pp. 83–84.
68. Ibid., p. 179.
69. Ibid.
70. Ibid., p. 225.
71. Ibid., p. 143; italics added in the last sentence.
72. Ibid., p. 44.
73. Ibid., p. 52.
74. Ibid., p. 53.
75. Ibid., pp. 396–97.
76. Ibid., p. 422.
77. Ibid., pp. 54–55.
78. Ibid., p. 256.
79. Ibid., pp. 79–80.
80. Ibid., p. 67.
81. Ibid., p. 173.
82. Ibid., p. 65.

Chapter 11

Neoclassical Theories of the Firm and Income Distribution: The Writings of Marshall, Clark, and Böhm-Bawerk

The utility perspective in economic theory was incomplete until the entire economic process, as envisioned and defined in this tradition, could be shown to be wholly the result of rational, calculating, maximizing behavior. The economic process is seen, in this perspective, as having two important focal points—the household and the business firm. There are two continuous circular flows between these points. First, there is what economics calls a "real flow." Households are viewed as the owners of the "factors of production" and as the consumers of final consumption goods. Based on a calculation of their marginal utilities, they decide how much to sell to business firms of each of their various factors of production and how much to buy of each of the various consumption goods. The real flow therefore is a flow of the use of productive factors from households to business firms and a return flow of consumption goods from business firms to households.

The second flow is a "monetary flow." Households receive money income from the sale of the use of their productive factors. This money then flows back to the business firms in payment for the consumption goods purchased by the households. The business firms make rational, calculating, maximizing decisions in a manner strikingly similar to the decisions of the households.

Whereas the household attempts to maximize the excess of the utility derived from the consumption goods purchased over the utility given up in the sale of productive factors, the business firm attempts to maximize the difference between the money it pays for productive factors and the money it receives from the sale of consumption goods. Therefore, the household is the focal point of the real flow, and utility is the thing being rationally maximized. Likewise, the firm is the focal point of the monetary flow, and profit is the thing being rationally maximized. Because the mathematical logic of maximization is the same regardless of the use to which it is put, the analyses of the household and the firm are highly similar in neoclassical economics.

Marshall's Contribution to Utility Theory and Demand Theory

Alfred Marshall (1842–1924) was a mathematician turned economist who taught economics at Cambridge University for several decades. Although he had developed and was teaching most of his ideas by the early 1870s, he did not publish a full version of them until 1890. His *Principles of Economics* gradually came to replace Mill's *Principles of Political Economy* as the dominant economics text used in English-speaking universities. Many of his formulations of neoclassical theory have continued to dominate the teaching of introductory neoclassical microeconomic theory in colleges and universities to the present.

In general, it may be said that Marshall was somewhat closer in spirit and ideology to John Stuart Mill than he was to Senior, Say, and Bastiat, although Marshall was decidedly more conservative than Mill. Marshall was the founder of that portion of the twentieth-century neoclassical tradition that tempers its advocacy of laissez-faire capitalism with a considerable latitude given to minor reforms designed to make the economic system function less harshly.

Because we have already discussed utility theory in the previous chapter, we will limit our discussion of Marshall's contributions to utility theory to those areas in which he went beyond Jevons, Menger, and Walras. Like the latter three theorists, he formulated the notion of diminishing marginal utility as well as the necessary conditions for consumer utility maximization through exchange. Neither Jevons nor Menger succeeded in directly linking their utility theory to demand theory. While Walras had shown such a link, Marshall was much more successful than Walras in rigorously deriving the contemporary neoclassical conclusions of demand theory from his notion of diminishing marginal utility.

Marshall deduced a negative demand curve in the following manner: first, as with all utility theorists, he assumed that during the period being analyzed the individual's schedule of marginal utilities remained unchanged. "We do not suppose," he wrote, "time to be allowed for any alteration in the character or tastes of the man himself."[1] We have already pointed out the importance of this assumption for the ethical theory underlying neoclassical economics. It was also a necessary assumption for Marshall's derivation of a demand curve. Second, he assumed that an individual's marginal utility of money was given and constant throughout the period of analysis. By assuming a fixed marginal utility of money, Marshall found a connecting link between utility schedules and price schedules.

For example, if a person has a marginal utility of two "utils" for $1 of money, and one additional loaf of bread would yield four utils while one additional pound of steak would yield six utils to that person, then he or she would be willing to give up $2 (i.e., four utils) for a loaf of bread and $3 (i.e., six utils) for a pound of steak. The utility of a second additional loaf of bread might fall to two utils and that of a second pound of steak to three. In that case, he or she would be willing to pay $1 (two utils) for the second additional loaf of bread and $1.50 (three utils) for the second additional pound of steak. This was because "the marginal utility of money to him is a fixed quantity, so that the prices he is just willing to pay for two commodities are to one another in the same ratio as the utility of those two commodities."[2]

From this Marshall derived an individual demand schedule. The total demand curve for any commodity was simply the summation of the individual demand curves. "Every fall, however slight in the price of a commodity in general use, will, other things being equal, increase the total sales of it."[3]

The phrase "other things being equal" was significant. Although Marshall briefly discussed the conditions necessary for a general equilibrium, most of his theories were *partial equilibrium* analyses, in which he examined only the markets for one or two commodities and ignored the mutual interconnections between these markets and the markets for all other commodities.

In addition to explaining the derivation of a demand schedule from a utility schedule, Marshall defined and elaborated the notion of the "price elasticity of demand,"[4] defined and discussed his notion of "consumer's surplus,"[5] and showed how exceptional circumstances could result in an upward sloping demand curve.[6] If we were concerned about elaborating the origins of every detail of modern neoclassical analysis, these notions would be explained. For our purposes this is unnecessary; the interested reader is advised to consult an appropriate text.[7]

Thus Marshall developed one-half of the utility-maximizing process of the household by extending and elaborating the ideas of Jevons, Menger, and Walras. The other half of the household-maximizing problem concerned the sale of factors of production. Of the three traditional factors of production— land, labor, and capital—Marshall believed that only the furnishing of labor and capital involved a negative utility, or disutility. His discussion of rent was basically similar to those of Ricardo and Mill. Rent was a surplus created by the differing fertilities of the soil and involved no social cost.[8] In this as in other cases, Marshall's defense of income from ownership was not as complete or as extreme as those of Malthus, Say, Senior, Bastiat, and most other neoclassical economists.

It was in selling the services of labor and capital that households had to make utility calculations. After stating certain qualifications to the principle, Marshall asserted that when labor was sold, there was always a point beyond which "the marginal disutility of labour generally increases with every increase in its amount."[9] This increasing disutility of labor might

> arise from bodily or mental fatigue, or from its being carried on in unhealthy surroundings, or with unwelcome associates, or from its occupying time that is wanted

for recreation, or for social or intellectual pursuits. But whatever be the form of the discommodity, its intensity nearly always increases with the severity and the duration of the labour.[10]

While it was always clear to all economists that labor was a social cost of production, conservative economists from Senior onward had argued that the capitalists' abstinence involved a similar social cost and a similar disutility. Marshall generally agreed with Senior but evidently was a bit embarrassed by the implications of this notion:

> Karl Marx and his followers have found much amusement in contemplating the accumulations of wealth which result from the abstinence of Baron Rothschild, which they contrast with the extravagance of a labourer who feeds a family of seven on seven shillings a week; and who, living up to his full income, practices no economic abstinence at all.[11]

Marshall hoped he could avoid this embarrassment by substituting the word *waiting* for *abstinence*:

> Human nature being what it is, we are justified in speaking of the interest on capital as the reward of the sacrifice involved in the waiting for the enjoyment of material resources, because few people would save much without reward. . . .
> The sacrifice of present pleasure for the sake of the future, has been called *abstinence* by economists. . . . Since, however, the term is liable to be misunderstood, we may with advantage avoid its use, and say that the accumulation of wealth is generally the result of a postponement of enjoyment, or a *waiting* for it.[12]

Thus, in Marshall's analysis of the household, people were always calculating the appropriate exchanges involved in minimizing the pains of labor or waiting against the pleasures received from acquiring consumption commodities. In doing so, "they strive to adjust their parings down so that the aggregate loss of utility may be a minimum."[13] The same utility calculations were made by laborers deciding how much painful exertion to endure as by capitalists deciding how much painful waiting to endure. "A prudent person will endeavor to distribute his means between . . . present and future in such a way that they will have in each the same marginal utility."[14] Therefore, utility-maximizing calculations controlled the real flow of the services of capital and labor from the household sector to the business sector and of the consumption commodities from the business sector to the household sector. To understand the monetary flow, however, it was necessary to examine the profit-maximizing behavior of the business firm.

Symmetry Between Neoclassical Theories of the Household and the Firm

Utility maximization through marginal adjustments of quantities of commodities bought and sold was possible in neoclassical theory because of the *substi-*

tutability of any commodity for other commodities. Commodities were purchased only because they produced utility in the consumer. In maximizing utility, the consumer could derive utility from any one of innumerable commodities. If the price of a given commodity increased, then the cost to the consumer of deriving utility from that commodity increased. Because utility was conceived of as qualitatively homogeneous (in accordance with Bentham's view but in opposition to Mill's), the only considerations of a consumer were the quantities of his marginal utilities produced by different commodities and the costs of these commodities. Therefore, when the cost of a commodity increased, the consumer *substituted* some amounts of *other commodities* for a part of his consumption of the more expensive commodity. In this manner, he reduced his purchases of the commodity from which the derivation of marginal utility was relatively more costly and increased his purchases of other commodities from which the derivation of utility was relatively less costly. Thus, after the price increase, these shifts in his sales and purchases would reestablish the conditions for utility maximization (i.e., $MU_a / P_a = MU_b / P_b$, and so forth for every commodity), because of the substitutability of commodities in producing utility.

In order for the theory of the business firm to be stated in terms of a maximization problem similar to the maximization problem of the household, it was necessary to see the factors of production as analogous to consumption goods and the revenues received from the sale of the output produced by these factors as analogous to utility. The household gave up utility in selling the services of the factors of production in order to pay the costs of consumption goods. The consumption goods produced utility. Households attempted to maximize the difference between the utility produced by their consumption of these goods and the utility lost in paying the costs necessary to acquire the goods.

The problem for the firm in Marshall's analysis was identical. A firm wanted to maximize the difference between the money revenue it received from selling commodities and the money costs it paid for acquiring the services of the productive factors that produced the commodities; that is, it wanted to maximize profit. The firm bought factors of production, which by producing sellable commodities, produced revenue for the firm. The maximization problem for the firm would be essentially identical to that of the household *if the factors of production were substitutable in the process of producing revenue, in the same way that consumption goods were substitutable in the production of utility.*

But most of the classical economists had assumed that production involved *fixed technical coefficients* of production. That is, they assumed that a given productive technology implied a "recipe" for producing commodities that dictated fixed proportions of the different productive factors to be used. They generally ignored the possibility of varying the proportion of productive factors by substituting one factor for another (although Ricardo had asserted that when inferior land was brought into cultivation, the more fertile land would be farmed more intensively through the use of relatively greater amounts of capital and labor on a given parcel of land).

Menger had also assumed fixed technical coefficients of production. This was why he had assumed that productive factors were complementary and why he had a difficult time explaining how each individual productive factor was priced in the market. In the first two editions of Walras's *Elements*, he also assumed fixed technical coefficients of production. Only in the third edition of the *Elements* (published in 1896) did Walras introduce the possibility of varying the proportions of productive factors by substituting one factor for another in response to changes in their relative prices.

Therefore, one of Marshall's most important contributions to utilitarian economic theory was his introduction of two closely related concepts: first, businessmen tried to reduce the costs of production by substituting one factor (or "agent," as Marshall sometimes referred to factors) for another factor:

> Every businessman . . . is constantly endeavouring to obtain a notion of the relative efficiency of every agent of production that he employs; as well as of others that might possibly be substituted for some of them.[15]

> And the sum of the prices which he pays for those factors which he uses is, as a rule, less than the sum of the prices which he would have to pay for any other set of factors which could be substituted for them.[16]

Second, when the firm increased the quantity used of one factor (e.g., labor) relative to the quantity used of another factor (e.g., capital), the marginal increment added to total production by each additional equal increment of the first factor (labor) would, beyond some point, begin to diminish in magnitude: "The notion of the marginal employment of any agent of production implies a . . . tendency to diminishing return from its increased employment."[17]

The substitutability of productive factors for the firm was thus analogous to the substitutability of consumption goods for the household. Similarly, the law of diminishing returns from the increased use of a productive factor was analogous to the law of diminishing marginal utility from the increased consumption of a commodity. From Marshall onward, the theory of the maximizing firm has been almost identical analytically to the theory of the maximizing household.

The firm purchased inputs and sold outputs. It attempted to maximize the difference between the costs of its inputs and the revenues from its outputs. The firm's maximization problem, therefore, could be viewed from either of two vantage points: the firm's outputs or its inputs. From the former perspective, one would examine the price at which the firm could sell various quantities of output and then calculate the firm's *total revenue* from the sale of its output, its *average revenue* per unit of output sold, and its *marginal revenue* arising from a small increase or decrease in the number of units of output sold. Similarly, one would calculate the firm's *total costs* of producing its output, its *average cost* per unit of output produced, and its *marginal cost* arising from a small increase or decrease in the number of units of output produced. From the perspective of a firm's inputs, one would examine the revenue resulting from the sale of the total produce of all of the units of a factor hired by the firm, the value of the average output resulting from one unit of the factor, and the value of the increment or decrement to production caused by a small increase or decrease in the quantity of the factor hired by the firm. Similarly, one would examine the firm's total cost of purchasing the services of the factor in question, the average cost per unit of the factor purchased, and the marginal cost of a small increase or decrease in the amount of the factor purchased.

Looking at the firm's maximization problem from the vantage point of output is usually associated with the theory of the firm in contemporary economic literature. It was this aspect of Marshall's analysis that was to become the basis for most subsequent elementary expositions of neoclassical microeconomic theory. We will therefore examine Marshall's explanation of the firm's attempt to maximize profits from this vantage point.

Looking at the firm's maximization problem from the vantage point of inputs has become the basis of the neoclassical theory of the distribution of income. This theory—called the marginal productivity theory of distribution—was inadequately developed by Marshall. Superior formulations of the theory were developed independently by an Englishman, P.H. Wicksteed, and an American, John Bates Clark. After indicating the nature of the deficiency in Marshall's distribution theory, we will examine Clark's version of the theory. Finally we will examine the difference between Clark's conception of capital and that of Böhm-Bawerk (a difference that has remained important in neoclassical theory to the present time).

Marshall's Theory of the Firm

Marshall's analysis of the firm was an integral part of his analysis of price determination. Prices were determined by supply and demand. Demand was determined by consumers' utility schedules, and supply was determined by firms' costs schedules. Although Marshall briefly discussed monopolies on the sale of particular products, most of his *Principles* was devoted to analyzing the situation in which an industry consisted of numerous competing firms. With competition, the price of a commodity produced in an industry was determined by the total demand and supply of the entire industry. The firm typically took the price as given (with an exception that we will discuss shortly) and adjusted its output and costs so as to maximize profits.

Marshall's theory depicted what he called a "representative firm" in a competitive industry. The representative firm was "in a sense an average firm."[18] It had no special advantages or disadvantages and hence its costs of production reflected the average costs of the various firms within the industry. His analysis was based on a distinction between three time periods. First, in the "market period," supply was fixed and prices depended entirely on the strength of demand in relation to the fixed supply. Second, in the "short period," capital (or the productive capacity of a factory or other productive facilities) was fixed, but supply could be increased or decreased by altering the number of workers laboring in conjunction with these productive facilities. Third, in the "long period," supply could be altered by increasing or decreasing both labor and capital. Any amount of productive facilities could be constructed in this period.

The market period was relatively unimportant in Marshall's analysis, so we will confine our discussion to the behavior of the firm in the short and long periods. Throughout the discussion, it was assumed that the firm had so many competitors that it could not itself directly influence either the prices that it had to pay for inputs or the price that it received for its output.

The Firm's Production and Cost Curves in the Short Period

In the short period, the size of the firm's productive facilities was fixed. It could therefore expand or contract output only by using a larger or smaller number of workers. But the factory (we will assume that the firm is a manufacturing firm) was constructed on the basis of a given technology of production. Therefore, average output per worker would be maximized when the firm hired the number of workers for which the factory was designed. The firm could alter the proportions of labor to capital (or the number of workers employed in the factory), but this alteration would affect the average productivity per worker. This meant that although labor and capital were substitutable, they were not *perfectly* substitutable. Therefore, as the capitalist hired more laborers, he or she would reach the point at which the factory was designed to function at optimum efficiency (that is, the point at which output per worker was maximized). Beyond that point, output per worker would decline.

Figure 11. 1 illustrates the so-called law of variable proportions, or the law of diminishing returns to a variable factor of production.[19] The *marginal product of labor* (MP_L) line shows the increment to total output that results from hiring the last laborer at various levels of employment of labor within the factory. The *average product of labor* (AP_L) line shows the average output per worker at various levels of employment. If the factory starts from no production at all, the marginal product of labor will increase until the firm employs the number of laborers depicted by L_0 in the graph. Beyond this point the marginal product of labor declines as more labor is employed. As long as the MP_L is above the AP_L, the average productivity per laborer is increasing. When the factory hires the number of laborers depicted by L_1 on the graph, the average product of labor is maximized (at O_1 on the graph). If it hires more laborers than this, then the MP_L will be below the AP_L line, and the average product per laborer begins to decline.

When the firm computes the costs per unit of output at various levels of output, its cost curves appear to be nearly an inverse reflection of the product curves illustrated in Figure 11.1. As long as the average productivity per laborer is increasing, the amount of labor embodied in a unit of output is decreasing. Therefore, in Figure 11.1 the firm's *average variable cost* (or average labor cost, insofar as we have assumed that labor is the only variable factor in the short period) per unit of output decreases continuously until it has hired L_1 number of laborers. As it hires laborers beyond that point, its average variable cost increases (reflecting the decrease in the average productivity of labor). Because the firm's capital is assumed to be fixed in the short period, its capital costs are fixed. As the firm hires more laborers and expands output, the *average fixed cost* per unit of output will decline continuously because the same level of total fixed costs is spread among ever larger quantities of output. The firm's *average cost is* simply the total of its average variable costs and average fixed costs.

The firm's cost curves are illustrated in Figure 11.2. Output level Y_1 corresponds to output per worker O_1 in Figure 11.1 (Y_1 is O_1 times the number of workers L_1 in Figure 11.1). At Y_1 average variable costs are minimized. At Y_2 average costs are minimized. Y_2 always involves a somewhat larger output than Y_1 because after average variable costs are minimized, there is a small range of output within which the declining average fixed costs more than offset the rising average variable costs. At outputs beyond Y_2, the rising average variable costs more than offset the declining average fixed costs, and, therefore, average costs rise continuously as output increases beyond Y_2. Marginal cost decreases continuously to output level Y_0, which corresponds to the output produced by L_0 number of laborers in Figure 11.1; it increases continuously beyond that point. The marginal cost curve intersects both the average cost and the average variable cost curves at their minimum point.

Equilibrium in the Short Period

The firm maximizes its profits by producing the level of output at which the price (as determined in the industrywide market) equals its rising marginal costs. If it produces at lower levels, then an increase in production will increase profits because the price that it receives for the additional output will exceed the marginal cost of the additional output. If it produces beyond that level, its rising marginal cost of the additional output will exceed the price that it receives for the additional output. Therefore, the marginal cost curve shows the amounts a profit-maximizing competitive firm will supply at various prices and is the firm's *supply curve.*

Figure 11.3 illustrates the supply curve for an industry (which is the summation of the marginal cost curves of every firm in the industry) and the

Figure 11.1 **Law of Variable Proportions**

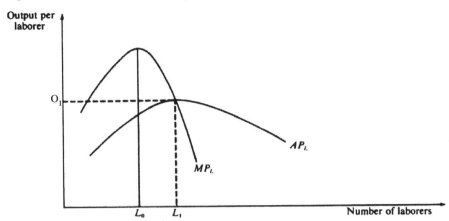

demand curve for the industry (which is determined by consumers' utility schedules). Part (a) of the figure shows the determination of the industry price by the intersection of the supply and demand curves. Part (b) shows the short-period equilibrium for the representative firm. The output for the industry is, of course, many times greater than the output for the representative firm. This is indicated in Figure 11.3 by using a capital Q for the industry's output and a small q for the firm's output, signifying the outputs are measured in different units (e.g., Q may be tons and q may be pounds of a product).

For the representative firm, the industry price equals its average cost. This does not mean that the representative firm earns no profit at equilibrium. Because neoclassical economists insist that a normal, or average, rate of profit on capital is a necessary part of the firm's capital costs, then such a profit would be included in average costs (as a part of its average fixed costs component). Any firm in this industry having higher costs than the representative firm will receive lower-than-normal profits. Any firm having lower costs than the representative firm will receive higher-than-normal profits, or excess profits.

Marshall believed that these latter firms have lower costs because they enjoy some natural advantage that other firms cannot acquire. He therefore called such excess profits "quasi-rents," and argued that they are similar to the "Ricardian rents" received by the owners of superior grades of land. In the long-period equilibrium, such quasi-rents will be incorporated into the firm's cost curves as ordinary rent costs, and every firm will ultimately receive only the normal rate of profit.

The Long Period and the Problem of Competition

In Marshall's long period, all productive factors could be varied, all costs were variable costs, and all quasi-rents disappeared. A long-period equilib-

Figure 11.2   **The Firm's Cost Curves**

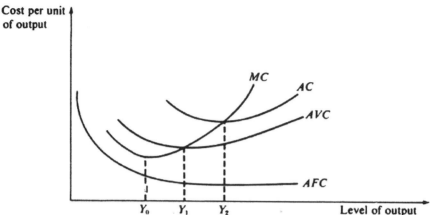

rium, similar to the short-period equilibrium for a representative firm as illustrated in Figure 11.3, obtained for all competitive firms in all industries. The principal difference between the equilibrium pictured in Figure 11.3 and the long-period equilibrium was that in the latter, the size of the factory or general productive capacity of the firm had been adjusted to reflect an optimum of productive efficiency.

Marshall's equilibrium solution showed what proponents of the "invisible hand" had argued since Smith: competition not only equalized the rates of profit for all firms, it also minimized the costs of production (i.e., it maximized productive efficiency) and resulted in the consumer being able to buy all commodities at the lowest possible price—a price that just covered the socially necessary costs of production and yielded no surplus for any class to expropriate from any other class. Marshall did posit what he called both a "consumer's surplus" and a "producer's surplus." These concepts had nothing in common with the notion of an economic surplus found in the writings of Smith, Ricardo, and Marx, however. They were merely restatements of a theme common to all utilitarian economic theories. Specifically, they showed the benefits—in terms of utility—that all exchangers received over and above the utility that they would have had if they had been unable to exchange. Like his theory of the equilibrium of the firm, Marshall's surplus theory merely showed the "universal advantages" and social harmony he believed to be inherent in the process of competitive exchange.

The question with which Marshall had to deal in his long-period analysis was whether proportionate increases in all productive factors resulted in proportionate, less than proportionate, or more than proportionate increases in the firm's output. The commonsensical conclusion (as well as the conclusion of many economic theorists from earliest times to the present) is that proportional increases in all inputs generally increase output proportionately (a situation defined as *constant returns to scale*, where average costs remain constant

Figure 11.3   **Short-Period Equilibrium for an Industry and Its Representative Firm**

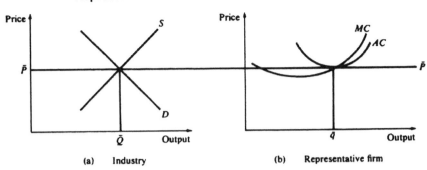

(a)   Industry   (b)   Representative firm

as the scale of productive operations expands). If such were the case, there would be no economic rationale (in terms of productive efficiency) for any particular sized firm in Marshall's long-period equilibrium. The emphasis on competition in the writings of the utility theorists would seem to suggest that they might favor legislated limits on the size of firms in order to maintain competition—particularly in view of the economic concentration that was developing in the late nineteenth century.

Marshall, however, did not believe that constant returns to scale would be the general rule. Following Ricardo, he believed that where land or natural resources were important in a production process, there was a tendency toward decreasing returns to scale (or increasing average costs over the long period). But when capital and labor were the primary factors of production, Marshall believed that there was a tendency toward increasing returns to scale (or decreasing average costs over the long period). He concluded that "while the part which nature plays in production shows a tendency to diminishing return, the part which man plays shows a tendency to increasing return."[20]

The increasing efficiency of greater size came from two sources. The first Marshall called "internal economies." Internal economies of scale were the result of improved organization of the firm: "An increase of labour and capital leads generally to improved organization, which increases the efficiency of the work of labour and capital."[21] The second source of increased efficiency Marshall called "external economies." External economies were due to benefits accruing to the firm (or the industry) from the output and pricing decisions of other firms (or industries). As examples of external economies of scale, Marshall discussed the benefits of industrial location and the benefits of closely interrelated secondary and tertiary industries.[22]

Marshall's notions of external economies (and the closely related notion of external diseconomies) were to become very important in neoclassical welfare economics, which we will discuss in a later chapter. The importance of external economies in Marshall's analysis, however, was clearly stated in the following quotation:

> The general argument of the present book shows that an increase in the aggregate volume of production of anything will generally increase the size, and therefore the internal economies possessed by . . . [a] firm; that it will always increase the external economies to which the firm has access; and thus will enable it to manufacture at a less proportionate cost of labour and sacrifice than before.[23]

It would appear, then, that in the manufacturing sector of the economy, the greater efficiency of large-scale production would lead inevitably to monopolies and oligopolies. It therefore seems that Marshall's theory would have led him to one of three conclusions: First, he could have abandoned the general utilitarian argument (that the invisible hand of the competitive market harmonized all interests and maximized the total social utility) and then defended capitalism on the basis of a new ideology stressing the social advantages of giant oligopolistic business corporations. Second, he could have argued that the social advantages of competition were more significant than the social advantages of the productive efficiency of large-scale production; thereby, he could have supported massive government intervention in the economy designed to break up large corporations and force them into perfectly competitive market structures where production inefficiencies were enforced by laws limiting the size of business firms. Third, he could have taken Marx's view that competition inevitably led to industrial concentration and that capitalist governments promoted rather than counteracted this tendency, and, therefore, advocated some form of socialism as the only possible means of taking advantage of the increased efficiency of large-scale production.

However, Marshall was unwilling to accept any one of these only possible practical conclusions. Like Mill, he wanted to retain the utilitarian ideology of the harmony of the invisible hand of the market. Also like Mill, he wanted to reject the notion (defended by Malthus and Senior, as well as most of the neoclassical economists within the more extreme laissez-faire utilitarian tradition) that the only hope for improving the plight of the poor was to promote the unfettered selfish quest for material gain by the rich. Not surprisingly, therefore, he proceeded in the same manner as Mill to incorporate into his intellectual system certain principles of moral and social philosophy that were quite incompatible with his utilitarianism.

Marshall's Ideological Defense of Capitalism

Marshall's ideological defense of capitalism was based on the incorporation of important elements of evolutionary social Darwinism into his theory. Unlike his American contemporary Thorstein Veblen, who was a thorough-going evolutionist, Marshall did not realize that the utilitarian social ethic was utterly incompatible with an evolutionary approach to economic theory.

Marshall set out "to consider the main bearings in economics of the law that the struggle for existence causes those organisms to multiply which are best fitted to derive benefit from the environment."[24] The principal conclusion he derived from his evolutionary approach was contained in the Latin phrase that appeared on the title page of the *Principles: "Natura non facit satum"* ("Nature contains no leaps"). All human progress, he argued, was very slow and proceeded only by minute *marginal* changes. Attempts to change society rapidly were doomed to fail and if undertaken would produce only misery. Social progress was generally a slow process of the hereditary improvement of a race or a nation. "This influence of heredity shows itself nowhere more markedly than in social organization. For that must necessarily be a slow growth, the product of many generations: it must be based on those customs and aptitudes of the great mass of people which are incapable of quick change."[25]

In this slow evolution of social institutions, a particular social structure might frequently appear to be exploitative on the surface. But the survival of that social structure for a long period of time was proof that, within its time and circumstances, its positive progressive features outweighed any of its defects:

> In early times . . . nearly all those nations which were leading the van of the world's progress were found to agree in having adopted a more or less strict system of caste: and this fact by itself proved that the distinction of castes was well suited to its environment, and that on the whole it strengthened the races or nations which adopted it. For since it was a controlling factor of life, the nations which adopted it could not have generally prevailed over others, if the influence exerted by it had not been in the main beneficial. Their pre-eminence proved not that it was free of defects, but that its excellences, relative to that particular stage of progress, outweighed its defects.[26]

The same argument, he believed, applied to modern capitalism. On the surface the capitalist system appeared as a "striking contrast" to the caste system. It also, however, offered "a no less striking resemblance to the system of caste."[27] While Marshall insisted that "the strength of . . . Marx's sympathies with suffering must always claim our respect,"[28] he nevertheless believed that these sympathies were misplaced: "The sacrifice of the individual to the exigencies of society as regards the production of material wealth seems in some respects to be a case of atavism, a reversion to conditions which prevailed in the far-away times of the rule of caste."[29] But in capitalism, as in the caste system, the benefits of the existing social structure far outweighed its defects.

Socialists had attacked the economic doctrines defending capitalism, but "the socialists did not study the doctrines which they attacked; and there was no difficulty in showing that they had not understood the nature and efficiency of the existing economic organization of society."[30] The socialists had not only wrongly perceived the economic doctrines that defended capitalism, they had wrongly perceived the motives of these economists:

> The fact is that nearly all the founders of modern economics were men of gentle and sympathetic temper, touched with the enthusiasm of humanity. . . . They were with-

out exception devoted to the doctrine that the well-being of the whole people should be the ultimate goal of all private effort and all public policy. But they were strong in courage and caution; they appeared cold, because they would not assume the responsibility of advocating rapid advances on untried paths, for the safety of which the only guarantees offered were the confident hopes of men whose imaginations were eager, but not steadied by knowledge nor disciplined by hard thought. . . .

It may be well therefore to note that the tendency of careful economic study is to base the rights of private property not on any abstract principle, but on the observation that in the past they have been inseparable from solid progress; and that therefore it is the part of responsible men to proceed cautiously and tentatively in abrogating or modifying even such rights as may seem to be inappropriate to the ideal conditions of social life.[31]

What was the most significant doctrine that the socialists had failed to understand and about which they should be "disciplined by hard thought?" It was none other than the invisible hand doctrine:

If a man had a talent for managing business, he would be surely led to use that talent for the benefit of mankind: that meanwhile a like pursuit of their own interests would lead others to provide for his use such capital as he could turn to best account; and that his own interest would lead him so to arrange those in his employment that everyone should do the highest work of which he was capable, and no other; and that it would lead him to purchase and use all machinery and other aids to production, which could in his hands contribute more than the equivalent of their own cost towards supplying the wants of the world.

This doctrine of natural organization contains more truth of the highest importance to humanity than almost any other which is equally likely to evade the comprehension of those who discuss grave social problems without adequate study: and it has a singular fascination for earnest and thoughtful minds.[32]

How then could "earnest and thoughtful minds" reconcile Marshall's belief in the greater efficiency of large-scale business firms with the perfect competition necessary for the working of the invisible hand? This was Marshall's most difficult problem, because he acknowledged that a capitalist owning an extremely large and growing firm "increases rapidly the advantages which he has over his competitors" and that this "process may go on . . . [until] he and one or two others like him would divide between them the whole of that branch of industry in which he is engaged."[33]

Once again Marshall was saved by his evolutionary theory of the life cycles of natural organisms. "Here," he insisted, "we may read a lesson from the young trees of the forest as they struggle upwards through the benumbing shade of their older rivals." Although these taller, better-established trees "have a better access to light and air than their rivals, they gradually lose vitality."[34]

As it was with trees, so it was with business firms:

Nature still presses on the private business by limiting the length of the life of its original founders, and by limiting even more narrowly that part of their lives in which their faculties retain full vigour. And so, after a while, the guidance of the business falls into the hands of people with less energy and less creative genius if not with less active interest in its prosperity. . . . But it is likely to have lost so much of its elasticity and progressive force, that the advantages are no longer exclusively on its side in its competition with younger and smaller rivals.[35]

Thus, Marshall was able to salvage his faith in the permanence of perfect competition by believing that an industry was like a forest. Just as trees are constantly growing and dying, so with business; [a] firm's "decay in one direction is sure to be more than balanced by growth in another."[36]

The productive efficiency of giant firms also was not a force in preventing workers from becoming capitalists, in Marshall's opinion. In capitalism, he proclaimed, "the social relations of classes . . . are now perfectly variable and change their forms with the changing circumstances of the day."[37] In answer to the socialist assertion that the separation of workers from the means of production resulted in the relative powerlessness of workers and the power of capitalists, he wrote:

> In speaking of the difficulty that a working man has in rising to a post in which he can turn his business ability to full account, the chief stress is commonly laid upon his want of capital: but this is not always his chief difficulty. . . . The real difficulty is to convince a sufficient number of those around them that they have the rare qualities [necessary to be a capitalist]. And the case is not very different when an individual endeavours to obtain from the ordinary sources the loan of the capital required to start him in business.[38]

The workers, if they had the appropriate moral virtues, could easily become capitalists. The existing English capitalists, or at least their forefathers, had achieved their position because they had "adopted a severe view of life; they took little delight in amusements that interrupted work, and they had a high standard as to those material comforts which could be obtained only by unremitting, hard work. They strove to produce things that had a solid and lasting utility."[39] Any worker with these character traits could still, he believed, become a capitalist.

But Marshall acknowledged that in its early phases capitalism was a harsh system for workers. In this period "free enterprise grew fast and fiercely, it was one-sided in its action and cruel to the poor."[40] Fortunately for the poor, Marshall reassured the reader, such cruelty was in the past. Capitalists, he believed, were becoming "chivalrous" and developing a benevolent concern for the poor.

> [Most social] evil may be lessened by a wider understanding of the social possibilities of economic chivalry. A devotion to public well-being on the part of the rich may do much, as enlightenment spreads, . . . in turning the resources of the rich to high account in the service of the poor, and may remove the worst evils of poverty from the land.[41]

Marshall cautioned "against the temptation to overstate the economic evils of our own age"[42] and against any impatience if economic chivalry took a long time to effect its social improvements. Social improvement ultimately depended on the elevation of human nature.

> But those elements of human nature which have developed during centuries of . . . sordid and gross pleasures, cannot be greatly changed in the course of a single generation.
> Now, as always, noble and eager schemers for the reorganization of society have painted beautiful pictures of life, as it might be under institutions which their imagination constructs easily. But it is an irresponsible imagination, in that it proceeds on the suppressed assumption that human nature will, under new institutions, quickly undergo changes such as cannot reasonably be expected in the course of a century, even under favourable conditions. If human nature could be thus ideally transformed, economic chivalry would dominate life even under the existing institutions of private property. And private property, the necessity for which doubtless reaches no deeper than the qualities of human nature, would become harmless at the same time that it became unnecessary.[43]

When Marshall spoke of some pleasures being "sordid and gross," he had of course completely abandoned the utilitarian premises underlying the invisible hand argument—an argument that he had asserted to be a "truth of the highest importance to humanity." In our previous discussions of the ideas of William Thompson and John Stuart Mill, we showed that social philosophies that discriminate among pleasures, calling some benevolent and lofty and others sordid and gross, contradict the very intellectual foundations of utilitarianism. We need not repeat that discussion here. Suffice it to say that this is another example of the general principle that a thinker's contradictions frequently furnish a revealing clue to his or her class orientation.

Clark and the Marginal Productivity Theory of Distribution

Earlier in this chapter, we made two important observations about neoclassical marginalism: first, when the principle of continuous marginal substitutability among the productive factors used in the production process is posited, the neoclassical theory of the firm becomes perfectly symmetrical analytically to the theory of household utility maximization. Second, given this factor substitutability, the theory of the firm's profit maximization can be viewed either from the standpoint of the revenue and expense per unit of output produced and sold or from the standpoint of the expenses of and the revenue resulting from the purchase and use of productive inputs. The latter standpoint represents the foundation of the neoclassical theory of income distribution.

While Marshall developed the neoclassical theory of the firm from the perspective of output, his development of distribution theory was inferior to that of John Bates Clark (1847–1938). This was because when Marshall analyzed the pricing of productive inputs, he assumed fixed technical coefficients of production and did not investigate the effects of marginal changes in the proportions in which the inputs were combined.[44] When he discussed the principle of substitution of productive factors, he analyzed only the substitution of different techniques of production, rather than investigating the effects of varying the proportion of the inputs used in a given production technique.[45]

For Clark, however, the principle of substitution of labor and capital was clearly developed. He argued that "in manufacturing and in transporting, too, the working force may often be varied perceptibly, with no change in the amount or in the character of the capital goods that are used in connection with it."[46] By holding the amount of capital constant and varying the quantity of labor, one could derive a schedule of the marginal product of labor for different levels of employment. From this schedule a graph showing the marginal product of labor, similar to Figure 11.1, could be constructed. If we assume that the marginal product of labor working with some fixed amount of capital declines continuously as more labor is added, then we get an MP_L curve as illustrated in part (a) of Figure 11.4.

In order to maximize his profits, the capitalist must know the *value of the marginal product of labor* and the price of labor. The value of the marginal product of labor in a competitive industry is merely the money value of the marginal product, or the marginal product times the selling price per unit. Thus, the VMP_L curve in part (b) of the figure is merely the MP_L curve from part (a) multiplied by the price of the output. The VMP_L tells the capitalist how much will be added to his revenues by hiring one more laborer at various levels of employment.

For a firm in a competitive industry, the price of labor is determined in the aggregate market for labor and that firm has no perceptible effect on either the price of labor or the price of the output that it sells. Figure 11.5 shows the labor market in part (a) and the level of employment of labor by a firm that will maximize the firm's profit, which occurs when the value of labor's marginal product is just equal to the wage rate as determined by the labor market. Therefore, at various wage rates, the VMP_L curve shows the corresponding amounts of labor that the firm will want to hire, that is, the VMP_L curve is the firm's *demand curve for labor*. Thus it follows that the aggregate demand for labor, shown in part (a) of Figure 11.5, is the summation of the VMP_L curves for all firms. The vertical supply curve for labor indicates that the supply of labor is, at any given time, fixed by the size of the population.

In Figure 11.5, the area of the shaded rectangle represents the total wages paid by the firm (the wage rate times the amount of labor hired, L_1) and the area of the triangle represents total interest (which is the residual of the value of the total product after wages are paid). The important point in this graph is that each firm hires labor until the value of labor's marginal product equals the wage. This is the necessary condition for the firm to maximize profits.

This was a very significant conclusion for Clark. The first page of the preface to *The Distribution of Wealth* began with this statement:

> It is the purpose of this work to show that the distribution of the income of society is controlled by a natural law, and that this law, if it worked without friction, would

Figure 11.4   **The Firm's Marginal Product and Value of Marginal Product Curves**

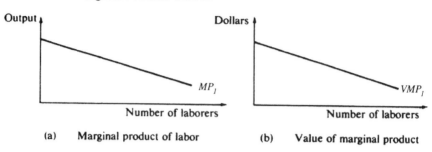

(a)   Marginal product of labor   (b)   Value of marginal product

give to every agent of production the amount of wealth which that agent creates. However wages may be adjusted by bargains freely made between individual men, the rates of pay that result from such transactions tend, it is here claimed, to equal that part of the product of industry which is traceable to the labor itself; and however interest may be adjusted by similarly free bargaining, it naturally tends to equal the fractional product that is separably traceable to capital. At the point in the economic system where titles to property originate—where labor and capital come into possession of the amounts that the state afterwards treats as their own—the social procedure is true to the principle on which the right of property rests. So far as it is not obstructed, it assigns to everyone what he has specifically created.[47]

Thus, Clark had completed the task, originated by Say and Senior, of showing that the rewards to capitalists and workers were based on exactly the same principle. There was no surplus and there was no exploitation. Capitalists were rewarded by receiving what they created just as were laborers.

If in Figure 11.5 it appears that interest is a surplus, this is an illusion based on the fact that we held capital constant and varied labor to generate the MP_L curve. Because capital and labor are substitutable in neoclassical economic theory, we can just as easily hold labor constant and vary the amounts of capital used in production. Figure 11.6 is identical to Figure 11.5 except for the substitution of capital for labor as the variable productive factor.

It can be shown that in competitive equilibrium, if the total output involved in Figures 11.5 and 11.6 is the same, then the wage share and the capital share portrayed in both figures are the same. That is, the shaded rectangle representing total wages in Figure 11.5 represents exactly the same amount of wages as the triangle in Figure 11.6. The interest in both figures is also the same.

Each factor receives an income that is equal to the value of its marginal product. Although Clark merely assumed it, later economists rigorously proved that under the conditions of equilibrium in a perfectly competitive market, if each factor is paid the value of its marginal product, then these factor payments *exactly exhaust the value of the total output.* There is absolutely no possibility of exploitation. Each person receives the value of what his factor produces, and there is no surplus for anyone to expropriate.

Figure 11.5   **Determination of the Wage Rate and the Firm's Level of Employment of Labor**

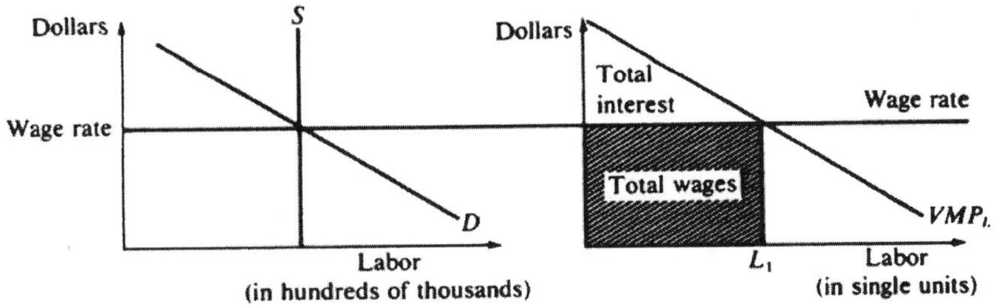

(a) Demand for and supply of labor in labor market

(b) Firm's profit-maximizing level of employment of labor, total wages paid, and interest received

Economics as Exchange and the Role of the Entrepreneur

In the exchange or utility perspective, profit disappears in equilibrium. Wages are the return to labor's contribution and interest is the return to capital's contribution. In the writings of the neoclassical economists, the distinction between classes—so important in the writings of Smith, Ricardo, Thompson, Hodgskin, Marx, and Mill—is completely eliminated. Most of the classical economists and Marx had defined profit as the residual surplus left after capitalists paid all the necessary costs of production. Neoclassical economists retained this definition of profit as a residual over and above costs. But in the neoclassical competitive equilibrium, *all income results from payments of the necessary costs of production. There is no residual*; *there is no surplus*; *and there is no profit.*

Neoclassical economics is the culmination of the tradition of Say, Senior, and Bastiat: *economics is exchange.* The entire economic process is seen in the following scenario: a population of egoistic, rational, utility-maximizing individuals, clustered in households, is originally endowed with inalienable private property rights to factors of production. To give up the use of these factors involves a sacrifice of utility. A strange minority of individuals has an assortment of talents and virtues qualifying them to be entrepreneurs. Entrepreneurs, as we will see, play the role of a fictional *deus ex machina* that performs a strange and contradictory—but absolutely necessary—function in the scheme.

Beginning with the initial endowments of productive factors, two sets of motives initiate a frenzy of rational, maximizing exchanges. First, households want to maximize utility. They do this by selling their factors and buying consumption goods to the point at which the ratio of marginal utility to price is the same for every factor that they sell and every commodity that they buy. Second, entrepreneurs want to maximize profits. They do this by buying factors and selling consumption goods. They combine the factors, and, by virtue

Figure 11.6   **Determination of the Interest Rate and the Firm's Level of Employment of Capital**

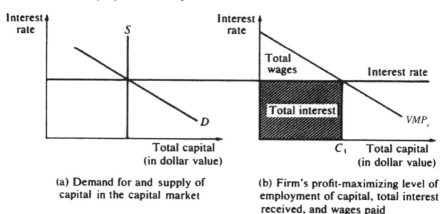

(a) Demand for and supply of capital in the capital market

(b) Firm's profit-maximizing level of employment of capital, total interest received, and wages paid

of a productive function, these factors are transformed into consumption goods. The production function permits smooth, continuous substitution of the factors so that the marginal productivity of each factor is ascertainable.

The entrepreneur maximizes profits, in competitive equilibrium, when he or she pays each factor the value of its marginal product and sells each unit of the output at its cost. Because the factor payments exhaust the value of what is produced, the income accruing to the factor owners is exactly enough to purchase all of the consumption goods. And so the circular process goes on and on. Each factor owner sacrifices less total utility in selling his or her factors than he or she acquires through the purchase of consumption goods. Therefore, exchange benefits everyone, increases everyone's utility, and ensures a just and equitable harmony of interests. No one exploits anyone else. Each sells commodities and buys commodities at their equilibrium values. Each maximizes individual utility through the beneficence of the invisible hand of exchange. A beautiful symmetrical harmony, which Bastiat and Clark believed could only be explained by the divine benevolence of God, prevails everywhere.

But two very important *deus ex machina* are needed for the analysis (not to mention innumerable unrealistic assumptions about people, production functions, and economic institutions, which we will discuss in our chapter on neoclassical welfare economics). We saw both these *deus ex machina* in our discussion of Walras's ideas, and they recur in nearly all neoclassical analyses. The first is the entrepreneur whose ceaseless drive for maximum profits makes the system go, which results in the transformation of productive factors into consumption goods and thereby renders utility maximization possible.

If there ever was a modern-day counterpart to the myth of Sisyphus, it is the neoclassical myth of the entrepreneur. As we saw in Walras's theory, the entrepreneur is the organizer of production. As a classless entity, the entrepreneur may be a capitalist, a worker, or a landlord. If a capitalist, the entrepreneur receives only the interest on his or her capital that any other capitalist would receive. If a laborer or a landlord, the entrepreneur receives only the wage or rent that these same factors provide for a nonentrepreneur. There are, of course, real entrepreneurs in capitalism, but the entrepreneurs of neoclassical theory are purely mythical entities.

Such entrepreneurs are perpetually motivated by the quest for profit. But in the neoclassical vision of competitive equilibrium, there are no profits. So the neoclassical entrepreneur is perpetually scheming, worrying, buying, and selling in the quest for an illusory, chimerical will-o'-the-wisp. He or she never learns but continuously and assiduously pursues the Sisyphean task. In Clark's words:

> Normal prices are no-profit prices. They afford wages for all the labor that is involved in producing the goods, including the labor of superintending the mills, managing the finances, keeping the accounts, collecting the debts and doing all the work of directing the policy of the business. They afford, also, interest on all the capital that is used in the business, whether it is owned by the *entrepreneur* or borrowed from someone else. Beyond this there is no return, if prices stand exactly at their normal rate; and the reason for this is that *entrepreneurs* compete with each other in selling their goods, and so reduce prices to the no-net-profit level.[48]

The second *deus ex machina* is Walras's crier. Without this omniscient auctioneer, neoclassical economists have never been able to show how, in a general equilibrium setting, the free forces of supply and demand would ever automatically establish this set of equilibrium normal prices, in which each person gets just what his or her factors have created, and in which depression and involuntary unemployment are no longer matters of concern.

Thus, with initial endowments of private property secured as just and natural, equilibrium prices established by a cosmic crier, and mythical entrepreneurs constantly striving for nonexistent profits, the invisible hand of exchange maximizes every person's utility as they ubiquitously and universally engage in tens of thousands of marginal utility and price calculations and exchange their goods having less utility per dollar's value for goods having more utility per dollar's value. Everyone's interest is in harmony with every other person's interest, and each maximizes his or her own utility. Such is the way that capitalism functions according to the exchange or utility perspective. It is of no consequence in this theory that some exchangers ride to their plush thirtieth-floor offices in their chauffeur-driven Rolls-Royces, while others trudge, lunch pail in hand, to the bus stop, and still others trudge with no lunch pail to the unemployment line.

Clark's Defense of Private Property

The benevolence of the invisible hand ultimately rested on the belief that the existing laws of and distribution of private property were just and fair.[49] Clark believed that owning private property derived from instinctive behavior: "The land-owning instinct is the most effective motive in attracting laborers into the wealth-owning class."[50] The laws of private property reflected a kind of social ethos that embodied the people's moral feelings: "In free countries the people's sense of right expresses itself in laws; and in modern states it has actually pronounced in favor of the private ownership of land . . . and the Federal government, reflecting the will of the whole people, has confirmed it."[51]

Clark felt it to be particularly important to defend the private ownership of land, because he thought that the claims of socialists were most persuasive concerning ownership of land. Therefore, he believed that a defense of the private ownership of land would ultimately be a defense of all kinds of private ownership of productive factors. "Whatever logic there is in the case against landed property," he declared, "merges it in a case against all property, or in radical socialism."[52]

Unfortunately, in Clark's opinion, the majority of people were not aware of "the will of the whole people" or of the "people's sense of right." Because of this ignorance, many people attacked the rights of private property: "It is to be expected that the assailants of private property should outnumber the defenders. This is usually true of an institution having great moral strength."[53] It was therefore of great importance that everyone understand the "natural law" that Clark had discovered: "The social procedure is true to the principle on which the right of property rests. . . . It assigns to everyone what he has specifically produced."[54]

Clark's Conception of Capital

The neoclassical marginal productivity theory of distribution explains the levels of wages and interest by positing a relationship between *physical quantities* of labor and capital used in production and corresponding *physical quantities* of marginal products attributable to these factors.

It is clear how one can aggregate physical quantities of labor. By defining one day's work by one laborer as a unit of labor, we can simply add the number of workdays to get the amount of labor expended in production. While there are differences among laborers, in most types of manufacturing these differences are quite unimportant:

> The men in an employer's services are thus interchangeable, it makes no difference to him which of them leaves his service. If the man who departs has been doing some kind of work that is quite necessary in conducting the business, the employer has only to put in his place the man who has been doing the work that is least needed.[55]

When entirely different skills and training are necessary, as we have seen in the chapters on Ricardo and Marx, the labor time spent in acquiring the necessary skills can be used to equate skilled labor to unskilled labor. Therefore, there are generally no insurmountable problems in summing physical quantities of labor.

It is an entirely different matter with capital. In summing the physical quantities of capital used in production, we must add together the most diverse set of objects. We must decide how, for example, to add screwdrivers to wheelbarrows to conveyor belts to blast furnaces to trucks and to innumerable other physical objects. The universal yardstick by which capitalists measure their capital is by its value. That is, each item is counted by adding its price to the prices of the other items constituting the stock of capital. While this method is perfectly appropriate for capitalists, who are only interested in making profit and not in providing an intellectual rationalization of profit making, it is absolutely inappropriate for the marginal productivity theory of distribution.

In neoclassical distribution theory, *the value of capital is determined by its productivity.* We cannot assume its value in order to ascertain its productivity. If we do this, then the productivity of capital will depend on its value. But in neoclassical theory, this line of causation must be reversed: the value of capital must depend on its productivity. Therefore, for the neoclassical marginal productivity theory of distribution to be consistent (i.e., for it to escape the charge of intellectual circularity), there must be some method, completely independent of prices, to quantify the capital used in production.

Clark's treatment of this problem was most puzzling—and yet we will see that some neoclassical economists have continued to use Clark's formulation down to the present time. Clark insisted that his theory could not be understood unless one understood the distinction between capital and capital goods. "Capital consists of instruments of production," Clark wrote, "and these are always concrete and material."[56] When productive instruments were considered in their individual, material, concrete forms, they were called capital goods. Therefore, capital consisted of capital goods—and yet, at the same time, capital had qualities that were very different from the qualities of capital goods:

> The capital of the world is, as it were, one great tool in the hand of working humanity the armature with which humanity subdues and transforms the resisting elements of nature.
> The most distinctive single fact about what we have termed capital is the fact of permanence. It lasts; and it must last, if industry is to be successful. . . . Yet you must destroy *capital-goods* in order not to fail. . . .
> Capital-goods, then not only *may* go to destruction, but *must* be destroyed, if industry is to be successful; and they must do so, in order that capital may last. Seedwheat must perish that wheat may abide.[57]

Another distinction was that "capital is perfectly mobile; but capital-goods are far from being so."[58] So capital was indestructible, perpetual, fluid, and mobile, while capital goods wore out and were concrete and immobile. Such a concept certainly is useful in the neoclassical theory of distribution but does not take us far in the quest to measure capital. Clark's example of wheat does not help. We can measure the quantity of wheat seed used up and compare it to our average inventories of wheat held over time. But wheat is wheat, and capital goods are incredibly diverse.

Clark answered that capital was an abstraction. It was "an abstract quantum of productive wealth, a permanent fund."[59] The word *quantum* certainly seems to name something quantifiable. But quantification is usually a concrete procedure directed at concrete things, not a quality of an abstraction. However, Clark never offered any definition of capital other than the following:

> A quantum of wealth, or a fund—if one of these be thought of apart from the concrete things that embody it, it is an abstraction; but if it be thought of as actually embodied in concrete things it is not an abstraction, but a material entity. . . .
>
> Guarding ourselves as carefully as we have done against the idea that capital ever lives in a disembodied state, we may safely use, for scientific purposes, the business man's formula. We think of capital as a sum of productive wealth, invested in material things which are perpetually shifting—which come and go continually—although the fund abides. Capital thus lives, as it were, by transmigration, taking itself out of one set of bodies and putting itself into another again and again.[60]

Clark appears to have been somewhat uncomfortable with his notion that abstract capital conceived of as "an abiding entity" could be measured. "Productive power measured in units," he admitted, "is abstract."[61] However, he assured the reader that "such an abstract formula as this for describing a concrete thing is common in every sphere of thought."[62] If the reader had any final doubts, Clark offered one last profundity: "Life in itself is an abstraction."[63] He never offered the reader any method of quantitatively measuring either life itself as an abstraction or capital, which, as an abiding entity, is an abstraction.

But from Clark's time to the present, many neoclassical economists have continued to use the aggregate quantity of capital as a measurable physical quantity in their production (and later their growth) theories. They could not, with any theoretical consistency, use the value of capital as a means of measuring its quantity, because its quantity determined its marginal productivity, which, in turn, was supposed to determine its value. But insofar as "life in itself is an abstraction," they continued to construct theories as though they had found such a measure, when in fact they had not.

Böhm-Bawerk's Measure of Capital

Eugen von Böhm-Bawerk (1851–1914), who imagined that he had formulated the definitive critique of Marx, made an effort to formulate a measure of capital that would be independent of any prices. Böhm-Bawerk was aware of the inadequacies of most conservative economists' definition of capital, but he was most concerned to show the inadequacy of Marx's view of capital:

> Marx . . . would confine the conception of capital to those productive instruments which are to be found in the hands of persons other than the labourers themselves, and are used to exploit the labourers. With him, therefore, capital is the same thing as "means of exploitation." This distinction would be quite an important and suggestive one if the exploitation theory itself were correct. But since, as has been shown in my former work, it is not, the justification of the distinction based on that theory falls with it.[64]

Böhm-Bawerk was not content to criticize Marx's theory; he also developed a theory of capital and interest. He felt "obliged again to tread the heated path of controversy, in the hope that impartial and sober inquiry into the matter in dispute may succeed in ending it."[65] He was convinced he could show that interest was inevitable. "Those, then, who demand its abolition may . . . not, as the Socialists do at present, [base this demand] on the assertion that this kind of income is essentially unjustifiable."[66]

There were, Böhm-Bawerk asserted, only two "original" factors of production—land and labor. Capital came into existence as soon as it was realized that production takes *time*. Labor cannot be applied instantaneously but must be spread through time. Furthermore, people soon discovered that there are many alternative methods of producing a good. Some are short and direct and require relatively little time. Others are more "roundabout," more indirect, and require more time. He believed that the lesson to be learned from this was obvious:

> It is—that a greater result is obtained by producing goods in roundabout ways than by producing them directly. Where a good can be produced in either way, we have the fact that, by the indirect way, a greater product can be got with equal labour, or the same product with less labour. . . .
>
> That roundabout methods lead to greater results than direct methods is one of the most important and fundamental propositions in the whole theory of production.[67]

With a given quantity of labor, Böhm-Bawerk believed that the longer the period of production, the greater would be the output of that labor, although diminishing returns would eventually develop. That is, if we continually increased the length of the production period by equal increments of time, production would continually increase but by smaller amounts with each successive increment.

It would seem, therefore, that if the only objective in producing were to maximize the amount produced, then people would always choose the longest possible production period. This was not so, Böhm-Bawerk argued, because just as people derived differing utilities from various goods in the present, so they derived differing utilities from having goods in the present and having goods in the future. That is, *people had time preferences.* Moreover, nearly all people preferred goods in the present to goods in the future. Böhm-Bawerk felt that there were several reasons for this preference. First, there were "cases of immediate distress and necessity,"[68] in which the present seemed more important than the future. Second, people had a tendency to "underestimate future pleasures" because of "the incompleteness of imaginations," or "a defect in the will," or "the shortness and uncertainty of life."[69]

It followed that the time pattern of production affected people's utilities in two separate and opposite ways. First, more goods would yield more utility, and the longer the period of production the more goods would ultimately be available for consumption. Second, the sooner people got their goods the more utility they would expect, and a longer period of production meant a longer postponement of consumption.

Now if we began with a very short production period with low labor productivity, increasing the time period would probably be beneficial (that is, increase utility) because the increased utility of more goods would outweigh the disutility of waiting slightly longer for the goods. But as we continued adding equal time increments to the production process, two things would happen. First, the marginal increment to output would continuously decline. Second, the disutility of a marginal increment of waiting time would increase. It is obvious that at some point we would have extended the production period to the length at which the utility of the marginal increment in output would just equal the disutility of the marginal increment in waiting time. At that point, society's utility is maximized over time.

In this conception, the quantity of capital is an index of three separate aspects of the production process: first, the amount of the original factors of production used; second, the length of the production period; and third, the temporal pattern of the usage of the original factors of production throughout the period of production. To lengthen the production process is to increase the amount of capital. In equilibrium, each person's time preference is given by the ratio MU_t / MU_{t+1} (where the subscripts t and $t + 1$ refer to two successive time periods). This ratio is also equal to the marginal productivity of capital (or the ratio of the value of inputs in time period $t + 1$ over their value in time period t). Both these ratios are equal to (and, in fact, they are the determinants of the equilibrium value of) one plus the interest rate.

Thus, in Böhm-Bawerk's analysis, the definition of the nature of capital was completely subsumed in the process of utility maximization simply by introducing time into the analysis. Böhm-Bawerk appeared to have provided a solution to Clark's problem of measuring capital, because the quantities of the original factors used in production, the length of the production period, and the time pattern of input usage could be ascertained independently of any prices. We will see in a later chapter, however, that this measure of capital is totally unsatisfactory because it is an index of several numbers, and, under certain conditions, the numbers yield indexes that contradict the premises of the marginal productivity theory of distribution. We will see that, although neoclassical economics has yet to find a consistent method of measuring capital that is independent of prices, the ideological value of the marginal productivity distribution theory is so great that the majority of neoclassical economists continue to defend the theory.

Capitalist Class Relations in Neoclassical Distribution Theory

Despite Böhm-Bawerk's insistence that his theory was completely different from that of Senior, it appears to be merely an extension and elaboration of the latter's theory. Böhm-Bawerk identified capitalist production with roundabout production. He thereby assumed that any production process that uses tools and intermediate products was a capitalist production process. The following quotation summarizes his view of the essential difference between capitalists and laborers:

> The adoption of capitalist methods of production is followed by two consequences, equally characteristic and significant. One is an advantage, the other a disadvantage. The advantage . . . consists in the greater technical productiveness of those methods. . . .
> The disadvantage connected with the capitalist method of production is its sacrifice of time. The roundabout ways of capital are fruitful but long. . . . In the overwhelming majority of cases we must tread the roundabout ways of capitalist production under technical conditions of such a nature that we have to wait, and often for a very long time, before we get the ripe final product. . . . In the loss of time which is . . . bound up with the capitalist process lies the sole ground of that much-talked-of and much-deplored dependence of labourer on capitalist. . . . It is only because the labourers cannot wait till the roundaboutness . . . delivers up its products ready for consumption, that they become economically dependent on the capitalists.[70]

In other words, only a difference in mental and emotional attitudes differentiated laborers from capitalists. They had different time preferences. Laborers wanted their reward now, while capitalists had the moral character that permitted them to wait. But Böhm-Bawerk's notion of waiting, as well as Marshall's notion of waiting, was essentially identical to Senior's notion of abstaining. Like Marshall, Böhm-Bawerk was somewhat embarrassed by the use of the word *abstinence*, because he was uncomfortable with Marx's critique of Senior's claim that abstinence was a unique social cost of production. Böhm-Bawerk quoted the following passage from Marx:

> It has never occurred to the vulgar economist to make the simple reflection, that every human action may be viewed as "abstinence" from its opposite. Eating is abstinence from fasting, walking abstinence from standing still, working abstinence from idling, idling abstinence from working, etc. These gentlemen would do well to ponder, once in a while, over Spinoza's *Determinatio est Negatio.*[71]

Böhm-Bawerk simply dismissed Marx's point by stating that "to my mind there is more dialectic than truth in this argument."[72]

We will conclude this chapter by repeating our earlier assertion. Neoclassical economics sees the economic process as simply a series of exchanges in which equivalent is exchanged for equivalent. Everyone benefits because, while each person gets exactly the value equivalent of what he or she gives up, each person derives more utility from what he or she gets than from what he or she gives up. The market therefore harmonizes everyone's interest and maximizes everyone's utility. There are no classes or class antagonisms in this theory. Some exchangers have a higher moral character than others (i.e., some practice abstinence and some do not), but each person receives, through exchange, the value equivalent of what his or her factors create. The marginal productivity theory of distribution is an integral part of the general neoclassical theory of exchange.

In discussing his distribution theory, Marshall expressed a conclusion that was shared by all three of the theorists discussed in this chapter (as well as most of the subsequent neoclassical theorists). After discussing his theory of input pricing (or income distribution), he concluded: "This statement is in close harmony with such common sayings of every-day life, as that 'everything tends to find its own level,' that 'most men earn just about what they are worth.'"[73]

While Marshall's statement summarized the moral conclusion inherent in the marginal productivity theory of distribution, the following quotation from Clark's *The Distribution of Wealth* most clearly illustrates the central concern that has motivated neoclassical developers of the marginal productivity theory of distribution from his own time to the present:

> The welfare of the laboring classes depends on whether they get much or little; but their attitude toward the other classes—and, therefore, the stability of the social state—depends chiefly on the question, whether the amount that they get, be it large or small, is what they produce. If they create a small amount of wealth and get the whole of it, they may not seek to revolutionize society; but if it were to appear that they produce an ample amount and get only a part of it, many of them would become revolutionists, and all would have the right to do so. The indictment that hangs over society is that of "exploiting labor." "Workmen," it is said, "are regularly robbed of what they produce. This is done within the forms of law, and by the natural working of competition." If this charge were proved, every right minded man should become a socialist; and his zeal in transforming the industrial system would then measure and express his sense of justice.[74]

Notes to Chapter 11

1. Alfred Marshall, *Principles of Economics*, 8th ed. (London: Macmillan, 1961), p. 79.

2. Ibid., p. 80.

3. Ibid., p. 83.

4. Ibid., pp. 86–97.

5. Ibid., pp. 103–9.

6. Ibid., pp. 109–14.

7. For example, M. Blaug, *Economic Theory in Retrospect*, rev. ed. (Homewood, IL: Irwin, 1968), pp. 327–430.

8. Marshall, *Principles*, pp. 120–43.

9. Ibid., p. 117.

10. Ibid.

11. Ibid., p. 193.

12. Ibid.

13. Ibid., p. 99.

14. Ibid., p. 100.

15. Ibid., pp. 336–37.

16. Ibid., p. 335.

17. Ibid., p. 337.

18. Ibid., p. 265.

19. The remainder of this section and some of the sections describing Clark's distribution theory and Böhm-Bawerk's capital theory are written in the present tense because these analyses have become standard in contemporary elementary economics textbooks.

20. Marshall, *Principles*, p. 265.

21. Ibid.

22. Ibid., pp. 222–31.

23. Ibid., p. 265.
24. Ibid., p. 201.
25. Ibid., p. 203.
26. Ibid., pp. 203–4.
27. Ibid., p. 204.
28. Ibid., p. 488.
29. Ibid., p. 204.
30. Ibid., p. 631.
31. Ibid., pp. 39–40.
32. Ibid.
33. Ibid., p. 263.
34. Ibid.
35. Ibid., pp. 263–64.
36. Ibid., p. 264.
37. Ibid., p. 204.
38. Ibid., p. 257.
39. Ibid.
40. Ibid., p. 615.
41. Ibid., p. 599.
42. Ibid., p. 600.
43. Ibid.
44. Ibid., p. 318.
45. Ibid., pp. 335–37.
46. John Bates Clark, *The Distribution of Wealth* (New York: Augustus M. Kelley, 1965), p. 101.
47. Ibid., p. v.
48. Ibid., p. 111.
49. For an excellent discussion of this and many other aspects of Clark's writings, see John F. Henry, "John Bates Clark and the Origins of Neoclassical Economics," Ph.D. diss., McGill University, 1974.
50. John Bates Clark, "The Ethics of Land Tenure," *International Journal of Ethics* (October 1890): 69.
51. Ibid., p. 62.
52. Ibid., p. 77.
53. Ibid., p. 62.
54. Clark, *Distribution of Wealth*, p. v.
55. Ibid., p. 103.
56. Ibid., p. 116.
57. Ibid., p. 117.
58. Ibid., p. 118.
59. Ibid., p. 119.
60. Ibid., pp. 119–20.
61. Ibid., p. 121.
62. Ibid.
63. Ibid.
64. Eugen von Böhm-Bawerk, *The Positive Theory of Capital* (New York: Stechert, 1923), p. 57.
65. Ibid., p. 23.
66. Ibid., p. 364.
67. Ibid., pp. 19–20.
68. Ibid., p. 249.
69. Ibid., pp. 254–55.
70. Ibid., pp. 82–83.
71. Ibid., p. 123.
72. Ibid.
73. Marshall, *Principles*, p. 335.
74. Clark, *Distribution of Wealth*, p. 4.

Chapter 12

Thorstein Veblen

During the late nineteenth and early twentieth centuries, capitalism underwent an important and fundamental transformation. Although the foundations of the system—the laws of private property, the basic class structure, and the processes of commodity production and allocation through the market—remained unchanged, the process of capital accumulation became institutionalized in the large corporation. In the earlier stages of capitalist development, individual capitalists had played a central role in the accumulation process. From their standpoint, the process had depended on organizational skills, cunning, business acumen, ruthlessness, and no small amount of luck. From the standpoint of society, however, the fortune of any particular capitalist was irrelevant—accumulation was an inexorable, ceaseless, spiraling process that had momentum and patterns of development that were quite independent of the actions of any particular capitalist.

The late nineteenth century saw the accumulation process rationalized, regularized, and institutionalized in the form of the large corporation. "Taylorism" and scientific management replaced the older, more individualistic mode of capital accumulation. A new managerial class became increasingly important. Ownership of the means of production remained the principal source of economic, social, and political power in capitalism. The new managerial class was primarily composed, at least in its highest echelons, of important and powerful owners of capital. The managerial class was clearly and decisively subordinated to the entire capitalist class.

Among the consequences of this institutional transformation were two changes of particular importance. The first was the internationalization of capital. We will discuss this in the next chapter. The second was a change in the structure of the capitalist class. While the social, political, and economic dominance of the capitalist class remained unchanged, the institutionalization of the accumulation process permitted the majority of capitalists to perpetuate their status merely through passive absentee ownership. The majority of capitalists became a pure rentier class, while a minority engaged in managerial functions (in both the economy and the polity) and acted as a kind of executive committee to protect the interests of the entire capitalist class. This committee performed its function by "managing the managers" of the new corporate structure.

These changes in economic organization and activities were reflected in diverse ways in the realm of economic theory. In chapter 10, we discussed the ways in which neoclassical marginalism reflected the social vantage point of the rational, absentee, rentier capitalist who is constantly readjusting his or her asset portfolio in order to maximize returns from ownership. In chapter 13, we will discuss the economic theories that sought to analyze the imperialist expansionism of this era. But the economic writings that most completely reflected and described the institutional and cultural transformation of this period were those of Thorstein Veblen (1857–1929). Veblen was probably the most significant, original, and profound social theorist in American history.

Many writers communicate their message as much by their writing style as by the cognitive content of their writings. This was particularly true of Veblen. Feigning a stance as a detached, neutral, disinterested observer of American capitalism of his era, he was in reality a profoundly passionate champion of the "common man" against the "vested interests," of reasoned, peaceable human relations against "predatory exploit," and of creative, constructive workmanship against the profiteering of "business sabotage." His writing had a biting, sardonic irony that cannot be recaptured by paraphrasing. One of his most-used rhetorical devices was to describe an institution or human practice in terms that leave no doubt as to his own moral indignation and then to add a phrase such as "but that is good and as it should be"; or we find another indignant passage followed by the sentence: "There is no fault to be found with all this, of course; but it is necessary to note the fact." Because Veblen's writing style was so unique, we have quoted longer passages in this chapter than in other chapters of this book.

While Veblen's personal life was most interesting and unusual, we will not discuss it here. Unlike some economic theorists, such as Nassau Senior, details about Veblen's life and activities contribute relatively little toward an understanding of his ideas. Suffice it to say that while Veblen felt very passionately about many social issues, in his personal life he was generally considered unconventional both academically and socially, and, thus, he led a lonely and alienated life. His alienation undoubtedly contributed to his writing style, which frequently had the tone of an outsider or of a social scientist who might have been socialized in a foreign culture that was more socially, intellectually, and morally advanced than the contemporary American culture, and who recorded and reported the strange and "barbarian" traits of American culture in much the same manner as the anthropologists of the time reported the mores of "primitive" cultures.

Veblen taught at the University of Chicago and at Stanford University, and was mistreated at both institutions, particularly the latter. He wrote prolifically, publishing ten important books and innumerable articles and reviews in journals and periodicals. His great genius and unusual writing style make all of his works enormously enjoyable and intellectually valuable.

Veblen's General Evolutionary Social Philosophy

During the late nineteenth century, Charles Darwin's theory of evolution had a deep and powerful impact on philosophy and social theory. This impact can be seen most clearly in the writings of Veblen. He viewed society as a highly complex organism, declining or growing, always changing, and adapting or failing to adapt to new situations. His analysis, like Marx's, was historically oriented in every aspect:

> Where, as in economics, the subject of inquiry is the conduct of man in his dealings with the material means of life, the science is necessarily an inquiry into the life history of material civilization. . . . Not that the economist's inquiry isolates material civilization from all other phases and bearings of human culture . . . but insofar as the inquiry is economic science, specifically, the attention will converge upon the scheme of material life and will take in other phases of civilization only in their correlation with the scheme of material civilization.[1]

Human history was, for Veblen, the history of the evolution of social institutions. Human conduct was based on certain discernible patterns that were common to all epochs of history. But these common patterns were very general and were expressed concretely in extraordinarily diverse ways within differing historical, social, and institutional settings. In many of his writings Veblen referred to these common patterns of human behavior as "instincts." Because twentieth-century science has dismissed as untenable any notion that human behavior is instinctive, many economists have believed that much of Veblen's theory is therefore scientifically invalid. This is not so. When he used the word *instinct* (the use of which was very common among social scientists of that era, who were under the influence of Darwin), he had no intention of implying that human behavior was instinctive in the same way as animal behavior. In fact, his whole theory is antithetical to this view.

Veblen explicitly disavowed any notion that human behavior was instinctive in the sense of being genetically determined:

> In economic life, as in other lines of human conduct, habitual modes of activity and relations have grown up and have by convention settled into a fabric of institutions. These institutions . . . have a prescriptive, habitual force of their own. . . . If the contrary were true, if men universally acted not on the conventional grounds and values afforded by the fabric of institutions, but solely and directly on the grounds and values afforded by the unconventionalized propensities and aptitudes of hereditary human nature, then there would be no institutions and no culture. But the institutional structure of society subsists and men live within its lines.[2]

It was only within a particular historical institutional framework that common patterns of human behavior took on concrete, particular characteristics.

> Like all human culture this material civilization is a scheme of institutions—institutional fabric and institutional growth. . . . The growth of culture is a cumulative sequence of habituation, and the ways and means of it are the habitual response of human nature to exigencies that vary incontinently, cumulatively, but with something of a consistent sequence in the cumulative variations that so go forward—incontinently, because each new move creates a new situation which induces a further new variation in the habitual manner of response; cumulatively, because each new situation is a variation of what has gone before it and embodies as causal factors all that has been effected by what went before; consistently, because the underlying traits of human nature (propensities, aptitudes, and what not) by force of which the response takes place, and on the ground of which the habituation takes effect, remain substantially unchanged.[3]

Veblen therefore stood somewhere between those theorists in the utility tradition who saw all humans in all historical situations as essentially identical (i.e., as calculating, rationalistic utility maximizers) and those theorists (including some disciples of Marx, but not Marx himself) who saw humans as having no nature, being indefinitely malleable, and as being totally and absolutely a product of their particular cultural and institutional settings. In Veblen's view, all humans had, as in any animal species, certain common, genetically inherited features, drives, propensities, and potentialities, regardless of the culture or historical epoch of which they were a part.

It was precisely culture and social institutions that differentiated humans from other animals. The traits common to all humans, which were much more malleable than those of animals, could be found in their concrete, actual expression only within a cultural setting. And there was a wide (but not indefinite or infinite) range of possible expression for these traits. Moreover, depending on the particular social institutions, certain traits might become exaggerated in importance while others might be repressed or stifled. Certain potentialities might be actualized, while others would remain unrealized.

It was in reference to these common traits and potentialities that Veblen used the word *instinct*. From the foregoing discussion we can agree with the following statement by one of Veblen's most important disciples:

> Thorstein Veblen was a social theorist of the first rank, and by far his most important contribution was his theory of instincts. I make this claim notwithstanding the fact that the very notion of instincts is now scientifically obsolete. It is on this account, of course, that a whole generation of hostile critics have focused their ridicule of Veblen upon this, seemingly his most vulnerable point. But in doing so they have demonstrated their own lack of understanding not just of Veblen but of human behavior. For even after we have rid ourselves of the false simplicity of "inborn," or genetically determined, behavior patterns, the fact remains that human behavior differs very substantially from that of any other creature and that such differences must have their taproots somewhere.[4]

It is difficult to summarize Veblen's views on the common human traits because his own classification and terminology differed in his various writings. One central feature of these traits, however, emerged clearly in all of his writings: all of the basic traits underlying human behavior were interrelated in a fundamental, antagonistic dichotomy that existed in some form in nearly all societies. All such traits could be classified into two clusters between which existed a perpetual conflict. Central to one of the clusters was Veblen's notion of the "instinct of workmanship." Central to the other cluster was his notion of the instinct of "exploit," or the "predatory instinct." Associated with workmanship were traits that Veblen referred to as the "parental instinct" and the "instinct of idle curiosity." These traits were responsible for the advances that had been made in productivity and in the expansion of human mastery over nature. They were also responsible for the degree to which the human needs for affection, cooperation, and creativity were fulfilled. Associated with exploit, or the predatory instinct, were human conflict, subjugation, and sexual, racial, and class exploitation. Social institutions and habitual behavior often tended to hide the true nature of exploitation and predatory behavior behind facades that Veblen referred to as "sportsmanship" and "ceremonialism."

The antithesis between these two sets of behavioral traits, and the social institutions through which they were manifested, was the central focal point of Veblen's social theory. Veblen was primarily interested in analyzing the capitalist system of his era within the context of this social theory. We will discuss Veblen's analysis of capitalism after discussing his critique of neoclassical economic theory.

Veblen's Critique of Neoclassical Economics

Veblen's fundamental criticism of neoclassical economics (he clearly recognized neoclassical theory as merely the working out of Bentham's utilitarianism) was that it had an utterly nonhistorical and simplistic view of human nature and social institutions. By attempting to explain everything in terms of rational, egoistical, maximizing behavior, neoclassical economics explained nothing.

At the heart of the failure of neoclassical economics was its conception of human nature:

> The hedonistic conception of man is that of a lightning calculator of pleasures and pains, who oscillates like a homogeneous globule of desire of happiness under the impulse of stimuli that shift him about the area, but leave him intact. He has neither antecedent nor consequence. He is an isolated, definite human datum in stable equilibrium except for the buffets of the impinging forces that displace him in one direction or another. Self-imposed in elemental space, he spins symmetrically about his own spiritual axis until the parallelogram of forces bears down upon him, whereupon he follows the line of the resultant. When the force of the impact is spent, he comes to rest, a self-contained globule of desire as before.[5]

Veblen had no doubt as to the principal issue toward which neoclassical economic theory was directed:

> Since hedonism came to rule economic, science, the science has been in the main a theory of distribution—distribution of ownership and of income. . . . And consistently with the spirit of hedonism, this theory of distribution has centered about a doctrine of exchange value (or price) and has worked out its scheme of (normal) distribution in terms of (normal) price. The normal economic community, upon which theoretical interest has converged, is a business community, which centers about a market, and whose scheme of life is a scheme of profit and loss.[6]

The ultimate purposes of neoclassical theory were: first, to justify the return to capital on the grounds that capital produced utility; second, to show that all incomes were equally representative of the productive contributions of ownership to society and hence socially, economically, and morally indistinguishable; and third, to show that in a competitive capitalist system, social harmony was the natural or normal state of affairs.

> [In neoclassical] theory the center and circumference of economic life is the production of . . . "pleasant feeling." Pleasant feeling is produced only by tangible physical objects (including persons), acting somehow upon the sensory. . . . The purpose of capital, is to serve this end—the increase of pleasant feeling—and things are capital, in the authentic hedonistic scheme, by as much as they serve this end.[7]

In this utilitarian theory, every source of income represented a useful, serviceable contribution to society. Nothing that gave rise to income could be socially useless or destructive:

> In the hedonistically normal scheme of life, wasteful, disserviceable, or futile acts have no place. The current competitive, capitalistic business scheme of life is normal, when rightly seen in the hedonistic light. There is not (normally) present in it anything of a wasteful, disserviceable or futile character. . . . The normal end of capital, as of all the multifarious phenomena, is the production of pleasure and the prevention of pain.[8]

Because all income, including all returns to capital ownership, derived from the creation of utility, the final conclusion toward which all neoclassical theory was oriented, was

> that the gain of each business man is, at the most, simply the sum of his own contributions to the aggregate of services that maintain the life and happiness of the community. This optimistic light shed on the business situation by the hedonistic postulate is one of the most valued, and for the wise quietist assuredly the most valuable, of the theoretical results following from the hedonistic taxonomy. . . . But while this light lasts the hedonistic economist is able to say that, although the scheme of economic life contemplated by him as normal is a competitive system, yet the gains of the competitors are in no degree of a competitive character; no one (normally) gains at the cost of another or at the cost of the community at large. . . . In this light, the competitive struggle is seen to work out as, in effect, a friendly rivalry in the service of mankind at large, with an eye single to the greatest happiness of the greatest number.[9]

The neoclassical economists had been able to achieve these ideological results by assuming that all human behavior in all societies in all times was utility-maximizing behavior. All efforts to attain more utility in all societies, places, and times could be reduced to the exchange of land, labor, and capital for commodities. All utility received and enjoyed by all persons in all societies, places, and times was therefore reducible either to wages, rent, or interest. The only way in which capitalism differed from any other society, in the neoclassical view, was that in capitalism these universal human activities and the universal modes by which the activities were rewarded functioned more effectively than in any other form of social organization.

The categories of wages, rent, and interest

> are hedonistically "natural" categories of such taxonomic force that their elemental lines of cleavage run through the facts of any given economic situation . . . even where the situation does not permit these lines of cleavage to be seen by men . . . ; so that, e.g., a gang of Aleutian Islanders slushing about in the wrack and surf with rakes and magical incantations for the capture of shell-fish are held, in point of taxonomic reality, to be engaged in a feat of hedonistic equilibration in rent, wages, and interest. And that is all there is to it. Indeed, for economic theory of this kind, that is all there is to any economic situation.[10]

In reality, Veblen insisted, production was always a social and cultural phenomenon in which output could never be said to be purely the result of any person or factor of production. Production was a social process in which human beings shared knowledge and skills, passed them on from generation to generation, and cooperated socially in a process of transforming nature to suit human needs and uses. The separation of this process and categorizing the different elements of the process as land, labor, and capital were simply a historical phenomenon peculiar to capitalism. The distribution of the fruits of human social endeavor by means of wages, rent, and interest was also simply a historical phenomenon peculiar to capitalism.

Veblen noted that in Clark's writings "much is made of the doctrine that the two facts of 'capital' and 'capital goods' are conceptionally distinct, though substantially identical."[11] It was, he added, difficult to understand the notion of capital as a general physical abiding entity" into which particular capital goods came and went. In fact, he insisted that the

> continuum in which the "abiding entity" of capital resides is a continuity of ownership, not a physical fact. The continuity, in fact, is of an immaterial nature, a matter of legal rights, of contract, of purchase and sale. Just why this patent state of the case is overlooked, as it somewhat elaborately is, is not easily seen. . . . [Not overlooking this obvious fact] would, of course, upset the law of the "natural" remuneration of labor and capital to which Mr. Clark's argument looks forward from the start. It would also bring in the "unnatural" phenomenon of monopoly as a normal outgrowth of business enterprise.[12]

Just as capital was not a universal physical substance that was present in every society but rather a result of the laws and institutions of capitalism, so interest income was a peculiarity of capitalism:

> In point of historical fact anything like a consistent rate of interest emerges into the consciousness of mankind only after business traffic has reached some appreciable degree of development; and this development of business enterprise has taken place only on the basis and within the lines of the so-called money economy. . . . But a money economy . . . can emerge only on the basis afforded by the mature development of the institution of property. The whole matter lies within the range of a definite institutional situation which is to be found only during a relatively brief phase of civilization.[13]

Similarly, wage labor and wages could exist only where capitalists had monopolized the ownership of the means of production in a commercial money economy. Only then would capital exist, and it was "only then that the term 'wages,' in the strict technical sense, can properly be employed."[14] This was true because, like most neoclassical economic categories, "wages" was a category growing out of and reflecting a social relationship peculiar to capitalism: "Wages is a fact incident to the relation of employer and employed. It is . . . an economic category whose scope is entirely within the theory of production as carried on by the method based on that relation."[15]

The function, therefore, of neoclassical economic theory was to obscure the nature of the most fundamental antagonism of capitalism, the conflict between owners and workers, first, by making the conflict seem only apparent and not real, and second, by making the worker-capitalist relationship seem timeless and eternal. One of the dominant, historically distinct, and distinguishing features of contemporary capitalism, Veblen insisted, was a "settled and malevolent hostility on the part of the embattled workmen against their employers and the absentee owners for whose ease and gain they are employed."[16] In that situation, the social harmony conclusions of neoclassical economic theory were most valuable and serviceable to businessmen, absentee owners, and the powerful and privileged "vested interests" of society generally:

> Many public spirited citizens, and many substantial citizens with an interest in business, deplore this spirit of division and cross purposes that pervades the ordinary relations between owners and workmen in the large industries. And in homiletical discourse bearing on this matter it is commonly insisted that such a division of sentiment is uncalled for, at the same time that it works mischief to the common good, that "the interests of labor and capital are substantially identical," that dilatory and obstructionist tactics bring nothing better than privation and discontent to both parties in controversy, as well as damage and discomfort to the community at large. Such homiletical discourse is commonly addressed to the workmen. It is a plain fact of common sense, embedded in immemorial habit, that the business men who have the management of industrial production must be free to limit their output and restrain employment with a view to what the traffic will bear. That is a matter of sound business, authentic and meritorious. Whereas unemployment brought to bear by collusion among workmen in pursuit of their special advantage will interfere with

the orderly earnings of business and thereby bring discouragement and adversity upon the business community, and so will derange and retard the processes of industry from which the earnings are drawn.[17]

This, then, was the inevitable end toward which all utilitarian, neoclassical theory ultimately led. Thus, Veblen went beyond a mere logical or empirical critique of neoclassical economics, showing within the framework of his own theory the historical and institutional functionality of neoclassical theory in serving the needs of absentee ownership and the "vested interests."

The Antagonistic Dichotomy of Capitalism

We stated above that Veblen believed that there were two generally antagonistic clusters of behavioral traits, which were manifested in different historical eras through the social institutions and modes of behavior peculiar to those eras. Veblen's principal concern was to analyze and understand capitalism. Just as Marx in the mid-nineteenth century had taken England as the prototype of capitalist society, Veblen, writing during the last decade of the nineteenth and first quarter of the twentieth centuries, took the United States as the prototype. The central question for him was how these two antagonistic clusters of behavioral traits were manifested in and through the institutions of capitalism.

The question could be approached from several vantage points; Veblen used at least three. From a social psychological point of view, he distinguished individuals and classes whose behavior was dominated by the propensity for exploit, or the predatory instinct, from those whose behavior was dominated by the instinct of workmanship, the parental bent, and the development of idle curiosity. From the standpoint of economics, Veblen saw the same dichotomy between the forces that he referred to as "business" and the forces that he referred to as "industry." From the standpoint of sociology, the dichotomy was manifested in the differences between the "ceremonialism" and "sportsmanship" characteristic of the "leisure class" and the more creative and cooperative behavior characteristic of the "common man." Each of these three levels of analysis tended to merge with the other two, for Veblen was in fact analyzing a society that was mainly constituted of two major classes, the capitalists (whom he variously referred to as the "vested interests," the "absentee owners," the "leisure class," or the "captains of industry") and the working class (whom he variously referred to as the "engineers," "the workmen," and the "common man").

Private Property, Class-Divided Society, and the Subjugation of Women

At the foundation of the class structure was the institution of private property. Veblen began his analysis by rejecting the "natural-rights" approach to private property.

> In the accepted economic theories the ground of ownership is commonly conceived to be the productive labor of the owner. This is taken, without reflection or question, to be the legitimate basis of property. . . . To the classical economists the axiom has, perhaps, been as much trouble as it has been worth. It has given them no end of bother to explain how the capitalist is the "producer" of the goods that pass into his possession, and how it is true that the laborer gets what he produces.[18]

This view of private property was, Veblen believed, fundamentally wrong, whether used by conservatives to defend capitalism or by socialists to attack capitalism. Its wrongness lay in the individualistic presuppositions regarding the production processes that were its foundations. Production, Veblen always insisted, was everywhere and at all times a social process and never an individual process:

> This natural-rights theory of property makes the creative effort of an isolated, selfsufficing individual the basis of ownership vested in him. In so doing it overlooks the fact that there is no isolated, selfsufficing individual. . . . Production takes place only in society—only through the co-operation of an industrial community. This industrial community may be large or small . . . but it always comprises a group large enough to contain and transmit the traditions, tools, technical knowledge, and usages without which there can be no industrial organization and no economic relation of individuals to one another or to their environment. . . . There can be no production without technical knowledge; hence no accumulation and no wealth to be owned, in severalty or otherwise. And there is no technical knowledge apart from an industrial community. Since there is no individual production and no individual productivity, the natural-rights preconception . . . reduces itself to absurdity, even under the logic of its own assumptions.[19]

But while production is always social, the laws of private property, which in capitalism determined the distribution of social production, were private and individual. This represented, in Veblen's view, a basic social antagonism. All human progress had been achieved through advances in social production. Such advances were, in general, the result of the "instinct of workmanship" and the working of "idle curiosity." Private property was the result of the "predatory instinct" and stood in opposition to the "instinct of workmanship."

Historically, Veblen believed, the instinct of workmanship was prior to and more fundamental than the predatory instinct. A proposition central to Veblen's entire social philosophy was that "man's life is activity; and as he acts, so he thinks and feels."[20] It was not people's ideas and feelings that primarily determined their activities; rather their life processes and activities determined their ideas and feelings. Moreover,

> throughout the history of human culture, the great body of the people have almost everywhere, in their everyday life, been at work to turn things to human use. The proximate aim of all industrial improvement has been the better performance of some workmanlike task.[21]

In the earliest stages of human society, low productivity made a predominance of the instinct of workmanship a social prerequisite for survival. During this period, "the habits of life of the race were still perforce of a peaceful and industrial character, rather than contentious and destructive."[22] During this early period, "before a predacious life became possible" and while society was still dominated "by the instinct of workmanship, efficiency [or] serviceability commends itself, and inefficiency or futility is odious."[23]

Only after production became substantially more efficient and technical knowledge and tools were socially accumulated did predatory exploitation become possible. Invidious distinctions among different members of society became possible only at that point. With greater productivity, it became possible to live by brute seizure and predatory exploitation. "But seizure and forcible retention very shortly gain the legitimation of usage, and the resultant tenure becomes inviolable through habitation."[24]

Private property had its origins in brute coercive force and was perpetuated both by force and by institutional and ideological legitimization. Class-divided societies inevitably came with the development of private property: "Where this tenure by prowess prevails, the population falls into two economic classes: those engaged in industrial employments, and those engaged in such nonindustrial pursuits as war, government, sports, and religious observances."[25] In precapitalist societies the class division was somewhat sharper and more clearly perceived than in capitalism. "Under serfdom and slavery those who work cannot own, and those who own cannot work."[26]

A class-divided society was a predatory society. In it the predatory instinct held sway over the instinct of workmanship, even though the dominant predatory class was always numerically small in relation to the ordinary people who worked. By subjecting the worker to innumerable indignities and oppressions, the predatory society tended to stint and thwart the instinct of workmanship, and in so doing it made most work irksome, even though pleasant feelings of self-realization were inherently involved in the instinct of workmanship. In class-divided societies,

> the irksomeness of labor is a spiritual fact; it lies in the indignity of the thing. The fact of its irksomeness is, of course, none the less real and cogent for its being of a spiritual kind. Indeed, it is all the more substantial and irremediable on that account.[27]

In a private property, class-divided society, the older values associated with workmanship were eroded and replaced by new values:

> As the predatory culture reaches a fuller development, there comes a distinction between employments. The tradition of prowess, as the virtue *par excellence*, gains in scope and consistency until prowess comes near being recognized as the sole virtue. Those employments alone are then worthy and reputable which involve the exercise of this virtue. Other employment, in which men are occupied with tamely shaping inert materials to human use, become unworthy and end with becoming debasing. The honorable man must not only show capacity for predatory exploit, but he must also avoid entanglement with the occupations that do not involve exploit. The tame employments, those that involve no obvious destruction of life and no

spectacular coercion of refractory antagonists, fall into disrepute and are relegated to those members of the community who are defective in the predatory capacity; that is to say, those who are lacking massiveness, agility, or ferocity. Occupation in these employments argues that the person so occupied falls short of that decent modicum of prowess which would entitle him to be graded as a man in good standing.

. . . Therefore the able-bodied barbarian of the predatory culture, who is mindful of his good name . . . puts in his time in the manly arts of war and devotes his talents to devising ways and means of disturbing the peace. That way lies honor.[28]

With private property and the predatory culture also came the subjugation of women:

Fighting, together with other work that involves a serious element of exploit, becomes the employment of able-bodied men; the uneventful everyday work of the group falls to the women and the infirm. . . . Infirmity, that is to say incapacity for exploit, is looked down upon. One of the early consequences of this depreciation of infirmity is a tabu on women and women's employments.[29]

From this came the view that excessive contact with women was "ceremonially unclean to the men." This "has lasted on in later culture as a sense of the unworthiness or Levitical inadequacy of women; so that even now we feel the impropriety of women taking rank with men, or representing the community in any relation that calls for dignity and ritual competency."[30]

Even though most men in a predatory culture were subservient to the fighters—who constituted only a minority of the men—the predatory traits were generally emulated by weaker common men in their relations with women. Women generally became subservient to men. "Men who are trained in predatory . . . modes of thinking came by habituation to apprehend this form of the relation between the sexes as good and beautiful."[31] This form of the oppression of women led to the peculiar form of the institution of marriage found in private property, class-divided societies. Such marriages originated in coercion and always involved some "concept of ownership."[32]

Veblen believed that only a reemergence of the instinct of workmanship to social dominance over the predatory instinct could finally end the subjugation of women. He believed that capitalism had spurred the development of the instinct of workmanship, even though, as we shall see, it was still controlled by those dominated by predatory behavior. The social forces "now apparently at work to disintegrate the institution of ownership-marriage may be expected also to work a disintegration of the correlative institution of private property."[33]

Class Structure of Capitalism and the Domination of Business over Industry

Private property and the predatory instinct led to the predatory, class-divided societies of the slave and feudal eras. Capitalism was the outgrowth of feudalism in western Europe. Whereas the predatory instinct totally dominated society in slavery and feudalism, in capitalism there had occurred an important, profound growth of the instinct of workmanship. Capitalism—or, as Veblen sometimes referred to capitalism, "the regime of absentee ownership and hired labor"[34]—had begun as a "quasipeaceable" society in which the forces of workmanship had originally developed very rapidly. But with the passage of time, the forces of workmanship and the predatory forces of exploit had become locked in a struggle.

This antagonism was expressed by Veblen as a conflict between "business" and "industry" or between "salesmanship" and "workmanship." Capitalism had originally evolved from feudalism in western Europe because in that culture the predatory instinct and its concomitant patriarchal culture had not fully developed. "For lack of sufficient training in predatory habits of thought (e.g., as shown in the incomplete patriarchalism of the north-Europeans) the predatory culture failed to reach what may be called a normal maturity in the feudal system of Europe."[35] In the ensuing period of "free labor," in which the compulsion to work was the necessity of earning a livelihood rather than a coercively imposed necessity, the instinct of workmanship thrived and the industrial arts showed great progress. In the nineteenth century, the predatory forces, which had been inherited from the slave and feudal societies, began to gain more power. This continued until the capitalist system had evolved, by the late nineteenth century, to the point where the forces of workmanship and the forces of exploit were both powerful social forces.

These two social forces were embodied in entirely different classes of people in capitalism. "The interest and attention of the two typical . . . classes . . . part company and enter on a course of progressive differentiation along two divergent lines."[36] The first class embodied the instinct of workmanship:

> The workmen, laborers, operatives, technologists—whatever term may best designate that general category of human material through which the community's technological proficiency functions directly to an industrial effect—these have to do with the work, whereby they get their livelihood, and their interest as well as the discipline of their workday life converges, in effect, on a technological apprehension of material facts.[37]

The second class embodied the predatory instinct:

> These owners, investors, masters, employers, undertakers, businessmen, have to do with the negotiating of advantageous bargains. . . . The training afforded by these occupations and requisite to their effectual pursuit runs in terms of pecuniary management and insight, pecuniary gain, price, price-cost, price-profit and price-loss;— that is to say in terms of the self-regarding propensities and sentiments.[38]

While the essence of success for laborers involved productive creativity, the essence of success for owners and businessmen involved exploitative advantage over others:

> Pecuniary gain is a differential gain and business is a negotiation of such differential gains; . . . commonly . . . it is a differential as between the businessman's outlay and his returns—that is to say, as between the businessman and the unbusiness like generality of persons with whom directly or indirectly he deals. For the purposes of such negotiation of differentials the weakness of one party (in the pecuniary respect) is as much to the point as the strength of the other—the two being substantially the same fact.[39]

This training fostered the predatory ideals, while the training of laborers fostered the workmanship ideals. But while the ideals of workmanship were highly serviceable to society as a whole, it was nevertheless true that if they ever came to dominate society completely, they would destroy the very institutional basis that supported the luxurious, idle, and parasitic existence of the absentee owner class. Therefore it was constantly necessary to counter the excessive growth of the ideals of workmanship:

> The standards of propriety imposed on the community by the better classes will have a considerable corrective effect on the frame of mind of the common man in this respect as in others, and so will act to maintain the effective currency of predatory ideals and preconceptions after the economic situation at large has taken on . . . a commercial complexion.[40]

Profit making, or business, created behavior that was totally removed from industry or workmanship. Increasingly, owners had less and less to do in the direction of production, which became entrusted to a "professional class of 'efficiency engineers.'"[41] But the concerns of this new managerial class of efficiency engineers was never with productivity itself or with serviceability to the community at large. "The work of the efficiency engineers . . . [is] always done in the service of business . . . in terms of price and profits."[42]

There had, in fact, evolved what Veblen called a "New Order" in which industry, where alone the instinct of workmanship was fostered and developed, was totally subordinated to business, where profit making was the sole concern. Business in turn was subordinated to and existed for the aggrandizement of the wealth of absentee owners.

> This new order of things in American business and industry may be said to have arisen so soon as a working majority of the country's industrial resources, including the transportation system, had been brought securely under absentee ownership on a sufficiently large scale, in sufficiently large holdings, to make these national resources and the industries which make use of them amenable to concerted surveillance and control by the vested interests that represent these larger absentee owners.[43]

The principal antagonistic contradiction of modern capitalism was, in Veblen's view, between the new social forms of production, which were oriented toward productive efficiency and serviceability to the entire community, and the laws of private property, which put control of industry in the hands of absentee owners, who directed industry for profit:

The New Order, therefore, is by way of being a misfit. It is an organization of new ways and means in the way of industrial processes and man-power, subject to irresponsible control at the hands of a super annuated general staff of businessmen moving along lines of an old-fashioned strategy toward obsolete ends.[44]

The nature of the control of business over industry was described by Veblen in one term: "sabotage." Business sabotaged industry for the sake of profit. Sabotage was defined as a "conscientious withdrawal of efficiency."[45] For businessmen, "a reasonable profit always means, in effect, the largest obtainable profit."[46] The problem in capitalism was that large-scale industry and the forces of workmanship were always increasing the quantity of output that could be produced with a given quantity of resources and workers. But given the existing, extremely unequal distribution of income, this added output could be sold only if prices were reduced substantially. Generally, the necessary price reductions were so great that selling a larger quantity at lower prices was less profitable than selling a lesser quantity at higher prices. Therefore, in modern capitalism

> [there] is an ever increasing withdrawal of efficiency. The industrial plant is increasingly running idle or half idle, running increasingly short of its productive capacity. Workmen are being laid off. . . . And all the while these people are in great need of all sorts of goods and services which these idle plants and idle workmen are fit to produce. But for reasons of business expediency it is impossible to let these idle plants and idle workmen go to work—that is to say for reasons of insufficient profit to the business men interested, or in other words, for the reasons of insufficient income to the vested interests.[47]

The sabotage of industry by business, of course, caused widespread suffering and privation on the part of the general public. But absentee owners never had to witness such suffering or even contemplate their role in causing this suffering, particularly when they were taught only the economic theories of the neoclassical economists. In the capitalist system in which business controlled industry,

> this control, and the running balance of sabotage which is its chief method of control and its chief material consequence, all takes effect in an impersonal and dispassionate way, as a matter of business routine. Absentee ownership . . . on this grand scale is immune from neighborly personalities and from sentimental considerations and scruples. . . . The absentee owners are removed out of touch with the working personnel . . . except such remote, neutral and dispassionate contact by proxy as may be implied in the continued receipt of a free income. . . . Thereby the absentee owners as well as their absentee business managers are spared many distasteful experiences, saved from reflecting on many dreary trivialities of life and death— trivialities on the balance sheet of assets and liabilities, although their material counterfoil in terms of life and death among the underlying population may be grave enough to those on whom their impact falls.[48]

Such a picture of capitalism was not, for Veblen, a picture of a crisis or an unusual situation. It was a picture of how capitalism functioned day by day.

Furthermore, this mode of functioning was not due to any inherent immorality on the part of the absentee owners. It was simply institutionally built into the essential structure of capitalism:

> It will be noted that all . . . businesslike strategy falls properly under the head of sabotage. It is, in effect, a traffic in privation, of course. It is also business-as-usual. No fault need be found with it, since there is no help for it. It is not a matter of personal preference or moral obliquity. It is not that these captains of Big Business whose duty it is to administer this salutary modicum of sabotage on production are naughty. It is not that they aim to shorten human life or augment human discomfort by contriving an increase of privation among their fellow men. Indeed, it is to be presumed that they are as humane as they profess. But only by shortening the supply of things needed and so increasing privation to a critical point can they sufficiently increase their . . . earnings, and so come off with a clear conscience and justify the trust which their absentee owners have reposed in them. They are caught in the net of business-as-usual, under circumstances which dictate a conscientious withdrawal of efficiency. The question is not whether this traffic in privation is humane, but whether it is sound business management.[49]

The normal state of modern capitalism, Veblen believed, was one of recurring depressions: "It may, therefore, be said, on the basis of this view, that chronic depression, more or less pronounced, is normal to business under the fully developed regimen of the machine industry."[50] Moreover, throughout the business cycle and at all times, capitalism necessarily involved a continuous class struggle between owners and workers:

> In the negotiations between owners and workmen there is little use for the ordinary blandishments of salesmanship. . . . And the bargaining between them therefore settles down without much circumlocution into a competitive use of unemployment, privation, restriction of work and output, strikes, shut-downs and lockouts, espionage, pickets, and similar manoeuvres of mutual derangement, with a large recourse to menacing language and threats of mutual sabotage. The colloquial word for it is "labor troubles." The business relations between the two parties are of the nature of hostilities, suspended or active, conducted in terms of mutual sabotage; which will on occasion shift from the footing of such obstruction and disallowance as is wholly within the law and custom of business, from the footing of legitimate sabotage in the way of passive resistance and withholding of efficiency, to that illegitimate phase of sabotage that runs into violent offenses against persons and property. The negotiations . . . have come to be spoken of habitually in terms of conflict, armed forces, and warlike strategy. It is a conflict of hostile forces which is conducted on the avowed strategic principle that either party stands to gain at the cost of the other.[51]

Government and the Class Struggle

The ultimate power in the capitalist system was in the hands of the owners because they controlled the government, which was the institutionally legitimized means of physical coercion in any society. As such, the government existed to protect the existing social order and class structure. This meant that in capitalist society the primary duty of government was the enforcement of private property laws and the protection of the privileges associated with ownership. Veblen repeatedly insisted that

> modern politics is business politics. . . . This is true both of foreign and domestic policy. Legislation, police surveillance, the administration of justice, the military and diplomatic service, all are chiefly concerned with business relations, pecuniary interests, and they have little more than an incidental bearing on other human interests.[52]

The first principle of a capitalist government was that "the natural freedom of the individual must not traverse the prescriptive rights of property. Property rights . . . have the indefeasibility which attaches to natural rights."[53] The principal freedom of capitalism was the freedom to buy and sell. The laissez-faire philosophy dictated that "so long as there is no overt attempt on life . . . or the liberty to buy and sell, the law cannot intervene, unless it be in a precautionary way to prevent prospective violation of . . . property rights."[54] Thus, above all else a "constitutional government is a business government."[55]

This did not mean that Veblen denied that the American government was democratic. He realized that there were different political parties and that Americans were free to vote for the party of their choice. He also realized that the government could not always represent all business interests equally. Conflicts among businessmen were reflected in the different political parties.

> The business interests domiciled within the scope of a given government fall into a loose organization in the form of what might be called a tacit ring or syndicate, proceeding on a general understanding that they will stand together as against outside business interests. The nearest approach to an explicit plan and organization of such a business ring is the modern political party, with its platform, tacit and avowed. Parties differ in their detail aims, but those parties that have more than a transient existence and superficial effect stand for different lines of business policy, agreeing all the while in so far that they all aim to further what they each claim to be the best, largest, most enduring business interests of the community. The ring of business interests which secures the broadest approval from popular sentiment is, under constitutional methods, put in charge of the government establishment.[56]

While the money of the absentee owners and businessmen was an important factor in their control of politics, Veblen did not have the simplistic view that businessmen simply bought corrupt politicians (even though they frequently did just that). The political control of capitalists rested far more fundamentally on their control of the socialization and indoctrination processes:

> Representative government means, chiefly, representation of business interests. The government commonly works in the interest of the business men with a fairly consistent singleness of purpose. And in its solicitude for the business men's interests it is borne out by current public sentiment, for there is a naive, unquestioning persuasion abroad among the body of people to the effect that, in some occult way, the material interests of the populace coincide with the pecuniary interests of those business men who live within the scope of the same set of governmental contriv-

ances. This persuasion is an article of popular metaphysics, in that it rests on an uncritically assumed solidarity of interests. . . . This persuasion is particularly secure among the . . . business men, superior and subordinate, together with the professional classes, as contrasted with those vulgar portions of the community who are tainted with socialistic or anarchistic notions. But since the conservative element comprises the citizens of substance and weight, and indeed the effective majority of law-abiding citizens . . . even including those who have no pecuniary interests to serve in the matter, constitutional government has, in the main, become a department of the business organization and is guided by the advice of the business men. . . . In most of its work, even in what is not ostensibly directed to business ends, it is under the surveillance of the business interests.[57]

This control of government by business pervaded all branches and phases of government. Americans were "practical" people, in Veblen's opinion. Given the central influence of business in American society, practical always meant businesslike. Hence, in all branches of government

the incumbents of office are necessarily persons of businesslike antecedents, dominated by the logic of ownership, essentially absentee ownership. Legislators, executives, and judiciary are of the same derivation in respect to . . . [this] bias. . . . There need of course be no question of the good faith or the intelligence of these responsible incumbents of office. It is to be presumed that in these respects they will commonly grade up to the general average, or something not far short of that point. . . . Doubtless in good faith and on sound principles, the ceaseless proliferation of statutes, decisions, precedents, and constitutional interpretations has run, in the main and with increasing effect, on these lines that converge on the needs and merits of absentee ownership.[58]

Thus, in the ceaseless class struggle between workers and absentee owners, the owners nearly always prevailed. Government, as the institutionally legitimized means of physical coercion, was firmly in their hands. Since workers greatly outnumbered owners, the maintenance of the owners' supremacy, that is, the maintenance of the existing class structure of capitalism, depended on the absentee owners being in control of the government. At any point in the class struggle when the workers of a particular industry might appear to have been gaining the upper hand, the government was called in.

At this point the national establishment, federal and local, comes into the case, by way of constituted authority exercising surveillance and punitive powers. . . . [The] intervention of government agencies in these negotiations between the owners and the workmen rebounds to the benefit of the former. Such is necessarily the case in the nature of things. . . . As things go in any democratic community, these governmental agencies are administered by a businesslike personnel, imbued with the habitual bias of business principles—the principles of ownership; that is to say, under current conditions, the rights, powers, and immunities of absentee ownership. In the nature of the case, the official personnel is drawn from the business community—lawyers, bankers, merchants, contractors, etc. . . . "practical men," whose preconceptions and convictions are such as will necessarily emerge from continued and successful experience in the conduct of business of that character. Lawyers and magistrates who have proved their fitness by their successful conduct of administrative duties and litigations turning on the legal niceties of ownership, and in whom the logic of ownership has become second nature.[59]

When these government officials, lawyers, and judges entered the case, it was certain that their prior training would have taught them that

> such collusion, conspiring, or coalition as takes the form of (absentee) ownership is right and good, to be safeguarded in all the powers and immunities of ownership . . . at any cost to the community at large. . . . Increased earnings on capital . . . will be defended by a suitable use of force in case of need.
>
> It is otherwise . . . with the collusive organizations of workmen. Being not grounded in ownership, their legal right of conspiracy in restraint of trade is doubtful at the best.[60]

The corporations generally won the struggle. Workers were more strongly embued with the instinct of workmanship, which was generally associated with peaceable habits of mind. Businessmen were strongly embued with the predatory instinct and the mores of competitive sportsmanship. The life habits of workers were creative and constructive. The life habits of businessmen were destructive and based on a mastery of the techniques of sabotage. The businessmen had the government and the courts on their side. Finally, the businessmen and their agents had a near monopoly on the use of deadly force.

> The presumption, in law and custom and official predilection, is against the use of force or the possession or disposal of arms by persons or associations of persons who are not possessed of appreciable property. It is assumed, in effect, that the use of weapons is to protect property and guard its rights; and the assumption applies to the use of weapons by private persons as well as to the armed forces of government. Under statutes regulating the possession and use of weapons . . . it will be found that permits to carry weapons are issued in the main to substantial citizens [absentee owners of much property], corporations, and to those incorporations of mercenaries that are known by courtesy as detective agencies; these latter being in the nature of auxiliary forces employed on occasion by corporations which may be involved in strikes or lockouts. All this is doubtless as it should be, and doubtless the intention of it is salutary.[61]

Whenever the rights and prerogatives of private property were threatened in any way, the property-owning class responded by force of arms. Property rights were the basis of this class's power and of its "free income," and it would protect them at any cost: "And it is well known, and also it is right and good by law and custom, that when recourse is had to arms the common man pays the cost. He pays it in lost labor, anxiety, privation, blood, and wounds."[62]

Capitalist Imperialism

During the last quarter of the nineteenth century and the early twentieth century, aggressive, imperialist expansion was one of the dominant features of industrial capitalism. In the next chapter we will discuss several economic theories of imperialism. Veblen also wrote extensively on this topic. He believed that the quest for profits knew no national boundaries. The absentee owners of business saw rich possibilities for profits in different areas of the world if those areas could be brought under the domination of capitalist countries or domestic governments that approved of foreigners extracting profits from their countries. The absentee owners' success in getting the population to believe that everyone's interests were identical to the corporations' interests extended into the realm of patriotism. Patriotism was a nationalist sentiment that could be used to gain support for the government's aggressive, imperialist policies on behalf of business interests. "Imperialism is dynastic politics under a new name," Veblen wrote, "carried on for the benefit of absentee owners."[63] He was convinced that there was "a growing need for such national aids to Business."[64] Imperialism was needed because

> the nation's business men . . . are interested in gainful traffic in foreign parts; that is to say, it is designed to extend and enlarge the dominion of the nation's absentee owners beyond the national frontiers.
>
> And by a curious twist of patriotic emotion the loyal citizens are enabled to believe that these extra-territorial gains of the country's business men will somehow benefit the community at large. The gains which the business men come in for in this way are their private gains, of course; but the illusions of national solidarity enable the loyal ones to believe that the gains which so come to these absentee owners at the cost of the taxpayers will benefit the taxpayers in some occult way—in some obscure way which no loyal citizen should inquire into too closely. . . . Should any undistinguished citizen, not an absentee owner of large means, hesitate to throw in his life and substance at the call of the politicians in control, for the greater glory of the flag and the greater profit of absentee business in foreign parts, he becomes a "slacker."
>
> By stress of this all-pervading patriotic bias and that fantastic bigotry which enables civilized men to believe in a national solidarity of material interests, it has come now to pass that the chief—virtually sole—concern of the constituted authorities in any democratic nation is a concern about the profitable business of the nation's substantial citizens. . . . So the constituted authorities of this democratic commonwealth come, in effect, to constitute a Soviet of Business Men's Delegates, whose dutiful privilege it is to safeguard and enlarge the special advantages of the country's absentee owners. And all the while the gains of the absentee owners are got at the cost of the underlying population. . . .
>
> It is perhaps needless to say that all this is said without malice. A description by simple enumeration will sometimes look like faultfinding.[65]

But the profits that imperialism brought to the absentee owners were not, in Veblen's opinion, its most important feature. Imperialism was a conservative social force of the utmost social importance. With the development of the techniques of machine production, human productivity had expanded rapidly during the capitalist era. The natural concomitant of the growth of productivity was the growth of the instinct of workmanship and its related social traits. As workmanship and its attendant traits became dominant in the culture, the social basis of absentee ownership and predatory business practices became endangered. The ethos of workmanship stressed cooperation rather than competition, individual equality and independence rather than pervasive relations of subordination and superordination, logical social interrelationships rather than ceremonial role playing, and peaceable rather than predatory dispositions generally. Thus, the traits associated with workmanship were subversive to the very foundation of the existing class structure. The absentee owners had to find some means to counteract the subversive effects of workmanship, cooperation, individual independence, and the quest for a peaceable brotherhood.

For this important task the absentee owners turned to imperialism. This social role of imperialism was so central to Veblen's view of the functioning of capitalism that we will quote him at length:

> The largest and most promising factor of cultural discipline—most promising as a corrective of iconoclastic vagaries—over which business principles rule is national politics. . . . Business interests urge an aggressive national policy and business men direct it. Such a policy is warlike as well as patriotic. The direct cultural value of a warlike business policy is unequivocal. It makes for a conservative animus on the part of the populace. During war time . . . under martial law, civil rights are in abeyance; and the more warfare and armament the more abeyance. Military training is a training in ceremonial precedence, arbitrary command, and unquestioning obedience. A military organization is essentially a servile organization. Insubordination is the deadly sin. The more consistent and the more comprehensive this military training, the more effectually will the members of the community be trained into habits of subordination and away from the growing propensity to make light of personal authority that is the chief infirmity of democracy. This applies first and most decidedly, of course, to the soldiery, but it applies only in a less degree to the rest of the population. They learn to think in warlike terms of rank, authority, and subordination, and so grow progressively more patient of encroachments upon their civil rights. . . . The disciplinary effects of warlike pursuits . . . direct the popular interest to other, nobler, institutionally less hazardous matters than the unequal distribution of wealth or creature comforts. Warlike and patriotic preoccupations fortify the barbarian virtues of subordination and prescriptive authority. Habituation to a warlike, predatory scheme of life is the strongest disciplinary factor that can be brought to counteract the vulgarization of modern life wrought by peaceful industry and the machine process, and to rehabilitate the decaying sense of status and differential dignity. Warfare, with the stress on subordination and mastery and the insistence on gradations of dignity and honor incident to a military organization, has always proved an effective school in barbarian methods of thought.
>
> In this direction, evidently, lies the hope of a corrective for "social unrest" and similar disorders of civilized life. There can, indeed, be no serious question but that a consistent return to the ancient virtues of allegiance, piety, servility, graded dignity, class prerogative, and prescriptive authority would greatly conduce to popular content and to the facile management of affairs. Such is the promise held out by a strenuous national policy.[66]

Social Mores of Pecuniary Culture

Where the instinct of workmanship held sway, the social tendency was toward the advancement of knowledge, cooperation, equality, and mutual aid. But the class division of capitalism depended on the continued social prominence of the traits associated with predatory exploit—the admiration of predatory skills, acquiescence in the hierarchy of subordination, and the widespread substitution of myth and ceremony for knowledge. The free and unearned income of the absentee owners ultimately depended on the cultural and social domination of the mores of the predatory, or, what in capitalism amounted to the same thing, the pecuniary or business aspects of the culture.

When the predatory instinct dominated society, the prevailing mores were those of the leisure class, which constituted the ruling element of society. Veblen believed that "the emergence of a leisure class coincides with the beginning of ownership. . . . They are but different aspects of the same general facts of social structure."[67] In all class-divided societies there had always been a fundamentally significant differentiation between the occupations of the leisure class and those of the common people. "Under this ancient distinction," he wrote, "the worthy employments are those which may be classed as exploit; unworthy are those necessary everyday employments into which no appreciable element of exploit enters."[68]

In all class-divided societies the predatory powers of a man or a group were held in the highest possible esteem. People who had developed the abilities associated with exploitation to a very high degree were given the most honorific status in society. Thus, in a capitalist society,

> economic institutions fall into two roughly distinct categories—the pecuniary and the industrial. The like is true of employments. Under the former head are employments that have to do with ownership or acquisition; under the latter head, those that have to do with workmanship or production. . . . The economic interests of the leisure class lie in the pecuniary employments; those of the working class lie . . . chiefly in the industrial. Entrance to the leisure class lies through the pecuniary employments.
>
> These two classes of employments differ materially in respect of the aptitude required for each. . . . The discipline of the pecuniary employments acts to conserve and to cultivate certain of the predatory aptitudes and the predatory animus. . . . So far as men's habits of thought are shaped by the competitive process of acquisition and tenure; so far as their economic functions are comprised within the ownership of wealth . . . and its management and financiering . . . ; [to that extent] their economic life favours the survival and accentuation of the predatory temperament and habits of thought. Under the modern . . . system . . . the pecuniary employments give proficiency in the general line of practices comprised under fraud.[69]

Under capitalism there came to be a hierarchy of occupations ranging from the most honorific—absentee ownership—to the most vulgar and repulsive—creative labor.

> Employments fall into a hierarchical gradation of reputability. Those which have to do immediately with ownership on a large scale are the most reputable. . . . Next to these in good repute come those employments that are immediately subservient to ownership and financiering—such as banking and law. Banking employments also carry a suggestion of large ownership, and this fact is doubtless accountable for a share of the prestige that attaches to the business. The profession of law does not imply large ownership; but since no taint of usefulness, for other than the competi-

tive purpose, attaches to the lawyer's trade, it grades high in the conventional scheme. The lawyer is exclusively occupied with the details of predatory fraud, either in achieving or in checkmating chicane, and success in the profession is therefore accepted as marking a large endowment of that barbarian astuteness which has always commanded men's respect and fear. . . . Manual labour, or even the work of directing mechanical processes, is of course on a precarious footing as regards respectability.[70]

But wealthy absentee owners usually lived in large cities and spent most of their time with lawyers, accountants, stockbrokers, and other advisers, buying and selling stocks and bonds, manipulating financial deals, and generally engineering schemes of sabotage and fraud. Therefore, whereas the predatory virtues in more barbarian cultures were so obvious and immediate as to easily incite the admiration of the populace, the predatory virtues in a capitalist society were largely hidden from view and could not so readily incite admiration.

In order to gain and to hold the esteem of men it is not sufficient merely to possess wealth or power. The wealth or power must be put in evidence, for esteem is awarded only on evidence. And not only does the evidence of wealth serve to impress one's importance on others and to keep their sense of his importance alive and alert, but it is of scarcely less use in building up and preserving one's self-complacency.[71]

Most of *The Theory of the Leisure Class* was devoted to a detailed description of how the leisure class displayed its predatory prowess through conspicuous consumption and the conspicuous use of leisure. For Veblen, conspicuous consumption often coincided with conspicuous waste. The housing of the rich, for example, "is more ornate, more conspicuously wasteful in its architecture and decoration, than the dwelling-houses of the congregation."[72] It was always necessary for the rich to have expensive, ornate, and largely useless—but above all, expensive—paraphernalia prominently displayed. For the wealthy, the more useless and expensive a thing was, the more it was prized as an article of conspicuous consumption. Anything that was useful and affordable to common people was thought to be vulgar and tasteless.

The beauty and elaborate dressing and display of one's wife was essential for a substantial citizen of good taste. Innumerable servants were indicators that a wife had to do none of the vulgar work of an ordinary housewife and that she was herself primarily an ostentatious trophy of beauty and uselessness that added to the esteem of her husband. Villas on the sea, yachts, and elaborate mountain chateaus, all of which were rarely used but prominently visible, were essential for respectability.

Veblen had much more in mind in describing the conspicuous consumption of the rich than merely giving an amusing anecdotal account. Pecuniary culture was above all else a culture of invidious distinction. When an individual's personal worth was measured primarily in a pecuniary system of invidious distinction, one of the most powerful forces in society was emulation, which was the most important guarantor of social, economic, and political conservatism.

The wealthy maintained their position by perpetuating the "principle of predation or parasitism."[73] Their activities automatically led to the belief that "whatever is, is right."[74] They were inherently and profoundly conservative. The extremely poor in society constituted very little threat to the predatory, pecuniary social order:

> The abjectly poor, and all those persons whose energies are entirely absorbed by the struggle for daily sustenance, are conservative because they cannot afford the effort of taking thought for the day after tomorrow; just as the highly prosperous are conservative because they have small occasion to be discontented with the situation as it stands today.[75]

It was generally the more economically secure elements of the working class that constituted a potential threat to the status quo. They had usually been successful in acquiring highly marketable productive skills. This meant that they usually had considerable pride of workmanship. There was a constant danger that the traits associated with the instinct of workmanship— clear, logical thinking, cooperation, mutual aid, and general humanitarianism —would increase to a point where such workers would turn to anarchism or socialism in order to promote the hegemony of workmanlike traits over pecuniary, predatory traits. Emulative consumption was a primary means of reducing this threat. Emulative consumption, however, represented a personal treadmill from which no progress was possible and escape was difficult if not impossible. When a person got on that treadmill, he gave himself up totally to the mores of predatory, pecuniary culture. Veblen's views on emulative consumption, together with his views on the social, psychological, and ideological importance of patriotism, militarism, and imperialism constituted the very heart of his theory of the social, economic, and political domination of capitalism by absentee owners and business interests.

While it was true that the "free income," privileges, and powers of the capitalists derived directly from the laws of property ownership, the concentration of property ownership in the hands of the absentee owners, and the control by the absentee owners of the government and all legitimized uses of deadly force, in the long run, their power to rule over society depended most on their ability to control the emotions, ideas, and ideological dispositions of the majority of working people.

If the majority of working people came to realize that capitalists contributed nothing to the production process, that the capitalists' business and pecuniary activities were the cause of depressions and other malfunctions of the industrial system, that the disproportionately large share of wealth and income going to the capitalists caused the impoverishment of the majority of society, that the degradation of the work process was the result of the prevailing predatory ethos of capitalists—if the workers came to realize these facts, then they would surely free the industrial system from the oppressive and archaic fetters of the laws, governments, and institutions of the pecuniary business culture. There would be a revolutionary overthrow of capitalism.

The capitalists relied on two principal means of cultural discipline and social control. The first, as we have seen, consisted of patriotism, nationalism, militarism, and imperialism. The second means of emotionally and ideologically controlling the population was through emulative consumption (or "consumerism," as this phenomenon later came to be called). The importance of this phenomenon in Veblen's total theory was so great that we will quote him at length:

> A certain standard of wealth . . . and of prowess . . . is a necessary condition of reputability, and anything in excess of this normal amount is meritorious.
>
> Those members of the community who fall short of this, somewhat indefinite, normal degree of prowess or property suffer in the esteem of their fellow-men; and consequently they suffer also in their own esteem, since the usual basis of self-respect is the respect accorded by one's neighbours. Only individuals with an aberrant temperament can in the long run retain their self-esteem in the face of the disesteem of their fellows. . . .
>
> So soon as the possession of property becomes the basis of popular esteem, therefore, it becomes also a requisite to that complacency which we call self-respect. In any community . . . it is necessary, in order to have his own peace of mind, that an individual should possess as large a portion of goods as others with whom he is accustomed to class himself; and it is extremely gratifying to possess something more than others. But as fast as a person makes new acquisitions, and becomes accustomed to the resulting new standard of wealth, the new standard forthwith ceases to afford appreciably greater satisfaction than the earlier standard did. The tendency in any case is constantly to make the present pecuniary standard the point of departure for a fresh increase of wealth; and this in turn gives rise to a new standard of sufficiency and a new pecuniary classification of one's self as compared with one's neighbours. So far as concerns the present question, the end sought by accumulation is to rank high in comparison with the rest of the community in point of pecuniary strength. So long as the comparison is distinctly unfavourable to himself, the normal average individual will live in chronic dissatisfaction with his present lot; and when he has reached what may be called the normal pecuniary standard of the community, or of his class in the community, this chronic dissatisfaction will give place to a restless straining to place a wider and ever-widening pecuniary interval between himself and this average standard. The invidious comparison can never become so favourable to the individual making it that he would not gladly rate himself still higher relative to his competitors in the struggle for pecuniary reputability.[76]

When people were caught on this treadmill of emulative consumption, or consumerism, they led a life of "chronic dissatisfaction," regardless of the amount of income they received. The misery of workers, in Veblen's view, arose predominantly from material deprivation only in the part of the working class that lived in abject poverty. For the remainder of the working class, the misery was caused by both the social degradation of labor and the "chronic dissatisfaction" associated with emulative consumption. The misery of the materially advantaged workers was spiritual. But Veblen insisted that this misery "is . . . none the less real and cogent for its being of a spiritual kind. Indeed it is all the more substantial and irremediable on that account."[77]

It seemed irremediable because the workers' response to the misery furthered and perpetuated the misery, the reaction being to believe that they would be happy if they acquired more and consumed more. So the workers went into debt, depended more and more heavily on moving up in their jobs and securing more income, and ultimately were convinced that their only possibility for transcending their chronic dissatisfaction was to please their employers and never do or say anything disruptive or radical.

But such a treadmill was endless. The harder one tried to overcome one's chronic dissatisfaction and misery, the more dissatisfied and miserable one became. In a system of invidious social ranking and conspicuous consumption, a worker rarely blamed the "system," the "vested interests," or the "absentee owners" for his or her plight. The worker generally blamed him- or herself, resulting in a further decline in self-esteem and self-confidence and a tighter clinging to the values of pecuniary culture.

Working against these values of pecuniary culture, however, were the values associated with the instinct of workmanship. The dignity and ultimate happiness of the majority of people depended on the eventual triumph of the values of workmanship over the predatory, pecuniary values of business. Veblen had no doubt about what would be necessary for the values of workmanship to triumph:

> Inasmuch as the aim of emulation is not any absolute degree of comfort or of excellence, no advance in the average wellbeing of the community can end the struggle or lessen the strain. A general amelioration cannot quiet the unrest whose source is the craving of everybody to compare favorably with his neighbor.
>
> Human nature being what it is, the struggle for each to possess more than his neighbor is inseparable from the institution of private property. . . . The criterion of complacency is, largely, the *de facto* possession or enjoyment; and the present growth of sentiment among the body of the people—who possess less—favors, in a vague way, a readjustment adverse to the interests of those who possess more, and adverse to the possibility of legitimately possessing or enjoying "more"; that is to say, the growth of sentiment favors a socialistic movement. . . . The ground of the unrest . . . that makes for socialism is to be found in the institution of private property. With private property, under modern conditions . . . jealousy and unrest are unavoidable.
>
> The corner-stone of the modern industrial system is the institution of private property. . . . It is, moreover, the ultimate ground—and, under modern conditions, necessarily so—of the unrest and discontent whose proximate cause is the struggle for economic respectability. The inference seems to be that, human nature being what it is, there can be no peace from this—it must be admitted—ignoble form of emulation, or from the discontent that goes with it, this side of the abolition of private property.[78]

In this quotation, written in 1892, Veblen believed the tide was going in favor of the forces of socialism, or the values of workmanship, and against the forces of business, or the pecuniary values and the predatory instinct. Still somewhat optimistic (but slightly less so) in 1904, he wrote that industrial employment "is particularly designed to inculcate such iconoclastic habits of thought as come to a head in the socialist bias."[79] The values of the predatory, pecuniary business culture were still very strong, however:

> Which of the two antagonistic factors may prove the stronger in the long run is something of a blind guess; but the calculable future seems to belong to the one or the other. It seems possible to say this much, that the full dominion of business enterprise is necessarily a transitory dominion.[80]

Over the next twenty years, Veblen witnessed the patriotic and imperialist orgy of World War I, its blind, fanatical national chauvinism, and its hysterically repressive aftermath—the Great Red Scare, the Palmer raids, and the blind acquiescence of the majority of people to the systematic government onslaught on all progressive and socialist movements. Veblen's mood changed from one of cautious optimism to one of despair and pessimism. He seemed to see little hope for capitalism ever being reformed into a decent, humane society; that is, he seemed to see little hope for socialism. But he still believed that private property and its pecuniary, predatory culture were anachronistic institutions that were destined to fall. The future looked very bleak:

> In the long run, of course, the pressure of changing material circumstances will have to shape the lines of human conduct, on pain of extinction. . . . But it does not follow that the pressure of material necessity, visibly enforced by the death penalty, will ensure such a change in the legal and moral punctilios as will save the nation from the death penalty. . . .
>
> Whether any given people is to come through any given period of such enforced change alive and fit to live, appears to be a matter of chance in which human insight plays a minor role and human foresight no part at all.[81]

Assessment of Veblen's Ideas

While Veblen cannot properly be considered a disciple of Marx, the parallels between the two great thinkers are striking. They both insisted on a historical approach to the study of capitalism; both saw capitalism as a historically unique and historically transient society based on the exploitation of the direct producers by a numerically small ruling class of parasitic owners. They both saw the laws of capitalist, private property ownership as the basis of capitalists' power and workers' degradation. Both saw the debilitating effects of capitalism on the lives of working people, and both saw this in very similar terms. Both saw increasing industrial concentration as the inevitable outcome of competition, and both saw economic crises and depressions as being inherent in the very functioning of capitalism. Finally, both saw capitalist governments as essentially the enforcers and guarantors of the profits and privileges of the capitalist class.

There were, of course, important differences in the theories of the two men. Veblen's emphasis on the historical and evolutionary nature of capitalism was so strong that it caused him to reject most forms of economic theory that were couched in equilibrium terms. Although Marx believed that a historical understanding of capitalism was essential, he nevertheless considered it quite proper to take many particular, historically changing circumstances of capitalism as fixed or given, in order to investigate the short-run functioning of the system. When Marx did this, he frequently utilized equilibrium analyses (if only, as in the case of his theory of crises, to show how improbable the continuous achievement of equilibrium would be). This difference constitutes one of the areas in which Marx's analysis was clearly superior to Veblen's. There are two principal consequences of this difference, both of which rendered Marx's theory superior.

First, although both Marx and Veblen saw the determination of wages and profits as the result of a protracted class struggle between capitalists and workers, Veblen was never able to translate the outcome of this struggle into a concrete theory of the determination of a wage rate and a profit rate. This was because, eschewing equilibrium theory, Veblen had no theory of value. Both the utility theory of value (which Veblen and Marx equally detested) and the labor theory of value (which Veblen rejected) are basically equilibrium theories. Marx had been able to show that at any particular time, the struggle between capital and labor resulted in some widely accepted, culturally defined minimum standard of living for workers. Taking this standard as given in the short term, Marx's labor theory of value permitted him to explain the nature and origins of profit, the value of labor power, and the magnitude and rate of profit. Veblen's theory was never addressed to these issues; he merely detailed (in a most perceptive and accurate fashion) the forces that would lead to changes in these magnitudes over time, without ever explaining the precise nature and magnitudes of profits and wages at any point in time.

Second, Marx's theory of crises and depressions was somewhat more comprehensive than Veblen's. Both thinkers had detailed and insightful descriptions of the manner in which waves of financial speculation would lead to unwarranted appreciation of capital values, which in turn would lead to financial and industrial crises. But because Marx did not reject equilibrium theory, he was able to show the equilibrium conditions that would be necessary for smooth, continuous "expanded reproduction," or economic growth. He was thereby able to show the practical impossibility of the continuous fulfillment of these conditions in a capitalist system as well as how a failure of the system to fulfill any of these conditions could easily result in a business crisis, or a depression. Veblen definitely needed a similar theory to reconcile an apparent (but not actual) contradiction in his theory: his perspicacious description of emulative consumption, or "consumerism," would appear to guarantee a perpetual sufficiency of aggregate demand, so that the persistent crises and general stagnation that he believed to be inherent in capitalism would never occur. Had he incorporated something like Marx's theory of sectoral imbalances into his theory, this apparent contradiction would have disappeared and both emulative consumption and depressions could have been shown to be ongoing, inherent characteristics of capitalism.

There were, however, areas in which Veblen's analysis was decidedly superior to Marx's. Whereas they both saw, in much the same terms, capitalism's pernicious effects on the material, spiritual, emotional, and esthetic well-being of workers, Marx erroneously believed that the time was close when the workers would revolt and overthrow capitalism. Marx's misperception seems to have resulted from his failure to consider with sufficient care social and cultural norms and mores and their effects in the workers' socialization. Workers embraced these socializing influences and thus promoted the interests of capitalists, even though these influences were ultimately destructive to the interests of the workers themselves. Veblen's analysis of the power of patriotic fervor and emulative consumption, which conditioned workers to accept these self-defeating attitudes, was extraordinarily perceptive and insightful. It remains to this day one of the most powerful and accurate explanations of why workers not only endure exploitation and alienation, but very frequently support the very institutions, laws, governments, and general social mores that create and perpetuate this exploitation and degradation.

Whereas Marx's insights have become central to nearly all socialist political movements, and Marx is almost universally revered by socialists of all political ideological varieties, Veblen's insights appear to have been consistently underestimated by a large number of socialists. It is, of course, impossible to give a full and adequate explanation of this relative neglect. However, two reasons might at least partially account for it. First, most socialists are political activists and tend to admire others who are politically active. Veblen might appear to have been politically detached and inactive, and thereby does not incite the same admiration as does Marx, who was very politically active. But such a view is somewhat shortsighted. The struggle between capitalists and laborers is not merely a struggle at the level of organizing and carrying out concrete political actions; it is also a struggle of ideas.

Viewed as a struggle of ideas, the conflict between the classes is a struggle to win the hearts and minds of workers and all other segments of society, as well as a quest to understand capitalism clearly enough so that it might someday be effectively transformed into a more humane society, conducive to the full realization of human potential. Insofar as the class conflict of capitalism manifests itself as a struggle of ideas, Veblen was a political activist of the first rank. He succeeded brilliantly in exposing the ideological elements of neoclassical economic theory and in promoting a clear and insightful understanding of both the historically transitory and the exploitative nature of capitalism.

Ironically, the second reason that many socialists neglect Veblen's insights stems from what we argued was a superiority of Veblen's insights over those of Marx. Many socialists dislike Veblen because of the pessimism that seems to be reflected in his last writings. But, as we have shown, that pessimism results from both a knowledge of the ways in which the capitalist culture socialized workers to promote interests contrary to their own and a witnessing of the patriotic fervor that pervaded the working class during and immediately following World War I. As a result of that patriotic fervor, the majority of the working class acquiesced to the harshly repressive governmental onslaught that followed in the aftermath of the war—an onslaught on the most progressive and militant of labor and socialist organizations of that period. But here again, Veblen fought back in the only way that he knew—with his condemning, biting, sardonic, and insightfully written attacks on these government policies.

In assessing the pessimism of Veblen, we can do no better than to quote the final two paragraphs of a book by the social philosopher and economist, Joan Robinson. We believe that these two paragraphs could just as well have been written by Veblen at the close of his career and that they accurately reflect the spirit and impact of his writings:

> Anyone who writes a book, however gloomy its message may be, is necessarily an optimist. If the pessimists really believed what they were saying there would be no point in saying it.
>
> The economists of the laissez-faire school purported to abolish the moral problem by showing that the pursuit of self-interest by each individual rebounds to the benefit of all. The task of the [new] generation . . . is to reassert the authority of morality over technology; the business of social scientists is to help them to see both how necessary and how difficult that task is going to be.[82]

Notes to Chapter 12

1. Thorstein Veblen, "The Limitations of Marginal Utility," in *The Place of Science in Modern Civilization, and Other Essays* (New York: Russell and Russell, 1961), p. 241.

2. Thorstein Veblen, "Fisher's Rate of Interest," in *Essays in Our Changing Order* (New York: Augustus M. Kelley, 1964), p. 143.

3. Veblen, "Limitations of Marginal Utility," pp. 241–42.

4. C.E. Ayres, "Veblen's Theory of Instincts Reconsidered," in *Thorstein Veblen: A Critical Reappraisal*, ed. Douglas F. Dowd (Ithaca, NY: Cornell University Press, 1958), p. 25.

5. Thorstein Veblen, "Why Economics Is Not an Evolutionary Science," in *Place of Science in Modern Civilization*, pp. 73–74.

6. Thorstein Veblen, "Professor Clark's Economics," in *Place of Science in Modern Civilization*, pp. 182–83.

7. Thorstein Veblen, "Fisher's Capital and Income," in *Essays in Our Changing Order*, p. 163.

8. Ibid., p. 164.

9. Ibid., pp. 166–67.

10. Veblen, "Professor Clark's Economics," p. 193.

11. Ibid., p. 195.

12. Ibid., p. 197.

13. Veblen, "Fisher's Rate of Interest," p. 142.

14. Thorstein Veblen, "Böhm-Bawerk's Definition of Capital," in *Essays in Our Changing Order*, p. 136.

15. Ibid., p. 135.

16. Thorstein Veblen, *Absentee Ownership and Business Enterprise in Recent Times* (New York: Augustus M. Kelley, 1964), pp. 402–3.

17. Ibid., p. 407.

18. Thorstein Veblen, "The Beginnings of Ownership," in *Essays in Our Changing Order*, p. 32.

19. Ibid., pp. 33–34.

20. Thorstein Veblen, "The Instinct of Workmanship and the Irksomeness of Labor," in *Essays in Our Changing Order*, p. 85.

21. Ibid., p. 84.

22. Ibid., p. 86.

23. Ibid., pp. 87, 89.

24. Veblen, "Beginnings of Ownership," p. 95.

25. Ibid., p. 43.

26. Ibid., p. 42.

27. Veblen, "Instinct of Workmanship," p. 95.

28. Ibid., pp. 93–94.

29. Veblen, "The Barbarian Status of Women," in *Essays in Our Changing Order*, pp. 51–52.

30. Ibid., p. 52.

31. Ibid., p. 55.

32. Ibid.

33. Ibid., p. 64.

34. Veblen, *Absentee Ownership*, p. 291.

35. Veblen, "The Instinct of Workmanship," p. 202.

36. Ibid., pp. 187–88.

37. Ibid., p. 188.

38. Ibid., pp. 189–90.

39. Ibid., p. 191.

40. Ibid., pp. 185–86.

41. Ibid., p. 222.

42. Ibid., p. 224.

43. Veblen, *Absentee Ownership*, pp. 210–11.

44. Ibid., p. 210.

45. Thorstein Veblen, *The Engineers and the Price System* (New York: Augustus M. Kelley, 1965), p. 1.

46. Ibid., p. 13.

47. Ibid., p. 12.

48. Veblen, *Absentee Ownership*, pp. 215–16.

49. Ibid., pp. 220–21.

50. Thorstein Veblen, *The Theory of Business Enterprise* (New York: Augustus M. Kelley, 1965), p. 234.

51. Veblen, *Absentee Ownership*, pp. 406–7.

52. Veblen, *Theory of Business Enterprise*, p. 269.

53. Ibid., p. 272.

54. Ibid., p. 278.

55. Ibid., p. 285.

56. Ibid., pp. 293–94.

57. Ibid., pp. 286–87.

58. Veblen, *Absentee Ownership*, pp. 405–6.

59. Ibid., pp. 404–5.

60. Ibid., pp. 409–10.

61. Ibid., p. 411.

62. Veblen, *Essays in Our Changing Order*, p. 413.

63. Veblen, *Absentee Ownership*, p. 35.

64. Ibid., p. 35.

65. Ibid., pp. 35–37.

66. Veblen, *Theory of Business Enterprise*, pp. 391–93.

67. Thorstein Veblen, *The Theory of the Leisure Class* (New York: Augustus M. Kelley, 1965), p. 22.

68. Ibid., p. 8.

69. Ibid., pp. 229–30.

70. Ibid., pp. 231–32.

71. Ibid., pp. 36–37.

72. Ibid., p. 120.

73. Ibid., p. 209.

74. Ibid., p. 207.

75. Ibid., p. 204.

76. Ibid., pp. 30–32.

77. Veblen, "Instinct of Workmanship," p. 95.

78. Thorstein Veblen, "The Theory of Socialism," in *Place of Science in Modern Civilization,* pp. 396–98.

79. Veblen, *Theory of Business Enterprise*, p. 351.

80. Ibid., p. 400.

81. Veblen, *Absentee Ownership*, pp. 17–18.

82. Joan Robinson, *Freedom and Necessity* (New York: Pantheon Books, 1970), p. 12.

Chapter 13

Theories of Imperialism: The Writings of Hobson, Luxemburg, and Lenin

Capitalism has always been an economic system that operated on an international scale. The capture and sale of Africans was an important source of the original accumulation of capital in the early stages of capitalism. Forceful conquest in the Americas and Africa was a major source of the inflow of precious metals into Europe. These precious metals made possible the monetization of much of the European economy—a necessary precondition for commodity production. And forced subjugation of innumerable colonial peoples created many privileged sanctuaries of profiteering for the many government-created or government-protected European trading companies during the early stages of capitalism.

During the late eighteenth and first half of the nineteenth centuries, however, the drive to industrialization seemed to occupy nearly all of the attention, time, and money of the capitalists. There was, during this period, a lull in the capitalists' drive to conquer, colonize, subjugate, and exploit the areas of the world lying outside the North Atlantic region where capitalism was born. This lull was temporary, however. During the last third of the nineteenth century, while industrial, financial, and commercial power was becoming concentrated in the hands of giant corporations and internal financial empires were being built within all of the major capitalist countries, there occurred a worldwide orgy of capitalist imperialism. The major industrialized capitalist countries brutally and forcefully subdued areas all over the earth for the profits or potential profits of giant corporations.

In Africa, for example, despite centuries of bloody and heinous slave trade, the European capitalist countries had hardly penetrated beyond the coastal areas by the early nineteenth century. By the early twentieth century, however, after a ruthless, barbaric onslaught, 10 million square miles, or about 93 percent, of Africa had been forcefully subjugated to foreign capitalist rule. France had conquered about 40 percent (much of it within the Sahara Desert),

England about 30 percent, and the remaining 23 percent had been seized by Germany, Belgium, Portugal, and Spain.

While the British East India Company had long engaged in exploitative commerce in India, during the latter half of the eighteenth and most of the nineteenth centuries this commerce gave way to brutal military conquest and harsh economic and social exploitation. In the late nineteenth century, this exploitation became so severe that over two-thirds of the population was badly undernourished; famine, disease, and misery were rife, and, in 1891, the average Indian lived less than twenty-six years and usually died in misery.

Also during the late nineteenth century, much of the remainder of Asia was divided among the European capitalist powers. In 1878, the British overran Afghanistan and placed it under the Indian government, which was ruled by Britain. In 1907, Persia was divided between Russia and Britain. By 1887, the entire territory of Indochina had been brought under the rule of France. The Malay Peninsula and the Malay Archipelago (which stretches for nearly 3,000 miles) were forcefully subdued and carved up. The British grabbed Singapore and the Malay states, the northern part of Borneo, and southern New Guinea. Another part of New Guinea was taken by the Germans and most of the remaining islands (an area comprising about 735,000 square miles) went to the Dutch.

American imperialism was also rampant during this period. Through a series of intrigues, invasions, and bloody military subjugation of native populations, the United States had, by World War I, gained control of Samoa, Midway Island, Hawaii, Puerto Rico, Guam, the Philippines, Tutuila, Cuba, the Dominican Republic, Haiti, Nicaragua, and the Panama Canal Zone.

During the imperialist frenzy of the last third of the nineteenth century, Great Britain forcibly grabbed 4.5 million square miles, which she added to her empire; France seized 3.5 million; Germany, one million; Belgium, 900,000; Russia, 500,000; Italy, 185,000; and the United States, 125,000. In all, one-fourth of the world's population was subjugated and put under the domination of the capitalist governments of Europe and North America.

To the capitalist governments, this subjugation and domination was desirable for two reasons. First, most of these conquered people had been living in traditional, noncapitalist, nonmarket societies, and hence their traditional nonpecuniary cultures represented barriers to the commercial exploitation and resource grabbing desired by the large capitalist corporations. Therefore, these cultures had to be coercively forced through something similar to what Marx had called "primitive accumulation" in order to create the extensive commercial relationships and universal dependence on the market that were necessary for systematic commercial exploitation. Forcefully destroying the institutions and bonds of traditional life in these societies was, of course, a brutal and bloody process, as it had been during the period of primitive accumulation in Europe.

Second, even after the traditional institutions and ways of life had been destroyed and widespread economic dependence on the market had been established in these underdeveloped lands, terms of trade that were much more favorable to the industrialized capitalist countries could be established if these capitalist countries effectively ruled the underdeveloped countries.

Neoclassical economists never addressed any of their theoretical inquiries to the issue of imperialism (and have not to the present). This is not surprising, because for them all economic theory was merely an extension and an elaboration of the theory of exchange. Aspects of imperialism that did not involve purely voluntary economic exchange were defined as "not economic" and therefore of no concern to these economists; aspects involving exchange were no different than any other exchange—both parties benefited and harmony prevailed. Within neoclassical economic theory, there came to be a special field of inquiry called "international economics." It was concerned almost entirely with a development of the ideas of Smith, Ricardo, and Mill, which showed that gains from international trade were essentially the same as gains from any form of specialization and exchange. Within neoclassical economic theory, the principal differences between international exchanges and exchanges within a nation were first, that governments might enact tariffs or other restrictions to free international trade, and second, that different currencies were involved. Neoclassical international economic theory consisted primarily of utilitarian proofs that all trade restrictions should be removed in order that free trade benefit everyone in all nations in its usual harmonious manner. It also consisted of elaborate deductive theories to show how exchange rates among different currencies would be determined under conditions of pure competition and international harmony.

Because neoclassical theory assumed that its theoretical categories—utility, exchange, rents, profits, and wages—were universal features of all societies, and that capitalism was "natural" and "eternal," neoclassical theorists could hardly have been expected to have formulated an analysis of the rapacious destruction of the traditional cultural institutions of previously noncapitalist societies. Frequently, the problem seemed to be that the people of these traditional societies simply failed to realize the "great benefit" and "harmony" with which the market would bless them once their societies were opened up for capitalist exploitation. Furthermore, just as the neoclassical utility theorists could see the great benefit to a propertyless worker when he or she exchanged his or her labor power for a subsistence wage rather than avoiding exchange and starving, so they saw that once the people of the imperialistically subjugated cultures were impoverished and made dependent on the market for their very existence, such exchange (regardless of the relative bargaining power of their foreign rulers) would also benefit them. After all, exchanging and living in poverty, deprivation, and destitution was certainly preferable to not exchanging and dying.

It must be said, in all fairness, that few important neoclassical theorists were actually direct and explicit apologists for military conquest. They simply ignored it as improper subject matter for economists, and then, once such conquest was accomplished, they ignored the relative bargaining power of the exchangers (as they did in virtually all their analyses of exchange) and extolled the universal beneficence and harmony that resulted from the exchange.

There were many economic theorists outside the neoclassical tradition, however, who were concerned with imperialism. They sought to understand it, hoping that such understanding would aid in the struggle to end imperialist exploitation. In the previous chapter, we discussed Veblen's view of the nature, causes, and consequences of imperialism. In this chapter, we will briefly discuss the theories about the nature and causes of imperialism of J.A. Hobson, Rosa Luxemburg, and V.I. Lenin.

Hobson's Theory of Capitalist Imperialism

John A. Hobson (1858–1940) was an extraordinarily productive intellectual whose writings run to more than thirty volumes. He was also a lifelong crusader for various progressive social causes. His book *Imperialism: A Study*, first published in 1902, was probably the most influential study of imperialism ever published. Almost all subsequent efforts to understand imperialism were significantly influenced by Hobson's pioneering work.

Hobson saw imperialism as a "social parasitic process by which a moneyed interest within the state, usurping the reins of government, makes for imperial expansion in order to fasten economic suckers into foreign bodies so as to drain them of their wealth in order to support domestic luxury."[1] He realized that imperialism was a complex, many-sided phenomenon. It was the outcome of many separate social forces such as nationalism, patriotism, religious fervor, and militarism, as well as of capitalists' ceaseless quest for more profits. He was therefore interested in investigating these various social forces to ascertain their relative importance in creating and perpetuating imperialism.

In the official propaganda that justified imperialism, it was generally described as a benevolent quest to "civilize" and "bring Christianity" to the "lower races." American President McKinley, for example, described the brutal, bloody, military crushing of the Filipino independence movement by American troops as a benevolent attempt "to educate the Filipinos and uplift and Christianize them." The same rationale was repeated in nearly every imperialist, capitalist country. Hobson believed that while this facade of "Christianizing" and "uplifting" the "backward people of the world" was not a purely propagandist lie, it was nevertheless a deceptive, fraudulent conceit behind which the real motives of imperialism were hidden:

> We are well aware that most British missionaries are quite untainted by admixture of political and commercial motives, and that they set about their work in a single spirit of self-sacrifice, eager to save the souls of the heathen, and not a whit concerned to push British trade or "sanctify the spirit of Imperialism."[2]

Such missionary work was encouraged, Hobson believed, because it furnished what appeared to be lofty motives for the politicians and businessmen engaged in imperialist exploitation: "The politician always, the business man not seldom, believes that high motives qualify the benefits he gets."[3] It was, in fact, this Christian element of imperialism that constituted one of its worst features:

> It is precisely in this falsification of the real import of motives that the gravest vice and the most signal peril of Imperialism reside. When, out of a medley of mixed motives, the least potent is selected for public prominence because it is the most presentable, when issues of a policy which was not present at all to the minds of those who formed this policy are treated as chief causes, the moral currency of the nation is debased. The whole policy of imperialism is riddled with this deception.[4]

Some theorists of the times had explained imperialism as simply the result of the militarism and jingoism that they felt were inherent in human nature. While Hobson admitted that the military "services are, of course, imperialist by conviction and by professional interest, and every increase of the [military forces] . . . enhances the political power they exert,"[5] he believed that this was universally a trait of all military people, and therefore could not account for the recent outburst of imperialist domination. Military officers did not constitute the leading political power in society. Moreover, patriotism and jingoism were not, he argued, inherent characteristics of human nature. Rather, they were socially learned: "Jingoism is merely the lust of the spectator, unpurged by any personal effort, risk, or sacrifice, gloating over the perils, pains, and slaughter of fellowmen whom he does not know, but whose destruction he desires in a blind and artificially stimulated passion of hatred and revenge."[6]

Such blind hatred was "artificially stimulated" because "the party, the press, the church, [and] the school mold public opinion and public policy by the false idealization of those primitive lusts of struggle, domination and acquisitiveness . . . whose stimulation is needed . . . for the work of imperial aggression, expansion, and . . . forceful exploitation."[7]

Other theorists attributed imperialism to the inherently blind and irrational nature of politics. Hobson disagreed:

> The disastrous folly of these wars, the material and moral damage inflicted even on the victor, appear so plain to the disinterested spectator that he is apt to despair of any State attaining years of discretion, and inclines to regard these natural cataclysms as implying some ultimate irrationalism in politics. But careful analysis of the existing relations between business and politics shows that the aggressive Imperialism which we seek to understand is not in the main the product of blind passions . . . or of the mixed folly and ambition of politicians. It is far more rational than at first sight appears. Irrational from the standpoint of the whole nation, it is rational enough from the standpoint of certain classes in the nation.[8]

The primary force promoting and directing imperialism, in Hobson's view, was the ceaseless drive to accumulate capital and then to invest the profits derived from this capital into new and equally profitable capital. The problem was that, as capital was accumulated, it became more and more difficult to find investment outlets:

> Aggressive Impérialism, which costs the taxpayers so dear . . . which is fraught with such grave incalculable peril to the citizen, is a source of great gain to the investor who cannot find at home the profitable use he seeks for his capital, and insists that his Government should help him to profitable and secure investment abroad.[9]

And investment, Hobson showed, was no longer dominated by individuals or even by manufacturing corporations (although they were certainly important). In advanced capitalist economies, giant banks and financial houses dominated foreign investment:

> These great businesses—banking, bill discounting, loan floating, company promoting—form the central ganglion of international capitalism. United by the strongest bonds of organization, always in closest and quickest touch with one another, situated in the very heart of the business capital of every State, controlled . . . chiefly by men . . . who have behind them centuries of financial experience, they are in a unique position to manipulate the policy of nations. No great quick direction of capital is possible save by their consent and through their agency. . . .
>
> Every great political act involving a new flow of capital, or a large fluctuation in the values of existing investments, must receive the sanction and the practical aid of this little group of financial kings. These men, holding their realized wealth and their business capital, as they must, chiefly in stocks and bonds, have a double stake, first as investors, but secondly and chiefly as financial dealers. . . .
>
> To create new public debts, to float new companies, and to cause constant considerable fluctuations of values are three conditions of their profitable business. Each condition carries them into politics, and throws them on the side of Imperialism. . . . A policy which rouses fears of aggression . . . and which fans the rivalry of commercial nations . . . evokes vast expenditures on armaments, and ever-accumulating public debts, while the doubts and risks accruing from this policy promote that constant oscillation of values of securities which is so profitable to the skilled financier. There is not a war, a revolution, an anarchist assassination, or any other public shock, which is not gainful to these men; they are harpies who suck their gains from every new forced expenditure and every sudden disturbance of public credit.[10]

Hobson, after examining the empirical data showing profits on foreign investments and profits derived from ordinary export and import trade, concluded "that the income derived as interest upon foreign investments enormously exceeded that derived as profits from ordinary . . . trade."[11] Given this enormous profitability, and given the enormous economic and political power of the great bankers and financiers, Hobson concluded that they—and not the Christian missionaries, or the irrational politicians, or the military, or the jingoistic segment of the population—were chiefly responsible for imperialism.

> In view of the part which the noneconomic factors of patriotism, adventure, military enterprise, political ambition, and philanthropy play in imperial expansion, it may appear that to impute to financiers so much power is to take a too narrowly economic view of history. And it is true that the motor-power of Imperialism is not

chiefly financial: finance is rather the governor of the imperial engine, directing the energy and determining its work; it does not constitute the fuel of the engine, nor does it directly generate the power. Finance manipulates the patriotic forces which politicians, soldiers, philanthropists, and traders generate; the enthusiasm for expansion which issues from these sources, though strong and genuine, is irregular and blind; the financial interest has those qualities of concentration and clear-sighted calculation which are needed to set Imperialism to work. An ambitious statesman, a frontier soldier, an overzealous missionary, a pushing trader may suggest or even initiate a step of imperial expansion, may assist in educating public opinion to the urgent need of some fresh advance, but the final determination rests with the financial power.[12]

While the great finance capitalists were the controllers and directors of imperialism, they were neither the sole beneficiaries of imperialism nor its ultimate cause. There were three main groups of capitalists who benefited from imperialism. First and most important were the financiers. Second were "certain big firms engaged in building warships, . . . manufacturing guns, rifles, and other necessary military supplies."[13] Third were "the great manufacturers for export trade, who gain . . . by supplying the real or artificial wants of the new countries we annex or open up."[14]

But pointing out who gained from imperialism was not sufficient. Hobson wanted to show why imperialism was required for these capitalists to make their profits—why they could not make their profits by investing at home and buying and selling either at home or with other capitalist countries. Why was it necessary to subjugate a noncapitalist culture, to destroy its traditional institutions, and to make it economically dependent on the market and politically dependent on its imperialist conqueror? What was the ultimate cause of imperialism? What was, in other words, the "economic taproot of imperialism?"

The answer, in Hobson's opinion, was to be found in the rapid and accelerating concentration of industrial power and wealth that had occurred in the last third of the nineteenth century. So much wealth had become concentrated in so few hands that the distribution of yearly income had become enormously unequal. The yearly income accruing to capitalists from their colossal wealth holdings was so large that even the most extravagant and luxurious of consumption expenditures would leave them with enormous amounts of excess income—or saving—for which they had no use but to invest in the accumulation of more capital.

> An era of cut-throat competition, followed by a rapid process of amalgamation, threw an enormous quantity of wealth into the hands of a small number of captains of industry. No luxury of living to which this class could attain kept pace with its rise of income, and a process of automatic saving set in upon an unprecedented scale. The investment of these savings in other industries helped to bring these under the same concentrative forces.[15]

This economic situation had an inevitable imbalance. The distribution of income was so unequal that even after workers had spent all of their income on consumption and capitalists had spent all that was practically possible on consumption (given the ultimate constraint that it takes time to buy and consume commodities), capitalists still had so much forced saving that if all of the saving was used to increase production facilities, then the growth of the productive capacity to produce consumer goods would inevitably exceed the growth in their demand (which was limited by the workers' incomes and the capitalists' maximum practical capacity for consumption). When productive capacity grew faster than consumer demand, there was very soon an excess of this capacity (relative to consumer demand), and, hence, there were few profitable domestic investment outlets. Foreign investment was the only answer. But insofar as the same problem existed in every industrialized capitalist country, such foreign investment was possible only if noncapitalist countries could be "civilized," "Christianized," and "uplifted"—that is, if their traditional institutions could be forcefully destroyed and the people coercively brought under the domain of the "invisible hand" of market capitalism. So imperialism was the only answer.

Some critics of Hobson have called him a "naive underconsumptionist," implying that he did not realize that production itself creates income of an exactly equivalent value—so that if all income is spent, then all production can be sold. Such critics have never bothered to read Hobson. He realized this simple fact as clearly as did any conservative defender of Say's law. Thus, he wrote:

> Whatever is, or can be produced, can be consumed, for a claim upon it, as rent, profit, or wages, forms part of the real income of some member of the community, and he can consume it, or else exchange it for some other consumable with someone else who will consume it. With everything that is produced a consuming power is born. If then there are goods which cannot get consumed, or which cannot even get produced because it is evident they cannot get consumed, and if there is a quantity of capital and labour which cannot get full employment because its products cannot get consumed, the only possible explanation of this paradox is the refusal of owners of consuming power to apply that power in effective demand for commodities.[16]

The wealthy capitalists did not, of course, refuse on principle to spend all of their income. They spent all that was practically possible on luxurious living. With their saving, they preferred to invest in capital that would yield them even more income in the future. The problem was the imbalance between the funds destined for consumption and those destined for investment. With consumption restricted by the grotesquely unequal distribution of income, there soon developed a shortage of profitable investment outlets. Capitalists could not go on expanding the capacity to produce consumption goods beyond demand and continue to make profits on the resultant unsold goods. Therefore, they had three choices: (1) continue to spend all of their income and stockpile unsold goods, (2) refuse to spend all of their income (i.e., hoard some of it) and thereby reduce effective demand, thus ensuring that some previously produced goods could not be sold and a general glut or economic stagnation would set in, or (3) find foreign investment outlets through an imperialist governmental policy.

As long as the present distribution of wealth continued, Hobson believed that "the rich will never be so ingenious as to spend enough to prevent overproduction."[17] The inevitable results of the inability of the rich to invest all of their surplus income profitably were business cycles, depressions, and an increasingly rapacious imperialism:

> Everywhere appear excessive powers of production, excessive capital in search of investment. It is admitted by all business men that the growth of the powers of production in their country exceeds the growth in consumption, that more goods can be produced than can be sold at a profit, and that more capital exists than can find remunerative investment.
> It is this economic condition of affairs that forms the taproot of Imperialism.[18]

Capitalism created the spectacle of widespread poverty and deprivation among the working class, which coexisted with the unused capacity to produce more goods. This inevitably led to the wealthy capitalist class living luxuriously by exploiting their own working class and also "to a larger extent every year . . . living on tribute from abroad."[19]

It seemed obvious to Hobson that imperialism did not benefit a capitalist nation as a whole. It benefited the wealthy at a very high price to ordinary workers, both in taxes and in blood. The existing system of ideological control and manipulation of the workers by the wealthy capitalists made British democracy a sham. The only hope in the fight to curb imperialism was for the workers to take more power into their own hands, to create a real democracy. In a real democracy (as opposed to the plutocracies that Hobson saw under capitalism), wealth and income would never be so concentrated. Therefore, the "taproot of Imperialism" would be removed. Hobson consistently argued that "Trade Unionism and Socialism are thus the natural enemies of imperialism, for they take away from the 'imperialist' classes the surplus incomes which form the economic stimulus of imperialism."[20] He was convinced that a "completely socialist State which kept good books and presented regular balance-sheets of expenditure and assets would soon discard Imperialism."[21]

Luxemburg's Theory of Capitalist Imperialism

One of the most insightful analyses of imperialism was that of Rosa Luxemburg (1870–1919). For many years one of the most important and influential of the political and intellectual leaders of the left wing of the German working-class socialist movement, she was attacked, severely beaten, and murdered by right-wing German soldiers in 1919. Her analysis of imperialism is contained in her best-known work, *The Accumulation of Capital* (first published in 1913), and a subsequent defense of that book entitled *The Accumulation of Capital—An Anti-Critique.*

In *The Accumulation of Capital*, Luxemburg's intention was to show, on the basis of Marx's two-sector model of capitalist expanded reproduction,[22] that in an economy consisting of only capitalists and workers, balanced economic growth was impossible. She attempted to show that as the two sectors grew (sector I producing the means of production and sector II producing consumer goods), imbalances between them were inevitably built into the very functioning of capitalism. In particular, she attempted to show that it would be impossible for the demand for the consumer goods produced in sector II to grow as fast as the growth in the capacity to produce them in that sector.

From this she hoped to show that it was absolutely necessary for capitalism to constantly and perpetually to capture new, noncapitalist markets in order to sell these surplus commodities so that capitalists could realize their profits. In the early stages of capitalism, she argued, there had survived many remnants of noncapitalist production within the boundaries of each capitalist country. Consequently, the necessary expansion of capitalism could be largely internal in this phase. That is, capitalism as an economic system could expand within the political boundaries of a single nation by constantly exploiting those areas of production based on handicraft or independent petty commodity production (where workers owned their own means of production) and thereby bringing them into the realm of capitalist production. But as capitalism grew, these potential sources of internal expansion had been exhausted. Therefore, foreign imperialist expansion had become essential to the survival of capitalism.

Luxemburg's demonstration of the logical necessity for this type of expansion was defective. Her results were achieved only because she based her theory on some unrealistic assumptions. In this book we will not present Luxemburg's theory attempting to show the logical necessity to expand capitalism, nor will we discuss the defects of her theory. The reader interested in understanding these should read Joan Robinson's admirably succinct introduction to Luxemburg's *The Accumulation of Capital*.[23] However, despite the flaws in Luxemburg's book, there remains a significant and persuasive theory of imperialism.

After studying *The Accumulation of Capital* carefully, Joan Robinson has concluded that, on the basis of many of the defensible theoretical and factual assertions made by Luxemburg, "we can substitute for a supposed logical necessity a plausible hypothesis about the nature of the real case, and so rescue the succeeding argument."[24] It was in her "succeeding argument" that Luxemburg made her lasting and profound contributions to our understanding of capitalist imperialism. We will therefore briefly mention what Robinson called Luxemburg's "plausible hypothesis" (and what we consider a convincing theory) about the nature and origins of capitalist imperialism and then discuss at somewhat greater length the contributions made in Luxemburg's "succeeding argument."

Luxemburg's argument showing the difficulties of maintaining sufficient consumer demand for the expanding productive capacity of the consumer goods sector of the economy was based on her view of wages and the behavior of capitalists. Workers, she believed, spent virtually all of their incomes, as a class even though not individually, on consumption (and the available data, from earliest times to the present, certainly show this to be a reasonable assumption). Capitalists could spend their profits on either consumption or investment.

For the capitalist, "workers are . . . simply the labour force, whose maintenance out of part of its own produce is an unfortunate necessity, reduced to the minimum society allows."[25] Therefore, as productivity increased, the gap between the purchasing power of the working class and the potential output of consumer goods continually widened. The capitalists, to be sure, had the potential to purchase this surplus of consumer goods. But the capitalist class, "even with its luxurious whims,"[26] would never do this, for two reasons. First, there was an upper limit, in both time and money, on what any individual could consume, and many of the capitalists received yearly incomes far higher than this limit. Second, and much more important to Luxemburg, the capitalists were not motivated primarily by the desire to consume but rather by the desire to accumulate more capital and make more profit. Furthermore, as Marx had shown, competition among capitalists made progressive accumulation absolutely necessary for any single capitalist if that capitalist was to avoid being destroyed by rivals. Therefore, there was a basic contradiction between how an individual capitalist would like (and need) a fellow capitalist to behave and how the competitive system forced that capitalist to behave. Any individual capitalist would view the enjoyment of fellow capitalists of "the luxury of 'high society' . . . [as] a desirable expansion of sales, i.e., a splendid opportunity for accumulation."[27] But, at the same time, the individual capitalist would know that his or her own excessive enjoyment of luxury "is sheer lunacy, economic suicide, for it is the destruction of accumulation at its roots."[28]

Therefore, capitalists would never expand their own consumption as fast as productive capacity was expanding, due to their ceaseless desire to accumulate capital. An imbalance between the two productive sectors would therefore be created, and capitalists would increasingly find it more difficult to find profitable investment outlets. Imperialism seemed to offer the only solution to this imbalance. Thus, when we abandon Luxemburg's indefensible claim to have demonstrated the logical necessity of imperialism, her resultant theory is very nearly the same as that of Hobson. Indeed, we agree with Joan Robinson's conclusion that "on the purely analytical plane her [Luxemburg's] affinity seems to be with Hobson."[29]

If that were all there were to the matter, we would have confined the discussion in this chapter to Hobson and Lenin. But Luxemburg went on to develop rich insights into the nature of imperialism that are not found in the writings of either Hobson or Lenin.

Luxemburg realized that within any given area in which capitalism predominated, there would eventually develop a glut of capital. The only way in which profitable investment outlets could be continually assured was through the forced destruction of traditional nonmarket economies (or "natural" economies, as she called them). By opening up these traditional economies to capitalist exploitation, rich new reserves of cheap raw materials and cheap labor power would become available for potential exploitation. But the development of these potential sources of exploitation would require extensive investment. These new investment outlets would reduce the glut of capital at home and stimulate a demand for the imperialist country's exports—that is, for the materials for building harbors, roads, railroads, and all of the necessary physical means for exploiting the conquered territory. As a result, the imperialist country's newly stimulated exports would not be offset by a corresponding volume of imports (because there was already a glut of consumer commodities in the imperialist country); rather, the exports would be offset by a growing ownership of the wealth of the conquered territory by the capitalists of the imperialist countries. In other words, imperialism was really an extension of what Marx had described as "primitive accumulation" (see chapter 9). This, we believe, was Luxemburg's most lasting and important contribution to an understanding of capitalist imperialism. We will therefore develop this aspect of her analysis more extensively, quoting important passages from *The Accumulation of Capital* to illustrate her insights.

Whereas Marx had seen the process of primitive accumulation as explaining only the historical origins of capitalism, Luxemburg saw primitive accumulation as an inherent characteristic of capital accumulation. Expanding the domain of capitalist social and economic relations had always, she believed, been a means by which accumulation of capital was made possible within existing capitalist areas. "Capitalism arises and develops historically," she wrote, "amidst a noncapitalist society."[30]

> The existence and development of capitalism requires an environment of non-capitalist forms of production, but not every one of these forms will serve its ends. Capitalism needs . . . a market for its surplus value, a source of supply for its means of production and . . . a reservoir of labour power for its wage system. For all these purposes, forms of production based upon a natural [that is, nonmarket] economy are of no use to capital. In all social organizations where natural economy prevails, where there are primitive peasant communities with common ownership of the land, a feudal system of bondage or anything of this nature, economic organization is essentially in response to the internal demand; and therefore there is no . . . urgent need to dispose of surplus products. What is most important, however, is that, in any natural economy, production only goes on because both means of production and labour power are bound in one form or another. The communist peasant community no less than the feudal corvee farm and similar institutions maintain their economic organization by subjecting the labour power, and the most important means of production, the land, to the rule of law and custom. A natural economy thus confronts the requirements of capitalism at every turn with rigid barriers. Capitalism must therefore always and everywhere fight a battle of annihilation against every histori-

cal form of natural economy that it encounters, whether this is slave economy, feudalism, primitive communism, or patriarchal peasant economy. The principal methods in this struggle are political force (revolution, war), oppressive taxation by the state, and cheap goods; they are partly applied simultaneously, and partly they succeed and complement one another.[31]

In the imperialist struggle to subjugate natural (nonmarket) economies, there were four objectives: first, to gain possession of the vast amounts of raw materials in these countries, either by taking ownership directly or by making cheap commodities of these raw materials; second, to destroy traditional methods of production, to separate every worker from having access to any means of production, and thereby to create economically dependent wage workers who must sell their labor power in order to live; third, to transform the natural economy into a commodity, or market, economy; and fourth, to separate industry, trade, and agriculture, all of which generally constitute an interconnected whole in a natural economy.

In other words, capitalists had to use coercive power in order to create the market commodity relations necessary for the extraction of surplus value. In its infancy capital forcibly had to create these conditions in Europe. This was the process of primitive accumulation, which most Marxists believed to have ended once capitalism had been firmly established. Luxemburg disagreed. She argued that while the task of primitive accumulation had been essential in the beginnings of capitalism,

> yet capital in power performs the same task even to-day, and on an even more important scale—by modern colonial policy. It is an illusion to hope that capitalism will ever be content with the means of production which it can acquire by way of commodity exchange. In this respect already, capital is faced with difficulties because vast tracts of the globe's surface are in the possession of social organizations that have no desire for commodity exchange or cannot, because of the entire social structure and the forms of ownership, offer for sale the productive forces in which capital is primarily interested. . . . Since the primitive associations of the natives are the strongest protection for their social organizations and for their material bases of existence, capital must begin by planning for the systematic destruction and annihilation of all the non-capitalist social units which obstruct its development. With that we have passed beyond the stage of primitive accumulation; this process is still going on. . . . Accumulation, with its spasmodic expansion, can no more wait for, and be content with, a natural disintegration of noncapitalist formations and their transition to commodity economy, than it can wait for, and be content with, the natural increase of the working population. Force is the only solution open to capital; the accumulation of capital, seen as an historical process, employs force as a permanent weapon, not only at its genesis, but further on down to the present day. From the point of view of the primitive societies involved, it is a matter of life or death; for them there can be no other attitude than opposition and fight to the finish—complete exhaustion and extinction.[32]

Luxemburg followed this analysis with a vivid, poignant, and scorching (but accurate) account of the actual imperialist destruction of traditional economies by conquest, force, fraud, theft, and trade. Some traditional cultures were taken over as colonies; others were reduced to market economies that were dependent on the imperialist, capitalist economies even though they nominally remained politically independent. After this forced transformation of a foreign economy, the internal economic imbalance within the imperialist, capitalist economy would be temporarily alleviated. The third-world people would become partially dependent on commodities produced within the consumer goods sector of the imperialist economy. In this situation, "capitalist production supplies consumer goods over and above its own requirements, the demand of its workers and capitalists, which are bought by noncapitalist strata and countries."[33] This meant that the export industries in the imperialist countries would require more of the capital goods produced in the capital-goods-producing sector. In addition, in order to exploit these new territories properly, many substantial investment expenditures, such as harbors, roads, and railroads, were required. In this situation, "capitalist production supplies means of production in excess of its own demand and finds buyers in noncapitalist countries."[34]

These exports were financed in two ways. First, the subjugated territories provided sources of cheap raw materials that were not readily obtainable at home. "The process of accumulation . . . requires inevitably free access to ever new areas of raw materials."[35] The second method of financing the imperialist country's exports was to increase the ownership of the resources and capital of the subjugated territories by the capitalists of the imperialist economies. Capital ownership in less developed areas was very profitable because the workers in these subjugated regions had been reduced to such a wretched condition that a very high rate of exploitation was possible:

> Untold masses of peasants were put to work; they were switched over from one job to the next as the need arose, and they were exploited to the limit of endurance and beyond. Although it became evident at every step that there were technical limits to the employment of forced labor for the purposes of modern capital, yet this was amply compensated by capital's unrestricted power of command over the pool of labour power, how long and under what conditions men were to work, live, and be exploited.[36]

But no single conquest or wave of conquests could permanently solve the economic imbalance of capitalism. Eventually the traditional, nonmarket economy would be totally assimilated into the capitalist system. Then the capitalist system—including the newly assimilated territories—would once again encounter the same problems that had originally led to the imperialist expansion. Therefore, capitalism ceaselessly had to attempt the expansion of its borders. Extended primitive accumulation, in the form of imperialist subjugation and the subsequent destruction of all noncapitalist social and economic structures, was a permanent feature of capitalism, in Luxemburg's opinion.

One last feature of Luxemburg's analysis of capitalist imperialism deserves mention—her discussion of militarism. She realized that militarism had always been an integral part of capitalism:

> Militarism fulfills a quite definite function in the history of capital, accompanying as it does every historical phase of accumulation. It plays a decisive part in the first stages of European capitalism, in the period of the so-called "primitive accumulation," as a means of conquering the New World and the spice-producing countries of India. Later, it is employed to subject the modern colonies, to destroy the social organizations of primitive societies so that their means of production may be appropriated, forcibly to introduce commodity trade in countries where the social structure had been unfavourable to it, and to turn the natives into a proletariat by compelling them to work for wages in the colonies. It is responsible for the creation and expansion of spheres of interest for European capital in non-European regions, for extorting railway concessions in backward countries, and for enforcing the claims of European capital as international lender. Finally, militarism is a weapon in the competitive struggle between capitalist countries for areas of non-capitalist civilization.[37]

In addition to recognizing this essential role of militarism in creating an expanding capitalism, she was also one of the first economists to see clearly that, in the twentieth century, militarism was rapidly becoming an important source for partially offsetting the chronic deficiency of demand that had plagued mature capitalism. The central thesis of the final chapter of *The Accumulation of Capital* was that "militarism has yet another important function. From the purely economic point of view, it is a preeminent means for the realisation of surplus value." It performed this function because it acted "as a buyer for the mass of products containing the capitalized surplus value."[38]

This was a most remarkable insight into the essential nature of capitalism in its mature phase. When Luxemburg wrote her book (1913), most of the capitalist countries had much smaller military establishments than they were to have in the decades following World War II. It was only after the writings of John Maynard Keynes (which we will discuss in chapter 15) had gained widespread influence in the 1940s and 1950s, and after the permanent "military-industrial complex" had become so colossal and so economically dominant in the post–World War II capitalist economies, that a large number of economists came to see clearly that Luxemburg was correct in her assessment of the importance of militarism.

However, in this, as in her analysis of imperialism, Luxemburg's acute and perspicacious insights outran her theoretical abilities. She argued that through indirect taxation, most of the costs of supporting the military were extorted from the working class.[39] But the working class, as she had recognized, spent virtually all of its income on consumption. Therefore, to the extent that militarism was financed through taxes extracted from the working class, it did not contribute to aggregate demand. Luxemburg's perceptive insights into the importance of militarism in sustaining aggregate demand could have been supported by firmer theoretical grounds if she had realized that a considerable proportion of profits go to the financing of militarism. In this respect, militarism functions much the same as the luxury expenditures of Malthus's landlord class—they represent a source of demand that channels some profits into an economically unproductive investment. This permits a maintenance of the existing inequalities of the distribution of wealth and income, bolsters aggregate demand, and, yet, does not add to the productive capacity of the economy, which constantly tends to grow faster than aggregate demand.

Luxemburg also had another unusually perspicacious and prescient insight into the manner in which militarism tended to mitigate the instability of capitalism. As many economic theorists from William Thompson onward had realized, even when there was no deficiency of aggregate demand in a capitalist economy, the anarchy of the market created economic instability and business cycles. This was because the profits of any particular capitalist depended on the buying and selling decisions of thousands of other capitalists and consumers, decisions that could not be known in advance by each capitalist. Consequently, capitalists inevitably guessed wrong at times, investing too much here or too little there. These mistakes frequently were compounded when other capitalists assumed that the mistaken capitalists would continue such faulty patterns of investment. Therefore, investment decisions were based on erroneous assumptions, and mistake compounded mistake. Not infrequently, the result was an economic crisis or an economic collapse (thus resulting in an irrational, wasteful use of society's resources).

Luxemburg realized this. And she also realized that this anarchy of the market was particularly costly in an era when giant corporations made investment decisions involving hundreds of millions (or later on, billions) of dollars. In this situation, militarism represented, to the giant corporations, a welcome and profitable relief from the anarchy of the market. In Luxemburg's words, when militarism prevails,

> the multitude of individual and insignificant demands for a whole range of commodities, which will become effective at different times, . . . is now replaced by a comprehensive and homogeneous demand of the state. And the satisfaction of this demand presupposes a big industry of the highest order. It requires the most favourable conditions for the production of surplus value and for accumulation. In the form of government contracts for army supplies the scattered purchasing power of the consumers is concentrated in large quantities and, free of the vagaries and subjective fluctuations of personal consumption, it achieves an almost automatic regularity and rhythmic growth. Capital itself ultimately controls this automatic and rhythmic movement of militarist production through the legislature and a press whose function is to mould so-called "public opinion." That is why this particular province of capitalist accumulation at first seems capable of infinite expansion. All other attempts to expand markets and set up operational bases for capital largely depend on historical, social and political factors beyond the control of capital, whereas production for militarism represents a province whose regular and progressive expansion seems primarily determined by capital itself. In this way capital turns historical necessity into a virtue.[40]

Needless to say, Luxemburg did not believe that capitalism could be reformed in any manner that both left capitalist property relations (and hence capitalist class relations) intact and simultaneously eliminated imperialism, militarism, oppression, and exploitation. These four evils were inherent in the very social and economic structure of capitalism as a system. But Luxemburg was convinced that capitalism would not continue indefinitely:

> At a certain stage of development there will be no other way out than the application of socialist principles. The aim of socialism is not accumulation but the satisfaction of toiling humanity's wants by developing the productive forces of the entire globe. And so we find that socialism is by its very nature a harmonious and universal system of economy.[41]

Lenin's Theory of Capitalist Imperialism

V.I. Lenin (1870–1924) was the most influential leader of the Bolshevik party, and his writings remain most influential within nearly all contemporary Communist parties. Among his most frequently read and quoted works is *Imperialism, the Highest Stage of Capitalism*, which was written in 1916. In the preface to this book, he acknowledged the influence that Hobson's book had exerted on him. In writing his book, Lenin told the reader, "I made use of the principal English work on imperialism, the book by J.A. Hobson, with all the care that, in my opinion, that work deserves."[42] In many essential respects, Lenin's account was strikingly similar to Hobson's, despite numerous assertions to the contrary by later disciples of Lenin. In our account, we shall summarize Lenin's theory of imperialism, showing its similarities to Hobson's theory and then discussing its differences from both Hobson and Luxemburg.

Lenin, like Hobson, began by emphasizing the massive industrial concentration that had occurred in all industrialized capitalist countries during the late nineteenth and early twentieth centuries. "The enormous growth of industry," he wrote, "and the remarkably rapid concentration of production in ever-larger enterprises are one of the most characteristic features of capitalism."[43] He then gave extensive statistics and descriptive data and accounts of the rise of monopolies, oligopolies, cartels, and trusts in the leading capitalist countries. Again like Hobson, Lenin stressed the importance of banks and finance capital in bringing about the phenomenon of capitalist imperialism:

> As banking develops and becomes concentrated in a small number of establishments, the banks grow from modest middlemen into powerful monopolies having at their command almost the whole of the money capital of all the capitalists and small businessmen and also the larger part of the means of production and sources of raw materials in any one country and in a number of countries. This transformation of numerous modest middlemen into a handful of monopolists is one of the fundamental processes in the growth of capitalism into capitalist imperialism.[44]

The importance of banks, or finance capital, in Lenin's opinion, grew out of the historical trend of capitalists' withdrawal from the day-to-day managing of industrial enterprises. Increasingly, such management had been turned over to a professional managerial class, and most capitalists had become a purely parasitic, functionless rentier class that lived in luxury. But the managerial class had to remain subservient to the capitalist class. Therefore, some capitalists had to manage and control the noncapitalist managers on behalf of the entire capitalist class. It was, in Lenin's view, the banking or financial sector that performed this function of overseeing the interests of all capitalists. This control of finance capital over industrial capital was, in his opinion, a distinguishing feature of the imperialist stage of capitalist development—a stage that Lenin believed was distinctly and importantly different from earlier stages of capitalist development:

> It is characteristic of capitalism in general that the ownership of capital is separated from the application of capital to production, that money capital is separated from industrial or productive capital, and that the rentier, who lives entirely on income obtained from money capital, is separated from the entrepreneur and from all who are directly concerned in the management of capital. Imperialism, or the domination of finance capital, is that highest stage of capitalism in which this separation reaches vast proportions. The supremacy of finance capital over all other forms of capital means the predominance of the rentier and of the financial oligarchy.[45]

The control exercised by the banks constituted a financial oligarchy because the banks created a complex, interwoven network of controls over industrial and commercial corporations through the ownership of stocks, and, more important, through the creation of interlocking boards of directors between the banks and the other corporations, as well as among the other various nonbanking corporations:

> A personal link-up, so to speak, is established between the banks and the biggest industrial and commercial enterprises, the merging of one with another through the acquisition of shares, through the appointment of bank directors to the Supervisory Boards (or Boards of Directors) of industrial and commercial enterprises, and vice versa.[46]

It was in this manner that "finance capital, concentrated in a few hands and exercising a virtual monopoly, exacts enormous and ever-increasing profits from the floating of companies, issue of stock, state loans, etc., strengthens the domination of the financial oligarchy and levies tribute upon the whole of society for the benefit of monopolists."[47]

Lenin's analysis of the economic foundation of capitalism was very nearly the same as Hobson's "taproot":

> On the threshold of the twentieth century we see the formation of a new type of monopoly: firstly, monopolist associations of capitalists in all capitalistically developed countries; secondly, the monopolist position of a few very rich countries, in which the accumulation of capital has reached gigantic proportions. An enormous "surplus of capital" has arisen in the advanced countries.
>
> It goes without saying that if capitalism could . . . raise the living standards of the masses, who in spite of amazing technical progress are everywhere still . . . poverty-stricken, there could be no question of a surplus capital. . . . But if capitalism did . . .

[this] it would not be capitalism. . . . As long as capitalism remains what it is, surplus capital will be utilized not for the purpose of raising the standard of living of the masses in a given country, for this would mean a decline in profits for the capitalists, but for the purpose of increasing profits by exporting capital abroad to the backward countries. In these backward countries profits are usually high, for capital is scarce, the price of land is relatively low, wages are low, raw materials are cheap.[48]

Therefore, Lenin and Hobson both concluded that the pressing economic necessity that led to imperialism was the need for profitable investment outlets for surplus capital. Both agreed that the export of capital was more important than the export of commodities, and both saw that the export of capital led to a related or induced increase in the volume of the exports of commodities.

Two quite separate and distinct "divisions of the world" resulted from this export of capital in the imperialist stage of capitalism. First, there was a "division of the world among capitalist associations," such as international business cartels or colossal multinational firms.

Monopolist capitalist associations, cartels, syndicates, and trusts first divided up the home market among themselves and obtained more or less complete possession of the industry of their own country. But under capitalism the home market is inevitably bound up with the foreign market. Capitalism long ago created a world market. As the export of capital increased, and as the foreign and colonial connections and "spheres of influence" of the big monopolist associations expanded in all ways, things "naturally" gravitated towards an international agreement among these associations, and towards the formation of international cartels.[49]

But the ultimate source of the power of any capitalist or capitalist enterprise, whether national or international, was the coercive power of the state. Thus, the rule of finance capital depended not only on control over industrial and commercial corporations but also on control of the government. "The 'personal link-up' between the banks and industry is supplemented by the 'personal link-up' between both of them and the government."[50] Because most international business cartels were dominated by a very few corporations with headquarters in one or two countries, it followed that the economic division of the world among business cartels would be reflected as well as promoted by the political "division of the world among the great powers."

The epoch of the latest stage of capitalism shows us that certain relations between capitalist associations grow up, *based* on the economic division of the world; while parallel to and in connection with it, certain relations grow up between political alliances, between states, on the basis of territorial division of the world, of the struggle for colonies, of the "struggle for spheres of influence."[51]

Thus, the second division of the world was among capitalist governments, and it both reflected and promoted the first division of the world among the great trusts and cartels. This led many apologists for imperialism (and a few mild critics of imperialism, such as the influential German Marxist Karl

Kautsky) to conclude that this political partitioning of the world would ultimately lead to a prolonged era of world peace. Lenin, writing during World War I, knew that this was not true. He clearly realized that the war was the consequence of imperialist conflicts among the great capitalist powers. Furthermore, such conflicts, he believed, were inevitably built into the very nature of imperialism.

The source of the conflicts was the fact that no capitalist, capitalist corporation, trust, or cartel was ever satisfied with the level of its profits. Capitalism always engendered an insatiable, ceaseless, frenetic obsession for ever increasing profits in every capitalist business enterprise. For this reason, any one of the great trusts would peacefully settle for a given share of the world market only when its directors were convinced that any attempt to take over a part of the territory of a rival trust would result in financial losses exceeding the financial gains involved. But in their rivalry, each trust was perpetually on guard for any indication of a shift in power that would make the seizure of rival territory profitable. Conflict was inevitable as long as there were at least two rival trusts dividing the world's market: "The division of the world between two powerful trusts does not preclude *redivision* if the relation of forces changes as a result of uneven development, war, bankruptcy, etc."[52]

Therefore, the claim that imperialism and the division of the world into "spheres of influence" would lead to a balance of power conducive to world peace was an ideological apology for imperialism and was based on sophistry:

> Certain bourgeois writers (now joined by Karl Kautsky, who has completely abandoned the Marxist position he had held, for example in 1909) have expressed the opinion that international cartels, being one of the most striking expressions of the internationalisation of capital, give the hope of peace among nations under capitalism. Theoretically, this opinion is absolutely absurd, while in practice it is sophistry and a dishonest defence of the worst opportunism. International cartels show to what point capitalist monopolies have developed, and *the object* of the struggle between the various capitalist associations. . . . The *forms* of the struggle may and do constantly change in accordance with the varying, relatively specific and temporary causes, but the *substance* of the struggle, its class *content*, positively *cannot* change while classes exist. Naturally, it is in the interests of . . . the . . . bourgeoisie . . . to obscure the substance of the present economic struggle (the division of the world) and to emphasize now this and now another *form* of the struggle. . . . The capitalists divide the world, not out of any particular malice, but because the degree of concentration which has been reached forces them to adopt this method in order to obtain profits. And they divide it "in proportion to capital," "in proportion to strength," because there cannot be any other method of division under commodity production and capitalism. But strength varies with the degree of economic and political development. In order to understand what is taking place, it is necessary to know what questions are settled by the changes in strength. The question as to whether these changes are "purely" economic or *non*economic (e.g., military) is a secondary one, which cannot in the least affect fundamental views on the latest epoch of capitalism. To substitute the question of the form of the struggle and agreements (today peaceful, tomorrow warlike, the next day warlike again) for the question of the *substance* of the struggle and agreements between capitalist associations is to sink to the role of a sophist.[53]

The substance of the struggle was the control of the earth and all of its resources as well as the labor power of all of its inhabitants. Capitalism, in Lenin's view, could not stop as long as the prospect for more profitable investment outlets still existed. Wherefore, recurring international conflicts and wars were inevitable in capitalism's highest, or imperialist, stage. Among the imperialist capitalist powers, "alliances, no matter what form they assume, . . . are *inevitably* nothing more than a 'truce' in periods between wars."[54]

Despite the then recent upsurge in the economic growth and the worldwide power of the capitalist countries, Lenin insisted that imperialism represented the last stage of capitalism—or, in Lenin's phrase, "moribund capitalism."[55] The leading capitalist powers were becoming what Lenin called "rentier states."[56] Furthermore, the "rentier state is a state of parasitic, decaying capitalism."[57] It is difficult to understand, however, precisely what Lenin meant by saying that capitalism was in a "decaying" and "moribund" state, because he wrote that it

> would be a mistake to believe that this tendency to decay precludes the rapid growth of capitalism. It does not. In the epoch of imperialism, certain branches of industry, certain strata of the bourgeoisie and certain countries betray, to a greater or lesser degree, now one and now another of these tendencies. On the whole, capitalism is growing far more rapidly than before; but this growth is not only becoming more and more uneven in general, its unevenness also manifests itself, in particular, in the decay of the countries which are richest in capital (Britain).[58]

Lenin seemed to be describing a worldwide capitalist system that was growing and that showed a changing balance of power among the different capitalist countries. Lenin insisted, however, that this was the last stage of capitalism and a prelude to the system's inevitable collapse.[59]

Comparison of the Theories of Hobson, Luxemburg, and Lenin

Rosa Luxemburg believed that her theory had shown the absolute, logical necessity of imperialist expansion for capitalism, but her theory contained both errors and unrealistic assumptions. When we disregard the indefensible aspects of Luxemburg's theory, her remaining explanation of the roots of imperialism was essentially the same as Hobson's. Moreover, Lenin's theory of the origins of imperialism added very little to the ideas of Hobson. There was, however, a crucial and important difference between the theory of Hobson, on the one hand, and of Luxemburg and Lenin, on the other. The difference was clearly seen and formulated by Lenin:

> The questions as to whether it is possible to reform the basis of imperialism, whether to go forward to the further intensification and deepening of the antagonisms which it engenders, or backward, towards allaying these antagonisms, are fundamental questions in the critique of imperialism.[60]

Both Lenin and Luxemburg believed that the forces of imperialism were inherent in the capitalist system and that no reform of capitalism that left its basis (the laws of private property, the market, and class division) intact could ever remove the evils of imperialism. Both believed that only a socialist revolution that did away with the foundations of capitalism could eliminate imperialism. While Hobson was a socialist and believed that under socialism there would be no motive for imperialist conquest, nevertheless, he believed that reforms of capitalism could mitigate the evils of imperialism and make capitalism a somewhat more humane society. In fact, Hobson actively supported social protest movements and reform movements designed to eliminate or reduce imperialism and to make capitalism a more just society.

The theories of both Luxemburg and Lenin contained errors. We have already stated the errors in Luxemburg's theory. Likewise, we have described Lenin's belief that capitalism was decaying and moribund, despite his admittance that it was growing faster than at any period in its history.

With Luxemburg and Lenin, as with so many other theorists whom we have examined in this book, such errors furnish us with an insight into the ideological preconceptions of their theories. Both Luxemburg and Lenin learned Marxism from their participation in the Second International (the worldwide, working-class, Marxist political organization of the late nineteenth and early twentieth centuries). The Marxism of the Second International tended to reduce the rich complexity and subtleties of Marx's ideas into a mechanistic, deterministic view of the inevitable and imminent demise of capitalism. Both Luxemburg and Lenin formulated their theories to show that this inevitable demise was indeed close at hand. And in this they were wrong.

Lenin's error was to prove costly to the members of the Third International (the international Communist movement formed shortly after the Bolshevik Revolution, of which Lenin was one of the most important leaders). In a precise and scholarly history of the Communist movement, Fernando Claudin has shown how Lenin's notion of moribund capitalism contributed to many important organizational and tactical errors on the part of the leaders of the Third International. These errors were, in Claudin's opinion, at least partly the consequence of the fact that "Lenin, like Rosa Luxemburg, . . . saw world capitalism in the monopoly imperialist stage as having reached a terminal situation."[61] Whenever this element of mechanistic, deterministic ideology has found its way into Marxism, the effect has been to weaken seriously the profound and insightful analyses of capitalism that were developed by Marx as well as by later thinkers within the Marxist tradition.[62]

Despite these weaknesses, however, we must conclude that both Luxemburg and Lenin added significantly to our knowledge of how and why capitalist imperialism functions. The principal strengths of their respective insights were quite dramatically different. Lenin improved Hobson's analysis of imperialism by convincingly demonstrating that the growth of giant corporations, trusts, and cartels as well as the extreme inequality in the distribution of income—factors that both Hobson and Lenin saw as being at the base of capitalist imperialism—appeared to be built into the very nature of mature capitalism. Lenin showed why in its mature stage capitalism was, in fact, a drastically modified social and economic system from what it had been in its earlier stages. While it cannot be said that Lenin demonstrated the absolute impossibility of reforming capitalism and thereby making it a more humane, less imperialistic economic system, he certainly demonstrated that such reform would have to affect the very foundations of the economic and social base of the entire capitalist system, which the existing capitalist governments and corporations—the capitalist class generally—would oppose and fight against by any means available.

The strength of Luxemburg's analysis was in many respects the opposite of the strength of Lenin's. Whereas he showed the unique features of the monopolistic stage of capitalism that accentuated and intensified the capitalist exploitation of economically less-developed areas of the world, she showed the continuity between the imperialism of the early twentieth century and the bloody and oppressive social upheavals in the earliest period of capitalist primitive accumulation. Whereas Lenin's analysis of imperialism offered no direct refutation to the dominant conservative neoclassical view that foreign investment in less-developed countries would benefit those countries by increasing their capital and thereby increasing their productivity and general economic well-being, Luxemburg convincingly showed that such investment was possible only after the traditional social institutions and patterns of human relationships had been devastated. Luxemburg, Lenin, and Hobson all showed that, in reality, capitalist investment in less-developed countries was coercively implemented, rarely conferred any immediate benefit on the majority of the people, was intended exclusively to take the raw materials of these countries and to give little in return, and exploited to an extreme degree the working people of these countries. Only Luxemburg, however, showed the extremes of social destruction that were inevitably involved in making these traditional societies into capitalist countries.

Notes to Chapter 13

1. J.A. Hobson, *Imperialism: A Study* (Ann Arbor: University of Michigan Press, 1965), p. 367.
2. Ibid., p. 203.
3. Ibid., p. 197.
4. Ibid., p. 198.
5. Ibid., p. 50.
6. Ibid., p. 215.
7. Ibid., p. 221.
8. Ibid., p. 47.
9. Ibid., p. 55.
10. Ibid., p. 53.
11. Ibid.
12. Ibid., p. 59.
13. Ibid., p. 49.
14. Ibid.

15. Ibid., pp. 74–75.

16. Ibid., pp. 81–82.

17. Ibid., p. 84.

18. Ibid., p. 81.

19. Ibid., p. 53.

20. Ibid., p. 90.

21. Ibid., p. 47.

22. See chapter 9.

23. Joan Robinson, "Introduction," in *The Accumulation of Capital*, by Rosa Luxemburg (New York: Monthly Review Press, 1964), pp. 13–28.

24. Ibid., pp. 25–26.

25. Rosa Luxemburg, *The Accumulation of Capital–An Anti-Critique* (New York: Monthly Review Press, 1972), p. 55.

26. Ibid., p. 55.

27. Ibid., p. 56.

28. Ibid.

29. Robinson, "Introduction," pp. 20–21.

30. Rosa Luxemburg, *The Accumulation of Capital* (New York: Monthly Review Press, 1964), p. 368.

31. Ibid., pp. 368–69.

32. Ibid., pp. 370–71.

33. Ibid., p. 352.

34. Ibid.

35. Ibid., p. 435.

36. Ibid.

37. Ibid., p. 454.

38. Ibid.

39. Ibid., p. 455.

40. Ibid., p. 466.

41. Ibid., p. 467.

42. V.I. Lenin, "Imperialism, the Highest Stage of Capitalism," in *V.I. Lenin: Selected Works*, by V.I. Lenin, 3 vols. (Moscow: Progress Publishers, 1967), vol. 1, p. 677.

43. Ibid., vol. 1, p. 685.

44. Ibid., vol. 1, p. 697.

45. Ibid., vol. 1, p. 721.

46. Ibid., vol. 1, p. 706.

47. Ibid., vol. 1, p. 716.

48. Ibid., vol. 1, pp. 723–24.

49. Ibid., vol. 1, p. 728.

50. Ibid., vol. 1, p. 706.

51. Ibid., vol. 1, p. 734.

52. Ibid., vol. 1, p. 730.

53. Ibid., vol. 1, pp. 733–34.

54. Ibid., vol. 1, p. 770.

55. Ibid., vol. 1, p. 776.

56. Ibid., vol. 1, p. 774.

57. Ibid., vol. 1, p. 756.

58. Ibid., vol. 1, p. 774.

59. Ibid., vol. 1, p. 776.

60. Ibid., vol. 1, p. 763.

61. Fernando Claudin, *The Communist Movement*, 2 vols. (New York: Monthly Review Press, 1975), vol. 1, p. 58.

62. For examples of how mechanistic determinism has weakened Marxist analysis, see Lucio Colletti, *From Rousseau to Lenin: Studies in Ideology and Society* (New York: Monthly Review Press, 1972), pp. 45–108; E.K. Hunt, "Socialism and the Nature of Soviet Society," *Socialist Revolution*, no. 32 (March–April 1977): 143–60; and J. O'Malley and K. Algozin, eds., *Rubel on Karl Marx: Five Essays* (Cambridge, UK: Cambridge University Press, 1981).

Chapter 14

Consummation, Consecration, and Destruction of the Invisible Hand: Neoclassical Welfare Economics

During the first half century after the publication of the books by Jevons, Menger, and Walras, capitalism underwent rapid change and experienced extraordinary turbulence. The first and most obvious change was the movement toward industrial concentration and giant corporations with worldwide trusts and cartels. The second change was the imperialist frenzy of the major capitalist countries. The third change was merely one of degree: whereas capitalism had always been an unstable economic system, constantly experiencing alternating periods of prosperity and depression, the length and severity of these depressions grew worse and culminated in the worldwide Great Depression of the 1930s. Combined with these changes, as well as with the chaos and social unrest that resulted from the increasing instability of capitalism, was the worldwide social turbulence that was manifested in the massive upheaval of World War I, the Soviet Revolution, and the emergence of fascism in Italy and Germany.

The theorists whose ideas we examined in the preceding two chapters all tried to understand these momentous changes. The increased economic instability, and particularly the Great Depression, also caused John Maynard Keynes (whose ideas we will examine in the next chapter) to reevaluate the neoclassical theories that he had been taught and to reorient his own thinking toward understanding the nature and causes of depressions in a capitalist system.

But if one examines the writings of the economists in the strict utilitarian, neoclassical tradition during this period, one seldom finds any recognition that capitalism was undergoing a period of turbulent change. Say, Senior, and Bastiat had sanitized the theories of Smith and Ricardo and rejected every element of the labor theory perspective in classical economics. Instead, they had focused entirely on the utilitarian perspective—emphasizing market exchange; calculating, rational, maximizing behavior; the essential similarity of all types of income (and hence the nonexistence of different classes in capitalism); and the universally beneficent harmony created by the "invisible hand" of free market exchange. Bastiat had declared that "political economy is exchange." With the discovery of the marginalist method of analysis by Jevons, Menger, and Walras, Bastiat's slogan became descriptive of nearly all orthodox neoclassical theory. Increasingly, neoclassical theory resembled medieval scholasticism, with innumerable scholars working endlessly to refine, develop, elaborate, and embellish the utilitarian vision of a society consisting of numerous, small, relatively powerless, rational utility maximizers, ceaselessly repeating the same harmonious social process.

Perhaps the three most obscurantist aspects of the theory were its conceptions of the entrepreneur, the nature of production, and the process by which competitive equilibrium prices were determined. We have already discussed the entrepreneur in chapter 11: the entrepreneur was the person who perpetually hired factors of production, transformed them into finished commodities, and sold these commodities; the entrepreneur was motivated entirely by the desire to maximize profits, although in the neoclassical scheme there were never any profits when the economy was at competitive equilibrium. The entrepreneur never learned this sad fact, however, and endlessly bought factors and sold commodities in search of these nonexistent profits. At the end of each production period (if equilibrium prevailed), the entrepreneur found that paying each factor owner the value of what that factor created in the production process exactly exhausted the total value of what had been produced. The entrepreneur's only remuneration was the normal return received for his or her own factors that were used in the production process. He or she got no profit and therefore would have been just as well off if he or she had passively hired out their factor to another entrepreneur and not bothered to be concerned with profits at all.

As obscurantist as the neoclassical conception of the entrepreneur was, the conception of the production process was equally so. When neoclassical economists wrote about production, they never mentioned bosses and workers, strikes, lockouts, struggles over safety conditions or the length of the working period, speedups of workers, factory discipline, assembly lines, work stoppages, Taylorism, or any of the many other negative features of the production process under capitalism. Production, in neoclassical theory, was a kind of alchemy. The entrepreneur had a complex mathematical recipe, called a "production function," which explained how various combinations of quantities of the factors of production could be transformed into different quantities of outputs of finished commodities. The entrepreneur looked at the prices of the factors (which were provided by the market or by Walras's "crier") and the prices of the finished commodities (provided from the same source), and selected the factors to hire and the commodities to sell accordingly. He or she always made this selection, within the above-described constraints, so as to maximize profits. Once such a choice was made, the problem of production was over. The alchemy of the production function simply transformed the inputs into outputs so that the cycle of exchanges could be completed. When competitive equilibrium prevailed, the profit-maximizing combination of inputs and outputs happened to yield no profit. Any other combination would result in a loss.

Such was the nature of the entrepreneur and the nature of the production process in neoclassical theory. They were useful fictions permitting the process of universally beneficial and harmonious market exchanges to perpetually repeat itself. For this reason we have said that, despite theorizing about production and production functions, neoclassical economic theory was the contemporary version of Bastiat's utilitarian vision. It was a theory of exchange, and, as such, it was an elaborate and esoteric version of Adam Smith's invisible-hand argument, in which there was very little concern with real production processes.

The third principal obfuscation of neoclassical theory was its conception of the process by which competitive equilibrium prices were determined. In this theory, each consumer, each owner of a factor of production, and each entrepreneur were passive "price takers." All prices were determined by the competitive market completely independently of the actions taken by any individual or business firm. Despite the considerable amount of attention that this problem received after the publication of Walras's *Elements*, the neoclassical theorists did not substantially improve on Walras's attempts to solve it. They could assert that these equilibrium prices were arrived at through a process of "groping," but they were never able to give any convincing empirical or theoretical argument to show that such groping would not take the economy farther away from equilibrium rather than closer to it. They could rely on Walras's useful fiction of the crier, but such an obvious resort to a useful fiction as a *deus ex machina* designed simply to hold the theory together reduced the effectiveness of the theory's ideological defense of free market capitalism.

In the more esoteric literature of professional journals, the neoclassicists demonstrated that the existence of such a set of equilibrium prices was not logically impossible, given their initial assumptions. This demonstration was taken as a reasonable justification for the textbook practice of simply assuming that this set of equilibrium prices existed and was known to all individuals and business firms.

This was a particularly critical assumption because the three pillars of the neoclassical ideological defense of free market capitalism were the marginal productivity theory of distribution (which will be discussed further in chapter 16), the invisible-hand argument, and the belief, *held purely on faith*, that the free market forces of supply and demand automatically and efficaciously take the economy to a full-employment equilibrium (although, as we will see, one branch of neoclassical economic theory, in response to the ideas of Keynes, at least partially abandoned this third point). None of these three ideological props for capitalism could be defended if the market did not automatically create equilibrium prices. Therefore, the third useful fiction of the crier was as important as the first two.

Before we proceed with a summary of neoclassical welfare economics—which is the final and most elaborate apotheosis of Adam Smith's invisible-hand argument—three comments must be made about the difference in style between this chapter and the preceding chapters, as well as the place of neoclassical welfare economics within the context of the entire neoclassical school. First, in this chapter we will rarely refer to the writings of any significant economic theorist. This is because neoclassical welfare economics is essentially an elaboration, with relatively minor modifications, of the analysis of Walras, and no particular theorist added so significantly to Walras's version of the theory as to merit individual treatment. If we were to make an exception to this statement, it would be for the refinements added by Walras's disciple, Vilfredo Pareto (1848–1923). Some economists have considered Pareto's contribution so significant that they refer to neoclassical welfare economics as "Paretian" welfare economics. Pareto's main achievement, however, was to recast Walras's ideas in terms of "indifference curves," which had first been developed by the Englishman Francis Y. Edgeworth (1845–1926).

In our explication of neoclassical welfare economics, we will follow Pareto (and most modern textbook presentations) and use indifference curves—and their analogue in neoclassical production theory, "isoquants"—to illustrate the concepts. We agree, however, with the statement made by the eminent historian of economic ideas Joseph A. Schumpeter, who wrote that "as pure theory, Pareto's is Walrasian—in groundwork as well as in most details."[1] Thus, Pareto, as well as all other subsequent theorists who refined Walras's version of the invisible-hand argument, were merely refiners and elaborators and will not be given separate treatment because of limited space. We will therefore simply present a general summary of neoclassical welfare economics without detailing the particular refinements made by different neoclassical economists.

Second, while most of the refinements of the theory had been made by the 1940s (with the exception of the treatment of "externalities," which was further refined in the 1950s and 1960s), we will generally use the present tense because this analysis still constitutes the heart of neoclassical analysis to this day.

Third, over the past century Walrasian welfare economics has become the dominant strain of neoclassical economics (particularly in the United States). Nevertheless, there are two somewhat different versions of neoclassical welfare economics. The one presented here is the dominant version. But there has also been an important minority strain that has persisted to this day and is heavily influenced (particularly on methodological issues) by Menger as well as by Walras. This strain has a somewhat different perspective, and it was known in the first few decades of the twentieth century as the "Austrian School," and then, during the 1950s and thereafter, as the "Chicago School." We will consider their ideas in chapter 17.

Utility Maximization and Profit Maximization

Neoclassical microeconomic theory serves as the foundation of neoclassical welfare economics and is generally divided into two separate (but analogous and symmetrical) parts—the "theory" of consumer utility maximization and the "theory" of profit maximization by the firm. Both "theories" are simple demonstrations of the logic of constrained maximization.

In textbook accounts, the theories yield several conclusions. The theory of consumer utility maximization, for example, shows deductively that a change in the price of a commodity usually (but not always) leads to a change in the opposite direction in the quantity demanded of that commodity. The theory shows how the change in the quantity demanded can be conceptually separated into one part caused by the "substitution effect" and another part caused by the "income effect." Students of economics are usually required to learn a somewhat esoteric mathematical proof of the conceptual identifiability of these two effects, but rarely, if ever, are they told why such a separation has any practical or theoretical importance. It is merely an analytical exercise by which one demonstrates one's competency as a neoclassical theorist. The same is true for most of the other analytical deductions made from the premises of the theories of utility and profit maximization.

There are, however, some conclusions of these microeconomic theories that are important. These are the conclusions that form the foundations of neoclassical welfare economics, and their importance is purely ideological. It is only these aspects of neoclassical theory that we will consider in this chapter.

The use of indifference curves permits the marginal utility analyses of consumer utility maximization to drop the assumption that utility can be cardinally quantified. All that is required is that the consumer be able to list a preference ranking for different commodities. This represents only an ordinal quantification (or ranking) of utility and requires no interpersonal comparisons of utility, which we have already argued are conceptually impossible. The only requirements necessary to get the neoclassical results are that indifference curves have the general configuration illustrated in Figure 14.1 and the consumers act "consistently." Consistency is defined in this manner: If an individual prefers X to Y and prefers Y to Z, then that individual must always prefer X to Z.

Indifference curves permit the neoclassical economist to illustrate graphically how the consumer maximizes his or her utility when there are only two commodities to purchase and consume. The same conclusions can be derived mathematically for many commodities, but the two-commodity case is much simpler and suffices to illustrate the point. In Figure 14.1 the axes of the graph measure quantities of goods A and B. The individual is presumed to be

Figure 14.1 **Consumer Utility Maximization**

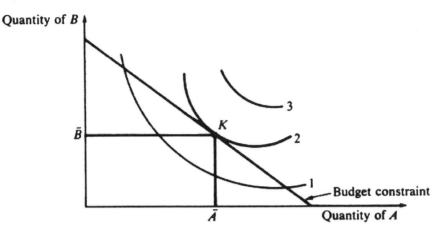

able to rank all possible combinations of A and B that he or she might consume. If the individual gets more of both A and B, his or her utility always increases. If the individual gets more of A and less of B (or vice versa), then it is assumed that he or she can always tell when the added utility from the extra A exactly offsets the utility lost from the decrease in B. The three curves in Figure 14.1 are indifference curves. On each curve are points representing "bundles" of A and B that give the same amount of utility. As we move from one point on a curve to another point on the same curve, the utility gained by getting more of one commodity is exactly offset by the utility lost in getting less of the other commodity. Therefore, the consumer is indifferent between all the bundles of A and B represented by the various points on a single indifference curve.

Any number of indifference curves could be constructed on the graph for one individual. In Figure 14.1 we have three indifference curves. Curve 1 represents the lowest level of utility; curve 2 represents a higher level of utility (insofar as more of both A and B can be gotten by moving from curve 1 to curve 2); and curve 3 represents an even higher level of utility.

The straight line in the figure is the consumer's "budget constraint" line, which shows what combinations of A and B the individual can buy with the income that he receives from the sale of his productive factors. The distance between the budget constraint line and the origin of the graph indicates the size or purchasing power of the individual's income. The slope of the budget constraint line gives the ratio of the prices of A and B (in Figure 14.1, the slope of the budget constraint line is P_a / P_b, or the price of A divided by the price of B).

It is clear that in the situation depicted in Figure 14.1, the consumer maximizes his or her utility by buying and consuming quantities A and B on indifference curve 2. Any higher indifference curve cannot be attained, given the consumer's budget constraint. Any other attainable point within his or her

budget constraint lies on an indifference curve below curve 2. Therefore, point
K maximizes the individual's utility, and the individual in neoclassical economic theory will always choose point K.

The slope of an indifference curve at any particular point measures the
ratio of the marginal utility of A to the marginal utility of B [MU_a / MU_b] at
that point. The slope of the budget constraint line measures the ratio P_a / P_b.
At point K, indifference curve 2 is just exactly tangent to the budget constraint line. Therefore, at point K for this individual, it must be true that ($MU_a
/ MU_b$) = ($P_a / P_b$), or what amounts to the same thing, (MU_a / P_a) = ($MU_b /
P_b$). We thus see that point K satisfies the utility-maximizing condition for-
mulated by Jevons and Walras.

Furthermore, because each individual, under a system of perfect competition, faces the identical prices for A and B, it follows that each individual will
move to a point on one of his or her indifference curves at which the same
maximizing condition is met. Therefore, the equilibrium market prices of A
and B, as determined by the competitive market (or by the crier), *perfectly
reflect the marginal psychic evaluation of A and B for every single consumer*.
That is, if the equilibrium price of A, for example, is twice the equilibrium
price of B, then every single individual psychically considers A to yield twice
as much marginal utility as B after he or she has achieved an optimum level of
consumption. Therefore, prices perfectly reflect marginal utility for every
consumer—and the attainment of this result in a free market is exactly what
neoclassical economists mean by the phrase "consumer sovereignty."

The demonstration of a firm's profit maximization is nearly identical to
that of an individual's utility maximization. In Figure 14.2, the axes of the
graph measure quantities of labor (L) and capital (C) used in a firm's production process. Curves 1, 2, and 3 are now isoquants, which show the various
combinations of labor and capital necessary to produce a given level of output
(the output could be either commodity A or commodity B). Each curve represents one level of output and is derived from the firm's production function;
the closer a curve is to the origin of the graph, the smaller the output represented. The straight line is an "isocost" line, showing various combinations of
labor and capital that a firm can purchase with a given outlay of money.

The firm in Figure 14.2 produces on isoquant 2 at point J. It hires quantities C and L of capital and labor. This solution can be interpreted in either of
two ways: first, if the firm decides to produce at the output level represented
by isoquant 2, then the isocost line shows the lowest cost at which it is possible to produce this amount. Second, if the firm decides to spend only that
amount represented by the isocost line, then isoquant 2 represents the maximum possible production for this level of expenditure, and C and L represent
the amounts of capital and labor, respectively, that can be purchased for this
given outlay and that will maximize the quantity of output that the firm can
produce with this outlay.

All firms in a perfectly competitive equilibrium situation will be faced

Figure 14.2 **Profit Maximization**

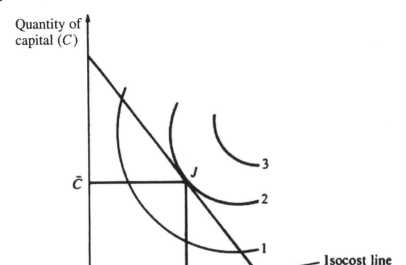

with the same prices for capital and labor (which, again, are determined by the market or by the crier). Hence, all firms will produce at a point such as J on their isoquant curves. The slope of the isocost line is P_L / P_C (or the ratio of wages to interest). The slope of the isoquant is MP_L / MP_C (or the ratio of the marginal product of labor to the marginal product of capital). Therefore, in equilibrium, for each and every firm it is true that $(MP_L / MP_C) = (P_L / P_C)$. It is relatively simple to demonstrate further that if perfect competition prevails, it will also hold true that both $VMP_L = P_L$ and $VMP_C = P_C$. That is, the value of the marginal product of each factor is exactly equal to the price of each factor. The marginal productivity theory of distribution holds true. Each factor gets the value equivalent to exactly what it produces at the margin. Production is maximized, and each factor owner receives as income just exactly the value of the marginal contribution of his or her factors.

The Beatific Vision and Eternal Felicity

On the basis of the conditions of utility maximization and profit maximization, neoclassical economists have built an elaborate, symmetrical, esthetically pleasing deductive and mathematical edifice; it "proves" that, given competitive conditions, utility-maximizing exchanging consumers and profit-maximizing exchanging entrepreneurs will automatically act and interact so as to maximize the social welfare. We will not go through either the mathematical or geometrical "proofs" of this conclusion but simply indicate verbally the nature of the steps involved and the intended importance of the analysis. The interested reader may wish to read an analytically elegant journal article in which Francis M. Bator gives a full demonstration of how a competitive, free market, capitalist society will reach a "bliss" point at which total social welfare is maximized.[2]

The demonstration begins by taking the total quantity of capital and labor available at a given time. Using isoquants derived from the production functions for each of the consumer commodities produced, the profit-maximizing condition described above can be proved to be a necessary and sufficient condition for society to reach what is called a "production-possibility frontier." A production-possibility frontier is a complex mathematical formula that shows all of the possible combinations of commodities that can be produced when all of society's labor and capital are *efficiently* utilized. Efficiency is attained when, for any combination of commodities produced, increasing the production of any one commodity necessarily entails a reduction in the production of other commodities.

Any point on the production-possibility frontier represents a total output comprised of a particular assortment of quantities of each of the commodities produced. At a given point, one can calculate the "marginal rate of transformation in production" for any two commodities. For example, the marginal rate of transformation of commodities A and B may be 2 : 1, which means that by giving up two units of A, one additional unit of B could be produced.

It can be proved that, under competitive conditions, the above mentioned point on the production-possibility frontier (where the marginal rate of transformation is 2 : 1) will be attained when the equilibrium market price of B is twice as high as the corresponding price of A. Therefore, under competition, the marginal rate of transformation in production for commodities A and B will always reflect their prices. Once this particular level and composition of output is produced, consumers will exchange and acquire that bundle of commodities that maximizes their utility. If the 2 : 1 price ratio is an equilibrium price ratio, then all consumers can exchange for any quantity of either commodity that they desire (given their budget constraint) and all markets will clear; that is, supply will be exactly equal to demand in every market.

We have seen that when consumers exchange so as to maximize their utility, the 2 : 1 price ratio for B and A will exactly reflect the ratios of the marginal utility of B to the marginal utility of A for every consumer. Therefore, under competition, the marginal rate of transformation of A and B, as well as the ratio of the marginal utilities of A and B for each consumer, reflects the price ratio of A and B. If this were not so, and if the rate of transformation and the ratio of marginal utilities were not equal, then at least one consumer's utility could be increased without decreasing anyone else's utility, either through more exchange or through a change in the composition of output. But because it can be proved that, under perfect competition, all of these ratios will be equal if the economy is in equilibrium, then this is proof that the equilibrium level and composition of production and the resultant exchange of that production have led to a point on society's *utility-possibility frontier.*

Each point on the utility-possibility frontier represents a situation in which no change in production and no additional amount of commodity exchange could possibly make a single individual any better off without worsening the position of some other individual. Given the initial "endowment" of ownership of productive factors (or the initial distribution of wealth), utility has been increased through production and exchange to the maximum possible level consistent with that original distribution of wealth.

This point on the utility-possibility frontier is what neoclassical economists call a "Pareto optimum." It represents the maximum welfare that society can derive from a particular distribution of wealth. Competitive utility and profit-maximizing behavior have been "demonstrated" to lead automatically to such a point. There is, however, a different Pareto optimum point for each possible initial distribution of wealth. So some individuals may judge other points on the utility-possibility frontier, representing other initial distributions of wealth, to be preferable to the one in question.

But such a judgment, as we saw in our discussion of Thompson's ideas, involves an interpersonal comparison of different individuals' utilities, something that is inherently impossible. It is, in the view of most neoclassical economists, merely a matter of personal bias or prejudice whether a person would like a more equal distribution of wealth or a less equal one. It is not a matter for "scientific economics." Not surprisingly, neoclassical economists have never been able to come up with an "objective" or "scientific" criterion for judging the appropriate distribution of wealth that is, at the same time, logically consistent with the individualistic assumptions of their utilitarian philosophy. To repeat what we have asserted numerous times in our discussions of utilitarian economics: Hedonism or utilitarianism gives one no basis whatsoever for making invidious comparisons among the desires and pleasures of different individuals.

However, if one likes the existing distribution of wealth, then the Pareto optimum point to which individual maximizing behavior automatically takes society is referred to, in neoclassical writings, as the "bliss point" or the "point of constrained bliss."[3] Insofar as most neoclassical economists tend to find very little that is fundamentally wrong with existing capitalist society, it can be fairly said that neoclassical welfare economics represents the contemporary version of Saint Augustine's "beatific vision" of "eternal felicity."[4]

Microeconomic Theory, Neoclassical Economics, and Welfare Economics

The previous section was necessarily terse and somewhat difficult to understand for anyone not already familiar with neoclassical welfare economics. The reason for this is that *contemporary orthodox microeconomic theory, as it is taught in most colleges and universities, is neoclassical economics. Moreover, the very heart of orthodox microeconomic theory, and the principal end toward which it is almost inevitably oriented, is neoclassical welfare economics.* This is a fact of such importance in understanding contemporary economic theory that it cannot be stressed too strongly. To give the careful reader a full and sophisticated understanding of neoclassical welfare economics would require one to write a complete text in intermediate-level contemporary orthodox microeconomic theory. Many such texts already exist that are coherently organized and reasonably well written, which those interested in pursuing this matter further can read.

In the meantime, in order to make our point, we will discuss one of these texts, chosen both because it is highly typical of the orthodox academic treatment of microeconomic theory (and hence represents an accurate summary of the current state of neoclassical utilitarian economics), and because it is very well organized and well written. The text is the revised edition of *Microeconomic Theory* by C.E. Ferguson, which consists of sixteen chapters. The last chapter is entitled "Theory of Welfare Economics,"[5] and it is obvious that most of the first fifteen chapters are designed to lay the analytical foundations for the last chapter on neoclassical welfare economics, which is the climax and denouement of the entire book. Early in the final chapter Ferguson has written:

> We now wish to show . . . that a perfectly competitive, free enterprise system guarantees the attainment of maximum social welfare. The proof rests upon the maximizing behavior of producers and consumers. To recall the dictum of Adam Smith, each individual, in pursuing his own self interest, is led as if by an "invisible hand" to a course of action that promotes the general welfare of all.[6]

There follow nine pages of summary explanation outlining what we have verbally summarized in the preceding section. The most important aspect of these nine pages is this: Ferguson is able to tie together his demonstration of neoclassical welfare economics and the attainment of bliss in a coherent and brief manner, because with each point he makes, he is able to refer his readers to earlier chapters or sections of his book. His standard explanation of orthodox microeconomic theory has developed the ideas and analytical tools *that inevitably lead to the conclusions of neoclassical welfare economics.* Indeed, in examining the previous fifteen chapters, we can see very little else to which they do lead. The nine-page demonstration of welfare economics ties the entire book together and then concludes: "This unique equilibrium . . . is called the point of 'constrained bliss' because it represents the unique organization of production, exchange and distribution that leads to the maximum *attainable* social welfare."[7]

Furthermore, the neoclassical school is the dominant (and probably the numerically largest) school in contemporary economics. For neoclassical economists, microeconomic theory (i.e., welfare economics) underlies every theoretical subfield of specialization and every theoretical, practical, and policy-oriented conclusion at which they arrive. All of their cost-benefit analyses, their demonstrations of the universal gains from foreign trade, their notions of market efficiency that are encountered in every branch of applied economics, as well as their notion of rational prices, *have absolutely no meaning whatsoever* other than that manifested in their faith that a free-enterprise, competitive market system will tend toward a Pareto optimal situation. Without a Pareto optimal situation in effect, these phrases and notions cannot be defended. In fact, in the absence of an optimal situation, these phrases *have no meaning whatsoever.* They are given meaning only when the neoclassical economists first posit the existence of a Pareto optimum; then, *by definition,* all exchangers are said to gain, resources are said to be "efficiently allocated," prices are said to be "rational" and therefore conducive to making accurate assessments—on utilitarian grounds—of the social costs and social benefits of various government projects. Utilitarian neoclassical welfare economics pervades and dominates nearly all neoclassical analyses on all theoretical and practical matters.

Neoclassical economic theory is the direct descendant of the portion of Smith's and Ricardo's ideas that was dominated by the utility or exchange perspective as developed and elaborated in the writings of Malthus, Say, Senior, Bastiat, Jevons, Menger, Walras, Marshall, and Clark. But neoclassical economics increasingly has taken the form of esoteric mathematical analyses, to the point where an economics student can spend years simply learning the analytical tools and techniques and easily become blinded to the philosophical and social values underlying the analysis. That is one of the reasons it is highly useful and important to examine the above writers' ideas, because the "smokescreen" of esoteric mathematics does not obscure these values. These philosophical, social, and moral values, which are obscured in, but nevertheless absolutely integral to, the writings of contemporary neoclassical economists, remain essentially identical to those unambiguously reflected in the writings of Malthus, Say, Senior, and Bastiat. The writings of Jevons, Menger, Walras, Marshall, and Clark initiated the progressive obscuration of these values, culminating in their being veiled behind an esthetically dazzling monument constructed with elaborate, esoteric mathematical elegance.

For this reason, it is important to construct a critique of contemporary neoclassical welfare economics that extends and refines many of our conclusions here, both explicit and implicit. The remainder of this chapter is devoted to such a critique.

Hedonistic Foundations of Welfare Economics

Neoclassical welfare economics rests squarely on hedonistic preconceptions. It contains both a psychological hedonism and an ethical hedonism. The psychological hedonism was, in the late nineteenth century, a rather crude theory of human behavior. Utility was conceived as a cardinally quantifiable relationship between a person and external consumable objects. This relationship was treated as though it were metaphysically given and fixed, and not a proper subject for further investigation. All human behavior was then reduced to attempts to maximize utility through the use or exchange of the commodities and productive resources with which the individual had been endowed (the source and propriety of the endowment, like the utility relationship, was beyond the purview of analysis).

Psychological hedonism, however, had been thoroughly discredited by the late nineteenth century. The development and refinement of the behavioral assumptions of welfare economics over the past half century represent attempts to obviate the objections against psychological hedonism while continuing to draw conclusions identical to those derivable from the discredited theory. Indifference curves permit the substitution of ordinal quantification of utility for cardinal quantification. Further, the word *utility* is frequently dropped in favor of the word *preference*. Preferences, argues the neoclassical economist, can be empirically observed, provided we assume that individual choices are consistent. The consistency, however, is merely the assumption that choices reflect a preexisting, metaphysically given "preference ordering" (empirical observation, of course, has continuously shown what common sense should have told these economists—that choices do not have this type of consistency). Cardinally quantifiable utility or ordinally quantifiable preferences have identical psychological and ethical import, and welfare economics remains a hedonistic theory of maximizing economic humankind behaving in a manner totally predetermined, or programmed, by two metaphysically given, and, by implication, immutable entities: the preference ordering and the initial endowment of assets.

The ethical hedonism of welfare economics has been called the "pig principle" by Professor S.S. Alexander. The "pig principle" is simply "that if you like something, more is better."[8] Thus, the ultimate normative principle of welfare economics can be stated several ways: More pleasure is ethically better than less (Benthamite version); more utility is ethically better than less utility (late nineteenth-century neoclassical version); and a more-preferred position on one's preference ordering is ethically better than a less-preferred position (contemporary neoclassical version). In each case, the isolated, atomistic individual is the sole judge qualified to assess the pleasure, utility, or preferability of an object because these welfare magnitudes are presumed to depend only on the relationship between the individual and the object of consumption. Individual desires, weighted by market purchasing power, are the ultimate criteria of social values. Whenever an individual's utility is not purely a personal, individual matter, that is, whenever the utility of one person is affected by the consumption of other persons (or the production of business firms), such interpersonal effects are labeled as "externalities." Externalities caused by interdependencies of preference orderings (i.e., consumption considered as a social activity) can be handled only by treating them as isolated exceptions (which will be elaborated below). Welfare economics ignores the fact that individual desires are themselves the products of a particular social process and the individual's place within that process. If neoclassical economists did not ignore this, they would have to acknowledge the fact that normative evaluations can be made of totally different social and economic systems and their resultant patterns of individual desires. Welfare economics is the direct descendant of the doctrines that Marx labeled as "vulgar economy," a point of view that "confines itself to systematizing in a pedantic way, and proclaiming for everlasting truths, the trite ideas held by the self-complacent bourgeoisie with regard to their own world, to them the best of all possible worlds."[9]

Essential Nature of the Norm of Pareto Optimality

Upon this foundation of psychological and ethical hedonism is constructed the norm of Pareto optimality—the core concept of welfare economics. We have already seen how neoclassical microeconomic theory inevitably culminates in the norm of Pareto optimality. This theory leads to the conclusion that a free market, competitive capitalist system inevitably allocates resources, distributes income, and apportions consumer goods among consumers so that no reallocation of resources through changes in consumption, exchange, or production could *unambiguously* augment the value of the commodities being produced and exchanged. This is Pareto optimality the fundamental norm of neoclassical economics.

The fundamental rule of Pareto optimality states that the economic situation is optimal when no change can improve the position of one individual (as judged by himself) without harming or worsening the position of another individual (as judged by that other individual). A Pareto improvement is a change that moves society from a nonoptimal position closer to an optimal position: "Any change which harms no one and which makes some people better off (in their own estimation) must be considered to be an improvement."[10]

The most significant point to note in the Pareto rule is its conservative consensual character. Defined away are all situations of conflict. In a world of class conflicts, imperialism, exploitation, alienation, racism, sexism, and scores of other human conflicts, where are the changes that might make some better off without making others worse off? *Improve the plight of the oppressed and you worsen the situation of the oppressor* (as perceived by the oppressor, of course)! Any important social, political, and economic situations where improving the lot of one social unit is not opposed by naturally antagonistic social units are indeed rare. The domain of this theory would, indeed, seem to be so restrictive as to hardly warrant serious investigation, were it not for the fact that the theory is considered important not only by the overwhelming majority of neoclassical economists but also by many unwary economists writing in the traditions of Marx and Veblen.[11]

Social Values Underlying Welfare Economics

We have already stated that the meaning of the neoclassical notions of efficiency and rationality is inevitably tied to Pareto optimality. Acceptance of the efficiency or rationality of the free-market solution to the problem of the allocation of resources demands that one accept the social values as well as the empirical and behavioral assumptions underlying this neoclassical analysis. The above discussion of hedonism alludes to some of these social values. All of these values should be made explicit.

The only values that count in Pareto analysis are the preferences of each isolated individual weighted by his or her purchasing power. The individualism and the distributional assumption will be separately considered.

The axiom of individual preferences is extraordinarily constraining. Because in the neoclassical analysis we have no way of evaluating the relative merits of different persons' preferences, we likewise have no criterion for evaluating changes in a given individual's preferences. To be able to do the latter would imply the ability to do the former. At the level of abstraction on which this theory is constructed, individuals only differ in their preference orderings; there is absolutely no difference between a change in a given individual's preference ordering, on the one hand, and the complete withdrawal from society of one individual and his or her replacement by a new individual, on the other. For this reason the theory can consider neither the historical evolution of social and individual values nor their day-to-day fluctuations. To do so would be to admit the normative incomparability of any two events or situations that are temporally separated, that is, to admit the necessity of excluding nearly all real-life phenomena from the domain to which the theory is applicable. Conversely, to permit such normative comparisons would be to return to the egalitarian conclusions of utilitarian radicals and socialists such as William Thompson and, hence, to weaken seriously neoclassical economics as an intellectual support of the status quo.

It is therefore obvious that this theory is applicable only where individual preferences or tastes do not change over time. It is equally obvious that every person, including fanatics, lunatics, sadists, masochists, mentally incompetent persons, children, and even newborn babies must always be the best judge of their own welfare. (It might also be added that all decisions must be made individually and never simply by heads of families or leaders of other social groupings.) Every person must have perfect knowledge of all available alternatives with no uncertainty about the future. Unless these conditions are realized, people will find that the utility that they expect before an act will have no necessary relation to the utility realized after the act, and individual choices or preferences will have no demonstrable connection to an individual's welfare. This extreme individualism also breaks down when we admit the existence of envy and sympathy, which make one individual's perception of his or her own welfare depend on his or her perception of the welfare of others (this is, of course, a special case of the general problem of externalities, which will be elaborated below).

The fact that any Pareto optimum can be defended only in relation to a specific distribution of wealth and income is perhaps the most decisive normative weakness of the theory. Although neoclassical economists usually admit the extremely restrictive relativity of any Pareto optimum, they tend to ignore this restriction and hurry on to safer topics. By using the normative assumptions of Paretian analysis, it can be shown that unless the existing distributions of wealth and income are socially optimal, a situation that is Pareto optimal may be socially inferior to many situations that are not Pareto optimal but have preferable distributions of wealth and income. Neoclassical economists skirt this issue by inserting one standard sentence: "Assume that the existing distributions of wealth and income are ideal *or that the government uses a system of taxes and subsidies to make them so.*"

After stating this standard caveat, the neoclassical economist proceeds to his or her policy analysis using cost-benefit techniques that assume the normative and empirical adequacy of standard Paretian analysis. The fact that the government has *never* used its taxing and spending powers to obtain a just distribution of wealth and power is never admitted. The lack of such an admission is not surprising, because it would force orthodox economists to discuss the nature of social, economic, and political power; and an analysis of vested economic interests and their relation to political power has always been taboo for neoclassical economists (and this is, of course, one of the many important differences between their theories and those of Smith, Ricardo, Thompson, Hodgskin, Marx, Veblen, Hobson, Luxemburg, and Lenin). The reason that no serious effort has ever been made to achieve a more just distribution of wealth and income—and the reason seems painfully obvious—is that the ordinary social, legal, and political means of making such a redistribution are themselves integral parts of the initial distribution of wealth. To possess wealth is to possess political power in a capitalist system. For those neoclassical economists who dislike the unequal distribution of wealth, the hope that those now holding political power will redress existing economic inequities is perhaps their most glaring blind spot.[12]

In practice, most neoclassical economists merely accept the existing distribution of wealth without question. Only rarely do they admit that accepting the existing distribution of wealth implies the acceptance of the existing system of legal and moral rules (including the laws of private property), and, more generally, the acceptance of the entire system of social power, all roles of superordination and subordination, as well as the institutions and instruments of coercion through which power is assured and perpetuated. Thus, most of the important issues that concern economists who are oriented toward a class-conflict approach are eliminated from the neoclassical economists' analyses by the initial assumptions of the Pareto approach.

Empirical and Analytical Assumptions of Welfare Economics

In addition to the assumptions of individualism and distributional justice, the neoclassical welfare theory requires many additional empirical and analytical assumptions. These make up the familiar intermediate microeconomic theory textbook recitation of the conditions necessary for equilibrium under pure competition (and no neoclassical economist has ever argued for any other means to achieve Pareto optimality in a capitalist economy). Among these are the assumptions that a capitalist economy includes:

1. a large number of buyers and sellers, none powerful enough to appreciably affect the market;
2. ease of any business firm to enter or exit any industry;
3. homogeneous inputs and outputs, each divisible into units of any desired size;
4. no uncertainty about the future;
5. perfect knowledge of all possible alternatives in production and consumption;
6. production functions having the "appropriate second-order optimality conditions" (i.e., being of smooth curvature, not having increasing returns to scale, and having diminishing marginal rates of substitution along any isoquant curve);
7. similarly appropriate utility functions that are stable over time;
8. productivity that is generally unaffected by the distribution of wealth, income, and power;
9. only those external economies and diseconomies (or "externalities") that can be corrected or nullified with taxes, subsidies, or the creation of new property rights; and
10. markets that are always in equilibrium, with all change represented as instantaneous shifts from one static equilibrium situation to another.

These assumptions do more than limit the domain of applicability of the neoclassical analyses of competitive equilibrium; they overwhelm the whole analysis. Assumptions 1 and 2 are the foundations of the orthodox concept of competition. But in the historical development of capitalism they were the first casualties of competition. Real capitalist competition, unlike the neoclassical textbook variety, is warfare, a deadly struggle to eliminate rivals and achieve monopoly. Competitive neoclassical equilibrium is often called "long-run equilibrium." Real capitalist development, however, moves inexorably in the opposite direction toward the more pervasive existence of monopoly and oligopoly.

Assumption 10 concerning the continuous existence of equilibrium is indicative of the general inability of neoclassical economics to deal with the historical development of economic phenomena. Despite innumerable attempts to formulate theories of economic growth, neoclassical economists have been unable consistently to integrate welfare and growth analyses. Once economic growth is admitted, the neoclassical analysis itself often shows that instability is the inevitable result.[13] When instability and unemployment are admitted, the Pareto criterion seems unimportant even to most neoclassical economists. Moreover, not only is there nothing in the system to insure smooth, balanced, full-employment economic growth, but the essential question of *what* maximizes welfare in a growing economy is not clear. Is it maximizing the rate of growth, maximizing profit, maximizing total consumption, or maximizing consumption per person? Moreover, none of the proposed answers to these questions helps to resolve the issue of the nature and significance of a method of considering, or giving the appropriate weight to, the welfare of unborn generations, which is being decisively affected by current consumption and investment decisions. Each possible criterion for judging welfare in a growing economy has no necessary connection to neoclassical welfare economics and no necessary consistency with the assumptions of the static theory.[14] The neoclassical Paretian criterion simply cannot handle such problems. It is, by its very nature, a static theory that cannot be extended to describe a growing or changing economy.

The remaining assumptions (3 through 9) all involve similar difficulties. Assumptions 4 and 5 about certainty and perfect knowledge abstract from two inevitable consequences of free-market capitalism that are of singular significance in understanding the human costs of the system's instability and misallocation of resources. Assumptions 3 on homogeneity of inputs (particularly capital) and 6 about "properly behaved production functions" have both been shown to be untenable by the recent theoretical work of Piero Sraffa (which will be discussed in chapter 16). Finally, assumption 9 about externalities is perhaps the most indefensible part of the entire analysis. We will examine it in greater detail below.

Neoclassical Welfare Economics as a Guide to Policy Making

Few neoclassical economists would argue that the assumptions underlying the theory of competitive equilibrium are realistic, but nearly all accept the social, moral, and philosophical foundations of the Paretian welfare criterion. This lack of realism, however, does not prevent neoclassical economists from advocating the theoretical model as a basis for policy making by government officials. The analysis should not, they argue, be considered as descriptive of reality but as a normative model that can be used to guide government interventions into the marketplace whenever any of the above assumptions necessary for competitive equilibrium are not met.[15] Two criticisms should be made regarding this view of government interventionism in a capitalist economy.

First, the neoclassical view gives government a shadowy existence. As long as Pareto optimality exists, it is never mentioned. When an imperfection occurs (which is generally regarded as an isolated occurrence in an otherwise perfect world), the government becomes a *deus ex machina* that restores the system to a state of bliss. It is an aloof, impartial arbitrator that descends on the scene and enacts an excise tax or gives a subsidy in order to restore Pareto optimality. If neoclassical economists are asked about vested interests, corruption (which is, after all, simply another aspect of the functioning of the market), economic and political power, or class control of government processes, they reply with disdain that these issues are the concern of sociologists and political scientists (although one searches in vain for such concerns in most conservative, orthodox social science).

The second criticism of Pareto optimality as a norm for government policy is even more damaging. Perusing the several necessary assumptions and contemplating the hundreds of thousands of interdependent markets in the contemporary capitalist economy, one is impressed by the certainty that at any moment there are innumerable departures from Pareto optimality. The neoclassical economists themselves, in response to the many criticisms about the lack of realism of the assumptions of their theory, modified the theory with the intention of making it more realistic. The modification was dubbed the "theory of the second best" and was still based squarely on the same utilitarian foundations as the original neoclassical version of welfare economics. But the modified version of the theory led to unexpected logical conclusions. According to "the theory of the second best," policies designed to remedy only some and not all of the defects (insofar as simultaneously remedying all would obviously be impossible) will often result in effects diametrically opposed to those intended. In the words of the eminent economic theorist William J. Baumol:

> In brief, this theory [of the second best] states, on the basis of a mathematical argument, that in a concrete situation characterized by *any* deviation from "perfect" optimality, partial policy measures which eliminate only some of the departures from the optimal arrangement may well result in a net decrease in social welfare.[16]

Where then does this leave the normative theory of Pareto optimality, on which the neoclassical notions of market efficiency and rational prices (not to mention the classical liberal argument for laissez-faire capitalism) are based? The answer is obvious: it is a normative ideal, constructed on the most implausible and unrealistic of foundations, whose adherents cannot show (even in theory) whether any given policy decision will move the economy closer to or farther from the ideal; it is riddled by even more acute contradictions than the economic reality from which it springs and for which it attempts to provide both an obscurantist veil and an ideological defense.

Welfare Economics and Externalities

The Achilles' heel of welfare economics is its treatment of externalities. Of all the unrealistic assumptions underlying neoclassical theory, those upon which this treatment are based are the most implausible. In the usual neoclassical approach, the processes of production and consumption are assumed to have "direct" effects on only one or a few persons who are doing the producing or consuming.[17] Externalities occur when the utility function of one consumer is affected by the consumption of another consumer; or the production function of one firm is affected by the production of another firm; or, most important, the utility of an individual is affected by a production process with which he or she has no direct connection. The traditional neoclassical approach is to assume that, except for a single externality, Pareto optimality exists everywhere. With all prices other than those in the market in question reflecting "perfect market rationality," the welfare economists claim to be able to simulate what would have been the correct, rational market price for the unpriced effect of the externality through a process of extrapolation or interpolation (commonly referred to as cost-benefit analysis).

The cost-benefit analysis that can be used to correct externalities is itself a mere extension of the Paretian theory of allocative efficiency. As an important contemporary neoclassical theorist has stated:

> A person who agrees to apply the principles of allocative efficiency needs no new assumption to extend his agreement to the application of existing cost-benefit analysis. In sum both the principles of economic efficiency and those of cost-benefit analysis derive their inspiration from the . . . Pareto criterion, and a person cannot with consistency accept the one and deny the other.[18]

The externality being analyzed is not really imagined to be the only actual deviation from Pareto optimality. Rather, it is asserted that this approach is only a tolerably close approximation to reality. The same neoclassical theorist further asserts that "although it is not expected that the economy at any moment in time, attains an optimum position, in its continuous adjustment to changes in the conditions of demand and supply, it may not be too far from an overall optimal position for any prolonged period."[19]

So when we find an externality, the beneficent, impartial government is called upon; this time to tax or subsidize in such quantities as to nullify or neutralize the lone externality. Pareto optimality is restored. But the cost-benefit analysis that forms the foundation of the tax-subsidy approach to externalities is as unrealistic as the simple statement that there are no externalities at all, because it rests on the assumption of Pareto optimum prices in all markets except the one in question.[20]

An even more devastating criticism results when we realize that externalities are totally pervasive.[21] When reference is made to externalities, a typical example considered is a factory that emits large quantities of sulfur oxides and particulate matter that can cause respiratory diseases to nearby residents or a strip-mining operation that leaves an irreparable, unesthetic scar on the countryside. The fact is, however, that most of the millions of acts of production and consumption in which we engage daily involve externalities. The lack of realism of welfare economics is but a manifestation of the individualistic hedonism of utilitarianism. As Veblen so convincingly demonstrated, production is a social and cultural process not a process of a single individual or even of an isolated group of individuals (even when the group numbers in the hundreds of thousands, as is the case with large modern corporations). Similarly, all human acts, including consumption, are social. Every individual's well being is affected in a thousand ways by the social patterns and institutions that determine who consumes what and in what manner. Human beings are predominantly social creatures, not isolated, unrelated atoms.

In a market economy, any action of one individual or enterprise that induces pleasure or pain in any other individual or enterprise and is unpriced by a market constitutes an externality in neoclassical welfare economics. Because the vast majority of productive and consumptive acts are social, that is, they involve many people to some degree, it follows that such acts will involve externalities. Our table manners in a restaurant; the general appearance of our house, our yard, or our person; our personal hygiene; the route we pick for a joy ride; the time of day we mow our lawn—all affect the pleasures or happiness of others. Furthermore, most of our productive activities have even more widespread and pervasive influences on multitudes of people who are not directly involved. The decision of a business enterprise to relocate a factory may leave an entire community economically destitute. The pollution of the air by a factory may inflict physical discomfort, large cleaning bills, illness, and even death on innumerable people who have no direct connection to the factory. The polluting of water and the practice of strip mining may destroy valuable social resources and disrupt the ecological balance of an entire geographical region in which people must live. But in the "invisible hand" world of the neoclassical utilitarians, each person is concerned only with his or her own actions, and, of course, the general welfare is promoted by all selfish actions.

With the recognition of the pervasiveness of externalities, the tax-subsidy solution is clearly seen as the fantasy that it is. This solution would require literally hundreds of millions of taxes and subsidies (in the United States alone). Moreover, the imposition of any single tax or subsidy would undoubtedly create totally new externalities because it would create new patterns of envy and sympathy. This envy and sympathy would constitute new externalities for which there would have to be new taxes and subsidies. The process would go on forever, with an infinitude of taxes and subsidies never getting us any closer to that most elusive of all individualistic, utilitarian chimeras— Pareto optimality.

But the more reactionary element of orthodox neoclassical theorists, the Austrian and Chicago schools (which we will discuss in chapter 17), has never accepted the principle of discretionary government intervention into any of the market processes. Therefore, for many years they simply ignored externalities. In the late 1950s and early 1960s, however, they devised new formulations of their doctrines that permitted them to enter the debates on externalities that came into vogue in the late 1960s, when even orthodox theorists could no longer ignore the degradation of the environment by American capitalism. During the decade of the 1960s, the Chicago School theorists formulated a policy recommendation to deal with externalities. This formulation remains unchanged in the 1990s.

The policy of the Chicago School neoclassicists was to create new property rights to pollute the environment and then to create new markets in which these rights to pollute could be freely bought and sold.[22] Presumably such trade would continue to the point where the marginal utility to the polluter of another dollar's added pollution would just equal the marginal disutility to the sufferers from the pollution. At this point, it would be impossible to effect a Pareto improvement by either increasing or decreasing pollution, and a new, laissez-faire, competitive Pareto optimum with pollution included would be attained.

One might ask these ultraconservative neoclassicists: to whom would the neutral, impartial government assign these rights to pollute? To the poor residents in the polluted slums? To people chosen randomly? Or to the giant monopolies and oligopolies who do the polluting? The answer to this question might be anticipated from a knowledge of the Austrian and Chicago schools' answer to every policy question of the past one hundred years: *If* we assume perfect competition; and *if* we assume perfect knowledge on the part of all producers and all consumers; and *if* we assume there are no transaction costs (e.g., if victims of a corporate polluter could organize themselves to bargain with the company without cost); then it can be demonstrated that the "initial allocation of property rights has no effect on allocative efficiency." With these assumptions, the inevitable conclusion is that within a laissez-faire capitalist market, the "failure to reach mutual agreement . . . can be regarded as *prima facie* evidence that . . . a net potential Pareto improvement is not possible."[23] This is, however, too obviously apologetic for the more candid neoclassical economists. One of the most important neoclassical theorists (who is not a member of the Chicago School), for example, writes: "Rationalizing the *status quo* in this way brings the economist perilously close to defending it."[24] Perilously close indeed! But what this neoclassical theorist fails to mention is that the more moderate neoclassical welfare theorists (such as himself) provide an even more effective rationalization of the status quo—more effective because it is so much less blatant and yet achieves nearly identical results.

The extremely individualistic orientation of the Austrian and Chicago schools is reflected in their view of the nature of externalities. They simply consider externalities, for which they advocate the establishment of property rights and markets, as being somehow metaphysically given and fixed. By ignoring the relational aspects of social life, their theory ignores the fact that individuals can create externalities almost at will. If we assume the maximizing economic man of utilitarian economics, and if we assume that the government establishes property rights and markets for these rights whenever an external diseconomy is discovered, then each person can purposefully impose external diseconomies on other people, knowing that the bargaining within the new market that the government will soon establish will surely make him or her better off. The more significant and unpleasant the social cost imposed on one's neighbor, the greater will be one's reward in the bargaining process. It follows from the orthodox assumption of maximizing economic exchangers that each person will create a maximum of repugnant and pernicious social costs that he or she can impose on others. This general process can quite appropriately be called the "invisible foot" of the laissez-faire capitalist marketplace. The invisible foot ensures us that in a free market, capitalist economy, each person pursuing only his or her own maximum gain will automatically and most efficiently do his or her part to maximize the general public misery.

To see why this principle has some validity, note that a self-seeking, calculating, maximizing individual will maximize the value of participating in these newly organized markets by devising a new production function that creates nonmarket commodities, or external diseconomies, that harm others. Taking this production-possibility set for creating external diseconomies or nonmarket commodities that annoy, harm, damage, or mutilate others, he or she will select only those diseconomies with a higher marginal return than the marginal return that he or she could earn by engaging in market transactions. But by so doing, he or she will maximize the suffering, pain, and misery, or simply the cost, to others, because his or her gain will always be someone else's loss. The recipient of these rationally calculated social atrocities, or external diseconomies, will immediately undertake defensive expenditures or pay bribes until the usual marginal conditions of Pareto efficiency are fulfilled. Thus, the recipient's cost will be minimized, and an efficient pattern of external diseconomies, or mutual social mutilation, will emerge.

But if these external diseconomies, in terms of value to the generator, are maximized in the society, and if they are efficiently contended with by recipients, then we have a completely reversed operation of the rational, maximizing individual and Pareto efficiency. That is, instead of getting those goods produced that have the highest utility and whose costs are minimized, we will have created goods that have a maximum of disutility, pain, and suffering and that are allocated such that they will have the most severe impact that the perpetrator can inflict, with the impact being minimized in terms of recipient cost as well as production costs. The economy, as the accepted principles of neoclassical microeconomic theory will confirm, is efficient, but only in providing misery. To paraphrase a well-known precursor of this theory: *Every individual necessarily labors to render the annual external costs of the society as great as he can. He generally, indeed, neither intends to promote the public misery nor knows how much he is promoting it. He intends only his own gain, and he is in this, as in many other cases, led as if by an invisible foot to promote an end that was no part of his intention. Nor is it any better for society that it was no part of it. By pursuing his own interest he frequently promotes social misery more effectually than when he really intends to promote it.* Such is the principle of the invisible foot of capitalism as it would work if the conservative Austrian and Chicago schools of neoclassical economists were ever to persuade the government to adopt their method of dealing with externalities.[25]

The utter failure of neoclassical economists to deal adequately with these problems stems from their failure to recognize that in capitalism, while all acts of production and consumption are social (as they are in every other type of economic system), the system of incentives that governs production and consumption is almost entirely individual (as it is not and need not be in other types of economic systems). It is, of course, an utterly impossible task to develop legal property rights to every type of physical, biological, and social interdependence, or to develop a rational taxation system that would eliminate the social aspects of production and consumption (or external diseconomies). Rather, in order to move toward an economic system that more adequately and more justly satisfies human needs, the incentive system that underlies capitalism itself needs alteration, as does the private-property system. Needless to say, however, this is a task that goes far beyond the purview of orthodox neoclassical economics.

The theory's absolute inability to handle pervasive externalities should more than suffice to convince any reasonable person of its irrelevance, particularly in the light of the conclusion of the theory of the second best, that attempts partially to achieve Pareto optimality may well have diametrically opposed effects. But the theory is much worse than irrelevant. A few of the more candid orthodox economists are themselves admitting this. One of the most eminent has written:

> The achievements of economic theory . . . are both impressive and in many ways beautiful. But it cannot be denied that there is something scandalous in the spectacle of so many people refining the analysis of economic states which they give no reason to suppose will ever, or have ever, come about. It probably is also dangerous. Equilibrium economics, because of its well known welfare economics implication, is easily convertible into an apologia for existing economic arrangements and it is frequently so converted. On the other end of the scale, the recent, fairly elaborate analysis of the optimum plans for an economy which is always in equilibrium has, one suspects, misled people to believe that we actually know how an economy is to be controlled. . . . It is an unsatisfactory and . . . dishonest state of affairs.[26]

The Normative Critique of Pareto Analysis

Some of the more progressive neoclassical economists regret this state of affairs. "Too bad," they say, "that the theory is so irrelevant. It is so elegant and analytically sophisticated, and seems to have such universal normative appeal." This lament, as we have tried to show throughout this book, is misguided. The normative objections to the neoclassical utilitarian theory are more damaging than all of the practical, empirical, and analytical objections raised to this point. Neoclassical welfare economics accepts as the ultimate ethical criteria of social value the *existing* personal desires, generated by the institutions, values, and social processes of *existing* society, and weighted by the *existing* distributions of income, wealth, and power. Thus, the theory becomes incapable of asking questions about the nature of an ethically good society and the ethically good person that would be its product. The plausibility of the normative criteria of the utilitarian theory probably derives from the widely felt moral repugnance toward the notion of an omnipotent central government arbitrarily and capriciously dictating the choices and behavioral patterns of individuals. Moral rejection of this Orwellian specter should not, however, lead to the illusion that existing society reflects that specter's antithesis. Orwell's *1984* was, after all, merely the extension of tendencies that he saw in the capitalist economies of his day, and it remains fairly descriptive of most industrial capitalist countries in the twenty-first century.

Since the existing desires of each person who is socialized under the capitalist system constitute the bases of all moral judgments in utilitarianism, we should begin by discussing these desires. Commenting on a lifetime of psychoanalyzing people afflicted by the system of desires generated by capitalist society, Erich Fromm has written:

> Man today is fascinated by the possibility of buying more, better and especially new things. He is consumption-hungry. The act of buying and consuming has become a compulsive, irrational aim, because it is an end in itself, with little relation to the use of or pleasure in the things bought and consumed. To buy the latest gadget, the latest model of anything that is on the market, is the dream of everybody in comparison to which the real pleasure in use is quite secondary. Modern man, if he dared to be articulate about his concept of heaven, would describe a vision which would look like the biggest department store in the world, showing new things and gadgets, and himself having plenty of money with which to buy them. He would wander around open-mouthed in his heaven of gadgets and commodities, provided only that there were ever more and newer things to buy, and perhaps that his neighbors were just a little less privileged than he.[27]

Human nature does not automatically produce the consumption-hungry, maximizing automaton, so necessary for the tranquil, profitable operation of our economic system. Capitalist humankind and most of his or her desires are created through an elaborate system of social control, manipulation, deception, and general verbal pollution.

In this economic and political system based on corruption and deception, each lonely, isolated individual is pitted against all other individuals in merciless competition. Is it any wonder that the result is nearly universal disorientation, apathy, and despair? A pervasive sense of the emptiness and futility of life is the foundation on which corporate advertising executives create the desires of the capitalist person. Such a person watches commercials in which bright, happy, vivacious people buy new cars, houses, and stereos. He or she then strives to overcome particular unhappiness and anxieties by purchasing. Purchase, purchase, purchase becomes his or her Moses and the capitalists' profits. But this gives him or her no relief, so he sets his or her sights on a bigger car, a more expensive house, and so on, and he or she is aboard the Alice-in-Wonderland treadmill of consumerism.

Such are the desires of the isolated, egoistic, alienated, manipulated capitalist person created by the capitalist social system. These desires form the moral foundation on which neoclassical welfare economics is constructed. And the moral weight given to each person's desires, of course, is determined solely by the wealth and income of that person. Many neoclassical economists, when confronted with the arguments of this chapter (as well as many other criticisms that could be made), will admit that welfare economics cannot be defended on normative, empirical, or analytical grounds. Nevertheless, they continue to use concepts that are only defensible when the Pareto analysis is accepted in most lines of applied economics. Pareto efficiency notions underlie (1) the theory of comparative advantage in international trade theory, (2) most normative conclusions in the neoclassical theory of public finance, (3) most cost-benefit analyses, and (4) nearly every other area in which neoclassical economics affects policy recommendations. Even worse are the rarely defended, sanctimoniously stated clichés and shibboleths about "rational prices" and "market efficiency" in that most ideologically tainted of all neoclassical academic specializations, comparative economic systems, or the analysis of socialist economies. Perhaps the most interesting aspect of the economic reforms in Eastern Europe in the late 1980s and early 1990s was the extent to which this neoclassical argument, despite the numerous weaknesses detailed above, had been naively and uncritically embraced by many of the reformers. It would appear as though the defects of Eastern European Communism induced many reformers to accept a theory that hides and obscures the defects of capitalism in a desperate hope that capitalism, with all its defects, might be preferable to their economic system. In the 1990s and early twenty-first century, every one of these economies has degenerated to a position of mass poverty, mass unemployment, massive organized crime, mass prostitution, and grotesque inequalities in wealth and income.

We conclude this chapter by repeating our earlier assertion that modern neoclassical welfare economics is the direct descendant of the views of Senior and Bastiat. Like those two nineteenth-century thinkers, neoclassical economists see the capitalist system as a system of natural harmony and universal beneficence. The price of maintaining such a view has always been to ignore or deny all significant social problems and all significant social conflicts. The reward for maintaining this view is, of course, that one can sit back and relax, forget all the unpleasantness of the world, and enjoy one's dreams of the beatific vision and eternal felicity.

Notes to Chapter 14

1. Joseph A. Schumpeter, *History of Economic Analysis* (New York: Oxford University Press, 1954), p. 860.

2. Francis M. Bator, "The Simple Analytics of Welfare Maximization," *American Economic Review* 47 (1957): 22–59.

3. The neoclassical critic may object to this statement. The "bliss point" in neoclassical literature is defined as that point on the utility-possibility frontier that lies at the highest possible point on some "social welfare function." But since neoclassical literature itself has shown that no such "social welfare function" can be formulated that contains a clear and unambiguous principle by which to judge the distribution of wealth, and which simultaneously does not logically contradict the foundational tenets of individualistic utilitarianism, we are justified in asserting that such "social welfare functions" in neoclassical theory reduce to mere statements of one's own biases.

4. The title of this section is taken from the titles of two chapters of the book *The City of God* written by the influential Christian philosopher Saint Augustine in the fifth century A.D. Because Bentham considered his own philosophy to be the "felicific calculus" and because the neoclassical elaboration of Bentham's views is a timeless, "eternal" model, the title seems appropriate.

5. C.E. Ferguson, *Microeconomic Theory*, rev. ed. (Homewood, IL: Irwin, 1969), pp. 442–66.

6. Ibid., pp. 444–45.

7. Ibid., p. 454.

8. S.S. Alexander, "Human Value and Economists' Values," in *Human Values and Economic Polity*, ed. S. Hood (New York: New York University Press, 1967), p. 107.

9. Karl Marx, *Capital*, 3 vols. (Moscow: Foreign Languages Publishing House, 1961), vol. 1, p. 81.

10. W.J. Baumol, *Economic Theory and Operations Analysis*, 2d ed. (Englewood Cliffs, NJ: Prentice-Hall, 1965), p. 376.

11. See E.K. Hunt, "Orthodox and Marxist Economics in a Theory of Socialism," *Monthly Review* 24, no. 8 (1973): 50–56.

12. This point is developed more amply in W.J. Samuels, "Welfare Economics, Power and Property," in *Perspectives on Property*, ed. Gene Wunderlich (Philadelphia: Pennsylvania State University Press, 1972).

13. F.H. Hahn and R.C.O. Matthews, "The Theory of Economic Growth: A Survey," in *Surveys of Economic Theory*, vol. 2, ed. American Economic Assoc. (New York: Macmillan, 1966), pp. 95–99.

14. Ibid., pp. 99–113. See also Richard Goodwin, *Elementary Economics from the Higher Standpoint* (New York: Cambridge University Press, 1972).

15. For a discussion of this view, see E.K. Hunt, "Orthodox Economic Theory and Capitalist Ideology," *Monthly Review* 19 (1968): 50–55.

16. William J. Baumol, "Informed Judgment, Rigorous Theory and Public Policy," *Southern Economic Journal* (October 1965): 138. For the definitive formulation of the theory of the second best, see R.G. Lipsey and Kelvin Lancaster, "The General Theory of the Second Best," *Review of Economic Studies* 24 (1956): 63, 64, 65.

17. By using the adjective *direct*, I am following E.J. Mishan, "The Postwar Literature on Externalities: An Interpretive Essay," *Journal of Economic Literature* 9, no. 1 (March 1971): 2. Excluded are "indirect effects," which are obtained through changes in relative prices in a Walrasian general equilibrium system.

18. E.J. Mishan, *Economics for Social Decisions: Elements of Cost-Benefit Analysis* (New York: Praeger, 1973), p. 17.

19. Ibid., p. 80.

20. Ibid., pp. 79–83.

21. For an analysis of the implications of pervasive externalities, see R.C. d'Arge and E.K. Hunt, "Environmental Pollution, Externalities, and Conventional Economic Wisdom: A Critique," *Environmental Affairs* 1, no. 2 (June 1971): 266–86.

22. For a clear formulation of this point of view, see Thomas Crocker and A.J. Rogers, III,

Environmental Economics (New York: Holt, Rinehart and Winston, 1971).

23. Mishan, *Economics for Social Decisions*, p. 17.

24. Ibid.

25. The principle of the invisible foot was first developed in E.K. Hunt and R.C. d'Arge, "On Lemmings and Other Acquisitive Animals: Propositions on Consumption," *Journal of Economic Issues* 7, no. 2 (June 1973): 337–53.

26. F.H. Hahn, "Some Adjustment Problems," *Econometrica* 38, no. 1 (1970): 1–2.

27. Erich Fromm, *The Sane Society* (New York: Fawcett, 1965), p. 123.

Chapter 15

Neoclassical Ideology and the Myth of the Self-Adjusting Market: The Writings of John Maynard Keynes

Utilitarian economics reached its highest, most complex, and most esthetically elegant state in the neoclassical ideological defense of laissez-faire capitalism. The three principal ideological elements of neoclassical utilitarianism were: (1) the marginal productivity theory of distribution, which pictured competitive capitalism as an ideal of distributive justice; (2) the "invisible hand" argument, which pictured capitalism as an ideal of rationality and efficiency; and (3) the faith in the automatic, self-adjusting nature of the market, which demonstrated that the principal functions of government should be to enforce contracts and to defend the powers and privileges of private property.

Each of these three tenets of utilitarian conservatism represented an obfuscation of the realities of capitalism, but each promoted the general acceptance of unfettered profit making. The first two tenets were a pure and unmixed blessing for capitalists. They obscured reality in a manner that promoted the public's faith in the beneficence of capitalism but did not hamper in any way the functioning of capitalism or profit making. The third tenet (the automaticity of the market) was a mixed blessing.

During the beginnings of capitalist industrialization, the capitalists' quest for industrial profits was frequently obstructed by governments that represented the older merchant and land-owning interests. Moreover, much of the antipathy of the early capitalists toward the existing governments stemmed directly from the many corrupt, despotic, capricious, and tyrannical actions of several European kings, as well as from the actions of the English Parliament, which was notoriously unrepresentative and often despotic. Therefore, under the banner of laissez faire, capitalists could campaign for governments that more effectively promoted unrestricted profit making and yet make these campaigns appear to be humanitarian efforts to promote the general public's freedom from tyrannical government abuse. The argument for self-adjusting markets (Say's law) was an effective argument for limiting the functions of existing governments. But the capitalist market system has never adjusted smoothly and automatically to full-employment equilibrium. There has never, in fact, been a Walrasian "crier," and the capitalist market system has always been anarchical: the history of capitalism is a history of economic instability.

Furthermore, during the late nineteenth century, the development of worldwide capital markets and improvements in production and transportation led to immense concentrations of industrial power in giant corporations, trusts, and cartels. There were two important consequences of this increased industrial concentration: first, unregulated competition became extremely costly and hazardous to these giant corporations. Second, the anarchy of the market became more severe because giant corporations significantly reduced whatever amount of flexibility and adjustability the market had previously possessed. Depressions became longer and more severe and occurred somewhat more frequently.

Therefore, the belief in the self-adjusting market, which influenced government policy, became increasingly costly to capitalists. Moreover, whereas during the late eighteenth and early nineteenth centuries, capitalists had not completely brought the existing governments under their control, all of this had changed by the late nineteenth and early twentieth centuries. The governments of the capitalist countries were quite firmly in the control of capitalists. Under these circumstances, it is not surprising that capitalists should turn to the government as the only possible means of escaping the ruinous competition of the late nineteenth century and the extremely costly depressions that resulted from the anarchy of the market.

In the United States, for example, the Interstate Commerce Act of 1887 established the Interstate Commerce Commission, which ostensibly was designed to regulate the railroads in order to promote the public interest. This was merely the first of a long line of government regulatory commissions supposedly created for the same purpose. In fact, the regulatory agencies were from the very beginning staffed primarily with former executives of the industries that were to have been controlled, and they thus became government agencies that promoted and protected the interests of these industries. Similarly, the Sherman Antitrust Act of 1890 (which passed both houses of Congress with only a single dissenting vote) was the first of a series of antitrust acts ostensibly designed to promote competition, but which, in fact, turned out to be merely the means of curbing labor organizations and rescuing corporations from what the courts came to label "unfair competition."

These extensions of the duties of government, however, could be rationalized very easily within the context of neoclassical, laissez-faire economics. In fact, these extensions of the duties of government could be used to demonstrate that the invisible-hand argument, which presupposed innumerable, small, relatively powerless competitors in each industry, was empirically relevant to an economic situation dominated by giant corporations. The regulatory agencies and the antitrust laws, so the argument went, forced these giants to act as if they were small competitors and created something called "workable competition," which was held to be a tolerably close approximation to perfect competition. The government, it was sometimes argued, intervened in the economic situation only to assure the harmonious and beneficent workings of the invisible hand.

Meanwhile, the instability of capitalism grew worse, and the faith in the self-adjusting market became more and more costly to capitalists (as well as the rest of society). During the first half of the nineteenth century, for example, the United States had only two severe economic crises (beginning in 1819 and 1837), and England had four (beginning in 1815, 1825, 1836, and 1847). During the last half of the century, the crises became more severe and increased in number to five in the United States (beginning in 1854, 1857, 1873, 1884, and 1893) and six in England (beginning in 1857, 1866, 1873, 1882, 1890, and 1900). In the twentieth century, the situation grew worse. Increasingly frequent depressions plagued capitalism, culminating in the Great Depression of the 1930s.

The Great Depression of the 1930s was a worldwide phenomenon, affecting every major capitalist economy. In the United States, for example, on October 24, 1929 (a day that came to be known as "Black Thursday"), the New York Stock Exchange saw security values plummet, a phenomenon that eventually destroyed all confidence in business. As a result, businessmen cut back production and investment. This decreased national income and employment, which in turn worsened business confidence even more. Before the process came to an end, thousands of corporations had gone bankrupt, millions were unemployed, and one of the worst national catastrophes in history was under way.

Between 1929 and 1932, there were over 85,000 business failures; more than 5,000 banks suspended operations; stock values on the New York Stock Exchange fell from $87 billion to $19 billion; unemployment rose to 12 million, with nearly one-fourth of the population having no means of sustaining themselves; farm income fell by more than half; and manufacturing output decreased by almost 50 percent.[1]

America had plunged from the world's most prosperous country to one in which tens of millions lived in desperate, abject poverty. Particularly hard hit were the blacks and other minority groups. The proportion of blacks among the unemployed was from 60 percent to 400 percent higher than the proportion of blacks in the general population.[2] Certain geographical areas suffered more than others. Congressman George Huddleston of Alabama reported in January 1932:

> We have about 108,000 wage and salary workers in my district. Of that number, it is my belief that not exceeding 8,000 have their normal incomes. At least 25,000 men

are altogether without work. Some of them have not had a stroke of work for more than 12 months, maybe 60,000 or 75,000 are working one to five days a week, and practically all have had serious cuts in their wages and many of them do not average over $1.50 a day.[3]

Many cities reported that they had enough funds to give relief payments for only a very short time, often one week. The executive director of the Welfare Council of New York City described the plight of the unemployed.

When the breadwinner is out of a job he usually exhausts his savings if he has any. Then if he has an insurance policy, he probably borrows to the limit of its cash value. He borrows from his friends and from his relatives until they can stand the burden no longer. He gets credit from the corner grocery store and the butcher shop, and the landlord foregoes collecting the rent until interest and taxes have to be paid and something has to be done. All of these resources are finally exhausted over a period of time, and it becomes necessary for these people, who have never before been in want, to ask for assistance.

The specter of starvation faces millions of people who have never before known what it was to be out of a job for any considerable period of time and who certainly have never known what it was to be absolutely up against it.[4]

The abject despair of these millions of people is suggested by a 1932 report describing the unloading of garbage in the Chicago city garbage dumps: "Around the truck which was unloading garbage and other refuse were about 35 men, women and children. As soon as the truck pulled away from the pile all of them started digging with sticks, some with their hands, grabbing bits of food and vegetables."[5]

What had happened to reduce the output of goods and services so drastically? Natural resources were still as plentiful as ever. The nation still had as many factories, tools, and machines. The people had the same skills and wanted to put them to work. Yet millions of workers and their families begged, borrowed, stole, and lined up for a pittance from charity, while thousands of factories stood idle or operated at far below capacity. The explanation lay within the institutions of the capitalist market system. Factories could have been opened and men put to work, but they were not because it was *not profitable* for businessmen to do this. In a capitalist economy, production decisions are based primarily on profits not on people's needs.

In this disastrous situation, it became clear to many neoclassical economists (but by no means to all of them) that the myth of the self-adjusting market had outlived its ideological usefulness. The unregulated anarchy of the market was becoming a threat to the very existence of capitalism. It was obvious to many economists of all persuasions that drastic measures were needed on a scale that could be undertaken only by the government.

But neoclassical economics, with its emphasis on the automaticity of the market, offered no cure for the malady of capitalism. In neoclassical theory depressions did not occur, so there was no need to remedy them. If neoclassical economics, with its elaborately developed defense of the status quo, was to be of any use in such a crisis, it had to be modified drastically. To this task came one of the most brilliant conservative economists of this century: John Maynard Keynes (1883–1946). In his *The General Theory of Employment, Interest and Money*, published in 1936, Keynes attempted to show what had happened to capitalism so that measures could be taken to preserve the system.

In his endeavor to understand depressions, Keynes could have examined the writings of either Malthus or almost any economist in the socialist tradition, particularly Marx. Although Keynes wrote about Marx several times, there is absolutely no indication in any of his writings that he ever read Marx. Keynes knew very well which side of the class struggle Marx was on and which side Malthus was on. Marx's ideas, Keynes concluded a priori, were "characterized . . . by mere logical fallacy.[6] Marxism held no interest for him as a scientific theory; it was interesting merely as a social phenomenon: "Marxian Socialism must always remain a portent to the historians of opinion—how a doctrine so illogical and so dull can have exercised so powerful and enduring an influence over the minds of men, and through them, the events of history."[7]

Keynes had no use for Marxism because of his horror of any doctrine with revolutionary socialist appeal:

> I do not believe that there is any economic improvement for which Revolution is a necessary instrument. On the other hand, we have everything to lose by methods of violent change. In Western industrial conditions, the tactics of Red Revolution would throw the whole population into a pit of poverty and death.[8]

Furthermore, to give Marx any credit for understanding the instability of capitalism would be, he believed, a promotion of the overthrow of capitalism, rather than a contribution to its salvation. He believed that "it is ideas, not vested interests, which are dangerous for good or evil."[9]

But Malthus had also constructed a theory of capitalist depressions, and he was a much safer economist than Marx. Malthus, it will be recalled, had shown in his theory the necessity of "a society divided into a class of proprietors, and a class of labourers, and with self-love the main-spring of the great machine."[10] Although Keynes definitely did not endorse all of Malthus's ideas, this belief in the inevitability of capitalism was comforting to him:

> For my own part, I believe that there is social and psychological justification for significant inequalities of income and wealth, but not such large disparities as exist today. There are valuable human activities which require the motive of money-making and the environment of private wealth-ownership for their full fruition. Moreover, dangerous human proclivities can be canalised into comparatively harmless channels by the existence of opportunities for moneymaking and private wealth.[11]

It is surprising that after rejecting Marx's ideas as hopelessly illogical, Keynes could exclaim: "If only Malthus, instead of Ricardo, had been the parent stem from which nineteenth-century economics proceeded, what a much wiser and richer place the world would be today!"[12]

Theoretical Setting of Keynes's Analysis

Keynes's theory was set in a conceptual context that was basically the same as Walrasian general equilibrium theory. It is an analysis of a continuous process of production, circulation, and consumption. In a given production period, a firm produces a certain dollar volume of goods. From the proceeds of the sale of these goods the firm pays its costs of production, which include wages, salaries, rent, supplies and raw materials, and interest on borrowed funds. What remains after these costs are paid is profit.

The important point to remember is this: a cost of production to the business firm represents income to an individual or another firm. The profit is also income—the income going to the owners of the firm. Because the value of production is exhausted by the costs of production and profits, and all these are income, it follows that the value of what has been produced must be equal to the incomes generated in producing it.

In terms of the entire economy, the aggregate picture is the same as that for the individual firm: the value of everything produced in the economy during any period is equal to the total of all incomes received in that period. Therefore, in order for businesses to sell all that they have produced, people must spend in the aggregate all their incomes. If an amount equal to the total income in society is spent on goods and services, then the value of production is realized in sales. In that case, profits remain high, and businessmen are willing to produce the same amount or more in the succeeding period.

This process can be seen as a *circular flow*: Money flows from businesses to the public in the form of wages, salaries, rents, interest, and profits; this money then flows back to the businesses when the public buys goods and services from them. As long as businesses sell all that they have produced and make satisfactory profits, the process continues.

But this does not happen automatically. When money flows from businesses to the public, some of it does not flow directly back to the businesses. The circular flow has leakages. To begin with, all people do not spend all of their incomes. A percentage is saved, usually in banks, and therefore withdrawn from the spending stream. There are also two other leakages: people buy goods and services from foreign businesses, so that the money spent on these imports is not spent on domestically produced goods, and the taxes that people pay are withdrawn from the income-expenditure flow.

These three leakages (saving, imports, and taxes) may be offset by three spending injections into the income-expenditure flow. First, imports can be offset by exports. They are exactly offset when foreigners buy goods produced in the United States in amounts equal in value to imports purchased by Americans. Second, the government uses taxes to finance the purchase of goods and services. If it uses all taxes for this purpose and balances the budget, then government expenditures will exactly offset taxes in the spending stream. Third, if businessmen wish to expand their capital, they can finance investment in capital goods by borrowing the funds that have been saved. Investment, then, may exactly offset the saving leakage.

If these three injections into the income-expenditure flow are just as large as the three leakages, then spending equals the value of production. Assuming that the structure of all relative prices apportions demand among the various industries so that demand and supply are equal in each industry, then everything that has been produced can be sold, and prosperity reigns.

This was the orthodox neoclassical vision of how competitive capitalism normally functioned. The levels of total employment and total output were determined by the production function and the free choices of owners of the factors of production. In a short-run period, with a given amount of capital in existence, the demand for labor was determined, as we saw in chapter 11, by the value of the marginal product of labor. With this given demand for labor, neoclassical theory explained both the wage rate and the amount of total output by the supply of labor. This analysis is illustrated in Figure 15.1, where *VMP* is the value of the marginal product of labor and *S* is the supply of labor.

In Figure 15.1, if 100 workers wish to work, then they must accept a wage (determined by the value of their marginal product) of $2.00 per worker. In this case, the total of wages is $200.00, and $50.00 goes to profits (for an explanation, see chapter 11). Total output in this example has a value of $250.00. Now if 125 workers wish work, then the value of the marginal product of labor will decline to $1.75. For more workers to find employment, *the wage rate must decline.* If 125 workers are employed, then the total wages are $218.75 (125 × $1.75), the total profits are $78.12, and the total output is $296.87. Thus, in the short-run neoclassical analysis, given a productive function and the resulting demand curve for labor (paying labor according to the value of its marginal product), the supply of labor determines the wage rate and the total level of production (as well as total wages and total profits). This was the standard analysis of the levels of output and employment advanced by most orthodox neoclassical economists in the 1930s.

If unemployment existed in this analysis, it was because workers refused to work unless they received *more* than the value of their marginal product. For example, in Figure 15.1, if the wage rate were $2.00, then only 100 workers would be employed. If 125 workers wished to work, then they would have to accept a wage rate of $1.75. If they were willing to do this, then profit-maximizing behavior of capitalists would assure that 125 workers would be employed. If the workers refused to take a wage cut and 25 remained unemployed, then neoclassical economists *defined* these workers as voluntarily unemployed and insisted that full employment prevailed.

Only when workers were willing to work at a wage equal to the value of their marginal product and could not find work at that wage rate were neoclassical economists willing to admit that involuntary unemployment existed. But capitalists maximized profits when they hired workers up to the point where the value of their marginal product equaled the wage rate. Therefore,

Figure 15.1   **Neoclassical Determination of the Wage Rate and Total Output**

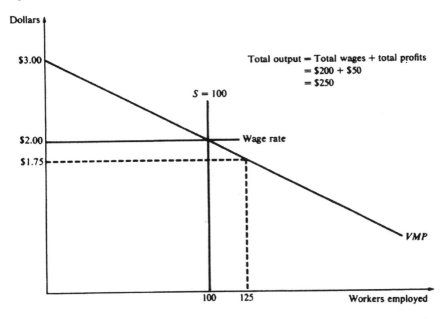

profit maximization, the neoclassicists concluded, insured that there would never be any involuntary unemployment. When unemployment appeared to exist, it was only because workers refused to take the wage cuts necessary to bring the wage rate into equality with the lower value of the marginal product that would result when more workers were employed.

If workers were willing to accept a wage that was equal to the value of their marginal product, then there would never normally be any problem of aggregate demand being equal to aggregate supply. All income would normally be spent. The three injections into the income-expenditure flow would normally equal the three leakages. This was because: (1) neoclassical theory showed that the free play of supply and demand would balance international transactions; (2) "sound fiscal policy," in the view of both neoclassical economists and most politicians, dictated that the government maintain a balanced budget in which taxes equaled government expenditures; and (3) the rate of interest would always bring saving and investment into equality.

The last point represented a crucial difference between the neoclassical economists and Keynes, so we will briefly elaborate the neoclassical view. In this view, people always preferred present consumption to future consumption (see chapter 11). Therefore people would only save when they received a reward for doing so, the reward being interest received on their saving. The higher the rate of interest, the more they would save; and the lower the rate of interest, the less they would save. People who invested in a new plant and equipment or other capital goods had to pay for the funds they invested. The amount they had to pay was determined by the rate of interest (if they had their own money, then the rate of interest would be a measure of the income that they would have to forgo by not loaning this money but choosing to invest it in capital goods). The lower the rate of interest, the cheaper would be the funds for investment and more investment would be undertaken. Figure 15.2 illustrates these two relationships between the rate of interest and saving and the rate of interest and investment.

In Figure 15.2, if r_1 is the prevailing rate of interest, then saving exceeds investment; savers cannot find sufficient investment to absorb all of the funds that they have saved. They will bid competitively to find borrowers for their funds and bid the interest rate down to $\bar{r}$. If r_2 is the prevailing rate of interest, then investors cannot find sufficient saving to finance their investments. They will competitively bid for the available funds and bid the rate of interest up to $\bar{r}$. At $\bar{r}$, saving equals investment.

Therefore, in neoclassical theory, competition automatically created an interest rate at which saving and investment were equal. This meant that all three leakages from the income-expenditure flow would automatically be brought into equality with all three injections into the flow, and aggregate demand would automatically equal aggregate supply.

The only conceivable cause of what appeared to be involuntary unemployment was, to nearly all neoclassical economists, the refusal of laborers to take sufficiently large cuts in wages. Thus, during the Great Depression, when neoclassical economists were consulted by governments regarding the most effective way to combat the depression, even those neoclassicists who were the most humane and sympathetic to the plight of workers could recommend nothing but a general cut in all wages.[13]

Keynes's Defense of the Marginal Productivity Theory of Distribution

Keynes basically agreed with the neoclassical marginal productivity theory of distribution (in fact, as we will see, he agreed with nearly every tenet of neoclassical theory except for the belief that aggregate demand would always equal aggregate supply at the full-employment level of income). He began the *General Theory* by stating that the neoclassical (or classical, as Keynes referred to it) "theory of employment" was based "on two fundamental postulates," the first being that the *"wage is equal to the marginal product of labour."*[14] In stating his disagreements with neoclassical economics, Keynes was careful to reassure the reader that he agreed with this first postulate—that laborers receive the value of their marginal product:

> In emphasizing our point of departure from the classical system, we must not overlook an important point of agreement. For we shall maintain the first postulate as heretofore, subject only to the same qualifications as in the classical theory; and we must pause, for a moment, to consider what this involves.
> It means that, with a given organization, equipment and technique, real wages

Figure 15.2 **Interest, Saving, and Investment**

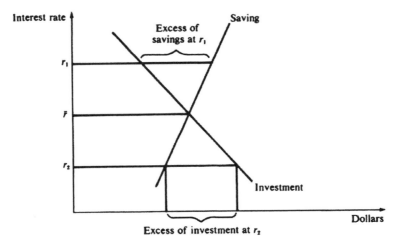

and the volume of output (and hence of employment) are uniquely correlated, so that, in general, an increase in employment can only occur to the accompaniment of a decline in the rate of real wages. Thus I am not disputing this vital fact which the classical economists have (rightly) asserted as indefeasible. . . . Thus if employment increases, then, in the short period, the reward per unit of labour in terms of wage-goods must, in general, decline and profits increase.[15]

It would seem that Keynes had a theory of employment identical to that of his neoclassical contemporaries and that his recommendation for increasing employment would be identical to theirs, that is, to decrease wages and increase profits. It was and it was not. Keynes was involved in a contradiction. As the neoclassicists did, Keynes argued that to increase employment, wages had to be decreased and profits increased (and many ignorant conservatives of the time considered Keynes a radical!). If profit-maximizing behavior motivated capitalists to hire laborers to the point where their wage equaled the value of their marginal product (as Keynes and all the neoclassical economists agreed), then lowering the real wage of workers was the only answer to unemployment. Keynes wanted to agree with the neoclassicists and simultaneously to disagree with them.

He did this in a most unconvincing way. He argued that real wages could be decreased in either of two ways. First, the money wage rate could be decreased while the prices of wage goods remained constant or decreased more slowly (which is what most neoclassical economists recommended). Second, the price of wage goods could be increased while the money wage rate remained constant or increased more slowly. Keynes argued that workers would never accept the first method of reducing their real wages but would accept the second method more or less peacefully.[16]

The argument is unconvincing because in their wage negotiations, workers are generally as concerned with the cost of living as they are with their money wages. When workers are in a strong bargaining position, they generally insist that money wage increases compensate them for any increase in the cost of living. Moreover, in their generally destitute condition in the 1930s, millions of workers aggressively searched for any job that would pay a livable wage.

If the workers employed in 1929 before the onset of the depression were receiving the value of their marginal product, as Keynes believed they were, then the sharp decline in employment in the 1930s with a relatively constant level of physical capital in existence *must have resulted in a sharp increase in the marginal productivity of labor* according to the logic of the marginal productivity theory of distribution, which Keynes fully accepted. But insofar as real wages had not increased in the 1930s, and in many cases had decreased, it logically followed from the marginal productivity theory that employed workers were *receiving real wages substantially below their marginal productivity.* Moreover, millions of workers were eager to work for the existing wage but could not find work.

Keynes's Analysis of Capitalist Depressions

Throughout the remainder of the *General Theory*, Keynes consistently assumed that the rate of utilization of the productive capacity of physical capital declined sharply in times of depression, and the number of employed workers declined sharply as well. Keynes's theory was addressed to those obvious realities of depression in an insightful and coherent manner. But because it is an equally obvious fact of capitalist depressions that the real wages of workers did not increase when employment decreased, Keynes's adherence to the marginal productivity theory that wages were always equal to the workers' marginal productivity contradicted the rest of his theory.

As we have frequently pointed out in this book, the contradictions in a great thinker's theory (and Keynes was a logician of the first order) give the best insights into the thinker's ideological orientation. Keynes wished to furnish capitalist governments with theoretical insights that would help to save capitalism. In doing so, it was necessary for him to abandon some tenets of neoclassical theory. But, as we will see, he wanted to retain as much neoclassical ideology as possible. So he adhered to both the marginal productivity theory of distribution and the belief that the free market efficiently allocated resources (once full employment was attained), despite the fact that both these tenets of neoclassical ideology were logically tied to the belief that the free market automatically created a full employment, Pareto optimal situation. Even with theorists having the extraordinary logical ability of Keynes, ideology very frequently wins out over logic.

Keynes rejected the notion that if a capitalist economy started from a situation of full employment, then the rate of interest would automatically equate saving and investment and thus keep aggregate demand equal to aggregate supply. His major departures from the doctrines that comprised the neoclassical theory of automaticity were twofold: First, although he accepted the neoclassical notion that saving was influenced by the rate of interest, he insisted that the level of aggregate income was a far more important influence on the amount of saving than was the rate of interest. Second, he argued that saving and investment did not determine the rate of interest. The interest rate was a price that equalized the demand and supply of money—something quite different from (although not unrelated to) investment and saving.

These were very important departures indeed, because, although Keynes was unaware of it, they destroyed not only the neoclassical theory of the automaticity of the market but also the two other pillars of neoclassical ideology—the marginal productivity theory of distribution and the theory that a free, competitive market will result in a Pareto optimal allocation of resources. Keynes wanted to achieve the first result (the destruction of the belief in the automaticity of the market) but leave the other two concepts intact.

The principle that underlay his departure from the neoclassical theory of saving was referred to by Keynes as the "consumption function." He insisted that the level of consumption and the level of saving were primarily a "function of the level of income," that is, they were determined primarily by the level of income. He admitted that "substantial changes in the rate of interest . . . may make some difference"[17] in the level of saving, but this influence was much less important than the influence exerted by the level of income:

> For a man's habitual standard of life usually has first claim on his income, and he is apt to save the difference which discovers itself between his actual income and the expense of his habitual standard. . . . It is also obvious that a higher absolute level of income will tend, as a rule, to widen the gap between income and consumption. For the satisfaction of the immediate primary needs of a man and his family is usually a stronger motive than the motives toward accumulation. . . . These reasons will lead, as a rule, to a greater proportion of income being saved as real income increases.[18]

The consumption function depicted the relation of saving and consumption to the level of income. The relationship between a change in income and the resultant change in saving (or the ratio of the change in saving to the change in income) was defined as the " marginal propensity to save." The relationship between a change in income and the resultant change in consumption (or the ratio of the change in consumption to the change in income) was defined as the "marginal propensity to consume." Neither the marginal propensity to consume nor the marginal propensity to save was primarily determined by or among the primary determinants of the rate of interest.

Keynes's second major departure from the neoclassical theory of the automaticity of the market was his rejection of the neoclassical theory of the determination of the interest rate.

> The *propensity to consume* . . . determines for each individual how much of his income he will consume and how much he will reserve [save] in *some* form of command over future consumption.

But this decision having been made, there is a further decision which awaits him, namely, in *what form* he will hold the command over future consumption. . . . Does he want to hold it in the form of immediate liquid command (i.e., in money or its equivalent)? Or is he prepared to part with immediate command for a specified or indefinite period of time . . . ? In other words, what is the degree of his *liquidity-preference*—where an individual's liquidity preference is given by a schedule of the amounts of his resources . . . which he will wish to retain in the form of money in different sets of circumstances? . . .

It should be obvious that the rate of interest cannot be a return to saving or wait-ing as such. For if a man hoards his savings in cash, he earns no interest, though he saves just as much as before. On the contrary, the mere definition of the rate of interest tells us in so many words that the rate of interest is the reward for parting with liquidity for a specified period. For the rate of interest is, in itself, nothing more than the inverse proportion between a sum of money and what can be obtained for parting with control over the money in exchange for debt for a stated period of time.

Thus the rate of interest at any time, being the reward for parting with liquidity, is a measure of the unwillingness of those who possess money to part with their liquid control over it. The rate of interest is not the "price" which brings into equilibrium the demand for resources to invest with the readiness to abstain from present con-sumption. It is the "price" which equilibrates the desire to hold wealth in the form of cash with the available quantity of cash. . . . If this explanation is correct, the quan-tity of money is the other factor, which, in conjunction with liquidity preference, determines the actual rate of interest in given circumstances.[19]

The rate of interest was determined, then, by the demand for and supply of money. At any given time the supply of money was constant at a level deter-mined by the actions of the central bank or the monetary authorities. The demand for money—which was the same as the liquidity preference—was, according to Keynes, determined by three motives:

(i) the transactions motive, i.e. the need for cash for the current transaction of per-sonal and business exchanges; (ii) the precautionary motive, i.e. the desire for secu-rity as to the future cash equivalent of a certain proportion of total resources; and (iii) the speculative motive, i.e. the object of securing profit from knowing better than the market what the future will bring forth.[20]

The portion of demand for money that arose from the speculative motive was related to the rate of interest. To understand this relationship, we must understand how the price of a bond (or a security, or any kind of interest-paying I.O.U.) reflects the rate of interest. If we purchase a bond that prom-ises to pay us $1,000 in one year, and the rate of interest is 3 percent, then the current value of that bond is approximately $970 (the extra $30 being the interest we will earn in one year). If, however, the day after we purchase that bond, the rate of interest rises to 6 percent, then the value of a $1,000 bond falls to approximately $940 (the extra $60 being the interest that can be earned at 6 percent). It is obvious that if we are then forced to sell the bond, we will suffer a loss. Moreover, even if we do not anticipate being forced to sell the bond, but we do expect the interest rate to rise to 6 percent, then we are better off not to buy the bond when the interest rate is 3 percent. If we instead hold the cash and wait for the interest rate to go up, then (if our expectation about the change in the interest rate proves to be correct) we can buy the bond for $940 rather than $970, and apply the extra $30 toward the purchase of another bond with which to earn more interest.

Therefore, in Keynes's view, a portion of the demand for money depended on expectations about what will happen to the interest rate in the future. When the interest rate was very high (in relation to previous rates), very few people would expect it to go even higher in the future; consequently, very few people would hold cash for speculative purposes. At lower interest rates, more people would be inclined to believe that the interest rate would increase; consequently, more money would be held for speculative purposes by those who expected the interest rate to rise in the future. Therefore, the amount of money demanded for speculative purposes declined as the interest rate rose, and increased as the interest rate fell.

Figure 15.3 illustrates Keynes's theory of the interest rate and its relation to saving and investment. It can be contrasted to the orthodox neoclassical view illustrated in Figure 15.2. In part (a) of the figure, the demand for money reflects in part the speculative motive and hence declines as the interest rate rises. With the original supply of money (determined by the monetary authorities) r_1 was the interest rate that equated the demand for and supply of money. But at r_1 there was an excess of saving over investment, as illustrated in part (b). If this situation persisted, then aggregate demand would be less than aggregate supply. All output could not be sold. Businesses, unable to sell all that they had produced, found that their inventories of unsold goods were increasing. Each business saw only its own problem: that it had produced more than it could sell. It therefore reduced production in the next period. Most businesses, being in the same situation, did the same thing. The results were a large reduction of production, a decrease in employment, and a decline in income. With the decline in income, however, even less would be spent on goods and services in the next period. So businessmen again found that even at the lower level of production, they were unable to sell all they had produced. They again cut back production, and the downward spiral continued.

Under these circumstances, businesses had little or no incentive to expand their capital goods (because excess capacity already existed), and, therefore, investment fell drastically. Expenditures of all types plummeted. As income declined, saving declined more than proportionately. This process continued until the declines in income had reduced saving to the point where it no longer exceeded the reduced level of investment. At this low level of income, equilibrium was restored. Leakages from the income-expenditure flow were again equal to the injections into it. The economy was stabilized, but at a level where high unemployment and considerable unused productive capacity existed.

But the problem, as posed in Figure 15.3, was easily remedied. The monetary authorities could increase the supply of money to the point where $\bar{r}$ was the prevailing rate of interest (in Figure 15.3). At that interest rate, saving

Figure 15.3   Determination of the Rate of Interest and the Inequality of Saving and Investment

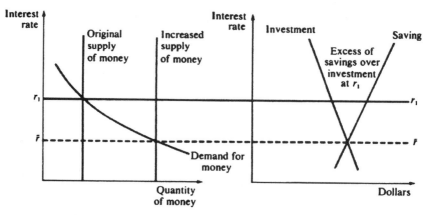

(a)   Determination of the interest rate   (b)   Inequality of saving and investment

equaled investment, aggregate demand equaled aggregate supply, and there was no problem. There were some situations, in Keynes's view, in which monetary policy (increasing or decreasing the money supply) was sufficient to maintain full employment. But there were also some situations in which monetary policy was not sufficient. Keynes was more interested in these situations because he believed them to be more realistic characterizations of the actual conditions that both precipitated and sustained depressions in capitalist economies.

The first such situation occurred when the distribution of income was so unequal (thereby increasing saving by putting more income into the hands of the wealthy, who saved much more than did workers) and the full-employment level of output and income was so high that, regardless of how low the rate of interest sank, saving and investment could not be equated. This situation is illustrated in Figure 15.4, which is self-explanatory.

But Keynes did not believe that it required such a drastic discrepancy between saving and investment to create a situation in which monetary policy was unable to prevent a disastrous depression. It was possible, he argued, that if the rate of interest that would equate the full-employment levels of saving and investment was very low, monetary policy might not be able to lower the interest rate sufficiently. If monetary authorities pushed the rate of interest so low that nearly everyone expected the interest rate to rise significantly in the future, then people would prefer to hold cash rather than securities even when the monetary authorities dramatically increased the amount of money in the system:

> Circumstances may develop in which even a large increase in the quantity of money may exert a comparatively small influence on the rate of interest. . . . Opinion about the future of the rate of interest may be so unanimous that a small change in present rates may cause a mass movement of cash [into private hoards].[21]

Figure 15.4   Situation in Which Rate of Interest Cannot Equate Full-Employment Levels of Saving and Investment

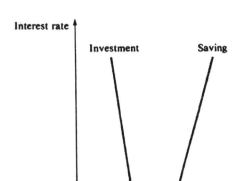

Such a situation is depicted in Figure 15.5. It can be seen that when the rate of interest approaches some minimum point, the demand for money flattens out, indicating that even with large increases in the supply of money, most of the increased money supply will be held in private hoards. In Figure 15.5, a large increase in the money supply results in a very small decline in the rate of interest and still leaves an excess of saving over investment.

In either of the situations depicted in Figures 15.4 and 15.5, the free, competitive market would lead society into a disastrous depression; monetary policy would be useless in preventing the social calamity. It was obvious that something more fundamental and more powerful was needed.

Keynes's analysis was not, in its essentials, drastically different from those offered by Marx (chapter 9) and Hobson (chapter 13). The principal cause of a depression was, in the opinion of all three thinkers, the inability of capitalists to find sufficient investment opportunities to offset the increasing levels of saving generated by economic growth. Keynes's unique contribution was to show how the relation of saving to income could lead to a stable but depressed level of income, with widespread unemployment.

Marx had believed the disease to be incurable. Hobson had prescribed measures to equalize the distribution of income and thereby reduce saving as a cure. Could Hobson's prescription work? This probably is not a very meaningful question. In most industrial capitalist countries, wealth and economic power determine political power, and those who wield power have never been willing to sacrifice it to save the economic system.

In the United States, for example, out of 300,000 nonfinancial corporations existing in 1925, the largest 200 made considerably more profit than the other 299,800 combined. The wealthiest 5 percent of the population owned virtually all the stocks and bonds and received in excess of 30 percent of the income. Needless to say, this 5 percent dominated American politics. In these circumstances, speculating about what would happen if the income and wealth were radically redistributed amounts to mere daydreaming. Keynes's answer

Figure 15.5   **Situation in Which Monetary Policy Cannot Equate Full-Employment Levels of Saving and Investment**

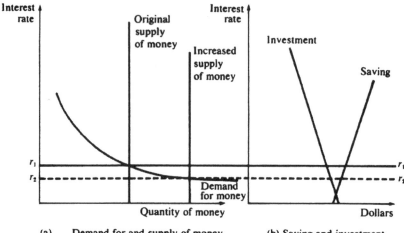

(a)   Demand for and supply of money   (b) Saving and investment

to the problem was more realistic. Government could step in when saving exceeded investment, borrow the excess saving, then spend the money on socially useful projects that would not increase the economy's productive capacity or decrease the investment opportunities of the future. This government spending would increase the injections into the spending stream and create a full-employment equilibrium. In doing so, it would not add to the capital stock. Therefore, unlike investment spending, it would not make a full-employment level of production more difficult to attain in the next period. Keynes summarized his position thus:

> Ancient Egypt was doubly fortunate, and doubtless owed to this its fabled wealth, in that it possessed *two* activities, namely, pyramid-building as well as the search for precious metals, the fruits of which, since they could not serve the needs of man by being consumed, did not stale with abundance. The Middle Ages built cathedrals and sang dirges. Two pyramids, two masses for the dead, are twice as good as one: but not so two railways from London to York.[22]

What type of expenditures ought the government to make? Keynes himself had a predilection toward useful public works such as the construction of schools, hospitals, parks, and other public conveniences. He realized, however, that this would probably benefit middle- and lower-income recipients much more than it would the wealthy. Because the wealthy had the political power, they would probably insist on policies that would not redistribute income away from them. He realized that it might be politically necessary to channel this spending into the hands of the large corporations, even though little that was beneficial to society would be accomplished directly.

> If the Treasury were to fill old bottles with banknotes, bury them at suitable depths in disused coal mines which are then filled up to the surface with town rubbish, and

leave it to private enterprise on well-tried principles of laissez faire to dig the notes up again . . . there need be no more unemployment. . . . It would indeed be more sensible to build houses and the like; but if there are political and practical difficulties in the way of this, the above would be better than nothing.[23]

Efficacy of Keynesian Policies

The depression of the 1930s dragged on until the outbreak of World War II. From 1936 (the year *General Theory* was published) to 1940, economists hotly debated the merits of Keynes's theory and policy prescriptions. When the various governments began to increase armament production rapidly, however, unemployment began to melt away. During the war years, under the stimulus of enormous government expenditures, most capitalist economies were rapidly transformed from situations of severe unemployment to acute shortages of labor.

The American armed forces mobilized 14 million people who had to be armed, quartered, and fed. Between 1939 and 1944, the output of the manufacturing, mining, and construction industries doubled, and productive capacity increased by 50 percent. The American economy produced 296,000 planes, 5,400 cargo ships, 6,500 naval vessels, 64,500 landing craft, 86,000 tanks, 2,500,000 trucks, and massive amounts of other supplies and materials of warfare.[24] In 1939, about 20 percent of the labor force was unemployed. Persistent and severe unemployment had lasted a full decade. With the outbreak of war, the problem was reversed almost instantaneously, and the American economy experienced a pressing and acute *shortage* of labor.

Most economists believed that this wartime experience proved Keynes's ideas. Capitalism could be saved, they proclaimed, by the wise use of the government's powers to tax, borrow, and spend money. Capitalism was, again, held to be a viable social and economic system. Public confidence had been restored.

After 1945, the majority of politicians joined economists in proclaiming the new Keynesian orthodoxy. In 1946, Congress passed the Employment Act, which legally obligated the government to use its taxing, borrowing, and spending powers to maintain full employment. Optimism reigned. Conferences were held to discuss the "social priorities" and "national objectives" that should guide government policy in this new Keynesian era in which depressions were to be abolished and prosperity was to be the normal state of affairs.

There is no question that the massive government expenditures of the war pulled the American economy out of a decade of stagnation and depression. But the optimism of Keynesian economists after the war has proved to be less than completely justified. To be sure, the depressions that have occurred in the United States since World War II have been substantially less severe than the Great Depression of the 1930s (thereby giving rise to the modern euphemism of *recession*, which has replaced *depression* in the vocabulary of most economists and politicians). In 1948–49, a "recession" lasted for eleven months; in 1953–54, for thirteen months; in 1957–58 for nine months; and in 1960–61 for nine months. While the Vietnam War gave added stimulus to the American economy in the 1960s, by the end of that decade the old pattern had set in again. The recession of 1969–71 lasted about two full years. Between 1973 and the early 1980s, a new, more severe, and much more perplexing crisis hit American capitalism. During that period, the American economy (and nearly every other advanced industrialized capitalist country) experienced both severe recession (with unemployment, according to the conservative statistics of the United States government, ranging from 6 percent to nearly 10 percent) and severe inflation (with the average price level in the United States increasing from 5 percent to 11 percent per year—with the prices of food, housing, medical care, and other working-class necessities rising at an even faster rate). The situation was even worse in many other capitalist countries.

After the recession of 1981–82, which was the worst recession since the 1930s, the inflation rate went down and economic conditions improved through the remainder of the 1980s. The 1990–91 recession lasted for eight months and was followed by a modest but lengthy expansion.

In the late 1980s, developments in the Soviet Union and Eastern Europe were widely acclaimed as the end of the cold war and it appeared that the stimulus for armaments expenditures might decline. Military expenditures, however, have remained, very high, with "rogue states" and "terrorist networks" having replaced the Soviet Union as the justification of massive military spending.

Still, since World War II, unemployment rates have not approached those of the Great Depression (which reached 20–25 percent by official figures and would probably have been closer to 30–35 percent had more realistic methods of defining unemployment and gathering statistics been used). Unemployment in the 1950s and early 1960s averaged 4.6 percent. With the stimulus of the Vietnam War, in the mid-1960s the rate fell to 3.5 percent. Through the 1970s and 1980s, it ranged between 5 percent and 10 percent. In the 1990s, the rate peaked at 7.9 percent just after the 1990–91 recession and steadily declined to 3.9 percent by the close of the decade. In late 2000 and throughout 2001, unemployment has been increasing as a new recession sets in.

Although the post–World War II record is certainly less impressive than the optimistic vision of many Keynesian economists writing in the 1940s, given the stagnation and near disintegration of capitalism in the 1930s, it may be said that for over six decades Keynesian policies have worked tolerably well. But as is sometimes the case in medicine, a new and previously untried cure has side effects that may be as bad as the original disease. When one looks beneath the surface of the gross national product (GNP) and employment statistics, one sees that Keynesian policies mitigated one form of capitalist crisis only to bring on two new forms, namely, a structural change to a permanent military or warfare economy and the creation of a precarious debt structure, on which the entire economy is based, that creates the possibility of an economic collapse more pervasive and severe than that of the 1930s. The Savings and Loan Crisis of 1989–91 is only a small tip of a potentially massive problem of the vulnerability of the debt structure. And the supposed "end of the cold war" has had no affect on the economy's reliance on military spending.

The Military Economy

Between 1947 and the mid-1970s, the American government spent nearly $2 trillion (numbers of that magnitude are hard to conceptualize: that figure is 2,000 billions of dollars) on military expenditures.[25] The total expenditures for wars and preparation for potential wars, past, present, and future, including both warfare and related expenditures, grew from $27.9 billion per year in 1947 to $112.3 billion in 1971.[26] These figures represent a total of 12.2 percent of GNP in 1947 and 11.1 percent in 1971. Moreover, if one analyzes the "multiplier" effect of further aggregate demand created by these military expenditures, the impact was much larger. The most careful study of these effects resulted in two estimates, constituting lower and upper limits. The conservative estimate showed that, in 1947, military expenditures accounted, directly and indirectly (through the induced or multiplier effect), for 24.4 percent of aggregate demand in 1947 and 22.2 percent in 1971. Using the higher estimate, militarism accounted for 30.5 percent of aggregate demand in 1947 and 27.8 percent in 1971.[27] In only a few of the intervening years was the figure very slightly lower, and in several of the intervening years the figure was higher. In the 1970s military spending grew at a somewhat lower rate but it virtually exploded in the 1980s. During the late 1970s many economists were predicting a severe recession was at hand. Indeed, the recession of 1981–82 was the worst since the 1930s. It was not, however, nearly as bad as most economists had predicted. The remaining years of the 1980s were years of economic prosperity. One does not have to look far to find the reason for this prosperity. Between 1980 and 1987, American military expenditures more than doubled. Defense spending was $134 billion in 1980 and had soared to $210 billion by 1983. During 1982 alone, the construction of two nuclear-powered aircraft carriers, two nuclear-powered attack submarines, and five warships; the procurement of the F-15 jet fighter; and the work of the B-1B and Stealth bomber and the MX missile created about 300,000 new jobs. General Dynamics hired 7,000 new employees to work on the M1 tank project. Rockwell International added 4,000 additional employees to work on the B-1B bomber. Boeing, Lockheed, Raytheon, McDonnell Douglass, United Technologies, and General Electric all substantially increased their workforces to produce new military hardware. The U.S. Defense Department increased its employment by 255,000 new jobs between 1981 and 1985.[28] There can be no doubt that the prosperity of the 1980s was due primarily to the huge growth in militarism. President Bush's budget proposal for the fiscal year 1991 included over $303 billion directly for defense and another $65 billion for "international affairs," "science, space, and technology," and "veterans' benefits," most of which are disguised military spending. Defense spending has remained high throughout the past decade, averaging $280 billion annually from 1990 to 2000, and seems destined to climb ever higher as the administration of George W. Bush prosecutes its new "war on terrorism."

Moreover, the correlation between changes in military spending and the cyclical instability of capitalism is very significant.[29] There seems to be little question that militarism has been the contemporary capitalist equivalent to the pyramids of Egypt and the cathedrals of the Middle Ages.

Has this militarism been a necessary response to international exigencies, or do military expenditures have unique features that make them particularly effective and desirable forms of government expenditures? A full answer to this question would necessitate an extensive discussion of the "cold war" and its putative demise—something that cannot be done within the scope of this book. A growing body of historical literature has amassed considerable evidence, however, to show that the cold war was the deliberate and fraudulent creation of American politicians, capitalists, and the capitalist-controlled press.[30] If this position is correct, then the cold war must be revived or a suitable substitute must be found. The wars in Iraq and Afghanistan might be the prototypes of a new world policing role for the United States. This could be our new cold war. Whatever position one takes on the nature of the cold war, however, two facts clearly emerge from the study of American militarism. First, militarism offers several unique and distinct advantages to capitalists over nearly any other form of government spending; and second, militarism has become so thoroughly enmeshed in the structure of the American economy that it is increasingly inconceivable that it can ever be extirpated short of a complete restructuring of the entire American social, economic, and political system.

Militarism offers innumerable advantages to large corporations. (1) It stimulates aggregate demand without redistributing income from the rich to the poor. (2) There can never be too much elaborate weaponry; government-financed research constantly renders military hardware obsolete, and horror stories convince most of the public that continued escalation of the arms race is absolutely necessary for survival. (3) The capital goods industry—the most volatile and unstable segment of a capitalist economy—is kept operating at near capacity by military production, and, yet, this does not increase the productive capacity of the capitalist economy. As a result, militarism does not worsen the persistent problem of excess aggregate productive capacity. (4) Because virtually all military production is done by giant private corporations or subcontracted to smaller private corporations, it does not compete with private profit making; on the contrary, it reduces the anarchy of the free market by giving corporations a stable core of demand not subject to the vagaries of the market. (5) Although precise statistics to substantiate this are unobtainable, most evidence points to military production being more profitable than production for the free market. (6) As Rosa Luxemburg pointed out, large military establishments are necessary to maintain and enlarge the worldwide "sphere of influence" of capitalist countries, in which profitable foreign investment and very favorable terms of trade can be assured. (7) As Veblen pointed out, jingoism, patriotism, and militarism are perhaps the most effective means of keeping workers docile and promoting the view among workers that their interests are in harmony with the interests of the capitalists.

The price that we have paid for this militarism, however, is reflected in the evolution of the military-industrial complex, in which militarism has become a permanent, thoroughly integrated cancer in the very heart of the structure of American industry.

Many of the largest and most powerful of American corporations are heavily dependent on military contracts. Equally important is the fact that a large number of cities, regions, and even whole states are heavily economically dependent on these corporations or on large military bases to support their local economies and maintain employment at a time when persistently high unemployment plagues the economy. A large reduction in the output of military hardware or in the number or size of these military bases can economically ruin whole communities. Therefore, the slightest hint of a reduction in militarism brings powerful protests from military leaders, large corporations, politicians, and labor union leaders.

In 1989 and 1990, there was a good deal of talk about the end of the cold war. Because most East European economies, including the Soviet Union, were undertaking reforms that were pushing their economies toward market capitalism, it became difficult to use the horror of communism as a pretense for massive military expenditures. Yet, there is a powerful built-in resistance to the reduction of these expenditures. If military expenditures are significantly reduced, the U.S. economy faces the prospect of stagnation and depression. It would appear as though the United States cannot allow the cold war to "cool off" to a very great extent without finding some alternative to the "dangers of communism." Iraq, Afghanistan, or any other nonindustrialized nation can never, by itself, replace the Soviet Union as the new enemy because they can be destroyed. The problem of finding an enemy to justify military expenditures is likely to grow worse.

The Debt Economy

The moderately improved performance of the American economy since World War II is in large measure attributable to a massive, ever accelerating expansion of debt. Keynes had shown how government expenditures financed by borrowing would be much more effective in stimulating aggregate demand than would expenditures financed by taxation (insofar as taxation removed some funds that would be spent anyway, part of the increase in government expenditures was offset by a decrease of private expenditures). Many of the enormous increases in government expenses have been financed by increasing government debt (at the federal, state, and local levels). In addition, while consumer debt was quite low in the period before the Great Depression (about 8.5 percent of consumer disposable income in the late 1920s), capitalists discovered that through massive advertising campaigns and a huge expansion of consumer credit, consumption demand could be effectively stimulated. By 1974, consumer debt had grown to about 17 percent of disposable income. If one includes mortgage debt in the calculation, then household debt as a percent of disposable income rose from 65 percent in 1955 to 93 percent in 1974.

In order to meet these debt-financed increases in government and consumer demand, businesses rapidly increased their debts. From 1946 to 1974, the total debt in the United States rose from $400 billion to $2,500 billion, doubling between 1960 and 1970 and accelerating even more in the 1970s and 1980s, reaching a figure of over $8,000 billion in 1988. This mushrooming of debt in the United States was merely a part of an intricately interrelated, massive increase in debt throughout all countries of the capitalist world. The debt has become so large, so interwoven, and so pyramidal that (1) it must continue to grow faster just to keep up with the growing interest charges; and (2) if a major multinational corporation or capitalist government should go bankrupt and be unable to pay its interest charges or the amortization of its debt, there is an extreme danger of a chain reaction of defaults that would be far more devastating than the worldwide financial panic of 1929. The following example illustrates this second point. Lending institutions have pyramided credit. One borrows from another in order to loan the money at a higher rate elsewhere. A major default of one borrower could render creditors (who are also large borrowers) unable to pay their interest and amortization payments. Because their creditors are also borrowers, and so on, a disastrous, worldwide chain reaction could set in.

This is not merely the nightmare of a radical alarmist. The leading conservative American business publication *Business Week* wrote in 1974 of a shocking "specter of a chain of defaults by borrowers and failures by lenders." The article continued by insisting that "the dangers are greater than in the 1930s. The amounts at risk are greater, and so is the leverage, here and abroad." The danger exists because huge amounts of money are "owed to banks whose own liquidity is all too often stretched dangerously thin."[31]

During the decade of the 1980s, the mushrooming of the debt accelerated. In 1981, the debt of the U.S. Government was $914 billion. When President Reagan left office in 1988, it was more than $2,600 billion—in eight years it had more than tripled the total prior accumulation in all of our history through 1981. The prosperity of the Reagan decade had been stimulated by government borrowing, during the 1980s, of more than $20,000 per family of four in the nation. One careful study of government debt in the decade of the 1980s has concluded that the "sense of economic well being was an illusion, an illusion based on borrowed time and borrowed money." This represented, in the opinion of the author of the study, "deliberate moral irresponsibility on a truly astonishing scale."[32] By 1990, despite a seemingly healthy economy, the federal government "bailed out" the troubled savings and loan industry. Some estimates place the cost of this rescue at $2,000 for every person in the United States. If this can happen in prosperous times, then the consequences of adverse economic circumstances leading to a collapse of the entire massive credit structure are so catastrophic that they are beyond economists' abilities to estimate. This prospect looms in 2001 as the economy enters a recession and the government has appropriated $15 billion for the airline industry and dozens of other industries are now asking for "bail outs."

Thus, we may conclude this section by repeating the fact that large increases in government expenditures, justified by their defenders on the grounds of Keynesian theory, have decreased the severity of the depressions since World War II. But this prosperity (if one can call rates of unemployment at times approaching 10 percent prosperity) has been purchased at a heavy cost. First, it has been erected on a foundation of a worldwide credit structure that constantly is in danger of a disastrous economic collapse. Second, it has resulted in a permanent war-oriented economy in which a substantial part of society's productive resources are devoted to ever more elaborate methods and means of destroying the human race.

If a capitalist government followed Keynes's prescription to create full employment, he could "see no reason to suppose that the existing system seriously misemploys the factors of production."[33] In retrospect, after more than sixty years of Keynesian-type policies, his optimism appears, shall we charitably say, ill-founded.

Ideological Foundations of Keynes's Ideas

We have already pointed out that the marginal productivity theory of distribution cannot logically explain sharp increases in unemployment in a capitalist society when real wages remain constant or decline. In addition, if wages do not reflect the marginal productivity of labor (which they cannot possibly do in this circumstance), and if there are unutilized factors of production (as there always are in a time of depression), then it is impossible, on the strictly logical grounds of neoclassical theory itself, to argue that the notions of a Pareto optimum, efficient resource allocation, and rational prices (in a word, the whole invisible-hand argument) have any actual or empirical meaning whatsoever.

At the beginning of this chapter we argued that the neoclassical ideological defense of capitalism had three principal elements: the faith that free markets would automatically adjust to a full-employment level of output; the marginal productivity theory of distribution as both a model of ideal distributive justice and a theory of how the distribution of income actually occurred; and the invisible-hand argument or the belief that a competitive capitalist economy would automatically attain a Pareto optimum in which prices were "rational" and resources were "efficiently allocated." We saw how propagating a belief in the latter two elements brought nothing but benefits to the capitalist class. The first element, however, was a mixed blessing. While teaching the universal beneficence of the capitalist market system was one thing, believing this ideology and passively standing by while the capitalist system moved through a series of convulsions toward its demise was quite another. But all three elements of neoclassical ideology form a logically integrated, mutually consistent intellectual system in which it is logically impossible to maintain any two elements without implying the third.

But this was exactly what Keynes attempted to do. He wanted to drop the assumption of the automaticity of the market in order to save capitalism from self-destruction. But he wanted to maintain faith in the marginal productivity theory of distribution and faith in the allocative efficiency of the market. He wanted government to intervene as little as possible into capitalists' quest for profits, and then only to avert disaster. However, he did mention as an aside that he personally preferred a less extreme degree of inequality in the distribution of wealth and income (but here again, with a sigh, we may repeat that universal dictum of utilitarianism—pushpin is as good as poetry).

Some neoclassical economists had expressed alarm at Keynes's ideas when they read his manuscript before its publication. So Keynes ended the *General Theory* with a note of ideological solidarity with the neoclassicists:

> If our central controls succeed in establishing an aggregate volume of output corresponding to full employment as nearly as is practicable, the classical theory [i.e., neoclassical theory] comes into its own again from this point onwards. If we suppose the volume of output to be given, i.e. to be determined by forces outside the classical scheme of thought, then there is no objection to be raised against the classical analysis of the manner in which private self-interest will determine what in particular is produced, in what proportions the factors of production will be combined to produce it, and how the value of the final product will be distributed among them. Again, if we have dealt otherwise with the problem of thrift, there is no objection to be raised against the modern classical theory as to the degree of consilience between private and public advantage . . .
>
> To put the point concretely, I see no reason to suppose that the existing system seriously misemploys the factors of production which are in use. There are, of course, errors of foresight; but these would not be avoided by centralising decisions. . . . Within this field the traditional advantages of individualism . . . still hold good.
>
> Whilst, therefore, the enlargement of the functions of government, involved in the task of adjustment to one another the propensity to consume the inducement to invest, would seem to a nineteenth century publicist or a contemporary American financier to be a terrific encroachment on individualism, I defend it, on the contrary, both as the only practicable means of avoiding the destruction of existing economic forms in their entirety and as the condition of the successful functioning of individual initiative [i.e., profit making].[34]

Some writers, who have misleadingly tried to portray Keynes as a radical reformer, have made much of an empty phrase coined by Keynes: "the euthanasia of the rentier." We have already seen that Keynes believed that there was "social and psychological justification for significant inequalities of incomes and wealth."[35] He had faith, however, that there were forces at work in a capitalist system that automatically tended, in the long run, to mitigate the extremes of inequality. Following the logic of the marginal productivity theory of distribution, he concluded that the rate of return to capital would inevitably decline as the quantity of capital accumulated. His belief that this would tend to lessen the degree of inequality on income was nearly identical to that of Bastiat (which we criticized in chapter 8). The fallacy of this view, as was pointed out by Marx in the context of his own theory of the tendency of the profit rate to fall, was that it was entirely possible for the share of income going to the owners of capital to increase even though the rate of return on capital declined (see chapter 9). This was the only hope for greater equality of income within capitalism that Keynes explicitly stated. Furthermore, as we have seen, Keynes believed that in the short run, in order to stimulate employment, real wages would have to fall and profits would have to increase.

Keynes's passage describing the "euthanasia of the rentier" is quoted below. The interested reader can reread the discussion in chapter 8 on the ideas of Bastiat—perhaps the most conservative economist of the nineteenth century—to compare this passage from Keynes's writings and an almost identical passage from Bastiat's:

> I feel sure that . . . it would not be difficult to increase the stock of capital up to a point where its marginal efficiency had fallen to a very low figure. This would not mean that the use of capital instruments would cost almost nothing, but only that the return from them would have to cover little more than their exhaustion by wastage and obsolescence together with some margin to cover risk and the exercise of skill and judgement. . . .
>
> Now, though this state of affairs would be quite compatible with some measure of individualism [i.e., capitalism], yet it would mean the euthanasia of the rentier, and, consequently, an euthanasia of the cumulative oppressive power of the capitalist to exploit the scarcity value of capital.[36]

It is hard to imagine a more obscurantist passage than this. Surely Keynes knew (being a logician of the highest order) that a diminution of the rate of return on capital was quite consistent with an increase in the share of income going to capitalists. Surely he knew that most capitalists and many conservative economists believed that capitalism had long since passed the point at which capitalists received only that return on their capital that would "cover little more than their exhaustion . . . and obsolescence together with some margin to cover risk and exercise of skill and judgment." Surely he knew that the use of the term *euthanasia* was pure ideological obscurantism. And how could Keynes write that under the present capitalist system "there is no objection to be raised against the classical analysis of . . . how the value of the final product will be distributed" and simultaneously speak of the "oppressive power of the capitalist to exploit the scarcity-value of capital?"

With such confusion and obscurantism it is not surprising that Keynes hastened to reassure the functionless, rentier capitalists "that the euthanasia of the rentier, of the functionless investor, will be nothing sudden, merely a gradual but prolonged continuance of what we have seen recently in Great Britain, and will need no revolution.[37] Still eager to convince these capitalists that he had their interests at heart, Keynes assured the rentier that there was no case to be made "for a system of State Socialism. . . . It is not the ownership of the instruments of production which it is important for the State to assume."[38] He only wanted the government to act in such a manner as to make possible continued profit making. And such government functions could, he promised them, "be introduced gradually and without a break in the general traditions of society."[39]

Notes to Chapter 15

1. Figures taken from Louis M. Hacker, *The Course of American Economic Growth and Development* (New York: Wiley, 1970), pp. 300–301.

2. See Lester V. Chandler, *America's Greatest Depression* (New York: Harper and Row, 1970), pp. 40–41.

3. U.S. Congress, *Senate Hearings before a Subcommittee of the Committee on Manufacturers*, 72d Cong., 1st sess. (Washington, DC: Government Printing Office, 1932), p. 239.

4. Quoted in Chandler, *America's Greatest Depression*, pp. 41–42.

5. Quoted in Leo Huberman, *We the People* (New York: Monthly Review Press, 1964), p. 260.

6. John Maynard Keynes, *Laissez-Faire and Communism* (New York: New Republic, 1926), p. 47.

7. Ibid., pp. 47–48.

8. Ibid., pp. 130–31.

9. John Maynard Keynes, *The General Theory of Employment, Interest and Money* (New York: Harcourt, Brace and World, 1936), p. 384.

10. T.R. Malthus, *An Essay on the Principle of Population and a Summary View of the Principle of Population*, ed. A. Flew (Baltimore: Penguin, 1970), p. 144.

11. Keynes, *General Theory*, p. 374.

12. John Maynard Keynes, *Essays in Biography* (New York: Norton, 1963) p. 120.

13. For examples of this, see Robert Lekachman, *The Age of Keynes* (New York: McGraw-Hill, 1975), pp. 59–61.

14. Keynes, *General Theory*, p. 5.

15. Ibid., p. 17.

16. Ibid., pp. 13–14.

17. Ibid., pp. 95–96.

18. Ibid., p. 97.

19. Ibid., pp. 166–68.

20. Ibid., p. 170.

21. Ibid., p. 172.

22. Ibid., p. 131.

23. Ibid., p. 129.

24. Hacker, *Economic Growth and Development*, p. 325.

25. The data on military expenditures are difficult to compute because much of this money is hidden in what are classified by government statisticians as nonmilitary expenditures. This figure, as well as much of the other data used in this section, is taken from the most thorough

and comprehensive study of American military expenditures yet undertaken by an American economist: James M. Cypher, "Military Expenditures and the Performance of the Postwar U.S. Economy: 1947–1971," Ph.D. diss., University of California, Riverside, 1973.

26. Ibid., pp. 136–37.

27. Ibid., pp. 164–65.

28. This data taken from Benjamin Friedman, *Days of Reckoning* (New York: Random House, 1988), pp. 273–74.

29. Cypher, "Military Expenditures," pp. 328–32.

30. See, for example D.F. Fleming, *The Cold War and Its Origins*, 2 vols. (New York: Doubleday, 1961); Gar Alperovitz, *Atomic Diplomacy: Hiroshima and Potsdam* (New York: Simon and Schuster, 1965); David Horowitz, ed., *Corporations and the Cold War*, (New York: Monthly Review Press, 1969); David Horowitz, *Empire and Revolution* (New York: Random House, 1960); Gabriel Kolko, *The Politics of War* (New York: Vintage, 1970); I.F. Stone, *The Hidden History of the Korean War* (New York: Monthly Review Press, 1952); Stephen E. Ambrose, *Rise to Globalism* (London: Penguin, 1971).

31. These data, as well as those of the following paragraph, are taken from Douglas Dowd, "Accumulation and Crisis," *Socialist Review* 5, no. 2 (1975): 27–30.

32. Friedman, *Days of Reckoning*, pp. 5, 24.

33. Keynes, *General Theory*, p. 379.

34. Ibid., pp. 378–80.

35. Ibid., p. 374.

36. Ibid., p. 375–76.

37. Ibid.

38. Ibid., p. 378.

39. Ibid.

Chapter 16

Annulment of the Myth of the Measurable Productivity of Capital: The Writings of Sraffa

The three fundamental tenets of neoclassical utilitarian ideology are: the faith that the invisible hand of the competitive market harmonizes all interests through free exchange, creates rational prices, and leads to an efficient allocation of resources; the faith that the free market will automatically create a full-employment equilibrium; and the belief that the wage rate is equal to the value of the marginal product of labor and that the profit rate (or interest rate) is equal to the value of the marginal product of capital; hence, by implication, each social class gets the value created by the factors it happens to own. In chapters 14 and 15 we discussed the first two of these tenets. In this chapter we will discuss the last—the marginal productivity theory of distribution.

Current State of Neoclassical Distribution Theory

Neoclassical economics thoroughly dominates contemporary, conventional academic economics. Orthodox Keynesian economics has become merely a branch of neoclassical theory, although, as we will see in chapter 18, another tradition, post-Keynesianism, strongly opposes neoclassicism. The marginal productivity theory of distribution is a settled, unquestioned article of faith among nearly all neoclassical economists (with qualifications that we shall discuss in the next chapter). The contemporary neoclassical distribution theory has not essentially changed from the formulations by Clark and Böhm-Bawerk (chapter 11), although it has received a much more mathematically elegant statement in the writings of contemporary neoclassicists.

    The current state of neoclassical distribution theory has been summarized in a book by Professor Martin Bronfenbrenner entitled *Income Distribution Theory*. The book is an accurate reflection of prevailing economic orthodoxy. The author begins the preface by stating:

> This is an old-fashioned income distribution book. It was written by a theoretical economist and concentrates on economic theory. It follows the tradition of John Bates Clark's *Distribution of Wealth* (1899). . . .
>
> What makes the book old-fashioned is, primarily, its content of reformulation and restatement. . . . I am unwilling to discard neoclassical economics, either marginalism or the production function either at the micro-economic or the macro-economic level.[1]

Bronfenbrenner does indeed follow the neoclassical orthodoxy, both in content and in sequence of argument. He begins with the theory of the profit-maximizing firm that buys inputs, mixes them to produce (in accordance with a standard, "well-behaved" neoclassical "production function") an output to be sold in the market. The production function allows for smooth, continuous substitution of the factors of production in order that the profit-maximizing combination of factors can be selected. At the level of microeconomics, there are no laborers or capitalists, only owners of inputs labeled a, b, c, and so on.

> A microeconomic production process carried on by a single firm will be represented by a production function:
>
> $$x = F(a, b, c \ldots)$$
>
> . . . The first partial derivatives of . . . [the production function] are the marginal products or marginal productivities of the inputs a, b, c, . . . It is ordinarily assumed that any two inputs a and b can be substituted for each other in production. . . . The second partial derivatives of the production function are ordinarily negative. . . . This is one form of the principle of *diminishing returns to inputs*.[2]

These assumptions give the familiar value of the marginal product (*VMP*) curves for each input. These curves, as we saw in our discussion of Clark, slope downward and constitute the profit-maximizing firm's demand curve for a factor. Then it is the case that "with all prices known, the optimum [i.e., profit-maximizing] employments of productive inputs are determined by equality between input prices and their respective v.m.p. values."[3] That is, each factor gets exactly what it creates, at the margin.

Then the analysis shifts to the macroeconomic level. The a, b, and c that, at the microeconomic level, had no social, political, or economic significance attached to their differentiation, now become capital and labor. Their rewards now become interest and wages. According to Bronfenbrenner, "Classical and neoclassical economists unite in treating the economy as a firm or industry writ large."[4] There is no problem of aggregate demand being sufficient to buy the output of this "firm writ large," because the ideological value of the marginal productivity theory of distribution is equally great within the automaticity tradition of Say, or the Keynesian tradition: "The maintenance of aggregate demand and expenditure either comes about naturally, according to Say's Law, . . . or is provided by some other branch of economic administration such as monetary or fiscal policy."[5]

In this circumstance, capital and labor are merely two factors of production to be used by our gigantic "firm writ large" in such a manner as to maximize profits. The demand for labor, like the *a, b,* and *c* of the microeconomic analysis, slopes downward and reflects the value of labor's contribution at the margin: "The labor demand function . . . slopes downward on marginal-productivity grounds."[6] It logically follows that laborers receive the value of their marginal product. The analysis for capital is identical. Either labor or capital could have been *a, b,* or *c* in the microeconomic analysis. Both receive the value of their marginal product.

A problem arises at this point, however. While it is perfectly clear what we mean when we aggregate the amount of labor employed (in order to ascertain its marginal productivity), it is by no means clear what we mean when we aggregate capital. If we say 100 laborers worked for one week, the meaning is unambiguous. But what does it mean to say 100 capitals worked for one week? One hundred factories? Of various sizes? One hundred shovels? Fifty factories and 25 shovels and 25 oil refining plants? This is obviously nonsensical. One piece of capital can be anything ranging from a screwdriver to a gigantic plant that employs tens of thousands of workers. The obvious answer for practically minded, profit-maximizing capitalists is to aggregate capital equipment according to the price of each item. If the screwdriver has a price of $1 and the gigantic plant has a price of $500 million, then together they constitute capital worth $500,000,001. This is all the practical capitalist needs to know in order to make his profits. But the capitalist makes the profit while the neoclassical economist constructs the ideology.

The capitalist's measure of total capital will not do for the purposes of the neoclassical ideology. In marginal productivity theory, *the price of capital is determined by its profitability, and its profitability depends on its productivity.* Thus, as Bronfenbrenner correctly points out, in the neoclassical theory of capital "we speak of an asset . . . price as the *capitalized value* of its income."[7] In other words, the price of a capitalized good is the present discounted dollar value (or capitalized value) of all of the income that will be yielded by that capital good. In neoclassical theory, however, the income that capital will yield is determined by its productivity.

Therefore, neoclassical economists must first aggregate capital in order to ascertain its productivity. But they cannot aggregate different capital goods according to their prices, because the price of capital depends on its productivity (which cannot be calculated until capital is first aggregated). The problem is identical to Clark's problem that was criticized by Veblen. Clark had said that there were both capital goods and the general capital that consisted of some "continuum" of a "physical abiding entity." Veblen correctly pointed out that the

> continuum in which the "abiding entity" of capital resides is a continuity of ownership, not a physical fact. The continuity, in fact, is of an immaterial nature, a matter of legal rights, of contract, of purchase and sale. Just why this patent state of the case is overlooked, as it somewhat elaborately is, is not easily seen. . . . [Not over-

looking this obvious fact] would, of course, . . . upset the law of the "natural" remuneration of labor and capital to which Mr. Clark's argument looks forward from the start.[8]

The amount of capital must be quantified totally independently of any resort to prices, or else the neoclassical marginal productivity theory of distribution, with its explanation of and rationalization for the existing wage and profit rates, is utterly defenseless. Böhm-Bawerk suggested using the "average period of production" as a measure of capital. Most neoclassical economists have declined to use this measure for two reasons: First, it is a complex index number consisting of four separate, disparate magnitudes—the quantity of land, the quantity of labor, the length of the time period, and the distribution of the usage of the land and labor over the different time segments making up the total time period. Böhm-Bawerk's solution was messy, and most neoclassical economists sensed from the very beginning that it involved insuperable "index number problems." Therefore, most neoclassical economists stuck with Clark's notion of capital as a continuum of some mysterious, physical abiding entity. Adding up this entity would give the neoclassicist the total quantity of capital, thus enabling him to compute the marginal productivity, income yields, and present value of capital.

The second reason for rejecting Böhm-Bawerk's solution was that it was dangerously close, in its basic conception of capital, to the labor theory perspective. In Böhm-Bawerk's view, only land and labor were originally or ultimately factors of production. Capital existed only because of the time element of production. It is but a short step from this conception of production to one that sees production as the transformation of preexisting natural resources, a transformation effected by labor and by labor alone.

Thus, Bronfenbrenner follows the dominant school of neoclassicists in rejecting Böhm-Bawerk's definition of capital: "We do not . . . follow the tradition that regards labor and land as 'original' inputs or factors of production, whose productivity is supposed to embody the productivity of 'derived' inputs like capital. In other words, the marginal productivity of capital has meaning apart from the productivities of labor and land."[9]

What then was the "continuum" or the "physical abiding entity" by virtue of which capital could be aggregated independently of any knowledge of prices? Clark had a faith that the entity was there but gave it no name. Later neoclassical economists continued to have Clark's faith but did venture to give the entity a variety of names. Bronfenbrenner lists four of the names that various neoclassicists have assigned to the entity—"putty," "jelly," "leets," and "meccano sets"—and then proceeds to argue as though conjuring a name (or even four names) for the entity actually creates it. His theory, he tells the reader, rests on several assumptions. Among these is the assumption that "capital instruments . . . will . . . be homogenized . . . into all-purpose machines—'putty' or 'jelly' or 'leets' or 'meccano sets'—with uniform lengths of life. That is to say, capital will be treated as malleable and plastic in the long run, and as having uniform marginal productivity."[10] On the basis of this assumption, capital is found to receive, like labor, a reward equal to its marginal productivity.

In the most complete and consistent mathematical and verbal summary of the neoclassical theory of production and distribution yet written, C.E. Ferguson follows exactly Bronfenbrenner's sequence of argument. Ferguson begins with microeconomic theory in which the factors of production are referred to as merely "x_i's." Then he moves to macroeconomic theory:

> The theory of derived input demand, developed in chapters 6, 8, and 9 [of Ferguson's book], constitutes the microeconomic theory of distribution. By analogy the macroeconomic theory of distribution is obtained, together with the conventional "rules," such as equality of the marginal product and real wage rate under perfect competition. To specialize the theory to two homogeneous inputs, labor and capital, one has only to substitute K and L for the x_i's in chapters 6 and 9.[11]

Once again (and the equivalent analysis could be quoted from hundreds of contemporary books by neoclassicists) Ferguson has simply shifted from the unspecified and undifferentiated x_i's of his microeconomic theory to an aggregate of pure, undifferentiated capital containing some "abiding entity" that permits its aggregation independently of any knowledge of prices.

The necessity of deriving a purely physical aggregate for capital lies at the heart of neoclassical aggregate distribution theories that attempt to show that interest (all profits are assumed to be interest when the economy is in a position of general equilibrium) is merely the return to capital—a return that reflects and is determined by the productivity of capital. But the aggregation of capital and the determination of its marginal productivity has an importance in neoclassical economic theory that extends far beyond the confines of the marginal productivity theory of distribution. In the previous chapter, when we discussed Keynes's attempts to reject the notion of the automaticity of the market while continuing to defend the invisible-hand theory and the distribution theory, we stated that one cannot reject any one of these ideological tenets of neoclassicism and logically maintain the other two. The three tenets are theoretically and logically interconnected, and the single most important theoretical interconnection among the three ideological tenets is constituted by the neoclassical theory of capital.

In distribution theory, the importance of aggregating capital (independently of prices) is obvious: without such an aggregation one cannot derive the marginal product schedules of either capital or labor (because, in this theory, labor's productivity depends in part on the quantity of capital in use). In the theory that the free market will automatically adjust to full employment, a central assertion is that, if saving were to increase sharply and thereby lower the rate of interest, then large amounts of investment would be necessary in order to increase the amount of capital, or to increase the ratio of capital per worker, to the point where the marginal productivity of capital is equal to the interest rate. In other words, the neoclassical theory of the automaticity of the market depends entirely on a universally present *inverse* relation between the interest rate and the ratio of capital per worker. Such a theory has no meaning if we cannot aggregate capital and determine its marginal productivity. Finally, in the invisible-hand theory, or neoclassical welfare economics, the notion of an efficient allocation of capital among different industries and the notion of an efficient allocation of resources over different points in time (both absolutely necessary to neoclassical welfare economics) have no meaning whatsoever and involve logical inconsistencies if (1) we cannot aggregate capital and determine its marginal productivity, (2) the marginal productivity of capital does not decrease as the quantity of capital (relative to the quantity of labor) increases, and (3) lower interest rates do not invariably lead to increased ratios of capital to labor.

Thus, the notion that capital represents a physical continuum containing an abiding entity is central to the entire neoclassical ideology. This is recognized and acknowledged by those neoclassical economists who really understand the meaning underlying the elaborate mathematical structure that constitutes their theory. Thus, Ferguson correctly states:

> The neoclassical theories of distribution and growth are clearly derivative theories, the former depending largely upon the theory of production, the latter upon capital theory. The theories of capital and production are more closely integrated and more fundamental. But in the last analysis neoclassical theory, in its simple and not-so-simple forms, depends upon the basic nature of the 'thing" called *capital*.[12]

What is the basic nature of capital? From the time of publication of Clark's *The Distribution of Wealth* through the 1950s, neoclassical economists were content to leave unexamined the question of the basic nature of the abiding entity of capital. All of this changed dramatically in the 1960s, when neoclassical economists were jolted from their conservative complacency and put on the defensive.

In 1962, Paul Samuelson, the most influential of all contemporary neoclassical economists (and whom we will discuss in the next chapter), found it necessary to label Clark's notion of capital as the "J.B. Clark neoclassical fairy tale." Samuelson admitted that Clark's notion of capital could not be logically or empirically defended but argued that it was an exceedingly useful "parable" that could, by analogy, illustrate "truths" that could not be directly formulated and defended. Samuelson's 1962 article was entitled "Parable and Realism in Capital Theory: The Surrogate Production Function."[13] It argued that neoclassical production and capital theories were not scientific truths but parables that could illustrate truths.

Ferguson, being one of the most astute and insightful of the neoclassical economists, recognized that Samuelson was right; these theories were mere parables. But he also recognized that these parables constituted the very heart of the entire neoclassical theory:

> To use Clark's analogy, capital is like a waterfall. Every second, different water passes over the fall; but the fall itself remains the same. That is, . . . there is a *real* substance called capital whose depletion is continuously replaced so that the substance itself remains homogeneous.
>
> Using this simple notion, a succession of economists too numerous to mention have developed the modern version of simple neoclassical theory, the "J.B. Clark neoclassical fairy tale." Of course, elaborate versions of the theory may be constructed. But the simple version yields the simple parables upon which we base our understanding of much of the real economic world. In particular, these parables give us a direct relation between the sphere of production and the market and establish the basis for all of microeconomic pricing theory, which is, of course, the heart of neoclassical theory.[14]

But neither Samuelson nor Ferguson is a critic of neoclassicism. On the contrary, they *defend* the theory. Ferguson states that his theory is "a generalized form of the (aggregate) neoclassical theory of production . . . and distribution, or what Samuelson calls the 'J.B. Clark neoclassical fairytale.' So far as production and distribution are concerned, the model seems to be a useful and satisfactory approximation to reality."[15]

What had occurred to put the neoclassical economists on the defensive in the 1960s? Why had the most capable defenders of neoclassical theory admitted that their truths were based on fairy tales and parables? The answer to these questions is that in 1960 one of the most important books in the history of economic thought was published—Piero Sraffa's *Production of Commodities by Means of Commodities.*[16] The original purpose of the book was to solve Ricardo's problem of finding an invariant measure of value, a problem that has always plagued the labor theory of value. The book had an incredibly long gestation period of nearly forty years,[17] but once it was published, it not only succeeded in fulfilling its original purpose (finding an invariant measure of value) but also provided a devastating and decisive critique of neoclassical capital theory and distribution theory—all in eighty-seven pages of text and three appendixes. Each of these two accomplishments is of great significance in the history of the development of economic theories. In the rest of this chapter, we will consider his critique of neoclassical theory, and in chapter 18, we will consider Sraffa's construction of an invariant measure of value.

Sraffa's Critique of Neoclassical Theory

The neoclassical economists have attempted to base their theory of distribution on the general propositions of market exchange and the technical conditions of production embodied in the production function. They believe that this makes their theory so general that it requires no knowledge of economic institutions, economic history, or social and political institutions to explain how income is distributed. On a microeconomic level, they have attempted to show how the valuation (based on utility) of final consumer goods creates a demand schedule for factors of production (based on their marginal productivities as determined by the production function). This demand for factors, in conjunction with the supply of these factors (usually taken to be fixed and constant), determines the prices of the factors—and hence the incomes of factor owners.

The most obvious criticism, which has been made for decades (and continuously ignored), is that the demand for commodities and the supply of factors are significantly influenced by the distribution of income. This involves a circularity from which the theory, on the micro-level, could never escape. Nevertheless, the theorists have not hesitated to aggregate the categories of marginal productivity distribution theory in order to provide a macroeconomic ideology justifying the class distribution of income between profit and wages.

Neoclassical distribution theory has been refined significantly since the time of John Bates Clark, but the guiding light is still, as it was with Clark, to demonstrate that in this, the most just of all possible worlds, "what a social class gets is, under natural law, what it contributes to the general output of industry."[18]

One of the first attacks on this theory came from Professor Joan Robinson.[19] While we must certainly give Robinson her due in this critical revival, she has acknowledged her indebtedness to Sraffa for some of her most important theoretical points.[20] The most important point made by Robinson was that it is impossible "to find a unit in which capital may be measured as a number, i.e., an index, which is independent of relative prices and distribution, so that it may be inserted in a production function where along with labour . . . it may explain the level of national output."[21]

Capital, as we have seen, must be reducible to a single homogeneous quantity if one is to be able to calculate its marginal productivity in the production function. G.C. Harcourt has written the most thorough and insightful survey of the contemporary economic literature in capital theory. He found, in accord with our statements in the first section of this chapter, that the neoclassical economists simply assume such a homogeneous entity or substance and give it a name. This substance is supposedly convertible, at will and without cost, into any and all concrete forms of capital. These patently absurd assumptions gave rise to the debate about methods of quantifying capital that begin with the recognition that capital is heterogeneous and that the production function is not a smooth, continuously differentiable function.[22]

The first step in investigating this issue is to substitute a list of "recipes"of all possible combinations of productive inputs and the resultant outputs in place of the neoclassical "production function." We then accept the notion that profit maximization is the motive force determining the choice of productive techniques that capitalists will use. This assumption is accepted by neoclassical economists and Marxist economists (and almost all others).

Profit maximization will lead to the choice of a single productive technique (where profits are maximized), which is determined, given the different recipes for production, by the rate of interest and the wage rate. The question arises immediately of what changes in productive techniques, or recipes of production, can be expected from changes in the wage rate and the rate of interest.

Sraffa first effectively demonstrated the answer to this question in part 3 of his book, entitled "Switch in Methods of Production."[23] This demonstration led to an avalanche of articles debating the issue of "switching techniques."[24] Although the arguments were very esoteric, the general principles established are rather simple and of monumental importance in the history of economic doctrines. They represent the logical and theoretical destruction of the entire intellectual tradition of utilitarian economics as embodied in the dominant, orthodox neoclassical theory of the past century.

Our demonstration of the switching (or, more properly, reswitching) of productive techniques will be in two parts. First, we will treat capital as a "period of production" concept following the definition of Böhm-Bawerk. In this case, our demonstration of reswitching can be purely verbal. Next we will consider existing commodity inputs as capital and demonstrate the phenomenon of reswitching. This demonstration will require simple mathematical formulas and graphs.

In demonstrating the logical inconsistency of Böhm-Bawerk's notion of the period of production as a measure of capital, we will first describe a possible situation in which Böhm-Bawerk's definition of capital can yield results that are consistent with the conclusions of the marginal productivity theory of distribution. Then we will describe a situation in which Böhm-Bawerk's definition of capital leads to logical contradictions within the marginal productivity theory.

Assume that there are two techniques by which a commodity can be produced. Technique A involves a large labor input, but this labor time is concentrated in the late stages of the productive process. Technique B involves a smaller labor input where the labor time is concentrated in the early phases of the productive process. If wages are very low and the rate of interest is very high, technique A will be most profitable and thus be chosen. If wages begin to rise and the rate of interest begins to fall, it is obvious that a point will be reached where technique B will become more profitable. As this trend in interest rates and wages continues, technique B will continue to be the most profitable, regardless of how high wages go (or how low the interest rate falls). This is the orthodox case and is perfectly consistent with the conclusions of neoclassical theory.

But now suppose that in technique A, the bulk of the labor is applied very early in the production process. In technique B, suppose we have a *longer* production period with a small amount of labor applied at the beginning of the period and a large amount of labor applied toward the end of the period. The total labor input in technique B exceeds that of technique A, but the labor input of technique A exceeds either the small, early labor input or the large, late labor input of technique B taken separately.

At very high interest rates (and low wage rates), the compounding effect of the interest rate makes the cost of the labor applied early in technique B (remember, it has a longer production period than technique A) grow so large that it is higher than the wage and interest costs involved in technique A. Therefore, technique A is the low-cost technique, and it will be used.

As the interest rate declines (and the wage rate increases), it will reach a point where the total cost of technique B will be less than that of technique A, because most of the labor in technique B is applied at the end of the period and the compounding effect of the small, early labor input is not so significant. Therefore, the profit-maximizing capitalist will switch to technique B.

But if the interest rate continues to decline and the wage rate continues to increase, the compounding effect of the interest rate becomes even less important. Conversely, the increasing wage rate becomes more important. The larger total labor input of technique B eventually must make it the more expensive productive process. The capitalist will reswitch to technique A. It is this reswitching of techniques that is impossible in neoclassical capital and distribution theory. Proof that reswitching is possible is proof that neoclassical capital and distribution theory is false; that is, none of the conclusions of neoclassical distribution theory can hold.

When the rate of interest decreases, the profit-maximizing firm will always, in neoclassical theory, employ more capital. Similarly, when the wage rate increases, neoclassical economics (and Keynesian economics) tells us that the profit-maximizing firm will always hire less labor. With a given level of output, as nearly all economists from Ricardo onward have clearly recognized, an increase in the wage rate always involves (or necessitates) a decrease in the rate of interest. According to the neoclassical marginal productivity theory (and neoclassical welfare economics and the neoclassical theory of self-adjusting markets), an increase in the wage rate accompanied by a decrease in the rate of interest *must always* lead the profit-maximizing firm to increase the ratio of capital to labor used in the production process; that is, they *must* substitute capital for labor and switch to a more capital-intensive technique of production.

In the example we have just described, the logical impossibility of using Böhm-Bawerk's definition of capital in neoclassical theory is obvious. As we have said before, Böhm-Bawerk's measure of capital, the average period of production, is an index measuring *both* the time involved in the production process and the amount of labor used at various points during that time period. For neoclassical theory to make any sense at all (using this measure of capital), it is absolutely necessary for the theory to tell us, in our example, which production technique, A or B, is the more capital intensive.

Technique B involves both a longer period of production and more labor. Does this make it more capital intensive or more labor intensive? The answer to this question must be given in a clear, logical, and unambiguous manner, or the entire elaborate structure of neoclassical economic theory disintegrates.

But the answer is anything but obvious. Neoclassical theory has never given any criterion whatsoever for judging whether technique A or B is more capital intensive *except* that, when the rate of interest decreases and the wage rate increases, the profit-maximizing firm will always switch from a less capital-intensive technique to a more capital-intensive technique. In our example, we saw that at very high interest rates (and correspondingly low wage rates) technique A involved lower costs and hence was the profit-maximizing technique. As the interest rate declined (and the wage rate increased), technique B became less costly. Therefore, the profit-maximizing firm switched from technique A to technique B. Because a decrease in the interest rate (and an increase in the wage rate) leads a profit-maximizing firm to switch from technique A to technique B, neoclassical theory *must*, if it is to make any sense or have any logical consistency, conclude that technique B is more capital intensive than technique A.

But we also saw in the example that as the interest rate continued to decline to very low levels (and the wage rate continued to increase), a point was reached where technique A once again became the profit-maximizing technique. The firm switched (or reswitched) from B to A. Now with a decline in the interest rate leading to a switch from B to A, it becomes absolutely necessary for neoclassical theory to define technique A as being more capital intensive than technique B.

During the entire process, techniques A and B remained unchanged. Yet, we have seen that neoclassical theory requires us to define B as being more capital intensive than A and also to define A as being more capital intensive than B. Neoclassical theory is thus shown to be built on a logical contradiction from which there is absolutely no escape.

The point is that the identical assortment of physical capital goods used at identical points in time under identical conditions creates widely divergent capital values depending on the prevailing rates of interest and wages. Furthermore, the relative costs of producing different commodities change even though the physical conditions of production may be identical. Sraffa correctly concluded that he had succeeded in

> showing the impossibility of aggregating the "periods" belonging to the several quantities of labor into a single magnitude which could be regarded as representing the quantity of capital. The reversals in the direction of the movement of relative prices, in the face of unchanged methods of production, cannot be reconciled with *any* notion of capital as a measurable quantity independent of distribution and prices.[25]

But while Böhm-Bawerk's measure of capital has been proved to involve logical contradictions, we must also look at Clark's conception of capital and consider only the immediate production period in which labor works with capital that consists of previously produced commodities in order to see if a logically consistent measure of capital is possible. We must use a few equations and a few simple graphs to illustrate this case.

For the utmost simplicity, we assume an economy producing only one capital good and one consumer good (the demonstration can be extended mathematically to include any number of capital goods and consumer goods). We also assume that there are two different techniques of production, each involving recipes by which both goods are produced.

In equilibrium, the price of each good will equal the wage cost plus the interest on the capital used in production plus an amount equal to the capital used up or destroyed in the production process. Therefore, we can write two price (or cost) equations for the two goods.[26] These equations will apply whichever technique of production is used:

$$1 = l_a w + c_a p_c (r + d),$$ (16.1)

and

$$p_c = l_c w + c_c p_c (r + d),$$ (16.2)

where 1 is the price of the consumption good (i.e., it is the *numeraire*); l_a and c_a are the amounts of labor and capital used in producing the consumption good; p_c is the price of the capital good; l_c and c_c are the amounts of labor and capital used in the production of the capital good; w is the wage rate and r is the interest rate; and d is the percentage of the capital that is actually used up or destroyed in the production process.

From these two equations, a mathematical relationship between the wage rate and the interest rate can be derived:

$$w = \frac{1 - c_c (r + d)}{l_a + (l_c c_a - l_a c_c)(r + d)}.$$ (16.3)

This mathematical relationship between the wage rate (w) and the interest rate (r) can be shown by a line on a graph. The line showing the relationship between r and w can have any one of three possible shapes, which are illustrated in three panels of Figure 16.1. Which shape the r-w line (the line showing the relationship between r and w) will have depends entirely on the ratios of physical capital to labor in the two industries (or, in Marx's terminology, the organic compositions of capital in the two industries). The ratio of physical capital to labor in the capital good industry is c_c / l_c; in the consumer good industry the ratio is c_a / l_a. When the ratios are equal, the line is straight, as is illustrated in part (a) of Figure 16.1. When the ratios are unequal, the line is either concave or convex, as is illustrated in parts (b) and (c).

Figure 16.2 illustrates how to tell which of two techniques will have the lower costs and hence will be chosen by the profit-maximizing firm. The curve that lies farther from the origin of the graph will always represent the least costly technique of production (because for any given wage rate, the curve farther from the origin yields a higher interest rate). In the figure, the

Figure 16.1   **Three Possible Relationships Between *r* and *w***

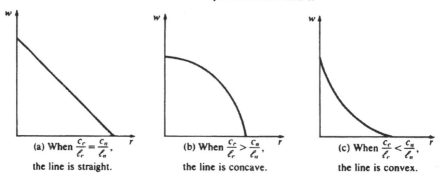

(a) When $\frac{c_c}{\ell_c} = \frac{c_a}{\ell_a}$, the line is straight.

(b) When $\frac{c_c}{\ell_c} > \frac{c_a}{\ell_a}$, the line is concave.

(c) When $\frac{c_c}{\ell_c} < \frac{c_a}{\ell_a}$, the line is convex.

two curves labeled M and N represent the two different production processes.

At interest rates above r_1 (and, correspondingly, wage rates below w_1), technique N is the less costly technique that the profit-maximizing firm will choose. That portion of line N representing interest rates between r_1 and r_0 is depicted by a heavy line, indicating that at these rates technique N will be chosen as the less costly, more profitable technique. The rate of interest can never get as high as r_0, because at that rate the wage rate is zero. That portion of line M representing interest rates between zero and r_1 is depicted by a heavy line, indicating that at these interest rates technique M will be chosen as the less costly, more profitable technique.

If we begin with an interest rate above r, in Figure 16.2, then technique N will be chosen. If the interest rate declines to any rate below r_1, then the profit-maximizing firm will switch to technique M. Point Q, with interest rate r_1, is called a switch point. At such a point, it becomes more profitable for a firm to switch techniques of production.

In Figure 16.2, neoclassical theory yields perfectly consistent results. Technique M is clearly and unambiguously more capital intensive than technique N (because as the interest rate declines, the firm switches from N to M). Both techniques of production are assumed to involve equal ratios of capital to labor in both industries. Hence, both techniques have straight r-w lines, as illustrated in part (a) of Figure 16.1.

But now consider Figure 16.3. In this figure, technique M is assumed to involve the conditions illustrated in part (b) of Figure 16.1; that is, $(c_c / l_c) > (c_a / l_a)$ and technique N is assumed to involve the conditions illustrated in part (c); that is, $(c_c / l_c) < (c_a / l_a)$. For the various possible interest rates, we have once again depicted the less costly technique by a heavy line. Now there are two switch points, Q and P. Reswitching occurs in this case. And, once again, the neoclassical theory is shown to be logically inconsistent.

At interest rates above r_1, technique N is chosen. When the interest rate drops below r_1, (but above r_2) technique M is chosen. Therefore, the logic of neoclassical analysis requires us to define technique M as more capital intensive than technique N (because the profit-maximizing firm will switch from

Figure 16.2 **Choosing the Less Costly Technique of Production**

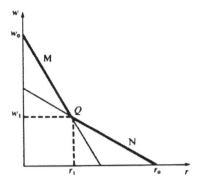

N to M as the interest rate declines). But if the interest rate continues to decline until it drops below r_2, then the profit-maximizing firm will switch (or reswitch) from technique M back to technique N. Therefore, the logic of neoclassical analysis also requires us to define technique N as more capital intensive than technique M, involving us in an insoluble contradiction: we must simultaneously define N as more capital intensive than M and M as more capital intensive than N.

The question now arises of whether this reswitching of techniques, which involves neoclassical economists in an insoluble logical contradiction, is an unusual, special case that can be treated as an isolated exception not covered by the theory, or whether the possibility of reswitching is the general case. If it is the general case, then all neoclassical theories that rely on the notion of the measurability of capital and the marginal productivity of capital (and all three of the main tenets of neoclassical ideology usually do rely on both notions) are logically contradictory and hence logically invalid.

In Figure 16.2 we showed the only case in which reswitching is impossible, which occurs when both techniques of production have equal capital-to-labor ratios in both industries. In all other cases reswitching is possible, and neoclassical economic theory is involved in a logical contradiction.

There is a supreme historical irony in this. Neoclassical economists have nearly always identified the labor theory of value with the proposition that prices are proportional to labor values. As we saw in chapters 5 and 9, when the organic compositions of capital (or the ratios of physical capital to labor) differ from industry to industry, the basic principle of the labor theory of value requires a modifying principle to show that prices actually deviate from such strict proportionality with labor values. But such a modifying principle has been quite consistently developed by proponents of the labor theory of value.

The irony of the Sraffa-inspired critique of neoclassical theory is this: neoclassicists have consistently refused to admit that the modifying principle to the labor theory of value is logically and theoretically valid; they have scoffed at and rejected the labor theory because it supposedly requires that equal or-

Figure 16.3 **Reswitching Productive Techniques**

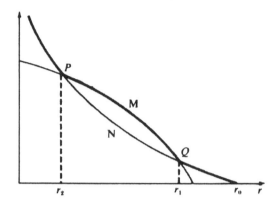

ganic compositions of capital exist in all industries; this assumption, the neo-classicists have (correctly) maintained, is ridiculous as a description of actual economic reality. But with Sraffa's critique the tables are turned. *The labor theory of value does not require equal organic compositions of capital, but neoclassical theory does.* Neoclassical economists can escape from the dilemma of reswitching only when the organic compositions of capital are equal in every industry. In this case, the basic principle of the labor theory of value (as used by Marx in volume 1 of *Capital)* requires no modifying principle and can be shown to hold true always. But labor theorists have always recognized that this will not hold true and have developed the modifying principle of the labor theory of value.

Because neoclassicists and Marxists alike have recognized that the organic compositions of capital are not ever going to be equal in all industries, we must conclude that the possibility of reswitching is the general case, and all neoclassical theory that relies on the notion of the marginal productivity of capital is invalidated.

In Figure 16.4, we illustrate why the possibility of reswitching is the general case. With two techniques of production, each depicted by any one of the three types of r-w lines illustrated in Figure 16.1, only that special case illustrated in Figure 16.2 has no possibility of two switching points (and hence no possibility of reswitching). All other possible cases are illustrated in the three panels of Figure 16.4. In each of these panels there are two switching points, reswitching can take place, and neoclassical theory is involved in a logical contradiction.

The neoclassical economists brought out their best mathematicians in an attempt to rescue their theory. But every attempt made merely reinforced Sraffa's point that it is *impossible* to make deductive conclusions about the relation of the aggregate capital-to-labor ratio and the ratio of interest rates to wage rates—the very heart of neoclassical value and distribution theory.

Paul Samuelson made a noble attempt to rescue neoclassical theory (and ideology) in his "Parable and Realism in Capital Theory: The Surrogate Pro-

Figure 16.4 **The Generality of Reswitching**

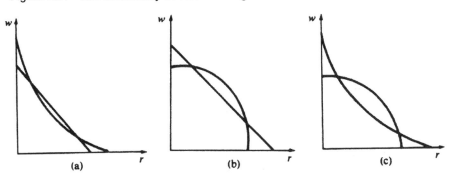

duction Function." He accepted the Sraffa criticism but believed he could construct a simple and admittedly unrealistic "parable" that would be logically consistent and could, by analogy, illustrate the "truths" of J.B. Clark. These truths could not, by themselves, stand either empirical or logical criticisms. On this point it is worthwhile to quote Harcourt:

> The neoclassical tradition, like the Christian, believes that profound truths can be told by way of parable. The neoclassical parables are intended to enlighten believers and nonbelievers concerning the forces which determine the distribution of income between profit-earners and wage-earners, the pattern of capital accumulation and economic growth over time, and the choice of the techniques of production associated with these developments.... [These] truths ... were thought to be established ... before the revelations of the false and true prophets in the course of the recent debate on double switching.[27]

Samuelson's parable was based on a series of assumptions and simplifications that were so extreme that they would have been ridiculed by everyone had not this been the last desperate attempt to rescue an ideology that so conveniently and elaborately justified the existing income distribution. Samuelson found, as we would expect from our discussion of reswitching, that his parable could be made logically consistent only if he assumed that the capital-to-labor ratios and the time patterns of inputs "are uniform throughout all the processes of productions," and hence all "prices are proportioned to labour-time."[28]

Samuelson grasped the gravity of the theoretical crisis, however, when he wrote a summary of the 1966 symposium on the reswitching controversy for the *Quarterly Journal of Economics.*

> Pathology illuminates healthy physiology. Pasinetti, Morishima, Bruno-Burmeister-Sheshinski, Garegnani merit our gratitude for demonstrating that reswitching is a logical possibility in any technology, indecomposable or decomposable. Reswitching, whatever its empirical likelihood, does alert us to several vital possibilities.
>
> Lower interest rates may bring lower steady-state consumption and lower capital/output ratios, and the transition to such lower interest rates can involve denial of diminishing returns and entail reverse capital deepening in which current consumption is augmented rather than sacrificed.

There often turns out to be no unambiguous way of characterizing different processes as more "capital-intensive," more "mechanized," more "roundabout," except in the *ex post* tautological sense of being adopted at a lower interest rate and involving a higher real wage. Such a tautological labeling is shown, in the case of reswitching, to lead to inconsistent ranking between pairs of unchanged technologies, depending upon which interest rate happens to prevail in the market.

If all this causes headaches for those nostalgic for the old time parables of neoclassical writing, we must remind ourselves that scholars are not born to live an easy existence. We must respect, and appraise the facts of life.[29]

But the ideological value of neoclassical theory is too great for its devotees to abandon it just because it is theoretically inconsistent. Harcourt, after convincingly demonstrating the logical inadequacy of neoclassical distribution and value theory, concluded: "It is *the general methodology* of neoclassical analysis, rather than any particular result which basically is under attack.... As a betting man, I know on whom I'd put my money; but then as a God-man, I have never expected virtue to triumph this side of the grave."[30]

C.E. Ferguson, in his preface to the book discussed earlier in this chapter, showed a candor seldom present among the devotees: "Placing reliance upon neoclassical economic theory is a matter of faith. I personally have the faith; but at present the best I can do to convince others is to invoke the weight of Samuelson's authority."[31]

Joan Robinson concluded her review of Ferguson's book with these words:

No doubt Professor Ferguson's restatement of "capital" theory will be used to train new generations of students to erect elegant seeming arguments in terms which they cannot define and will confirm econometricians in the search for answers to unaskable questions. Criticism can have no effect. As he himself says, it is a matter of faith.[32]

Notes to Chapter 16

1. Martin Bronfenbrenner, *Income Distribution Theory* (Chicago: Aldine-Atherton, 1971), p. xi.

2. Ibid., p. 122.

3. Ibid., p. 134.

4. Ibid., p. 268.

5. Ibid., p. 271.

6. Ibid., p. 269.

7. Ibid., p. 301.

8. Thorstein Veblen, "Professor Clark's Economics," in *The Place of Science in Modern Civilization, and Other Essays* (New York: Russell and Russell, 1961), p. 197.

9. Bronfenbrenner, *Income Distribution Theory*, p. 299.

10. Ibid., p. 298.

11. C.E. Ferguson, *The Neoclassical Theory of Production and Distribution* (Cambridge, UK: Cambridge University Press, 1969), p. 235.

12. Ibid., p. 251.

13. Paul Samuelson, "Parable and Realism in Capital Theory: The Surrogate Production Function," *Review of Economic Studies* 29, no. 3 (1962): 193–206.

14. Ferguson, *Neoclassical Theory*, p. 252.

15. Ibid., p. 250.

16. Piero Sraffa, *Production of Commodities by Means of Commodities* (Cambridge: Cambridge University Press, 1960).

17. Ibid., p. vi.

18. John Bates Clark, "Distribution as Determined by Rent," *Quarterly Journal of Economics* 5 (1891): 313.

19. Joan Robinson, "The Production Function and the Theory of Capital," *Review of Economic Studies* 21, no. 2 (1953–54): 81–106.

20. Joan Robinson, "Capital Theory up to Date," *Canadian Journal of Economics* 3, no. 2 (1970): 309–10.

21. G.C. Harcourt, "Some Cambridge Controversies in the Theory of Capital," *Journal of Economic Literature* 7 (1969): 370.

22. Ibid., pp. 369–405.

23. Sraffa, *Production of Commodities*, pp. 81–88.

24. Many of the articles are mathematically formidable. It is recommended that the interested reader rely on Harcourt, "Some Cambridge Controversies," pp. 386–395. The following discussion benefited substantially form Harcourt's account.

25. Sraffa, *Production of Commodities*, p. 38.

26. The following demonstration, involving principles first proved by Sraffa, is based on a very important extension of Sraffa's analysis by P. Garegnani, "Heterogeneous Capital, the Production Fund and the Theory of Distribution," in *A Critique of Economic Theory*, ed. E.K. Hunt and Jesse G. Schwartz (Baltimore: Penguin, 1972).

27. Harcourt, "Some Cambridge Controversies," p. 387.

28. Robinson, "Capital Theory up to Date," p. 311.

29. Paul A. Samuelson, "A Summing Up," *Quarterly Journal of Economics* 80, no. 4 (1996): 582–83.

30. Harcourt, "Some Cambridge Controversies," p. 398.

31. Ferguson, *Neoclassical Theory*, pp. xvii–xviii.

32. Robinson, "Capital Theory up to Date," p. 317.

Chapter 17

Contemporary Economics I:
The Bifurcation of Orthodoxy

During the period between World Wars I and II, two major historical developments powerfully influenced the course of economic ideas for the remainder of the twentieth century. The first was the Bolshevik Revolution of 1917 (and the ensuing civil war) and the unprecedentedly rapid industrialization of the Soviet Union over the next several decades. The pace of industrialization in the Soviet Union was particularly impressive because it occurred despite the impediments of what was tantamount to a second civil war in the 1930s in addition to the staggering devastation inflicted on the Soviet Union by Germany in World War II. The second major event that had a significant impact on subsequent economic theory was the Great Depression of the 1930s. In this chapter, we will briefly examine each of these historical developments and then, in this and the final two chapters, we will show the impact they had on subsequent economic theorizing.

The Bolshevik Revolution and Soviet Industrialization

World War I so weakened the economic and political structure of Russia that the tsarist government collapsed in 1917. It was replaced by a provisional government, which also proved unable to cope with the chaotic situation. In October 1917, the Bolsheviks led by Lenin seized power, in the name of Marxism, in an almost bloodless coup. The problems that had overcome the tsar and the provisional government, however, were of an overwhelming magnitude, and the Bolsheviks, who were mostly political activists with no experience in governing, had enormous difficulties confronting them when they first assumed power.

The new government found itself in the midst of a war that had devastated the foundations of the economy, slowed transportation and communication almost to a halt, and created something approximating social anarchy. The counter-reactionary forces were supported by the major capitalist powers. Not only did their army, called the White Army, receive financial and material aid, but most of the major capitalist governments also sent armed troops to destroy the Soviet government. Few Americans realized it at the time, but President Wilson sent thousands of American soldiers and spent millions of tax dollars on a war that, like the Vietnam War nearly a half century later, was undeclared. The army of the Bolsheviks, called the Red Army, eventually won the war, but only after three years of hard and very costly fighting.

Marx had believed that communism would be created on the industrial base of an already industrialized capitalist system. The Russian economy was, however, a preindustrial mixture of decaying feudalism and nascent capitalism. It was the type of economy that Marx had believed could not possibly sustain a communist society. The communists all agreed that rapid industrialization was a necessity. Despite this agreement, following Lenin's death, a debate raged in the late 1920s over the most efficient method of financing this industrialization. In order to feed and clothe the workers producing capital goods and to spare the material resources necessary for the construction of factories and machinery, large surpluses had to be appropriated by the government. Foreign capital goods could also be purchased if the surpluses could be marketed in the West. With the overwhelming majority of the Soviet workforce employed in agriculture (a large percentage of these in subsistence agriculture), it was obvious that most of the surplus would have to come from agriculture. But Soviet economists and political leaders were divided on the question of how best to appropriate this agricultural surplus.

One group of conservative Communists was led by the economist Nikolai Bukharin. He believed that industrial planning should emphasize increased production of agricultural machinery and consumer goods to be sold to the peasants. The peasants should be paid high prices for their grain and should be offered consumer goods and agricultural machinery at low prices to induce them to expand output and market a continually larger surplus. Industrial development, Bukharin believed, was limited by the rate of expansion of agricultural production.

A second group, consisting of more radical Communists, was led by Leon Trotsky, ex-commander of the Red Army and Lenin's chief lieutenant during the civil war, and Eugenii Preobrazhensky, the leading Marxist economist of the period. They favored extracting a maximum surplus from agriculture by paying peasants low prices for farm produce, charging them high prices for manufactured goods, and putting heavy taxes on farm profits. Agriculture should be more efficiently organized, they believed, by consolidating private plots of land into large-scale collective farms. Many sectors of the economy should be purposely neglected or shortchanged in order to devote a maximum of resources and labor power to the rapid expansion of heavy industry, which, when fully operational, would efficiently produce the capital necessary to catch up in the industries neglected in the initial phases of industrialization.

Josef Stalin used the antagonisms created in the debates as a means of achieving power for himself. At first he aligned himself with the conservatives to form a coalition that ousted Trotsky and his left-wing sympathizers. He then turned on Bukharin and his followers and successfully stripped them of their power, leaving himself in full control. Having thus gained power, he began to move along lines that had been advocated by Trotsky and Preobrazhensky, although he moved more rapidly and more harshly than they had ever advised.

In November 1929, the government announced a policy of promoting collectives as a means of increasing agricultural production. At first the collectivization was to have been voluntary. Suddenly, however, in early 1930, the government decided to force collectivization as widely as possible and to eliminate the richer peasants as a class by turning their holding over to collectives. The resulting change was profound. The events of 1929–34 constituted one of the great dramas of history.

Only the poor peasants could be persuaded to join the collectives voluntarily; but they owned so few animals and so little capital that collectives could not succeed with them alone. The middle-income and rich peasants resisted forced collectivization with bitterness and ferocity. At times this resistance was so widespread as to constitute what could almost be called a second civil war. When the richer peasants realized they could not defeat the government directly, they began to burn buildings, destroy equipment, and slaughter animals. By 1931, one-third of Russia's cattle, half of its sheep and goats, and one-fourth of its horses had been slaughtered.

The drama of the battle over collectivization was one about which many books have been written. Here it will suffice to say that while an immense social cost was incurred, it did bring about the revolution in Soviet agriculture that made industrialization possible. Collectivization succeeded in drastically increasing the government's collections of grain. The 22.1 million tons from the 1930–31 harvest amounted to more than twice the tonnage collected by the government in 1928–29.

When collectivization placed a large economic surplus in government hands, Soviet industrialization proceeded very rapidly on the basis of successive five-year plans during the 1930s. Industrial growth at such a rapid pace was, in fact, unprecedented in history. Official Soviet figures for the 1930s show an average annual growth rate in industrial production of about 16 percent. Studies by Western economists using different methods of arriving at indexes of industrial production show somewhat lower rates (ranging from about 9 percent to about 14 percent), but, by any of these estimates, the performance was without historical precedent.

The major Soviet achievement was not simply a higher rate of industrial growth; it was a significant transformation of the whole society so that industrial growth could begin and continue. Before 1928, the Soviet Union was mostly rural; by 1938, the urban population had tripled—there was a constant flow of people from country to city and a constant flow of ideas from city to country. Before 1928, there was 80 percent illiteracy; by 1938, over 90 percent could do some reading and writing, there was a very large adult education movement, and all young people were in school. In other words, the Soviet Union changed from a less developed country in 1928 to one of the main developed countries in 1938. This spectacular rate of growth was interrupted by World War II, during which the Soviet Union suffered unparalleled losses. Estimates of the number of Soviet citizens killed in World War II are generally around 20 million, although some experts place the figure as high as 30 million. Early in the war, Hitler rapidly conquered an area that contained more than half of the Soviet Union's prewar productive capacity. The German occupied territory had accounted for 70 percent of Soviet coal mining, 60 percent of iron ore production, 50 percent of steel capacity, and 33 percent of the area sown in grain.

When the Soviet army retreated, it destroyed many productive facilities to prevent their use by the Germans. When the Germans were subsequently pushed back, they also pursued a scorched-earth policy, destroying everything of value as they retreated. Especially hard hit were factories and houses. In addition to killing more than 20 million Soviet people, the Germans destroyed the homes of another 25 million, totally razing about 2,000 towns and 70,000 villages.

The destruction of these millions of people, homes, factories, untold millions of animals, and railroad, transportation, and communications systems left the Soviet Union an almost totally devastated "victor" in World War II. The economic progress of the 1930s, purchased at high social and human cost, was in large measure erased by the Nazi attempt to conquer the Soviet Union.

Despite these losses, however, the Soviets retained their economic organization and general skills, and with their experience in economic planning during the 1930s, they recovered with miraculous speed. By 1950, gross industrial production was much higher than its prewar level and agriculture had recovered to its prewar level. Because the Soviet economy was so underdeveloped in relation to the advanced capitalist societies that Marx believed to be the only possible foundation for the building of communism, that economy cannot, either in its performance during that era or more recently, serve as any real test of the possibility of constructing Marxian socialism. Nevertheless, this rapid industrialization had a powerful demonstration effect in third-world, economically underdeveloped economies. The speed of Soviet industrialization was unprecedented. When one considers the obstacles that were overcome in this industrialization, it becomes obvious that the Soviet experience would serve as a desirable model for industrialization in poor third-world countries that were experiencing a powerful, nationalistic, anticolonial, and anti-imperialist upheaval in the years following World War II.

The Great Depression

During the period just discussed, defenders of capitalism were very concerned over the example that Soviet industrialization gave to third-world capitalist countries. This concern was increased however, by the second major historical development mentioned above—the Great Depression of the 1930s.

During the first three decades of the twentieth century, the worldwide capitalist economy experienced several business cycles. The depression phases of these cycles, however, were relatively mild, and, in general, these were prosperous decades for most capitalist countries.

This era came to a halt in the 1930s, however. In the United States there were over 85,000 business failures between 1929 and 1932, as the American economy collapsed into a devastating depression. During those three years, more than 5,000 banks suspended operations; stock values on the New York Exchange fell from $87 billion to $19 billion; 12 million workers lost their jobs, and fully one-fourth of the American population had no means of sustaining themselves; farm income fell by more than half; and manufacturing output decreased by nearly 50 percent.

The depression struck the United States first but quickly spread to the entire capitalist world. Real income fell from an index of 100 in the United States in 1929 to a low of 68 in 1931. Similar declines were experienced in the capitalist countries of Western Europe. Unemployment in Western Europe rose from just over 3 million to an unprecedentedly high figure of 15 million unemployed in 1932. In Germany, 43 percent of the labor force was without work in 1932. World trade declined precipitously and the entire capitalist world experienced a crisis of poverty, starvation, and general economic desperation.

The economic suffering of the period was worse than it had been during most wars and natural disasters, yet, natural resources were as plentiful as ever; the workforce was as numerous as ever and as desirous of productive employment; factories, shops, and other productive facilities were all as abundant as ever and stood ready for use; peoples needs and desires for commodities were certainly as numerous and strong as ever. Yet, resources, factories, tools, and machines remained idle while unemployed workers lost their homes and could not feed themselves or their families.

Faith in the automaticity of the free market, capitalist economy plummeted. Millions turned to the right and advocated nazism or fascism or turned to the left and advocated socialism or communism. Laissez-faire capitalism had very few enthusiastic supporters. Nearly every economist and politician favored extensive government intervention into the market. This is reflected in the spectacular success of Keynes's *The General Theory of Money, Interest and Employment* when it was published in 1936.

The capitalist economy was, however, rescued from this precarious state of affairs by World War II. Nearly every major capitalist economy experienced massive government intervention into the market system as the production of weapons, ammunition, and war-related materials increase sharply and continuously for several years. In the United States, for example, military-related expenditures were $3.2 billion or 3.2 percent of GNP in 1940. In 1943, at the height of World War II, military spending was almost 40 percent of a much larger GNP. Profits rose to unprecedented heights and capitalists became aware of how rapidly massive military expenditures could end a depression and ensure large returns to their capital.

By the early 1950s, neoclassical economic theory was on the defensive. We have seen that neoclassical economic theory contained three basic ideological defenses of capitalism. The first was the invisible-hand argument that free market exchange harmonized all people's interests, created "rational prices," and resulted in an efficient allocation of resources. Theoretical work in welfare economics that formed the basis of the critique of welfare economics (see chapter 14) was done mostly in the 1930s and 1940s. This work had put the neoclassical ideologists on the defensive. The second ideological tenet was the neoclassical faith that the free market would automatically adjust to a full-employment equilibrium. The Great Depression of the 1930s and the work of Keynes had cast profound doubt on this proposition. The third ideological pillar was the belief that the distribution of income was determined by the marginal productivity of the different factors of production and that each individual received as income only that value created, at the margin of production, by that individual's own factors. While this proposition did not receive its theoretical *coup de grâce* until 1959 with the publication of Sraffa's *Production of Commodities by Means of Commodities*, the marginal productivity theory of distribution had never been convincing to critics of capitalism. In third-world capitalist countries, the abject poverty of the majority of people and its stark contrast with the opulence of the wealthy elite was so extreme that hardly anyone believed the theory to be applicable to these economies. The ideology was therefore in a state of intellectual disarray and capitalism (particularly in the third world, but in the industrial countries as well) was in danger of a severe crisis of legitimation.

The precursors of neoclassical theory—Say, Senior, and Bastiat—used each of these ideological doctrines to argue for a policy of extreme laissez faire. These writers wanted the government to use its power only to protect the existing inequalities of power and wealth by enforcing the laws of contract and the laws of private property. Once these existing inequalities were coercively protected by the government, free market exchange was sufficient to perpetuate them. If workers had no way to exist except by selling their labor power in the market, and if a substantial pool of unemployed workers could be kept in a state of constant competition for the available jobs (as has almost always been the case under capitalism), then the free market would perpetuate the extreme wealth and power of the numerically tiny capitalist class. Under these basic conditions of capitalism, however, the free market was merely a financial slaughterhouse, where the rich increased their wealth by chopping up the poor.

Neoclassical economists have always adopted these three ideological defenses of capitalism. During the past century, however, neoclassical economics has split into two quite separate (and not infrequently hostile) traditions. This split has been the result of both the force of existing social, economic, and political circumstances and the persistent barrage of criticisms leveled at the neoclassical ideology. The split has existed since at least the 1870s. The social, political, and economic consequences of the Soviet industrialization, the Great Depression, the cold war, and the anti-imperialist movement in the third world significantly exacerbated the split, however.

The problem was that while neoclassical economics continued to constitute the intellectual foundation for intellectually sophisticated ideologies of capitalism, most economists and politicians had lost faith in the free market, laissez-faire policy conclusion that is derived from the theory. This loss of faith can be seen most clearly in the rapid development during the 1940s and 1950s of two important trends in economic theory. The first was the nearly instantaneous and almost unanimous acceptance of Keynesian economics and the second was the birth and virtually explosive growth of a vast literature in the new field of "development" economics. The new Keynesian economics and the new development economics shared a general abandonment of faith in laissez-faire capitalism and both advocated policies that involved widespread and profound extensions of government into economic processes.

The neoclassical arguments for laissez faire remained important throughout the entire period, however. They have always constituted the most elaborate, and seemingly scientific, ideological defense of capitalism. There is another important reason for the persistence of the neoclassical laissez-faire doctrine during the period in which confidence in free market capitalism was at a low ebb. Government intervention, in the United States economy, for example, has usually taken the forms of either various government regulatory agencies or the "military Keynesianism" of expenditures on space programs and on the military. These interventions affect the various capitalist enterprises very differently. Regulatory agencies have generally acted in a manner that protected and expanded the power of giant oligopolistic business firms, not infrequently at the expense of medium- and small-sized firms. The overwhelming bulk of the profits from space contracts and military contracts has gone to corporations that were among the largest and most powerful in the economy. Moreover, the profits reaped from the worldwide American economic empire have generally gone to the largest and most powerful of the multinational corporations.

For many thousands of medium- and small-sized capitalist firms, the expansion of government into the economy has steadily undermined their ability to compete with the corporate giants. They typically see themselves as reaping few, if any, of the benefits of government's expanding economic activities. To them, bigger government means a deteriorating competitive position compared with the giant firms, mountains of "red tape," bureaucratic hassles, and ever increasing taxes. These medium and small firms are generally controlled by people who are ardent supporters of an ultraconservative, laissez-faire political philosophy that advocates a decrease in the magnitude and extent of government's role in the economy. Giant corporations, however, are usually controlled by people who are more "realistic" and "liberal" in their economic and political philosophy. In the cant and jargon of American politics, advocacy of more government is usually associated with liberalism and advocacy of less government is usually associated with conservatism. The economic base for both of these political tendencies, within both the Democratic and Republican parties, is primarily the business community.

Big corporations, with the backing of labor union bureaucrats, generally support liberals in both parties. Small businesses, with the backing of independent professional people and other middle-class elements, generally support the conservatives. In American politics, neither liberals nor conservatives ever question or criticize the institutional foundations of capitalism; that is, they are both profoundly conservative, but represent differing—and frequently hostile—groups within the capitalist class.

The common threads in the writings of all of the neoclassical economists, by virtue of which they can still be called a "neoclassical school" despite their differences are these: (1) they all defend, or simply take for granted, the capitalist system of private property and all of the fundamental institutions of capitalism; (2) their conception of economic behavior remains that of the isolated, egoistical, calculating utility maximizer, or Veblen's "homogeneous globule of desire of happiness"; and (3) they all defend some version of, or close substitute for, the three basic tenets of neoclassical ideology. Therefore, despite their differences, their general view of the individual and society continues to reflect the social perspective of the absentee rentier (as discussed in chapter 10).

In the remaining pages of this chapter, we will briefly examine the ideas of three recent economic theorists, each of whom has won the Nobel Prize in economics and each of whom has had a profound influence on orthodox economics. W. Arthur Lewis was one of the prime movers in creating the subdiscipline of development economics. Milton Friedman utterly ignored the Great Depression and the crises of confidence in the neoclassical policy of laissez faire and remained an ardent champion of an extreme version of that economic ideology. Perhaps the most significant of the three theorists was Paul A. Samuelson, who did much to establish neoclassical theory as an esoteric discipline, understandable only to the highly trained neoclassical economist. More important, he created what was to become the standard orthodox neoclassical reconciliation of the polar bifurcation between the traditional neoclassical ideology and the newer Keynesian and development economics.

W. Arthur Lewis and the Origins of Development Economics

Before 1945, there was almost never a mention of "development economics." The standard view was that economic theory was universal and applied to all economies in all times and places (see Veblen's critique of neoclassical economics in chapter 12). In less than ten years, economic development in what theorists of that period termed "backward" countries had become the most widely researched and written about field in academic economics.

In the late 1940s, there was a vast and powerful movement in the third-world countries of Asia, Africa, and Latin America. The movement combined nationalism with opposition to imperialism and colonialism. The charter of the United Nations proclaimed the goal of colonial emancipation. By 1950, India, Pakistan, Ceylon, Burma, the Philippines, Indonesia, Jordan, Syria, Lebanon, and Israel had all become nominally independent nations. During the 1950s, the trend continued with nominal independence given to or promised to Cambodia, Laos, Vietnam, Malaysia, Libya, Somaliland, Sudan, Morocco, Tunisia, Egypt, Ghana, Togoland, the Cameroons, and Guinea. While imperialism had not generally taken the form of outright colonialism in Latin America, the nationalistic tide of anti-imperialism was as strong there as it was in the former colonial empires of Asia and Africa.

The citizens of these third-world countries reacted against the racism and political and economic exploitation that they saw as responsible for the grueling poverty that prevailed in most of the countries. It became immediately obvious, however, that nominal and actual independence were not the same thing, that economic exploitation could take new forms, and that significant barriers were retarding if not preventing the desired independence and increase in living standards. Most politicians and economists living in third-world countries felt certain that simply relying on the free market would never improve their situation. The example of the rapid industrialization of the Soviet economy held a powerful attraction. It was the task of orthodox economics to suggest some formula for planned, forced industrialization that could give the hope of higher standards of living to third-world countries while simultaneously making sure that these countries retained the necessary legal, economic, and governmental institutions that would assure safe, profitable investments in these countries for the large multinational corporations of the industrialized capitalist world.

W. Arthur Lewis provided the necessary theoretical framework for this task in a series of articles and books, the most famous being a 1954 article entitled "Economic Development with Unlimited Supplies of Labour" and a 1955 book entitled *Theory of Economic Growth*.[1] Lewis began with what was already common knowledge among historians and economists: industrialization requires a reorientation of an economy's production capacity. The economy must substitute the production of producer goods such as factories, machines, and tools, for consumer goods such as food, shelter, clothing, and other necessities. In other words, the economic surplus, over and above the necessary consumption goods, had to be increased by finding a large segment of society that could be forced to subsist on more meager provisions.

In England, in the classic case of capitalist industrialization, this deprivation was forced upon both the urban and rural working class in a pitiless onslaught of upper-class greed that has been amply chronicled by numerous historians. In the Soviet Union, by contrast, while working people definitely suffered during industrialization, nevertheless, much of the economic surplus that was necessary for industrialization was attained by expropriating the assets and enormous incomes of the capitalist and wealthy land-owning classes.

In most third-world countries, the peasant and working classes were wretchedly poor because they were already creating a large economic surplus that was being divided by indigenous elites and foreign capitalists. The problem was that the foreign capitalists made most of their profits through their control of agriculture and resource extraction and appeared to show no interest in spending any of these profits in promoting industrialization in other sectors of these economies. The local elites were often "precapitalist" in their mentality, resembling feudal lords more than they did industrial capitalists. Thus, it appeared that the working classes were already subjected to the maximum possible exploitation and that the recipients of the resultant economic surplus would never use it as a means of general industrialization. The great appeal that the Soviet model had in this period is certainly easy to understand.

Lewis changed the focus of the debate, however. Lewis argued that in industrialized capitalist countries with nearly full employment the neoclassical marginal productivity theory of distribution was correct and that the wages of workers reflected their marginal productivity. He argued that in third-world economies capitalism had not developed fully and that wages were not determined by marginal productivity. Wages were, he argued, determined by tradition: "In economies where the majority of the people are peasant farmers . . . the minimum at which labor can be had [by capitalist employers] is now set by the average product of the farmer."[2] He believed, however, that "earnings in the subsistence sector set a floor to wages in the capitalist sector, but in practice wages have to be higher than this, and there is usually a gap of 30 percent or more between capitalist wages and subsistence earnings."[3]

The cause of poverty in third-world countries, in Lewis's view, was a shortage of capital. Because most workers worked in the subsistence sector, Lewis asserted that the marginal productivity of labor in these traditional economies was "negligible, zero, or even negative."[4] Lewis got this result because he defined workers who were not working for capitalists as "unproductive." Committing the essential error of which Marx accused the classical economists, Lewis confused previously produced (or reproducible) means of production, which are used by all people in all times and places, with capital. Capital comes into being only with the capitalist mode of production and hence cannot be identical with all previously produced means of production. This is a confusion that affects almost all ideological defenders of capitalism. Lewis showed that he saw matters strictly from the point of view of the capitalist when he asserted that laborers not working for capitalists were unproductive:

> The subsistence sector is . . . that part of the economy not using reproducible capital. Output per head is lower in this sector than in the capitalist sector because it is not fructified by capital. . . . As more capital becomes available more workers can be drawn into the capitalist from the subsistence sector, and their output per head rises as they move from one sector to the other.[5]

The problem, then, was simple. Third-world countries needed more savings to be invested in capital that would draw unproductive workers from the traditional sector, where they had "negligible, zero, or even negative" marginal productivity, into the capitalist sector, where their marginal productivity would be much higher and where they would increase the economy's output, and, eventually, increase everyone's economic welfare.

> The basic problem in these countries was low savings. Increased capital, in a capitalist economy, comes from savings out of the profits of capitalists: the reason why savings are low in an underdeveloped economy relatively to national income is not that people are poor, but that capitalists' profits are low relatively to national income. As the capitalist sector expands, profits grow relatively, and an increasing proportion of national income is re-invested.[6]

The problem was to promote what Marx had labeled "primitive accumulation"; that is, to expand the sector controlled by capital and reduce and eventually destroy the traditional economy. This became the central problem of development economics in the 1950s and 1960s. Nearly every orthodox "development economist" saw the problem in these terms, and, to combat the spread of socialism and communism, nearly every development economist advocated extensive government involvement—on the part of both third-world and first-world capitalist governments—as the only solution to the problem.

That this anticommunist concern dominated most development economics can be detected from a study of nearly any of the important texts of the period. It can, perhaps, be most clearly seen in the writings of Walt W. Rostow, whose *The Stages of Economic Growth: A Non-Communist Manifesto* was published in 1960 and was arguably the most influential book by a conventional development economist in the 1960s. Writing in 1983, Rostow recalled his commitment to combating communism. He had believed that "the struggle to deter and contain the thrust for expanded communist power would be long and that new concepts would be required to underpin U.S. foreign policy."[7] He also forthrightly admitted, with a candor that is uncommon among conservative economists, that his intellectual attacks on communism were financed by the United States Central Intelligence Agency.[8]

While development economics, like Keynesian economics, seemed to be an abandonment of neoclassical laissez-faire conservatism, most development economists argued that this situation would be temporary. Once these third-world economies fully attained a capitalist system, then the neoclassical theory would be applicable.

Liberal and Conservative Neoclassical Economics

From the late nineteenth century to the present, there has been a split in the neoclassical intellectual tradition between a liberal wing and a conservative wing. These terms are sometimes confusing because the nineteenth century doctrine of laissez faire was then known as "liberalism" whereas today the more extreme advocates of laissez faire are now called conservative and the neoclassical economists who temper their analysis and advocate government intervention to correct "market imperfections" or "market failures" are now called liberals.

In the two decades immediately following World War II, both branches of neoclassicism were equally ardent in their advocacy of a foreign policy dedicated to destroying communism wherever it existed and to preventing third-world economies from experimenting with any form of socialism. Thus, even the staunch conservative advocates of a laissez-faire policy supported a huge military and an aggressive foreign policy.

The conservatives were not, however, very deeply impressed with the great depression. They retained their faith in laissez-faire capitalism. The liberals had a number of reservations about laissez-faire capitalism, however. The inherent instability of capitalism, as seen by Keynes, was only one of four general areas in which they believed that the government should actively intervene to promote national economic well-being. With an active fiscal and monetary policy, liberals believed that capitalism could, if not eliminate, then certainly mitigate this inherent instability.

Second, liberals recognized the existence of powerful, giant corporations that would not, if left alone, behave in the manner depicted in the theory of perfect competition. Here the liberals believed that government antitrust laws and regulatory agencies could force these giants to act in the general public interest. So, with a little help from government, the invisible hand still basically did its beneficent, harmony-creating task.

Third, liberals recognized that some commodities were "socially consumed" and are desirable, even though a private capitalist could not make a profit on the production of these commodities. Once again, they believed the government could solve this problem. It could produce and distribute these commodities in order that society's general well-being would be maximized.

Fourth, liberals recognized that "externalities" (see chapter 14) would cause private costs and social costs (which include costs such as pollution) to diverge. The government could cure this problem too, they argued, with a system of taxes and subsidies that would bring the private costs and social costs into equality.

Thus, from the 1950s to the present, liberal neoclassical economists not only do not advocate extreme laissez faire, they enthusiastically embrace government intervention in the economy. Government becomes a *deus ex machina* that conveniently allows liberals to recognize the validity of many of the objections to neoclassical theory while still defending their faith in the three fundamental ideological tenets of neoclassicism. They concede that the invisible hand is not by itself sufficient. They give what frequently appears to be a fair hearing to the many objections to laissez faire, but they always end up defending all three tenets of neoclassical ideology. They conclude, more frequently implicitly rather than explicitly, that although the invisible hand, helped along by the visible fist of government, is not perfect, it is the closest thing to perfection that current levels of human knowledge allow. Those difficulties that remain appear to be resolvable by a mere continuation of the reforms of the past century.

Paul A. Samuelson Versus Milton Friedman and the Conservative Neoclassicists

In the liberal and conservative traditions of neoclassical economics, two thinkers have had the greatest influence during the period since World War II, Paul A. Samuelson and Milton Friedman, respectively. Samuelson's impact has been more powerful than that of any other economist. He has dominated the course of development of, as well as the teaching of, liberal neoclassical economics. Because liberal neoclassical economics has dominated the academic economics profession, Samuelson can be said to have been the most influential economist since World War II.

Friedman's influence on the extreme laissez-faire tradition of neoclassical economics, although very great, has not been as decisive as has Samuelson's influence on the liberal tradition. For that reason, in the next section we will discuss the ideas of Samuelson as our only representative of contemporary liberal neoclassicism, and in the following section we will discuss the ideas of Friedman as well as those of other advocates of extreme laissez faire.

The relationship between Samuelson and conservative neoclassicists is strikingly similar to the relationship in the mid-nineteenth century between John Stuart Mill and Frédéric Bastiat (discussed in chapter 8). Samuelson, like Mill, is an eclectic, which accounts for many of his strengths as well as some of his weaknesses. Like Mill, he has an urbane, flexible, and nondogmatic style. He considers and generally grants some validity to many of the objections to neoclassicism. When one reads Samuelson, as with Mill, one cannot help but be aware that he would prefer capitalism to be a somewhat more humane system than it in fact is. Like Mill, he does not hesitate to admit many of the inequities as injustices of capitalism. But also like Mill, he has a faith in gradual reform within the institutions of capitalism, and when one sorts out the eclecticism of his approach, his neoclassical ideas culminate in a general acceptance of some version of the three main ideological tenets of utilitarian economics.

The laissez-faire neoclassicists, conversely, display the single-minded consistency of Bastiat in their defense of utilitarianism. Like Bastiat's, their writings are rigid, dogmatic, and doctrinaire. They simply deny reality where it does not fit their theory, and they lack entirely Samuelson's flexibility and open-minded admission of difficulties, which exist in both the realities of capitalism and the neoclassical theories of capitalism. But just as Bastiat, while clearly inferior to Mill intellectually, presented a more logically consistent defense of the conclusions inherent in the utilitarian premises than did Mill, so are the conservative laissez-faire neoclassicists clearer, more logically consistent devotees of utilitarianism than is Samuelson.

Samuelson's Defense of Utilitarianism

While still a very young man, Samuelson exerted significant influence on the economics profession by systematizing and putting into mathematical formulations the various strands of neoclassical analysis in his *The Foundations of Economic Analysis*.[9] In 1947, primarily on the basis of this book, the American Economics Association awarded him the first John Bates Clark Medal for the most outstanding contribution to economic theory made by an economist under forty years of age. The book was also instrumental in securing the Nobel Prize in economics for Samuelson in 1970.

His greatest influence on the economics profession, however, has come from his text *Economics*, which was first published in 1948, has gone through seventeen editions (the past few being coauthored by William Nordhaus), has been translated into almost every major language, and has sold many millions of copies. The first edition set out mainly to explain and simplify Keynes's ideas. But, as we saw in chapter 15, Keynes was a neoclassical economist who merely wanted to extricate the utilitarian ideology from the untenable faith in the automaticity of the self-adjusting market. Samuelson has succeeded admirably in carrying out Keynes's intentions. Each subsequent edition of *Economics* has tended to bring in more of the traditional neoclassical ideology of capitalism. In 1955, Samuelson offered his "grand neoclassical synthesis," an integration of Keynesian with neoclassical economics. The Keynesian theory was to provide the knowledge necessary to maintain a full-employment economy, and the market system was to operate within this Keynesian framework to allocate resources and distribute income according to the time-honored principles of neoclassical ideology.

Samuelson clearly recognizes, as do most liberal neoclassical economists, that, in at least four areas, the laissez-faire ideology is clearly inadequate: (a) the free market capitalist system seems to be inherently unstable; (b) the existence of oligopolies and monopolies makes the neoclassical vision of competitive efficiency utterly unrealistic; (c) there are "public" goods that must be consumed socially and cannot be efficiently produced for individuals; and (d) a closely related problem to public goods is the issue of pervasive external economies and diseconomies whereby individuals are everywhere and always effected by thousands of acts of production and consumption over which they have no control. Samuelson believes, however, that these four problem areas should not undermine our faith in the neoclassical ideology.

First, laissez-faire capitalism is economically unstable. But the extension of government has, he argues, created a "mixed economy—the mixture being one of the invisible hand of the market and the visible fist of the government." The mixed economy has not totally eliminated instability but has rendered it moderate and tolerable:

> The business cycle has been tamed, even if not completely made a thing of the past. Although democratic mixed economies are unlikely to experience old fashioned, prolonged depression ever again, recessions and periods of relative stagnation will no doubt still occur even though fiscal and monetary policies can moderate their frequency, intensity, and duration.[10]

So some tolerable version of Say's law, enforced by government fiscal and monetary policies, can be maintained.

Second, Samuelson recognizes the existence of giant oligopolistic business firms. "In appraising oligopoly," he writes, "we must note that the desire of corporations to earn a fair return on their past investments can at times be at variance with the well being of the consumer."[11] As we would expect, he assures the reader that "government regulation and government antitrust laws are the principal weapons a mixed economy uses to improve the workings of the price system."[12] So, on this second qualification of the utilitarian laissez-faire doctrine, he concludes:

> We cannot expect competition to become everywhere "perfectly perfect," in the strict sense of the economist. But what we must strive for is what the late J.M Clark years ago called "workable competition." . . . But laissez faire cannot be counted on to do this. Public vigilance and support for antitrust will be required.[13]

So the second objection is once again obviated by the *deus ex machina* of government, and something called "workable competition" is achieved through "public vigilance" and government intervention.

Third, Samuelson recognizes the existence of "public goods" that are socially needed but are not profitable for capitalists to produce and sell. In the mixed economy, he writes, we express our needs for these goods by the way we "vote on election day and in the way we acquiesce to the coercive fiats legislated by our responsive government, rather than in *our day-to-day* private purchasing."[14] Once again, the utilitarian ideology is rescued by the impartial and benevolent government.

Fourth, Samuelson does not ignore the fact that acts of consumption and production have important effects on people who are not directly involved in these acts. These externalities result in what neoclassical economists call a divergence between private costs and social costs. As we saw in chapter 14, the more that such divergences exist, the more impossible it is to argue that the invisible hand of the market creates rational prices and an efficient allocation of resources (we also saw that it is impossible on numerous other grounds as well). Not surprisingly, Samuelson argues that "since no one profit maker has the incentive, or indeed the power, to solve problems involving 'externalities,' here is a clear case for some kind of public intervention."[15] Once again, however, the benevolent *deus ex machina* can restore the economy to an acceptably close approximation of the "bliss point" of neoclassical welfare economics (see chapter 14) by "subsidy or public control, to expand situations fraught with external economies; and . . . to contract, by tax or fiat, activities involving external diseconomies."[16] Samuelson does not, of course, tell the reader that this would involve literally millions of different taxes and subsidies, as we saw in chapter 14. He simply has the faith that the government can and will create a situation tolerably close to Pareto optimality.

Having thus recognized the absolute necessity for literally millions of instances of government intervention into the economy and having a faith in the impartial benevolence of capitalist governments, Samuelson defends some variation of each of the three fundamental tenets of neoclassical ideology.

First, as we have seen, the market can be guided by a government armed with Keynesian insights to a situation tolerably close to automatic full employment.

Second, with millions of discrete, benevolent interventions into the market, something reasonably close to Pareto optimal rational prices and efficient allocation can be achieved. Samuelson writes:

> Adam Smith, in his talk about an Invisible Hand which leads the selfish actions of individuals toward so harmonious a final result, did have some point. Smith never could state or prove exactly what the point was, but modern economics can state this property of ideal competitive pricing: under perfectly perfect competition, where all prices end up equal to all marginal costs, where all factor-prices end up equal to values of marginal products and all total costs are minimized, where the genuine desires and well being of individuals are all represented by their marginal utilities as expressed in their dollar voting—then the resulting equilibrium has the efficiency property that "you can't make any one man better off without hurting some other man."
>
> What does this mean exactly? It means that a planner could not come along with a slide rule and find a solution, different from the laissez-faire one, which could improve the welfare of everyone.[17]

But Samuelson, as we have seen, does not hold that the free market can automatically achieve this benevolent, harmonious state of bliss. It requires the help of his benevolent *deux ex machina*—the government. The reader should review the discussion in chapter 14 of the present book to see the incredibly unrealistic and spurious assumptions underlying neoclassical welfare economics and then to judge whether Samuelson's *deus ex machina* can do the job (or even if it would be desirable to have the job done). In the early part of *Economics*, before he has yet demonstrated that benevolent government actions can result in tolerable corrections of every deviation from perfect competition, Samuelson writes:

> Needless to say, the requirements for absolute perfect competition are as hard to meet as the requirements for a perfectly frictionless pendulum in physics. We can approach closer and closer to perfection, but can never quite reach it. Yet this fact need not do serious damage to the usefulness of our employing the idealized concept. . . .
>
> To be sure, not all today's markets are anywhere near to being perfectly competitive in the economist's sense. We shall see later . . . that elements of monopoly power or of market imperfection may enter in, and these imperfections will require us to modify the competitive model. After we have learned how to handle such cases [by calling in the benevolent *deus ex machina* of government], we shall recognize . . . that the competitive analysis, properly qualified, is still an indispensable tool for interpreting reality.[18]

The third tenet of neoclassical ideology is the marginal productivity theory of distribution. Here it would seem that Samuelson's recantation in the reswitching debate (see chapter 16) would require him to abandon this theory. But he, like Ferguson, has the faith that his "fairy tales" and "parables" illustrate profound truths of capitalism. So he tells the reader that "the demand for capital is its *net productivity* curve."[19] Similarly, the demands for all factors are derived from the productivity of each factor, where capitalists "will want to hire more and more of . . . [any factor] up to the point where its marginal-revenue-product is equal to its market rental."[20]

True to his "fair-mindedness" and eclecticism, Samuelson has two pages of a brief appendix devoted to a discussion of reswitching.[21] He concludes this appendix with a statement that is a total obfuscation of the issue: "The science of political economy has not yet the empirical knowledge to decide whether the real world is nearer to the idealized polar cases represented by (a) the neoclassical parable, or (b) the simple reswitching paradigm."[22]

This is a deliberate confusion of the issue for two reasons: first, as we saw in the previous chapter, Samuelson himself admitted that the reswitching controversy proved that in many cases (and, as we saw, these cases are the general rule) there is no logically consistent method of even *defining* which of different production techniques is more capital intensive. This means that no amount of empirical evidence will show that "greater capital intensiveness" leads to the results predicted by the neoclassical parable. This was, in fact, admitted by Samuelson in his esoteric journal article. But in his *Economics*, through which he influences untold millions of readers, he denies it. Samuelson's second obfuscation, again contrary to his recantation in the esoteric journal article, is his failure to show the reader that the reswitching demonstration utterly destroyed the foundation of the neoclassical parable, as well as most neoclassical versions of the invisible-hand argument.

Unquestionably, however, Samuelson's most significant and pervasive obfuscation of reality lies in his treating of government as a benevolent, neutral, *deus ex machina* that patches up every departure from competitive bliss in a tolerable, even if not perfect, manner. He fails to discuss the fact that government regulatory agencies have generally promoted the interests of the oligopolistic industries that they are supposed to regulate. He fails to mention the fact that imperialism and militarism have been the principal tools of Keynesian policy. He fails to mention the fact that these tools have created the potential for a crisis that could be worse than the crises that they have avoided. He fails to mention the fact that the government has never attempted to equitably nullify externalities through a system of taxes and subsidies. The list could be continued, but we will end with one last failure: he fails to mention the fact that the government has rarely, if ever, taken any action that would significantly decrease the extreme inequalities of income and wealth.

All of these failures lie at the heart of the liberal neoclassical obfuscation—their view of the nature of government in a capitalist system. These failures and this faulty conception of government mask the extreme conservatism that actually underlies the liberal analysis. Let us illustrate this by taking only the last failure mentioned—the issue of government creating an equitable distribution of wealth and income.

Throughout his book, Samuelson repeatedly qualifies his enthusiastic praise for the market by stating that "market efficiency" ignores the question of the fairness of the distribution of wealth and income. But he never explains to the reader how this unfairness totally vitiates the normative significance of free market efficiency—even if the concept of market efficiency could be defended, which we argued in chapter 14 was not the case. Furthermore, Samuelson never makes any concrete recommendations of specific measures that would significantly redistribute wealth, power, and income. Rather, he merely states his faith that "when a democratic society does not like the distribution of dollar votes under laissez-faire, it uses redistributive taxation to rectify the situation."[23] When, we may ask, has the government done this in any systematic and significant way? The answer is never.

But it may be asked whether Samuelson recognizes the fact that it is only because wealth (and particularly the means of production) is monopolized by a tiny segment of the population that people can amass gigantic incomes solely from the interest on their assets. Only when the majority of people who produce have no independent means of sustaining their own consumption or exerting any control over the process by which they produce, can they be forced to pay a large part of what they produce in interest to those who have monopolized ownership. These elementary facts of capitalism are totally obscured by Samuelson.

In a section of his book entitled "Fairness and Inevitability of Interest,"

Samuelson asks if the payment of interest is not a fair payment to an individual for a valuable service performed. His answer is this:

> Let us make the realistic assumption that when I borrow money from you, my purpose is not to hold onto the cash: instead, I use the borrowed cash to buy capital goods; and, as we have seen, these intermediate capital goods are so scarce as to create a net product over and above their replacement cost. Therefore, if I did not pay you interest, I should really be cheating you out of the return that you could get by putting your own money directly into such productive investment projects![24]

Fairness indeed! When we look behind the liberal verbiage, we see why Samuelson does not discuss the class monopolization of the means of production and why he conceals the importance of the reswitching demonstration—so that he could defend as fair the nature of the class distribution of income in a capitalist society. Samuelson's ideological defense of income from ownership is not essentially different from those of Say, Senior, Bastiat, Clark, and the conservative neoclassicists in general.

The Austrian and Chicago Schools

The school of neoclassical economists that advocates extreme laissez-faire capitalism represents the contemporary counterparts of Senior and Bastiat. In a sense this group really represents two separate but similar schools—the Austrian School and the Chicago School. The Austrian School traces its lineage directly back to Carl Menger (see chapter 10). Menger's extreme methodological individualism is the basis of the social philosophy of the Austrian School.

While Menger's first generation of disciples included both social reformers and conservatives, the ultraconservative nature of the Austrian School is more properly thought of as the product of two of Menger's second-generation disciples, Ludwig von Mises and Friedrich A. Hayek. Both von Mises and Hayek taught at various times at the University of Chicago. Together with Frank H. Knight, who taught for many years at the University of Chicago, they were the most important influences in the formation of the Chicago School. For the past generation, Milton Friedman has been the most influential member of the Chicago School. In 1976, Friedman was awarded the Nobel Prize in economics.

The problem with classifying the Austrian and Chicago schools together is that, although they both emphasize the universal beneficence of exchange, extreme individualism, and a doctrinaire advocacy of laissez faire, they have methodological differences. The Austrians generally advocate a rationalist approach to economic theory, while Milton Friedman and his followers generally advocate an empiricist approach. Although it is currently very common in the academic economics profession to hear all extremely individualistic advocates of laissez faire referred to as the "Chicago School," it is probably more accurate to say that the more conservative wing of contemporary neo-classicism is about evenly divided between those who, on methodological grounds, follow the Austrian School and those who follow Friedman's Chicago School. We do not believe these methodological differences to be terribly significant,[25] so we will consider these contemporary advocates of extreme laissez faire together.

One of the most frequent claims of these schools, which is nearly identical to the claim made by Senior and Bastiat, is that their theory is pure, value-free science that contains no normative judgments at all. Friedman, for example, argues "that, in principle, there are no value judgments in economics."[26] Similarly, Richard McKenzie and Gordon Tullock have written: "The approach of the economist is *amoral*. Economics is not concerned with what *should be*, . . . but rather with understanding why people behave the way they do."[27] They maintain that their "analysis is devoid (as much as possible) of our own personal values."[28] In a widely used textbook written from the Austrian and Chicago perspective, Armen Alchian and William Allen have stated: "Economic theory is 'positive' or 'non-normative.'"[29]

Not only is the theory of these schools purported to be pure value-free science, it is claimed that only their theory merits the name *economics* and that their theory is equally valid for all people, in all social systems, in all times. In their introductory chapter, for example, McKenzie and Tullock proclaim: "In fact, it is the thought process or the mental skill developed below [in their book] that defines an economist."[30] The modesty of the devotees of these schools is matched only by the purported scope of their theory. Their theory "is a valid core of economic theory applicable to *all* economic systems and countries."[31]

Before the reader becomes overawed by the claim of the Austrian and Chicago schools as constituting the only value-free economic theory that explains all behavior, in all societies, in all places, and in all times, we suggest a careful consideration of the following statement by Joan Robinson (who made many original theoretical contributions to neoclassical theory—admittedly of the liberal variety—in the 1930s, before she abandoned neoclassicism):

> There has been a good deal of confused controversy about the question of 'value judgments' in the social sciences. Every human being has ideological, moral and political views. To pretend to have none and to be *purely objective* must necessarily be either self-deception or a device to deceive others. A candid writer will make his preconceptions clear and allow the reader to discount them if he does not accept them. This concerns the professional honour of the scientist.[32]

A reading of the literature of the Austrian and Chicago schools shows their analyses to be about as value free as the writings of Senior, Bastiat, and Menger (who also made that claim). In fact, it shows that the values that have always been at the base of the most extremely conservative, utilitarian, laissez-faire tradition clearly form the foundations for these schools. The writings of these schools could be quite accurately characterized as the ideology of Bastiat stated in terms of the maximizing marginal calculus.

The Austrian and Chicago schools are generally not particularly bothered by the four major areas (listed previously) in which liberal neoclassicists believe that the competitive laissez-faire theory is not a good representation of reality, and so, unlike the liberal school, they see very few reasons to extend the proper scope of government activity beyond the protection of the existing system of market power (i.e., the protection of private property and the enforcement of contracts). They generally reduce, as we will see, all human behavior to acts of exchange. As Marx said of Bastiat and the other precursors of these schools, when one looks only at exchange, one is struck with the illusion that capitalism is a veritable Eden of the rights of man—freedom, equality, property, and Bentham (see the quotation by Marx in chapter 9).

The four liberal neoclassicist objections to extreme laissez-faire are summarily disposed of by the Austrian and Chicago schools.

First, they maintain their faith in Say's law of the automaticity of the market. They simply assert that what instability has been observed in capitalism is wholly the fault of *too much government*. Thus, Friedman writes: "The fact is that the Great Depression, like most other periods of severe unemployment, was produced by government mismanagement rather than by any inherent instability of the private economy."[33]

Second, they simply deny that the gigantic corporations generally have any significant or meaningful monopoly power. Again, Friedman writes: "The most important fact about enterprise monopoly is its relative unimportance from the point of view of the economy as a whole."[34] The small and insignificant amount of monopoly power that does exist is almost never due to the actions of capitalists. Any attempts on the part of private capitalists to secure monopoly power, Friedman assures the reader, "are generally unstable and of brief duration unless they can call government to their assistance."[35] Once again, government, not the capitalist, is the culprit (although the evil is small and insignificant): "Probably the most important source of monopoly power has been government assistance."[36]

Third, the only "legitimate" socially consumed good that these schools generally feel the government should provide is defense. "I cannot get the amount of national defense I want and you, a different amount."[37] In this particular case, the government can provide us with defense, but in nearly all other cases "government intervention limits the area of individual freedom"[38] and is therefore undesirable.

Fourth, we have already discussed these schools' reaction to externalities (see chapter 14). Their answer is to create property rights to pollute and then to establish a market for the free buying and selling of these rights. We saw that this recommendation is based on these schools' individualistic belief that externalities are simply metaphysically given. Once one recognizes that individuals can, in fact, create externalities at will (because, in reality, we do live in a social world, not millions of individual worlds), then one sees that the recommendation of these schools would guarantee us that the free market would become an "invisible foot" that would automatically maximize human misery (see chapter 14).

So the Austrian and Chicago schools dismiss all of the liberal neoclassical economists' concerns and then advocate extreme laissez faire. In *Capitalism and Freedom*, for example, Milton Friedman advocates the elimination of (1) taxes on corporations, (2) the graduated income tax, (3) free public education, (4) social security, (5) government regulations of the purity of food and drugs, (6) the licensing and qualifying of doctors and dentists, (7) the post office monopoly, (8) government relief from natural disasters, (9) minimum wage laws, (10) ceilings on interest rates charged by usurious lenders, (11) laws prohibiting heroin sales, and nearly every other form of government intervention that goes beyond the enforcement of property rights and contract laws and the provision of national defense. Such are the conclusions of the value-free science of the intellectual descendants of Bastiat. The invisible hand, they believe, will do very nearly everything rationally and efficiently while preserving a maximum of freedom.

Most of the theorists of these schools escape from the devastating conclusions of the reswitching demonstration (see chapter 16), but they do so at a very high intellectual cost: They deny the existence of capitalism. There is, in their view, no general thing called capital, and, therefore, they do not need to calculate the productivity of capital. These schools have completed the process, started by Say, Senior, and Bastiat, of obscuring the difference between labor and capital. In their theory there are no laborers and no capitalists; there are only exchanging individuals. Alchian and Allen, for example, write: "Every person . . . is a form of capital good. And almost every physical good is a form of labor, in the sense that someone's labor was involved in making it as valuable as it is now."[39]

The utilitarian social perspective of each individual or household as an autonomous, calculating, rational undertaker of maximizing exchanges is most fully and consistently developed in the Austrian and Chicago schools. According to Friedman:

> A working model of a society organized through voluntary exchange is a *free enterprise exchange economy*—what we have been calling competitive capitalism.
>
> In its simplest form, such a society consists of a number of independent households—a collection of Robinson Crusoes, as it were. Each household uses the resources it controls to produce goods and services that it exchanges for goods and services produced by other households, on terms mutually acceptable to the two parties to the bargain.[40]

How quaint and nice. Each independent household is a little factory run by a family. No capitalists, no laborers—only individuals in households maximizing their utility through exchange. No strikes, no lockouts, no conflict at all; only harmonious maximizing individuals.

What, then, is the rate of interest? According to these schools, the rate of interest is merely a price that governs exchange. Individuals exchange commodities at a point in time and they exchange commodities over time, that is, they buy and sell commodities now, for which delivery will be taken in the future. The rate of interest is a measure of two quantitative magnitudes (which are equal, in equilibrium): the subjective measure of the individual's preference for present consumption over future consumption and the objective measure of the ability commodities have (this verges on magic) to increase over time if not consumed at present. Thus, in this view, there is no need to aggregate capital because, depending on one's perspective, either everything is capital or nothing is capital.

Bastiat's dictum that "political economy is exchange" is carried out to its logical extreme in this theory: *all human actions and interactions are reduced to simple, rational, utility-maximizing exchanges.* The world is, by the definitions and assumptions of their theory, always in a state of Pareto optimum bliss. Everything is always rational and efficient.

This reduction of all human action and interaction to simple exchange begins with these schools' conception of the firm and the process of production. The most definitive version of this theory of interest, J. Hirshleifer's *Investment, Interest and Capital*, begins by Providence (or perhaps Malthus's great lottery of life) giving to each individual an "initial endowment," that is, "a combination of goods that provides a starting point [how convenient!] for optimizing choice."[41] The individual can then acquire those goods that will maximize the individual's utility—or enable the individual to reach bliss point—either by exchanging this "initial endowment" of goods directly with other maximizing exchangers or by producing.

A business firm is defined as "a grouping of one or more individuals specialized to productive activities (transformation of commodity combinations effected through dealing with nature rather than through exchange with other economic agents)."[42] Thus, of the two principal divisions of neoclassical theory—consumption and production theory—consumption involves merely exchanges among persons, while "production is 'exchange' with nature."[43] So all economic activity is merely exchange. As we have seen many times throughout this book, the great "profundity" of utilitarian economics consists entirely in the observation that if exchange is voluntary, then both parties to the exchange must benefit and harmony must prevail. The theory, of course, entirely overlooks how the capitalist system creates a situation in which some exchangers have great bargaining power (while, doing little that is socially useful) and other exchangers exchange from a position of powerlessness or even desperation. But given the "initial endowments"—what a mystifying phrase this is in utilitarian economics—both exchangers do benefit; that is, working for any wage, under any working conditions, is usually preferable to starvation. In the approach of the Austrian and Chicago schools to capital and interest, there are both present prices and future prices for all commodities;

the wage rate (for labor applied either now or in the future) is a price like any other commodity price. Investment is merely an exchange, with nature or with other exchanging individuals, of present goods for future goods. Interest is merely an element in the price ratio between present and future goods. Capital is defined as merely the present value of all future consumption goods (their future value discounted by the interest rate over the length of time into the future before the individual can consume them). Thus, by definition, every individual must have capital (if he or she is ever to enjoy any good in the future), and, hence, everyone is a capitalist because everyone makes the same intertemporal, utility-maximizing exchanges.

The essential nature of this theory has been best described by a critic of neoclassicism, D.M. Nuti:

> The limitation of this approach can be summed up in one sentence: "production is 'exchange' with nature," productive investment being treated as forward exchange with nature. This restricts the validity of the analysis to the following cases: a technology where production is the growth in time of a seed effortlessly dropped on earth and equally effortlessly harvested; a slave economy where workers are like horses [i.e., they can be bought and sold both at present and for future delivery]; an economy of working and self-breeding robots; an economy of individual or cooperative producers [i.e., an economy in which labor power is not bought and sold and where producers control their own means of production]. Outside these cases, workers are hired and no labour other than one's own can be a part of the initial endowment; hence the production possibility set corresponding to a given initial "endowment" (whether this is a bundle of goods or "finance") will itself change with [a change in] the wage rate of dated labour. If, on the other hand, one's own labour is part of the initial endowment, it should be remembered that of all commodities labour power is the one for which in a capitalist system there are no conceivable forward markets. This is due to the special feature of labour as an input: workers—unlike bondsmen, slaves, horses and robots—can leave their job whenever they like.[44]

This criticism devastates the theory of the Austrian and Chicago schools. The existence of the "free" laborer is, as we have seen, one of the defining features of capitalism. The "freedom" of labor consists in the facts that the laborer can sell his or her labor power only for limited, contractually defined periods—the laborer cannot sell him or herself into slavery—and that most laborers are "free" of any controlling connection to the means of production; that is, they must sell their labor power in this limited, one-period-at-a-time manner in order to live. This is not only one of the defining features of capitalism, it is also the necessary condition, in neoclassical theory, for a "perfect" labor market in each time period.

So the cost of avoiding the devastating criticism contained in the reswitching demonstration (see chapter 16) is that the theory of these schools is not only *not* universal, it is inapplicable to capitalism. It can describe only a slave economy that is commercially oriented, or an economy comprised entirely of small, independent producers who own their own means of production. It is this latter vision of innumerable, small, independent producers that characterizes these schools' view, as we saw in our previous quotation from Friedman.

But these schools wish their readers to believe that capitalism is being described. The way out of this dilemma is usually to obscure this inapplicability of the theory to capitalism. This is illustrated by the following passage from Alchian and Allen:

> We shall find it convenient to speak of just two general kinds of inputs, even though there is in reality an infinite variety of types. Rather than identify the particular inputs in each case, we could call the inputs A and B. More commonly, the standard names given to the two broadest classes of inputs are *labor* and *capital*.[45]

It is particularly "convenient" for Alchian and Allen to use "standard names" of labor and capital because in their discussion of distribution, which follows this quotation, they show capital as a magnitude that can be aggregated, has a definable marginal product, and has a "reward" determined by its marginal productivity.[46]

Alchian and Allen end their discussion by making "a few precautionary comments." Among these comments is this: "The present analysis does not require the assumption that there be sets of different but internally homogeneous . . . resources."[47] What they neglect to tell the reader is that if you drop the assumption that capital contains some homogeneous "abiding" entity, then the theory no longer applies to capitalism. And if you retain the assumption, then the devastating reswitching critique is applicable.

Rather than face this issue forthrightly, Alchian and Allen, on the next page following this discussion, dogmatically assert that "the marginal productivity theory is valid in every economy."[48] If, when reading Veblen's critique of John Bates Clark, the reader thought that Veblen's mocking example (in which "a gang of Aleutian Islanders slushing about in the wrack and surf with rakes and magical incantations" could be understood as harmonious neoclassical maximizers) was a little extreme, then one should read Alchian and Allen, or any of the writers of the Austrian or Chicago schools who piously announce the universality of their value-free science.

Their science applies everywhere because it applies nowhere. Most theorizing by these schools is purely tautological. The argument goes like this:

1. All human behavior involves choice.
2. In any choice situation, whichever alternative is chosen involves gains and costs (whether explicit costs or implicit "opportunity" costs).
3. Therefore, all human behavior involves exchange, insofar as it involves acquiring gains in exchange for costs.
4. All human beings choose rationally; that is, they exchange in such a manner as to maximize the excess of the utility of the gain over the disutility of the cost (or the utility forgone in the opportunity cost).
5. Therefore, all choices are rational and represent the best possible alternatives

among those available in the exchange process (the utilitarian neoclassicists have always avoided facing the issue of how capitalist society gives some individuals so many alternatives and others so few).

6. Because all choices, or exchanges (they amount to the same thing), are rational and maximize each chooser's or exchanger's utility, then total utility is always maximized.

7. Therefore, free exchange in a capitalist society harmonizes all interests, maximizes utility, results in rational prices, results in efficient resource allocation, and, in general, automatically creates the best of all possible worlds.

8. Furthermore, because all human activity is in reality exchange, each and every aspect of a capitalist society is rational and blissful.

Perhaps the foregoing eight points might seem exaggerated to some readers. Do the theorists really believe that every exchange between a capitalist and a laborer greatly and significantly benefits the laborer? Do they really believe that every human action is a calculating, rational utility maximization? We will use quotations to let the Austrian and Chicago schools answer these questions in their own words.

To discuss the great benefits that come to the laborer because capitalists have monopolized the means of production, we turn to one of the founding fathers of the Austrian and Chicago schools, Ludwig von Mises. This economist believed there were three "progressive" classes that were responsible for all progress in human welfare—the savers, the investing owners of capital, and the innovators. He wrote:

> Everyone is free to join the ranks of the three progressive classes of a capitalist society. . . . What is needed to become a capitalist [a saver], an entrepreneur [an investor, or owner of capital goods] or a deviser of new technological methods is brains and will power. The heir of a wealthy man enjoys a certain advantage as he starts under more favorable conditions than others. But his task in the rivalry of the market is not easier, but sometimes even more wearisome and less remunerative than the newcomer's.[49]

Pity the poor inheritor of capitalist wealth whose task is more "wearisome" and "less remunerative" than the tasks faced by the rest of us. Somehow (undoubtedly because of genetic superiority) families like the Rockefellers seem to make it generation after generation despite such odds. Because the workers are able to exchange their labor power, selling it to these "progressive" possessors of "brains and will power," the workers derive great benefit. In fact, you might even say, reversing Adam Smith's dictum, that the workers reap where they do not sow. The workers are able, through the harmonious beneficence of the market, to "enjoy the fruits" of capitalists' "achievements." Von Mises wrote:

> The characteristic feature of the market economy is the fact that it allots the greater part of the improvements brought about by the endeavors of the three progressive

classes—those saving, those investing the capital goods, and those elaborating new methods for the employment of capital to the nonprogressive majority of people. . . . The market process provides the common man with the opportunity to enjoy the fruits of other peoples' achievements. It forces the three progressive classes to serve the nonprogressive majority in the best possible way.[50]

How fortunate for common people, who do all of the producing, that they as workers are able to "enjoy the fruits" of the "achievements" of coupon clippers, dividend receivers, and other functionless rentiers, whose lavish incomes are simply the "just returns" to the "wearisome" exercise of their "brains and will power." Indeed, how could the workers get along without this beneficent, functionless rentier class? Von Mises did not believe that they could. Thompson, Hodgskin, Marx, Hobson, Luxemburg, Lenin, and Veblen knew differently.

Finally, the Austrian and Chicago schools reduce all human behavior to rational maximizing exchanges and hence are able to prove that, in every respect, economic and noneconomic, a free market, capitalist system is the best of all possible worlds.

McKenzie and Tullock, who, it will be recalled, let us know that only their ideas constituted economics, demonstrate these profound and everlasting truths for us. In a section of their book entitled "Why People Walk on the Grass," they describe an individual about to make the choice of (or engage in the exchange that will result in) stepping on the grass: "Before stepping onto the grass he must quickly reflect on the benefits and then calculate the cost involved. . . . Consequently, the calculated benefits exceed the costs, so he walks—and he does so rationally!"[51] How comforting to know that, in capitalism, even walking on the grass is a rational, maximizing action that contributes to our harmonious bliss.

But do these utilitarians really believe that humans are nothing but rational, calculating pleasure machines, even when people act from what most of us regard as passion? McKenzie and Tullock assure us that everything is the result of rational maximizing exchange. They take sexual behavior as another example. We are told that "sex is a service that is produced and procured [i.e., gotten in exchange]. Like all other production processes . . . sexual experience entails costs."[52] Therefore, for all of us rational, utility-maximizing automatons,

> it follows that the quantity of sex demanded is an inverse function of price. . . . The reason for this relationship is simply that the rational individual will consume sex up to the point that the marginal benefits equal the marginal costs. . . . If the price of sex rises relative to other goods, the consumer will "rationally" choose to consume more of other goods and less sex. (Ice cream, as well as many other goods, can substitute for sex if the relative prices require it.)[53]

McKenzie and Turlock are referring to "ordinary sexual relationships" as well as prostitution. In prostitution the payment is "monetary," and in "ordinary sexual relationships" the payment is "non-monetary."[54] All sex, in principle, is identical for rational, maximizing pleasure machines. The authors go on to tell us how we make the same type of rational, maximizing exchanges in choosing a marriage partner and also in what they call "child production." "Children," we are told, "are also economic goods."[55] All child rearing—including child beating—is merely a series of rational, utility-maximizing exchanges.

Smith and Ricardo, in the grandeur of their general vision of capitalist society, saw the economy, as we have seen, from both a utility (or exchange) perspective and a labor (or production) perspective. Neoclassical economics represents the final, ultimate extension of the utility perspective. In the development of this perspective, we have seen throughout this book an intellectual degeneration from Ricardo onward. Only eclectics such as Mill, Keynes, and Samuelson could escape the force of this degeneration, because they had enough common sense to combine more realistic perspectives with their utility perspective. The degeneration is now complete, however. The banalities of McKenzie and Tullock can be said to be the ultimate triumph and the inevitable result of the development of pure, logically consistent, individualistic utilitarianism.

There seems to us to be a profound sadness in the inimical banalities of McKenzie and Tullock, not simply because they are banalities—there have always been and perhaps will always be people espousing insipid ideas—but because of what these banalities represent. The sadness is that alienation in our society is so intense that McKenzie and Tullock's "theories" are actually partially descriptive of the behavior of some people under capitalism—people who have suffered such psychic repression that they come close to being merely rational, calculating automatons.

Utilitarian marginalism is surely a social symptom of this intense alienation. It is a philosophy that takes, the most alienated, repressed, emotionally fragmented, and pathologically damaged of human behavior and then both assumes this behavior to be universal human nature and elevates it to an apotheosis of human potential.

This issue, as seen in the tradition of Marx and Veblen, is not how to make the most advantageous purchase of sex or how to make the most astute investment in "child production." The issue is how to create a society in which people will reach their full potential emotionally, esthetically, intellectually, and physically; and in this process the people will surely have to treat themselves as well as all others as unique, valuable humans, that is, as ends in themselves and not as commodities. Human interaction that would adequately fulfill our most truly human needs is the very antithesis of the commercialized, rational treatment of humans as commodities that is extolled in the Austrian and Chicago schools. The sadness also is that alienation has reached such proportions that these schools thrive and constitute a major segment of academic economics. Only in a society in which acute and chronic alienation is extensive could such a contumelious assessment of human worth be passed off as pure, value-free science.

Notes to Chapter 17

1. W.A. Lewis, "Economic Development with Unlimited Supplies of Labour," Manchester School, May 1954; and W.A. Lewis, *Theory of Economic Growth* (London: Allen and Unwin, 1955).

2. Lewis, "Economic Development," p. 148.

3. Ibid., p. 150.

4. Ibid., p. 141.

5. Ibid., p. 147.

6. Ibid., p. 190.

7. W.W. Rostow, "The Marshallian Long Period," in *Pioneers in Development*, ed. G.N. Meier and D. Seers (New York: Oxford University Press, 1983), p. 240.

8. Ibid., p. 241.

9. Paul A. Samuelson, *The Foundations of Economic Analysis* (Cambridge, MA: Harvard University Press, 1947).

10. Paul A. Samuelson, *Economics*, 10th ed. (New York: McGraw-Hill, 1976), p. 267.

11. Ibid., p. 521.

12. Ibid., p. 523.

13. Ibid., p. 531.

14. Ibid., p. 160.

15. Ibid., p. 811.

16. Ibid., p. 479.

17. Ibid., p. 634.

18. Ibid., pp. 69–79.

19. Ibid., p. 603.

20. Ibid., p. 560.

21. Ibid., pp. 617–18.

22. Ibid., p. 618.

23. Ibid., p. 47.

24. Ibid., p. 605.

25. See E.K. Hunt, "Rationalism and Empiricism in Economic Theories of Value," *Social Science Journal* 14, no. 3 (1977): 11–26.

26. Milton Friedman, "Value Judgments in Economics," in *Human Values and Economic Policy*, ed. S. Hook (New York: New York University Press, 1967), p. 86.

27. Richard B. McKenzie and Gordon Tullock, *The New World of Economics, Explorations in Human Experience* (Homewood, IL: Irwin, 1975), p. 6.

28. Ibid., p. 7.

29. Armen A. Alchian and William R. Allen, *University Economics* (Belmont, CA: Wadsworth, 1964), p. 5.

30. McKenzie and Tullock, *New World of Economics*, p. 5.

31. Alchian and Allen, *University Economics*, p. 5.

32. Joan Robinson, *Freedom and Necessity* (New York: Pantheon, 1970), p. 122.

33. Milton Friedman, *Capitalism and Freedom* (Chicago: University of Chicago Press, 1962), p. 38.

34. Ibid., p. 121.

35. Ibid., p. 131.

36. Ibid., p. 129.

37. Ibid., p. 23.

38. Ibid., p. 32.

39. Alchian and Allen, *University Economics*, p. 433.

40. Friedman, *Capitalism and Freedom*, p. 13.

41. J. Hirshleifer, *Investment, Interest and Capital* (Englewood Cliffs, NJ: Prentice-Hall, 1970), p. 2.

42. Ibid., p. 12.

43. Ibid.

44. D.M. Nuti, "Vulgar Economy in the Theory of Income Distribution," in *A Critique of Economic Theory*, ed. E.K. Hunt and Jesse G. Schwartz (Baltimore: Penguin, 1972), pp. 230–36.

45. Alchian and Allen, *University Economics*, p. 433.

46. Ibid., pp. 433–51.

47. Ibid., p. 452.

48. Ibid., p. 453.

49. Ludwig von Mises, *The Anti-Capitalistic Mentality* (New York: Van Nostrand, 1956), pp. 40–41.

50. Ibid., p. 40.

51. McKenzie and Tullock, *New World of Economics*, p. 28.

52. Ibid., p. 52.

53. Ibid., pp. 51–52.

54. Ibid., p. 52.

55. Ibid., p. 108.

Chapter 18

Contemporary Economics II: Institutionalism and Post-Keynesianism

When the Great Depression of the 1930s and the rapid industrialization of the Soviet economy of that era created a crisis of confidence in neoclassical theory, alternative, heterodox theories prospered. We have already mentioned the fact that Keynesian economics gained such rapid acceptance that its influence among economists came close to, or perhaps even surpassed, that of neoclassicism.

One of the significant accomplishments of Paul Samuelson was to obviate the struggle between advocates of these two theoretical perspectives for the hearts and minds of economists by convincing them that neoclassical economics (now known as microeconomic theory) and Keynesian economics (now known as macroeconomic theory) were not competitors at all. They were the twin pillars of orthodoxy. The differences between them—indeed, in many instances, the contradictions between them—could safely be ignored if, when one looked at microeconomic issues, one ignored Keynesian ideas, and when one looked at macroeconomic issues, one ignored neoclassical ideas. Samuelson's *Economics* enshrined macroeconomic (Keynesian) and microeconomic (neoclassical) theories as the twin pillars of orthodoxy.

Not everyone was content with this reconciliation, however. Indeed, it was attacked from the beginning by many defenders of, and critics of, neoclassical economics. Institutionalist economists and Marxist economists rejected neoclassical theory almost in its entirety. They substituted entirely different social visions of the nature and functioning of a capitalist market economy for the neoclassical vision and their rejection of the neoclassical vision rested on profound and (if accepted) devastating criticisms of neoclassicism.

And while most Keynesians were content to be elevated to one of two pillars of orthodoxy (Joan Robinson was an outstanding exception to this), many conservative neoclassicist advocates of laissez-faire capitalism were very unhappy about Samuelson's merging of their theoretical tradition with another tradition that they saw as a logically and theoretically inconsistent and politically and ideologically hostile.

Ironically, the origins of the neoclassical attack on Keynes came from the pen of a professed socialist, Oscar Lange. Immediately after the publication of Keynes's *General Theory*, Lange made an effort to reconcile Keynes's ideas with the prevailing Walrasian general equilibrium approach to neoclassicism. Keynes had sought to explain an economic equilibrium in which a significant amount of involuntary unemployment existed, that is, a general equilibrium in which one very large and economically significant market—the labor market—was in disequilibrium.

Lange concluded that the Keynesian notion of equilibrium was incompatible with the Walrasian notion—in the latter, a general equilibrium implies an equilibrium in each and every market. In 1940, Lange published his *Price Flexibility and Employment,* in which he attempted to recast Keynes's arguments within the context of a Walrasian general equilibrium model. Basically, Lange argued, Keynes had identified special situations that involved involuntary unemployment—and hence were disequilibria in a Walrasian system—in which market forces would not tend to establish equilibrium and the disequilibrium would persist. Lange's influence can be traced through a line of theorists that included Don Patinkin, Robert Clower, and Axel Leijonhufvud all from the 1940s through the 1970s. In the 1970s and 1980s, orthodox Keynesian theory lost its favored standing and the ideas of these theorists had a significant impact on the economics profession. Many economists began to see Keynesian economics as merely a special case of neoclassical economics. Macroeconomics increasingly became simply the study of the general conditions in which a market would more or less automatically attain a general Walrasian equilibrium and the special conditions under which problems might arise. The dominant approach to macroeconomics, known as "rational expectations theory," stressed the automaticity of the market. The implications of this for a renewed defense of the laissez-faire ideology are obvious. Although some college texts continued to devote a chapter or two to traditional Keynesian economics, by 1990 it no longer occupied the privileged place as one of the twin pillars of orthodoxy. Neoclassical theory once again totally dominated orthodoxy.

Throughout the period after World War II, two heterodox economic traditions—Marxist and institutionalist economics—continued their developments more or less independently from neoclassical or Keynesian economics. Marxist economics will be discussed in the next chapter. In the first half of this chapter, we will discuss one tendency or branch of the several somewhat different streams of economic theory that fall under the general heading of institutionalist economics. We will discuss the tradition that has its foundations in the theories of Thorstein Veblen, John Dewey, and Clarence E. Ayres. In the second half of the chapter, we will discuss "post-Keynesian" economics—a new tradition of heterodox economists founded in the 1970s and 1980s by the disciples of Keynes who were unsympathetic to neoclassical economics and resisted the incorporation of Keynes into the neoclassical framework.

The Institutionalist Economics of Clarence E. Ayres

Veblen's break with traditional economic theory had been sharp and extreme. He had rejected equilibrium analyses and he had rejected the neoclassical vision of a society filled with utility-maximizing exchangers. He had sought to understand the biological nature of human beings and had emphasized that this biological nature always rendered human beings interdependent social creatures. The social nature of human beings did not imply social relationships or social behavior that was biologically determined, however. People existed under a very wide variety of social conditions. And individual human beings were very malleable. This malleability permitted human beings to become conditioned and habituated to the radically different attitudes, values, and actions that were required for the social behavior appropriate to, or consistent with, radically different social institutions.

As the neoclassical theory of utility-maximizing individuals became more and more esoteric, it also became much more difficult to master. It required a strong background in mathematics and years studying the esoteric analytical constructs of neoclassical economics to receive a doctorate in economics at most universities. For most graduate students of economics this left little or no time for the study of philosophy, anthropology, history, and sociology—the disciplines from which many of Veblen's ideas were drawn. Moreover, in many economics departments, the ideological domination of conservative neoclassical economists resulted in a situation in which the study of Veblen's writings became personally, politically, and ideologically "unwise" as did the study of Marx's writings. Evidence that a young economist took either Marx or Veblen seriously was often construed as evidence of intellectual incompetence. Consequently, the institutionalist and Marxist schools of economic theory have remained small—but they have also remained influential.

Clarence E. Ayres (1891–1972) received a Ph.D. in philosophy from the University of Chicago in 1917. Ayres was a "grand" systematic thinker interested in all facets of human existence. From the beginning, he showed as much interest in economics as he did in philosophy. One year after receiving his Ph.D., he published a thought-provoking article entitled "The Function and Problems of Economic Theory."[1] In his first teaching position, at Amherst College, he was significantly influenced by Walton Hamilton, a brilliant young economist who coined the term *institutionalism*. Ayres had learned standard neoclassical economics as a student and was assigned to serve as a teaching assistant to Hamilton. Ayres has described the early impact that Hamilton had on his thinking:

> As Professor Hamilton discoursed to Amherst freshman . . . I began to wonder when he was going to get around to unfolding to these freshman such basic ideas as "marginal utility." Finally I mustered up my courage to ask him, and through the 44 years that have since elapsed I have never forgotten the gleam of amusement in his eyes as he replied, "I'd do so at once if only I understood them myself!" Like Henny Penny, I felt the heavens falling, for already I had conceived a tremendous admiration for the mental processes of this extraordinary young professor. Could it be that all the elaborate apparatus of marginal analysis was actually without meaning?[2]

Ayres did indeed conclude that neoclassical theory was meaningless. He recognized that the concept of utility and the theory that in market capitalism utility-maximizing individuals *automatically* create an optimal situation were the intellectual heart of neoclassical economics. He also recognized the hollow, tautological nature of the foundations of this theory:

> . . . the concept of utility is peculiarly open to criticism on the ground of tautology. . . . It is all very well to say that utility is the want—satisfying quality, whatever wants may be. But if we have no way of knowing, let alone measuring, wants, how can we know utility—let alone measure it? It is all very well to say that price is the measure of utility. But if we have no independent measure of utility (and we have none), that only means that we have equated price and utility by definition. Such being the case, nothing can be inferred from the correspondence.[3]

Neoclassical economics was, in Ayres's view, merely folklore designed to preserve the status quo of social, political, and economic power.

In one of his earliest books, *Holier Than Thou*, Ayres's ideas showed the distinct influence of Veblen. He asked how seemingly intelligent people adopted ideas, attitudes, mores, and folkways that were based on superstition and that a more detached rational individual would find impossible to accept. The answer, he believed, could be seen in the functionality of these ideas, attitudes, mores, and folkways in sustaining the power of the wealthy, dominant social class.

Ayres's point of departure was a discussion of Veblen's account of the reasons for the rapid changes in clothing styles. Veblen had argued that the clothing of the rich had to set them distinctly apart from the poor. The motive of the clothing designers was merely to create sharp, stark differences in the clothing of the rich and the poor. The designers were rarely motivated by any genuinely aesthetic concerns or standards. The aesthetic ugliness of this year's styles would provoke a revolt that would lead to drastic changes next year, the year after that, and so on. As long as invidious distinction and not beauty was the motivating force, there would continue to be such revolts leading to perpetual changes in the styles of clothing for the rich.

Ayres, while obviously strongly influenced by and enormously respectful of Veblen, objected to this analysis on two grounds. First, he denied that there was any inherent or transcendent aesthetic standards by which the styles could be judged to be ugly. Second, he argued that the rate of change in the clothing styles of the rich depended entirely on the rate at which capitalists selling low-cost clothing to working people could imitate these styles and sell these cheaper imitations to poor people seeking to emulate the rich. This would reduce the distinction between the rich and the poor if the rich failed to make new and drastic changes in their styles.

Ayres went on to argue that not only were there no general standards of beauty but there were no general standards of moral rightness or goodness. People's attitudes on these matters were merely the accidents of the mores and folklore of their society. Moreover, most people's attitudes toward truth or science were also simply superstitions.

But Ayres was not interested in being nihilistic or in promoting some form of extreme cultural relativism. There was still a question of whether there were understandable reasons for people's beliefs in cultural folklore and superstitions and also whether some beliefs had more truth value than others. Here the second great influence on Ayres becomes obvious—the philosophy of John Dewey.

Dewey had rejected the view, dominant in philosophy and the social sciences of his era, that ends and means are qualitatively different and can always be clearly distinguished. Ayres was influenced by Dewey's argument that means and ends are never entirely separable. Means are chosen, Dewey argued, because they promote some desired end. But if one investigates the reasons why the end in question is the object of desire, one nearly always finds that it is desired because it is seen as a means to some further end. Thus, if my end is getting to the grocery store, I have a number of means of conveyance from which to choose. These means of conveyance are "means" and yet they are valued as ends because I know that regularly I am going to need them to enable me to travel to the store (and elsewhere). Going to the store appears to be the end. It does not, however, have intrinsic value. Getting to the store is the *means* by which I can attain food. The attainment of the food then appears to be the end. But again this does not have intrinsic value. It is valued only as a means of satisfying my hunger. Dewey argued that if you examine most ends you find that they are desired because they serve as means toward other ends. Moreover, most means, for the same reasons, are also perceived as ends. Life, Dewey argued, is constituted by a continuum of causes and effects and means and ends. Any event is the effect of prior causes and the cause of subsequent consequences. No particular event can be called a cause only or an effect only but, rather, must be seen as both an effect and a cause. Similarly, things, circumstances, situations, and actions are almost never seen by people solely as ends or solely as means. If they are a means toward something valued, then they are valued. Similarly, the value of nearly every end derives from the fact that it serves as a means toward another end or ends.

Ayres adopted this view: "Day to day experience reveals no generic difference between 'ends' and 'means.' Every item of our experience is both an end and a means. There is no difference of 'substance' or 'essence' by which, in the continuum of day to day experience, 'means' and 'ends' can be distinguished."[4]

Ayres followed Veblen in believing that most human actions and values fell into two dichotomous and antagonistic categories. At one extreme were superstitions, ceremonial values and actions. These values and actions had as their social function the creation and preservation of hierarchical distinctions of social and economic status and were the foundations of all invidious distinctions based on social status. At the other end of the dichotomy were technological values and actions. These values and actions were instrumental in providing the means necessary to further what Ayres called the "general life process."

Ayres rejected absolutism and nihilistic relativism in both epistemology and ethics. He believed that, following Dewey, he had found a middle ground that preserved the advantages of both absolutism and relativism with the disadvantages of neither.

> We know that social development is a continuous process, and it is in terms of this continuity that value and welfare can be quite objectively defined and understood. For not only is the social process a continuous one in the chronological sense; on the technological side it is a logical continuum, a time progression each item of which implies succeeding items by the same process by which each has been itself derived from preceding items in the series. It is this technological continuum which is the locus of truth and value.[5]

Truth and value were derived from technological mastery of nature in furthering the "general life process." "When we judge a thing to be good or bad, or an action to be right or wrong, what we mean is that, in our opinion, the thing or act in question will or will not serve to advance the life process in so far as we can envision it."[6] In his last major work, Ayres argued that "it is the dissociation of truth and value that defines the moral crisis of the twentieth century."[7] When this dissociation occurred, truth was replaced by superstition. Most widely held superstitions were, he believed, the results of ceremonial values and actions that functioned to preserve hierarchical distinctions of social status. While the dichotomous nature of technological and ceremonial values persuades Ayres's writings, it is, perhaps, most succinctly stated and explained by a leading contemporary disciple of Ayres:

> The value structure . . . derives its social warrant from one of two systems of value formation. Values are either ceremonially warranted or instrumentally warranted. The essence of the institutional dichotomy is contained in this distinction between the two modes of social valuation existing within the society.
>
> Ceremonial values are warranted by those mores and folkways that incorporate status hierarchies and invidious distinctions as to the relative "worth" of various individuals of classes in the community. They rationalize power relationships and patterns of authority embedded in the status quo.
>
> Accordingly, patterns of behavior correlated by ceremonial values are observed to be those social practices that manifest their use of power and coercion in the conduct of human affairs: social practices that require invidious distinctions and status relationships to justify their existence. On the other hand, patterns of behavior cor-

related by instrumental values are manifest in those problem-solving activities upon which the life processes of the community depend."[8]

The ideas of Veblen and Ayres have been developed, refined, and extended by a number of contemporary economists, including, but by no means limited to, Paul D. Bush, Thomas R. DeGregori, William M. Dugger, David Hamilton, F. Gregory Hayden, Louis Junker, Phillip Klein, Anne Mayhew, Walter C. Neale, Baldwin Ranson, Warren Samuels, Robert Solo, and Mark Tool. Bush and Junker developed an important extension of this basic institutionalist analysis with their concept of "ceremonial encapsulation." In Bush's words:

> The dynamic force that brings about institutional adjustment is an expansion of the knowledge fund through the problem-solving processes of the community. According to the principle of ceremonial encapsulation, the new knowledge will be incorporated into the institutional structure only to the extent that it can be made ceremonially adequate; that is, only to the extent that its incorporation can be accomplished without upsetting the existing degree of ceremonial dominance embedded in the value structure of the community.[9]

In other words, the ability of a given society to use new problem-solving knowledge is limited by the patterns of social, political, and economic domination that are exercised by the powerful and wealthy individuals of that society. And because the vested interests of the ruling elites come to be embodied in the dominant institutions of a society, millions of ordinary individuals who derive their livelihood from these institutions come to be defenders of these ceremonial values that preserve the status quo. Bush points to the example of the military-industrial complex in the United States:

> The demilitarization of the American economy poses a grave threat not only to the vested interests of the giant corporations of the military-industrial complex, but also to the economic base of hundreds of communities, large and small, throughout the nation that have become heavily dependent on military contracts.
>
> The economic waste that is inherent in ceremonial encapsulation of resources and technology by the military-industrial complex is also the source of secure income for millions of Americans as long as the Cold War ideology dominates the American *Weltanschauung*. The economic continuity of the lives of millions of Americans is encapsulated by the ceremonial nexus of anticommunist demonology, guaranteed profits of military contracts, and self-serving patriotism.[10]

Similarly, F. Gregory Hayden has shown that giant enterprises in the chemical, farm machinery, and agribusiness industries have gained control of science and technology in their fields for the purpose of increasing their profits and industrial control. The increases in profits have often come at the expense of land conservation and the preservation of vital social and ecological systems.[11]

William M. Dugger has shown that in the United States today the large corporation is the central bastion of ceremonialism. It is the main institution that secures and preserves the social relations and individual behaviors necessary to maintain and perpetuate the American hierarchy of power, privilege, and invidious distinction. As a result, the large corporation tends to dominate all other institutions in American life. This corporate hegemony is maintained through four social mechanisms: subordination, contamination, emulation, and mystification. In Dugger's words:

> Subordination ties all institutions together so that noncorporate institutions are used as means to corporate ends. Contamination puts corporate role motives into noncorporate roles. Emulation allows corporate leaders to gain acceptance, even respect, in noncorporate leadership roles. And mystification covers the corporate hegemony with a protective (magic) cloak.[12]

Through these mechanisms, corporations are able to gain control of technology and to discard what they cannot use while subordinating the remaining aspects of technology to their own use. As a result, ceremonial encapsulation subordinates technological values to ceremonial values that perpetuate the structure of power and privilege.

In this process, propaganda and thought control are of crucial significance. In this regard, Dugger shows how colleges and universities are subordinated to corporate interests. The university's instrumentally warranted goals of free inquiry and the expansion of the intellectual horizons of faculty and students are generally subordinated to the teaching of ceremonially warranted conservative ideology, vocational training, and the promotion of research needed by specific industries. Thus, the social mission of the university is subordinated to the needs of industry to the detriment of the community.

The academic world is, in fact, a rigidly hierarchical system infused and pervaded by invidious distinctions—an ideal system for perpetuating the ceremonial propaganda of conservative ideology. At the top of the hierarchy are the elite Ivy League universities together with a few other elite private and state universities. These schools determine what ideas will be "respectable" within academia. They also train the professors who teach at the principal state universities and other private research universities. These latter schools train the professors who teach at the bottom of the hierarchy in state colleges and private teaching colleges.

At the top of the hierarchy, ideological purity is maintained. Conservative ideology is academically and intellectually pronounced as "scientific" while critical theory is ignored. One clearly sees this when one examines the profession of academic economics. The dissident schools of thought such as Institutionalism, post-Keynesianism, and Marxism go virtually untaught in the elite Ivy League universities. On the other hand, the majority of the most influential theorists and writers in the conservative neoclassical school teach at these elite universities. Institutionalists, post-Keynesians, and Marxists teach at the middle and lower levels of the hierarchy and hence are always struggling to maintain "respectability." Thus, as the academic hierarchy promotes the dominance of ceremonial values over instrumental values, it also promotes and defends the social, economic, and political hierarchies on which differential power and privilege rest, and on which the socially important invidious distinctions among individuals rest.

Finally, John Munkirs has shown that corporate dominance in the United States rests on what he calls the system of centralized private sector planning (CPSP). This system of economic planning is dominated by giant financial and industrial corporations. Munkirs argues that it is the function of conservative capitalist ideology to conceal this dominance. Munkirs writes:

> Unfortunately, in America, the real choices that our technological knowledge make possible (choices between different production and distribution systems, for example, centralized versus decentralized) have been circumscribed by, or encapsulated within, our capitalistic ideology and, in particular, by the values of self-interest, profit seeking, and laissez-faire. In brief, the particular type of centralized planning that exists in America today is due neither to technological determinism not to conspiratorial machinations. Rather CPSP is a direct result of combining the values of self-interest, profit seeking, and laissez-faire with certain technological possibilities.[13]

In this short account of the ideas of C.E. Ayres and several of his contemporary disciples, we have discussed only a few of the many facets of contemporary institutionalism. Institutionalist economists seek to understand much more than the simple workings of supply and demand in the market. They are interested in the evolution of the entire society. They examine the institutional foundations of economic, social, and political power and how this power is affected by, but also exerts powerful controls on, the market. As this brief account has shown, institutionalist economists see the economy as a part of a greater social valuation process that is far larger and far more important than the process of commodity pricing. Again, they depict two dichotomous social bases of valuation—the instrumental and the ceremonial. While human progress depends on the ascendance of instrumental values, the present economic order is characterized by a dominance of the ceremonial valuation process. Orthodox neoclassical economics will be of little help in this regard because most of its tenets have the social function of reinforcing the ceremonial values that underlay and protect the status quo with its emphasis on differential power and invidious distinction.

Institutionalists have also done a great deal of research in fields such as labor economics, industrial organization, law and economics, comparative economic systems, public choice, agricultural economics, and government regulation of business. As a contemporary school of economics, institutionalism remains alive and healthy.

Post-Keynesian Economics

Keynes saw his theory as a critique of neoclassical economics. In the 1940s and early 1950s, people spoke of the "Keynesian revolution." As we saw in the beginning of this chapter, however, the neoclassical economists selectively chose a few ideas from Keynes's *General Theory* and elaborated and

developed these ideas until, by the 1970s, Keynes's ideas were seen by orthodox neoclassical economists as merely a special case of the more general
neoclassical theory.

During the 1970s and 1980s, a group of economists revived the ideas of
Keynes that were not compatible with neoclassical economics. They com-
bined these ideas with the theories of Michal Kalecki, Joan Robinson, and
Piero Sraffa and reasserted the radical side of the Keynesianism tradition in
what has now become a new school of economics known as "post-Keynesian
Economics."

Post-Keynesians have a central concern with economic growth. Nearly all
theories of economic growth begin with the "Harrod-Domar" growth formula,
$G = s/v$, where G is the rate of growth, s is the average propensity to save (or
the ratio of saving to national income and production) and v is the capital/
output ratio (or the average number of units of capital required to produce one
unit of output). To explain this formula we can begin with a simplifying assumption that demand is equal to supply in each market as well as in the
aggregate economy. This would mean that all saving in the economy would
automatically become embodied in newly produced capital goods. Under this
assumption the ratio of saving to income, s, would automatically be the same
as the ratio of investment to income, or the same as the ratio of the increase in
the capital stock (i.e., investment) to income.

The increased capital stock, however, increases the economy's productive
capacity. Therefore, if all markets are to remain in equilibrium, all of the
productive capacity must be utilized and production and income will have to
be larger than they were in the previous period. The rate of growth expresses
the size of this necessary increase in production and income, expressed as a
percentage of the total income.

If v, the capital/output ratio were *one*, that is, if every dollar of new investment would result in an increase in the capital stock just sufficient to produce
one dollar of additional output, then the total dollar amount of additional productive capacity (and hence, under our assumptions, of new production and
income) would be just equal to the total saving. Therefore, under this assumption, the rate of growth would be the same as the average propensity to save.

If v were *two*, that is, if for each two-dollar increase in the capital stock the
capacity to produce would increase by only one dollar's worth of new commodities, then the total amount of saving would increase productive capacity
by only one-half of its dollar amount. Thus, under this assumption, the average propensity to save would have to be divided by two to get the rate of
growth of the economy.

The Harrod-Domar formula is not a theory. It is merely a conceptual framework within which economists can examine quantitatively the relationships
among the variables of saving, investment, the capital stock, output, income,
and the rate of growth. The general framework is used by economists of nearly
all schools of thought. The neoclassical economists, for example, use this

framework to show that the pillars of capitalist ideology at the core of their theory (i.e., automaticity, efficiency, and the marginal productivity theory of distribution) are all valid for an economy that is growing through time. Given exogenously determined preferences (which, together with income distribution, determine saving) and exogenously determined production functions and resource endowments (which, together with preferences and income distribution, determine the amount and composition of production), with an array of unrealistic assumptions, one can show how the economy automatically adjusts to the proper full-employment rate of growth. One can also show how this growth rate utilizes resources efficiently and how each category of productive factor (natural resources, labor, and capital) earns a reward that is equal to its marginal productivity.

The entire demonstration is an abstract exercise in analytical logic. The "time" involved is "logical time" not real time. The time period is defined as just long enough for all of the logical and mathematical relationships to work out the way the neoclassical economists want them to work out.

Post-Keynesian theory, by contrast, is concerned with a real economy that exists in a concrete historical situation and adjusts to disequilibrating forces with a process that occurs in real, historical time. The adjustment depends, among other things, upon how economic agents interpret the past and what they expect in the future. The accuracy of their expectations depends not only on the adequacy of their assessment of the past and present but also on the compatibility or incompatibility of their decisions, based on these expectations, with the decisions of the hundreds of thousands of other economic agents with whom they are economically interdependent. Thus, an entrepreneur can be very knowledgeable, make very careful, precise calculations and very cautious investments, but the success of these investments will always depend in part on the decisions being made simultaneously by competitors, suppliers, and customers, as well as other factors that are unforeseeable. Competitors, suppliers, or customers may act upon expectations based on less knowledge, or may act totally irrationally. In these cases, even an entrepreneur's most carefully constructed projections about the future may be wrong.

One of the most distinguished post-Keynesian economists, Professor J.A. Kragel, has summed this aspect of the theory as follows:

> The methodology that Keynes chose in confronting the analysis of an uncertain world was in terms of alternative specifications about the effects of uncertainty and disappointment. . . . In fact, Keynes argued that his approach could not assume perfect foresight and full information, for under such an assumption his main theoretical contribution, the theory of effective demand, had no meaning.
>
> Further, Keynes' own view of his general theoretical approach was that it could be used to analyze a range of problems in addition to that which he found most pressing, i.e., the determination of the level of output and employment. Different problems would, however, require different basic assumptions about the dependent, given and independent variables of the system.

Finally, . . . what has come to be called . . . "post-Keynesian" theory can be viewed as an attempt to analyze various different economic problems, e.g., capital accumulation, income distribution, etc., through the methodology of Keynes.[14]

In particular, following the theories of both Keynes and Kalecki, the post-Keynesians have analyzed the relationship between income distribution and economic growth. In the formulation of N. Kaldor, we again assume that saving equals investment. In Keynes's formulation, "s" was the "propensity to save, while S and Y were the saving and income for one period." Thus, $S = sY$ was the "saving function," specifying how saving varied with variations in income. Kaldor divided an economy's income into two categories: the income of workers, consisting of wages and salaries received for their labor performed, and the income of capitalists, consisting of rent, interest, dividends, and profits received from their ownership of the means of production.

Now, in place of the Keynesian saving function, we have

$$S = s_w Y + (s_p - s_w)P. \tag{18.1}$$

where s_w is the propensity to save of workers and s_p is the propensity to save of capitalists. Assuming investment is equal to saving, as it must be in equilibrium, we have

$$1 = s_w Y + (s_p - s_w)P. \tag{18.2}$$

We can divide this equation by Y and rearrange the terms and we have

$$\frac{P}{Y} = \frac{1}{(s_p - s_w)} \cdot \frac{1}{Y} - \frac{s_w}{(s_p - s_w)} \tag{18.3}$$

The classical economists had argued that workers live at or near subsistence and hence must consume all of their income. Thus, they believed that capitalists do all of the saving. If we assume this, then $s_w = 0$. If we assume further that capitalists receive so much income that consumption is an inconsequential part of their income and that they therefore save nearly all of their income, we can approximate this assumption when $s_p = 1$. If $s_w = 0$ and $s_p = 1$, then equation (18.3) reduces to

$$\frac{p}{Y} = \frac{1}{Y} \tag{18.4}$$

This formulation has the advantage of showing the basic relationship in a capitalist economy between the rate of investment and the capitalists' share of national income. The higher the level of investment the larger will be the income share of capitalists and the lower will be the income share of workers.

A more realistic formulation is to assume that the capitalist propensity to save is less than one. In this case, equation (18.3) becomes

$$\frac{P}{Y} = \frac{1}{s_p} \cdot \frac{1}{Y} \tag{18.5}$$

With this formulation we see one of the most significant conclusions of post-Keynesian economics. For a given level of investment, the lower the capitalists' propensity to save, the higher will be their share of national income and the lower will be the workers' share. This flies in the face of the old myth that capitalists enjoy a high income due to the pain that is necessary for them to save. In this formulation, we see that the less they save, the higher will be their share of the income. This paradoxical result follows from the post-Keynesian views of the determinants of investment and saving. Investment, it is argued, is determined by capitalists' expectations about the future profitability of investment projects as well as their general optimism or pessimism about the future. Saving, on the other hand, changes somewhat passively in response to changes in the level of income.

Thus, we see that if capitalists are very optimistic about the future and decide to increase the level of investment, then this investment will stimulate a growth in production and income (and in the income share of the capitalists). As the capitalists' income grows, their saving grows. This process will continue until the growth of capitalists' income has been sufficient to bring forth new saving that will just offset the increase in investment to create a Keynesian equilibrium. If the capitalists' propensity to save is very high, then it will require only a relatively small increase in their income to bring forth the requisite amount of saving. If their propensity to save is very low, then it will require a relatively large increase in their income to result in an equilibrium in the level of saving.

Thus, given expectations about the future and resultant level of investment, the more profligately capitalists spend their income on their own consumption the higher will be their share of that national income. Frugal and abstemious behavior lowers their share of the national income. The neoclassical view, dating at least back to Nassau Senior, that the disutility of abstemious behavior morally justifies the high incomes of capitalists is turned on its head here.

In addition to their emphasis on distribution and growth post-Keynesian economists have done extensive work in monetary theory. They stress the fact that real commodity and labor flows are expressed in the economy as monetary flows. Money has, for them, a unique characteristic: It possesses a negligible elasticity of substitution with respect to either any other store of value or any other medium of exchange. These assumptions differentiate post-Keynesian economists from neoclassical monetary theorists and permit the former to show, with considerable sophistication, how the range of financial institutions from commercial banks to investment brokers can collectively either sterilize or activate the available monetary stocks and in doing so increase or lessen the severity of exogenous shocks to the economic system. Post-Keynesian economists have shown how these monetary adjustments may lead to a situation in which the money wage rate varies independently of the real wage rate.[15]

Sraffian Price Theory

In the area of value theory the post-Keynesian economists build on the foundation created by Piero Sraffa. In chapter 16 of this book we examined Sraffa's powerful critique of the neoclassical theories of capital, growth, destruction, and efficiency. Had Sraffa done nothing but develop this critique he would have made a monumental contribution to economic theory. He went beyond this, however, to provide a new, more sophisticated version of classical value theory. Sraffa's principal purpose in writing *Production of Commodities by Means of Commodities* was to develop Ricardo's price theory as an alternative to neoclassical marginal utility theory. In doing so, he solved Ricardo's problem of finding an invariant measure of value.

Sraffa's analysis starts with a simple model of subsistence economy producing only two commodities.[16] Each of the commodities serves as a necessary input in the production of both commodities. The two commodities, wheat and iron, are produced in quantities barely sufficient to serve as inputs in producing the same quantity of each in the succeeding period. "Suppose that, all in all, and including the necessaries of the workers, 280 quarters [qr.] of wheat and 12 tons [t.] of iron are used to produce 400 quarters of wheat; while 120 quarters of wheat and 8 tons of iron are used to produce 20 tons of iron."[17] One period's production is summarized as follows:

$$
\begin{array}{llll}
280 \text{ qr. wheat} & + & 12 \text{ t. iron} & \rightarrow & 400 \text{ qr. wheat} \\
120 \text{ qr. wheat} & + & 8 \text{ t. iron} & \rightarrow & 20 \text{ t. iron} \\
\hline
400 & & 20 &
\end{array}
\qquad (18.6)
$$

The total amount produced must be used as productive inputs to perpetuate the same level of production.

It is evident that in order for this process to continue, the wheat growers must exchange 120 quarters of wheat for 12 tons of iron. The price of a ton of iron must therefore be ten times the price of a quarter of wheat. Neither utility nor any type of marginalism enters the calculation. It is not immediately obvious, however, how labor enters the analysis. We have already mentioned that the commodity inputs included the necessities of labor. In a later chapter, entitled "Reduction to Dated Quantities of Labour,"[18] Sraffa shows us how the analysis can be shifted from commodities as the only inputs to labor as the only input.

To make this shift, we begin with the amount of labor used directly in the production of a commodity. The commodities that enter directly into production can themselves be broken down to the direct labor and other commodities used to produce them. Those commodities, in turn, can be similarly broken down. The process can be continued back to a point where the remaining commodities in the calculation represent only an insignificantly small part of the value of the commodity in question and can be eliminated. What remains are only quantities of dated labor, which have culminated in the production of the commodity in question. The argument is simpler and easier to understand, however, when it is stated in terms of commodities. The analysis can be easily generalized for a subsistence economy producing n products, each of which serves as an input in at least some of the other products. Unique price solutions for each commodity will be determined by n equations similar to those for iron and wheat.

Sraffa next considers an economy in which a surplus above subsistence is produced. The following hypothetical production conditions might exist:

$$
\begin{array}{rcrcl}
280 \text{ qr. wheat} & + & 12 \text{ t. iron} & \rightarrow & 575 \text{ qr. wheat} \\
120 \text{ qr. wheat} & + & 8 \text{ t. iron} & \rightarrow & 20 \text{ t. iron} \\
\hline
400 & & 20 & &
\end{array} \tag{18.7}
$$

Again, assuming labor's subsistence is contained in the 400 quarters of wheat and 20 tons of iron, there is a surplus of 175 quarters of wheat. Assume that the total surplus is distributed as profits and that competition equates the rate of profit in both industries. If the price of wheat is 1 and the price of iron is p_i and the rate of profits is r, the above equations become:

$$
\begin{aligned}
(280 + 12p_i)(1 + r) &= 575 \\
(120 + 8p_i)(1 + r) &= 20p_i
\end{aligned} \tag{18.8}
$$

The solutions to these equations are $p_i = 15$ and $r = 0.25$.

Again we can generalize. With n commodities we have n equations to determine n unknowns (one price is unity; this leaves $n - 1$ prices and the rate of profits as unknowns). This is the "classical and Marxian solution," in that wages are predetermined at the subsistence level.

The problem, however, is more complex than this. In Marx's theory, the subsistence wage is determined socially and not biologically. In the class struggle between capitalists and workers, the real wage level that constitutes the subsistence wage varies according to shifts in the balance of power between workers and capitalists. Moreover, since workers do not consume any part of some of the commodity inputs, a change in the conditions of production among the various commodities (and hence a change in the relative prices of the commodities) may require a change in money wages to keep the workers at the same level of real wages. Therefore, in Marx's theory, the money wage rate can vary from either a variation in the real wage rate or a variation in the relative prices or other commodities when the real wage rate remains constant.

Changes in the rate of wages have a particular significance in the Marxist labor theory of value. In the above example, all prices are stated in terms of wheat; that is, wheat is the *numeraire*. If, however, wheat is not produced with the socially average organic composition of capital, then a change in the wage rate will have two effects: first, it will cause the price of wheat to diverge from its labor value. Second, it will cause the money profit in the wheat industry to diverge from the surplus value in labor terms that is produced in the wheat industry (both of these effects are due to the differences in the organic compositions of capital in the various industries, which were discussed in chapters 5 and 9).

This creates a problem for the Marxist labor theory of value, because the secondary principle by which the divergence of prices from labor values can be explained (see chapter 9) requires that such divergences be explainable in terms of the differences in the organic compositions of capital among the various industries. But *if* the price of wheat does not simply reflect its labor value, and *if* all other prices are stated in terms of wheat, *then* divergence of prices from labor values will not simply reflect differences in the organic compositions of capital in the various industries. In this case, divergences of prices from labor values reflect both divergences in the organic compositions of capital and the extent of the divergence of the price of wheat from the labor value of wheat (because all other prices are stated in terms of the price of wheat). In this case, it would become impossible to ascertain to what degree the divergences of prices from labor values can be explained by the secondary principle of the labor theory of value and to what degree such divergences are caused by a change in the measuring rod—the price of wheat. Thus, we are led back to the conclusion reached in both chapters 5 and 9 that the labor theory of value appears to require an invariant measure of value whose price always perfectly reflects its labor value, or (as we will see in chapter 19) the labor theory value must abandon one of the two specific linkages between labor values and prices that were suggested by Marx (i.e., total value equals total price, and total surplus value equals total profit) and find a new way of linking the analysis in labor value terms to the analysis in price terms.

At this point, however, Sraffa departs from both Ricardo and Marx. He abandons the notion of a socially defined subsistence wage:

> We have up to this point regarded wages as consisting of the necessary subsistence of the workers and thus entering on the same footing as the fuel for the engines or the feed for the cattle. We must now take into account the other aspect of wages since, besides the ever-present element of subsistence, they may include a share of the surplus product. In view of this double character of the wage it would be appro-

priate, when we come to consider the division of the surplus between capitalists and workers, to separate the two component parts of the wage and regard only the 'surplus' part as variable; whereas the goods necessary for the subsistence of workers would continue to appear, with the fuel, etc., among the means of production.

We shall, nevertheless, refrain in this book from tampering with the traditional wage concept and shall follow the usual practice of treating the whole wage as a variable.[19]

With this passage, Sraffa departs drastically from Marx. Labor power is not, for Sraffa, a commodity whose value is determined the way the value of any other commodity is. Because there can be no division of labor into necessary labor and surplus labor, surplus labor cannot be shown to be the source of surplus value. Sraffa defines the total of both wages and profits as surplus. All production in excess of the replacements for the material commodities used up in production is defined as the surplus. Therefore, not only does Sraffa not have a Marxist theory, he does not have a Ricardian theory (in this respect, at least) or even a labor theory of value. But he does, as we will see, provide the labor theory of value, in either its Ricardian or its Marxist version, with an indispensable analytical tool.

Having defined the surplus as including both wages and profits, the rate of wages w now becomes an unknown, and the system has one more unknown than it has equations. We must assume a fixed magnitude for one of the variables before the system can be made determinate. "The system," Sraffa concludes, "can move with one degree of freedom; and if one of the variables is fixed the others will be fixed too."[20]

Sraffa then examines what happens to relative prices and profits as the wage rate moves from a point where labor receives none of the surplus to a point where labor receives all of the surplus. This section of Sraffa's book is absolutely crucial for the labor theory of value, because here Sraffa encounters the traditional logical nemesis of the labor theory—the effects of differing ratios of labor to the means of production, or, in Marx's terms, differing organic compositions of capital. It is obvious that as wages increase, the relative effects on the costs of production of different commodities will depend on the proportions of labor and commodity inputs used in their production (see chapters 5 and 9 for a more complete discussion of this point). The cost of commodities using relatively more labor will increase by a larger percentage than the cost of commodities using relatively less labor. But commodities are also productive inputs for other commodities. If a given commodity is labor intensive but its major commodity inputs are capital intensive, the wage increase will increase the labor costs of the commodity in question but cheapen the relative costs of the commodity inputs used in its production. It is obvious that the price will depend upon the net result of these opposing forces. It is thus impossible to decide a priori what effect an increase in the wage rate will have. As such, a knowledge of the labor inputs and commodity inputs of all commodities will not itself be sufficient to determine relative prices.

It is also obvious that even if we were to find a commodity that was produced with the socially average ratio of labor to the means of production, changes in the wage rate would affect the values of the commodities used as the means of production for this commodity unless these inputs were also produced under socially average conditions. Therefore, for the prices of a commodity to reflect only its labor inputs and not to change when the wage rate changes, it is necessary for the commodity (1) to be produced with a socially average ratio of labor to other commodity inputs, (2) to use as commodity inputs only other commodities produced under these same socially average conditions of production, and (3) to have the same average conditions of production extend back to all commodity inputs that, at any point in time, formed a part of the chain of commodity productions culminating in the production of the commodity that is to serve as the invariant measure of value.

Sraffa demonstrates that the difficulty in finding a commodity to serve as an invariant measure of value is much more severe than had been imagined by Ricardo, Marx, or any of the later theorists in the labor theory tradition. Sraffa's method of handling this difficulty is the most ingenious contribution of this book. Unfortunately, details of the argument are too involved and lengthy to review here.[21]

The end product of Sraffa's theoretical manipulations is a proof that, regardless of the proportions in which labor and various commodities are combined in the production processes of various industries, there always exists what is called a "composite," or "standard," industry that enables us to solve the system of equations. In Meek's words: "the rate of profit *over the economy as a whole* is determined as soon as we know R (the ratio of net production [surplus] to the means of production in the 'standard' industry), and w (the proportion of the net product of the 'standard' industry going to wages)."[22] It is this determination of the rate of profit *over the economy as a whole* that is crucial for the labor theory of value. In chapters 5 and 9 we saw that both Ricardo and Marx believed that "natural prices" and "prices of production" were arrived at by individual, competitive capitalist firms summing their costs and adding a profit margin determined by the rate of profit prevailing in the economy as a whole.

However, these costs and profits could not, as both Ricardo and Marx realized, be explained simply on the basis of preexisting prices, or else one would not have a real theory of value. The costs of production include labor costs and the costs of the capital goods used in production. Labor costs are determined, as we saw in chapter 9, by the amount of labor necessary to produce the subsistence goods for the laborers. Capital, as we have seen in all of our previous discussions of the labor theory, can be reduced to a time-dated sequence of previously expended labor exertions. But in order to aggregate this past labor so as to arrive at present capital costs, it is necessary to compound past labor costs at the prevailing rate of profit over the period of time separating their occurrence and ultimate completion of the production process. Finally, to the labor costs and the capital costs we must add the profit (as determined by the overall, competitive rate of profit) accruing to the capitalist in the final period of the production process. Only after making all of these calculations do we arrive at the final equilibrium price (or natural price, or price of production) of a given commodity.

It is obvious that if this final equilibrium price is to be explained by the quantity of labor and its time sequence in the production process, then we must be able to explain the rate of profit on the basis of the technical conditions of production (i.e., on the basis of the quantity and time sequence of labor in the production process). This is precisely what Sraffa did (at least, within the model in which he considered the consumption of laborers to consist of necessary commodity input in the production process). The technical conditions of production in his standard industry permit us to determine the rate of profit over the economy as a whole without any prior knowledge of prices. Obviously the existence and identifiability of the standard industry is crucial to the theory. One of the most significant highlights of Sraffa's book is his elegant proof that such an "industry" (it is really a composite of industries) exists and is identifiable in any actual economy.[23]

To construct his standard industry Sraffa isolates what he calls "basic commodities." A basic commodity enters directly or indirectly into the production of all commodities. From the technical coefficients of production for all of the basic commodities, Sraffa identifies portions of each basic commodity so that, within the standard industry, each commodity enters as a means of production in the same proportion as it appears as output.

Within this standard industry, the ratio of the value of the surplus to the value of the means of production will remain unchanged as wages increase. This is because the increase in costs (due to labor-intensive production processes) are exactly offset by decreases in costs (due to capital-intensive production processes). Thus, Sraffa has a technically determined ratio of surplus to means of production that is independent of fluctuations in wage and profit rates.

The important point is that the entire economy contains the same basic equations as the standard industry but in different proportions. Thus, a knowledge of the labor and commodity inputs in the various industries, together with a knowledge of labor's share of the surplus in the standard industry, permits us to determine the rate of profit prevailing over the economy as a whole, and consequently to determine all prices without ever considering utility or marginal analysis. The system has the added advantage that it does not depend on any particular assumptions about productive returns to scale.

Sraffa's standard commodity would thus appear to function as the ideal "average commodity" for which both Ricardo and Marx searched in vain. While Sraffa's contribution is important for the labor theory of value (as we will see in chapter 19), it does not furnish a solution to the transformation problem in precisely the same manner or context as Marx's proposed solution. This is because the standard commodity is invariant only in a limited, specific sense. When the price of the standard commodity is expressed in terms of its own means of production, then that price is invariant to changes in the wage and profit rates. The price of the standard commodity, when stated in terms of any other commodity, changes when the income distribution changes. Moreover, technological changes result in a modification of the form of the standard commodity. Sraffa's method of construction of the standard commodity did, however, furnish the key to establishing the link between Marx's analysis of the nature and origins of profit (an analysis undertaken in volume 1 of *Capital* solely in terms of labor values) and his analysis of the prices of production (an analysis undertaken in volume 3 of *Capital* in money price terms). We will briefly describe this link between labor values and prices of production in chapter 19.

It is not clear what direct theoretical connection, if any, exists between Sraffa's price theory and the macroeconomic theories of post-Keynesian economics. Not all post-Keynesians espouse Sraffa's theory, but many of the individuals who have developed, elaborated, and extended Sraffa's theory are the same individuals who have made major contributions to post-Keynesian analysis. Perhaps the connection is simply that both developments occurred within a common intellectual tradition centered around Cambridge University.

Notes to Chapter 18

1. C.E. Ayres, "The Function and Problems of Economic Theory," *Journal of Political Economy* 26 (January 1918): 69–90.

2. C.E. Ayres, *Toward a Reasonable Society* (Austin: University of Texas Press, 1961), p. 28.

3. C.E. Ayres, *The Industrial Economy* (Boston: Houghton Mifflin, 1952), pp. 337–38.

4. C.E. Ayres, "Instrumental Economics," *New Republic*, October 1949, p.19.

5. C.E. Ayres, "The Significance of Economic Planning," in *Development of Collective enterprise*, ed. S. Eldridge (Lawrence: University of Kansas Press, 1943), p. 477.

6. Ayres, *Toward a Reasonable Society*, p. 113.

7. Ibid., p. 49.

8. Paul D. Bush, "An Exploration of the Structural Characteristics of a Veblen-Ayres-Foster Defined Institutional Domain," *Journal of Economic Issues* 17, no. 1 (March 1983): 36–37.

9. Paul D. Bush, "On the Concept of Ceremonial Encapsulation," *Review of Institutional Thought*, 3 (December 1986): 30.

10. Paul D. Bush, "The Concept of Progressive Institutional Change and Its Implications for Economic Policy Formation," *Journal of Economic Issues* 23, no. 2 (June 1989): 460, 461.

11. F. Gregory Hayden, "A Geobased National Agricultural Policy for Rural Community Enhancement, Environmental Vitality, and Income Stabilization," *Journal of Economic Issues* 18 (March 1984): 181–221.

12. William M. Dugger, *An Alternative to Economic Retrenchment* (New York: Petrocelli Books, 1984), p. 57.

13. John Munkirs, *The Transformation of American Capitalism* (Armonk, NY: M.E. Sharpe, 1985), p. 179.

14. J.A. Kragel, "Economic Methodology in the Face of Uncertainty: The Modelling Methods of Keynes and the Post-Keynesians," *Economic Journal* 86 (June 1976): 222.

15. Some of the most important post-Keynesian works in monetary theory include Paul Davidson, *Money and the Real World* (London: Macmillan, 1972); J.A. Krege, *The Reconstruction of Political Economy: An Introduction to Post-Keynesian Economics* (New York: Wiley, Halsted Press, 1973); and Hyman Minsky, *John Maynard Keynes* (New York: Columbia University Press, 1975).

16. This account has benefited significantly from Ronald Meek's excellent exposition of Sraffa's theory: Ronald Meek, "Mr. Sraffa's Rehabilitation of Classical Economics," in R. Meek, *Economics and Ideology and Other Essays* (London: Chapman and Hall, 1967).

17. Piero Sraffa, *Production of Commodities by Means of Commodities* (Cambridge, UK: Cambridge University Press, 1960), p. 3.

18. Ibid., pp. 34–42.

19. Ibid., pp. 9–10.

20. Ibid., p. 11.

21. The interested reader will find a concise mathematical proof of Sraffa's conclusion in Peter Newman, "Production of Commodities, a Review" in *The Subtle Anatomy of Capitalism*, ed. Jesse Schwartz (Santa Monica, CA: Goodyear, 1977), pp. 346–62.

22. R. Meek, *Economics and Ideology*, p. 173.

23. Sraffa, *Production of Commodities by Means of Commodities*, pp. 26–33.

Chapter 19

Contemporary Economics III:
The Revival of Critical Political Economy

The fifteen years immediately following World War II constituted a period of profound conservatism in nearly all capitalist countries. The capitalist countries most heavily damaged by the war made what were widely described as miraculous economic recoveries. The victorious capitalist countries made more or less steady (and, by comparison to the Great Depression, quite satisfactory) economic progress. There was a widespread and powerful political movement in most of the third-world colonies of the capitalist powers that resulted in nominal political independence for most of these colonies, and it was widely heralded as the end of capitalist imperialism.

In most European countries, the Labor, Socialist, Social Democratic, and Communist parties became more conservative, adapting themselves to the basic social and economic institutional structure of capitalism and becoming primarily advocates of reforms designed to improve the lot of working people within the capitalist system. In the United States, the rapid spread of virulent anticommunism, the cold war, and the pervasive social, political, and intellectual repressiveness of McCarthyism all resulted in the near destruction of the radical and socialist movements in organized labor, colleges and universities, and nearly every other area of American society in which these movements had exerted influence.

The era was one of both pessimism and optimism. On the one hand, cold-war propaganda convinced most people that a destructive Armageddon between the communist and capitalist countries was inevitable. On the other hand, most people were convinced that, if left alone, capitalism was well along a road leading to and inevitably culminating in the elimination of poverty, class distinctions, imperialism, and economic instability. Liberal intellectuals argued that the term *capitalism* no longer had any meaning. The countries of the North Atlantic region, they argued, were rapidly becoming universally beneficial political and economic democracies with no social classes and hence no class interests. They heralded the era as marking the "end of ideologies." Political and economic debate was largely confined to liberals defending the reforms of the 1930s, which had become an integral part of the structure of capitalism, and conservatives arguing for a repeal of these reforms and a return to the general conditions prevailing prior to the Great Depression. The liberals predominated.

In academic economics, this general social situation was reflected in the overwhelming dominance of the ideas of Keynes and Samuelson. The theorists writing and teaching in the tradition of Marx and Veblen were reduced to a very small number, and they frequently had to conceal their ideas in order to retain their academic positions.[1] The Austrian and Chicago schools, while much larger than the radical school, dominated only a few departments in a few universities, but their members were generally considered to be extremists, if not eccentrics. The elite universities were dominated by individuals who followed Samuelson in his synthesis of liberal neoclassical economics in the area of microeconomics and Keynesian economics in the area of macroeconomics.

All of this changed dramatically in the 1960s and 1970s. These were decades of chronic, if not acute, social, economic, political, and ideological crises. These crises affected all capitalist countries, although the effects were not always the same. Internal economic crises, with the concurrence of high unemployment and chronic inflation, as well as recurring international monetary crises, severely eroded what had been a nearly universal faith in the efficacy of Keynesian policies. Social crises, as typified in the United States by the civil rights movement, the urban ghetto revolts of the 1960s, and the antiwar movement, undermined the faith in the social harmony of capitalism. Innumerable clandestine acts of subversion and military invasions of third-world countries weakened people's faith that the era of capitalist imperialism was really over. The American defeat in Vietnam severely disturbed the public's faith in the cold-war ideology. Finally, innumerable revelations of the government's deceptions, lies, and frauds throughout the entire period, culminating in the Watergate scandal, destroyed many people's faith that capitalist governments were neutral, benevolent, democratic servants of the people, interested only in maximizing everyone's welfare and promoting peace, harmony, and brotherhood worldwide.

These economic, social, and political crises contributed to and were reflected in a severe crisis of liberal cold-war ideology. In academic economics, the crisis of liberal ideology led both to a rapid increase in the number and influence of the Austrian and Chicago schools and to a revival of the critical traditions of Marx and Veblen. This final chapter presents a brief survey of a few of the developments in the revival of critical political economy.

Revival and Development of the Labor Theory of Value

Despite the fact that a conceptually adequate solution to the "transformation problem" was worked out early in the twentieth century, the labor theory of value was nearly universally dismissed (and usually treated very contemptuously) by orthodox academic economists well into the 1960s. For the less knowledgeable orthodox economists, this dismissal was based on an ignorance of the literature. For them, the labor theory of value simply asserted that prices would always be proportionate to labor values—an assertion that they scornfully dismissed. They therefore mistakenly believed that the theory could not be taken seriously.

The more knowledgeable orthodox economists, however, were aware that a conceptually adequate solution to the transformation problem had been formulated. They dismissed the labor theory on the grounds that it required the identification of an invariant measure of value. As we saw in chapters 5 and 9, the need to identify an invariant measure of value was a difficulty that plagued labor theorists from the time of Ricardo until the 1950s. But as we saw in chapter 18, Piero Sraffa, working within the context of Ricardo's formulation of the labor theory of value, demonstrated both the actual existence and the identifiability of an invariant measure of value in any capitalist economy.

While the importance for Marxist economic theory of Sraffa's demonstration was immediately obvious to some economists, the precise nature (as well as the importance) of the difference between Sraffa's theoretical formulation and the Marxist formulation has been debated by both orthodox and Marxist economists. Alfredo Medio, in a 1972 article entitled "Profits and Surplus-Value: Appearance and Reality in Capitalist Production,"[2] argued that there was an important relationship between Sraffa's formulation of the theory and the Marxist formulation.

Medio isolated the most essential distinction between Marx's theory and the "neo-Ricardian" (i.e., Sraffa's) theory. He then pointed out that

> the derivation of prices from values, the solution of the "transformation problem" is only subsidiary and a formal proof of consistency of Marx's theory of *value*. Even when this is worked out it remains to be explained how it is that profit exists at all. In a sense, the neo-Ricardian theory has pushed economic analysis back to a pre-Marxian stage—though in much more sophisticated and rigorous form. However, profit plays an essential role in a capitalist society and *some* theory of profit is required—just as in a state based on apartheid some theory about race is necessary. In this respect, Marx's theory of *surplus-value* is significant and still constitutes the only valid alternative to the neoclassical explanation of the origin and nature of capitalists' gains.[3]

But Sraffa's approach was to define as surplus all output in excess of the physical means of production used up in the production process and then to show how, given the technical conditions of production, changes in the rates of wages and profits affected prices. Therefore, Sraffa had no need for labor values in his analysis, and hence he had no transformation problem. If one accepts the view "that the object of a 'proper' theory of value is to study the quantitative relations between wages, rate of profit and relative prices, value analysis and the related concepts of value and surplus-value become an unnecessary detour and all the discussion about the 'transformation problem' is 'much ado about nothing.'"[4]

But, as we saw in chapter 9, Marx's analyses of the nature of the class structure of capitalism and the nature and origins of profit required the concepts of value and surplus value. Hence, unlike Sraffa's analysis, Marx's theory requires the transformation of values into prices because it is a much broader theory, concerned with more important issues. Medio succinctly stated his view of the relationship between the ideas of Sraffa and Marx when he wrote that Sraffa's "theory, while providing the analytical tools for a correct solution to the 'transformation problem,' at the same time denies its relevance."[5]

Medio then presented a mathematical demonstration that a solution to the transformation problem, having most of the characteristics of traditional solutions, can be formulated so that Sraffa's standard commodity (which, as we saw in chapter 18, is identifiable in any economy) provides a crucial link between Marx's analysis of the nature and origins of profits in labor value terms and Marx's analysis of the prices of production.

Both Ricardo and Mill showed that, given a wage rate and an average rate of profit, the technical conditions of production would determine prices. Prices would include the costs of production plus profit at the going rate. Marx realized that neither Ricardo nor Mill had explained the nature and origins of profit. Considering commodities as merely labor values, Marx developed a penetrating and insightful analysis of the social and economic basis of profits.

Marx believed that the cost-of-production theory of prices, as developed by Ricardo and Mill, was the best analysis of the determination of the prices of production if, and only if, one had previously developed a theory of the value of labor power and a theory of profits. Both of these prerequisites were developed in volume 1 of *Capital* by considering commodities as labor values. But Marx was also aware that he had to link his analysis in value terms to his analysis of prices. In chapter 9 we saw that Marx realized that prices would deviate from values whenever the organic compositions of capital differed among the various industries. Following Ricardo, he showed that the size of the divergences of price ratios from value ratios would depend on the differences in the organic compositions of capital among the various industries.

Marx attempted to establish the link between prices and values in two ways: first, he posited that total prices would equal total values. Second, he posited that total profit would equal total surplus value. In his demonstration of the solution to the transformation problem, however, Marx neglected to transform the values of inputs into prices. This oversight was corrected by subsequent theorists. These theorists discovered, however, that the problem generally could not be solved in a manner that left both of Marx's links between labor values and prices intact. If the problem was solved so that total labor values equaled total prices, then total surplus value generally would not be equal to total profit. Similarly, if the solution left total surplus value equal to total profit, then total prices generally would not equal total labor values. Moreover, we saw in chapter 9 that in order for either of these equalities to obtain after labor values were transformed into prices, it was necessary to find a *numeraire* for making the aggregations. This measure could only be a commodity whose price always equaled its value after the transformation.

In chapter 18, we saw that Sraffa's standard commodity was, in a limited sense, an invariant measure of value (i.e., when the price of the standard commodity was expressed in terms of its own means of production, it would be invariant to changes in the wage and profit rates). Now this very specific and limited invariance is too restrictive to permit Sraffa's standard commodity to serve as the ideal *numeraire* in terms of which either total labor values are equal to total prices or total surplus value is equal to total profit (except under the most restrictive and unrealistic of assumptions). Therefore, Medio's approach is forced to reject both of the two equalities by which Marx linked labor values to prices.

Marx, however, suggested a third method for linking prices to labor values. Within the context of this third method, Medio demonstrated that Sraffa's standard commodity provides an important analytical tool for the Marxist labor theory of value. Marx realized that if a commodity could be found that was produced with the socially average organic composition of capital (and, following Sraffa's insights, we must add the condition that each of the inputs that culminates in the production of this average commodity must also be produced under the same socially average conditions), then the rate of profit that would obtain in the production and sale of that commodity would be identical whether all commodities were sold at their labor values or at their transformed money process. Therefore, the rate of profit on that commodity would be determined entirely by labor values. Moreover, because competition tended to equalize all profit rates, it could be shown that the socially average rate of profit (by virtue of which all price calculations could be made within a cost-of-production theory of prices) would correspond to the rate of profit on the average commodity—a rate determined entirely by labor value calculations.

Medio believed this to be the only link between labor values and prices needed in the Marxist theory of value. The labor analysis is intended only to show the nature and origins of profit as surplus value. The cost-of-production theory of prices then shows how competition tends to redistribute surplus value among capitalists (through price changes) so as to equalize the rates of profit in different industries. If a *numeraire* that equates aggregate profit and aggregate surplus value (or equates the aggregate of values and prices) cannot be found, then an average industry whose rate of profit is determined by labor values suffices to connect the labor value analysis and the price analysis.

Medio demonstrated that in the industry producing Sraffa's standard commodity, the Marxian formula for the rate of profit, $p = (s / v) / (c / v + 1)$, always holds true. In Medio's demonstration the profit rate (p) is the money profit rate by which capitalists mark up their money costs to arrive at prices.

The rate of exploitation, or rate of surplus value (s / v), is defined in labor value terms. It is the rate at which surplus value is created in the sphere of production, and hence it is equal in all industries. The organic composition of capital (c / v), however, has a special meaning in Medio's formulation. It is determined by labor values alone, but it is a kind of weighted average of all of the production processes making up the industry that produces the standard commodity. Each process is given a weight determined by the mathematical multiplier by which that process was incorporated into the standard industry producing the standard commodity. The standard industry is, of course, notional and not actual. But Sraffa demonstrated that the procedure for arriving at a computation of what constitutes the standard industry is applicable in any actual economy. Therefore, Medio's computation of the weighted average of the organic composition of capital in the standard industry has provided us with an index of the aggregate organic composition of capital for the entire economy (defined strictly in labor value terms) and has provided the labor theory of value with the extremely important link between labor value analysis and price analysis. This completed the last step in the chain of the argument of the labor theory of value—a step that remained only partially completed for about a century and a half after Ricardo's *Principles* was first published.

Sraffa's analysis was significant for Marxist economic theory because it made the labor theory of value more rigorous and persuasive, and also showed the neoclassical theory to be defensible only when the organic compositions of capital were equal in all industries. Thus, the principle that had been erroneously used to debunk Marx's theory was demonstrated to be a necessary condition for neoclassical theory. This meant that academic economists could no longer discriminate in the hiring or firing of Marxist economists on scientific or impartial grounds. Such discrimination will always be, on the grounds of the admissions made by the neoclassicists themselves, a reflection of ideological prejudice and bigotry.

In the 1980s, other solutions to the transformation problem were suggested. One of the most influential was proposed by Anwar Shaikh. His solution was published in two important papers in 1977 and 1984.[6] In his 1977 paper on the transformation problem, Shaikh was concerned with establishing a link between Marx's method and what he considered the "correct" prices obtained by Ladislaus von Bortkiewicz in a classic article written in 1907. In his article, Bortkiewicz had assumed that all gold was produced in an industry in which conditions were such that its value was equal to its price of production, serving therefore as the *numeraire*. With this assumption he showed how a consistent solution to the transformation problem could be calculated. His solution was one in which the total surplus value was always equal to the total money value of profits but the total value of production was not necessarily equal to the total price of production.

Instead of developing a new mathematical apparatus, all one had to do, according to Shaikh, was to take Marx's procedure and to calculate a number of successive iterations using that procedure. If one took Marx's prices of production and used them as inputs, and then used Marx's procedure again to obtain new prices of production, and so on, one converged on the set of Bortkiewicz prices. Shaikh's actual procedure, however, made a number of assumptions that were found in Bortkiewicz but may not have been in Marx. He set the sum of prices equal to the sum of values in each step, and adjusted the money wage at every step so that the workers consumed a certain bundle of commodities at the previous period's prices. Shaikh's procedure did obtain the set of prices consistent with the Bortkiewicz method, but also like Bortkiewicz, he obtained only one of Marx's aggregates. In Shaikh's solution, total surplus value was not equal to total profit. This was the issue discussed in his 1984 paper.

In his 1984 paper, Shaikh argued that the transformation solution should not adopt ad hoc assumptions to obtain both of Marx's aggregates. Instead, he reasoned, we should actually expect total surplus value and total profit to differ. This difference is due to the price-value deviations and the size of the luxury sector. When price-value deviations exist in the luxury section, surplus value can be gained or lost through the circuits of revenue. Shaikh's proof of this argument utilizes the assumption of balanced growth. In a situation of balanced growth he shows that the difference between surplus value and profit can be shown to be proportional to the price-value deviation in the sector producing luxury products.

A third new approach to the transformation problem is being called the "new solution" by a small but growing group of Marxist economists. It was first introduced to English-speaking readers by Lipietz in 1982, but the original solution was formulated by Duménil in 1980, and later "discovered" independently by Duncan Foley in 1982.[7] The new solution entailed two important assumptions that were traced back to Marx. The first was that "the sum of prices equaled the sum of values" should be modified to read: "the sum of the prices of the net product (defined as the value added) should be the sum of the values of the net product." The second assumption was that distribution must be defined ex post, as either the value of the money wage that workers receive, or the bundle of consumption goods that the workers buy valued at existing prices. Once these two assumptions are made, any set of values can be transformed into any set of prices with the property that both of Marx's aggregates hold.

Duménil and Foley made two arguments for the adoption of their unique normalization procedure on the net product. First, they claimed that such a normalization avoids double counting. In addition, they both argued that such a normalization conforms to Marx's view of what value is. Value "is the linking of the total labour expended in a given period with the production associated with it, that is, the net product."[8] Furthermore, they argued that wages must be evaluated on the basis of prices and not as the value of a wage bundle.

This view of distribution avoids the problem that when prices deviate from values, the rate of exploitation in price terms depends on the particular set of goods that workers buy and is not settled in the production process. They further argued that, in the previous formulations, if any part of the wage is saved, the rate of surplus value becomes incalculable. Foley, in contrast to Duménil, went on to argue that the wage should not be considered as a bundle at all. Wages, Foley claims, are a sum of money that can be used to buy any goods at the existing set of prices. In addition, unlike a wage bundle, the money wage conceals the exploitative nature of capitalist relations and thus confirms Marx's claim that the normal functioning of the market tends to conceal the real nature of capitalist social relations.

One argument posed against this view is that, in the set of "new solution" prices of production, the sum of the values of constant capital does not equal the total sum of its prices. A convincing argument justifying this result must be established. In addition, the distribution assumption requires ex post knowledge. The actual set of prices must be known before the rate of wages can be established. One cannot move step by step from values into prices. The two realms must be considered separately while the new solution only provides a mapping procedure from one to the other.

These developments in the labor theory of value occurred during a period when a major revival of Marxist economic theory was taking place (some parts of which will be briefly discussed in this chapter). This general revival also led to major improvements in another element of the labor theory of value—the problem of reducing skilled labor to unskilled, "simple" labor. Although several Marxist economists developed more rigorous and systematic approaches to this problem, perhaps the most analytically sophisticated is contained in an article by Bob Rowthorn entitled "Skilled Labour in the Marxist System."[9] This article demonstrated, both verbally and mathematically, that skilled labor can be regarded as simply a combination of unskilled labor and educational and training activities. In this manner, skilled labor can be regarded as a produced commodity, with the expenses of training and education being an integral part of the costs of production. Rowthorn demonstrated that the Marxist theory of value can explain the value of skilled labor (and, hence, reduce skilled labor to unskilled labor) in exactly the same fashion that it explains the values of other commodities.

Changes in the Labor Process Under Capitalism

Marx's theory of capitalism rested on his labor theory of value, which posits that there is no meaningful way to speak of separate, independent, metaphysically given factors of production. Production is a purely social, human activity of transforming an unusable environment into usable products of human labor. Human life, of course, presupposes an environment. The earth, which predates human existence by unknown millions of years, is where people exist. It furnishes the raw material that must be transformed by human labor in order to sustain life. This statement would be self-evident and even banal if it were not for two centuries of utilitarian ideology. This ideology has trained us to think that land and capital produce commodities in exactly the same way that labor does and that landowners and capitalists deserve the value equivalent of the output of their factors in exactly the same way that laborers deserve their wages.

The utilitarian view totally obscures the self-evident fact that production is a process of human labor that transforms the preexisting unusable crust of the earth into products capable of sustaining humanity and of giving enjoyment. The notion that land produces or in some manner transforms itself is ludicrous. When capital is seen as a physical means of production, it is obviously merely the product of past labor. The notion that there is some mystical "abiding entity" in the means of production by virtue of which capital's productivity can be measured is absurd. The very notion that capital produces is equally absurd, and when examined closely it simply reduces to the notion that roundabout, time-consuming processes of human labor are frequently more effective than shorter, more immediate processes of human labor.

Only in a society such as capitalism, where human labor is debased to the status of a commodity, could other commodities be elevated to a human plane and be considered to produce in the same way that humans produce. But such is the obscurantism that results from utilitarian economics.

Capital, as Marx insisted, is a social relation—the power of an unproductive segment of society to extort from the direct producers a large part of what is produced. The emergence of capital as a social relation required several historical, social, and technological prerequisites. Of these prerequisites, the extensive division of labor was extremely important. If the division of labor has progressed to a point, for example, where shoemakers do not produce leather or shoemaking tools, weavers do not produce wool and looms, and most other production processes are similarly interrelated and interdependent, then workers can be rendered unable to produce if they are systematically denied access to the physical means (produced by other workers) that are necessary for production. Capitalist ownership of the means of production constitutes such a denial. The power to deny workers the ability to produce gives capitalists the power to extort from workers a part of what is produced. Most incomes in a capitalist society that are classified as profits, interest, or rent are simply the fruits of this extortion.

Income to the capitalist class derives entirely from the coercively created and coercively maintained state of dependence and helplessness of workers. In the beginning of capitalism the forceful, bloody seizure of all the means of production (primitive accumulation) was sufficient to give capitalists this power. But as long as laborers retained their knowledge and skills, they retained some vestige of power and independence. The ultimate power of the capitalist class necessitated the separation of this knowledge and these skills from those who did the work. The industrial revolution and the rise of factory production furthered the process of rendering workers helpless and dependent.

In volume 1 of *Capital*, Marx described the process of capitalist industrialization as involving a dramatic and historically unprecedented change in the nature of the division of labor in the production process. Before capitalism, the division of labor corresponded to the skills and knowledge necessary to produce one or two products. The shoemaker had all of the knowledge and skills necessary to produce shoes, for example, but depended on other specialized producers to create clothing, food, and other necessities. Work in any specialized endeavor was a combination of the exercise of both the mental and physical faculties. In capitalist factory production, however, a drastically different form of specialization occurred—mental work was separated from physical work.

The work in factories that produced only one kind of commodity was subdivided into many short, repetitious tasks. One worker would do the same monotonous operation every minute of every hour of every working day. This kind of production was doubly beneficial to capitalists. First, it enabled them to exercise far harsher and more effective discipline. Second, it stripped the worker of the knowledge and skills necessary to produce a commodity and greatly reinforced the worker's helplessness and dependence on the capitalists. There can be little wonder about why the Luddites went on their factory- and machine-wrecking rampages and why capitalist governments passed laws making machine wrecking an offense punishable by death.

As this process of specialization separated mental work from physical work, it degraded many forms of factory work to a subhuman level. It also gave rise to the notion that white-collar or mental workers were a privileged stratum of the working class. While this notion had a considerable element of truth in the capitalist factory system of the early nineteenth century, by the early twentieth century, the privileged status of clerical workers had become a myth.

In the revival of Marxist economic theory from the late 1960s through the 1980s, Harry Braverman's *Labor and Monopoly Capital, The Degradation of Work in the Twentieth Century* was exemplary.[10] Surveying different studies of various types of work processes and collecting innumerable data on the changing nature of work processes in the twentieth century, Braverman found that in white-collar (or mental, or clerical) work, most productive endeavors had reduced the working day to an endless repetition of minute, monotonous tasks, as degrading in its way as the alienation suffered by factory workers. In addition, clerical workers usually received less pay than did factory workers. Braverman wrote:

> In the beginning, the office was the site of mental labor and the shop the site of manual labor. . . . Scientific management gave the office a monopoly over conception, planning, judgement, and the appraisal of results, while in the shop nothing was to take place other than the physical execution of all that was thought up in the office. Insofar as this was true, the identification of office work with thinking and

educated labor, and of the production process proper with unthinking and uneducated labor, retained some validity. But once the office was itself subjected to the rationalization process, this contrast lost its force. The functions of thought and planning became concentrated in an ever smaller group within the office, and for the mass of those employed there the office became just as much a site of manual labor as the factory floor. With the transformation of management into an administrative labor process, manual work spreads to the office and soon becomes characteristic of the tasks of the mass of clerical workers.[11]

Thus, Braverman extends Marx's analysis and shows that, as capitalism develops, the degradation of industrial workers (which Marx had described in historical detail) becomes the norm and spreads to all occupations. In Braverman's words:

> The transformation of working humanity into a "labor force," a "factor of production," an instrument of capital, is an incessant and unending process. The condition is repugnant to the victims, whether their pay is high or low, because it violates human conditions of work; and since the workers are not destroyed as human beings but are simply utilized in inhuman ways, their critical, intelligent, conceptual faculties, no matter how deadened or diminished, always remain in some degree a threat to capital.[12]

The threat from the inner core of the indestructible human potential of workers must be continuously combated by the capitalist system. And the struggle takes place in the home, in the schools, in society at large, as well as in the workplace. The goal of capitalists must always be to create mindless, docile, compliant, obedient, producing automatons out of workers. The struggle for workers is to protect and nurture the emotional, physical, esthetic, and intellectual qualities that make them human. When workers perceive this entirely as a struggle of warring elements within themselves, as the inevitable outcome of the "human condition," or as a purely individual quest to escape from the emptiness, boredom, anxiety, frustration, and feelings of inferiority that plague them, the capitalists have the upper hand in this struggle—that is, when the struggle is viewed by workers as purely an individual rather than a class struggle.

One of the most striking differences between neoclassical economists and radical economists is that the former tend to believe either that the economic aspects of society can be fully understood independently of any understanding of sociology, psychology, or politics, or that the notion of rational, maximizing "economic man" explains all aspects of human behavior, while the latter recognize that even though economists specialize in the study of the economic aspects of society, in reality the economic, psychological, sociological, and political aspects of society are interrelated. No aspect of society can be adequately comprehended or understood in isolation from its place in the organic totality of the entire society.

Thus, while Braverman's book analyzes the impact and effects of the class struggle in the workplace, it immediately raises the issues of this struggle as manifested in the home, in the schools, in government, and in society generally. We will briefly consider some of these aspects of the class struggle as it occurs outside the workplace and then return to Braverman's analysis of the effects of the struggle in the workplace.

Building on the pioneering work of Wilhelm Reich, which was written in the early and mid-1930s (and ignoring the writings of the late 1930s and 1940s in which Reich appears to have suffered a kind of mental breakdown), contemporary Marxist theorists have attempted to show how the cultural mores that dominate family life, especially sex role socialization, systematically deny many of the deepest human needs. This denial, they argue, leads to psychic repression that is profoundly useful to capitalism. In Reich's view, the most fundamental form of repression was sexual. He believed that in capitalism sexual repression, which had its roots in the sex role socialization of family life, created a passive, submissive type of personality. This type of personality was necessary in capitalism in order that there could exist the institutional and ideological facade of democracy to cover and obscure the essentially coercive, undemocratic, and authoritarian functioning of the capitalist system. According to Reich:

> The repression of sexual needs creates a general weakening of intellectual and emotional functioning; in particular, it makes people lack [a capacity for] independence, willpower, and critical faculties. . . . In this way, the compulsive, patriarchal family, through the anchoring of sexual morality and the changes it brings about in the organism, creates that specific psychic structure which forms the mass-psychological basis of any authoritarian social order. The vassal-structure is a mixture of sexual impotence, helplessness, longing for a Fuhrer, fear of authority, fear of life, and mysticism. . . . People with such a structure are incapable of democratic living.[13]

Over the past few decades, some Marxist theorists have gone beyond Reich's emphasis on sexual repression and attempted to show that many aspects of the dominant cultural mores governing family life in a capitalist system tend to create an alienated, passive, and submissive personality, which is essential to the successful functioning of capitalist production processes. Representative of these writings are Bruce Brown's *Marx, Freud, and the Critique of Everyday Life* and Eli Zaretsky's essay entitled "Capitalism, the Family and Personal Life."[14]

Marxist theorists have also studied the capitalist educational system extensively. They have found that schooling in a capitalist system systematically stifles curiosity, inculcates passive, submissive, and obedient attitudes in students, and continuously creates the type of personality and the knowledge and skills necessary to perpetuate the existing class structure of capitalism as well as the subdivisions that exist within it. Representative of this literature is Miriam Wasserman's *Demystifying School*[15] and Samuel Bowles's and Herbert Gintis's *Schooling in Capitalist America*.[16] The school system is extremely important in perpetuating and inculcating the various intellectual defenses of the status quo of capitalism. Much of the analysis of the present book represents an attempt to show how the dominant academic tradition in one field of study, economics, systematically furthers the acceptance of the ideological defense of capitalism.

Equally important in the formation of accepting attitudes toward capitalism are the mass communications media. The corporations controlling the media are, of course, directly interested in maintaining the status quo, as are the major advertisers who furnish most of the revenue for these industries. Many radical writers have given extensive, detailed accounts of how the mass communications media have distorted and censored news stories and other material in order to manipulate public opinion. Representative of such writings are James Aronson's *The Press and the Cold War*[17] and Robert Cirino's *Don't Blame the People*.[18] Undoubtedly the most thorough and scholarly of these studies is Edward S. Herman's and Noam Chomsky's *Manufacturing Consent: The Political Economy of the Mass Media*.[19]

Finally, radical intellectuals have studied and documented the extent to which the government, despite the guise of its democratic basis, is controlled by capitalists and thus promotes their interests. One of the principal means of perpetuating capitalist social relations is to limit legitimate political debate to those issues that do not challenge the authoritarian control of economic and social processes that capitalists exercise. Representative of radical research in this area are G. William Domhoff's *Who Rules America?* and Howard L. Reiter's *Parties and Elections in Corporate America*.[20]

Such noneconomic methods of conditioning and controlling the working class reinforce the class structure of capitalism. But the most important foundation of capitalists' power, and, therefore, the ultimate end toward which each of these forms of control leads, is the control over the process of production. Braverman's study is an effort to show how such control, beginning in the industrial workplace and then spreading to all areas of work, has systematically stripped work of all its emotionally, esthetically, and intellectually satisfying aspects. It has reduced even most white-collar jobs to monotonous, repetitious, mechanical exertions and debased nearly all workers to the subhuman role of an appendage to a machine, whether that machine is gear driven or it is a digital simulation of certain aspects of human intelligence. To maintain such an extreme degree of economic control, numerous other forms of emotional and intellectual control are absolutely necessary.

Capitalism represents, at the level of the individual corporation, an economic system characterized by a most intricate, rationally calculated form of economic planning. In Braverman's words:

> The concept of control adopted by modern management requires that every activity in production have its several parallel activities in the management center: each must be devised, precalculated, tested, laid out, assigned and ordered, checked and inspected, and recorded throughout its duration and upon completion. . . . Just as labor in human beings requires that the labor process take place in the brain of the worker as well as in the worker's physical activity, so now the image of the process,

removed from production to a separate location and a separate group, controls the process itself.[21]

But while capitalism is characterized by rational, calculated planning at the level of the individual corporation, at the aggregate level, the entire economy remains, as it has always been, subjected to the anarchy and irrationality of the market.

Performance of Capitalism at the Aggregate Level

The class structure of capitalism rests on the capitalists' monopolization of the ownership of the means of production. This monopolization inevitably results in extreme inequality in the distribution of income. Many economists, from Malthus to Marx to Keynes, have been aware that this inequality contributes to the overall instability, tendency toward stagnation, and irrationality and chaos that have always characterized the functioning of capitalism. After Keynes, most orthodox economists believed that this instability and irrationality would be significantly mitigated, if not eliminated, by government interventionism. With the revival of critical political economy in the 1960s, however, many economists began to perceive that Keynesianism had not and could not remove this elemental irrationality of capitalism.

In 1966, Paul A. Baran and Paul M. Sweezy's influential book, *Monopoly Capital*, was published. In their book, Baran and Sweezy argued that under capitalism the economic surplus (defined as "the difference between what a society produces and the costs of producing it"[22]) has a persistent tendency to rise over time. Due to the enormous inequality of income distribution in capitalism, business firms have a continually difficult time finding sufficient aggregate demand. When there is insufficient aggregate demand, the surplus cannot be sold (or "absorbed," or utilized). According to Baran and Sweezy,

> the size of the surplus is an index of productivity and wealth, of how much freedom a society has to accomplish whatever goals it may set for itself. The composition of the surplus shows how it uses that freedom: how much it invests in expanding its productive capacity, how much it consumes in various forms, how much it wastes and in what ways.[23]

Much of *Monopoly Capital* is an effort to understand how American capitalism absorbs its economic surplus. The first and most obvious source of absorption is capitalists' consumption and investment. In an analysis similar to those of Malthus, Marx, and Hobson, Baran and Sweezy find that the institutional inequality that supports the class structure of capitalism is so great that as capitalism grows, the expenditures of capitalists on consumption and investment fall short, by increasingly greater amounts, of being sufficient to absorb the surplus.

> Twist and turn as one will, there is no way to avoid the conclusion that monopoly capitalism is a self-contradictory system. It tends to generate ever more surplus, yet it fails to provide the consumption and investment outlets required for the absorp-

tion of a rising surplus and hence for the smooth working of the system. Since surplus which cannot be absorbed will not be produced, it follows that the *normal state of the monopoly capitalist economy is stagnation. . . .* And this means chronic underutilization of available human and material resources. . . . Left to itself—that is to say, in the absence of counteracting forces which are no part of what may be called the "elementary logic" of the system—monopoly capitalism would sink deeper and deeper into a bog of chronic depression.

Counteracting forces do exist. If they did not, the system would indeed long since have fallen of its own weight. It therefore becomes a matter of greatest importance to understand the nature and implications of these counteracting forces.[24]

The first of these counteracting forces is the "sales effort" of the giant corporations: "In an economic system in which competition is fierce and relentless and in which the fewness of rivals rules out price cutting, advertising becomes to an ever increasing extent the principal weapon of the competitive struggle."[25] By "advertising," Baran and Sweezy mean all efforts to promote sales. Such methods include "advertising, variation of the products' appearance and packaging, 'planned obsolescence,' model changes, credit schemes, and the like."[26]

The principal way in which the sales effort results in greater absorption of the surplus is not that it induces a significantly higher rate of expenditure among people or institutions that might otherwise have saved a substantial amount of money (although it does, to a limited extent, have this effect); the most important effect is that it creates massive waste. Large expenditures on planned obsolescence, expensive and needless model changes, millions of laborers working in sales promotion and advertising, all contribute nothing to the production or actual serviceability of commodities. From a social point of view, all of these expenditures are pure waste. Yet in a capitalist system, such massive and wasteful expenditures are "rightly called 'a must for survival' for many a corporate enterprise."[27] All of these forms of economic waste absorb a portion of the surplus: "Unlike the component of surplus which takes the form of net profits, the fraction which takes the form of selling costs calls for no counterpart in capitalists' consumption, no investment outlets. It provides, as it were, its own offsets and outlets."[28]

A second counteracting force is government. According to Baran and Sweezy, in most capitalist countries, "votes are the nominal source of political power, and money is the real source: the system, in other words, is democratic in form and plutocratic in content."[29] Because of the overwhelming influence of capitalists in government, the government spends and thereby absorbs the surplus in ways that will promote, or at least not interfere with, the existing structural inequalities of wealth and income. This, in Baran and Sweezy's view, severely limits the scope of "civilian government expenditures."

Government expenditures on things such as public parks, libraries, slum clearance, and general welfare payments must be limited to the level that assures an emotional state of docility on the part of the poor and the unemployed while at the same time preserving the existing distribution of wealth and income. According to Baran and Sweezy, "*given the power structure of United States monopoly capitalism, the increase of civilian spending had reached its outer limits by 1939. The forces opposing further expansion were too strong to be overcome.*"[30] After this time, the bulk of the increases in government expenditures, considered as a percentage of GNP, came in the areas of militarism and imperialism.

The significance of government expenditures on militarism is obvious and was discussed in chapter 15. Baran and Sweezy's important discussion of capitalist imperialism, however, should be discussed. Because their book appeared at the height of the Vietnam War, it provoked a resurgence of interest in the topic of capitalist imperialism. Their account was short, but powerful and persuasive. It led to renewed research and writing on the topic, and we will mention a few representative examples of this research.

Baran and Sweezy concluded that while these counteracting expenditures have been sufficient to avoid a major depression or social disaster, their sufficiency in the future is highly questionable. In their opinion, the most significant forces opposing the continual expansion of these expenditures are the national liberation movements in third-world countries. These movements are usually dominated by socialists, and their aim is to withdraw their countries from the domain of profit making of the multinational corporations.

But even if the end of capitalism is not in sight—and Baran and Sweezy do not predict its imminent collapse—these counteracting forces, which prevent capitalism from sinking into a bog of stagnation and depression, sharply increase the waste and irrationality of capitalism. Baran and Sweezy conclude that the

> contradiction between the increasing rationality of society's methods of production and the organizations which embody them on the one hand and the undiminished elementality and irrationality in the functioning and perception of the whole creates that ideological wasteland which is the hallmark of monopoly capitalism. But we must insist that this is not, as some apologists for the status quo would have us believe, "the end of ideology"; it is the displacement of the ideology of rising capitalism by the ideology of the general crisis and decline of the world capitalist order. That its main pillar is anti Communism is neither accidental nor due to a transient conjunction of political forces, any more than is the fact that the main content of the political and economic policies of modern capitalism is armaments and Cold War. *These policies can only be anti; there is nothing left for them to be pro.*[31]

Baran and Sweezy contributed to a widespread revival of interest among economists in the phenomenon of capitalist imperialism. Perhaps the most influential work in this revival was Harry Magdoff's *The Age of Imperialism: The Economics of U.S. Foreign Policy*, published in 1969.[32] Magdoff's contribution was not so much in advancing the theory of capitalist imperialism beyond the theories reviewed in chapter 13, but in gathering and interpreting a massive amount of data to demonstrate the continuing relevance and applicability of these theories. Magdoff clearly demonstrated that much of the data on imperialism may seem relatively insignificant when compared, for example, to total GNP, but can be seen to be of crucial and strategic importance when evaluating the resource needs of the American economy and the profits of the giant multinational corporations.

In evaluating the economic and political relationship of American capitalism to the third-world economies, Magdoff drew attention to the fact that the United States depends on imports as the principal source for most of the sixty-two types of materials that the Defense Department classifies as "strategic and critical." For thirty-eight of these, 80–100 percent of the new supplies are imported; for fourteen more, 40–79 percent are imported. Moreover, he cites a study of third-world economies that shows that each of thirty-seven underdeveloped countries earns 58–99 percent of its export receipts from the sale of six or less commodities.[33]

In this situation, the United States forces extremely favorable (to the United States) terms of trade on these economies and hence assures itself of cheap raw materials and profitable investment outlets. A large and increasing percentage of U.S. corporate sales and profits results from exports and sales of the foreign subsidiaries of American corporations, many of which, of course, are in third-world countries.[34] But the favorable terms of trade are usually gotten at the expense of the living standards of the general population of these countries. Hence, most of the national liberation movements of these countries are anti-American and anticapitalist. So the U.S. government must impose and maintain governments in these countries that protect and further the interest of American corporations. Magdoff pointed to fity-three different "U.S. defense commitments and assurances" that commit the United States to the use of military force to maintain existing governments in these countries, most generally against their own people.[35]

Magdoff cited the following quotation from an officer of General Electric Company: "Thus, our search for profits places us squarely in line with the national policy of stepping up international trade as a means of strengthening the free world in the Cold War confrontation with Communism." Then Magdoff concluded: "Just as the fight against Communism helps the search for profits, so the search for profits helps the fight against Communism. What more perfect harmony of interests could be imagined?"[36] In the 1890s, imperialism was called an attempt to "Christianize, uplift and educate" the people living in third-world countries. In the post–World War II period, it is now called an attempt to save these people's souls from communism. Either facade is equally obscurantist and serves to justify morally American economic exploitation of third-world countries.

During the 1970s, innumerable case studies and theoretical discussions of imperialism were written by radical economists. For a fine representative sample of such writings, the interested reader can consult three special issues of the *Review of Radical Political Economics* (Spring 1971, Winter 1972, and Spring 1973). In the 1980s, numerous articles and books were written that detailed the extent and the methods of U.S. imperialism. One of the most convincing, as well as the most shocking, was Edward S. Herman's *The Real Terror Network: Terrorism in Fact and Propaganda.*[37] Herman cites innumerable data and produces pages and pages of descriptions based upon official reports of various organizations as well as careful descriptions by reliable sources, all of which show, with depressing consistency, the following general conclusions: the United States installs and maintains (economically and militarily) unpopular, corrupt, and brutally vicious governments in numerous third-world countries; these governments represent the interests of tiny indigenous elites and multinational corporations; these governments pursue policies that frequently worsen the already obscenely unequal distributions of wealth and income that prevail in these countries; they maintain their unpopular and repressive control by the widespread and systematic use of terror, torture, and murder committed against any citizen who is suspected of having views that are critical of the government. The U.S. government directly and indirectly aids and abets (and even occasionally directs and supervises) this terror, torture, and murder, all in the name of fighting "communism" and protecting "democracy." The people who are killed are only rarely communists (although even when they are, a democratic country would presumably defend their right to any political philosophy), and the totalitarian, militaristic governments that are defended are almost never democratic. In a word, the United States supports profits and profit making by any means necessary, including torture and murder.

Comments on the Social Perspective Underlying the Present Book

The revival of radical economics over the past forty years has been a widespread phenomenon, with a great many economists making substantial contributions. The foregoing survey is not intended to be at all comprehensive, but merely illustrative of a few of these contributions. To write an adequate survey of contemporary radical economics would require a work at least as long as this entire book. I would like to close this chapter and this book with a few reflections on the general methodological, social, and ethical perspective that underlies this book. Needless to say, all of my views may not be shared by different economists writing in the radical tradition.

All social theory rests on some preconceptions about the psychology of human behavior and on some preconceptions about what human situations are possible and ethically desirable. The claim that utilitarian economics is value free, which has been frequently made by thinkers such as Senior, Bastiat, Menger, and Friedman, is preposterous—as a reading of the works of these authors will readily reveal. All social theory, if studied carefully, is seen to rest on a particular psychological and ethical theory, whether the theory is explicitly stated or implicitly assumed. Most classical economists and all neoclassical economists rest their economic theory on the utilitarian, hedonistic conception of human psychology and ethics.

Utilitarian psychology and ethics are particularly well suited to the task of furnishing a conservative ideology for capitalism. The great strength of capitalism, viewed historically, is that it has immeasurably increased human command over nature, revolutionized human production, and, in doing so, opened the real possibility that, for the first time in human history, all people can live in material security and comfort. Yet, at the same time, it is a social system that inflicts such social, psychological, emotional, and esthetic damage that we are incapable of organizing and using this increased productivity in a socially or personally fulfilling manner.

Utilitarianism provides an ideal intellectual defense for such a social system for two reasons. First, in utilitarianism the individual's feelings, emotions, ideas, patterns of behavior, and desires are simply taken as metaphysically given. Patterns of socialization, as well as the social limits imposed on people's growth and development as human beings, are excluded from the domain of inquiry, and a normative critique of capitalism based on humanist concerns becomes meaningless—because it is outside the bounds of any social science based on utilitarian psychology and ethics. Second, utilitarianism not only takes human desires as being independent of social interaction, it identifies human well-being with the satisfaction of those desires, and it identifies this satisfaction with the consumption of commodities. It is not surprising that capitalism—which has, on the whole, been enormously successful in perpetually expanding the production of commodities—appears to be an economic system that is most conducive to the promotion of human well-being, insofar as human well-being is so narrowly conceived by utilitarian economic theory.

Throughout this book, the critique of utilitarianism has been based on the beliefs that human desires are largely socially determined, and, as such, their satisfaction may or may not augment human welfare; and that human production is a social phenomenon in which no individual (much less an inanimate object, such as a piece of land or a machine) can be said to be solely responsible for a specific amount of what is produced, and in which the destination and use of the fruits of production are socially determined and may be either beneficial or harmful to human well-being.

If we as a citizenry had not been so thoroughly indoctrinated with utilitarianism, both of the above statements would appear as immediately self-evident. We all know that the fulfillment of some of the desires of drug addicts or pathologically insane people does not promote human welfare. We also know that people are not simply metaphysically determined to be drug addicts or pathologically insane. While I have illustrated my point with extreme examples, the logic of the argument has a universal applicability for assessing human welfare. We can, must, and do ethically evaluate desires themselves as well as the social means by which they are satisfied. Utilitarianism, despite its pervasive influence in most of our thinking, is rejected every day by nearly every person in the recurring practical necessities of ordinary life. Human beings always function, think, and write on the basis of, among other things, moral feelings, precepts, and concepts. In spite of the pervasive indoctrination of utilitarianism, which is so valuable in maintaining the status quo of capitalism, reflection on the essential feelings underlying everyday behavior reveals that most of us do not function or think in a manner consistent with utilitarianism. For these reasons, I would like to make explicit some of the psychological and ethical preconceptions that form the foundation of this book. Given the limitation of space, they can be stated only briefly and not at all adequately defended, as I believe they could be in a lengthier discussion.

The ethical view underlying this book is based on the three following beliefs. First, following Veblen and Marx, I believe that all people in all societies have some common needs simply because they are human. Veblen gave the unfortunate label of "instincts" to these universal needs and thereby inadvertently invited the obscuration of the essential difference between these needs and animal instincts. Universal human needs inevitably and profoundly affect all of us throughout our lives, but they are separate and distinct from conscious human desires. For example, the conscious desire of the alcoholic to consume very little other than alcohol in no way lessens the needs of his or her body for essential nutriments. Basic human needs, however, are translated into conscious desires only in a social setting and as a consequence of an individual's participation in social processes.

Socialization may, in fact, so condition a person that this person remains unaware of any conscious desires that stem from, and might lead to the satisfaction of, an innate universal need. Such a situation generally culminates in the individual having neurotic anxiety. Socialization may also lead to conscious desires that systematically thwart the fulfillment of universal human needs. Again, the result is neurotic anxiety. According to the social psychologist Karen Horney, such anxiety reveals itself as "a feeling of being small, insignificant, helpless."[38] But in some sense, the world, in the form of capitalist society, is abusing, cheating, attacking, humiliating, and betraying the humanity of the individual. Such feelings are neurotic only because the individual feels that the situation is "natural" and "inevitable," and stems from that individual's own "essence" as a human being and from the "essence" of society, both of which are fixed and immutable. Such feelings would not be neurotic if the individual realized that they grow out of the social denial of that individual's real essence and that a society that denies human beings their humanity can in fact be changed by collective human action.

Second, I believe that there is a hierarchy of universal human needs. The fact that some needs tend to take precedence over others is the only reason for classifying them as "higher" or "lower." All universal human needs have an irreducible, basic, and autonomous integrity, and the proper satisfaction of each universal need is absolutely vital and essential to the fulfillment of human life.[39]

In the hierarchy of human needs, the lowest, or most basic, are the physiological needs for food, water, shelter, clothing, rest, exercise, and sex. At the next higher level are the needs for safety and security. Both these levels of needs must be relatively adequately satisfied for the mere existence and survival of the body. If they are not minimally satisfied, it will generally significantly interfere with the gratification of higher needs. In fact, the interference may be so great that the higher needs will remain "often largely unconscious."[40] Thus, Abraham Maslow wrote that "undoubtedly these physiological needs are the most prepotent of all needs."[41] If they go unsatisfied, then at the level of conscious desire "all other needs may become simply nonexistent."[42]

The third level of needs consists of what Maslow calls "belongingness and love needs." These are the needs for human warmth, affection, and love. Satisfaction of these needs demands that we be loved for our own essence and strictly as an end, and not as a *means*, or as a commodity, which is so frequently the case in capitalism (as apotheosized in the vulgar assessment of human worth in the writing of McKenzie and Tullock). In capitalism, the pervasiveness of commodity relations so militates against the satisfaction of these needs that few of us are able to have them fully or even adequately fulfilled. Moreover, according to Maslow, "in our society the thwarting of these needs is the most commonly found core in cases of maladjustment and more severe psychopathology."[43]

The fourth level consists of the needs for recognition, appreciation, and esteem from others. These are not needs for fame or celebrity status but are based on the importance to the individual of developing the traits that Veblen associated with the "instinct of workmanship." Such needs are present in the desire "for mastery and competence, for confidence in the face of the world, and for independence and freedom."[44] Only when such traits are developed can the esteem of our fellow human beings be consistent with healthy self-esteem, which is based on "deserved respect from others rather than external fame or celebrity and unwarranted adulation."[45] As we saw in our chapters on Marx and Veblen, as well as in the writings of Braverman discussed in this chapter, the history of capitalism has been characterized by the progressive decreasing of the possibility to achieve this form of self-esteem and social esteem for the vast majority in our society.

The fifth and highest level of needs consists of the need to experience and apprehend esthetic beauty for its own sake and to acquire and appreciate knowledge for its own sake, and not as a means to the achievement of further ends. Needless to say, these are needs that almost always go unfulfilled under capitalism.

Also underlying the ethical perspective of this book is my belief (the third to be discussed) that the good for human beings, or human well-being, consists of structuring our social life so that every human being is viewed by all other human beings as an end in him- or herself and never as simply a means, or as a commodity. Viewing each person as an end can only mean that it is universally desired that every individual achieves a maximum of self-fulfillment, or that each individual develops to the fullest possible extent his or her biological, emotional, intellectual, creative, and esthetic potential. Such individual development is attainable only through interaction with other human beings in a particular social setting. In fact, it is attainable only through a unified concern for oneself as well as for all other human beings in an appropriate social setting where self-concern and social concern are mutually promoted by the normal functioning of society. It follows that the good for any individual can be pursued only through the simultaneous pursuit of his or her personal fulfillment and the participation in a collective restructuring of society so as to make this social and personal fulfillment of all human beings ultimately possible.

Of course, underlying this entire book is the conviction that value-free social science is impossible—and even if it were possible, it would be undesirable. We are all human beings, and, as such, none of us is an objective, detached, disinterested observer of other human beings or of society in general. We cannot ask a writer to do the impossible, that is, to be an impartial, disinterested spectator. Any claim of having achieved this status is always either self-deception or a conscious effort to deceive others. The most that we can ask of a writer is that he or she be intellectually honest.

I have endeavored to communicate honestly to the reader what I consider to be the most important aspects of the writings of the various thinkers whose ideas I have summarized and criticized. But I have not tried to fulfill the impossible role of an impartial, disinterested spectator. I am partial and I am interested. In order that the reader may decide for him- or herself which, if any, of my critiques to discount, I wish to make explicit my views about the nature of capitalism, which result from the sum total of my life experiences, empirical observations, introspections, readings, discussions, thinking, and feeling during a lifetime spent entirely within the context of American capitalism.

First, capitalism is a social system whose very foundations are based on conflict and exploitation.

Second, the social relationship between capitalists and laborers is the most fundamental of all social relations in capitalism. This means that for the vast majority of us to fulfill the most basic, or lowest level, of our universal human needs, our creative productive potential must be reduced to a commodity, labor power, that we sell in the market.

Third, because our very life-creating activities generally necessitate selling our labor power as a commodity, we view others and are viewed by them as commodities, that is, as being means only and not ends. In capitalism, the pressures of socialization are almost entirely directed toward the universal application of commodity relations to all aspects of human relations. To the extent that our basic humanity rebels (whether consciously or unconsciously) against this dehumanization, the writings of utilitarian economists like McKenzie and Tullock are reduced to vulgar contumely. To the extent that our commodity-oriented socialization prevails, their ideas are sadly descriptive of some aspects of our behavior.

Fourth, the anarchy of the market and the continuous existence of millions of unemployed workers constantly create economic insecurity in most of us and thus systematically work against the fulfillment of many of our higher universal human needs.

Fifth, the reduction of human relations to commodity relations persistently thwarts our needs for genuine and fulfilling human warmth, affection, and love. The fact that these qualities do exist in capitalism is testimony to the strength of the vital spark of humanity that exists in each of us and that prevents our ultimate reduction to mere commodities.

Sixth, the reduction of the process of creative production to a series of rigidly controlled, unfree, tedious, repetitive exertions robs most of us of the satisfaction of our need for creative mastery and competence and the self-esteem and social esteem that go with such creativity.

Seventh, this alienation, with its attendant social and emotional fragmentation, creates a general anxiety, fear, and distrust in most of us that is often channeled into feelings that give rise to racism and sexism, which are used, as we know, to justify and contribute to the systematic exploitation of racial minorities and women. It also leads to patriotic, nationalistic, and jingoistic sentiment that is used to justify and contributes to economic imperialism, which harshly oppresses millions of human beings in third-world countries. All of these psychological attitudes create further barriers to the full development of the essence of common humanity in each of us.

Eighth, our alienation and fragmentation also render us vulnerable targets for the manipulation by corporate advertising managers that leads to what Veblen termed "emulative consumption." We experience aloneness, fear, anxiety, and boredom as needs to consume more commodities, to catch up to and pass the Joneses. This causes us to see our unhappiness not as the result of the endless capitalist treadmill of consumerism, but as a result of our failure to run fast enough on the treadmill, to consume enough commodities, and to work conscientiously enough on our job to get another raise in pay.

Ninth, the domination of the production process by the profit motive systematically denies us the use of our resources and our human productive capacities for the satisfactory creation and defense of parks, recreation centers, child-care centers, and mass transit systems, which are all socially used and hence generally not profitable for capitalists to produce and sell.

Tenth, because the sale of labor power is the only way in which most people can live decently in capitalism, our system relegates those who cannot sell their labor power—the young, the old, the handicapped, the single parents who must take care of small children, and so on—to a life of grueling poverty.

Eleventh, the needs of the capitalist system turn our educational system and other cultural institutions from being centers in which people can develop their inherent esthetic and intellectual potentials independently of external constraints into agencies for the propagation of ideas, training, and emotional patterns conducive to the maintenance and perpetuation of the social and economic structure of capitalism.

Twelfth, in their single-minded pursuit of profits, corporations pollute our water, air, and general environment, thereby rendering our living space esthetically repugnant, damaging to our health, and potentially unlivable.

Utilitarian economics teaches us that whatever our senses tell us, whatever our feelings tell us, capitalism is a rational, efficient, and fair system. It tells us that it will always be in the best interests of all people to have our resources, activities, and social interactions significantly influenced, if not rigidly controlled, by a tiny minority of wealthy individuals who are solely motivated by the pursuit of accumulating more wealth.

In writing this book, I have tried to present honestly what seem to me to be the most important ideas of the various economic theorists. But I am not neutral or impartial. I do not believe that capitalism is the apotheosis of human rationality. I believe that historically it served a most important and progressive function by increasing human control over nature. But in doing so, what was progressive and rational in capitalism eventually became regressive and irrational. The system as it now exists systematically thwarts the full development of the potential of human beings. For this reason the system is inefficient and irrational.

I believe, with Veblen and Marx, that capitalism is not the highest stage of human development and that if human beings ever assert their collective humanity against the irrationality of capitalism, they will open a vista of passionate possibilities hardly dreamed of during the reign of capitalism.

Notes to Chapter 19

1. Paul Baran, for example, was an influential Marxist economist teaching at Stanford University. In the 1950s he was forced to do much of his writing under a pseudonym. Leftist journals and periodicals of this era very frequently had articles written by academics under fictitious names.

2. Alfredo Medio, "Profits and Surplus-Value: Appearance and Reality in Capitalist Production," in A *Critique of Economic Theory*, ed. E.K. Hunt and Jesse G. Schwartz (Baltimore: Penguin, 1972), pp. 312–46.

3. Ibid., p. 326.

4. Ibid., pp. 325–26.

5. Ibid., p. 326.

6. A. Shaikh, "Marx's Theory of Value and the 'Transformation Problem'" in *The Subtle Anatomy of Capitalism*, ed. J. Schwartz (Santa Monica: Goodyear, 1977); and A. Shaikh, "The Transformation from Marx to Sraffa," in *Ricardo, Marx, Sraffa*, ed. E. Mandel (London: Verso, 1984).

7. A. Lipietz, "The So-called 'Transformation Problem' Revisited," *Journal of Economic Theory* 26, no. 1 (1982); G. Duménil, *De la valeur aux prix de production* (Paris: Economics, 1980); D. Foley, "The Value of Money, the Value of Labor Power and the Marxian Transformation Problem," *Review of Radical Political Economics* 14, no. 2 (Summer 1982): 37–49.

8. G. Duménil, "Beyond the Transformation Riddle: A Labor Theory of Value," *Science and Society* 47, no. 4 (Winter 1983): 442.

9. Bob Rowthorn, "Skilled Labour in the Marxist System," *Bulletin of the Conference of Socialist Economists* (Spring 1974): 25–45.

10. Harry Braverman, *Labor and Monopoly Capital, The Degradation of Work in the Twentieth Century* (New York: Monthly Review Press, 1974). For some examples of the scholarship that was stimulated by Braverman's book, see the articles contained in Samuel Bowles and Richard Edwards, eds., *Radical Political Economy*, vol. 1 (Hants, UK: Edward Elgar, 1990).

11. Ibid., pp. 315–16.

12. Ibid., p. 139.

13. Quoted in Bruce Brown, *Marx, Freud, and the Critique of Everyday Life* (New York: Monthly Review Press, 1973), p. 56.

14. Eli Zaretsky, "Capitalism, the Family and Personal Life," *Socialist Revolution* 3, no. 3 (January–April 1973): 69–125.

15. Miriam Wasserman, comp., *Demystifying School* (New York: Praeger, 1974).

16. Samuel Bowles and Herbert Gintis, *Schooling in Capitalist America* (New York: Basic Books, 1976).

17. James Aronson, *The Press and the Cold War* (Indianapolis, IN: Bobbs-Merrill, 1970).

18. Robert Cirino, *Don't Blame the People* (New York: Vintage, 1971).

19. Edward S. Herman and Noam Chomsky, *Manufacturing Consent: The Political Economy of the Mass Media* (New York: Pantheon Books, 1988).

20. G. William Domhoff, *Who Rules America?* (Englewood Cliffs, NJ: Prentice-Hall, 1967), and Howard L. Reiter, *Parties and Elections in Corporate America* (New York: St. Martin's Press, 1987).

21. Braverman, *Labor and Monopoly Capital*, p. 125

22. Paul A. Baran and Paul M. Sweezy, *Monopoly Capital* (New York: Monthly Review Press, 1966), p. 9.

23. Ibid., pp. 9–10.

24. Ibid.

25. Ibid., pp. 115–16.

26. Ibid., p. 115.

27. Ibid., p. 119.

28. Ibid., p. 126.

29. Ibid., p. 155.

30. Ibid., p. 161.

31. Ibid., p. 341.

32. Harry Magdoff, *The Age of Imperialism: The Economics of U.S. Foreign Policy* (New York: Monthly Review Press, 1969).

33. Ibid., pp. 99–100.

34. Ibid., p. 57.

35. Ibid., pp. 203–206.

36. Ibid., pp. 200–201.

37. Edward S. Herman, *The Real Terror Network: Terrorism in Fact and Propaganda* (Boston: South End Press, 1982).

38. Karen Horney, *The Neurotic Personality of Our Time* (New York: Norton, 1937), p. 92.

39. In my discussion and classification of universal human needs, I am generally following A.H. Maslow, *Motivation and Personality* (New York: Harper, 1954). However, on the question of the best means of ultimately fulfilling these needs, I disagree with Maslow.

40. Ibid., p. 101.

41. Ibid., p. 82.

42. Ibid.

43. Ibid., p. 89.

44. Ibid., p. 90.

45. Ibid., p. 91.

Suggestions for Further Reading

This list is intended as a supplement to the material in this book. The principal works by the economists discussed in the book are listed in the footnotes in the various chapters. This list contains only secondary sources that should complement the material in the text. The list is not a comprehensive bibliography, but merely a few suggestions that I believe will be useful in acquiring an understanding of some of the issues discussed in the book.

Chapter 1

Dobb, Maurice. *Studies in the Development of Capitalism.* New York: International Publishers, 1963.
Edwards, Richard C.; Michael Reich; and Thomas E. Weisskopf, eds. *The Capitalist System.* 2d ed. Englewood Cliffs, NJ: Prentice-Hall, 1978.

Chapter 2

Letwin, William. *The Origins of Scientific Economics.* London: Methuen, 1963.
Meek, Ronald L. *Studies in the Labour Theory of Value.* 2d ed. New York: Monthly Review Press, 1976, ch. 1.

Chapter 3

Dobb, Maurice. *Theories of Value and Distribution since Adam Smith.* Cambridge, UK: Cambridge University Press, 1973, ch. 2.
Macfie, A.L. "The Scottish Tradition in Economic Thought." *Scottish Journal of Political Economy* 2 (June 1955): 81–103.
Meek, Ronald L. *Studies in the Labour Theory of Value*, ch. 2.
Rogin, Leo. *The Meaning and Validity of Economic Theory.* New York: Harper and Row, 1958, ch. 3.
Samuels, Warren J. "Adam Smith and the Economy as a System of Power." *Review of Social Economy* 31 (October 1973): 123–37.

Chapter 4

Blaug, Mark. *Economic Theory in Retrospect*. 3rd ed. New York: Cambridge University Press, 1978, ch. 3.
Rogin, Leo. *The Meaning and Validity of Economic Theory*, ch. 5.

Chapter 5

Blaug, Mark. *Ricardian Economics*. New Haven, CT: Yale University Press, 1958.
Dobb, Maurice. *Theories of Value and Distribution since Adam Smith*, chs. 3 and 4.

Chapter 6

Bowley, Marian. *Nassau Senior and Classical Economics*. London: George Allen and Unwin, 1937.
Halevy, Elie. *The Growth of Philosophical Radicalism*. Boston: Beacon Press, 1955.
Hutchison, T.W. "Bentham as an Economist." *Economic Journal* 66 (June 1956): 288–306.
Schumpeter, Joseph. *History of Economic Analysis*. Oxford: Oxford University Press, 1954, pp. 615–25.

Chapter 7

Blaug, Mark. *Ricardian Economics*, pp. 140–150.
Halevy, Elie. *Thomas Hodgskin*. London: Ernest Berm, 1956.
Hunt, E. K. "Value Theory in the Writings of the Classical Economists, Thomas Hodgskin and Karl Marx." *History of Political Economy* 9 (Fall 1977): 322–45.
Pankhurst, R.K.P. *William Thompson*. London: Watts, 1954.

Chapter 8

Blaug, Mark. *Economic Theory in Retrospect*, ch. 6.
Mitchell, Wesley C. *Types of Economic Theory*. New York: Augustus M. Kelley, 1967, ch. 5.
Rogin, Leo. *The Meaning and Validity of Economic Theory*, ch. 8.

Chapter 9

Catephores, George. *An Introduction to Marxian Economics*. New York: New York University Press, 1989.

Dobb, Maurice. *Theories of Value and Distribution since Adam Smith*, ch. 6.

Hunt, E.K. "Philosophy and Economics in the Writings of Karl Marx." In *Marx, Schumpter and Keynes, A Centenary Celebration of Dissent*, ed. S.W. Helburn and D.F. Bramhall. Armonk, NY: M.E. Sharpe, 1986.

Hunt, E.K. "Joan Robinson and the Labour Theory of Value." *Cambridge Journal of Economics* 7 (1983).

Hunt, E.K., and Jesse Schwartz, eds. *A Critique of Economic Theory*. Baltimore: Penguin, 1972, ch. 13.

Meek, Ronald L. *Studies in the Labour Theory of Value*, chs. 4 and 5.

Meek, Ronald L. "Some Notes on the Transformation Problem." *Economic Journal* 66 (March 1956): 94–107.

Schwartz, Jesse, ed. *The Subtle Anatomy of Capitalism*. Santa Monica, CA: Goodyear, 1977, chs. 6 and 7.

Sweezy, Paul M. *The Theory of Capitalist Development*. New York: Monthly Review Press, 1956.

Chapter 10

Dobb, Maurice. *Theories of Value and Distribution since Adam Smith*, ch. 7.

Rogin, Leo. *The Meaning and Validity of Economic Theory*, chs. 10–12.

Spengler, Joseph J., and William R. Allen. *Essays in Economic Thought*. Chicago: Rand McNally, 1960, pt. 6.

Chapter 11

Blaug, Mark. *Economic Theory in Retrospect*, chs. 911.

Rogin, Leo. *The Meaning and Validity of Economic Theory*, ch. 13.

Stigler, George. *Production and Distribution Theories*. New York: Macmillan, 1941.

Chapter 12

Dorfman, Joseph. *The Economic Mind in American Civilization*, vol. 3. New York: Viking Press, 1949, ch. 19.

Dowd, Douglas, ed. *Thorstein Veblen: A Critical Reappraisal*. Ithaca: Cornell University Press, 1958.

Chapter 13

Fieldhouse, D.K. *The Theory of Capitalist Imperialism*. London: Longmans, 1967.

Kemp, Tom. *Theories of Imperialism*. London: Dobson, 1967.

Chapter 14

Carter, Michael. "To Abstain or Not to Abstain (Is That the Question?)." In *The Subtle Anatomy of Capitalism*, ed. Schwartz, pp. 36–50.

E.K. Hunt, "A Radical Critique of Welfare Economics." In *Growth, Profits & Property*, ed. E.J. Nell. New York: Cambridge University Press, 1980.

Nath, S.K. *A Reappraisal of Welfare Economics*. New York: Augustus M. Kelley, 1969.

Chapter 15

Blaug, Mark. *Economic Theory in Retrospect*, ch. 15.

Minsky, Hyman P. *John Maynard Keynes*. New York: Columbia University Press, 1975.

Rosen, Sumner. "Keynes Without Gadflies." In *A Critique of Economic Theory*, ed. Hunt and Schwartz, pp. 397–419.

Shaw, G.K., ed. *The Keynesian Heritage*. Vols. 1 and 2. Hants, UK: Edward Edgar, 1988.

Chapter 16

Harcourt, G.C. *Some Cambridge Controversies in the Theory of Capital*. Cambridge, UK: Cambridge University Press, 1972.

Hunt, E.K., and Jesse Schwartz, eds. *A Critique of Economic Theory*, pts. 3 and 4.

Chapter 17

Samuels, Warren J., ed. *Institutional Economics*. Vols. 1, 2, and 3. Hants, UK: Edward Elgar, 1988.

Sawyer, Malcolm C., ed. *Post-Keynesian Economics*. Hants, UK: Edward Elgar, 1988.

Chapter 18

Ricketts, Martin, ed. *Neoclassical Microeconomics*. Vols. 1 and 2. Hants, UK: Edward Elgar, 1988.

Littlechild, Stephen, ed. *Austrian Economics*. Vols. 1, 2, and 3. Hants, UK: Edward Elgar, 1990.

Chapter 19

Bowles, Samuel, and Richard Edwards, eds. *Radical Political Economy*. Vols. 1 and 2. Hants, UK: Edward Elgar, 1990.

King, J.E., ed. *Marxian Economics*. Vols. 1, 2, and 3. Hants, UK: Edward Elgar, 1990.

Index

About the Author

E.K. Hunt is professor of economics at the University of Utah. He has taught at five universities where he has won numerous awards for both his teaching and his research. His research has been concentrated in the areas of the history of economic thought, Marxian economic theory, and theoretical welfare economics. Dr. Hunt is the author of several books and dozens of scholarly articles.